Dim-Remembered Stories

Robert H. Barlow

Massimo Berruti

DIM-REMEMBERED STORIES

A Critical Study of R. H. Barlow

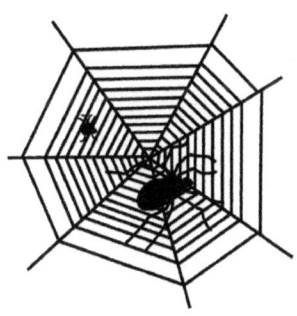

Hippocampus Press
New York

Copyright © 2011 by Massimo Berruti.
Foreword © 2010 by S. T. Joshi.

Illustration for "The Night Ocean" by R. Saunders, from the *Californian* (Winter 1936). Photograph of the Barlow homestead by Vance Pollock, used by permission.

Published by Hippocampus Press
P.O. Box 641, New York, NY 10156.
http://www.hippocampuspress.com

All rights reserved.
No part of this work may be reproduced in any form or by any means without the written permission of the publisher.

Cover illustration by Pete Von Sholly.
Cover design by Barbara Briggs Silbert.
Hippocampus Press logo designed by Anastasia Damianakos.

First Edition
1 3 5 7 9 8 6 4 2

ISBN 978-0-9846386-3-5

FOREWORD

The creative work of Robert Hayward Barlow has been neglected for far too long. Barlow has long been recognised as an important figure in the ultimate recognition of his great friend and mentor, H. P. Lovecraft: in his role as Lovecraft's literary executor, he donated a substantial amount of his friend's manuscripts, letters, and other materials to the John Hay Library of Brown University, thereby laying the foundations for serious critical work on Lovecraft's life and work. He assisted, as best he could, in the publication by Arkham House of the landmark volume *The Outsider and Others* (1939), which began the process of establishing Lovecraft as a canonical writer in the field of supernatural fiction. But Barlow's own fiction and poetry—the former never collected into a book in his brief lifetime, the latter issued in two or three fugitive volumes that attracted little notice—seemed doomed to the oblivion that would have overtaken Lovecraft's own work without the efforts of Barlow and others. It is for that reason that David E. Schultz, Douglas A. Anderson, and I took such great pleasure in assembling *Eyes of the God: The Weird Fiction and Poetry of R. H. Barlow* (2002). But we had no idea that the publication of this volume would lead to the impressive work of scholarship that you hold in your hands.

Massimo Berruti has already proved himself to be a perspicacious scholar of Lovecraft's own writing, as the several essays he has published in academic journals such as *Semiotica*, *Studi Lovecraftiani*, *Lovecraft Studies*, and *Studies in Fantasy Literature* attest. But Berruti has now composed what could well be the definitive study of Barlow as a weird fictionist and poet. While largely adhering to his chosen methodology of semiotics, Berruti also uses other approaches to paint an extraordinarily detailed portrait of the textual and philosophical richness of Barlow's writing—a richness that is by no means evident on the surface, even if such tales as "A Dim-Remembered Story" and "The Night Ocean" proclaim their brilliance to every reader. The meticulousness and subtlety of Berruti's analysis brings many hidden riches of Barlow's work to the surface, showing that this young writer, scarcely out of his novitiate when he died tragically at the age of thirty-two, had already achieved a level of literary brilliance that authors twice his age would envy.

Berruti's treatment of such significant themes in Barlow's work as vagueness, time, cosmicism, and nature is skillful and vibrant, illuminating many features of the text that a casual reading would overlook. The remarkable fusion of academic rigour with aesthetic sensitivity makes this work a model for intelligent and penetrating literary criticism. Every literary artist would be grateful to be the subject of the luminous and searching analysis that Massimo Berruti has devoted to R. H. Barlow.

—S. T. Joshi

Contents

Foreword 5
Abbreviations..9
1. Some Notes on an Entity 11
    1.1   Life and achievements of an undiscovered genius....................11
    1.2   The controversial choice of a career..40
    1.3   The categorization of Barlow's fiction...45
    1.4   The seven themes of Barlow's fiction..50
2. Dunsanianism 52
    2.1   Some critical remarks 52
    2.2   The nature of Barlow's Dunsanianism...55
        2.2.1   The formal aspects of Barlow's Dunsanianism................ 56
        2.2.2   The content aspects of Barlow's Dunsanianism: the Barlow Mythos 60
3. Vagueness...72
    3.1   Vagueness of communication 73
    3.2   Vagueness of perception...78
        3.2.1   Reality versus appearance, or the "deluding plot".......... 94
        3.2.2   The *Book of Garoth*.. 95
    3.3   Vagueness of the object of perception 98
    3.4   Vagueness of the narrating voice...100
        3.4.1   The lonely and paranoid narrator: "The Night Ocean"... 101
        3.4.2   The diseased and frantic narrator: "Origin Undetermined"............ 116
            3.4.2.1 The framing narrative of the first-level narrator 117
            3.4.2.2 The manuscript of the second-level narrator 121
    3.5   Vagueness as a literary technique 126
    3.6   Cumulative vagueness: "The Summons" 131
4. Cosmicism..144
    4.1   Silence, Emptiness, Desolation 144
    4.2   Mankind's existential condition and bleak fate.........................147
        4.2.1   "'Till A' the Seas'" and other dreadful ends 147
        4.2.2   Inanity of experience and deterministic compulsion 157
            4.2.2.1 Inanity and meaninglessness of the human experience.......... 157
            4.2.2.2 Deterministic compulsion and its impact on free will............ 180
    4.3   Vastness of the universe and cosmic Outsideness 187
5. Time 205
    5.1   The fictional mysteries of "Time" 205

| | | 5.1.1 Cosmic Time: an introduction .... 205 |
| | | 5.1.2 Human Time: an introduction .... 207 |

- 5.2 Cosmic Time 208
  - 5.2.1 "A Dim-Remembered Story" and the transcendent present 209
  - 5.2.2 Cosmic Time, still 220
- 5.3 Human Time 228
  - 5.3.1 "A Memory": caring for the future of civilization 228
    - 5.3.1.1 Memory, still 233
  - 5.3.2 The everlasting presence of the Past 242
- 5.4 "The Night Ocean": the hybridism of "existential" time 252

6. Nature 257
   - 6.1 The "conflict" between nature and culture 258
   - 6.2 The personification of nature 262
   - 6.3 The spiritualization of nature 269
   - 6.4 Nature and the sacred: "The Night Ocean" 272

7. Irony 287
   - 7.1 Tales of socially committed and bitter irony 290
   - 7.2 Tales of true humor and parody 295

8. Forbidden / Furtive Search 309

9. Poetry 333
   - 9.1 Barlow's poetry: an introduction 333
   - 9.2 The five nuclei of Barlow's poetry 336
     - 9.2.1 "Sense": Light and Darkness 337
     - 9.2.2 "Memory": Time and Memory 348
       - 9.2.2.1 Personal 348
       - 9.2.2.2 Historical 361
       - 9.2.2.3 Cosmic and Existential 362
     - 9.2.3 "Dream": Sleep and Wake 372
     - 9.2.4 "Essence": Internal and External 377
     - 9.2.5 "Nature": Nature and Culture 381

Conclusion 394
Bibliography 397

Abbreviations

CC	H. P. Lovecraft, *The Call of Cthulhu and Other Weird Stories* (1999)
CE	H. P. Lovecraft, *Collected Essays* (2004–06)
DW	H. P. Lovecraft, *The Dreams in the Witch House and Other Weird Stories* (2004)
EG	R. H. Barlow, *Eyes of the God* (2002)
FF	H. P. Lovecraft, *O Fortunate Floridian* (2007)
OLL	R. H. Barlow, *On Lovecraft and Life* (1992)
Joshi, "Recognition"	S. T. Joshi, "R. H. Barlow and the Recognition of Lovecraft" (1988)
LAL	S. T. Joshi, *H. P. Lovecraft: A Life* (1996)
SL	H. P. Lovecraft, *Selected Letters* (1965–76)
UL	Kenneth W. Faig, Jr., *The Unknown Lovecraft* (2009)
WG	R. H. Barlow, "The Wind That Is in the Grass" (1944), in Peter Cannon, ed., *Lovecraft Remembered* (1998)
CAS	Clark Ashton Smith
HPL	H. P. Lovecraft
JHL	John Hay Library, Brown University (Providence, RI)
RHB	R. H. Barlow

Illustration for "The Night Ocean."

1. Some Notes on an Entity

"We have learned to hold teacups so artfully that no one detects the absence of tea"
Robert H. Barlow, "Rainy-Day Pastime"

1.1 Life and achievements of an undiscovered genius

It can hardly be denied that Robert Hayward Barlow's early reading of Clark Ashton Smith, Lord Dunsany, and H. P. Lovecraft, as well as his association with the Providence writer, had a decisive impact on the development of his own literary production. This is not the place for a lengthy discussion of the biographical events that led Barlow (1918-1951) to his association with the fantastic and its masters; it may suffice to say that when Barlow first started to correspond with Lovecraft, with a letter dated 18 June 1931,[1] Barlow was barely thirteen, but already an avid consumer and collector of pulp magazines publishing weird fiction and poetry. Born in Leavenworth, Kansas, on 18 May 1918, Barlow as a teenager was an omnivorous reader and enthusiast of fantasy and horror fiction;[2] after starting his correspondence with Lovecraft, Robert E. Howard, Clark Ashton Smith, and other renowned authors of the genre, Barlow also requested and received from them autograph manuscripts of their stories. Gradually, a working relationship with Lovecraft developed whereby Barlow, despite his bad eyesight, would provide typewritten copies of his master's tales in exchange for the original manuscripts,[3] which he treasured together with impressive collections of weird books

---

1. HPL received the letter as forwarded by *Weird Tales*, while he was in Charleston, South Carolina, during a trip. (At the time RHB was living with the family in Fort Benning, Georgia.) HPL answered quite promptly, on 25 June, though he did not know how young his admirer was. He may have had some inkling about RHB's age before meeting him, but clearly "he was taken aback when he first stepped off the bus in DeLand on 2 May 1934" (Joshi and Schultz, "Introduction," in *FF* xiii). Thus HPL discovered RHB's age only during their first meeting in Florida in the summer of 1934; see HPL's letter to Helen V. Sully, 26 May 1934: "He always evaded statements regarding his age, but it now turns out that he *only turned sixteen last Friday*. The little imp! Thus he was scarcely 13 when he first corresponded with me" (*SL* 4.411).
2. Faig remarks that "Because of his family's frequent moves, Barlow had had little formal schooling, but in the world of *Weird Tales* and the science fiction pulp magazines the brilliant youth found a fascinating preoccupation" (*UL* 238).
3. HPL used to prepare typescripts of his stories, with one or more carbons (though he hated using the typewriter and composed in longhand, because he believed that high-value prose could not be written on the typewriter); then the originals would be sent to magazines, while the carbons would circulate among his friends and colleagues for years, even

and magazines, often duplicate and even triplicate copies of some of the pulps of his day,[4] in a locked closet called Yoh-Vombis, "after a story by Clark Ashton Smith" (WG 358) about caverns of horror on Mars. It is thanks to this habit of Barlow's that it is still possible to read Lovecraft's original versions of masterpieces such as *The Case of Charles Dexter Ward* (1927) and "The Shadow out of Time" (1934-35), which otherwise might have been destroyed by Lovecraft.[5] As an amateur, Barlow in fact considered "bibliophily a serious occupation, filing autographs of Wells and Verne with those of popular magazine writers, and searching for old *Weird Tales* along with out-of-print Cabell. It was indeed this bibliophily which led me to write to Lovecraft first, in 1931, when I was not quite thirteen" (WG 358). Barlow had "one of the finest and most distinctive fantasy collections in history" (*UL* 196) and "must have acquainted himself with book lore from some of the books on the subject which were popular in the 1920s and 1930s" (*UL* 200).[6] Barlow did not limit himself to collecting books, but picked up the art of bookbinding, "at which he became a superb craftsman. [. . .] By 1935 Barlow was a collector

---

after the story was published, until some deteriorated completely due to constant handling. "Barlow, willing to lend any assistance he could to an author whose work he admired, offered to prepare new typescripts to replace the battered carbons, and even to prepare typescripts of stories that remained unpublished in HPL's spidery handwriting. By early 1933 Barlow proposed a formal deal: 'Since I would like to make copies of all I lack of your work, I shall be glad to kill two birds with one stone [. . .] and make you a copy in return for the typescript'" (Joshi and Schultz, "Introduction," *FF* ix; RHB's letter dates to 10 February 1933). RHB could thus store many HPL's stories (including "The Doom That Came to Sarnath," "The Transition of Juan Romero," "The Quest of Iranon," "The Other Gods," and "The Strange High House in the Mist") in his own collection.

4. As Joshi remarks, "Barlow had singular perceptiveness: he did not collect hacks like Edmond Hamilton or Seabury Quinn, but only those writers who—as we can see through hindsight—were genuine artists in the weird tale" ("Recognition" 45).

5. "We owe much of modern Lovecraft scholarship to the efforts of Robert H. Barlow" (Joshi, "Introduction," *OLL* 6), because "Lovecraft was in the habit of destroying manuscripts once a reliable (or, sometimes, even an unreliable) printed copy was at hand" (Joshi 1988, 45). RHB even copied a few letters that HPL wrote to Winifred Virginia Jackson (*LAL* 200). "[RHB's] preservation of Lovecraft's manuscripts and personal effects [. . .] will be eternally remembered as making possible the ultimate textual restoration of Lovecraft's work" (Joshi, "Recognition" 51). After 1932, HPL handed to RHB all the surviving manuscripts of his own weird stories, with five exceptions: "The Shunned House," "Under the Pyramids" and "The Horror at Red Hook" (all given to Samuel Loveman), "The Haunter of the Dark" (to Donald A. Wollheim) and "The Thing on the Doorstep" (given to Duane W. Rimel, who after HPL's death lent the manuscript to RHB, who microfilmed it and stored it in the John Hay Library).

6. Faig also wonders whether RHB's "fondness for the words biblio-this and biblio-that" means he was familiar "with Holbrook Jackson's *The Anatomy of Bibliomania* [Scribner's, 1930], which deals at length with these phenomena. RHB also possessed a stamp reading 'R. H. Barlow: Bibliomaniac', which appears on some of his early papers in the Lovecraft collection" (*UL* 200).

and bookman of some sophistication, perfectly cognizant of the value of manuscripts, proofs, presentation copies, and the like" (*UL* 200). As an amateur, Barlow also displayed a strong interest in publishing projects: most of them failed to materialize;[7] but among those that saw the light, under the label of the "Dragon-Fly Press," a limited edition of 42 copies of Lovecraft's short tale *The Cats of Ulthar* as a surprise gift given to Lovecraft for Christmas, and a collection of Frank Belknap Long's poetry, *The Goblin Tower*, both issued in 1935, deserve mention.[8] Barlow

---

7. Such as the plan to issue a volume of Henry S. Whitehead's letters upon his death, in 1932, and whose tentative title was *Caneviniana*, or the plan to issue a collection of C. L. Moore's tales, and one of Clark Ashton Smith's poetry, whose tentative title was *Incantations* (a section with this very title, including an expanded selection of RHB's aborted book, appeared in Smith's *Selected Poems* [1971]), or even the ambitious project to publish HPL's complete *Collected Poetical Works* (HPL went as far as to provide RHB with a "sample table of contents," as an enclosure to a letter dated 13 June 1936, now in *FF* 348), an enterprise that actually required more than sixty years to be accomplished (through the Night Shade edition of *The Ancient Track: The Complete Poetical Works of H. P. Lovecraft*, in 2001). De Camp incisively summarized this quality of RHB, stating that "He was much given to starting more things than he could finish" (392). Joshi reinforces the argument, pointing out RHB's youthful impatience and restlessness as the main causes of the failures of these projects: "He no sooner started one project than he became filled with enthusiasm for another" (Joshi, "Recognition" 49). And HPL himself, in a letter to RHB dated 25 March 1935, exclaims, clearly referring to RHB's inconclusiveness: "I think I'll have to found a sort of efficiency cult based on the idea of *one thing at a time!*" (*FF* 232). In another epistle to RHB dated 24 May 1935, HPL writes: "I certainly hope you'll issue that amateur paper. [. . .] When *will* Grandpa be able to teach you to *finish what you start?*" (*FF* 275). And with reference to the planned *Collected Poetical Works* of HPL, this is how the latter expressed himself in a letter to RHB, dated 4 June 1936: "I'll consider it when I have a finished copy of Klarkash-Ton's 'Incantations' in my hands. One thing at a time! [. . .] I'm more interested in *finishing* jobs than in *starting* them!" (*FF* 338–39). Again, in a letter of a few days later (June 13), HPL reinforced the point: "You get me wrong about that *one-thing-at-a-time-&-finish-what-you-start* advice. I'm not urging you to *do anything more.* Indeed, I'm urging you to do *less!* My main point is that you ought to *stop starting new things* until you've finished up what's already under way. Not that you ought to hurry with the latter. Go easy, & avoid overstrain. But simply *choose the existing jobs to work at when you feel like working at anything at all.* That's the only way they'll ever get done. It's better to *finish one job* than to get a dozen started & have them all stalled at various stages. Starting an excessive number of new ventures prevents *any* of them from ever really materialising. [. . .] What's the use of getting things printed if they never circulate? Don't do *more* work. *Do less!* Simply limit your plans to things you know you can finish" (*FF* 343).

8. RHB had already started to work on *The Cats of Ulthar* in October 1935, when he asked HPL whether the *Weird Tales* publications of the work (in the issues for February 1926 and February 1933) were textually accurate. HPL, without suspecting anything, replied that they were, and when he then saw RHB's edition of *Ulthar*, he immediately expressed, in a postcard dated 2 January 1936, his enthusiastic appreciation for the idea and the quality of the work—without renouncing his usual humble underestimation of his own literary work: "Have seen Belknap's copy of 'Ulthar' & must express my overflowing appreciation! I had

undertook also the publication of two issues[9] of an amateur magazine of his own, the *Dragon-Fly*,[10] through the National Amateur Press Association, to which he was introduced by Lovecraft himself.[11] A Lovecraft letter even reveals that Barlow contemplated establishing a literary and publishing colony in Florida: Lovecraft did not fail to encourage this ambitious project on Barlow's part.[12]

---

no idea you were preparing anything of the sort. [. . .] No misprints that I can see—& the taste in format is ideal. Good stuff! A credit to the Dragon Fly Press—except for the trivial subject-matter. Thanks for the copies which I suppose are at home" (FF 313). Regarding *The Goblin Tower*, HPL helped set the type while visiting RHB in the summer of 1935 (see SL 5.182, 216). In a letter to Richard Ely Morse, dated 25 April 1936 (ms., JHL), HPL commented upon this volume: "Certainly, the book is extremely uneven. [. . .] There was no *selection* at all—the idea being to preserve safely every scrap of Belknap's scattered verse which had any claim to literacy & meaning. [. . .] But at any rate it formed good material for typographical practice. Neither Barlow nor I had ever done any real printing before, & in the numerous crudities one may trace a record of stumbling apprenticeship. It is also forming—for Barlow—an exercise in the binder's art. [. . .] Belknap has a couple of really bound copies, & they certainly represent very creditable work" (quoted in FF 348-49, n. 1). Long showed surprise and delight upon receiving the unexpected gift: "The printing suffers from being his first job, but the binding is more representative. Long himself was delighted & astonished—the existence of the book having been kept a perfect secret till a completed copy was mailed to him" (HPL, letter to Elizabeth Toldridge, 15 December 1935; SL 5.216).

9. The first is dated 15 October 1935, the second 15 May 1936. The quality of the selected material (the two issues include works by J. Vernon Shea, Clark Ashton Smith, August W. Derleth, Elizabeth Toldridge, E. A. Edkins, Eugene B. Kuntz, and RHB himself) attests RHB's refined literary judgment.

10. HPL praised highly this publishing endeavor on RHB's part. Soon after receiving a copy of the first issue, HPL expressed his enthusiastic comments to RHB in a letter dated 21 October 1935: "The magazine is a splendid contribution to amateurdom, & ought to evoke a lustily unanimous chorus of praise & enthusiasm. Nothing so close to the old Golden-Age standard has appeared in aeons. [. . .] The various items are splendidly balanced—fiction—essay—poetry. [. . .] Certainly, the appearance of the *Dragon-Fly* is *the* amateur event of the year. Your editorial is excellent, & very much to the point. [. . .] Typographically, too, the journal is surprisingly good. You seem to be getting better & better impressions with the press, while the text has a remarkably low error-percentage. [. . .] Altogether, this is certainly a magnificent start, & I hope devoutly that you'll keep right along issuing it. A few journals like that would be the regeneration of amateur journalism!" (FF 296-97). Also, HPL wanted to make sure the magnificent first issue of the magazine could reach the highest possible number of his gang members: "Before starting on any new printing, for Yuggoth's sake *circulate the Dragon-Fly!* Lots of people to whom I've mentioned it say they haven't received a copy," and then HPL even goes on listing names and addresses of possible recipients to whom RHB should send copies (HPL, letter to RHB, 13 December 1935; FF 304).

11. See Faig, *UL* 199, who remarks that, according to a note by F. Lee Baldwin in the *Fantasy Fan* issue of September 1934, RHB won the 1933 story laureateship for "Eyes of the God."

12. "Your idea of getting a small press is a very good one. It will be especially useful in the National Amateur Press Assn.; enabling you to issue a paper at intervals at little cost, & thus giving you a ready means of circulating your writings & opinions" (HPL, letter to

In his adolescence, Barlow the precocious fan was interested in becoming a writer in his own right, and he solicited Lovecraft's opinions on his own efforts. Barlow found in Lovecraft a master readily available to provide him with practical advice on the techniques of the weird tale. For the first year or two, "[. . .] the correspondence between Lovecraft and Barlow is somewhat routine and perfunctory, but Lovecraft's willingness to befriend a fellow enthusiast of the weird is always evident" (Joshi and Schultz, "Introduction," *FF* viii). However, their association grew increasingly closer: in the spring of 1934, Lovecraft spent nearly two months, from May 2 to June 21, with Robert and his mother Bernice[13] at their remote homestead eighteen miles outside DeLand,[14] Florida, near a hamlet called Cassia. The offer

---

RHB, 14 March 1933; *FF* 56). And again: "Your idea for a literary colony certainly sounds alluring. [. . .] If you had any idea of founding a *publishing* colony, the guy you would want to rope in is W. Paul Cook—who is not only an expert professional printer with publishing experience, but is more than ordinarily unattached & disposed toward radical migrations. [. . .] But it surely would be idyllic if a select bunch of weirdists, printers, & bibliophiles could be rounded up under the live-oaks & palmettos of His Hispanic Majesty's ancient province of Florida Orienta" (letter to RHB, 10 April 1934; *FF* 127-28). Again in a letter to RHB dated 19 March 1934, HPL encouraged RHB on the colony project, in part as a way of combating his restlessness at living in a place like DeLand, whose "social milieu" was not considered lively enough by RHB: "It would be a delightful idea if you could assemble a hand-picked literary colony after your own heart" (*FF* 118). HPL also encouraged young RHB in the establishing an amateur press in DeLand, the one that would ultimately be labeled the Dragon-Fly Press. HPL went as far as to suggest to RHB different possible names for the printing enterprise: "[. . .] the name of some heraldic or decorative symbol is perfectly suitable [. . .]. Do you think it necessary to have something familiar—something, that is, within the range of a standard literary allusion? It might be even more effective to use some title known only to the gang, & give the outside public the zest of guessing. How about the *Averoigne Press?* A staunch Klarkash-Tonite like you ought to favour that. Or if you want alliteration, how about the *Poseidonis Press?* Poseidonis, you know, was the last part of Atlantis to sink. The *Naacal Press* would evoke mystical reflections from those familiar with Churchward's 'Mu' canards. If you have any 'Golden something' press, make it less common than a dragon. You *could* make Two-Gun's fictitious *Golden Goblin* press a reality—or have a Golden Wyvern or Afreet or Djinn or something. Or you could borrow names from the cosmic fables of the theosophists—so extensively studied by Sultan Malik a couple of years ago. *Plaksha Press* is quite a phrase! Also *Pushkara Press.* As you may know, Pushkara is the future final land—corresponding to Klarkash-Ton's 'Zothique'. Which reminds me—what would be the matter with *Zothique Press* or *Tsathoggua Press?* At any rate, you ought to consult CAS for suggestions. He would be more than ordinarily fertile in that direction" (letter to RHB, 25 March 1935; *FF* 229-30).

13. RHB's father was away recovering from a nervous breakdown. And Robert's older brother, Wayne, in the army, was in Texas at the time of HPL's visit. The household consisted just of RHB, his mother, a housekeeper, and the housekeeper's son, Charles Blackburn Johnston.

14. Where the Barlows had moved sometime in 1933, after the retirement of RHB's father, Col. Barlow, from the army. Apparently the preferred spelled is *DeLand*, but both HPL and RHB spell it *De Land* throughout their correspondence.

had been made as early as in November 1933, and was "tempting for more than one reason: not only had Lovecraft richly enjoyed his 1931 visit to Florida, but the genial heat of the region was a balm to him" (Joshi and Schultz, "Introduction," *FF* ix). In addition, the area was replete with Spanish antiquities. All these features contributed to making the sojourn highly pleasant for Lovecraft, who repeatedly in his correspondence declared his wish (or dream) to settle in Florida.[15] During his guest's first visit, aside from typing some of Lovecraft's manuscripts, Barlow kept a running diary,[16] gathering sparse notes recording the episodes and anecdotes of those days, and from which he drew raw material when writing, in July 1944 in Mexico City, the celebrated memoir "The Wind That Is in the Grass," prepared for *Marginalia*. From both pieces, the picture of a lively, close relationship emerges, portraying two friends completely at ease in discussing any kind of topic and in sharing their own experiences in literary fields, as well as in their everyday habits (such as in one of their favorite pastimes—playing with the beloved cats). They also had walks until sunset, idle times spent in writing letters and rhymes in rowboats, searching for obscure stories in the archives of Yoh-Vombis, as well as long, exciting conversations on the most wide-ranging topics, from weird literature to history, from Dunsany to the *Fantasy Fan* to aesthetics and politics,[17] from the New Deal to the Abyssinian War, reinforcing their friendship and association until the very end of Lovecraft's life. "Life was all literary then; that is, all I cared to accept as life" (WG 358), Barlow would remark in his 1944 memoir. Lovecraft used to read his own stories aloud, "always with sinister tones and silences in the proper spots" (WG 359). Barlow delighted in the discussions about weird and fantasy fiction: "My own absorption in dreams and dream-tales kept the conversation along those lines" (WG 359). They also visited numerous sites of antiquarian and historical interest, such as "the Spanish Sugar Mill at DeLeón Springs, the Franciscan Mission at New Smyrna Beach, and rode on a glass-bottom boat at Silver Springs" (Jordan 33). In particular, DeLeón Springs must have been a very interesting site for Lovecraft the antiquarian: the small town, eight miles north of DeLand, was probably traversed by the Spanish forces under the leadership of Ponce DeLeón in the early sixteenth century (see Jordan 42) and hosted a well-preserved eighteenth-century Spanish windmill. Barlow and Lovecraft visited also New Smyrna (where portions of a mission stood) and St. Augustine, "where Lovecraft was genuinely enthralled by the authentic Hispanic atmosphere of the old town," which listed high among

---

15. HPL once even cited Florida as "the only state really fit to live in the year round" (letter to RHB, 25 November 1932; *FF* 43).

16. Later edited by August Derleth in an expurgated version published, with the title "The Barlow Journal," in *Some Notes on H. P. Lovecraft* (Arkham House, 1959). The definitive, uncensored version saw the light, under the title "Memories of Lovecraft," only in the 1992 pamphlet *On Lovecraft and Life*, edited by S. T. Joshi for Necronomicon Press.

17. "He & I are having a splendid time—motoring to various points, rowing on the lake behind the house, & having reading, writing, & discussing sessions all over the nearby countryside" (HPL, letter to Elizabeth Toldridge, 22 May 1934; *SL* 4.407–8).

his favorite ancient sites on the American continent (*UL* 199). And in his memoir, Barlow adds that "we visited the Chapel of Nuestra Senora de la Leche, and a mosquito-cursed graveyard full of tombs of young people who died of plague a hundred years before" (*WG* 359).

But what most captivated Lovecraft's admiration during his first sojourn at the Barlows' was young Robert's enthusiasm and precocity, his early achievements in arts as diverse as fiction, poetry, painting, sculpture, collecting, bookbinding,[18] and printing: "Never before in the course of a long lifetime have I seen such a versatile child. He is a writer; painter; sculptor; printer; pianist; marionette designer, maker, & exhibitor; landscape gardener; tennis champion; chess expert; bookbinder; crack rifleshot; bibliophile; manuscript collector; & heaven knows what else!"[19] That "Lovecraft was taken with Barlow" (*LAL* 507), a "truly brilliant kid" (*SL* 5.107), can hardly be questioned: he "recognised the youth's zeal and incipient brilliance, and nurtured his youthful attempts at writing weird fiction" (*LAL* 507), regarding him as a "child prodigy" (ibid.). Barlow even succeeded whereas other friends and correspondents of Lovecraft had failed: for instance, Lovecraft allowed him to prepare a typed copy of *The Dream-Quest of Unknown Kadath*, while other colleagues' similar attempts had been rejected by the Providence writer.[20]

During Lovecraft's first visit to Barlow, they also engaged in the writing and the secret printing and distribution of "The Battle That Ended the Century." The work is a spoof of the weird fiction community and was typed and mimeographed by Barlow, who distributed it (sending the copies from a non-Floridian address,

---

18. RHB bound a copy of *The Fantasy Fan*, now preserved at the John Hay Library of Brown University, and surprised HPL with his own ability at shooting snakes in order to use their skins as bookbinding material.

19. HPL, letter to Helen V. Sully, 26 May 1934 (*SL* 4.411). F. Lee Baldwin left a similar brief description of the teenage RHB in the July 1934 issue of the *Fantasy Fan*, the magazine where most of RHB's early Dunsanian fantasies appeared (in particular, nine episodes of the *Annals of the Jinns*): "R. H. Barlow is a very talented youth. He is a pianist, painter, sculptor in clay, landscape gardener, and book collector. He has completed a clay bas-relief of Cthulhu and a statuette of Ganesa, the Hindoo Elephant God. One of his favourite bindings for his books is snake skin. He shoots many snakes around his home in Florida and tans the skin" (quoted in *UL* 199). L. Sprague de Camp claimed, in his biography of HPL, that RHB was "a delicate little person of lively intellect and varied artistic talents," though "handicapped by his very versatility" (392). Elizabeth Toldridge, a New York friend and correspondent of both RHB and HPL, held young RHB in high regard: she "said she thought you were about the nicest boy she had even encountered. She marvels at the maturity of your mind" (HPL, postcard to RHB, 1 September 1935; *FF* 289).

20. The anecdote is told in *LAL* 417–18. RHB was particularly insistent with HPL on this matter, requesting him in early 1934 to unearth the manuscript for this and another story (*The Case of Charles Dexter Ward*), and had to overcome HPL's reluctance to let anyone read these repudiated words. But RHB, and only he, succeeded, and HPL sent him the manuscripts in October 1934. RHB then prepared partial typescripts for the two novels.

in order to deflect suspicion) to their colleagues after Lovecraft had left Florida. Lovecraft and Barlow would maintain an air of secrecy about the piece, for example in their correspondence with the people mentioned in the tale, never letting the truth about the actual authors of the work appear.

Lovecraft and Barlow briefly met again in New York City at the end of 1934 during the traditional reunion of the Kalems at Christmastide, on which occasion the other members of the Lovecraft circle had the opportunity to appreciate Barlow's brilliance and promise.[21]

Lovecraft's visit to Florida was repeated in the summer of 1935, when he stayed an even longer period (June 9–August 18). These summer invitations were probably intended by Barlow in part as a way to please his master with warm southern weather, since Lovecraft had complained with Barlow, in letters, about the distress he felt in Providence during the cold weather.[22] At the time of Lovecraft's first visit, Robert's father, Lieutenant-Colonel Everett D. Barlow, was recovering from a nervous breakdown with relatives up north. But in 1935 Barlow's father was in DeLand with his wife and sons, though showing some mental instability.[23] Lovecraft and Colonel Barlow seemed to get to each other: they "sang

---

21. Since 1932 HPL had developed the habit of spending the post-Christmas days with his New York friends, and especially with Frank Belknap Long. HPL arrived on December 31, while RHB had reached New York a few days earlier. After having lately surprised Long with a copy of *The Goblin Tower*, during this Christmas reunion he did the same with HPL "with a 42-copy edition of his early tale 'The Cats of Ulthar'" (*UL* 239). On New Year's night, HPL and RHB stayed up until 3 A.M. revising RHB's tale "'Till A' the Seas'" (see Joshi and Schultz, "Introduction," *FF* xv).

22. In February 1934, HPL lamented to RHB: "The minimum so far has been 17 *below zero* . . . I can't go out at all—for 20 above is the lowest temperature at which it's physically safe for me to be out for any length of time" (10 February 1934; *SL* 4.374-75). And RHB's invitation to HPL to visit him in Florida "was in the mail within a month of his [HPL's] writing RHB of the record-breaking cold temperatures besieging Providence" (Jordan 41).

23. Everett D. Barlow presents a quite interesting subject for psychological investigation, especially for the influence he might have exerted on his son's temperament and personal development. De Camp describes RHB's father as somewhat "cracked on religion and on sex" (393), so much so that "Lovecraft had been forewarned by R. H. Barlow to avoid these topics when conversing with his father" (Jordan 44). De Camp describes Everett Barlow as "a mental case. Subject to moods of intense depression, he suffered from delusions of having to defend his home against the attacks of a mysterious Them" (393). According to De Camp, RHB ultimately came to hate his father, "although later, after his parents had been divorced, he carried on a friendly correspondence with him" (393). The extent to which RHB suffered for his father's mental distress is also testified by the frequent references HPL made to the issue in his correspondence to RHB. Everett Barlow showed the traits of a paranoid personality, and HPL constantly tried to allay Robert's discomfort at his father's malaise. In a letter of 13 July 1933, HPL defined Mr. Barlow as "melancholically inclined" (*FF* 67). In a letter dated 8 August 1933, HPL suggested that RHB's father might be put to rest in bed to fight his "low spirits" and "turn the tide & start a gradual recovery," although in RHB's father's case "there may be an upswing when he sees that he is not dead on the

turn-of-the-century songs together, and it was presumably with the colonel's blessing that Lovecraft's repeated overtures to returning to Providence were met with protest, with the result that, by choice or not, the June 9 to August 18 visit with the Barlow family in 1935 would be the longest of his life."[24] Lovecraft was virtually adopted by the Barlows as a new family member, and the "super-hospitality of the Barlovii" made him seriously doubt "whether I'm a guest or a prisoner!" (SL 5.187). Lovecraft was even invited to stay down all winter, but he strove to find a tactful way to refuse the offer and move back to Providence before the chilling autumn would fall,[25] mainly protesting that he would be "lost without my books and files and familiar home things after a certain length of time" (SL 5.187). As in the previous summer, the two friends engaged in reading, writing, revising literary works, planning printing projects, and visiting the country (a trip to the gloomy and suggestive area of the Black Water Creek, about three miles southwest of the Barlow property, was especially remembered by Lovecraft as a landmark of his sojourn). Lovecraft also helped Barlow to build a cabin across the lake, where the latter would transfer "his press, desk, and various accessories" (SL 5.186). During this summer visit, the literary activity they engaged in was not particularly significant: they wrote the fragmentary "Collapsing Cosmoses" (a parody

---

date he now predicts. That will tend to destroy his belief in the illusion now gripping him, & leave the field clear for more realistic thinking" (FF 72). HPL's comments and sincere will to help never failed: in the July 1933 letter, he auspicated that Mr. Barlow, to ease his sense of oppression, might find an *"intense external interest"* (FF 67), something to keep his "consciousness fixed on objective things, & to forestall the introspection on which the trouble usually hinges" (ibid.). In a letter of September 1933 HPL expressed his regret at Mr. Barlow's continuing "melancholy" (FF 79), and wished "some nerve-specialist could get at the core of the trouble & prescribe a feasible way out" (FF 79). HPL even pushed himself to suggest a new hospitalisation, and the "acquisition of some new & absorbing interest, if such could be hit upon" (FF 79). In a letter of February 1934, HPL, probably in an attempt to ease RHB's distress, compared himself to RHB's father ("I've had just enough experience with nervous exhaustion in earlier years to realise how devastating it is, & how little the sufferer can help himself till things get better": FF 106); HPL even suggested to RHB that the ideal place for his father to live, would be a large Floridian town, "with busy urban life with something always going on" (FF 106). But it is surely in a letter dated 10 April 1934 that HPL provided the best picture of Mr. Barlow's depressive moods and "melancholy," as well as of his own sincere preoccupation for the gravity of the situation in his correspondent's household: in order to assuage his friend's distress, HPL told of his own juvenile nervous breakdowns and of their destructive impact on his physical health and intellectual endeavours. Aware of the gravity of the situation, HPL asked RHB not to hesitate to postpone or even cancel HPL's visit to DeLand in the summer of 1934, should the event "disturb him [RHB's father] & increase his depression" (FF 127).

24. Jordan 44. After the sojourn ended, HPL continued traveling and on August 20 RHB reached him in St. Augustine, to celebrate HPL's forty-fifth birthday.

25. HPL even "received an invitation to become a permanent resident on the Barlow property, possibly by making his home in the cabin across the lake where he and Barlow worked on various projects" (Jordan 44).

of the science fiction space opera), and "Bouts Rimés," two poems in which Barlow wrote the end-rhymes and Lovecraft filled the rest of the verses.

It was during these sorts of meetings that Lovecraft revealed to Barlow the tremendous inspirational power that dreams held for him in literary composition[26] (a feature that would have a strong impact on Barlow's own literary efforts, as we will see). Lovecraft also trained his young pupil in the rudiments of the aesthetics of the weird tale. From this first-hand evidence, the teenage Barlow emerges as a sensitive and dreamy young, whose lonesome adolescence led him to reading weird pulps as his favourite activity: "I had neither friends nor studies except in a sphere bound together by the U.S. mails and the magazines of fantastic stories for which Lovecraft wrote" (WG 358).[27] Kenneth W. Faig, Jr., in his invaluable biographical and critical study on Barlow, remarks how the solitude and the frequent moves of Barlow's childhood shaped a particularly sensitive personality: "he is mentioned in several places as having been a bright, introverted, and sensitive child, not much suited to the life of a military family. He was probably driven to reading for companionship because of his family's frequent moves" (UL 195).

The last meeting of the two friends occurred in the summer of 1936 (July 28–September 1), when Robert visited Lovecraft in Providence after the splitting of the Barlow household in Florida.[28] Barlow took lodge at the boarding house behind Lovecraft's residence at 66 College Street, and was "unremitting in his demands on Lovecraft's time" (Joshi and Schultz, "Introduction," FF xvii).[29] On August 8, Lovecraft and Barlow, along with Adolphe de Castro, held the celebrated Poe-session in the spectral atmosphere of St. John's Churchyard, off Benefit Street (a Providence landmark frequented in 1847–48 by Poe during his

---

26. Apart from several accounts (usually occurring at breakfast) of his own personal dreams, HPL confessed to RHB "to having cold-bloodedly invented Wilbur Whateley of Dunwich—but in many other tales—Cthulhu, for example—actual dreams are the bases" ("Memories of Lovecraft," OLL 16).

27. Joshi defines RHB's early life as "a sequestered, lonely life of the mind" (in "Introduction," OLL 5).

28. In mid-1936 RHB's parents separated, because of the "long-standing illness of Barlow's father" (UL 205), and young Robert was forced to move to Kansas City, to stay with his mother's family. In spite of this phase of acute distress, which marked the end of the idyllic days of the "Moon-Pool" (as RHB and HPL had dubbed the small lake on the Barlow property in Florida), RHB invited HPL to visit him in Florida also for the summer 1936; HPL had to decline, mainly because of "my aunt's illness, the lamentable state of the treasury, & the utter disorganisation of my writing programme" (letter to RHB, 29 April 1936; FF 327).

29. In writing to a revision client, Anne Tillery Renshaw, and probably trying to making excuses for his being late with a revision work for her, HPL would lament that "the kid [. . .] was a constant responsibility. He must be shewn to this or that museum or bookstall [. . .] he must discuss some new fantasy or chapter in his future monumental novel [. . .] & so on, & so on. What could an old man do—especially since Bobby was such a generous & assiduous host himself last year & the year before?" (letter to Anne Tillery Renshaw, 19 September 1936; quoted in Joshi and Schultz, "Introduction," FF xvii).

courtship of the poet Sarah Helen Whitman, who lived in a house close to the graveyard), writing rhymed acrostic poems on the name of Edgar Allan Poe. The idea of writing acrostics was suggested by Barlow (SL 5.360). De Castro's sonnet was published in *Weird Tales* in May 1937, while Barlow's and Lovecraft's appeared in the *Science-Fantasy Correspondent* of March–April 1937.[30] On August 20, Lovecraft and Barlow visited Salem and Marblehead, two of Lovecraft's favorite antiquarian sites, to celebrate Lovecraft's forty-sixth birthday, his last;[31] they also discovered they were sixth cousins, both descending from a John Rathbone or Rathbun, born 1658 (SL 5.300).

During their nearly six years' association, Barlow and Lovecraft worked on (or planned) several projects together, including literary collaborations (so far as is known, six fictional pieces can be counted overall[32]) and publishing enterprises of Lovecraft's own works. For instance, Barlow asked Lovecraft to prepare a definitive version of the poetic collection *Fungi from Yuggoth*, suggesting that he insert into it, as third to last, the sonnet "Recapture" (written by Lovecraft in November 1929, before the *Fungi* proper), which was not originally intended as part of the

---

30. Faig (*UL* 205) takes note of a letter de Castro sent to HPL on 12 August 1936, and which describes de Castro's impressions on young RHB: "And the greatest fun was dear young Barlow. Bob actually desires to be old, not knowing what treasure he owns in his youth and brains and his overindulgence in imagination, and good memory of what he reads."

31. The visit was planned in advance by HPL, who in a letter to RHB of 4 June 1936 discussed their possible travel programs during RHB's imminent sojourn in Providence: "Well—in view of the dimmed travel prospects at this end, I certainly hope you can get to Providence during the good weather! The local landscape can certainly keep you busy, & I think I could manage to raise enough cash to go the Boston-Salem-Marblehead rounds with you if you could (& would like to) arrange for a glimpse of the Arkham-Kingsport-Innsmouth countryside. You might like to do some digging at that genealogical joint in Boston, too. If your trip happened to be in late August or early September you might coincide with Moe or Morton, & thus ensure some pleasant sessions of general debate" (*FF* 339).

32. The collaborations undertaken by the two friends during their summer meetings in Florida are the literary spoof "The Battle That Ended the Century" (July 1934) and the fragmentary "Collapsing Cosmoses" (Summer 1935; later published by RHB in the second issue of *Leaves*, Winter 1938). The former was typed and mimeographed by RHB on his own press and distributed to mutual colleagues. HPL then provided the title and a substantial revision of "The Slaying of the Monster" (February 1933) and worked extensively on "The Hoard of the Wizard-Beast" (December 1933), probably a sequel to "The Sacred Bird," the fourth episode of RHB's *Annals of the Jinns*. The last two collaborations are the most mature and "cosmic" in flavor: "'Till A' the Seas'" was completed in January 1935 in New York by both authors, while "The Night Ocean" (1936) represents the second-to-last fictional piece on which HPL worked, during his last meeting with RHB in Providence in August 1936. (HPL wrote in his "death diary" a note dated 27 January 1937, concerning a "Rimel story" titled "From the Sea," which HPL returned to Duane W. Rimel in mid-February, with minor changes. However, "From the Sea" is non-extant, and likely was not published: therefore "The Night Ocean" can be considered the last *extant* fictional piece on which HPL held his revisory hand.)

cycle.[33] Barlow typeset many of the *Fungi*, with the intention to issue a booklet, but the project ultimately came to nothing.[34]

The reader of Lovecraft's correspondence to Barlow[35] realizes how impressed the Providence writer was with Barlow's promising qualities, and how much he felt at ease in disclosing to his pupil his innermost thoughts and beliefs. What emerges is the "unaffected friendship between a middle-aged man who already thinks of himself as a 'grandpa' and a teenage boy who could easily have been his son, and the literary and personal maturation of both under the influence of a multifaceted congeniality and mutual respect" (Joshi and Schultz, "Introduction," in *FF* xxiv). Their association grew consistently closer, and "Lovecraft's letters to Barlow are far more revelatory and intimate than those to many other colleagues"

---

33. It is remarkable to notice how HPL gave serious consideration to RHB's suggestions (let us remember that RHB was at the time seventeen years old). Not only did HPL, following RHB's advice, include the sonnet into the cycle, but he moved it from the last position (where he had placed it) to the third to the last (before "Evening Star" and "Continuity"), again complying with RHB's recommendation.

34. After almost a year had elapsed since RHB's proposal to publish the poetic cycle as a booklet, in late 1935 he presented HPL with a specimen page of the first sonnet. Later on, in 1936, RHB began to print the booklet of the *Fungi* under the imprint of the Dragon-Fly Press in DeLand, and went as far as compiling two sets of sheets, now preserved at the John Hay Library of Brown University. The first set of sheets—what Faig terms "Variant A"—contains HPL's corrections in pencils and was donated to the library by RHB himself, while the second sheet—"Variant B"—was presented to the library by August Derleth in 1961. For a detailed account of the various editorial events related to RHB's publication of the *Fungi* and of other weird books (notably of a planned collection of Clark Ashton Smith's poetry, *Incantations*), see Faig 1975. RHB also had in mind to publish "two additional slim volumes of HPL's verse—one of his best macabre poems apart from the 'Fungi' to be entitled *The Ancient Track* and another comprising a selection of his eighteen-century verse. Needless to say, RHB never began work on either project, but it might be noted that the organization of the ultimate *Collected Poems* published by Arkham House parallels precisely RHB's plans for the three volumes from his press" (Faig, "HPL: The Book That Nearly Was" 119). Another project that failed to materialize was RHB's attempt to bind sheets from HPL's tale "The Shunned House" (1924), which had been printed in 1928 by W. Paul Cook but not bound or distributed. The active role RHB played in the arrangement of HPL's works is also testified by the fact that it was RHB who provided the title for HPL's cycle of essays labeled "In Defence of Dagon" (*LAL* 212), for his series of advertising copy called "Commercial Blurbs" (*LAL* 356), and for his fictional fragment "The Book" (*LAL* 542). RHB even urged HPL to affix dates to the entries of the latter's *Commonplace Book* (*LAL* 232). In editing them, RHB often manipulated HPL's pieces: when he came to publish HPL's "Cats and Dogs" in the second issue of *Leaves* (1938), RHB "felt obligated to tone down some of HPL's more provocative (and only half-joking) political allusions" (*LAL* 412). From this brief overview alone, one can already easily infer how deep a connoisseur RHB was of HPL's work.

35. Now collected and published in full by S. T. Joshi and David E. Schultz in *O Fortunate Floridian: H. P. Lovecraft's Letters to R. H. Barlow* (Tampa, FL: University of Tampa Press, 2007).

(*FF* xxiii), perhaps also because the two friends were true lovers of the weird tale, so that they "could engage in unaffected discussion of the merits of authors and works all apart from the *business* of literature" (*FF* xxiii). About one hundred and sixty letters of Lovecraft's letters to Barlow are preserved (only seven from Barlow to Lovecraft survive), some of them particularly intimate, thoughtful, and revelatory. One dated February 1935 involved the sixteen-years-old Barlow in a mature discussion on the nature of art and aesthetics, on the value of subjectivity in aesthetic judgements, and on the notion of artistic pleasure or "enjoyment."[36] Lovecraft also held Barlow's imagination in high regard: in a letter of May 11, 1935, he mentioned having had a dream probably influenced by a plot-idea Barlow had submitted to him, and claimed he would probably use that idea in a story of his own.[37] Lovecraft, then, was convinced that young Barlow was mature enough to nurture brilliant ideas for serious aesthetic efforts in the weird field. However, their association was by no means a mainly professional one: though at the beginning their correspondence was "essentially one between teacher and pupil" (*UL* 196), the letters Lovecraft sent gradually became "longer and longer as the correspondence develops rapidly towards more of a dialogue than an instruction" (*UL* 196). Thanks to Lovecraft's generous availability and friendliness, Barlow gained confidence and even offered to provide his master with diverse services (such as the binding of an entire volume of *Weird Tales* [see *FF* 40]) and items, especially weird books and magazines.[38] And it must also be remarked that "the broadening of personal relationships did not work entirely in one direction: Barlow himself, taking the initiative to write to noted figures in the pulp world, occasionally introduced a new colleague to Lovecraft" (Joshi and Schultz, "Introduction," in *FF* xxiii), such as Catherine L. Moore and Wilson Shepherd. Increasingly complex subjects were discussed in their correspondence, upon topics as diverse as psychology (*FF* 362-68) and the future of the capitalistic system

---

36. Letter dated 10 February 1935 (*FF* 211). In the very same letter, HPL praised RHB's aesthetic tastes and sensitivity, equating the youth's education to that of his own older friends, Frank Belknap Long and James F. Morton.

37. "I had a very vivid dream fragment last night—perhaps in part derived from that extremely clever plot idea outlined toward the end of your letter. [. . .] Upon rising I made a note of the dream in my Black Book (whose present edition you so assiduously started)—& some day I may employ either that or your unadulterated suggestion in a story. Thanks for the idea—whether or not it caused the dream!" (*FF* 261).

38. Such as S. Fowler Wright's *Deluge: A Romance* (*FF* 74-75), Gustav Meyrink's *The Golem* (*FF* 216), A. Merritt's *The Metal Monster* (*FF* 104), etc. It was RHB who made HPL discover this last work, a masterpiece of cosmic horror that did not fail to arouse HPL's enthusiasm: "'Metal Monster' duly recd. & read—thanks a thousand times! [. . .] You are dead right about its merit—it surely *is* poignant & wondrous, & then some![. . .] I can see why Merritt believes it is in some ways his most powerful work [. . .] Altogether, the tale is one of the most striking evocations of absolutely unearthly conditions and experiences that I have ever seen. Perhaps the *most* striking [. . .] Again—profuse thanks!" (HPL, postcard to RHB, 3 March 1934; *FF* 113).

(FF 394-97). And, curiously, Lovecraft's correspondence to Barlow clearly reveals how both underwent a similar evolution in their political views: over the years Lovecraft gradually turned from the reactionary and conservative views of his youth to a moderate socialist and supporter of Franklin D. Roosevelt's New Deal, while Barlow went even further and became for a time a communist, as did several other of Lovecraft's younger colleagues, notably Frank Belknap Long.[39] Proof of the growing intimacy of their association is also supplied by the fact that Lovecraft began addressing Barlow with affectionately playful nicknames,[40] as was his habit with his closest correspondents.

In time, Barlow came to appreciate Lovecraft the man above all, more than the fantaisiste and the author of weird stories. In the final lines of the memoir "The Wind That Is in the Grass," he wrote:

> The fantasies he wrote have become models. As an unobtrusive guide treads knowingly the stair to an Etruscan tomb or a Zapotec chamber, Lovecraft conducts us by means of his dexterous prose to doorways of awe and wonder and flings them suddenly wide to us. But he was much more than a story writer [. . .] He is more important as a man who had the integrity to ignore the Machine Age and its levelling-out-to-rubble of life's rich irregularities, who had the courage to study and think and converse and write, in accordance with the deeper traditions of a more orderly age [. . .] His intimate acquaintance with astronomy, history, and literature, as well as a host of other interests, made him a civilizer among barbarians. (WG 362-63)

Lovecraft's choice, then, was not casual when, shortly before his death, in his "Instructions in Case of Decease," he appointed Barlow his literary executor and let him dispose of his papers and some personal effects. It is quite important to quote the exact words employed by Lovecraft in the document, in order to clarify

---

39. HPL poked fun at this attitude, which he considered a juvenile "weakness" of his "adopted sons." In two late letters to RHB, HPL addresses the issue of his pupil's and Long's adherence to Marxism and communism in a playful way: "The young rascal [Frank Belknap Long] seems to be rejoicing (in theory, whilst he piles up the capital) in your drift toward orthodox Marxism! Boys, boys!" (3 January 1937; FF 393). And in his last letter to RHB, dated 27 January 1937, before engaging in a lengthy discussion on the current world politico-economical situation and its possible future scenarios, this is how HPL refers to the issue of "bolshevism": "As for the bolshy business—you and Sonny [Frank Belknap Long] and Leedle Meestah Stoiling [Kenneth J. Sterling] will have to go some to make Grandpa swallow all the dogmatic blah which accompanies 'Marxist ideology'" (FF 395). RHB was also probably an active reader of the New Masses (1926-48), a leftist magazine founded by Piet Vlag and successor to the Masses (1911-18) and the Liberator (1918-24). RHB even tried to get HPL to read the magazine, but the latter found its contents "a bit too freakish & extreme to suit an old gentleman" (letter to RHB, 27 December 1936; FF 386).

40. Such as "Lord Ghu" (from the character of a Barlovian short tale, "The Fidelity of Ghu"), "Ten-Thousandth Incarnation of Garoth" (from RHB's episodic cycle "The Adventures of Garoth"), "Chief Apprentice of Maal Dweb," "Little Whiskerando," "Seventh Eye of Krang," adding the ineluctable qualifications "Invincible," "Mighty," "Venerable," "Omnipresent," etc.

the legitimacy of Barlow's subsequent actions concerning Lovecraft's literary "inheritance": "All files of weird magazines, scrap books not wanted by A. E. P. G. and all original mss. to R.H. Barlow, my literary executor" (CE 5.237).[41] After this opening statement (which conveys actual ownership on Barlow's part, not just provisional possession), there follows a short list of books and publications to be given to other people, and then we read: "After the preceding, first choice of all books, pictures, curios, and other articles to be had by R. H. Barlow" (CE 5.237). Lovecraft's decision to appoint Barlow his literary executor may have seemed incomprehensible to others, like Donald Wandrei, August W. Derleth, or Frank Belknap Long. In particular, August Derleth might have expected to be named Lovecraft's literary executor, "but it was Barlow who exhibited utter fascination with the full range of Lovecraft's work as a poet, essayist, and fiction writer, and his collector's instinct may have recommended itself to Lovecraft as well" (Joshi and Schultz, "Introduction," FF xxiv). An authoritative opinion on the matter was expressed by Clark Ashton Smith right after the news of Lovecraft's somehow "shocking" choice was revealed. Smith was convinced that the choice was dictated by exclusively "professional" reasons:

> [. . .] I believe it can be very readily explained. I do not believe it occurred to HPL that there was any prospect of his work being brought out by a professional publishing firm; and from this angle he would have felt that he was imposing a thankless and futile task on Belknap, Loveman, or any of the older friends. On the other hand, he would have felt that Barlow, with ambitions toward the establishment of a fine private press, might some day be in a position to print his work. This sounds logical to me. Certainly the choice shouldn't be taken as a slight to Belknap or others: HPL could only have thought that he was sparing them an embarrassment.[42]

Faig believes a major role was played by affection and personal esteem. In fact, the conclusion Faig draws is that the association between Lovecraft and Barlow had gone so far that "Barlow became something very close to a son for H. P. Lovecraft."[43] What is certain is that Lovecraft had detected in the still young Barlow a genial precocity and a remarkable "intuition" for literary matters. Lovecraft

---

41. A.E.P.G. stands for HPL's last surviving aunt, Annie E. Phillips Gamwell.

42. Letter to Donald Wandrei, 17 May 1937 (in Smith, Selected Letters 303). George Wetzel's essay "Lovecraft's Literary Executor" provides an illuminating discussion on the legal issues and quarrels following HPL's death and involving, for the resolution of the deceased's literary executorship, Robert Barlow, August Derleth, Donald Wandrei, HPL's aunt Annie Gamwell, and the HPL family lawyer Albert Baker.

43. Faig, UL 247. Perhaps we could also state that, given their similarities in temperament, HPL "saw in Barlow the same shy, awkward, bookish youth that he himself had been thirty years earlier" (Joshi and Schultz, "Introduction," FF xxiv). I also agree that personal affection, stemming from a "mutual love of fantasy, horror and science fiction, and some singular commonalities in character traits (love of cats, fondness for travel, and perhaps most significantly a shyness and social awkwardness that caused them to lead largely solitary lives)" (Joshi and Schultz, "Introduction," FF vii) played a major role in molding HPL's decision.

was convinced that Barlow could achieve a notable literary career and become one of the most prominent figures in the fantastic genre in American literature,[44] as well as a distinguished publisher and promoter of the genre,[45] had he not chosen to pursue another career.

On 12 March 1937, Mrs. Gamwell had informed Barlow by letter of Lovecraft's illness and entrance into the Jane Brown Memorial Hospital two days earlier. She lamented her nephew's poor state of health and remarked on his stoic bearing of the pain. Barlow received the letter on March 14 and immediately telegraphed to Mrs. Gamwell that he would come to help and provide assistance. On the evening of March 15 she sent him a reply telegram announcing Lovecraft's death early that morning.[46] Barlow, informed that he had been appointed Lovecraft's literary executor, shortly thereafter traveled to Providence by bus. Lovecraft had, on March 18, been interred in Swan Point Cemetery. Mrs. Gamwell handed to Barlow a longhand copy she herself had made of the "Instructions" document Lovecraft had compiled, naming Barlow his literary executor. She wished to keep the original draft.[47] While still in Providence in late March 1937, Barlow faithfully fulfilled his master's "Instructions," sending one book as far as Polynesia. Then he packed for shipment to Kansas City some of the Lovecraft manuscripts he had not yet copied (mostly notes and juvenilia, which he found in a metal box under an armchair), together with about 150 books from Lovecraft's library (which overall comprised about 2000 volumes). By April 2 Barlow had gone back to Kansas City, where he was studying. In the following years, legitimately performing the tasks ensuing from his "position," Barlow systematically deposited the bulk of Lovecraft's papers and manuscripts in the John Hay Library of Brown University (which at the beginning was not very enthusiastic about the acquisition of materials belonging to a then obscure pulp fiction writer), simultaneously urging other colleagues to donate their letters from Love-

---

44. "He is one of the most brilliant youths I have ever met; & as soon as maturity enables him to centralise his abundant scattered energies in one definite field (& I tend to think more & more that *literature* is the one best adapted to him, despite his many other aptitudes), he will begin to produce notable work" (HPL, letter to Elizabeth Toldridge, 6 October 1936; SL 5.316).

45. According to Joshi, RHB's brilliance as a connoisseur of the weird genre showed also in his "mature awareness of the importance of preserving literary documents, even those that might not then appear to have value" ("Introduction," OLL 5–6).

46. See "The Last Days of H. P. Lovecraft. Four Documents," *Lovecraft Studies* No. 28 (Spring 1993): 36: "HOWARD DIED THIS MORNING NOTHING TO DO THANKS."

47. Only the longhand copy by Mrs. Gamwell survives, preserved at the John Hay Library of Brown University. She rendered the phrase "literary executive," an apparent mistake. As RHB himself retold, Mrs. Gamwell already discovered this document as HPL was writing it: "When I arrived in Providence in March of 1937 [. . .], Mrs. Gamwell showed me a group of personal papers kept in a cabinet in his room, and took out one which she had been horrified to see him [HPL] write by chance a few months before" (WG 361).

craft to the library. In fact he believed that, though Lovecraft had given him actual ownership of his own manuscripts, they should be housed in a public repository. He also felt that his "many removals were endangering the papers" (WG 362) and therefore decided to deposit them in the library, together with microfilm materials and Lovecraft's file of *Weird Tales* (1923-37), augmented with his own copies of the magazine to fill in any gaps in Lovecraft's holdings, as well as issues published after Lovecraft's death. Moreover, in the late 1930s and early 1940s Barlow never failed to lend as much assistance as he could to editors August Derleth and Donald Wandrei with their pioneering Arkham House editions of Lovecraft's work,[48] though several regrettable misunderstandings occurred concerning the respective roles the two parties were intended to play in the preservation, publication, and promotion of Lovecraft's oeuvre. The origin of these misunderstandings must be at least partly looked for in the events immediately following Lovecraft's death. Barlow started to be perceived by those—such as Donald Wandrei and to a less degree August Derleth—who did not know him well (and whom he apparently failed to notify of the existence of the "Instructions" document), as an opportunist: they felt "he should not have taken the books from HPL's library, but instead have let them be so that HPL's aunt might benefit financially from their sale."[49] In particular Wandrei, who was a longtime friend of Smith and had previously met Barlow, "developed a strong dislike for [Barlow], which [he] made evident in his correspondence with [Clark Ashton Smith], warning [Smith] against future dealings with [Barlow],"[50] and spreading

---

48. Both Derleth and Donald Wandrei got written permission (a sort of blanket grant) from RHB to both pursue *The Outsider and Others* and to sell HPL's stories to other venues. However, probably Derleth and Wandrei dealt mostly with Mrs. Gamwell, since the checks for these sales went directly to her.

49. See Smith, *Selected Letters* 324n1. Of course RHB had the right to do what he did, but Derleth felt he should have left the books.

50. Ibid. In fairness to Donald Wandrei, we should acknowledge that even today the issue of the legality of RHB's own position within the Lovecraft estate has not been clarified. "Executor" is in fact a clearly defined legal position within an estate, and in this case it was Mrs. Gamwell. "Literary executor" is another matter altogether, one probably not recognized by Rhode Island probate law. Even if such a position did exist, normal state law would likely require it to be held by someone who lived within the State—at least that is true of "executors." Moreover, at the time he was appointed, RHB was a minor and, as such, not permitted to sign or be bound to contracts, the very job for which a literary executor would be needed. In any case, on 26 March 1937, the document was made legally cogent by an affidavit probated in a Providence court: this affidavit and its terms seem to prove that the document was considered legally valid by Rhode Island courts. However, what likely happened was that the Lovecraft Circle chose to accept RHB as literary executor (that is, not challenge the title) while simultaneously stripping him of all authority. Derleth was a central figure in this development. He worked with RHB, but only as it would further his own ends. At the same time, he bore RHB no animosity and was content to let him remain a figurehead and give him a boost to his ego whenever he needed him. Derleth actually "pushed Barlow out of the way and became HPL's de facto literary executor, claiming (with doubtful legality) that *he*

"numerous rumours about Barlow's supposed nefariousness to many colleagues" (Joshi and Schultz, "Introduction," *FF* xix). Certainly Wandrei succeeded in alienating Clark Ashton Smith's sympathies from Barlow, in spite of an early admiration the Auburn writer nurtured toward the young Robert.[51] Already in a letter of mid-May 1937, Smith wrote to Wandrei that "Barlow's delays in turning over mss. must have been provoking" (Smith 303). Smith did not seem to hesitate as to what side to take in the Derleth/Wandrei-Barlow "controversy": he even wrote of "rascality" on Barlow's part (Smith 323), and expressed his incredulity at Groo Beck's involvement in Barlow's dishonest plots: "What shocks and astounds me, however, is the thought that Beck, who, from what I have seen of him, struck me as being an honest, somewhat naïve and dreamy youth, should be implicated in such scullduggery [*sic*]. Isn't there a chance that he has been used as a sort of cat's paw by Barlow, and does not realize the moral obliquity involved in taking from Mrs. Gamwell the books, magazines and other matter that would be of such value to her in her present need?" (Smith, *Selected Letters* 323). And re-

---

owned Lovecraft's literary rights" (Joshi and Schultz, "Introduction," *FF* xix). The only problem was represented by Donald Wandrei. His hatred of RHB was intense and he lost perspective. Even when RHB was fully cooperating, Wandrei was insistent that RHB get no credit; that his name not even appear inside the covers of an Arkham House book. Derleth walked the tightrope between them, and did it well. Sadly, Wandrei did succeed in turning many people, including Clark Ashton Smith, against both RHB and the Beck Brothers. The result is that neither RHB nor the Becks were ever able to contribute to the field in the way they could have. The exact reasons for Wandrei's personal hatred for RHB are still open to speculation, but two important reasons are certainly the mishandling (more perceived than real) of Howard Wandrei's artwork during an ill-fated reprint venture, and the actions of a Beck boy (probably Claire) who had kept a Providence visit of his a secret even though he had been socializing with Wandrei, Derleth, and the New York gang just a few days before. Though sharing the same long-term goals as Wandrei, Derleth was much more professional—and at least successful—in his dealings with RHB, who in a couple of years turned over almost all the HPL materials in his possession. According to Dwayne Olson, "Barlow got a raw deal, but I also think he brought a lot of it on himself. Bob was a naïve, not terribly well-adjusted 17 year-old when he was named 'literary executor'. He wandered into a hornet's nest of people who were much older, didn't know him personally, and didn't trust him (and, one might add, felt some jealousy towards the exalted position he had attained in HPL's life). Sadly, he did not acquit himself well. Within days, the whole of the NY crew saw him as a danger to HPL's legacy and wanted him out of the way. An older Barlow could have probably finessed the situation, but 17-year Bobby could not" (personal communication). Regarding Howard Wandrei, he was alternately appalled by RHB and hopeful that he might turn out all right given his age and experience. Overall though, naturally he tended to side with his brother. When asked to provide a cover for an issue of the *Acolyte*, Howard hesitated when he saw that RHB's name was somehow associated. He wrote to Derleth to ask his opinion, and then, only after Derleth's approval, provided the artwork.

51. For example, in an early letter to RHB dated 30 October 1932, HPL mentions Smith's admiration toward RHB's pictorial skills: "Smith spoke of seeing your drawings, & said he thought they showed genuine promise" (*FF* 42).

garding the publication of his own volume of verse, *Incantations*, Smith began to feel uneasy: "The whole business finds me in a very awkward situation, since I had consented to the issuing of a small edition of my unpublished verse volume, *Incantations*, by the Beck brothers. It is, in fact, possible that work has already begun on this project by Groo Beck. [. . .] I do not relish the idea of having the book brought out by people who could, knowingly, be guilty of such turpitude as you have indicated" (ibid.). As the last words of this quotation show, Smith's opinion of Barlow was certainly influenced by Wandrei's negative propaganda.[52] Smith even decided to withdraw his *Incantations* manuscripts from the Becks with the excuse of a need for revision, and, fearing the possibility of Barlow's "looting" his own items,[53] ensured through an holographic will that his own collections of books, manuscripts, pictures, and art objects were going to be bequeathed to Mrs. Genevieve K. Sully after Smith's death.[54] In December 1938, once he got his verse manuscripts back, Smith had apparently to say a last word about Beck and Barlow. He did not want to hear from them anymore: "I [. . .] have no intention of communicating with them, or replying to any possible communications of theirs. Barlow wrote me a card some days ago, saying that they were now ready to

---

52. A major role in Smith's early acceptance of Wandrei's negative views on RHB was also played by the fact that Smith had known Wandrei longer than he had known RHB: "Knowing you as I have known you all these years, I cannot but believe that you have incontrovertible reasons for what you say" (Smith, letter to Wandrei, 30 September 1938; *Selected Letters* 323).

53. A fear certainly unfounded, since not only had RHB never really "looted" any Lovecraftian item, but he had always shown honesty and fairness in dealing with the items of his "masters." For instance, one could mention the exchange RHB had had with A. Merritt in the summer of 1937, when asking the famous writer permission to reprint his story "People of the Pit" in the first issue of *Leaves*. Merritt gave the permission but advised RHB to contact the Munsey editor Albert J. Gibney, who still held the rights to the tale, which was printed in 1918 in a Munsey magazine. Merritt himself offered to send RHB a note in support of his request. This is how RHB, in a very correct and honest way, addressed Gibney in letter: "Dear Sir, I am enclosing a letter from Mr. Merritt, in which he gives me permission (so far as he is concerned) to republish the People of the Pit [. . .] which appeared in All Story in 1918, in an anthology or annual magazine of fantastic stories by various writers. [. . .] It is being issued in an edition of 100 copies, for private circulation. If you would be so kind as to give me permission to use the story in question, I should be infinitely obliged" (RHB's letter to Albert J. Gibney, July 1937; Moskowitz 308). Not surprisingly, RHB secured permission to reprint Merritt's tale.

54. Mrs. Sully, in her turn influenced by the general opinions on RHB, started to develop a suspicious attitude toward him: "She has, by the way, expressed repeatedly her suspicions of RHB, and an antipathy toward him, and was in no way surprised when I read your letter to her last night" (Smith, letter to Donald Wandrei, 30 September 1938; *Selected Letters* 324). Mrs. Sully was a longtime lover and patron of Smith: they originally met in 1919, when she was living in Auburn, and had an affair that lasted more than thirty years. For some time Sully even provided Smith "with a regular stipend" (Ruber 58). Smith also dedicated to Sully his short story collection *Out of Space and Time* (1942). Mrs. Sully was the mother of Helen V. Sully, a correspondent of HPL.

begin work on the book. This card I consigned to the stove. I hope sincerely that neither Barlow nor Beck will try to see me in person" (*Selected Letters* 325). And in order to make sure this wish could become true, Smith, in reply to Barlow's repeated attempts to arrange a meeting,[55] sent him a lapidary message: "R. H. Barlow: Please do not write to me or try to communicate with me in any way. I do not wish to see you or hear from you after your conduct in regard to the estate of a late beloved friend. Clark Ashton Smith" (quoted in *OLL* 21n33). Barlow literally "gasped" (*OLL* 21) at reading these unexpected and shocking words by his erstwhile idol. Further developments certainly occurred in the Barlow-Smith relationship that helped to straighten it out, though little evidence is available for their detailed reconstruction. Yet what we do know is that Barlow finally visited Smith in Auburn not much later, on 28 December 1941, "a reconciliation having been arranged by E. Hoffmann Price."[56]

However, Barlow's life was to take other directions, because of the death of his mentor[57] and of Barlow's own uprooting from Florida due to family troubles. Already in the winter of 1938 Barlow virtually "removed himself from the scene" (Joshi, "Introduction" to *OLL* 7) of Lovecraft executorship, though it is hardly questionable that had Lovecraft survived longer, Barlow would have pursued either a literary or a publishing career, or both: the influence of his mentor, as we will see in the textual analysis, was a truly conspicuous and significant one, as the adult Barlow candidly admitted in his memoir "The Wind That Is in the Grass," where Lovecraft is described as "the man who virtually moulded my intellectual life and many of my tastes and habits" (*WG* 362). Thus, Barlow's professional and private life can be roughly split into two halves, the watershed being represented by Lovecraft's death, which occurred on 15 March 1937. At this time Barlow was studying at the Kansas City Art Institute. Faig agrees that "a break with the past was apparent almost immediately after Lovecraft's death" (*UL* 209), since Barlow ceased quite soon to buy the pulps he once used to collect for Yoh-Vombis.

Nevertheless, after Lovecraft's death Barlow published two large issues of his mimeographed amateur journal, *Leaves* (the first while in Leavenworth, Kansas, in the summer of 1937, and the second while in Lakeport, California, in the win-

---

55. "I had written him three times hoping to visit him at non-very-distant Auburn, and had lain out on the hillside memorizing Coleridge to recite to him" ("Autobiography," *OLL* 21). At the time, RHB was living in Lakeport, California, with the Beck brothers.

56. Smith, *Selected Letters* 338n2. RHB was supposed to have gone to Auburn on December 27 with Paul Freehafer, Robert A. ("Rah") Hoffmann, Henry Hasse, and Emil Petaja, all fans from Los Angeles. But RHB was delayed in Berkeley, where he was studying at the time, and made it up the next day on his own. So far, it has not been ascertained what happened on that day, but Smith did allow RHB to take photographs of many of his paintings, of which Rah Hoffmann has the negatives (Scott Connors, personal communication).

57. According to Joshi, "the death of Lovecraft in 1937 significantly curbed RHB's enthusiasm both as a writer and as a publisher" ("Recognition" 49), and "it was this, as much as his later inability to work harmoniously with Derleth and Wandrei, that caused Barlow's retreat from fantasy" (ibid.).

ter of 1938/39),[58] the second of which contained Barlow's outstanding story "Origin Undetermined" and "probably marks the definitive end of Barlow's activity within fandom as editor and publisher" (*UL* 204). In fact, Barlow "had been railing against the low quality of the pulps for some years, and made quite a strong attack in the first issue of *Leaves*, but the cessation of collecting activity definitely heralds a significant break with the past." (*UL* 209). However, Barlow's activity as Lovecraft's literary executor continued in time: after returning to Kansas City from Providence in April 1937, Barlow "seems to have launched into a determined preparation of H.P.L.'s remaining manuscripts for publication" (*UL* 207). In the period 1937–42, new deposits of Lovecraft materials that Barlow and others had transcribed continued to flow into the John Hay Library. With Mrs. Gamwell, Barlow exchanged an extensive correspondence until 1940 (Mrs. Gamwell died in 1941), concerning the arrangement of Lovecraft's literary estate. In March 1939, Barlow signed an agreement with the John Hay Library according to which, at Barlow's death, the library would come into possession of the Lovecraft manuscripts deposited there. According to Faig, "By October 1942, Barlow was completely cleaned out of Lovecraft manuscripts, with the exception of 'The Shadow Out of Time'" (*UL* 207).[59] Also, as we have seen, Barlow took care that Lovecraft's file of *Weird Tales* reached the John Hay Library.[60]

---

58. These issues were a sort of posthumous homage RHB paid to HPL, since the contents of the journal had been planned together with HPL "during the balmy Florida days" (*UL* 236). The first issue of *Leaves* contained about eighty pages "of closely typed fiction and poetry" (*UL* 204), including fantasy material written by RHB himself, Clark Ashton Smith, Robert E. Howard, Edith Miniter, A. Merritt, Frank Belknap Long, August Derleth, Donald Wandrei, C. L. Moore, and others, as well as Lovecraft's essay "Cats and Dogs" (published under the pseudonym "Lewis Theobald, Jr.").

59. But it was indirectly thanks to RHB that, in 1995, the original manuscript for "The Shadow out of Time" was rediscovered and made available for the first time. RHB had received the manuscript from HPL during the latter's second visit to DeLand in 1935, after HPL had given up any attempt to submit the tale for serious publication, due to his professional doubts about the tale's merits. HPL had already destroyed the first draft of the story and threatened to destroy also the second. Thus RHB secretly typed it and gave HPL the typescript in exchange for the original notebook in which the story had been pencilled. RHB produced an 88-page typescript that was, however, full of errors. RHB's transcription then circulated among HPL's colleagues, and Donald Wandrei took pains to deliver the text to *Astounding Stories*, where the tale was promptly accepted for publication. Years passed and RHB took the original Lovecraft manuscript with him in Mexico, because he felt he had some rights on it, since his preparation of the typescript led directly to its publication. In fact in his 1944 memoir, RHB felt the urge to justify his decision to retain this manuscript: "He [HPL] agreed that under certain circumstances manuscripts could justifiably be taken away from their authors, and this was certainly the case with the 'Shadow', for I had it copied, and later on Donald Wandrei submitted it for publication, both without consulting Lovecraft" (*WG* 362). Shortly before RHB's death, he entrusted the manuscript to a student in Mexico City College, one June Evelyn Riply, who had entered the college in 1950 in a postgraduate program to study Náhuatl language. RHB and Riply developed a

Barlow also supervised, when visiting the Beck brothers in Lakeport, California, the publication of Lovecraft's *Notes and Commonplace Book* under the imprint of the Futile Press (May and June 1938),[61] as well as a collection of George Sterling's poetry, *After Sunset*,[62] in 1939.

---

short though intense professional relationship. Riply remained another seven years in Mexico, where she taught English, and then moved back to California and taught at the Marin College of Kentfield from 1981 to 1993, when she retired. Only upon her death, which occurred on 28 December 1994, and thanks to the good offices of Riply's brother-in-law, Mr. Nelson Shreve, was it possible to unearth HPL's manuscript and read the original text, which was then donated to the John Hay Library in January 1995. It was an important discovery, since, by HPL's own testimony, the version published in *Astounding Stories* was corrupt. Initially, upon reading the published version, and in contrast to what he had done for the printed version of *At the Mountains of Madness*, HPL surprisingly told RHB he was satisfied of the version of "The Shadow out of Time" as published by *Astounding*: "It doesn't seem even nearly as badly mangled as the Mts. . . . . . so you may congratulate yourself on *your* story!" (letter to RHB, 4 June 1936; *FF* 335). However, HPL later admitted to other correspondents that "I fear Barlow's text had many errors, some of which greatly misrepresent my style—since I recall doing quite a bit of correction on my copy" (letter to August Derleth, 23 October 1936; *Essential Solitude* 2.711). In truth, the version of the tale published by Tremaine in *Astounding* was severely altered even in comparison to the text typed by RHB and corrected by HPL: for example, in the paragraphing, in a few stylistical choices, and in the punctuation (but no cuts had been made, as indeed had happened for the *Mts.*). It is likely that HPL did not complain too much of the corrupted version of the "Shadow" in *Astounding* out of the sheer gratitude he felt toward RHB (for having typed the long tale) and Wandrei (for having sold it). However, HPL corrected the text published on *Astounding* (as he had already done for *At the Mountains of Madness*) directly in his copy of the issue, but was able to remove only a fraction of the mistakes, since he did not have access to his original manuscript, which was entrusted to RHB: his corrections were made from memory. The discovery of the original manuscript allowed Hippocampus Press to publish the corrected text of "The Shadow out of Time" in 2001.

60. At the time of his death, RHB still had with him in Mexico many of those books he removed from HPL's library in 1937, his correspondence from HPL, and probably many manuscripts and other Lovecraft items. Other fantasy material was stored in the Florida family house, where his mother had returned after RHB's college days in California. George T. Smisor, appointed RHB's literary executor, took possession of the RHB materials in Mexico and contacted Mrs. Barlow regarding the Florida collection. Already in January 1951, he also wrote to the John Hay Library to offer the entire collection, but no arrangement was made (for these and more details, see *UL* 208).

61. 75 numbered copies were printed, but half of them remained unbound. Actually RHB just edited the text. Faig claims that "Derleth was not pleased by the appearance of the Futile Press edition of HPL's *Commonplace Book*" ("HPL: The Book That Nearly Was" 122n3), and "the bitter controversy over HPL's books and magazines worsened the personal relations between Barlow and Derleth" (ibid.). As a matter of fact, Donald Wandrei and Derleth were trying to get HPL's work published by a major New York firm, and to do that they needed to be able to present themselves as having the legal authority to do so. Unfortunately, they didn't have this, RHB did, and he was not only not in a position to

In the spring of 1939 Barlow went to San Francisco, where he got in touch with a group of "activist" poets led by Lawrence Hart in the Bay Area. Barlow was still quite unsure about what he wanted to do with his life; he was classified 4F for U.S. military service, and thus was freed from that obligation. According to George T. Smisor, Barlow began to focus his attentions on ancient Mexican anthropology, as a result of a brief study-tour he had made in Mexico in the summer of 1938. In the spring of 1939, while in San Francisco, Barlow was advised by a psychologist, Dr. Barbara Mayer, a member of the National Youth Administration, to enroll in a course in Mexican anthropology at the local Polytechnic Institute. Mayer had understood Barlow's maladjustment and advised him to pursue scholarship in the anthropological field—an "activity congenial to him from his publishing and bibliophile days"[63]—his life's work. Barlow was immediately fascinated with the study of the native peoples of Mexico and thus began serious study at the Polytechnic Institute in San Francisco in order to gain the prerequisites of his chosen career. In the summer of 1940 he enrolled in the National University Summer School in Mexico City, studying Náhuatl, the ancient Indian language of the Valley of Mexico, under the guidance of the scholar Wigberto Jimenez Moreno. While attending this course, Barlow first met Smisor as a fellow student.[64] In 1941 Barlow obtained a B.A. degree in anthropology at the University of Cali-

---

effect this, he was in effect passing away HPL into the fan press. When the Futile Press published the *Notes and Commonplace Book*, over Derleth's objections, RHB wrote the Beck brothers to ignore any screechings from Sauk City, since he, RHB, called the shots, not Derleth or Wandrei. Wandrei was concerned that RHB might screw up the deal with Scribner's or some other New York publisher by writing and asserting his literary executorship: in other words, just by existing as HPL's literary executor, RHB could sabotage *The Outsider and Others*. Wandrei was especially concerned with getting Albert Baker, HPL's executor, to revoke RHB's status and give it to Wandrei and Derleth, and to this end he turned Smith against RHB (and the Beck brothers), culminating in the withdrawal of the *Incantations* manuscript. However, according to Faig, RHB and Derleth "quickly acted to make clear their co-operation in the issuance of HPL's surviving aunt Mrs. Gamwell, who had been badly distressed by the controversy" (ibid.). According to Faig, "By the mid-forties cordiality seems to have been restored between Barlow and Derleth" (ibid.).

62. This book was actually simply compiled by RHB from a manuscript owned by John Howell, a bookseller. RHB candidly stated that "ninety percent of the work" on this edition was made by Groo Beck ("Autobiography," *OLL* 23), though RHB provided a brief introductory note to it. The book bore the imprint of John Howell, but RHB and Beck considered it the first publication of their "Druid Press," which never actually published anything else (*UL* 231).

63. *UL* 216-17. According to Smisor, Mayer "even suggested Mexican anthropology, introduced him [RHB] to the leading California professors in this field, and encouraged him to pursue such courses at the local junior college" (quoted in *UL* 217).

64. RHB and Smisor recalled how the Náhuatl course met at 8 o'clock in the chilly Mexican morning, and of how "we forgot the cold drafts in our classroom in the enthusiasm to learn a half-legendary and difficult language from an eminent scholar" (RHB and Smisor, "Introduction" to *Nombre de Dios Durango* [1943]; quoted in *UL* 217).

fornia at Berkeley, and in the fall he began working at the anthropology department of the same institution, under Dr. Alfred L. Kroeber, soon achieving the status of research assistant. Meanwhile, after working with Barlow in some Mexican libraries, Smisor and his wife followed Barlow to Berkeley. By 1942 Barlow was conducting full-time research on Mexican native peoples, and in a letter of 25 February 1942 to Professor S. Foster Damon of Brown University concerning Lovecraftian matters, Barlow complained of the press of academic affairs and compared himself to the lonesome academe living in an ivory tower and suffering from "agoraphobia," or fear of open and crowded spaces.[65] In 1942 Barlow published his first scholarly article, in *American Notes and Queries*, and made frequent trips to Mexico to consult rare documents and hunt for undiscovered materials. By the end of 1943 he had moved permanently to Mexico City, where he resided until his untimely death. It was in Mexico, in 1944, that Barlow wrote his fragmentary "Autobiography," covering the period between the winter of 1938 and the summer of 1940, an effort undertaken as a complement to the psychoanalytic sessions he took in San Francisco under the guidance of Dr. Emanuel Windholz. In these autobiographical pages, Barlow, besides openly revealing his sensitive nature and the torments of his life,[66] faced his homosexuality quite frankly (an ori-

---

65. For this and following information, see *UL* 218.

66. "I have still many of the deep doubts and unhappinesses which have made my heart a Warsaw since earliest childhood" ("Autobiography," *OLL* 19). In his account, almost every activity RHB tried to start and pursue, even the most rewarding and satisfying, is described as being troubled by psychological obstacles: when asked by Dr. Mayer to "compile a guide book on free recreational activities in San Francisco" (*OLL* 24), RHB was brought to see "much in San Francisco I had not known" (ibid.), and "it amused me more than any other job I had had" (ibid.). However, "The actual writing was difficult: as always psychological obstacles intervened" (ibid.). We will probably never be completely sure whether the following words already adumbrate suicidal intentions on RHB's part in 1944, but they unquestionably hint at a sense of distress: "a subtle feeling that my curious and uneasy life is not destined to prolong itself" (*OLL* 19). What is certain is that, already in spring 1939, while living in San Francisco, RHB was troubled by a strong depression, even though he enjoyed the company of Clyde Beck, the most cultivated of the Beck brothers. And according to RHB's words, "it was Clyde's company, perhaps, that kept me from suicide" (*OLL* 22). And in a letter dated 3 March 1939, and addressed to the John Hay Library of Brown University, RHB—then a young man of not even twenty-one—was already thinking over his own death: "All manuscripts of whatever nature, deposited by me in the Harris collection (Manuscript division) at the John Hay Library, are in the event of my death to become the property of that institution" (quoted in Joshi, "Recognition" 50). In his "Autobiography," RHB drops several hints, perhaps only half-consciously, as to his psychological distresses. One aspect of the social maladjustment he must have felt during his entire life is revealed by his fear of loneliness, and the related attitude that he describes as "mood of gregariousness": "A chasm of loneliness opens alongside my paths of study, and a pebble is enough to betray my foot. I delight in the presence of many people; I can end a conversation only by effort, can never get rid of a visitor, and when I have seduced people by wining and dining them into cheering the house with their voices, I hope they will never leave" (*OLL* 20).

entation he never manifested to Lovecraft),[67] allowing an insight on his particularly sensitive and depressive personality, which he perhaps inherited from his father. Tellingly, the account ends at the time of Barlow's heading toward Mexico, where he was to inaugurate the most professionally successful and prolific period of his short life, though during the 1940s he did not cut himself completely out of the weird fiction community.[68]

In Mexico, Barlow devoted himself to teaching in various schools and colleges, and to anthropological research concerning the local native cultures and languages, in particular the ethno-history and ancient history of the Valley of Mexico. Barlow's career as a scholar was much more than promising: he came to master the Náhuatl language and became researcher and professor at the Universidad Nacional Autonoma de Mexico and subsequently at the Universidad de las Americas (then known as Mexico City College). In the latter institution he served as chair-

---

67. See *LAL* 582, according to which Barlow's homosexuality "had presumably not yet made itself evident," and de Camp 392 ("His sexual aberration [sic] [...] may not have developed until near the end of Lovecraft's life"). The somewhat disturbing use of the word "aberration" in this context is of course revelatory of de Camp's mindset. In a letter to August Derleth dated 16 February, 1933, Lovecraft explicitly condemned homosexuality, on the basis of its being "naturally (physically and involuntarily—not merely 'morally' or aesthetically) repugnant to the overwhelming bulk of mankind" (*Essential Solitude* 2.546). In the *Gaylactic Gayzette* of Winter 1991, dedicated to the analysis of the homosexual element in Lovecraft's fiction, Franklin Hummel discusses the HPL-RHB relationship from the latter's viewpoint. Hummel, in contrast with Joshi and de Camp, claims that it is likely that Barlow "was aware of his homosexuality while Lovecraft was alive" (27a), though certainly Lovecraft "had no knowledge that Barlow was homosexual." However, had that been the case, Hummel believes that Lovecraft and Barlow "would have remained friends" (ibid.), since although Lovecraft "repeatedly demonstrated a great deal of prejudice [...] he also showed an unquestioning acceptance of and loyalty for his friends" (ibid.). Hummel's most interesting—and controversial—point is that "the emotional relationship between Barlow and Lovecraft was one which, for Robert Barlow, was love" (28). However, Hummel's arguments are too thinly supported by any evidence (not a single line by Barlow in his available fiction, poetry, or memoirs points in this direction) to be credited with more than a passing reference. Whatever Barlow's feeling toward Lovecraft was, we cannot but agree with Faig that Lovecraft's attitude toward Barlow was that of a father to a son ("Robert H. Barlow became something very close to a son for H. P. Lovecraft": *UL* 247).

68. For instance, in 1940 some short prose poems RHB wrote in spring 1939 appeared in the fanzine *Polaris*. Moreover, in the years 1942-46 RHB contributed stories and articles to the *Acolyte* (edited by Francis T. Laney), *Golden Atom* (ed. by Larry B. Farsaci), and others. In 1943 he assisted in the preparation of the first HPL bibliography by Francis T. Laney and William H. Evans. In 1944 he even wrote the introduction to the Arkham House edition of Henry S. Whitehead's *Jumbee and Other Uncanny Tales* (RHB had admired Whitehead since his teen years and long discussed this Floridian author's work with HPL). In the same year he also contributed the memoir "The Wind That Is in the Grass" for the Arkham edition of the Lovecraftian miscellany volume *Marginalia*.

man of the Department of Anthropology from 1948 until his death. At that time, the institution was still quite young, but already able to attract leading scholars in the field such as Pablo Martinez del Rio, Ignacio Bernal, Wigberto Jimenez Moreno, and Fernando Horcasita Pimentel. Barlow gave courses on topics as diverse as the ancient history of Mexico, Mexican anthropology, modern Náhuatl, codices, source materials in ancient Mexican history, and bibliography. He also lectured to scholarly societies and worked temporarily at libraries such as the Benjamin Franklin in Mexico City (where, thanks to Barlow's recommendation, Smisor was appointed head of the Microfilm Laboratory in 1945). Barlow's achievements in the field were widely recognized and appreciated,[69] to such an extent that his research work was funded by grants from the Rockefeller Foundation in 1944-45, the Guggenheim Foundation for the following two years, and the Division of Historical Research of the Carnegie Institution of Washington, which also allowed him to study the Mayan culture in the Yucatan peninsula. In the course of his scholarly activity, Barlow published about 150 books,[70] articles, pamphlets—many of which written in collaboration with George T. Smisor—and "is still regarded as a pioneer in the study of Náhuatl and the native Indian cultures of Mexico" (Joshi, "Introduction," OLL 8-9). Nonetheless, while in Mexico Barlow did not forget his former master H. P. Lovecraft: on 30 June 1946, he corresponded with the John Hay Library of Brown University, proposing to send the library "the entirety of his remaining fantasy collection—including the 150 or so books he selected from Lovecraft's library at the time of H.P.L.'s death and the vast holdings of Yoh-Vombis stored in Florida—in return for a printing press and type for a Náhuatl newspaper he was at the time undertaking in Mexico" (UL 208). But the project, of course telling of Barlow's "shift in his intellectual perspective,"[71] ultimately came to nothing, since Barlow found the press outfit elsewhere.

---

69. "His ability to gain a rapid competence in any area he set out to investigate was almost phenomenal. He had a fluent speaking knowledge of Náhuatl, an accomplishment rare even among Mexican scholars. In the last year of his life, he began to investigate the Mayan culture and language, and after a very brief period of book study and a trip to the Yucatan he returned with a good, if imprecise, knowledge of Mayan. In preparation for a trip to Europe in 1948 to investigate codices in Paris and London, he provided himself with a working knowledge of French in but a few days" (UL 225).

70. One of his most groundbreaking monographic works is *The Extent of the Empire of the Culhua-Mexica*, researched from March to December 1943 thanks to the grant received from Berkeley. This scholarly masterpiece gave voice to RHB's interest in the study of the native peoples of the Valley of Mexico, those once ruled by the Aztec Empire (which RHB more correctly termed "Culhua-Mexica"). The book was extensively revised by RHB over the years before finding final publication in 1949 under the imprint of the University of California Press; it was reprinted in 1978 by AMS Press (see UL 224-25).

71. Joshi, "Recognition" 50. In his letter to the library, RHB admitted he had built his fantasy collection "with such pains and enthusiasm, unconsciously building it around HPL's personality, *& leaving it almost at once on his death*" (UL 209; italics added).

And in fact, Barlow and Smisor were committed to various publishing projects. Within their plan to issue at least a representative sample of the Indian codices scattered in many libraries in and out of Mexico, they also published a small book titled *Nombre de Dios, Durango: Two Documents in Náhuatl Concerning its Foundation* (1943), which contained two valuable original testimonies on the foundation of the town of Nombre de Dios in Durango (the English versions of the Náhuatl and the index were by Smisor, while the footnotes and the map were by Barlow). The project resulted in a 130-copy edition under the imprint of the "House of Tlaloc," from the name of the ancient god of rain. Smisor had been a printing teacher in the Sacramento City Schools, and probably arranged for the issuance of the publication. He also provided the English translation from the Spanish and Náhuatl text (1845) of the Indian lawyer Chimalpopoco Galicia, who copied it from the earlier Indian texts of the sixteenth century. The book was quite unorthodox, with the text in Náhuatl, Spanish, and English on each pair of facing pages. Prior to the twentieth century, the great bulk of material that had been published in Náhuatl consisted of utilitarian grammars and religious texts; Barlow and Smisor selected the documents to publish in their book as representative of the numerous historical texts that remained unprinted. The book was well received and encouraged Barlow and Smisor to undertake the more ambitious project of issuing scholarly journals that would have as their principal purpose the publication of such texts. In fact, they also founded a journal, *Tlalocan* (meaning "Tlaloc's kingdom or domain"), devoted to the publication and study of source materials in the Náhuatl language on the native cultures of Mexico, which continued after Barlow's death and still constitutes an invaluable standard reference for researchers in Mexican antiquities, and in particular for scholarly work dealing with the Aztec empire and the Náhuatl language. A first volume of *Tlalocan* appeared in 1943-44, printed and coedited by Smisor, while a second one dated 1945-48 was run, with unfailing passion in spite of the financial straits, by Barlow alone. The journal featured many of Barlow's early articles and plenty of his scholarly notes and queries. Along with the footnotes in *Nombre de Dios, Durango*, the notes by Barlow in *Tlalocan* provide a genuine flavor of his interest and erudition. Thirty-four issues of another journal written in Náhuatl, *Mexihkayotl*, were published directly by Barlow, with the collaboration of professor Miguel Barrios E., through a small press located in Barlow's Azcapotzalco home at Santander 27, acquired in 1945 or 1946. According to Joshi, "Barlow's career as anthropologist was clearly the pinnacle of his life achievement" ("Introduction," *OLL* 8); George T. Smisor, later appointed Barlow's literary executor, had similar words of appreciation,[72] and Professor Kroeber, Barlow's teacher, is reported to have once said "Barlow is a born historian."[73]

---

72. According to Smisor, RHB's mind was "keen, nimble, and retentive" ("R. H. Barlow and 'Tlalocan'," *Tlalocan* 3, no. 2 [1952]: 97-102; quoted in "Introduction," *OLL* 9). "He had an intellectual driving force that never seemed to relax [. . .] He had a facility of expression that brought life to long-dead happenings. This happy facility was a carry-over

His last year, 1950, saw Barlow developing his studies on the Mayan civilization and founding a third journal in the field of Mexican anthropology, *Notas Mesoamericanas*, of which Barlow handset and printed the first two issues from his private home press.74 But by this time, the "strain of overwork was beginning to tell" (*UL* 226), and in the summer of 1950 Barlow was given a leave of absence from scholarly activity because of health problems. Moreover, his later years were a period of growing dissatisfaction, of torment and unease, especially on a personal level, probably because of a never-overcome maladjustment due to his lack of social contacts and because of distress due to the incompatibility he perceived between his homosexuality and his public role. Barlow committed suicide on 1 or 2 January 1951, with an overdose of Seconal.75 The contingent cause that pushed him to the tragic gesture was the fear that "his homosexuality was about to be revealed, apparently by a disgruntled student" (Joshi and Schultz, "Introduction," *FF* xx). However, in the course of this study there will be more opportunities to discuss the motives of Barlow's uneasiness with his personal and social condition and with life itself: we will see how both his fiction and his poetry bear the marks of the acute maladjustment of their creator.

In the next section I will discuss the conflict Barlow must have felt between his different artistic inclinations, a conflict that bore an enormous impact on his choice of a career. Then I will introduce the Barlovian artistic expression that is the object of this study: his weird work, starting from his fiction. Finally a textual analysis will be presented, and it will offer possible insights into both Barlow's life experience and the controversial reasons of its untimely and tragic conclusion. I also propose to demonstrate that both Barlow's fiction and poetry share a more than passing interest in forms and themes similar to Lovecraft's, significantly stemming from, and expressing, the tormented personality of their author.[76]

---

from his years of reading and writing fantasy fiction and composing poetry" (ibid.).

73. Quoted in *UL* 221. RHB was not only interested in investigating the customs and languages of the ancient peoples of Culhua-Mexica, but their history too, as many of the articles published in *Tlalocan* attest.

74. Around 350 copies of the first issue, and 500 of the second, circulated. This journal was similar to *Tlalocan* in flavor and content. After RHB's death, the journal was continued by his colleagues of the Department of Anthropology of the Universidad de las Americas.

75. His body was cremated and the ashes buried in the Desierto de Leones. Dr. Martinez del Rio was named executor and took charge of RHB's scholarly papers, while his literary books, magazines, and papers were entrusted to RHB's old friend and collaborator George T. Smisor—then still working at the Benjamin Franklin Library in Mexico City—since he was the only person in Mexico familiar with RHB's literary work. The bulk of the unpublished scholarly papers were classified by anthropologists Charles Wicke and Fernando Horcasita Pimentel, who deposited them in the Archivio Barlow of the Universidad de las Americas (the last institution where RHB was working, then named Mexico City College). For these and more details, see *UL* 227.

76. As we saw in this biographical sketch, in the second part of RHB's life, dating approximately from the time of HPL's death, his main interests became progressively de-

Yet before moving onward, it seems appropriate to reprint here the original obituary that appeared at page 3 of the *Mexico City Collegian* issue for 18 January 1951, as a testimony to the heartfelt admiration that the contemporaries of Robert Haywood Barlow felt toward a brilliantly gifted personality who had left them too soon, but whose exceptional talents and achievements would last longer in their memories and appreciation.

STUDENTS AND FACULTY MOURN PASSING OF PROFESSOR BARLOW

FROM THIS TREE

From this tree
No further fruit.
Search the boughs,
look where the ant looks;
Only as cold-veined snakes
knotting on the mud,
Daggering their bird heads
at a shadow,
Will they respond.
A fire has bounded past
And the bark is blistered.

(From a collection of poems by Robert Barlow)

Mexico City College today mourns the untimel·· death, on January 2, of Professor Robert Barlow, head of MCC's anthropology department. The brilliant young man gave much during his short lifetime to the college and American-Mexican culture.

In his 33 years Robert Barlow was a practicing teacher, anthropologist, linguist, author, poet, and painter, and was both a Guggenheim and Rockefeller Fellow. He did well in everything he touched, and won laurels all along the way.

He came to Mexico first in the spring of 1938, owned his own home here and intended to live in Mexico permanently. He left the country only twice. In 1941 he went to the University of California, where he studied for his A.B. degree and taught on the Berkeley staff. While in Berkeley he won the Ina Galbraith award for poetry.

The only other time he left Mexico was the summer of 1948, when he travelled to Europe to supplement his already vast knowledge by studying Mexican manuscripts in the Paris and London libraries.

During his short life Barlow published more than 100 articles, pamphlets, notebooks, and full-length works, most of them concerned with Mexican culture before and since the conquest.

Mexico itself recognized Professor Barlow's amazing mastery of Spanish and the Indian languages by appointing him in 1945 to organize literacy classes for the Nahuatl-speaking Indians of Puebla and Morelos, an honor especially rare because Barlow was an American with English his native tongue.

As a professor at MCC since 1948, he did a great deal toward developing the college's pre-eminence in anthropology.

Faculty, students, and friends join in regretting his loss.

---

tached from literature and concentrated on anthropological research on native Mesoamerican cultures. However, as we will see, RHB did not cease composing literary work, especially poetry, pouring into it a new set of images and themes derived from his scholarly acquaintance with native Mexican cultures and traditions.

1.2 The controversial choice of a career

Barlow's early decision to write weird fiction was by no means an easy one. His personality, from his teenage years, showed an authentic many-sidedness: several different artistic interests and abilities competed to find expression and supremacy over the others, and at different times in his life Barlow had to ponder over what career to undertake—producing literary work (fiction and poetry), painting, drawing, sculpting, or printing. Within this picture, Lovecraft always played the part of the elderly advisor trying to stir his young pupil to pursue a literary career, though never forgetting to praise and encourage Barlow also in his other promising artistic endeavors. Apart from any consideration of the distinction of Barlow's work as a scholar and an anthropologist, a sense of unfulfilled promise is what we are left with when reflecting over Barlow's decision to give up writing weird fiction at the end of the 1930s. It is both impossible and futile to try to conjecture what means of expression Barlow would have chosen had he decided to pursue an artistic career; certainly his acquaintances' testimonies point to the remarkable versatility and excellence of Barlow's artistic talents. And perhaps it is not by chance that Barlow strongly admired the multifaceted personality of William Blake, probably the most versatile of the artists who blossomed in Western civilization.[77] Blake excelled in arts as diverse as poetry, drawing, engraving, and printing, and the seventeen-year-old Barlow dedicated to him, in the December 1935 issue of the *Southern Amateur* (1, no. 2), an enthusiastical article titled "Blake and 'The Songs of Innocence,'" which won second place in the Essay Laureate contest of the NAPA for 1936. What Barlow admired in Blake was precisely his versatility as an artist, and his capability to reconcile diverging artistic inclinations under the unifying umbrella of personal genius:

> The overwhelming genius of William Blake could not be confined to a single art. Its wild spontaneity took form both pictorially and poetically. Equally master in whichever field he chose, he thought of them in unity. Referring once to a creative work that he planned, Blake spoke of it as a "poem or a picture". Once his genius was free of the limitations of ordinary printing, he merged the arts more than anyone else had ever done. As soon as Blake perfected his obscure process, wherein text and drawings were executed on a single plate and printed in rich colours, the stream of his genius gathered force, released by this new freedom of style. (7-8)

---

77. RHB also paid a homage to Blake mentioning him inside one of his own poems, "Chili Sin Carne (For W.)" (from his collection *View from a Hill*, 1947), where RHB imagines having a conversation with a figure painted by Blake: "Where Imhotep's words on plant nutrition / Bound up with Mrs. Hemans lie awake / On shelves in prim Platonic juxtaposition, / A figure from the brush of William Blake / Debates with me an indicated planet: / Is it the sun or moon which sank or rose? / And then ordains, as one who surely knows / 'But can it be? It cannot be! But can it?'" (EG 187).

It has not been yet ascertained when exactly Barlow started to write weird fiction—though his collecting of weird material certainly dates back to his early teens (in 1931, at age thirteen, Barlow sent his first letter to Lovecraft manifesting his enthusiasm over the master's and other weird writers' stories). What is certain is that Barlow's first published story, "The Black Tower" (episode 1 of the *Annals of the Jinns*), appeared in the *Fantasy Fan* for October 1933, i.e. when Barlow was just fifteen. In the period 1934-36, the products of Barlow's art—fiction, poetry, drawings, sculptures, engravings—were widely circulating among the members of the Lovecraft circle, arousing a lively discussion over Barlow's artistic abilities and the possible outlets of his career,[78] as is testified at least by the Lovecraft side of the Lovecraft-Barlow correspondence. In fact, besides offering advice and criticism over the pupil's literary efforts, Lovecraft provided Barlow with unfailing support concerning artistic expression in general, though "Lovecraft inevitably felt less able to offer criticism of Barlow's artwork" (*UL* 203). However, according to Faig, the final proof that Lovecraft appreciated Barlow's artwork lays in the fact that "'Barlovian' art shortly began making the rounds of Lovecraft's correspondents" (*UL* 203). While Lovecraft showed pleasure and enthusiasm in receiving Barlow's drawings depicting the creatures from his own tales, Barlow continued writing and publishing weird fiction capable of surviving the changeable fortunes of the amateur journals hosting his tales (the *Fantasy Fan*, for instance, folded in February 1935).

The perseverance with which Barlow kept on writing weird fiction should, at least partially, be explained by the inexhaustible encouragement Lovecraft provided: the perusal of Lovecraft's correspondence to Barlow shows that, apart from his often enthusiastic comments on Barlow's fiction, which we will have occasion to discuss in detail, Lovecraft offered his protégé support ranging from a "technical" assistance over literary matters to a philosophical and emotional backing, always aiming at encouraging his pupil to undertake a literary career. There are countless evidences of this attitude in Lovecraft's correspondence. As an example of the assistance Lovecraft provided Barlow in writing weird fiction, we may even mention the master's words regarding what he thought the ultimate goal of a weird tale should be. In a letter tentatively dated 11 May 1935, HPL expressed to RHB (after his pupil's solicitation) his own key idea that the writer of a weird story should give preference to the *depiction of a mood* rather than to the devising of a denouement or even the construction of a *plot*: "[To have a denouement] is a tempting trick, but essentially artificial & mechanical. Indeed—all formal *plot* in the sense praised & demanded by conventional commercial editors is basically inartistic. A weird story, to be a serious aesthetic effort, must form primarily a *picture of a mood*" (*FF* 262). In a letter of November 1933, Lovecraft described to Barlow the infinite reward and the pure pleasure of feeling oneself be(com)ing a writer, and claimed that "It is curious how one gets turned to such things as writ-

---

78. "By 1935, indeed, discussions of writing or artwork as a career were occupying the attention of Lovecraft and his young correspondent" (*UL* 197).

ing (I was so turned at the age of 6)—but I don't think the step is ever regretted. Even if one doesn't become a Poe or Machen or Dunsany, one gets a peculiar type of imaginative satisfaction which nothing else can quite replace" (FF 87). The goal of Lovecraft's words was almost unfailingly to infuse his young friend with trust and enthusiasm in his own writing skills, as well as to give advice on how to improve, and to suggest the most important readings useful to reach the aesthetic goals Barlow was aiming at. In a letter Lovecraft introduced Barlow to the world of the amateur press, encouraging him to submit even his very early fiction and poetry, for example, to the NAPA:

> I'd advise you to send all these sketches in to the NAPA—perhaps letting "The Slaying of the Monster" be your official "credential". Don't worry about merit—remember that this is an *amateur* organisation which includes writers & would-be writers of *every* grade, from the frankly illiterate small boy up. You will see things in the amateur papers which will make your own work stand out like a classic! I really think you will find the association very pleasant & encouraging, & hope you will cooperate fully in its activities. (FF 51)[79]

Lovecraft urged Barlow to send his works not only to the amateur associations, but also to professional publishers and the pulp magazines. After reading Barlow's "A Dim-Remembered Story" (published in the summer of 1936), Lovecraft sent him a letter of enthusiastic praise of the tale and did not fail to encourage his pupil to submit the tale to Farnsworth Wright, editor of *Weird Tales*, in spite of the work's previous appearance in an amateur journal, the *Californian*. These are Lovecraft's words, in which is also easily detectable the attempt to make Barlow gain confidence in his own writing skills and thus guide him toward the choice of a literary career: "But *literature* is certainly your forte, say what you will! Have you tried this on Wright? Of course, he rejects some of Klarkash-Ton's best things as 'too poetic'—but there's no harm in taking a chance. Previous amateur appearance is no barrier to WT publication. You've rung the bell this time! [. . .] Keep it up! Keep 'em coming! If this story doesn't get into WT, you must send it to one of the fan magazines—perhaps Hill-Billy's revived MT if he ever gets it started" (9 July 1936; FF 351).[80] In order to steer Barlow toward a literary career, Lovecraft often mentioned and compared Barlow's different artistic skills, certainly showing a substantial psychological understanding: "You'll gradually acquire care in the selection & collocation of words—when you come to regard modelling in prose in the same light as that in which you regard modelling in Florida clay [. . .] or laying colours on a picture [. . .] or scratching copper with your new Manhattan stylus" (10 February 1935; FF 207). Lovecraft was perfectly aware that a conflict was taking place in young Barlow's personality between different artistic inclinations. Each one was

---

79. As Joshi and Schultz note, "A 'credential' was a work submitted to an amateur press association as a testimonial of competence in literary composition" (FF 54n1).
80. "Hill-Billy" is the nickname for William Crawford (1911–1984), editor of *Marvel Tales* (the "MT" of HPL's letter) and *Unusual Stories*.

striving to overcome the others, and Lovecraft made an effort to persuade his pupil to give literature a better chance. On this significant issue, a passage from a letter of July 1936 deserves full quotation:

> As to the question of whether literature is after all your most natural medium of expression—of course one can't fully tell as yet. I'm not forgetting your splendid drawing & painting & sculpture—& indeed, it is possible that the graphic & literary talents might advantageously develop side by side, as in a few other cases. Possibly your recent writing impresses me so particularly merely because I can appreciate the fine points of writing more readily than those of other arts. [...] The fact that writing is hard & even uncongenial labour to you is no proof that you are not naturally creative in that line. Many eminent writers have maintained that composition was very difficult for them—& yet their preëminent creativeness has been attested by every line of their work. If I recall aright, Flaubert & George Moore fall within this category. But of course it is well to give your other talents a chance, & to let other creative urges have free play. *By all means* finish your oil painting—for your present misgivings are more likely to be unfounded than are your original hopes! At the same time, don't neglect writing. You have demonstrated real talent there, & incessant practice may remove some of the drawbacks & give you a greater sense of the inevitableness of composition. (FF 354)

One cannot help inferring, from the reading of these and other lines, that Lovecraft would have been especially proud had Barlow finally decided to let literature become his favorite artistic means of expression. Lovecraft would have probably perceived Barlow the (professional or semi-professional) weird fiction writer as, at least partially, his own product—and certainly as the token of a personal achievement. To reinforce this point, a quite telling passage from a Lovecraft letter might prove decisive. This is in fact Lovecraft's comment upon Barlow's winning of the 1933 story laureateship of the NAPA for the short tale "Eyes of the God": "Congratulations on your laureateship, of which I hadn't heard before. [...] Your story in the *Sea Gull* was really delightful, & I think the honour well earned. As your sponsor in the National, I feel a reflected pride!" (13 July 1933; FF 70).

However, after his removal from the Florida estate in 1936, Barlow studied at the Kansas City Art Institute and at the Polytechnic Institute in San Francisco, since his interest in art had been growing for some time. Already by 1936, Barlow seemed to have decided upon art as his career. His course work at the Kansas City Art Institute included instruction under the famous painter and muralist Thomas Hart Benton (1889-1975). Lovecraft sent his encouragement,[81] but his words betrayed "a note of regret that the happy Florida days were ended" (*UL* 206). Lovecraft soon realized that Barlow's inclination would probably be to

---

81. "Glad you're getting worked into a tolerable modus vivendi in Kansas City, & that your art course is proving fruitful. The race betwixt literature & pictorial art for adoption as your chief medium of expression is interesting to watch; & I fancy the present course, with its distinguished instructors, will do much toward helping you decide which candidate to vote for" (letter dated 30 November 1936; *FF* 370).

choose art and not literature, and his words of a later date, besides the apparent, predictable appreciation, allow one to infer the probable discontent from which they stemmed: "Glad the art work continues to be congenial, & that your instructors are proving encouraging. It may indeed be that painting & sculpture will nose out literature as your primary forte—at least, there's nothing to do now but experiment. Certainly, I think that pictorial art offers much quicker commercial returns—& with much less sacrifice of one's own personality & standards—than any ordinary form of writing" (11 December 1936; *FF* 380). Of the excellence of Barlow's artistic efforts, we have the testimony not only of Lovecraft[82] but also of Faig, who actually saw a painting Barlow presented to Lovecraft on 3 May 1934, representing "a squatting monster (with snout and tentacles) glaring into the night on a moon-litten blue-green plain" (*UL* 208).[83] And in 1969, a notebook containing about 130 of Barlow's drawings (both Aztec-Mayan subjects and personal interpretations of a few Lovecraftian creatures) was offered for sale by Roy A. Squires: the bookbinding was made also by Barlow and stands out as a further proof of his artistic versatility. However, we certainly agree with Faig that "these interests were not to hold Barlow's central attention for long. He seems to have had a strong drive to attain intellectual and personal maturity through a career, and evidently concluded that his prowess in art could not support such ambitions. Summer 1937 finds him in Leavenworth; by winter 1937–38 he is back in Kansas City, apparently still pursuing his studies" (*UL* 209). It may be useful to observe that also other considerations, of a practical if not "medical" type, certainly played a part in convincing Barlow to abandon literary and artistic activities as his major endeavors. Already at the time of his new sojourn in Kansas City in winter 1938, Barlow wrote these words to the Becks, revealing his own will—or should we say *need*—to abandon the literary career:

> The doctors here confirm what I have long expected—my eyesight will give out unless I stop all literary and artistic work (This means being a farmer or a mountain climber, I fear!). As a consequence, our current job [the planned edition of Smith's *The Hashish-Eater*] will probably remain my swan-song. When it is done I'm going to leave this environment for a more physical one. [. . .] I know [. . .] that a phase of my life is being shoved into the past.[84]

---

82. For instance, upon receiving from RHB, as a gift, the "sleeping figurine" of the late Sam Perkins, a beloved cat, HPL voices his enthusiasm over RHB's sculpting skills: "The more I look at that statuette, the more its grace & naturalness appeals to me. You have certainly caught the exquisitely distinctive lines of feline relaxation—not for nothing have you been the friend & associate of noble beasts like Doodle Bug, High, Low, Jack, Henry Clay, Cyrus, Darius, & Little Mr. Knopf! It is interesting to know that this is your first effort in the given medium—a decided success, if you ask me!" (3 January 1937; *FF* 391).

83. The painting is now preserved in the Lovecraft Collection of the John Hay Library of Brown University.

84. RHB's letter to the Beck brothers of 14 February 1938 (quoted in Faig, "HPL: The Book That Nearly Was" 120).

Of course, one is left with much speculation as to whether and to what extent Barlow's eyesight could indeed benefit from the choice of a scholarly career—instead of an artistic or literary one. In any case, "A trip taken in Mexico in the summer of 1938 seems definitely to have marked the end of his artistic studies" (*UL* 209), and one cannot help agreeing with Faig when he claims that for a man of Barlow's genius, to "spread his own wings, to make his own career, was a virtual necessity" (*UL* 247).

1.3 The categorization of Barlow's fiction

Barlow's short story output, which was almost entirely published in amateur journals affiliated with the NAPA or in fantasy magazines, dates almost entirely to the 1930s. There will probably be no certainty as to when Barlow actually started to write fiction; but when, in 1931, he first wrote to Lovecraft, the thirteen-year-old boy was already familiar with the works of weird writers published in pulp magazines—and had himself begun writing narratives in the same vein. We know that Barlow was, as early as in 1935, planning to write a novel, and that he had been intensively working on this project. On different occasions, Lovecraft's letters to Barlow drop hints as to the latter's efforts in novel-writing. In a missive of October 1935, Lovecraft wishes his pupil "Good luck with the novel [. . .] how far have you progressed into that blue pad?" (*FF* 299). The year 1936 saw Barlow committed—among other projects—to the writing of the novel, which was assuming fairly big proportions. In fact, in a letter dated 19 September 1936, commenting to a revision client on Barlow's recent visit to Providence, Lovecraft speaks of the youth's "future monumental novel" (quoted in *LAL* 614). Lovecraft has left another testimony of the size of Barlow's novelistic effort, in a letter addressed to his pupil and dated late November 1936: "Glad the novel goes along well—at this rate, it will be a five-foot shelf full by the time it's done!" (*FF* 370).

However, the year 1937 signaled a halt in Barlow's fiction writing. The reasons for this sudden change have been, at least partially, discussed in the previous pages: the most relevant contingent causes may still be the death of his friend and master Lovecraft, and Donald Wandrei's and Clark Ashton Smith's personal and professional hostility. With reference to the former cause, perhaps more telling than any biographical or psychological discussion to convey the sense of loss and bewilderment into which Barlow was thrown by his mentor's death, may be the quotation of the last rhyming couplet of Barlow's sonnet "March 1938," composed to commemorate the first anniversary of Lovecraft's demise:[85] "But I upon this beach, perplexed by night, / Dare not advance bereft of your keen sight" (*EG* 154). It is difficult not to refer also to this "perplexity" and inability to advance

---

85. Not only in 1938, but for several years to come, the anniversary of HPL's death called forth a poetic tribute from RHB, later published by Derleth in the Arkham House edition of *The Shuttered Room and Other Pieces* (1959).

without the master's guidance that Barlow felt, especially considering how big an impact Lovecraft had had on his growth and refinement as a fiction writer. And as a further proof of the relevance, for Barlow's decision to give up weird fiction, borne by Wandrei's and Smith's hostility, and specifically by the shocking letter from Smith that he received, we can mention Barlow's revelatory remarks in his own "Autobiography": "If I had not received this letter, and other blows of the same sort, originating with the half-informed and antagonistic Wandreis, and which continued for various years after, I should not have worked out new orientations. Its immediate effect was of cutting my entrails out with a meat cleaver, but its eventual effect was perhaps salutary, though I am even today wounded" (*OLL* 22). The short and partial autobiographical sketch from which this extract is quoted was written in Mexico City in 1944, thus six full years after the receipt of Smith's letter. Barlow's mention of being still "wounded" after so much time (and after having already met Smith in person, and apparently reconciled) cannot but attest to his extraordinary sensitivity. A third concomitant cause that might have had an impact on Barlow's progressive estrangement from weird fiction is represented by his own uprooting from Florida (where he held the Vaults of Yoh-Vombis), which already occurred in mid-1936, due to family troubles.

However, Barlow's writing career continued, albeit sporadically. He kept on publishing fiction well after 1937: the second issue of the amateur magazine *Leaves* (Winter 1938-39) featured Barlow's masterpiece "Origin Undetermined." Some of his prose poems, as "The Swearing of an Oath," "The Artizan's Reward," and "The Questioner," appeared in the fantasy magazine *Polaris* in 1940, and his last published story, "Return by Sunset," written between August 1938 and June 1939 and inspired by a drawing by his erstwhile idol Clark Ashton Smith, appeared in the *Acolyte* for Summer 1943. According to Joshi and Anderson, "A good number of fragmentary manuscripts of weird tales survive among Barlow's effects,"[86] and they are still unpublished.

Barlow's short story output may be roughly grouped into three broad categories, which reveal—at least partially—the influence of the writers he admired in his teenage years. They are as follows:

1—Dunsanian narratives: This category includes much of Barlow's early production, chiefly influenced by his readings of fantasy texts—not only by Dunsany, but also by Clark Ashton Smith and, in part, Lovecraft. Among the compositions that can be ascribed to this group are such tales as "The Inhospitable Tavern" (*Perspective Review*, Fall 1934), "The Adventures of Garoth" (*Perspective Review*, Summer 1935), "The Fidelity of Ghu" (probably written in June 1934 and first published in *EG*), "Eyes of the God" (*Sea Gull*, May 1933), and the fantasy cycle *Annals of the Jinns*, whose first nine episodes were published on the *Fantasy Fan* between Octo-

---

86. Joshi and Anderson, "Introduction," *EG* 11. RHB also published a few non-weird tales (e.g., "My First Cacomixtli" and "A Glimpse of Euterpe," in the *Californian Pelican* for November 1941 and April 1942), but they have not been reprinted.

ber 1933 and February 1935, when the magazine folded. The tenth episode ("The Theft of the Hsothian Manuscripts") was included in the *Phantagraph* for August 1936, edited by Donald A. Wollheim of New York City. The eleventh and last episode, "An Episode of the Jungle," probably composed in February 1934, was published for the first time in EG.[87] However, I would tend to include within this category of the Dunsany-inspired narratives two of the six collaborations Barlow wrote with Lovecraft, "The Slaying of the Monster" (written probably in 1932 or the beginning of 1933) and "The Hoard of the Wizard-Beast" (written in September 1933 and revised by Lovecraft after December of the same year).

2—Cosmic horror tales: To this category belongs the bulk of Barlow's fiction. Many themes and stylistic preoccupations typical of Lovecraft's work found an original reworking in Barlow's narratives. The sheer extent and variety of this reworking is impressive, since it covers almost all the most significant concerns of Lovecraft's writing. Just to mention a few, such tales as "The Experiment" (*Unusual Stories*, May–June 1935), "The Summons" (*Californian*, Fall 1935), "A Memory" (*Californian*, Winter 1935), "A Dim-Remembered Story" (*Californian*, Summer 1936), and "Origin Undetermined" (*Leaves* 2, 1938) all bear the imprint of Lovecraftian themes, atmospheres, and style. Also, the influence of other writers is detectable here and there. All these influences can be brought under the label of *cosmic horror*, although for different reasons in each case (a particular theme, a specific linguistic usage, the building of a certain atmosphere and mood, etc.). The analysis will ascertain the modalities and specificities of Barlow's aesthetic treatment, rendering, and interpretation of the theme of cosmic horror. In particular, I will strive to point out, as a mark of originality in Barlow's treatment of the theme, the notion of *sensitivity* (an element so pervasive in his personality that it showed itself in both his fiction and poetry), one that Barlow did not share with Lovecraft but was entirely his own, and perhaps detectable at its best in the collaboration "The Night Ocean" (*Californian*, Winter 1936): the unearthing of the original typescript of this last tale, recording Lovecraft's corrections in pen, has allowed scholars to consider it almost entirely Barlow's work.[88]

3—Ironic and spoof pieces: This group contains works like the Lovecraft collaborations "The Battle That Ended the Century" (written in Florida in July 1934, during Lovecraft's first visit to the Barlows, and published in the *Acolyte*, Fall 1944) and the incomplete spoof "Collapsing Cosmoses," of which Barlow and Lovecraft wrote alternate segments in the summer of 1935, during Lovecraft's second visit to DeLand. Though Lovecraft did not disdain to write ironic pieces and spoofs of his own, I am inclined to think that the stimulus to write this kind of narrative came primarily from Barlow—and we will see how, also in his corre-

---

87. For the editorial history of this cycle, see Joshi and Anderson, "Introduction," EG 9.
88. The discovery was made by Douglas A. Anderson, and a facsimile of the document reporting HPL's interpolated corrections is now available as an appendix in Faig, *R. H. Barlow*.

spondence to Barlow, Lovecraft tried to dissuade his pupil from infusing the touch of irony in his "serious" literary efforts.

In effect, Lovecraft's influence was so pervasive that, despite its more direct impact on the second group of Barlow's narratives outlined above, it is easily detectable in all the three categories. Lovecraft and Barlow did not simply collaborate in writing six tales (to the five mentioned above must be added "'Till A' the Seas,'" completed in January 1935 in New York and published in the *Californian* for Summer 1935); Lovecraft contributed significantly to the molding of Barlow's literary style and inclinations, constantly providing his pupil with technical advice over the most effective strategies to adopt in writing weird fiction. Lovecraft's letters to Barlow are replete with suggestions concerning writing techniques: Lovecraft certainly saw his protégé as a young yet raw writer, but one in possession of potentially excellent qualities that only needed to be refined and made more sophisticated with the guidance of a more expert hand and mind. For instance, in an early letter Lovecraft expressed his appreciation of the fifteen-year-old Barlow's narrative skills, though kindly noting the inevitable shortcomings of a beginner's work: "I read your stories with a great deal of interest, & really think that they display a gratifying degree of merit & promise. You have a good idea of what a dramatic situation is, & seem to be distinctly sensitive to the nuances of style. Of course, there are at present many marks of the beginner's work—but these are only to be expected. Emphatically, I think you are headed in the right direction" (*FF* 51). In the very same letter, apart from this quite generic praise, Lovecraft did not hesitate to delve into more sophisticated aesthetic matters. Having detected, in Barlow's early literary efforts, a strong inclination toward *imitation* of the style of the masters he was reading on magazines such as *Weird Tales*, Lovecraft addressed the question very plainly: "Don't mind the element of *imitativeness*, which is inevitable at the start. The only way to *begin* to acquire a good style is to copy those who seem to be saying about what you want to say. That's the way I did myself—copied Poe & Dunsany until their styles fused into something at least outwardly original" (18 February 1933; *FF* 51). What is perhaps even more interesting in this letter is Lovecraft's comment on the type of intervention he exerted over Barlow's prose in "The Slaying of the Monster": "Of the stories enclosed, I think I like best the little volcano sketch[89] (for style & atmosphere) & the tale of the man who became a satyr[90] (for plot possibilities). There is also,

---

89. Here HPL refers to "The Slaying of the Monster."
90. Likely, episode 1 of the *Annals of the Jinns*, published as "The Black Tower" in the *Fantasy Fan* (October 1933). In this short tale, the protagonist Castor has a peculiar ancestry, namely a satyr as father and a witch woman as mother. It is only by conjecture that we infer that HPL is here referring to "The Black Tower" when he writes of "the tale of the man who became a satyr," since no other narrative piece by RHB tells of a character who is somehow related to satyrs.

however, great cleverness in the idea of 'The Little Box'[91] [. . .] Again—congratulations on your interesting & promising tales" (FF 51).

In accomplishing the duties of his literary protectorate over Barlow, and in order to assist in the promotion of his literary efforts, Lovecraft, as we have seen, also persuaded him to join the NAPA (the UAPA had collapsed in 1926).[92] Moreover, Lovecraft did not simply offer technical assistance and revision (we will examine in greater detail the nature and scope of his intervention in some of Barlow's narratives); he considered the young Barlow a competent and well-prepared interlocutor on weird writing. They often engaged in discussions concerning the aesthetics of weird fiction, and Lovecraft took these debates as an occasion to provide Barlow with his own views on the genre. For example, in a postcard of 15 April 1934, Lovecraft commented upon some remarks Barlow had made in the column "Your Views" of the *Fantasy Fan* issue for April 1934. Barlow had written: "I should venture that the fascination of the weird is through a vaguely masochistic pleasure that derives delight from frightening one's self! I believe the simile is ancient that our gaze will often return to the ugliest person in a room rather than the most handsome. Perhaps it is that constant saccharine palls. I claim it is untrue that 'the beautiful, the good, is the aim of every true artist'." Lovecraft replied in his postcard to this view of Barlow's, expressing, very politely as usual, his own position, slightly contrasting with Barlow's: "It is very possible that you're right in many ways—the seat of the pleasure of the weird is certainly tremendously obscure. My own view is that tales of the supernatural give one a sense of a greatly expanded ego—a conquest of the galling limitations of time, space, & natural law—but that may be only part of the story. It would hardly explain why the *terrible* is preferred to other forms of the supernatural" (FF 131-32).

Another example of Lovecraft's interest in building a discussion with Barlow over the fundamentals of fiction writing is contained in a letter dated 21 October 1935, where Lovecraft faces the topic of single-plotness in literature, analyzing both the merits and the shortcomings of this textual strategy:

> As to the single-plotness of your principal tastes—that's nothing remarkable. We all tend to ride certain ideas or situations into the ground unless we're on our guard. Particular scenes or types of events impress us strongly—so we keep on depicting them under various guises. *I do the same thing*—being excessively fond of such stock happenings as a person or expedition uncovering the ruins of a prehuman civilisation; a descent down the ladder of communal decay; a late survival

---

91. Episode 7 of the *Annals of the Jinns*.
92. However, despite gaining prominence by winning the 1933 story laureateship for "Eyes of the God," RHB did not dedicate much energy to amateurdom, perhaps because he considered it too much "detached" from his favorite literary genres, weird and fantasy fiction. Anyway, RHB did assist HPL in some of the latter's amateur ventures, for example when he mimeographed, probably in late June 1936, HPL's broadside, *Some Current Motives and Practices*, in which the Providence writer defended NAPA president Hyman Bradofsky against attacks and actual litigation among some of the members.

of a hellish pre-human cult; a groping odyssey of horror in some subterrene realm, &c. &c. &c. (FF 299; italics added)

What is particularly striking in all these letters is the attempt Lovecraft made to constantly compare Barlow to himself: it seems almost as if Lovecraft tried to encourage his pupil in his writing efforts by letting him see that the very same problems, doubts, and difficulties he was facing at this early stage of his career as a writer were already met (and overcome) by Lovecraft during his own juvenile years. And the implicit statement was that if Lovecraft had the same problems and overcame them—finally becoming the skillful and distinguished author Barlow so strongly admired—then he, Barlow, was treading the right path and likely to follow the master's steps—and hopefully parallel a similar career.

1.4 The seven themes of Barlow's fiction

Barlow's narrative production displays a coherent though expanding set of thematic and stylistic features, which it is possible to describe under a few main headings. My analysis of Barlow's fiction will be conducted by defining and exemplifying seven themes that I identify as its most representative: my discussion by no means claims exhaustiveness, nor are these themes intended as identifying neatly separate aspects of Barlow's fiction. Thus, a few methodological elucidations are needed before proceeding to the discussion of each theme.

The first specification concerns the very usage of the label "theme": in the context of the present work, the notion of "theme" must be deprived of its merely "thematic" content. In other words, "theme" is not employed simply to refer to a content matter, but it acquires a wider signification in defining a more general feature of the literary work under analysis—a feature that might include the reference to a theme proper (thus, for instance, the recurrence of a fixed plot element or of a literary, aesthetic, or philosophical view on Barlow's part), as well as the reference to elements of form, narrative strategies and techniques, syntactic constructions, lexical choices, etc. In fact, a content matter or a formal issue, in itself, can rarely be analyzed as an isolated topic within a literary work of art, ignoring its impact on, respectively, formal issues and content matters. Thus, in the light of this specification, "theme" becomes an umbrella- or container-term, meant to hold a more comprehensive and functional definition of a literary issue.

A second specification is needed with regard to the nature of these "themes" in Barlow's fiction as they are discussed in the present study. Namely, these seven "themes" are not meant as neatly separable, and must *not* be intended as *impermeable* to each other. There are at least two significant reasons to justify my claim:

1. Each of the "themes" refers, to a greater or lesser extent, to both formal and content-thematic aspects;
2. The thematic aspects of the "themes" under examination only seldom can be discussed in isolation from the thematic aspects of other "themes."

This is of course the inevitable consequence of the work of art—and, specifically, the literary work of art—as the product of unique mind and imagination that, due to their own peculiar functioning, work as compact and coherent units. As a consequence, the occasional overlapping between different "themes" will be unavoidable, both in their formal and content-thematic aspects.

These clarifications made, it is now time to begin the discussion of Barlow's weird fiction. Therefore, I proceed now with the listing and the subsequent examination of the seven "themes" of his narrative production:

1. Dunsanianism
2. Vagueness
3. Cosmicism
4. Time
5. Nature
6. Irony
7. Forbidden and Furtive Search

2. Dunsanianism

It is certainly agreeable that "Barlow's fiction writing clearly was inspired by his early readings in fantasy—notably Clark Ashton Smith and Lord Dunsany—and his association with H. P. Lovecraft" (Joshi and Anderson, "Introduction," *EG* 9), and this is why the element of Dunsanianism is pre-eminent in Barlow's production. His early fiction, dating to the years 1933-35 in particular, maintains a strong Dunsanian flavor, which Lovecraft himself, as we will see, encouraged Barlow to pursue.

Before delving into the specific analysis of Barlow's narratives written in the Dunsanian vein, it may be fruitful to report and shortly comment on a few critical opinions on Barlow's fantasy tales, and in particular on the worth of their imitative nature.

2.1 Some critical remarks

Although I will attempt to show the authentic merit and originality of Barlow's fantasy tales, his narratives written in the Dunsanian vein have not met with general appreciation. For instance, S. T. Joshi once labeled the cycle *Annals of the Jinns* as "embarrassingly crude" (Joshi, "Recognition" 46), and, on another occasion, referred to Barlow's early tales—including the *Annals*—as "decidedly juvenilia" ("Introduction," *OLL* 6). However, Faig's claim that "the earliest pieces were somewhat clumsy and crude, but by 1935 or so it is clear that Lovecraft was very serious in his praise" (*UL* 197) introduces us to the issue of Lovecraft's opinion on Barlow's fantasy tales, and in particular to that of the nature and extent of Barlow's self-conscious imitation of the Dunsanian model. It must be noted that, upon reading the first manuscripts that Barlow submitted him, Lovecraft immediately recognized Dunsany as the most suitable model for the young's early attempts in fantasy and weird fiction:

> What you need is simply more practice—which the years will readily supply. Read the weird classics with a closely analytical eye, observing just how Dunsany & others handle the details of language in order to produce certain finely-calculated emotional effects. I recommend Dunsany especially, because so far your fancy seems to follow his more than that of any other standard author. If you'd like at any time to re-read Dunsany, & can't find his tales in DeLand, I'll be glad to lend you whatever items you'd care to see. The cream of Dunsany, of course, is in "A Dreamer's Tales". I'm going to re-read this & other Dunsaniana myself before long. My current work dissatisfies me profoundly—giving me the feeling that my imagination needs re-fertilisation. Of all the imaginative stimuli I have ever experienced, my first reading of Dunsany was the most powerful. (17 December 1933; *FF* 90)

Shortly after this missive, Lovecraft renewed his offer to help Barlow familiarize himself with Dunsany's style, immediately adding another suggestion on the most appropriate prose style to imitate: "I'll lend you Dunsany whenever you wish.

Meanwhile the good old King James Bible is certainly an excellent thing to absorb—or its stylistic purity & rhetorical eloquence are almost without a parallel" (13 January 1934; *FF* 101).

The first (in chronological order) of the six Lovecraft-Barlow collaborations, "The Slaying of the Monster," is an early short tale—whose title was provided by Lovecraft—that Barlow created when he was probably less than fifteen years old. The tale narrates of the superstition of the people of Laen, who, mistaking the eruption of a volcano as the "Stirrings of the Monster," decided to slay It in order to save their town and land from a "fearful doom." No slaying actually occurred, because no dragon was ever sighted, but the people of Laen set up a stone tablet proudly announcing their brave and heroic slaying of the monster. The concluding line of the tale reports the narrator's comment, claiming that the tablet has lately been discovered under its "deep, ancient layers of encrusting lava."

Barlow submitted the original draft of the tale to Lovecraft, who read it in February 1933, provided a revision of the manuscript, and supplied its title (see *LAL* 530). According to Joshi, Lovecraft's revisory hand contributed just 30% of the story (*LAL* 531). However, it is interesting to examine Lovecraft's words apropos of this tale, and in particular on the nature of his own revision:

> I have added a few pencil touches to these MSS. which you may possibly find helpful. In "The Slaying of the Monster" I have taken the liberty of changing many words in order to carry out fully the Dunsanian prose-poetic effect which you are obviously seeking. You will note that I have sought extreme *simplicity*—cutting out all words & constructions which primarily suggest prose, & confining the text as far as possible to the simple, familiar, largely Saxon words which we associate with poetry & which are especially prominent in the King James Bible. (Dunsany's chief model.) I have also tried to improve the *rhythm*. Doubtless you realise that good prose (& especially poetic prose) has just as distinct (though subtler) a rhythm as verse, & that a sketch of Dunsany's can almost be sung or chanted. In changing parts of your text I have sought to give it some of the smoothness or rhythm which this kind of writing demands. (18 February 1933; *FF* 51)

What is first worth noting in this epistolary excerpt is the plainness with which Lovecraft recognizes Barlow's narratives' attempt to obtain a *prose-poetic* effect reminiscent of Lord Dunsany's. Lovecraft's words are also revealing because they do not simply identify Barlow's tastes, but teach him how to colour a narrative style with a poetic flavor. Giving Barlow advice, Lovecraft is unconsciously offering valuable suggestions on how writing prose-poetry:

- to seek simplicity: avoiding too prosastic expressions and locutions in favor of the familiar Saxon prose largely used in King James Bible. Especially important is also the notion of "smoothness," i.e. the necessity for the narrative to allow a fluent and dream-inspiring reading;
- to pay attention to rhythm: poetic prose needs to be balanced and harmoniously wrought, so that the narrative may sound like the verses of a popular song.

As we will see from the analysis of Barlow's Dunsanian tales, he certainly demonstrated to know how to put Lovecraft's suggestions into practice.

Having fully realized Barlow's early fiction writing as a sort of imitative work, Lovecraft did not fail to offer his pupil his own opinions and suggestions on the general habit of "imitativeness":

> I am sure that "Annals of the Jinns" will prove a pleasing & interesting series, & wish you luck with its composition. Practice & perseverance will certainly give you a mature & adequate style in the end. At the outset, the moderate & judicious imitation of good models is a great help. The early Wells was tremendously clever with *ideas*, though I'd hardly say he ever had a really distinguished style. Dunsany's style, on the other hand, is admirable—as also is Machen's. Blackwood's is generally poor & journalistic—although his marvellous & unique command of the exact & serious psychology of the unreal makes one forget all this & place him at the very head of all fantastic novelists. [. . .] All told, Dunsany has probably influenced me more than any other writer save Poe. In 1919-22 he was so exclusively my model that the results are palpably imitative. (14 March 1933; FF 54-55)

However imitative Barlow's early pieces were, Lovecraft did not fail to encourage his correspondent by recognizing his own early debt toward Dunsany, thus once again comparing himself to Barlow. In any case, Lovecraft displayed strong and sincere admiration of Barlow's Dunsanian pieces, as many attestations of this sort may be found in his correspondence: in a letter of November 1933, and referring to the first two episodes of the *Annals* ("The Black Tower" and "The Shadow from Above"), Lovecraft writes: "Glad you're keeping [Charles D.] Hornig [editor of the *Fantasy Fan*] & other editors well supplied. I enjoyed both of your Annals of the Jinns, & believe you are laying the foundations for some extremely vivid & effective writing" (FF 87). While commenting on Barlow's fantasy tales, Lovecraft insisted on the element of imitativeness; the publication of the fifth episode of the *Annals*, "The Tomb of the God," was celebrated by Lovecraft with the usual enthusiasm: "By the way—let me congratulate you on 'The Tomb of the God' in the new *Fantasy Fan*. It is really splendid—redolent of such masters as Dunsany & Klarkash-Ton. Keep it up!" (3 March 1934; FF 113).[1]

---

1. Klarkash-Ton is one of the nicknames Lovecraft coined for his friend and colleague Clark Ashton Smith. "The Tomb of the God" appeared in the *Fantasy Fan* for February 1934. In a letter of 16 March 1935, Lovecraft even let himself express a judgment comparing Barlow and Derleth, to the full advantage of the former: "In the final (alas!) FF, I think your 'The Mirror' easily dominates—& this in spite of the tale by Comte d'Erlette" (FF 223). Lovecraft refers to Barlow's tale "The Mirror," the ninth episode of the *Annals*, the last to be published in the *Fantasy Fan* (in the February 1935 issue), as the magazine had folded. The work by Derleth mentioned here is "The Slanting Shadow." In a slightly later latter, dated March 25, Lovecraft wrote: "As for 'The Mirror'—I'm glad it did get printed. I like it very much, as I said when I read the MS. Hope you'll let the amateur press have other Garothian items" (FF 232).

It is now time to examine concretely the merits of Barlow's early fantasy tales, and to what extent and in what terms they might be truly considered "Dunsanian."

2.2 The nature of Barlow's Dunsanianism

The eleven episodes of the cycle *Annals of the Jinns* (all short narratives in which Lovecraft did not have a revisory hand),[2] tales like "The Fidelity of Ghu," "The Adventures of Garoth," "The Inhospitable Tavern," "The Temple," and a few others, all display some traits that are referable to the prose style and the contents of Dunsany's fantasies. In fact, the "theme" of Dunsanianism in Barlow's fiction concerns both formal and content aspects; of the many aspects of Barlow's Dunsanianism that would deserve attention, it seems appropriate—for their effectiveness and sheer pervasiveness in Barlow's oeuvre–to discuss the following:

1. **Formal aspects**: Following Dunsany's (and, as a matter of fact, at least partly Lovecraft's and Clark Ashton Smith's) models, Barlow strives to achieve a "poetic" prose style, in order to depict a "dreamy" atmosphere particularly appropriate for a fantasy tale. In order to do so, Barlow makes peculiar though coherent lexical choices, which can be summarized as follows:
   - use of adjectives. The words placed in adjectival positions are often *compounded words*, i.e. made of two or even more hyphenated words, sometimes in the accentuation of mythical epithets of Homeric memory. This is done in order to better depict (and convey the sense of) a suspended and "detached" realm, a scenery of fantasies properly "distanced" from the actual lifeworld, a sort of epic kingdom;
   - use of archaisms. Whenever a choice between a modern, current word and an older one is at hand, Barlow resorts to the latter, thus reinforcing his effort to "distanciate" the fictional world from the reader's;
   - use of unearthly names. The effect of distanciation is obtained also by resorting to a peculiar naming of peoples and lands, i.e. one employing words utterly alien from any human flavor, thus generating a strong sense of "otherworldliness."

2. **Content aspects**: Barlow's most significant aim in his "Dunsanian" narratives is to create from scratch a coherent set of tales displaying mythical cross-references to each other. Therefore, his attempt is clearly to build up an *artificial mythology* on the model of Dunsany's and Lovecraft's self-conscious literary efforts. What Barlow's fantasy tales aim at, is then the building of a coherent *Mythos*.

---

2. "Barlow's 'Annals of the Jinns' do not bear many revisory touches by HPL, and in many cases Lovecraft does not appear to have seen these items until after they were published" (LAL 531).

2.2.1 The formal aspects of Barlow's Dunsanianism

Barlow devotes particular care to the lexical and adjectival choice in the composition of his tales. As a proof of this attitude, countless examples can be detected inside his fiction of the distinctive selection of words Barlow made. The list of compounded adjectives or names present in his prose-poetic creations is virtually endless. Let us mention the most striking examples, with restriction to the tales that can be included in the "Dunsanian" or Smithian vein: *pall-like* and *new-risen* ("The Slaying of the Monster"), *crab-like* ("The Black Tower," episode one of the *Annals of the Jinns*), *toad-like* and *white-faced* ("The Shadow from Above," episode two of the *Annals*), *devil-things* and *slave-men* ("The Tomb of the God," episode five of the *Annals*), *jewel-encrusted* ("The Flower God," episode six of the *Annals*), *octopus-thing* ("The Little Box," episode seven of the *Annals*), *monster-things*, *fungi-masters* and *fast-gathering* ("The Fall of the Three Cities," episode eight of the *Annals*), *tree-things* and *frog-like* ("An Episode in the Jungle," episode eleven of the *Annals*), *wyvern-thing* and *man-bear* (Chapter 10, "The Castle in the Desert," of *The Adventures of Garoth*),[3] *woman-thing* (Chapter 11, "The Erring Knight," of *The Adventures of Garoth*), *wyvern-creatures* and *jelly-like* ("The Hoard of the Wizard-Beast," where the wizard-beast itself is another compounded word), *worm-like* ("The Misfortunes of Butter-Churning"), *goblin-torches* ("The Bright Valley"), *fungus-haunted* ("A Memory"), *time-assaulted* ("A Dim-Remembered Story"), etc. What can be noted quite easily is that many of these compounded expressions recall the inability of denotative language to successfully define the objects of its description. In other words, it is as if rational language admitted to being at a loss in defining its object positively, and, in absence of the proper word to describe the real-world referent, resorted to a substitutive lexeme in order to "humanize" an experience that is utterly non-humanlike: the compounded words following the pattern "x-thing" or "x-like" (devil-things, monster-things, tree-things, woman-thing, octopus-things, pall-like, crab-like, toad-like, etc.) all point to a comparison, to an "as if" that reveals the indescribability of the experience, one that in its turn points to a vagueness and unreliability of perception—on which more in the discussion of the second "theme" of Barlow's fiction, *Vagueness*.

Another very typical device of poetic prose is the employment of the rhetorical device of the *epic simile*. Although Barlow did not resort with particular frequency to this device, a few cases remain in his fiction to attest to its importance and effectiveness. Let us mention a couple of examples from the eminently prose-poetic style of "The Night Ocean": "I had eaten my luncheon at Ellston, and though *the heavens seemed the closing lid of a great casket*...." (EG 111; italics added).[4] The sec-

---

3. According to Joshi and Anderson, Barlow conceived *The Adventures of Garoth* in 1935, as a "lengthy episodic work [...] very much in the spirit of Dunsany's *Book of Wonder*" ("Introduction," EG 10). Only two segments appeared in the *Perspective Review* issue for Summer 1935: "The Temple," containing Chapters 3 and 4, and "The Adventures of Garoth," containing Chapters 10, 11, and 12.

4. The analysis of the original ms. with Lovecraft's corrections, reported in Faig, *R. H. Bar-*

ond example is a proper simile and even more striking, for both its sheer length (which truly configures it as "epic") and the vivid suggestiveness of the image involved: "Upon the beach and me alike had fallen a shadow, like that of a bird which flies silently overhead—a bird whose watching eyes we do not suspect till the image on the ground repeats the image in the sky, and we look suddenly upward to find that something has been circling above us hitherto unseen" (EG 117). Occasionally, in order to reinforce the poetic flavor of his prose Barlow employs another typical figure of the epic, namely the *syntactic inversion* or *anastrophe*, as in "*Whispers were* that he was drugged or hypnotized by the strange plant" ("The Flower God," episode six of the *Annals of the Jinns* [EG 20; italics added]).

Among the archaisms Barlow disseminates in his fantasy fiction, again a very long list of possible examples can be readily prepared: "ere" for "before" ("The Slaying of the Monster," EG 13), "fain," "hearken," and "wielded" (this last referred to the blade Gra, the counsellor of king Luud, brandishes so "judiciously") (all these examples are taken from "The Flower God," episode six of the *Annals of the Jinns*, EG 20-21), "spake" for "spoke" ("The Fidelity of Ghu," EG 41), "beldame" ("The Temple," EG 50), "thyself . . . thy god . . . thou hast" ("The Priest and the Heretic," EG 64-65), the use of "without" as "outside" in "[. . .] men might have unbarred the Door and gone without to see [. . .]" ("A Memory," EG 75).

As a third trait of the formal aspect of Barlow's Dunsanianism, the use of exotic and unearthly lexemes reinforces the depiction of a fantastic realm, alternative to that of the real world. The list of place and characters' names having a nuance of fantastic flavor is again potentially endless. Limiting our survey only to the short tales composing the cycle *Annals of the Jinns*, among the place-names or the names indicating natural elements (mountains, rivers, seas, etc.) we could mention: the river Olaee, the hamlet of Droom, the towns of Leek, Ullathia, Phoor, Saaldae, Yondath, Zath, Zaxtl, the cities Naazim, Zo, and Perenthines (the three titular cities of "The Fall of the Three Cities," episode eight of the *Annals*), the planet Loth, the isle of Hin, the sea-bed of Innia, etc. Among the names of characters like kings, wizards, sorcerers, counsellors, would-be heroes, etc., in the *Annals* Barlow drops exotic or weird-sounding ones such as Krang, Alair, Luud, Gra, Hsuth, Volnar, Sarall, Khalda, Malyat, Morla, Loman, etc. And even outside the *Annals*, quite popular in the recognition of Barlow's fictional trademark have become names as lord Ghu and Garoth,[5] which inspired Lovecraft to address his pupil in letters with nicknames such as "Lord Ghu" or "Invincible Garoth."

The word "Jinn" itself deserves a separate discussion. In fact, it may sound exotic and otherworldly, but the reasons that led Barlow to choose it probably are not merely phonetic. First, as an epitaph at the beginning of the *Jinns* cycle, Bar-

---

low, makes it possible to acknowledge this and the following simile as the exclusive product of Barlow's pen.

5. Protagonists, respectively, of the sarcastic "The Fidelity of Ghu" (published for the first time in EG 40-41) and *The Adventures of Garoth* (*Perspective Review*, Summer 1935; rpt. in EG 52-57).

low appended a quotation from William Beckford's "Story of Prince Barkiarokh," one of *The Episodes of Vathek*. The quotation reads as follows: "[. . .] Thither Ganigul often retired in the daytime to read in quiet the marvellous annals of the Jinns, the chronicles of ancient worlds, and the prophecies relating to the worlds that are yet to be born" (*EG* 14). The quotation is revelatory, since it both points to Beckford as one of the possible models of Barlow's prose-poetic style and also because it provides a possible explanation to Barlow's adoption of the word "Jinn," suggesting it was not, like the others of the fantasy cycle, an invented word. However, another, perhaps more suggestive reason may be at the basis of Barlow's lexical choice, a reason that would also significantly link his fiction even more to Lovecraft's and in particular to the *Necronomicon*.

As is well known, the original Arab title of Lovecraft's grimoire is *Al Azif*. In "History of the *Necronomicon*" (1927), Lovecraft writes: "Original title Al *Azif–azif* being the word used by Arabs to designate that nocturnal sound (made by insects) suppos'd to be the howling of daemons" (*Miscellaneous Writings* 52). Lovecraft derived this information precisely from Beckford's *Vathek* (French edition, 1782),[6] which claims that Muslims believe that the rumor of the buzz of those nocturnal insect is to be interpreted as a bad omen. In 1786 Samuel Henley translated Beckford's text into English, and in a note to the novel he remarks that, in the Bible, at the fifth verse of Psalm 95 (Psalm 91 in the Catholic version of the Bible), the locution "the *terror* by night" is rendered, in Old English, with "the *bugge* by night." In American colonial times, any potentially dangerous nocturnal insect was generically labeled a "bug." And *Beelzebul*, or "Lord of the Flies," was one of the Oriental names attributed to the Devil, while the nocturnal sound called *azif* by the Arabs was believed to be the howling of demons. It is not clear whence Henley derived his information: probably it had to do with the tradition according to which the ancient pre-Islamic mystics, known as *kahin* (prophets or mad poets), were rumored to get their ultramundane knowledge from listening to the nocturnal whispers, similar to the humming of insects, of the *Jinns* haunting the desert. In Middle Eastern folklore, the *Jinns* were inferior and demonic spirits (see Lock and Khaldun): therefore, *Al Azif*, the Arab title of the *Necronomicon*, may stand for "Revelations of the Jinns," or "The secrets of the demons."

However, the picture would be incomplete without a mention of the opinion of Richard Cavendish, historian of magic and demonology, according to whom the Jews, in the Middle Ages, identified the "nocturnal terrors" of Psalm 95 with the demon-woman Lilith. She had human form, but also wings and long ruffled hair. According to the legend, Lilith had been Adam's dissolute first wife, before Eve was created. Refusing to submit to Adam, Lilith left him and copulated with lascivious demons, with which she generated hordes of demonic beings. Cavendish reports another Hebraic legend, whereby Lilith would have been the *second* of Adam's

---

6. ". . . the original title was Al *azif –azif* (cf. Henley's notes to *Vathek*) being the name applied to those strange night noises (of insects) which the Arabs attribute to the howling of daemons": letter to Clark Ashton Smith, 27 November 1927 (*SL* 2.201).

wives, at the time when he, after Cain and Abel's births, did not lie with Eve for about 130 years. During this period, Adam engendered with Lilith several demons, grouped under the three classes of Shedim, Lilin, and Rouchin. All these creatures that Lilith would have produced by mating with Adam or the demons are precisely the titular *jinns* of Barlow's *Annals*, and responsible for the nocturnal sound that in the Arabic deserts is mistaken for the humming of insects, but that in reality derives from much more powerful sources: in fact, Lilith's sons had been taught by their mother to communicate, through their whispers, obscene secrets and pre-human abominations. Thus Abdul Alhazred, who listened to that sound, decided to write down its message and teachings, gaining madness as a reward.

In addition to these analytic traits which objectively testify the epic "Dunsanianism" of Barlow's prose style, other, more general remarks may be made in this sense. The prose-poetic quality of Barlow's style is also generated through the occasional resort to a device typically employed in poetry (and of which Barlow himself made abundant use, as we will see in discussing his poetry): alliteration. One example may suffice for all: it is particularly striking, since the alliteration involves the initial phoneme of six words in rapid succession within the same sentence: "I was sick with weariness when we stood at last before the gated wall" ("A Dim-Remembered Story," *EG* 94).[7] It seems as if Barlow tried, in this phrase, to insert a poetic line within an otherwise prose tale. Coloring a prose style with poetic nuances involves also the occasional resort to typical poetic devices such as *synaesthesia*.[8] In the perfectly calibrated "The Root-Gatherers," the reader encounters a "bluish silence," which is a textbook example of the combination of two different sensory fields (sight for "bluish" and hearing for "silence").

However, it is not simply due to these rhetoric devices that the overall flavor of Barlow's fiction often reveals a poetic nuance. Barlow consciously strove to achieve it in conjunction with his attempt to depict the "dreamy" atmosphere and mood necessary for a weird tale to be effective—something he had learned from his early readings of Lovecraft, Dunsany, and Smith. Poetic words occur frequently in Barlow's fiction: let us mention for instance the "rills of wax" (*EG* 96), the "hoar" and the "sundering" (*EG* 101) of "A Dim-Remembered Story," the "athwart" (*EG* 107) of "The Night Ocean," and the "runnels" (*EG* 139-40) of

---

7. A similar though shorter alliteration focusing on the sound *w* can be found in "The Night Ocean," where one reads "prisoned emotions which are hastily stifled when we would translate them" (*EG* 105).

8. From the Greek "perceiving together," it can be defined as "The description of a sense impression in terms more appropriate to a different sense; the mixing of sense impressions in order to create a particular kind of metaphor" (Gray 205) or as "the practice of associating two or more different senses in the same image. It speaks of one sensation in terms of another" (Murfin and Ray 473). In other words, this rhetorical figure simultaneously appeals to more than one sense. Probably the word *synaesthesia* "was first used by Jules Millet in 1892" (Cuddon 889), when the figure was theorized after its intense and conscious use by the French Symbolists (Baudelaire and Rimbaud in particular), though synaesthetic effects had been employed, more or less consciously, already by Homer, Aeschylus, and Horace (ibid.).

"Return by Sunset." Within this strategic insistence on the poetic quality of his prose, Barlow often introduces the devices of *personification* of natural elements: the effect and the purpose of this rhetorical device are in fact manifold, and some of them will be discussed in the analysis of the fifth "theme" of Barlow's fiction, "Nature." However, what one might call a collateral effect of this device is to reinforce the poetic quality of his prose, helping to depict an extraordinary scene, where animals or even inanimate objects are provided with human qualities and feelings. For instance, again in "A Dim-Remembered Story" we read: "It was the dirge of water-steeped Atlantis, or the cry of a tortured lover in the night. Long after the voice of passionate despair had ebbed into oblivion, the silence rippled with its memory" (*EG* 97).[9] The personification of silence here configures a peculiarly hazardous image: silence is not only solidified (the quality "to possess a surface" is attributed to it), but it is imagined that its surface may be "rippled" by the intervention of "memory," which is thus personified in its turn. It would be hard to conceive another delicate and suggestive image more able than this one to contribute to the creation of a poetic atmosphere.

2.2.2 The content aspects of Barlow's Dunsanianism: the Barlow Mythos

In his fantasy tales, one of the most significant of Barlow's aims is to depict a wholly coherent fantastic universe. In order to do so, and taking as a model Dunsany, Smith, and Lovecraft himself, Barlow carefully strives to build up an artificial mythology, in which the same invented characters, locations, events, and books are recalled from one tale to another. In particular—and this is the most evident but by no means unique case—the *Annals of the Jinns* were conceived by Barlow as a coherent fantasy cycle, and cross-references are present everywhere in the text. This is probably one of the most striking features of Barlow's Dunsanianism from the content viewpoint, and the one I have chosen to discuss here.[10]

In particular, the models represented by Dunsany and Lovecraft were extremely important to Barlow on this regard. As Lovecraft stated, he himself took Dunsany as his model when building up the artificial pseudomythology of his own fiction: "[. . .] Lord Dunsany—from whom I got the idea of the artificial pantheon and myth-background represented by 'Cthulhu', 'Yog-Sothoth', 'Yuggoth', etc." ("Some Notes on a Nonentity" [1933], *CE* 209-10). But why did Lovecraft decide to follow Dunsany's model and build up a mythology of his own? Essentially, in order find a way to express the impulses of his own imagination:

---

9. Let us note here, incidentally, another (not certainly casual) dropping of a compounded word, almost an epithet: "water-steeped."
10. Other elements of RHB's Dunsanianism will appear in passing along with the analysis of the other six "themes" of his fiction. This will prove, once more, the interconnectedness and non-separability of the "themes" of his fiction.

In my own efforts to crystallise this spaceward outreaching, I try to utilise as many as possible of the elements which have, under earlier mental and emotional conditions, given man a symbolic feeling of the unreal, the ethereal, & the mystical—choosing those least attacked by realistic mental and emotional conditions of the present. Darkness—sunset—dreams—mists—fever—madness—the tomb—the hills—the sea—the sky—the wind—all these, & many other things have seemed to me to retain a certain imaginative potency despite our actual scientific analyses of them. Accordingly I have tried to weave them into a kind of shadowy phantasmagoria which may have the same sort of vague coherence as a cycle of traditional myth or legend—with nebulous backgrounds of Elder Forces & trans-galactic entities which lurk about this infinitesimal planet (& of course about others as well), establishing outposts thereon, & occasionally brushing aside other accidental forms of life (like human beings) in order to take up full habitation. This is essentially the sort of notion prevalent in most racial mythologies—but an artificial mythology can become subtler & more plausible than a natural one, because it can recognize & adapt itself to the information and moods of the present. The best artificial mythology, of course, is Lord Dunsany's elaborate & consistently developed pantheon of Pegana's gods. (SL 4.70)

Dunsany had created his artificial pantheon essentially in his first two books: *The Gods of Pegāna* (1905) and *Time and the Gods* (1906).[11] A passage from Joshi's *A Subtler Magick* may prove fruitful in order to realize the scope and the importance of the creation of an artificial mythology for authors like Dunsany and Lovecraft, while at the same time illuminate the reasons themselves because of which Barlow decided to do the same:

The mere act of creating an imaginary religion calls for some comment: it clearly denotes some dissatisfaction with the religion (Christianity) with which the author was raised. Dunsany was, by all accounts, an atheist, although not quite so vociferous a one as Lovecraft; and his gods were, like Lovecraft's, symbols for some of his most deeply held philosophical beliefs. In Dunsany's case, these were such things as the need for human reunification with the natural world and distaste for many features of modern civilization (business, advertising, and in general the absence of beauty and poetry in contemporary life). Lovecraft, having his own philosophical message to convey, used his imaginary pantheon for analogous purposes. (131-32)

However, the major and original modification Lovecraft brought to the Dunsanian "pattern" was that of transferring the latter's imaginary pantheon from a fantastic realm like that of Pegāna into the real world:[12]

---

11. See Joshi, *The Weird Tale* 190: "Subsequent works by Dunsany utilize imaginary gods from time to time, but no longer in a systematic and interrelated manner."
12. Another work depicting a *terrestrial* mythology that probably influenced the genesis of HPL's pseudomythology was that by Arthur Machen, "[. . .] who wrote about a stunted and debased race of primitive beings still secretly existing beneath the lonely Welsh hills [. . .]. Lovecraft was much impressed with this concept, but he alone expanded the notion

The momentousness of this transference cannot be overemphasized: Lovecraft's own "Dunsanian" fantasies evolve their own series of interconnected gods and places—Ulthar, Sarnath, and the like—but they remain in an otherworldly never-never land with dim and insubstantial relations to the real world; these tales accordingly remain pure fantasies. When Cthulhu suddenly emerges from the depths of Pacific, he effects an unprecedented union of horror and science fiction unlike anything that went before. Cthulhu is a real entity—it may be a symbol, as Nyarlathotep and Azathoth are very largely symbols (and as Dunsany's gods, caught in their imagined universe, are entirely symbols), but it is first and foremost a real, dangerous, and malignant entity. It is also material, albeit with certain anomalous properties such as the ability to recombine disparate parts of itself. (Joshi, *The Weird Tale* 190-91)

Barlow shared the Lovecraftian decision to create an artificial mythology, namely to become a myth-maker,[13] and not to rely upon those already devised by human folklore and traditions. In Lovecraft, this choice was not simply dictated by the desire to comply with Dunsany's model, but had deeper roots in Lovecraft's own thought. In other words, this choice adhered to a specific vision on the writer's part: "But I consider the use of actual folk-myths as even more childish than the use of new artificial myths, since in employing the former one is forced to retain many blatant puerilities & contradictions of experience which could be subtilised or smoothed over if the supernaturalism were modelled to order for the given case" (letter to Frank Belknap Long, 27 February 1931; *SL* 3.293).

Of course, Barlow's Mythos, as it configures in its fantasy tales, had a much lesser readership than Lovecraft's, but the principles guiding its creation were certainly analogous. In fact, Lovecraft's reasons for why he was deliberately creating a coherent artificial mythology, by dropping names and cross-references (taken from his own tales or, as we shall see, borrowed from other writers' works) in his original narratives as well as in his revisionary work, were essentially two: sheer fun, and the attempt to give the mythology an appearance of verisimilitude. This is how Lovecraft expressed his viewpoint on the matter in a 1934 letter: "It rather amuses the different writers to use one another's synthetic demons & imaginary books in their stories. This pooling of resources tends to build up quite a pseudo-convincing background of dark mythology, legendry, & bibliography—though of course none of us has the least wish actually to mislead readers" (*SL* 4.346).[14]

---

of a localized prehuman survival into a vast cosmology of his own creation" (Robert Bloch, "Heritage of Horror," xvii).

13. Dirk W. Mosig was the first to employ the locution "myth-maker" with reference to the Providence writer (see "H. P. Lovecraft: Myth-Maker," in Mosig 21-29).

14. There are other passages of similar tenor in Lovecraft's correspondence: "For the *fun* of building up a convincing cycle of synthetic folklore, all our gang frequently allude to the pet demons of others [...] Thus our black pantheon *acquires an extensive publicity and pseudo-authoritativeness it would otherwise not get* [...] All this gives it a sort of *air of verisimilitude*" (letter to W. F. Anger, 14 August 1934; *SL* 5.16; italics added).

How then may the operation of creating an artificial mythology take place? Important roles are played by conscious deliberation, and also by sheer chance. Lovecraft was very careful in the insertion of Mythos elements within his original tales, on the basis of how many tales dealing with them had already become familiar to the readers of *Weird Tales*. Not only this, but the employment of Mythos elements in the tale "The Whisperer in Darkness" (completed in September 1930 and published in *Weird Tales* for August 1931) shows that Lovecraft had in mind the readers' reactions toward his developing pseudomythology. In fact, in this tale it is possible to detect an approach to the use of Mythos names very different from that of the previous "original" stories. The text presents more than two dozen names, and Lovecraft for the first time drops other names, taken from the works of at least other five past or contemporary authors, such as Robert E. Howard, Lord Dunsany, Clark Ashton Smith, Ambrose Bierce, Frank Belknap Long, and Robert W. Chambers.[15] Probably the reason behind this decision should be traced to an episode involving a reader, J. O'Neail, whose letter had appeared in *Weird Tales* for March 1930, in the letter column "The Eyrie":

> I was very much interested in tracing the apparent connection between the characters of Kathulos, in Robert E. Howard's "Skull-Face", and that of Cthulhu, in Mr. Lovecraft's "The Call of Cthulhu". Can you inform me whether there is any legend or tradition surrounding that character? And also Yog-Sothoth? Mr. Lovecraft links the latter up with Cthulhu in "The Dunwich Horror" and Adolphe de Castro also refers to Yog-Sothoth in "The Last Test". Both these stories also contain references to Abdul Alhazred the mad Arab, and his Necronomicon. I am sure this is a subject in which many readers besides myself would be interested; something which could be reviewed in a series of articles similar to those [on common folks beliefs] written by Alvin F. Harlow. (Joshi and Michaud, *H. P. Lovecraft in "The Eyrie"* 31)

Therefore, Lovecraft had achieved his goal: readers began to link the Mythos elements dropped in different tales—written by different authors—into a coherent set: the Mythos began to grow, both in popularity and verisimilitude, assuming that "pseudo-authoritativeness" which led O'Neail to question the shared folklore and legendary roots of apparently unrelated tales such as those by Lovecraft and Howard he had read in *Weird Tales*. O'Neail's letter may be considered an impor-

---

15. In an early letter to RHB, HPL revealed the deliberateness of the contribution of different writers in the gradual establishment of their fictional and sometimes intertwined mythologies: "Cthulhu & his myth-cycle are purely fictitious, & of my own invention. Various authors of my acquaintance, however, are beginning to employ references to them in their tales; so that we are really creating quite a synthetic pantheon! *Tsathoggua* is a similar creation of Clark Ashton Smith's—which we are also taking up for general mystical reference." (letter dated 13 July 1931; *FF* 4). Tsathoggua was introduced by Smith in "The Tale of Satampra Zeiros" (written 1929), but paradoxically it was HPL who first mentioned it in print (in "The Whisperer in Darkness" [*Weird Tales*, August 1931], while Smith's tale saw publication only in the November 1931 issue).

tant moment, almost a turning point, for the deep impact it had on the ways in which Lovecraft would later develop the Mythos. At the time the letter was published, Lovecraft had just begun his correspondence with Robert E. Howard (whom O'Neail mentions in his letter). Five months later, Lovecraft addressed Howard in this way: "[Frank Belknap] Long has alluded to the *Necronomicon* in some things of his—in fact, I think it is rather good fun to have this artificial mythology given an air of verisimilitude by wide citation. I ought, though, to write Mr. O'Neail and disabuse him of the idea that there is a large blind spot in his mythological erudition!" (SL 3.166).

If Lovecraft's borrowing of elements of other writers' pseudomythologies in his own fiction represented a deliberate act, he certainly had no part in Long's doing the same: thus, even chance contributed to the development and the enlargement of Lovecraft's artificial mythology. Other writers did the same, inserting elements derived from Lovecraft's Mythos in their own narratives, and the "favor" was in a sense reciprocal, since Lovecraft continued the borrowing. His artificial mythology was becoming very plausible and "believable"—without this having been planned in advance: readers like O'Neail even began to wonder about its actual "historiographic" and anthropological roots. But Lovecraft had certainly no desire to delude or mislead his readers: the profusion of Mythos names, for instance, in "The Whisperer in Darkness" (including the mentioning of "Kathulos," in homage to O'Neail himself and to the new correspondent Robert E. Howard, who invented it) attests to Lovecraft's regard for the impact his work produced on the public.

Of course, Barlow's own Mythos could not bear comparison with Lovecraft's, since the sheer scope and impact of the two artificial mythologies are significantly different. Barlow could not count on an audience quantitatively comparable to Lovecraft's—but this reflection does not threaten my conviction that the principles Barlow followed to devise his pseudomythology were analogous to those guiding his master: the scope, the range of their operations are different, but the goals and the technical realization are similar. In fact, according to Joshi, an artificial mythology is built upon literary devices or techniques that, for instance in Lovecraft's case, can be grouped in three categories: "first, the invented 'gods' and the cults or worshippers that have grown up around them; second, an ever-increasing library of mythical books of occult lore; and third, a fictitious New England topography (Arkham, Dunwich, Innsmouth, etc.)" (Joshi 2001, 245). With the possible but only partial exception of the "ever-increasing library" of mythical books, we will see that Barlow's artificial mythology reflected all the traits of Lovecraft's own Mythos.

Let us now examine in greater detail the characteristics and the nature of Barlow's Mythos. First of all, it must be noted that Barlow's literary mythology does exceed the borders of the fantasy cycle *Annals of the Jinns* and covers a wider bulk of narratives. Cross-references are in fact present all over Barlow's fantasy production, not only among the eleven installments of the cycle, and involve a wide variety of elements such as (human and non-human) characters, locations, objects, and plot elements. A peculiar element Barlow introduces in his fiction, following the model of Lovecraft's Mythos (and in particular of the obscure grimoire, the *Necronomicon*, and of the enigmatic book of ancient lore, the Pnakotic Manuscripts), is that of the forbidden text receptacle of a blasphemous knowledge, the only difference from Lovecraft being that Barlow's library of books of occult lore is not "ever-increasing," since, as already noted, the scope and range of Barlow's Mythos is not as wide and articulated as Lovecraft's. The name Barlow chose to define the source of forbidden knowledge for the protagonists of his fantasy tales is Hsoth. Not much is told about the nature of the fabled Hsothian manuscripts, consistent with the purpose to wrap them in a halo of vague legend. Very scarce information about these manuscripts, their source and their content, is provided in "The Tomb of the God," the fifth episode of the *Annals*: in the tomb of the dead monster-god Krang, together with other inestimable treasures, there were sealed up "the strange manuscripts with the Hsothian chants upon them, and other equally desirable objects" (EG 19). In "The Fall of the Three Cities," episode eight of the *Annals*, the story is told of sorcerer Volnar who, in order to effect his revenge against the citizens of Perenthines, who forced him to leave the town, frequently consulted "the parchments that were said to have been copied from the Hsothian manuscripts by a slave of the Lord Krang, very long ago" (EG 24). What strikes in particular is the vagueness of these hints: the reader is only told that these manuscripts are strange and very old, and that they contain some chants, while in episode ten, "The Theft of the Hsothian Manuscripts," they are simply described as "a scroll of tattered papyrus" (EG 29). This vagueness is of course intentional, but already points to a sort of coherence of the whole mythical fabric, since the Hsothian manuscripts are not only mentioned in different locations, but are often connected to the figure of the fabled Lord-God Krang, whose repeated presence then attributes a stronger degree of coherence to the Barlow Mythos (and let us remember that "invented gods" are, according to Joshi, one of the elements reinforcing the impression of a coherent mythology in Lovecraft's own work). Toward this very same goal, several other recurring elements contribute, among which the following could be mentioned:

- the town (or better, location, since the nature of this toponym is deliberately left vague) of Phoor appears in "The Tomb of the God" as well as in "The Fall of the Three Cities";
- the location of Phargo appears in "The Little Box," seventh episode of the *Annals*, and in "The Fall of the Three Cities" (these two short episodes were published at a two-month distance, on the June and August 1934 issues of the *Fantasy Fan*);
- the "hamlet" of Droom is the location of the uncanny events retold in "The Shadow from Above," second episode of the *Annals*: an invisible, portentous flying monster had appeared inside the village, spreading, during a fearful night, death, panic, and destruction over the peaceful inhabitants. While writing, in "The Fall of the Three Cities," about Zo,

- one of the three "cities of the plain" (together with Naazim and Perenthines), Barlow states that the rule in Zo had been to keep the city-gates "fast closed till full dawn, ever since the Night of the Monster in neighboring Droom, close unto the mountains" (EG 23). Thus, the nature of the cross-reference here is particularly interesting, due to its doubling: it does not simply refer to a plot element present in another tale (the "Shadow from Above"), but also hints at the geographic closeness of the two cities—suggesting that topographic coherence which Joshi recognizes as one of the trademarks of a carefully built artificial mythology;
- another, similar topographic cross-reference can be found comparing "The Fall of the Three Cities" (episode eight of the *Annals*), "The Mirror" (episode nine of the *Annals*, published in the last issue of the *Fantasy Fan*, February 1935) and "An Episode in the Jungle" (episode eleven, first published in *EG* 29-31): the location of Yondath, again left vague, the most likely hypothesis being that it is a complex of towns or, more likely, a kingdom bordering on (or immersed into) a forest; moreover, river Oolae appears in both episode eight, "The Fall of the Three Cities," and episode ten, "The Theft of the Hsothian Manuscripts";
- the character of Volnar, the sorcerer, is the protagonist of the revengeful doom that hits the three cities of "The Fall of the Three Cities"; but he comes back, though indirectly, in "The Mirror" (episode nine), whose protagonist is his similarly revengeful pupil Khalda;
- the terrible events retold in "The Mirror," in which Khalda avenges himself against the Emperor of Yondath, who had condemned him to the tortures of the Green Fungi, are reprised in the tenth episode of the *Annals*, "The Theft of the Hsothian Manuscripts."[16] In fact, we apprehend that Khalda happens to have escaped the tortures the Emperor of Yondath had intended to inflict upon him, through his servant, head torturer Malyat (events described in the eight episode, "The Mirror"), and is now dwelling in a huge hidden black palace he has built after his untold escape from Malyat's tortures. To reinforce the coherence of the Mythos, Barlow now makes Khalda preserve, in his castle, the fabled Hsothian manuscripts mentioned elsewhere in the cycle.

That Barlow was trying to concoct a parallel, coherent fantastic realm inside a single fantasy cycle is not particularly surprising. What is more striking is that he deliberately chose, again on Lovecraft's and Dunsany's models, to insert frequent references to the artificial mythology devised inside the cycle in disparate tales that were not part of the *Annals of the Jinns*. A few examples: "The Hoard of the

---

16. First published in *The Phantagraph*, August 1936. This tenth episode of the fantasy cycle was published a year and a half after the last installment, "The Mirror," saw the light in the *Fantasy Fan*, because of the folding of the latter magazine. Barlow, heedless of the time elapsed between the two publications, did not fail to link the two episodes by several elements, probably because they had been initially composed in rapid succession.

Wizard-Beast,"[17] the second of the six collaborations with Lovecraft so far ascertained, mentions the city of Ullathia, whose inhabitants are protagonists of the grotesque events of "The Sacred Bird," fourth episode of the *Annals*. Moreover, the same tale mentions the "Lord of Worms, Sarall," to which the protagonist of "The Hoard," Yalden, asks help in order to find his way to the cave of Anathas, the wizard-beast: it happens that this very same Sarall, Lord of Worms, plays a role in "The Fall of the Three Cities," where he/it is in fact the one to whom sorcerer Volnar sends a messenger "to obtain a certain ingredient most accessible to maggots" (*EG* 24). There are countless other possible examples: in "The Fidelity of Ghu," the protagonist is described as the "last of the priests that had served Krang" (*EG* 40), the Lord-God who had already been abundantly present in the *Annals*, while the 14,000-year-old demon Garoth appears in the *Book of Garoth*, "The Adventures of Garoth," as well as in the lesser-known "The Misfortunes of Butter-Churning."

Another interesting element Barlow uses in the attempt to depict a coherent, parallel fantastic universe is the introduction of peculiar elements, typical of the world in question, to which the author attaches invented words of exotic flavor. These names are not personal names, but define common objects or creatures existing only in the specific universe of Barlow's fantasies—and this is the reason why I would consider these elements as a content-aspect, and not a mere lexical-formal one. In other words, this is not a matter of simple vocabulary choice: in fact, the (living or non-living) objects described by these lexemes are integral parts of the alternative universe Barlow depicts; they are their constitutive and founding elements, and their names are not simply labels (chosen among the most exotic and otherworldly) attached to beings that exist also in the real world. What is also interesting is that in most cases the reader is not told what these fantastic objects precisely are: Barlow leaves the description vague, in order to reinforce the sense of mystery and alterity attached to these fantastic creations. Of course, this expedient is consistent with the model represented, for instance, by Lovecraft's fictional fantasy realms, which adopt a similar technique featuring recurring creatures such as the shoggoths and the night-gaunts.

Among the possible examples of this aspect of Barlow's fantasy fiction, we could mention the following:

- ridna-zat: this term appears in "The Little Box," episode seven of the *Annals of the Jinns*. It tells of Hsuth, a "brown tailed man from Leek," a very inquisitive savage living on the planet Loth. Hsuth had been made a captive in his youth and subsequently serviced in the "ridna-zat works." The reader may only suppose what they could be: perhaps factories or craftsmen's workshops, since the only thing she is told is that the activity carried on there was the manufacture of "first class ornaments to be worn in the nose" (*EG* 21);

---

17. Joshi recognizes the "pseudo-Dunsanian" flavor of this story, which Lovecraft revised extensively, though "it nonetheless remains the work of an apprentice" (*A Subtler Magick* 201).

- rogii: these are defined as "six-legged and grotesque monster-things" (*EG* 22) roaming freely in fields of waving grass; moreover, in the very same tale the reader is told that the rogii can be used as beasts of burden, are capable of climbing on mountainous paths, and can attain remarkable speed for their bulk (*EG* 24). Thus they are certainly domesticated creatures, and of remarkable size—the reader is left free to conjecture the physical aspect of the rogii, for instance whether they may be similar to cows, camels, or perhaps more likely horses (a rogii is defined as "steed");
- glortups: these "slave-things" are described as "squat, brownish-green little monsters that mimicked the aspect of humans and the features of toads" ("A Memory," *EG* 75); the history of the race of glortups follows closely that of the Lovecraftian shoggoths, in that they were both created by ancestors' experiments and passed through alternate phases of segregation and rebellion against their masters (imitating the parable of the Lovecraftian shoggoths of *At the Mountains of Madness*, the only difference being that in Lovecraft's novel the masters are the Old Ones, while in Barlow's "A Memory" they are humans). The glortups make their first appearance in "A Memory" and are mentioned again in the short tale "Pursuit of the Moth";
- mondal: this is a curious creature that makes its first appearance in "The Fall of the Three Cities," as sorcerer Volnar's pet. The only information about it is that it is "highly edible," it is able to "moan inconsolably" for the loss of his owner, and is much regretted by Volnar himself. The mondal seems then a creature capable of both giving and receiving affection—as a pet of the real world is commonly intended to do. In another episode of the Jinns cycle, the eleventh and last, "An Episode in the Jungle," the impression that the mondal is a quite remarkable and interesting creature is reinforced: it is mentioned together with elk and leopards as an inhabitant of forests, and thus meant as an animal. But, above all, it is described as the possible and much sought-after trophy of a hunt: everybody tries to return with a specimen of this "rare and delectable beast" (*EG* 29). Summarizing, the reader can then infer that a mondal is an animal friendly to humans, highly edible, and quite rare and difficult to capture. Any consideration about its physical aspect and/or its behavioural traits is left to the reader's imagination.

Thus most of Barlow's fantasy tales are deliberately set in a fantastic realm very similar to that of Dunsany's and Lovecraft's tales, a realm whose most significant features all concur to convey the impression of a coherent and carefully built artificial mythology. However, the discussion of the "Dunsanianism" of Barlow's fantasy fiction would not be complete without a final hint to another remarkable aspect. As in Dunsany's, Lovecraft's, and Smith's fantasies, Barlow's fantasy fiction also occasionally presents pure horrific elements—from this viewpoint too, Barlow's goal to deliberately imitate his masters is successful. A couple among the most significant examples may be sufficient to illustrate this point. In "The Fall of the Three Cities," episode eight of the *Annals*, sorcerer Volnar takes vengeance on the cities of Zo, Naazim, and Perenthines, by elaborating an obnoxious magic concoction, a bubbling substance he seals into a cylinder of unglazed pottery and then lets slide, at night, into the pool at the center of Zo. This is the description of the slow growing of the substance, and of its protoplasmic nature:

> [. . .] the strange substance grew and distended in size and weight until it restlessly filled the large pool. It had assumed no definite shape, but life was unquestionably within the vast prehensile tissue that groped at the edge of its confines. It was as yet unable to release itself and venture in search of food, but the time was not distant. A chance pedestrian [. . .] went slowly by and did not fully realize what was happening when he saw the thing droolingly emerge from the pool. The hundred evil eyes peered loathsomely as it extended an awful limb and seized him, intent upon the process of absorbing nutrition. Nor was that the end, for it roved the streets unsated, growing, devouring throughout the night, and in a few horrible hours had depopulated the cities that were so hostile to sorcerers. (EG 25)

This description reminds of the slowly growing ectoplasmic and vampiric creature, actually many-eyed and "absorbing nutrition" from other creatures, of Lovecraft's "The Shunned House" (1924): "One might easily imagine an alien nucleus of substance or energy, formless or otherwise, kept alive by imperceptible or immaterial subtractions from the life-force or bodily tissues and fluids of other and more palpably living things into which it penetrates and with whose fabric it sometimes completely merges itself" (*DW* 106). And again: "Out of the fungus-ridden earth steamed up a vaporous corpse-light, yellow and diseased, which bubbled and lapped to a gigantic height in vague outlines half-human and half-monstrous [. . .] It was all eyes—wolfish and mocking—and the rugose insect-like head dissolved at the top to a thin stream of mist which curled putridly about and finally vanished up the chimney" (*DW* 111).

And in "The Temple," Chapter 3 of the *Book of Garoth*, the demon protagonist of this other cycle Barlow never completed participates in quite unexpected, horrific events. A group of eight priests wondrously dressed drags forth from a temple a "lovely young girl," and each of them bewitches her with a "malignant curse." The descriptions of the torments to which the girl is subjected are purely in a horrific vein: the first curse caused her "to become a living torch as if a thousand little painful fires had blazed within her, and these fires shot forth and vanished, and she shrieked and fell to the ground" (EG 50). The second curse summoned "a hideous fiend in the form of an evil green thing with soft scales and puffy limbs ending in cruel claws. This abhorrence of perverted sorcery leered at her, and made great scratches on her smooth flesh; and then clutched her, with ease tearing off her head, though it bled not, and Garoth knew this was magic. It cast the corpse and head aside and vanished at its master's command" (EG 50). However, the most horrific touches have yet to come: "The third priest bewitched her decapitated body, and she writhed in terror. The head rolled most horribly back to its original position, and she was again living. The girl moaned fearfully at the thing that was being done to her. Her limbs and body withered, shrivelled as if a hundred years of desiccation had become compressed into a moment; and she became an ancient and repulsive beldame" (EG 50).

Therefore, already in the discussion of this first "theme" of Barlow's fiction, we see at work a blend of elements typical of his narrative strategies: the Dunsanian, suspended tone of his prose-poetic style often cannot do without horrific nuances. And of course, if within a single "theme" the combination of different elements is a consistent trait of Barlow's fiction, this attests to the possibility of the overlapping of different "themes," as the discussions about them in the next chapters will make clear.

H. P. Lovecraft, Robert H. Barlow. Mrs. Bernice Barlow, and Wayne Barlow.

3. Vagueness

The "theme" of vagueness constitutes an essential aesthetic aspect of Barlow's narratives, because it crosses all the major categories of his fiction (fantasy and cosmic horror), with the only possible exception of the ironic and spoof pieces. The importance of the "theme" of vagueness is underscored by the titles themselves of some of Barlow's narratives, like "A *Dim*-Remembered Story" or "Origin *Undetermined*." Not surprisingly, it was again Lovecraft who taught Barlow the importance of vagueness—and of the depiction of a mood—when writing weird fiction: "A plot in a weird story he called 'excess baggage'—mode and atmosphere being all" ("Memories of Lovecraft," OLL 17). In a letter to Barlow dated 11 May 1935, Lovecraft reinforced his aesthetic point by claiming that "Indeed—all formal *plot* in the sense praised and demanded by conventional commercial editors is basically inartistic. A weird story, to be a serious aesthetic effort, must form primarily a *picture of a mood*" (FF 262). And in *Supernatural Horror in Literature*, Lovecraft wrote—apropos of some of Algernon Blackwood's works: "Plot is everywhere negligible, and atmosphere reigns untrammelled" (67). As a matter of fact, Barlow's narratives do have a plot, as Lovecraft's own works do—but the insistence on aesthetic and literary vagueness in the depiction of fictional atmosphere and events represents a predominant trait for both. Of course vagueness should not be seen as a merely narrative or linguistic device: it reflects a particular vision of life, the pessimism of an observer/perceiver who is aware to have only a vague, and insufficient, possibility of grasping the (allegedly objective) reality around him, and finally the meaning of life itself. This is where the notion of aesthetic "vagueness" links to that of "cosmicism": an apparently "technical" theme that stems from (and consistently represents) a content concern on the author's part.

Altogether, in Barlow's fiction five levels of *vagueness* may be identified, according to an increasing narratological complexity. Barlow often operates a joining of different levels on the same narrative plane, in order to achieve a specific aesthetic effect: the analysis will elucidate when this union occurs and what impact it exerts on the narrative. The five-level vagueness of Barlow's fiction can be schematized as follows:

1. Vagueness of communication
2. Vagueness of perception
3. Vagueness of the object of perception
4. Vagueness of the narrating voice
5. Vagueness as a literary technique

Now I proceed to discuss each of the five levels of Barlow's fiction's vagueness.

3.1 Vagueness of communication

This level of vagueness is the most formal one, and pertains just the surface narrative level. "Vagueness of communication" essentially involves a difficulty and an uncertainty of the communication. Very often, Barlow's fiction tells of events of a very far past, which still bear an impact on the present time, when the actual narrative unfolds. However, these events of the past belong to an epoch so remote to be recorded only in ancient lore and traditions, in fables, in vague rumors and manuscripts, or in people's memories—with all the unreliability this causes on the communicative level. Communication is difficult, not clear nor convincing. The protagonists of the first-level narrative, and the reader with them, are left with no certainty pertaining the reliability or even the reality of the events handed down through legends, myths, manuscripts, or dim memories: the lifeworld into which Barlow's fictional characters are immersed often seems not to offer concrete points of reference, nor to present definite and identifiable characteristics. Barlow's fictional world is left, in a word, vague, and its characters move in it as in a bewildering, chaotic scenery.

The device is of course functional to the establishment of the vagueness of the whole narrative, and of an atmosphere wrapped in mystery. The striking aspect of this technique is that Barlow employed it not only in the fantasy tales, where the depiction of a mood and an atmosphere of vagueness might easily be recognized as a conscious aesthetic aim, but also in less predictable narratives. The few examples given below will point to the pervasiveness of this effort in the whole corpus of Barlow's fiction:

- "Before him loomed a tremendous door; beyond which, *rumour said*, dwelt Khalda" ("The Theft of the Hsothian Manuscripts," episode ten of the *Annals of the Jinns*, EG 28; italics added)
- "At the heart of its cave, *legend said*, Anathas had concealed an enormous hoard of jewels, gold, and other things of fabulous value" ("The Hoard of the Wizard-Beast," EG 33; italics added)

An important characteristic reinforcing the impression of vagueness and unreliability of old rumors and tales is that they must already look, at the outset, quite unbelievable and unrealistic. Of course, the effect is more fully achieved when the narrator himself defines the status of these rumors as unreliable and expresses his own skeptical opinion on them: in order to be convincing, these statements must be uttered by a narrating voice that the author has built as *reliable* within the tale.[1] A case of a reliable narrating voice, evaluating the trustworthiness of the rumors, is certainly that of the tale "A Memory":

---

1. In RHB's narratives, one of the most important tasks assigned to the reader is to discern the nature of the narrating voice: one of the author's aesthetic goals in dealing with vagueness is in fact to depict an ambiguous narrator (see 3.4. "Vagueness of the narrating voice").

> At times there were rumours among our people that the thick metal wall lying between our city and that of our slaves had been pierced in a hidden place, and that glortups went in secret throughout our city during the night [. . .] Other *incredible* tales said that the glortups went by dark into the outer world, that they had chipped the masonry from hidden doors, and at certain times made curious trips into the obscure realms lying beyond. *I did not think that this was so* [. . .]. (EG 76; italics added)

Through the cooperative effort the text solicits, the reader is now induced to give credit to the narrator—who up to now has proved reliable in his role—and to discard the rumors as mere "fables."

Especially when the final hour of mankind is approaching, the accounts of the splendid times of past prosperity and of places where the last humans are still able to survive assume the dim contours of fables: "[. . .] none had ever seen the tiny, *fabled* spots of ice left close to the planet's poles—if such indeed remained"; "There was naught to stay for, so he determined at once to seek out those *fabled* huts beyond the mountains and live with the people there" ("'Till A' the Seas,'" EG 46, 47; italics added). However, in the face of a reality that escapes comprehension and an active cognitive role on man's part, the character can only rely on what is *told* to him through legends, fables, and rumors: the only available knowledge is a second-hand one ("It was nearly before him, this land where men were *rumoured* to have dwelt; this land of which he *had heard tales* in his youth" [EG 48; italics added]). Even important events of mankind's past are not recorded anymore, except in dim memories. Memory of the history and achievements of mankind is left to vague records: to legends, whispers, and rumors ("Man had believed from ancient tales that once he had the gift of flight, but now there were many who did not credit this" ["A Memory," EG 74]).

However, this is not enough: the mere existence of old tales and rumors is a spur to action, perhaps the *only* spur to take an active role on reality: "*Because* old tales spoke of a land amid those dark enormous cliffs rising to the east of his village, Cern set out to find it" ("The Bright Valley," EG 61), also because a character of Barlow's fiction is seldom able to resist the fascination of old legends ("I did not mind seeing ruined buildings; in truth rumours of the corpse-town had fascinated my young ears" ["The Root-Gatherers," EG 83]). And when referring to an *active role on reality*, stimulated by rumors and fables, one should think of "active" as any sort of *activity*: in Barlow's fictional world, even an activity such as the pursuit of knowledge, essential to mankind's development, is carried on thanks to the spur of vague rumors and whispers ("When I was a child I had heard queer whispered tales of old, and had sought to learn more concerning the hinted marvels" ["A Memory," EG 75]). This represents of course a pessimistic hint to the inability of humankind to be an autonomous protagonist on the stage of history: human decadence is double, since not only need men to be stimulated in order to *act*, but they are not even able to verify the reliability of the rumor or legend working as a stimulus. In fact, again in "The Bright Valley," the character Cern does not bother to verify whether the rumors concerning the existence of the fabulous bright valley are true: he is convinced that beyond a barrier he is scaling, a "fragrant place," where he "might rest and refresh himself with fruit" (*EG* 62), awaits him. As in an allegorical tale, Cern's imprudence will be properly met with punishment—death. That the reader is often facing an allegorical tale is hardly deniable in most of Barlow's fiction. It is important to recognize the presence of an allegory or of a markedly metaphorical narrative, since this identification allows the interpreter to realize the fictive nature of the communication involved. In other words, the interpreter understands that she is not dealing with a narration that pretends to a mark of truth: though fictional, it posits itself on the meta-level of an allegory. For instance, tales like "The Priest and the Heretic" and "The Fidelity of Ghu" are so clearly intended by their author as open parodies of religion and superstition that the reader may nurture no doubt as to the communicative intent on Barlow's part. These tales are in fact not to be studied as literally (or even fictionally) true; they simply communicate the theoretical stance (the rejection of religion and superstition) by resorting to narrative images: a few characters meeting each other, their dialogues, all instrumental to the disclosure of the final apologue. No actual narrative communication occurs in these tales: they simply exploit narrative conventions in order to convey a moral.

Sometimes, Barlow's characters do not simply have to overcome the vagueness of the information they possess; they are left with no information at all. Old accounts, tales, and legends are simply silent about some aspects of reality ("What was said unto Ghu in that far lonesome place is not recorded" ["The Fidelity of Ghu," *EG* 41]), or the other characters with whom they deal do not provide—as a conscious choice—essential information: "She did not say whence she came, but stumbled into the cabin while the young suicide was being buried" ("'Till A' the Seas,'" *EG* 47). Already from these few hints, it appears as if Barlow's narrative world is one of delusion and disengagement, where humans have lost faith in each other and in the productivity of their rational association.

Communication proves to be uncertain, not only because its tools are vague or missing, but also because its reports turn out in the end to be actually false. In Barlow's fiction, communication frequently fails to convey the truth: Anathas, the wizard-beast, is finally seen by the seeker Yalden, and the monster reveals himself as a "shadow infinitely more hideous than anything hinted in any popular legend" (*EG* 35). Falsity, or at least unreliability, of communication may be represented also through a literary technique Barlow had seen at work in the works of several masters of weird fiction, including of course Edgar Allan Poe and Lovecraft: the resort to a manuscript, incorporated in the actual narrative as a significant, if not decisive, part of the tale. In truth, Barlow does not employ this device very often, but at least one striking example deserves mention: "Origin Undetermined," where the diary of the protagonist, Heywood Roberts, contains the core of the story and is introduced by an "editor's note" written by another character, a friend of Roberts's who remains unnamed. This device had been used by Lovecraft in collaborative tales such as "The Diary of Alonzo Typer," "Winged Death," and "In the Walls of Eryx"; since the tale told at the second-level narrative, namely the one in the manuscript, always contains the weird events and particulars, the introduction of the "diary" is a device adopted to gradually insinuate the doubt on the second-level narrator's reliability, and thus on the actual truth of the events he accounts. In fact, the appearance of second-level narrations always solicits in the reader an additional interpretative effort concerning the decision about their reliability. Naturally, the presence of an unnamed editor, a doctor who deals with the manuscript and defines Roberts as a person affected by an "uncommon sort of mental disorder," suffering a real and terrible "delusion" that brought him to choose "such a fearsome method of escape" (EG 121), adds to the suspicion that the whole manuscript and the tale in it are not trustworthy. In a story such as "Origin Undetermined" (already in the title a suggestion of vagueness is present), the word of the only unnamed character certainly has more weight than any other's: each character is named in this tale, even the nurse and the doctor's cat, while the doctor himself is not.

In order to strengthen this technique, Barlow often resorts to the *presentation of different perspectives and viewpoints* on the same event or description, a quite modernistic strategy. For example, when dealing with the description of Anathas, the wizard-beast, the narrator reports the different opinions he has come to know about the monster's appearance:

> Of the true aspect of Anathas none could be certain; tales of a widely opposite nature being commonly circulated. Many vowed it had been seen from afar in the form of a giant black shadow peculiarly repugnant to human taste, while others alleged it was a mound of gelatinous substance that oozed hatefully in the manner of putrescent flesh. Still others claimed they had seen it as a monstrous insect with astonishing supernumerary appurtenances. (EG 35)

The joined effect of the vagueness of communication together with the conflict of perspectives on a supposedly "objective" reality is so pervasive in Barlow's fiction that it adumbrates and verges toward a key theme of twentieth-century literature: *incommunicability*. Communication between human beings is often shown as a dead end: we as people are not able to convey our emotions, thoughts, or even descriptions of events and supposedly "objective" realities to others. Striking in this sense is a passage taken from the masterpiece "A Dim-Remembered Story"; this remarkable tale, for which even Lovecraft expressed an enthusiastic opinion, will be analyzed in greater depth in the section devoted to the "theme" of "cosmicism." For now, what concerns us is a telling passage showing how the difficulty in human communication may eventually lead to actual incommunicability. The protagonist of the tale, after finding himself, to his utter astonishment, in an epoch and a place totally alien to him, is confronted by two women, clad in queer and out-of-date clothing, who lead him—only through gestures—to an even more bizarre building rising in the forest, a sort of castle of medieval flavor. Inside it, the protagonist meets a person who seems to be the lord of the place, who finally addresses the unexpected guest:

He spoke to me in a voice of great suspicion. Since I comprehended nothing of his words I shook my head wearily, and the two women burst into shrill chatter. From their gestures I judged they told of how I had been found in the shadowed wood, and of my ignorance regarding their tongue. At any rate, the man did not attempt to speak to me again. Instead, he gave me a strange look and indicated that I was to stay in this room. Then, [. . .] he left me. The women followed, looking back at me in a secret triumph for which *I was at a loss to account*. It was as if they were pleased at having trapped *some malignant but valuable animal*. (EG 95; italics added).

Humans are here reduced to the status of animals belonging to different species, unable to convey any meaning to each other. Even other forms of communication, such as the aesthetic and artistic, are useless: "I went to look at those dim hangings, and found that pale designs were worked in threads that tiny spiders might have webbed. The scenes depicted were of great strangeness, and seemed to form a series commencing at the curtained door. But when I tried to catch their theme, I was unable to follow the narrative unfolded. [. . .] The tapestry [. . .] dealt with various subjects whose relationship was vague" (EG 96). The character is left silent and despairing, with no information about the people around him, their intentions,[2] their history, and above all, his condition and role in that place. That this was intended by Barlow again as a metaphorical trait, aiming at the depiction of the overall plight of mankind on the earth, in absence of the author's explicit words, is something pertaining the interpreter's aesthetic judgement.

Vagueness of communication is such a central theme in Barlow's fiction that it involves also the "active" side of communication: not only *what is communicated* to the characters is uncertain and vague, but also what narrators and characters *communicate* is not clear. This fact is related with the inadequacy of the rational language to properly and satisfactorily convey an experience that goes beyond human (and rational) comprehension.[3] Barlow's characters constantly highlight the enormous difficulties they encounter in translating their experiences into rational words.[4] Almost always "it is difficult to put such things in words" (EG 87), and of their confused experiences, Barlow's characters "can hope to convey but little" (EG 93). They candidly recognize their inadequacy to retell their experience: "I have little doubt but that I shall fail in my attempt to convey the peculiar shock of my knowing that to be a reality" (EG 97); "How am I to tell of the lunar magic wrought before me?" (EG 94). Nonetheless, Barlow's characters invariably (and bravely) strive to accomplish their epistemic task, writing down their narrative "in the hope that someone may understand, or at least believe, it" (EG 94).

In conclusion, the subject Barlow places in his fictional world has no reliable source of information, and even in the face of an objective manifestation he

---

2. "I had no idea of what these people intended" (EG 96).
3. "The incongruities of this narrative are due only to my faulty comprehension [. . .] I was inarticulate and lost" (EG 98).
4. "How may I convey to you the mysterious beauty of this afternoon wood?" (EG 88).

seems unable to convey his perceptive experience to others or even to undergo a reliable perceptive experience at all. At precisely this point there intervenes the second aspect of vagueness in Barlow's literary aesthetics.

3.2 Vagueness of perception

At this level, vagueness concerns the inability of human rational instruments—namely language and senses, in particular sight—to grasp the core and the truth of the representation. Barlow's fiction stages the insufficiency and ultimate failure of our five senses in their cognitive task: human perceptions are affected by a structural impairment. Where the five senses fail the perceiver and reveal themselves as unreliable, only *doubt* may arise concerning his cognitive approach to the external world. As we will see, Barlow's fiction often expresses a conflict: the one between *appearance* and *truth*, where appearance is what the senses perceive and communicate to the brain, while truth is the "thing in itself": the ability humans have to identify and perceive the truth is ultimately questioned in Barlow's narratives. The five senses and language

- are the only means available to human beings to obtain knowledge: this involves of course pessimism on mankind's chances to seize a satisfactory knowledge;
- are disparaged in their cognitive task to grasp the truth, or "thing in itself."

Barlow's fiction subtly suggests that the "thing in itself" is indeed unknowable, even if human beings had more sophisticated perceptive and gnoseologic tools at their disposal. The emerging picture is thus one of utter insufficiency for mankind, a species doomed to live in ignorance and never to realize its supposed meaning—first because it is not equipped to grasp that meaning (should it exist), and second because that meaning is non-extant. Let us see how Barlow's narratives express this articulated position.

Difficulties of perception are detectable almost everywhere in Barlow's narratives. He carefully depicts a universe where humans are at a loss in their search for knowledge or even for a reliable perception of the external world. There are countless examples of the failure of the senses in providing a credible grasp of external reality (and often, as we will see, of internal reality also): in the fantasy cycle *Annals of the Jinns*, the vagueness of perception is a theme on which Barlow insists regularly. For example, in episode two, "The Shadow from Above," a midsummer day in the hamlet of Droom is doomed by the sudden appearance of a dark and huge shadow—already a very vague entity, not perceptible since the creature casting the shadow is invisible—that casts itself all over the village: "Soon the whole population was out of doors looking upwards at that which could not be seen yet which cast a deep shadow. Nothing was to be perceived [. . .] yet upon the square cobblestones of the quaint little village an irregular black form wavered back and forth. Then it grew larger. Whatever it may have been, it was settling" (*EG* 15-16). Barlow here masterfully portrays a situation in which the human senses prove unable to identify the creature responsible for the shadow: neither sight nor smell nor touch can detect it. Only "A deep, heavy panting was distinctly audible, much like that of a great beast" (EG 15-16). Since the creature is an "unseen monster" and only the sense of hearing seems able to somehow perceive its presence, one can argue that the entity must be something really unseeable and untouchable—a creature coming from beyond, and one that human sensory apparatus is not equipped to sense. Humans can only grasp a "manifestation" of the entity, its auditive impact: the "thing in itself," in other words, i.e. the entity's outlook and nature, cannot be known—or, even worse, are *not knowable* through the human epistemic system. Not that hearing is a privileged sense in Barlow's works: in episode ten of the cycle, "The Theft of the Hsothian Manuscripts," protagonist Morla traverses the secret palace of the ancient sorcerer Khalda and, while crossing a long dark passage, cannot identify "sounds of strange nature" (EG 28) that come from the darkness, and his sight does not recognize a "vast fluttering thing" (EG 28) flying snortingly from his path; and also when Morla finally encounters Khalda lying in his chair, sundry "vague subtleties of physiognomy and contour made it clear that sorcerer Khalda was no longer entirely human" (EG 29), though what exactly these subtleties might be is left to the reader's imagination.

Barlow's characters move in a world where no certainty is available, but where *doubt* dominates any human perception; and this not only holds true for the dreamscapes of the fantasy narratives, but may be claimed to represent a substantial element of Barlow's entire fictional production. It is the rule to doubt, for instance, even the existence of some actual beings, because they are only rumored at in vague whispers or legends: "he was openly afraid of the monster Anathas, as were all the inhabitants of Ullathia and the surrounding land. Even those who doubted its actuality would not have chosen to reside in the immediate neighborhood of the Cave of Three Winds wherein it was said to dwell" ("The Hoard of the Wizard-Beast," EG 32-33).

Words, not only senses, are at a loss in describing the creatures inhabiting these fantasy realms: Oorn itself is hardly describable, not only because sight does not fully identify its nature, but also because language is insufficient ("It was a large pudgy creature very hard to describe, and covered with short grey fur" [EG 33]). Knowledge, Barlow argues, is almost confined to an act of faith, since it is continually marked by the presence of an overwhelming *doubt*: really few are the things humans may claim to know with certainty—and this is especially true in those "last-man stories," such as "'Till A' the Seas,'" where notions of the magnificent past of mankind survive in dim tales wrapped in mystery: "Only a sparse remnant of humanity survived the aeons of change and peopled those scattered villages of the later world. How many millennia this continued is not known" (EG 45). In tales like "'Till A' the Seas,'" Barlow exploits the effect of joining vagueness with the sense of the passing of vast cycles of time: the more time passes (and aeons are involved), the more vague and imprecise are the memories and the tales of the human survivors—thus the synergy of time and vagueness is employed for effective aesthetic purposes (and this shows, incidentally, another overlapping between two of the "themes" of Barlow's fiction: "vagueness" and "time"). But the passing of long eras does not simply affect the effectiveness of memory: what becomes vague is also man's capability to *describe*, to use language rationally in order to take a stance on reality and "dominate" it, at least cognitively. What is, in fact, a description if not an act of possession the human mind exerts on the reality it claims to describe? And thus again in "'Till A' the Seas'" the narrator states that "It cannot be described, this awesome chain of events that depopulated the whole Earth; the range is too tremendous for any to picture or encompass" (*EG* 46).

However, doubt and vagueness of perception are not strictly connected with, or even caused by, the passing of time: that would be too optimistic. If the passing of aeons may increase the vagueness of our memories, Barlow is aware that doubt characterizes any form of human knowledge. Often his characters erupt in series of unanswerable questions as to the experiences they are undergoing and the sights they are seeing: "The place was built to withstand prodigious attacks—yet I had seen no garrison, nor any man save this scarlet-cloaked figure. In what tumultuous halls were the fighting men, and who served this cryptic lord? Were the women menials, or did they share his rank and dignity?" ("A Dim-Remembered Story," *EG* 96). And again: "A thousand useless questions torment me, but speculation is the only thing to distract me from pain. Is the bond between the Maya urn and that stark mountain-bordered plain something hidden even from death? [. . .] How much was anciently known of the thousand-mile plain, and of the lights behind those scowling peaks? (Was it indeed a city? A city—or what?)" ("Origin Undetermined," *EG* 131-32). Or simply, Barlow's characters candidly admit their bafflement and incapability to comprehend, due to an insufficiency of proofs and elements to prefer one interpretation: "Now I am doubtful. Perhaps what he made me do was necessary; I do not know. The initial lie he told me has shaken my trust in him. So little proof exists!" ("Origin Undetermined," *EG* 124). And even in Earth's fortunate ages, when the planet and mankind were young and not long eras had passed since mankind's birth, there were people who doubted. They doubted the final outcome of mankind's history, the desolate end to which the race would come and that is depicted in a "catastrophic" tale as "'Till A' the Seas'": "billions of years before, only a few prophets and madmen could have conceived that which was to come—could have grasped visions of the still, dead lands, and long-empty sea-beds. The rest would have doubted [. . .] doubted alike the shadow of change upon the planet and the shadow of doom upon the race" (*EG* 46). Human knowledge, or even only human epistemic hypotheses, are always doomed because imperfect and not exhaustive, Barlow claims. The knowledge man can attain is at best doubtful, and at worst assumes the contours of a sheer lie: "Although you surmised that much of my story was a lie, I could not have said anything else. [. . .] What I will say must inevitably seem a greater lie than the lies I have told you, but I think that writing it out will be a relief to me" ("Origin Undetermined," *EG* 124). But there is more: not believing in a supernatural, teleological, and omniscient principle, Barlow extends his *epistemic pessimism* to other races besides the human. Divine or semi-divine creatures like the demons also fail to possess full knowledge nor enjoy reliable perceptions: in Chapter 3 of "The Temple," the 14,000-year-old demon Garoth, approaching the titular shrine, sees in its courtyard four carven statues, representing something of which he knows nothing, "for they were at best indistinct" (*EG* 49); Garoth is again told not to "clearly distinguish" (*EG* 51) the aspect of the creatures he encounters. Thus it seems that, in Barlow's fictional worlds, epistemic failure is a condition affecting all living creatures—and this represents of course a direct reflection of the author's disbelief in the existence of powerful entities superior to man.

Epistemic fallacy, both human and non-human, is thus a central theme in Barlow's fiction. Senses actually deceive their owners with a surprising—and almost unfailing—precision. Characters seldom have a clear perception of the experiences they pass through: "In what manner had I come to be there? Alien and inscrutable, my surroundings gave no clue" ("A Dim-Remembered Story," *EG* 89). Barlow's characters seem to move in worlds alien to them, and are constantly dazed and confused by something they do not fully comprehend and thus cannot actually define. In particular, they often feel or "sense" the presence of something wrong in their surroundings, but are unable to recognize its nature: "There was something unusual in the short body—something that troubled me, though what it was, I did not know" ("A Dim-Remembered Story," *EG* 90), and again: ""Not even the countless trees seemed normal, though what was unusual about them I could not decide" (*EG* 91). When facing the complicated mechanical devices built on an ancient and forgotten plane of their futuristic "city," the narrator of "A Memory" candidly reveals his astonishment and the confusion of his perceptions. He is utterly unable to identify the nature of what lies in front of him and his companion, the young girl Nalda:

> Upon this anciently built plane we came on ponderous machines. The glortups were trusted for their care, as there was little to go wrong, and no damage might be done to them. They occupied a vast *dim* room, and flashed amidst incessant grindings. There was a tremendous creaking and groaning and clashing of bright wheels, and clattering noises echoed through the sound-filled air. From an *unseen* source came endless tumbling sounds of maddening duration. *I was dazed and confused* by these contrivances. Hurrying cables intermeshed into a meaningful rhythm, dynamos spat their glittering fire; wheels and cogs and clashing metals were everywhere about us. As I stood with my companion there was a small movement across the cellar. *Something other than the machines had shifted, but it may have been a guard.* (*EG* 78-79; italics added)

Not only do the senses fail, human memory also shows its inadequacy: the narrator and his companion Nalda undertake a descent along the lowest levels of the "city," down to the forbidden planes inhabited by the slaves, the horrid *glortups*. While he is writing his account of the descent, the narrator cannot but recognize the fallacy of his recollection: "All that I recall is our certainty at the time, the assuredness that we should not fail in that dim quest. Of its nature I can tell nothing but that it was forbidden to us, and that we risked much to go. My weary memory holds little more [...] the dreams are fading rapidly; and I recall but a small part of that phantasmagoric descent" (*EG* 80).

However, this is not all. The recognition of the limits of mankind's cognitive apparatus (comprehending the sensory equipment, the workings of mind and memory, and rational language) is not simply an epistemic stance on Barlow's part, closed in itself. The author is in fact fully aware of the potentially catastrophic impact this faltering cognitive condition may bear on the human mind. One of the most immediate psychological consequences of man's awareness of his epistemic limits in facing reality is *fear*. Barlow's discourse on this point is particularly complex, since fear is not seen only as a *consequence* of human epistemic fallacy (and especially of its awareness on man's part), but also as a *cause* of the fallacy: the human being is a much too imperfect creature, there are simply too many factors influencing and provoking the fallacy of his perceptions to hope for any form of reliable knowledge. Again in "A Memory," this is how fear participates in the alteration and the weakening of human perceptions: "And once I thought that I had found a sign of something living. But I knew that it could not be, that I had seen some fungus, and that it was not a crust of bread that lay within the shadow; but cold fears crept into my heart" (*EG* 80).[5] Humans are sometimes aware that fear is provoking the confusion of their perceptions, and intensely hope that fear may be the *only* cause of it: ascribing their epistemic fallacy to fear, they would theoretically restore a reassuring dominion on reality, since the disappearance of fear would be enough to allow the restoration of clear perceptions. But this is not the case; Barlow's position is far more pessimistic—epistemic inadequacy is an ingrained, inescapable condition of mankind: "For a brief moment I hoped, wildly and incredulously, that all my fears had been the result of a weary body and a mind depressed by unknown surroundings. I wanted dreadfully to believe this, yet in the end I knew that I was unable" ("A Dim-Remembered Story," *EG* 92). A central question we should address is the following: what is Barlow's view of knowledge? In other words, is knowledge an unalloyed good, or is it perhaps *merciful* that man is unable to achieve a full comprehension of the (hideous) truth? This epistemic concern is of course highly significant in Lovecraft's work, where the dialectics between knowledge and ignorance is addressed in almost all the mature tales. Barlow's fiction does not develop a coherent and articulated discourse on this topic; but in a story as "Origin Undetermined," we can find a hint as to the mercy of the one who is unable to understand and *see*: the body of the protagonist is devoured by a corrupting disease, and he is grateful that his mental and bodily faculties are being slowly impaired and annihilated: "This was my body, these were my hands. What body and hands are now I cannot describe with sufficient loathing. Thank God for the mist

---

5. Of his "weakened senses" the narrator himself writes a few paragraphs later (*EG* 80).

which dims my sight. Flesh which is no longer flesh but corruption instead, cannot long support a reasoning brain" (*EG* 132). The character cannot stand truth anymore: he has achieved a too full knowledge, and this has doomed him. Of course this stance of Barlow's is reminiscent of the celebrated opening of Lovecraft's "The Call of Cthulhu."

All these observations justify our claim that Barlow's discussion of the epistemic limits of mankind deserves a more detailed analysis: the unreliability and actual falsity of our perceptions are two topics on which Barlow frequently insists. In particular, the perfectly calibrated narrative titled "The Bright Valley," first published in *Eyes of the God*,[6] contains a quite revelatory passage, in which Barlow momentarily digresses from the narrative flux and pauses to make a short but incisive reflection on the nature of fear, brilliantly connecting it with humanity's awareness of the inadequacy of its sensory and epistemic equipment in the face of the unknown:

> [Cern] sensed a malignancy about him, and shrank against the trunk of a thick pine. Fear comes to man in subtle ways. Her servant is less the blood-hungry animal, which he may combat, than the elusive spirit of an unknown sight or an unforeseen noise. But the greatest terror is in the abrupt facing of a thing which he cannot comprehend—like that fear introduced by the fragments of a sea creature found upon a silent beach, or by the darkness which seems to move in the night before him. (*EG* 63)

This telling passage underscores how the *inability to comprehend* is a source of fear for humanity, especially when two particular senses fail to convey the correct impulses to the brain: sight ("the elusive spirit of an unknown sight") and hearing ("an unforeseen noise"). Specifically, the dialectics between light and darkness, and between sight and blindness, hold a specific importance in Barlow's narrative discourse on human perception. In fact, the dialectics is complex, since sight—as a part of an inadequate sensory equipment—is portrayed by Barlow as a fallible means of perception, on which man cannot rely properly; but contextually, sight remains the only means man has at his disposal to perceive reality visually. Thus, the sensations sight may convey, though insufficient, are the only means man may have not to go adrift in the meaningless cosmos of blind confusion: in other words, darkness is even worse than the approximate information our sight provides, because the latter at least guarantees a form—however imperfect—of relationship with the external world. Barlow's fiction is rich in representations of the chromatic opposition between light and darkness, sight and blindness: the latter element of the opposition almost inescapably signals an epistemic and sometimes even a moral deprivation or negativity.

---

6. The tale was written in July–September 1935, and though scheduled to appear in James Blish's and William H. Miller's fanzine *Planeteer* (in the September 1936 issue), it did not do so (see Joshi and Anderson, "Introduction," *EG* 10, and *UL* 204).

Since in Barlow's narrative discourse the dialectics between light and darkness may be assimilated to that between salvation and damnation—with the two poles, as we will see, often exchanging their roles (light and darkness being alternatively the poles of salvation and damnation), his fiction is replete with passages showing how light/sight proves valuable in order to fight the darkness and blindness of a seething cosmos and an unexplainable reality. In "A Memory," light is clearly interpreted as saving. In the world of the far future, when humans will be confined into an isolated "city" redolent of the Great Redoubt of William Hope Hodgson's *The Night Land*, the narrator tells the story of a mankind congregated into huge, vertically developed feudal towns completely self-sufficient in the satisfaction of human basic needs (such as the provision of food and energy supply). The "creation" of light inside the enormous tower-towns is saluted by the narrator as another essential step toward the achievement of a full independence: "And then one day some forgotten *genius* mastered the secret of light, and created an artificial radiance more powerful than the sun, and as inexhaustible. The last need of the old world was gone, for dazzling synthetic beams lit and warmed our tiny world" (*EG* 74). But of course not even light is able to perfect the clearness of perceptions, which maintain their vagueness. It is as if Barlow's narrative discourse claims that the human sensory grasp of outside reality is by no means easy, and that not even the presence of light is a guarantee of a clear perception:

> [. . .] there were things which led the people in our Tower to believe that life must persist elsewhere. Curious lights as of many torches in a procession were once seen winding against the dark horizon [. . .] a writhing maggot of light which no telescope could resolve. [. . .] those who had seen these things could not be sure that the night had not deluded them, for of such nocturnal happenings no traces could be glimpsed by those who looked afterward, by day, from the high windows. (*EG* 75)

Not only is perception vague, but it invariably entails doubt on the actuality of what it revealed.

However, Barlow's fiction builds on light and sight as the positive poles of the opposition in several occasions, so much so that when sight fails man, he feels lost.[7] Nonetheless, Barlow's "epistemic pessimism" is such that even when sight works properly, this does not mean that perception and knowledge are clear. In fact Barlow, in order to metaphorically represent the epistemically confused condition of mankind, strives to place his characters within worlds whose experience and perception utterly baffle them.[8] Thus, even the sight of a rabbit may be disturbing for an inadequate epistemic equipment:

---

7. "I had never anywhere before seen the place, yet now I stood upon the grass within a strange, faintly sinister forest, searching with confused eyes for some familiar sight" ("A Dim-Remembered Story," *EG* 89).

8. The frequent occurrence in RHB's fiction of the verb "to baffle" and the adjective "baffling" points to the epistemic concern of his narratives.

> It was, I am certain, a rabbit; though of what breed I hesitate to say. There was only a glimpse of the round grey body before it plunged into the underbrush, but I was greatly disturbed by that sight. When I speak of it, there exists no comparable experience whereby to judge. The little animal was not visibly deformed: it moved with reassuring naturalness, yet there was something definitely wrong about those short, thick legs, and the flattened tail. It was a rabbit, but such a rabbit as might have lived in the years before man's existence. ("A Dim-Remembered Story," EG 90)

When his pessimistic epistemic concern is less urgent, Barlow associates light and sight with images of peace and familiarity, especially when he is dealing with full, strong "enchanted sunlight" (EG 89) and the summer season: in "Pursuit of the Moth," we read "[. . .] the golden haze of a summer noon there comes surcease to all the enmity of life [. . .] The sun was obscured by no cloud, and the day was fortunate" (EG 81). The same tale shows how the more light becomes dim and imperceptible, the more it moves toward the negative pole of the opposition: "Beyond the trunks of cypresses a faint illumination came, as if some horrid rottenness were glowing in putrescent filth" (EG 82). A *faint* light is no good, since dimness and vagueness are always associated with negativity: in fact, Barlow recognizes them as the principal characteristics of human epistemic equipment, contributing to the doom of man's cognitive acts. Thus there is a condition possibly worse than fear (a feeling man must experience, as we have seen, since fear is both a cause and a consequence of human epistemic fallacy): worse than "fear" is of course "dim fear" ("The Root-Gatherers," EG 83). When it comes, the human mind is completely overwhelmed and loses even the few and feeble faculties of comprehension left: "As I have said, the antiquity of this ruin began to trouble me. The fact alone that I was so far from any road seemed disquieting. Perhaps this is the best time to speak of those dim, unshaped fears that crowded my dazed mind [. . .] there was some dim barrier [. . .] a veil enshrouding whatever lay immediately before my wakening" ("A Dim-Remembered Story," EG 91).

Another dialectics, parallel to that between light and darkness, is the one between sight/non-sight, or to be seen/not to be seen. In Barlow's fiction, the success of the characters' endeavors often depends on their ability *to see* and *not to be seen*—since their discovery by their enemy may signify death or mental derangement. As we have seen, in "A Memory" the narrator and his companion Nalda try to reach the lower levels of the huge, autarchic "city" they live in a far future. Their attempt is risky, since the deepest levels are the exclusive dominion of the *glortups*, hideous slave-creatures capable of any sort of evil. The two seekers need to conceal themselves accurately, otherwise their mission will be met with certain failure: in other words, in order *to see* they need *not to be seen*. The success of their descent toward the unexplored, gloomy bottom of the city depends on finding a delicate equilibrium between the poles of the dialectics *to see/not to be seen*:

> The white metal walls shone clearly with a frosted silver glow, so that *we were ill-concealed*. Our cloaked forms must have been *easily visible* from the main hall

where folk were hurrying by, and anyone chancing to look *would easily have seen us there*. We did not wish this, even though no one could know what we intended. There were few places where one *might remain unseen* in the glowing city, and although no one had entered the passage in which we stood, Nalda was apprehensive. (*EG* 73; italics added)

For the narrator and Nalda, concealing themselves properly is equivalent to throwing the potential enemies of their quest into a metaphorical, impenetrable perceptive darkness. Contextually, the success of their expedition means to let the light and sight of the civilized world (and of rationality) triumph against the blackness and dimness of the underworld. The steps of their search are thus punctuated with the voluble outcomes of the light-vs.-darkness struggle: "The chief impression that remained was one of night-steeped crypts, all the blacker *through contrast with* the dazzling, man-made radiance which poured from hidden sources to give the upper world a ceaseless day" (*EG* 77; italics added). That the success of the expedition—and, metaphorically, the achievement of knowledge and sight—depends upon making light triumph against darkness is particularly evident along the whole narration of "A Memory": "Standing there in pale gloom lit by many torches, we hesitated, for neither knew the way, and it was grimly dark before us. But we must penetrate the shifting gloom" (*EG* 78).

Darkness is almost invariably placed on the negative pole of the dialectics, especially because it represents a contingent cause worsening the refinement of our sensory perceptions, already impaired, as we have seen, by structural limitations. Darkness works, as it were, like an additional "hampering veil" ("A Memory," *EG* 81) enshrouding our cognitive efforts. Darkness works against sight in a powerful way, adding to the confusion of visual perceptions and to the blurring of the contours of shapes: "By the curbing of a stone well there was a figure, blurred in the dark" ("A Dim-Remembered Story," *EG* 92), and again: "it was very dark, and objects were melting into a blurred unity" (*EG* 92); "The stairs before me writhed; grew dim in a blur of floating colours. Then came a wave of darkness, and a shock that tore my vitals, wrenching each cell of my flesh" (*EG* 100). In "A Dim-Remembered Story," Barlow offers several masterly descriptions of the blurring powers of darkness, and of its capacity to enshroud perception with a vague, confounding veil—in particular, the dialectics light/darkness and sight/blindness shows here all its relevance to create narrative transition and proves crucial for the advancement of the story:

> [. . .] all things merged before my sight, and a great radiance supplanted the hall and the many dark steps. A blur of light, as if some god crouched before me, so glorious that my eyes were dimmed. Vibrating, throbbing, this glow set up a curious rhythm which passed to my inmost tissues and was echoed there. I was enslaved by the pure and glowing energy of the hueless light [. . .] My heart jerked dizzily, and I felt an expectant lightness. Then I was devoured by the live, hungry radiance, so that in the final vertigo of consciousness my body was distant and my flesh numb. (*EG* 100)

Another telling passage of the same narrative shows how crucial is the opposition between sight and blindness, how their dialectics does not only influence the perceiver's moods and inner world; in fact, Barlow provides light and darkness with an almost concrete nature, and thus makes them capable of taking part in the narrative as tangible objects, scenarios, even sentient entities or "characters": "So I was left in ages of black so great that only blindness might conceive it. It was not an absence of light [. . .] it was a tangible negation, an unending hue like the shadows of a demon wing. Or it was a crypt—the burial ground of forgotten orbs whose brief lives were glut in the maw of that triumphant abyss" (EG 101). Not only darkness, also light assumes a concrete status and plays a revealing role in "A Dim-Remembered Story." Toward the end of his inexpressible experience in an epoch out of time, the protagonist is confronted with a phantasmagoric "galactic" vision, of the "aeonian past or vague futurity" (EG 103) of the universe—it is not possible to ascertain exactly what. At first, his "searching eyes" find, amidst the thick darkness of intergalactic space, a "dim light" pulsating far beyond the "limit of vision." Gradually the light grows and shows itself to be composed of "many separate glowing objects." They move at unimaginable speed through space, but since the galactic distances are huge, the objects seem to approach the observer slowly. When the lights are close enough, the perceiver understands their nature: they are globular forms of racing lights, colored in green, red, and purple. Their shape is "beyond ken," but "there was no complexity, no kin in their forms to the forms of Earth." Then, amazingly, the observer realizes that the light-balls are "living" and shifting "like phantasmal sea-things"; they even possess a consciousness, though the observer is of course unable to describe of what nature this consciousness could be: "their sentience was too different from my own for one to comprehend the other." Each ball radiates a faint glow, and they all group in front of the perceiver; everything is gone. This is Barlow's vision of the universe's end. And it is highly significant that, according to Barlow, the only thing left after everything has disappeared will be *light*: "My world was gone, and with it all worlds. Yet here before me, in the ultimate chill of a naked void, there clustered a group of living lights." The light-globes moved and played, gamboled in deformed symmetries, and built themselves in shapes of an unearthly geometry; above all, they possessed sentience and a goal, like any other "character." But this is not enough: the nature of the light (and of the observer's sight) would not be fully revealed, had it not been contrasted with that of its necessary opposite, darkness. Thus, the narrator-observer immediately claims that the vision of the spectacular light-balls made him wrench a "painful memory *from darkness*,"[9] and when his mind is overwhelmed by an indecipherable emotional illness in response to the vision, he loses sight. And it is crucial to underline how blindness, signaling the overcoming of darkness, entails the beginning of man's ruinous end:

---

9. This and the few preceding quotations from "A Dim-Remembered Story" are taken from *EG* 102.

> [. . .] it was like seeing *black* cliffs rise and curve away overhead. I lost all sense of vision, and seemed pressed on every side by a buzzing darkness. Then, slowly, deliberately, everything wheeled about me, so that I hung like a perishing wretch upon the edge of a great chasm. A chasm deeper than the pits of hell, and more evil. Again, with swifter motion, my surroundings revolved; and then life became a series of hideous revolutions backward through time and space. I seemed to experience anew each joy and pain that I had ever known: again and yet again I lived a tortuous life, and the dark years sped in rhythm with a lurching cosmos. (EG 103)

And to Barlow, the hypostatization of damnation for man consists in his realization of being thrown into utter darkness, into a "nighted world in no sense like our earth-wrought planets [. . .] a world upon the black Rim—a world that no mind can believe or even dimly picture" (EG 103).

Barlow's narrative discourse is thus revealed as quite articulated regarding the dialectics between light and darkness. Darkness is the harbinger not only of veiled perceptions, but of a diminished grasp on reality itself: "There is a dim, elusive spirit in the new evening, when the naked realities of day are veiled, and hidden things steal forth to caper with the bat in pearl-grey shadow. The sunlit, familiar aspect of nature is concealed, and mystery breathes in each sentient tree" (EG 93). The titular "Night Ocean" is revealed as a receptacle of invisible and unpredictable horrors for the protagonist, mainly intimate and psychological horrors. "The Night Ocean" is a complex and masterly piece of literature, so rich in themes and effects that it offers itself to a multi-layered analysis, as my discussion will hopefully demonstrate.[10] Among the most interesting features of this tale (in addition to the ambiguity of the narrating voice, discussed in paragraph 3.4.1 of this chapter), certainly the chromatic opposition between light and darkness, day and night, is aesthetically significant. The unnamed narrating voice begins his account by stating, already at the outset, that his tale is the result of a fight with darkness: his being a narrator makes him "like one who peers into an unlit realm and glimpses forms whose motion is concealed" (EG 105). Thus, already from the start, the (external or internal) events that are the object of the act of narration are configured as wrapped into darkness, and the act of narration as a "revealing," an "unveiling" act aiming at subtracting them from the obscurity concealing them. Though relying on imperfect perceptions and comprehension, the narrator strives to shed light on reality and truth: his is a hermeneutic role, he offers his own interpretation on the "unlit realm" of human experience. Perhaps his interpretation is fallacious and unreliable, but the narrator has at least the courage to defy his own imperfect ("dim") perception and offer an account that aims at approximating the actual truth. The issue is again epistemical: "The Night Ocean" stages a struggle between light and darkness in order to win the prize of comprehension and truth. Thus, the narrator fights in order to *achieve light*, firstly in his external surroundings (the beach, and the house in which he alone dwells on the

---

10. Joshi defines the tale a "richly interpretable story that produces new insights and pleasures upon each rereading" (A *Subtler Magick* 202).

solitary beach), and secondly in his own interiority. Since he is aware that perceptions are vague, the only way he has to achieve comprehension is—metaphorically but also literally—to *shed light* on his dim perceptive worlds. Therefore, manifestations of light are always welcomed as an epistemic "plus," almost as magic weapons or helpers in the subject's fight for knowledge—and they in fact are awarded concrete substance, almost as if they were material objects, namely weapons or creatures: "There was an effect of bright sun upon a shifting sea of waves whose mysteriously impelled curves were strewn with what appeared to be rhinestones. Perhaps a watercolour might have caught the *solid masses of intolerable light* which lay upon the beach where the sea mingled with the sand" (EG 106; italics added). In his search for light (and thus truth), the narrator—whom Barlow, not by chance, chooses to depict as a professional painter, therefore a man particularly careful to seize the nuances of light and color—seems even to consciously assign chromatic attributes to entities normally not endowed with them. He is looking for helpers in the fight against his own dim sensory perceptions: "Each of my senses was touched in a different way, but sometimes it seems that the roar of the sea was akin to that great brightness, or as if the waves were glaring instead of the sun" (EG 107). Thus the protagonist salutes each sunny day as a useful ally, or weapon, for his fight. Humphreys correctly remarks that the narrator fights a personal battle against darkness, employing different symbolical weapons—among which sunlight is certainly felt as the most valuable: "A number of beacons, or symbolic attempts at survival within the encroaching darkness of the outside are used in the story. The sun is one of the most important of these beacons [. . .] Thus the narrator places great emphasis on both the healing and the soothing powers of the sun" (18-19). Gradually, the narrator comes to perceive his struggle for comprehension, for a shedding of the light of knowledge on the darkness of ignorance, as a prophetic task—so that each manifestation of light assumes the shape of an omen of final success. To reinforce this impression of a "sanctity" investing his mission, the narrator resorts to an increasingly poetic prose-style: "There was a succession of sun-filled days at first. I rose early, and beheld the grey sky agleam with promise of sunrise; a prophecy fulfilled as I stood witness. [. . .] That great light, so apparent the first day, made each succeeding day a yellow page in the book of time" (EG 108). The protagonist is not afraid to declare plainly his debt to light, and the positivity he attaches to it as an instrument to attain knowledge and even to ensure survival: "I spent all my time outdoors in sunlight. . . . *As darkness is akin to death, so light is to vitality*" (EG 108; italics added). Humphreys too underscores the light-and-darkness imagery of the tale and insists upon the narrator's instinctive search for—and reliance on—light: "The most common images in 'The Night Ocean' involve darkness and light, from the title of the story through until the final words of the tale. The two images are juxtaposed throughout, as the narrator instinctively craves the light of the sun while he recoils from the darkness of the ocean" (18). For the protagonist, darkness is "akin to death" because it "[. . .] represents the unknown, the outside, and the narrator's primal fears and ignorance" (18). Instead, light is perceived as a reassuring, inalienable, primal element that helps fight against the fearful sense of displacement induced by darkness. However, the protagonist's condition on Ellston Beach is far from remaining idyllic. Fewer and fewer tourists attend the beaches, the chilly autumn winds approach, and the days become shorter. Of course, the narrator senses, in particular, the shortening of the days as a prelude to a *darkening* that hardly represents only an atmospheric event:

> I had been there perhaps a week when the weather began a gradual change. Each stage of this progressive darkening was followed by another subtly intensified, so that in the end the entire atmosphere surrounding me had shifted from day to evening. [. . .] The sun was displaced by long intervals of cloudiness—layers of grey mist beyond whose unknown depth the sun lay cut off. Though it might glare with the old intensity above that enormous veil, it could not penetrate it. (*EG* 109)

This is not simply an atmospheric event, but bears an impact on the narrator's own mood, as he himself candidly admits: "This was more obvious to me in a series of mental impressions than in what I actually witnessed" (*EG* 109). The protagonist's fight for truth gradually loses its best ally, light. His perceptions grow increasingly dim, since darkness begins to lay its enshrouding and obfuscating veil on his external and internal milieus. The protagonist sees, or believes he sees, an unidentifiable object emerging from the sea in front of his house. On the nature of this creature, he cannot be precise—his sight is dimmed by darkness, and the battle for comprehension appears already more problematic than previously thought during the sunlit days: "I did not see any such creature from the realm of imagining, but as the chill wind veered, slitting the heavens like a rustling knife, there lay in the gloom of merging cloud and water only a grey object, like a piece of driftwood, tossing obscurely on the foam. This was a considerable distance out, and since it vanished shortly, may not have been wood, but a porpoise coming to the troubled surface" (*EG* 112). The contours of the surroundings start to become blurred, and the enshrouding darkness mercilessly overcomes both the external and the internal light of the protagonist's house, blurring them into a confusing halo: "I was prisoned on all sides by an unnaturally increased dusk which had filtered down at some undefined hour under cover of the storm. [. . .] I half guessed the hour from the dimly seen hands, which were only slightly less indecipherable than the surrounding figures" (*EG* 112). The battle for clear perception is infuriating, but the enemy to overcome, material and spiritual darkness, is a tough one:

> [. . .] that night [. . .] when I looked again from the window there appeared surely to be figures blotting the grime of the wet evening. I counted three moving about in some incomprehensible manner, and close to one another—which may not have been a person, but a wave-ejected log, for the surf was now pounding fiercely. I was startled to no little degree, and wondered for what purpose those hardy persons stayed out in such a storm. (*EG* 113)

But when the protagonist steps outside, emerging on the porch, and salutes those "people," offering his hospitality, they too seem not to understand his purposes, nor to make any returning signal: "Dim in the evening, they stood as if half-surprised, or as if they awaited some other action from me [...] Abruptly there came to me a feeling that a sinister quality lurked about those unmoving figures [...] and I closed the door with a surge of annoyance which sought all too vainly to disguise a deeper emotion of fear" (EG 113). Thus *fear* appears again as the feeling resulting from man's acknowledgment of his own inability to understand, of his own impotence in the face of the unknown. Darkness finally launches its powerful attack on man's understanding faculties, and ultimately on his sanity. The narrator tries to overcome his powerful enemy by resorting to any available means: since darkness has turned into a concrete and material adversary, it has gained substance:

> Fighting away the prevalent gloom with a soiled lamp [...] I prepared my food, since I had no intention of going to the village. The hour seemed incredibly advanced, though it was not yet nine o'clock when I went to bed. Darkness had come early and furtively, and throughout the remainder of my stay lingered evasively over each scene and action which I beheld. Something had settled out of the night—something forever undefined, but stirring a latent sense within me. (EG 113)

Man clings to sight in order to orient himself in the chaos of perception induced by material and moral darkness. Artistically masterly are the pages in which Barlow describes this fight for clarity of sight, though the prevailing sensation underlying these pages is one of resignation for a fight doomed to fail. This is the protagonist's chaotic flow of perceptions (and thoughts) when he finds a piece of rotten flesh returned by the sea:

> I saw [...] tangled in a glimmer of sunlit moisture that was poured over it like a yellow vintage, a small object like a hand, some twenty feet ahead of me, and touched by the repetitious foam. The shock and disgust born in my startled mind when I saw that it was indeed a piece of rotten flash overcame my new contentment and engendered a shocked suspicion that it might actually be a hand. Certainly, no fish, or part of one, could assume that look, and I thought I saw mushy fingers wed in decay. [...] The thing, whose shape was nearly lost, held too much resemblance to what I feared it might be; and I pushed it into the willing grasp of a seething wave, which took it from sight with an alacrity not often shown by those ravelled edges of the sea. (EG 115)

Baffled by his finding, the man cannot decide what to do. Even his will is paralyzed: "Perhaps I should have reported my find, yet its nature was too ambiguous to make action natural" (EG 115). Confronting an *unclear, obscured perception* (the sight of a piece of rotten flesh not unequivocally identifiable), the human mind proves unable to rationalize and makes in turn *unclear, obscured suppositions*:

> The numerous drownings, of course, came into my mind—as well as other things lacking in wholesomeness, some of which remained only as possibilities. Whatever the storm-dislodged fragment may have been, and whether it were fish or some

animal akin to man, I have never spoken of it until now. After all, there was no proof that it had not merely been distorted by rottenness into that shape. (EG 116)

The character's epistemic, rational faculties begin to realize their utter bafflement and their ultimate defeat; with them also the reader's comprehension is stretched, and of course Barlow employs a reticent narrator who spurs the reader to formulate his own questions, and to side with him in his own battle for truth: Was it really a hand? If so, whose hand was it? Did it belong to a person who committed suicide, or was murdered? By whom was s/he murdered? Perhaps by the (reticent) narrator himself? And if it was not a hand, what did the protagonist actually see? These questions are strategically made to arise in the reader's mind, and this is a result of Barlow's weaving of an effective narration: he succeeds in transferring the ambiguity of perception and of sight from the character to the reader. Since the reader has no other source of information, his judgment must be founded exclusively on the narrator's account: the reader relives the narrator's fight for truth, the same doubts and epistemic efforts. Of course, he may come to formulate interpretative hypotheses more articulated and convincing than the narrator's; however, the reader, in order to formulate his own interpretations, is bound to follow the narrator's account on what he (thought he) experienced—and especially on what he saw. The reader's battle for truth replicates the narrator's, and in particular doubles the latter's attempt to overcome the darkness and dimness wrapping his cognitive efforts.

However, the dialectics between light and darkness is a fluid one: from an axiologic viewpoint, as anticipated above in this paragraph, each of the two poles of the opposition may revert into its opposite. Therefore, to light may also be attached a negative value, or, in semiotic terms, a *disvalue*. The sememe of light may thus be invested with a negative polarization, which identifies light as a potential source of evil and even of death. In fact, in the peculiar dialectics between light and darkness, we have seen how light may prove positive and essential, but it may also occupy the negative side of the opposition and become a source of evil and perdition: no certainty is available even about the nature of light—is it saving or condemning? The most extraordinary narrativization of the evil of light—now become a full character, capable of sentiment and of actual "actions," such as even killing a human being—is presented in "The Bright Valley": this narrative tells of a lethal light. In this tale's fictional world, the titular valley is renowned for being a haven of undreamed-of natural treasures, unexplainably abandoned by man in ancient times. The protagonist, Cern, sets out to find it and is at first dazed by the contemplation of the heavenly richness of life forms, both animal and vegetal, the valley reveals. But gradually, Cern becomes aware of the reason why the valley has been depopulated. Something is wrong in this valley: it is inhabited by an evil, killing *light*:

> Far away, in the heart of the valley, danced curious shimmerings that waxed in brilliancy. Pallid veils of light, borne by no creature. These webs wove a phosphorescent tapestry, and shifted as no lights should. They were phantasms: forms

more pale than the stars, and hung upon the breeze as if they had no weight or substance. They swung and soared before the man, and dropped like dying torches everywhere within the valley. The things had come out to feed, and they swirled and netted and spread apart, roving and searching among old trees and drifting across small lakes. The whole expanse of the valley was alight with their cold, deliberate forms, a misty glimmer beneath the stars. They swarmed over little hills and thronged on gentle upward slopes to the edge of that accursedly beautiful valley. Cern saw the procession of goblin-torches blotted out for a moment as they drifted through a little wood. In dull fear he watched them waver brightly again, inevitably towards him, and yet he made no effort to escape. [. . .] the light was strange and glorious. It poured upon him with the freshness of a mountain spring. [. . .] Sparkling, exhilarating, like the bleak wind that slithers upon a day of perishing winter, it merged into his very body, as if he were but a phantom of a man in the moon-rivalling glow. [. . .] His face and limbs were transfigured into a semblance of divinity by the glowing silver vapors. No man perished there, but a god. Like a flame-enamored moth, he was poisoned and consumed by the billowing crystal. . . A miasmatic halo that sucked and clustered like vampire moths on carrion, the radiance enshrouded him, and his body was limned with brightness. Under the dark pines the place was evil with feeding light. (EG 63-64)

In conclusion, we may claim that the only possible solution Barlow suggests to overcome the perceptive and epistemic fallacy of man's cognitive apparatus is, first of all, to accept it. Without the recognition and the serene acceptance of the limits of our cognitive faculties, no existence or peace of mind is left. Another suggestion Barlow provides in order to survive the inescapable vagueness and inadequacy of our epistemic efforts is to recognize that perception may occur *not only through rational means*. Reason shows its enormous limits and man can do nothing to correct them; he needs to accept them—though this may require a dramatic rational stretching and effort: "I realized wholly; and realizing, accepted the fact, that something—God knows what, for even yet I am uncertain—had precipitated me into realms that only madness can accept" ("A Dim-Remembered Story," EG 97). However, madness is not the necessary path to walk, once man realizes that reason cannot cope with the utter incomprehensibility of his condition. What is left to do is simply to give up the pretension to rational thinking and comprehension, but this does not entail a full faith in dreams: they might be as chaotic and deceiving as rational investigation is ("my dream was chaos, like reflections in a pool vexed with stones" ["Origin Undetermined," EG 130]). Barlow's proposed solution is instead to let one's soul flow freely in the streams of (irrational and unutterable) feelings and emotions ("I knew an emotion that mixed ecstasy and terror, and yet other things for which there are no words" ["A Dim-Remembered Story," EG 101]), or to abandon oneself to the aesthetic pleasure, or even *rapture*, and the delicate contentment they may provide:

What she sang I shall not ever know, but it was lonely and thin, and pierced my very soul with rapture. The round moon with its burden of ancient death was not so tragic as this melody; lamenting the inevitable doom of loveliness, like a mournful Pierrot in autumn's garden. It remembered dimly the scents and colours and the ecstasy of paradise. It was the dirge of water-steeped Atlantis, or a cry of a tortured lover in the night. Long after the voice of passionate despair had ebbed into oblivion, the silence rippled with its memory, and I scrutinized the black horizons to find a key to the singer and her melody. ("A Dim-Remembered Story," EG 97)

Giving up any effort at rational comprehension, Barlow's poetic and dreamy prose seems to claim here, does not necessarily entail doom and damnation: it is left to discover, and conquer, an entire universe of qualitatively different, but by no means less satisfactory, sensations, perceptions, and *raptures*.

3.2.1 Reality versus appearance, or the "deluding plot"

One of the ways in which Barlow's fiction develops the "theme" of vagueness of perception is by staging the narrative conflict between *supposed* truth and *actual* truth, namely between appearance and reality. Barlow chooses to represent, literarily and metaphorically, his philosophical distrust in the human epistemic equipment and his conviction of the unreliability of man's interpretative efforts on reality, showing that man is not allowed to attain ultimate knowledge of the real truth. In the previous paragraph, it has been discussed how the whole of Barlow's work is pervaded by this theoretical awareness. The "epistemic" theme is in fact a central concern of Barlow's fiction, but of course it can be metaphorically rendered in a myriad of different literary ways. Those discussed in the previous paragraph, such as the conflict between different perspectives on the same events or the opposition between light and darkness, are only a few possible ways of facing the same theme. In order to achieve more effectively the aesthetic thematization of his epistemic concern, Barlow devises a consistent group of stories in which characters and narrators are constantly deceived by their own senses as to the interpretation to assign to reality and to the events they experience. In this type of story, which may be labeled the "deluding plot," the character's impressions and suppositions induce him to formulate certain hypotheses on the chain of events he experiences, while final proof and verification invariably show his perceptions to have been wrong—and above all, that what *appeared* to his senses and mind never corresponds to what it actually *is*. The conflict between (objective) reality and (subjective) appearance is a truly central theme of Barlow's literature, and it is employed as another way to demonstrate the fallacy and unreliability of the human cognitive apparatus. A few examples of the "deluding plot" as a literary technique (inspired in any event, as we have seen, by a theoretical concern) will reveal how the "delusion" involved always entails a conflict between the *positivity* of the appearance and the *negativity* of reality, since human senses tend naturally to deceive their owner by making him believe that reality is much more rewarding, attractive, positive—in a word, *better*—than it actually is.

"The Theft of the Hsothian Manuscripts," episode ten of the *Annals of the Jinns*, tells of the hazardous, frightful mission youth Morla is assigned by his city:

to enter the giant, secret palace of Khalda, the ancient sorcerer, and steal the legendary manuscripts from the custody of Khalda's guards. While penetrating the last chamber, the one where the merciless wizard rests, Morla realizes how lucky he has been so far: "He [. . .] saw a pale greenish figure slumped in a chair of antique carving. The wrinkles of the flesh, and sundry other vague subtleties of physiognomy and contour, made it clear that sorcerer Khalda was no longer entirely human. [. . .] the old one did not move, and Morla thought his fortune fine indeed" (EG 29). However, after slaying an unwholesome creature that arises at his passage and is guarding both the sorcerer and the treasures of his palace, Morla is soon going to discover that he is under a delusion, and that his fortune will not ultimately be so fine. Cleverly opening, with a stratagem, the carven red chest containing the manuscripts, Morla can finally extract, from the interior of the chest, "a scroll of tattered papyrus on which was written that which he desired. Then, turning, he thought to leave while Khalda yet slumbered" (EG 29). But again Morla is deceived, his perception erroneous—and the hope of a safe escape deluded, since "Khalda, it would appear, was no longer asleep" (EG 29). This is a simple tale and a simple plot, but it stages a basic opposition between appearance, resulting from the character's perceptions (his senses, especially sight, tell Morla that Khalda is asleep) and his subsequent inferences ("Thus I can escape with the manuscripts and save my life"), vs. the actual reality ("Khalda may well be asleep, but he is a powerful and terrible sorcerer, and would certainly not allow his precious manuscripts to be stolen scot-free"). In this case, the price to pay for the delusion of the senses is very high for the character: nothing more is told of Morla's fate (Barlow of course does not say anything, since vagueness may be employed, as we will see, also as a literary technique), but the reader is induced to guess that Morla's must not have been a wholesome end. Also in "The Bright Valley," as we have seen, the protagonist Cern finally dies attacked and devoured by alien fires and "goblin-torches," after having searched and found a valley which, it was rumored, was rich and hid unthinkable natural beauties and fruits. Instead of prosperity and happiness, Cern finds death in the bright valley: "That place which Cern had thought beautiful became to him accursed" (EG 63). Again, a doxastic error on a character's part earns him a tragic end.

However, Barlow is not always so severe in punishing the "interpretative" mistakes his characters commit.

3.2.2 The *Book of Garoth*

For instance, the mistake in evaluating reality may become a reason for diversion, besides constitutively being a powerful spur for the narration. In Chapter 4 ("A Moral Explanation") of the *Book of Garoth*, the demon Garoth encounters an apparently hideous genie, a supposedly evil creature resting close to a black pool. Garoth asks the genie for some explanation regarding the awful tortures a "lovely young girl" (EG 50) had been subjected to inside a temple, by a group of eight luxuriously clad priests. The girl had been bewitched with malignant curses, and each priest had caused her to suffer the most painful tortures: she was first turned into a living torch, then scratched by an evil green creature that even tore off her head—afterwards restored to its original position by another priest, so that the lovely girl was again living. After an almost endless series of tortures, the priests "summoned up a fiend of green flame that gleefully carried his victim to some unseen Draalstrand" (EG 51). Then, looking for information about the otherwise unexplainable events he saw, Garoth talks to the awful-looking genie, only to find out, upon "critical inspection," that he "was neither terrible nor hideous as he had first thought" (EG 51). Garoth's first impression is then upturned: the hideous appearance of the genie (actually an "objective" fact) does not correspond to an evil "interiority." However, the most striking reversion is still to come. The genie guards a sort of hellish cavern, lit by pillaring flames: a few demons are engaged in torturing people placed amidst the flames. The "lovely young girl" so painfully abused by the apparently evil priests is over in one flame, and "Garoth saw the young lady just as she had looked before the priests began" (EG 51). The girl lies half-turned on the moss-covered bank of a small river, her eyelids nearly closed, and immersed in a musing speculation. She seems not fully aware of her surroundings. But then Garoth is distracted by a new sight: along the edge of the river, amidst a thicket of clustered flowers, a giant spider-thing advances, its pulpy tentacles covered with thick fur. The creature is moving with care, as if stalking some prey; and Garoth realizes that the giant spider's prospective victim is the girl "who lay oblivious." Of course, Garoth regards this as a "shocking truth" (EG 52) and "strove frantically to warn her and at the same time was conscious of the futility" (EG 52). He realizes he can do nothing but watch, taut and hopeful that "some intuitive sense would prompt the girl to turn and see the thing now close upon her. Yet she lay still unmoving as the thing rushed forward with its awful limbs extended menacingly" (EG 52). At this point, the fate of the girl seems sealed, and both Garoth and the reader are ready to witness her awful demise. But here, the most unexpected reversion occurs:

> She sprang to her feet, and whirling about showed for the first time her whole face. And it was such that even the demon shuddered and was afraid, for the girl was not wholly human. Her lips were too small and roundly vermilion, and behind them lay a split tongue like that of the serpent; she possessed many little teeth of surpassing sharpness. Moreover, her slim arms were like twin flexible rods of steel that clutched her adversary and held the thing while her tiny teeth sank into the fur of the throat. A wound was made, and with evident satisfaction the girl applied her mouth to it, drawing foul nurture from the weakening creature. And Garoth knew the girl for what she was, and he would have fled shrieking but for the lethargic trance that forced him to witness both this and other equally hideous obscenities. (EG 52)

Barlow's epistemic pessimism is clear: not only do appearances deceive, and polarities are unknowable (what is good? what is evil?), but even a demon like Garoth—a creature supposedly superior to human beings—is unable to distinguish truth from falsity. The truth, the "thing in itself," escapes comprehension—no matter how evolved and perfected is the epistemic equipment applied to its investigation.

Garoth is protagonist of another adventure in which the "deluding plot" is employed. This time, the old demon decides to go and rescue a maiden called Sasta, taken prisoner into a castle called Alair. An odd creature, a man-bear, gives Garoth the instructions necessary to reach the castle, depicting the demon's mission as a worthy and romantic one. Once arrived at his destination, Garoth enters the castle and starts exploring the gloomy prisons; each room has a tightly bolted portal and small eyeholes with sliding covers. Garoth begins looking into each chamber, searching for the beautiful maid to rescue. After peeping into a few rooms, Garoth comes upon one whose surprising occupant is a "tremendous monster-woman, whose pulpy green expanse filled the entire chamber. Her form was obese, and her sleep was accompanied by odd roaring sounds not pleasing to the ear. This woman-thing had numerous unclassifiable limbs of extremely plump size, and her face was distinguished by the fact that in its horned scaliness no nose was apparent" ("The Erring Knight," *EG* 55). The woman-thing has a huge flabby mouth, a hairless head, and four large eyes. Garoth wishes to close the opening and proceed further, but the prisoner wants to converse with him. Thus Garoth, thinking it impolite to refuse the request of even so peculiar a lady, consents and they start to talk. During their dialogue, Garoth even notices that the creature possesses big sharp teeth; he apprehends that the woman is prisoned because she was a victim of a bad sorcery and now waits for some brave one to break the spell and set her free. She invites Garoth to release her, but the demon, quite nervous, replies that he is already on a similar quest and cannot agree to save two ladies—who certainly would afterwards dislike each other and squabble for his favors. Thus Garoth says he is seeking a prisoner called Sasta: by now the reader has already realized that the woman-thing and Sasta are the same person, and that the beautiful maiden whose romantic rescue was Garoth's goal is instead a repulsive monster. When the woman-thing joyfully proclaims her identity, Garoth flees and is pursued by the hideous maiden; the demon succeeds in escaping her, by diving into a fathomless well-abyss. This short tale allegorizes once again on the deceiving nature of appearance and of the hypotheses built on it: nothing is really what it appears to the human (or even demonic) senses. However, perhaps a further reflection is possible here: in both the two "Garothian" tales here discussed, a feminine creature is featured, and in both cases she/it is revealed to be much different (and much more menacing and actually hideous) than she/it at first appears. Barlow was still a teenager when he wrote these tales—he was seventeen or eighteen, and the issue whether the disquieting view of females and women present in these narratives might already hint to an homosexual tendency—or at least to a distrust of the feminine universe—on Barlow's part may configure a fertile ground for further investigation.

3.3 Vagueness of the object of perception

The world in which the protagonists of Barlow's fantasy tales move is shown as one of unidentifiable nature, one where sheer landscapes, towns, and their inhabitants appear outlandish: the city of Zeth "lies on a planet of strange beasts and stranger vegetation" ("The Hoard of the Wizard-Beast," EG 31), and is ruled by Oorn, a "creature of extremely doubtful nature" (EG 32). In the tenth episode of the *Annals of the Jinns*, titled "The Theft of the Hsothian Manuscripts," brave Morla intrudes in the secret palace where the fierce and revengeful sorcerer Khalda sleeps his aeonian slumber. While Morla is approaching the chest where the Hsothian manuscripts are kept, "a monstrous creature, one of the pets of the old man [Khalda], arose hissing, and launched its brilliantly striped body at the intruder" (EG 29). Morla fights with the monster and severs its head, but only then "he was able to view the hideous creature which merged something of the dog with something of the winged snake; whose mouth, extending into a pair of writhing tentacles, yet softly snarled" (EG 29). The creature, defined "the thing" by the narrator, apparently defies (and defeats) definition, comprehension, and categorization, since its nature appears actually indefinable. Another possible example of a creature whose nature is presented as objectively chaotic and confused is the "man-bear" in Chapter 10 of *The Adventures of Garoth*, "The Castle in the Desert": "Garoth directed his gaze to the source of the words, and saw that an androcephalus-being was before him. Its body was *like that of a bear*, but curiously pied with spots of greenish yellow; the hairless face was ugly in the extreme. There was a *suggestion of hands* in the paws it awkwardly walked upon; and though the shaggy creature was tailless, it bore a spiked knob in *loco caudae*" (EG 52; italics added). To stress the impression of indescribability of the creature, the narrator employs terms that can be called "comparative," namely words that strive to retrace an unspeakable phenomenon back to a (humanly) recognizable and accepted canon. Thus Barlow writes of an "androcephalus-being" to say that the creature had a vague resemblance to a human being, then he writes that its body was "*like that* of a bear," that there are a "*suggestion* of hands," and the protuberance on its back is compared to a tail. Barlow is simply using some humanly recognizable referents ("bear," "hands," "tail," etc.) in order to account for a creature that escapes description according to human canons: he can only *approximate* through comparative terms what the creature *looks like*, not say what it really *is*. And again, in "The Experiment," a tale in which the influence of the Lovecraftian theme of the "expanded consciousness"[11] is particularly evident (and Barlow will address it again, as we will see, in "A Dim-Remembered Story"), we read

---

11. As present in tales such as "From Beyond" (1920), *The Dream-Quest of Unknown Kadath* (1926-27) and "Through the Gates of the Silver Key" (1932-33), where the disembodied consciousnesses of the protagonist characters, respectively Crawford Tillinghast in the first and Randolph Carter in the last two, experience "cosmic" voyages or levitations that reveal to them shocking truths about mankind, the universe, and its place therein.

of "foul creatures" that are vaguely told to be "*Like* jellyfish *emulating* humanity" (*EG* 59; italics added). There seems to be no way to describe an utterly alien entity without inevitably resorting to comparisons with human categorizations: these creatures are said to be not jellyfish, but *like* jellyfish—thus the reader is induced to think that their nature is not that of actual jellyfish; moreover, the creatures are said to be *emulating* humanity, and the attentive reader notices here that Barlow—who has learned the lesson of Lovecraft's and Smith's relativistic literature—is criticizing the anthropocentric attitude of so much fiction, not only of the weird field, that unfailingly—and childishly—refuses to acknowledge its inability to grasp the essence of *any* sort of phenomena and remedies the human epistemic inadequacy by referring the indescribable phenomenon to a human canon, no matter how inappropriate and inadequate that canon is.

In general, in Barlow's early tales the interpreter is induced to nurture no doubt as to the *objective* indescribability and incomprehensibility of some of these fantasy worlds' constitutive elements. However, it is obvious, already in the fantasy tales, that what the narration wants to pass off as the "objective" vagueness of the observed object may be a result not of its actual non-perceivability, but of the inadequacy of the human epistemic and linguistic equipments, respectively, to comprehend it and describe it: the creature killed by Morla, for instance, is not properly described by the omniscient narrator, who fumblingly provides the shadow of a description by referring to a "creature which merged something of the dog with something of the winged snake." Of course, the same holds true for the description of the entity queerly defined as a "man-bear" in the Garothian episode. But the approximations of the narrators' description may well be due not to an actual indescribability of the creatures, but to the insufficiency of the human episteme and scientific categorizations—as well as of the linguistic and lexical faculties (taking for granted, of course, that the narrator is a human being).

This epistemologically pessimistic approach to the description of (fictionally) real and extant objects is a trademark of all Barlow's work, not merely of his fantasy tales. In fact, if in discussing the second aspect of vagueness we have seen how the human sensory and epistemic equipment was shown to be utterly inadequate to grasp reality and thus to achieve a stable and reliable form of knowledge, in this third aspect of the theme of "vagueness" Barlow deepens his analysis of this issue, central in his fiction: human perception. His literature aims at showing how, even when the human subject apparently possesses all the epistemic, sensory, and linguistic faculties necessary to *describe* and *understand*, it is the object target of his efforts that, constitutively, escapes description and comprehension. In a sense, Barlow's work communicates in this way an utter and bleak pessimism concerning man's cognitive efforts; in fact, no real knowledge is possible, since always something is missing in the process: either the epistemic faculties of the observer, his five senses and his rationality, are insufficient, or the observed object, due to its intrinsically ungraspable nature, defeats comprehension.

However, in Barlow's fiction the situation is not always so simple and clear. In fact, the decision whether the nature of the observed object appears doubtful because of a fault in the observer's eye or because of an actual, "objectively" chaotic nature of the object is often left to the interpreter as a matter open to speculation. In other words, the resolution of the aporia cannot be inferred merely from reading the narrator's statements—especially because, in most cases, the narrator himself is unable to solve the conundrum, and the reader is not given enough information to solve it on his own: the reader is, as it were, provided with too few and too vague details to decide upon the most likely interpretation to assign to the story told.

3.4 Vagueness of the narrating voice

Another very relevant aspect of Barlow's treatment of vagueness consists in his introduction, in a significant amount of his narratives, of a specific figure of narrator. In these tales, the author's goal is to characterize the narrating voice as *unreliable*, therefore adding to his account a nuance of *ambiguity*. It is in fact this *ambiguous narration* that plays a major role in the building up of the aesthetic vagueness that most of Barlow's tales retain: the unreliability of the narrator is in fact a condition slowly constructed by the author, through the careful dissemination of details and particulars—concerning a myriad of elements about the narrator: his past, his psychology, his manner of narrating, the idiosyncrasies of his style, etc.—that are strategically meant to induce the reader to question the reliability of the narrator himself, and consequently the credibility of his account. In this way, Barlow doubles the impact of vagueness in his narratives: the queerness and implausibility of the events narrated are in fact joined and redoubled by the mistrust in the narrator's dependability. Of course the aesthetic goal Barlow aims at is very difficult to achieve: he must tactfully balance the information he conveys about the narrator and dose the way in which he conveys it, in order not to reveal too much. In fact, Barlow's proposition is not to take a definitive stance about his narrator, namely neither to present him as totally reliable nor to completely discredit him; for this would give the reader a certainty, not a doubt: this narration is reliable/unreliable. Instead, Barlow's aim is to maintain vagueness and uncertainty till the very end—and more—of the reading process: when the buyer of the pulp or fanzine ended reading the tale, he still had to wonder about the narrator's reliability and the actual truth of his account. Only in such a way may "hesitation" and vagueness be preserved as the main ciphers of the fantastic.[12]

---

12. This is in fact the opinion of Tzvetan Todorov, an important theoretician of the fantastic in literature. He believes the essence of the fantastic dwells in the reader's hesitation between a natural and a supernatural explanation of a fictional event. This suspended state "lasts only as long as a certain hesitation: a hesitation common to the reader and the character, who must decide whether or not what they perceive derives from 'reality' as it exists in the common opinion" (41). Todorov goes on to explain that if the reader "decides that the laws of reality remain intact and permit an explanation of the phenomena described, we say that the work belongs to another genre: the *uncanny*. If on the contrary,

How does Barlow proceed in the realization of this delicate and demanding artistic task? Does he succeed? Probably the best way to evaluate his treatment of the narrating voice is to discuss a couple of cases, among the most significant ones: I am going to introduce the narrators of "The Night Ocean" and "Origin Undetermined."

3.4.1 The lonely and paranoid narrator: "The Night Ocean"

Thanks to the recent discovery, by Douglas A. Anderson, of Barlow's original typescript (it had been microfilmed by Barlow's literary executor, George T. Smisor), reporting Lovecraft's pencil interpolations and corrections, "The Night Ocean" has been finally recognised as an almost fully Barlovian product:[13] Barlow's typescript, with Lovecraft's revisions, has been published (in Faig 2000), and the document reveals that the entire plot comes from Barlow, with Lovecraft limiting himself to "revising the language throughout but contributing perhaps less than 10% to the overall story" (Joshi and Schultz, *H. P. Lovecraft Encyclopedia* 189), in spite of Lovecraft's declaration to Hyman Bradofsky (editor of the *Californian*) that he "ripped the text to pieces in spots."[14] That the original idea—and writing—of the tale were entirely Barlow's is also proved by Lovecraft's words in a letter addressed to Barlow and dated 23 July 1936, where the Providence writer admits: "I am eager to see the items I haven't yet seen—'The Bright Valley', 'The Root-Gatherers', & 'The Night Ocean'" (*FF* 353). "The Night Ocean" is the sixth and last of the Barlow-Lovecraft collaborations, certainly the one in which the latter's revisory hand has been the least heavy—and probably the last extant fictional piece to which Lovecraft has put hand. It is likely that the two friends worked together on the tale during Barlow's sojourn in Providence in summer 1936. The tale was published by Hyman Bradofsky in the winter 1936 issue of the *Californian*, and right after the appearance of the work, Lovecraft expressed his praise to Barlow's merits: "The kid is coming along—indeed, the N.O. is one of the most truly artistic weird tales I've ever read."[15] Lovecraft's open praise for the tale represents a further proof that he had not had a very large hand in it (it would have been uncharacteristic of Lovecraft to applaud a tale in which he had intervened heavily). I hope my discussion will ultimately add to the correctness of Joshi's opinion, according to which "That this mature, atmospheric work was

---

he decides that new laws of nature must be entertained to account for the phenomena, we enter into the genre of the *marvellous*" (41). According to Todorov, in the moment when the hesitation is solved by the reader and/or the character in favor of the "uncanny" or the "marvellous," the narrative exits the dimension of the fantastic proper.

13. According to Joshi and Anderson, "Lovecraft did little more than smooth out the prose throughout, only occasionally rewriting a passage" ("Introduction," *EG* 10).

14. Letter dated 4 November 1936 (ms., JHL).

15. Letter to Duane W. Rimel, 20 February, 1937 (ms., JHL; quoted in *LAL* 615).

written by a young man who had just turned eighteen ought to make us marvel anew at Barlow's precocity."[16]

Joshi is correct in claiming that "The Night Ocean" is "one of the most pensively atmospheric tales in the Lovecraft canon" and in comparing this story to "The Colour out of Space" regarding its success in capturing the "essential spirit of the weird tale" (A *Subtler Magick* 201, 202),[17] since the atmosphere and the sense of vagueness are the dominant traits of this narrative. Barlow's development of the figure of an unreliable narrator certainly contributes to the aesthetic achievement of this sense of indecipherable vagueness and suspended atmosphere. Joshi does not fail to notice the essential role played by vagueness to ensure the efficacy of the tale: "The plot of the story—an artist occupies a remote seaside bungalow for a vacation and senses strange but nebulous presences on the beach or in the ocean—is indeed negligible, but the artistry is in the telling: *the avoidance of explicitness*—one of the besetting sins of Lovecraft's later works—*is the great virtue of the tale*" (LAL 616; italics added). The peculiar construction of the narrator's figure as an essential means adopted by Barlow to convey the aesthetic sense of "avoidance of explicitness" is precisely the object of the following discussion.

"The Night Ocean" is certainly an "atmospheric marvel" (Joshi and Anderson, "Introduction," *EG* 10), a beautiful tale revealing Barlow's "startling maturity, restraint, and subtlety that would make it a landmark even if it were not the work of an eighteen-year old" (Joshi, "Introduction," *OLL* 7). The tale is full of prose-poetic passages, the expression of the sensitive and tormented personality of its author: a complex tale, dealing with essential themes such as the relationship between life and death, man and nature. This latter topic will be addressed and discussed at length in the chapter dedicated to the theme of "Nature" in Barlow's fiction. But "The Night Ocean" is also a textbook example of the extreme sensitiveness and poetic attitude of Barlow's personality. The peculiar prose-poetic style of this one-man narrative certainly deserves an in-depth study, and this alone may grant this tale a full appreciation. However, my aim here is to concentrate on the specific way in which Barlow builds the figure of an ambiguous and unreliable narrator. The story of "The Night Ocean" in fact is told by a lonely narrator who—perhaps just because of his loneliness—progressively loses control of his mental faculties, as well as his grip on reality. This is the story of an unconscious degeneration, told by an unaware narrator who is himself the protagonist of the degenerative process. Once the interpreter recognizes this, he must automatically

---

16. "Afterword" (page 707) to the 2004 reprinting of Joshi's *H. P. Lovecraft: A Life* (originally released in 1996).

17. Joshi mentions, as Lovecraft's definitive words on the "essential spirit" of the weird tale, his aesthetic judgment on Algernon Blackwood's work: "Here art and restraint in narrative reach their very highest development, and an impression of lasting poignancy is produced without a single strained passage or a single false note [...] Plot is everywhere negligible, and atmosphere reigns untrammelled" (in *Supernatural Horror in Literature* 67).

also re-examine the figure of this narrator and especially reconsider the judgment on his account's alleged reliability.

The tale opens with the narration of the first days of the protagonist's sojourn in the house on Ellston Beach. Barlow is careful to show how this experience started positively for his character, a painter who at the end of August rented a small solitary cottage on a beach isolated from the tourist resorts of the nearby village. However, already at the outset Barlow drops a few hints—deserving of attentive consideration in light of the following events—about the peculiar mental and physical condition of the protagonist: "I went to Ellston Beach not only for the pleasures of sun and ocean, but to rest a weary mind" (EG 105). Therefore the reader is already informed about the "weariness" of the narrator's mind: he is a painter who lately has been working hard in order to finish a canvas to be presented in a contest. He has now rented the cottage on the beach in order to rest for a while—and wait for the results of the contest. He needs to "find rest and seclusion for a time" (EG 105), since he has

> no longer the old concern with a hundred complexities of colour and ornament; no longer the fear and mistrust of my ability to render a mental image actual, and turn by my own skill alone the dim-conceived idea into the careful draught of a design. And yet that which later befell me by the lonely shore may have grown solely from the mental constitution behind such *concern and fear and mistrust*. For I have always been *a seeker, a dreamer*, and a ponderer on seeking and dreaming. (EG 105; italics added)

Barlow's slow attempt to disrupt, in the reader's mind, the narrator's reliability starts already in these very first lines, through hints as to the narrator's dreamy personality and his natural inclination toward *fear* and *mistrust*, which contributes to the delineation of a reflexive and probably apprehensive and distressed soul. However, these are only passing notations: Barlow is careful to convey to the reader the picture of an initial situation of pleasure and contentment for his character. There are countless hints in this direction: he spends days "in the enjoyment of sun and restless water" (EG 106) and candidly admits he has been "content for many days, and glad that I had chosen the lonely house which sat like a small beast upon those rounded cliffs of sand" (EG 108). However, also within an apparently "positive" sentence as this last one, Barlow does not fail to highlight a decisive aspect of the narrator's personality: his extremely solitary nature, his love for loneliness and quiet. While observing the variable hues of the mighty ocean, and the reflections of the sunrays glaring on it, the narrator does express his enjoyment of the scene but adds a significant detail: "There was no other person near me, and I enjoyed the spectacle without the annoyance of any alien object upon the stage" (EG 107). The scenery is particularly appealing to him just because he is alone and no other person or object shares the same vision. Carefully avoiding sounding too dramatic, Barlow nevertheless drops another clue to push the reader's questioning of the narrator's reliability—if not of his overall mental sanity. And again, in the balmy first days of his sojourn, the narrator's revealing of his abnormal love for light—especially for sunlight—is a hint toward his likely sickness, which by the way the narrator himself recognizes: "I noticed that many of the beach-people were displeased by the inordinate sun, whereas I sought it. After grey months of toil the lethargy induced by a physical existence in a region governed by the simple things—the wind and light and water—had a prompt effect upon me; and since I was anxious to continue this *healing process*, I spent all my time outdoors in sunlight" (EG 108; italics added). His sojourn at the beach is thus meant as a healing process, as a means to recovery from an ill-identified illness—we could properly label it a "vague" one.

And in fact, the symptoms of the narrator's illness gradually begin to manifest themselves. This coincides with the progressive darkening of the atmosphere, one week after the man's arrival on the beach. The sun begins to be displaced by long intervals of cloudy weather and obscured by a veil of gray mist that it is unable to penetrate. Simultaneously with this atmospheric change, the protagonist starts to perceive one in his house's surroundings:

> That the place was isolated I have said, and this at first pleased me; but in that brief evening hour when the sun left in a gore-splattered decline and darkness lumbered on line an expanding shapeless blot, *there was an alien presence about the place*. [. . .] At these times I felt an uneasiness which had no very definite cause, although my solitary nature had made me long accustomed to the ancient silence and the ancient voice of nature. [. . .] all the while a gradual consciousness of the ocean's immense loneliness crept upon me, a loneliness that was made subtly horrible by intimations—which were never more than such—of some animation or sentience *preventing me from being wholly alone*. (EG 109; italics added)

The narrator feels presences around him, something spiritual and indefinite that accompanies his days: he cannot properly define it—not in words and not even in images. The reader is now led to attribute the mention of these "presences" to the narrator's solitary broodings, and to an invention—or suggestion—taking place in his fertile mind. That the protagonist's mental state is increasingly deteriorating is an impression that gradually but inescapably dawns upon the reader: "The noisy, yellow streets of the town, with their curiously unreal activity, were very far away, and when I went there for my evening meal (mistrusting a diet entirely of my own ambiguous cooking) I took increasing and quite unreasonable care that I should return to the cottage before the late darkness, although I was often abroad until ten or so" (EG 109). The narrator's sense of uneasiness grows, and is revealed not only by his plain statements (he defines his behavior as "quite unreasonable," i.e. unjustified), but also by this apparently unimportant notation: he does not trust his own cooking skills. Thus he admits he is already losing some sort of trust in himself: the narration induces the reader to perceive a progressive loss of faith in the narrator's reliability. And the protagonist is aware of this process, he understands he is slowly losing his reader's trust—and therefore with a sudden stylistic change he addresses the reader directly, through an invocation that wants to sound like an attempt to regain a credit progressively lost, but that ends up being a further admission of his own precarious mental state and mysterious illness:

> You will say that such action is unreasonable; that if I had feared the darkness in some childish way, I would have entirely avoided it. You will ask me why I did not leave the place since its loneliness was depressing me. To all this *I have no reply*, save that whatever unrest I felt, whatever of remote disturbance there was to me in brief aspects of the darkening sun or in the eager salt-brittle wind or in the robe of the dark sea that lay crumpled like an enormous garment so close to me, was something which had an origin half *in my own heart*, which showed itself only at fleeting moments, and which had no very long effect upon me. In the recurrent days of diamond light, with sportive waves flinging blue peaks at the basking shore, the memory of dark moods seemed rather incredible; yet only an hour or two afterward *I might again experience those moods*, and descend to a dim region of despair. (EG 110; italics added)

This passage reveals that part and parcel with the narrator's mysterious illness is certainly a psychological disorder affecting his mind and soul, and that one of its main manifestations is certainly the *volubility* of his temper—testified at least by two important clues Barlow drops here. First of all, the very loneliness that a week or less before has been pleasant and welcome to the character now "depresses" him; he even defines it a "hideous loneliness (something I did not even wish assuaged, so deeply was it embedded in my heart)" (EG 116), revealing in this way another proof of his disease: in fact, even though he is aware of the negative effect his loneliness is having upon him, he does not wish to heal. Secondly, his readiness to be prey to "dark moods" without any acceptable reason—and especially the continuous unjustified *changes* in his mood—represent a powerful hint toward the character's mental instability and, probably, depressive state.

The protagonist's progressive loss of control over his own faculties and memories—when seen in the light of the mysterious deaths occurring on the beaches at that summer's end—may even be a hint, subtly but disturbingly introduced by Barlow, to the eventual part the character may have had in those unexplained events. People are in fact found dead at sea, and Barlow carefully disseminates details about the inexplicability of the casualties—making the reader suspect the narrator's involvement:

> There were drownings at the beach that year, and while I heard of these only casually [...] I knew that their details were unsavoury. The people who died—some of them *swimmers of a skill beyond average*—were sometimes not found until many days had elapsed, and the hideous vengeance of the deep had scourged their rotten bodies. [...] No one seemed to know what had caused these deaths. Their frequency excited alarm, *since the undertow at Ellston was not strong*, and since *there were known to be no sharks at hand*. Whether the bodies showed marks of any attacks *I did not learn*. (EG 110; italics added)

If my interpretation is even only partially correct, it would also justify reading the tale on a second or meta-level, that of a *mystery* tale. After all, the reticence the narrator shows in regard to these deaths certainly adds to his ambiguity and unreliability: the weakening of his credibility is in fact a slow process, and Barlow takes particular pains in developing it. Even watching the shores and the cliffs upon them is, for this narrator, a pretext to blur dream and reality, and to superimpose the scene of an underwater realm, deposited in the back of his memory by a fairy tale he heard in his childhood, on the present observation of the actual shore in front of him. The narrator blurs reality with the colors of his (artistic) imagination—and ends up confounding "a grey object, like a piece of driftwood, tossing obscurely on the foam" (EG 112), with the ape-faced creature emerging from the depths of his childhood fable. The protagonist's perceptions are thus slowly losing reliability, and this is testified also by his acknowledgment that the piece of driftwood was probably not a piece of driftwood at all: "since it vanished shortly, may not have been wood, but a porpoise coming to the troubled surface" (EG 112).

Surprised by a heavy and cold rain, the protagonist returns home, only to discover that darkness is now approaching and seems almost attacking him, confounding his senses and perceptions: "I was prisoned on all sides by an unnaturally increased dusk which had filtered down at some undefined hour under cover of the storm. How long I had been on he reaches of wet grey sand, or what the real time was, I could not tell" (EG 112). Therefore Barlow's narrator, after a time—whose length he is not able to remember—spent in fancies (and perhaps also other, less wholesome activities) on the rock cliffs, is now wrapped in darkness inside his house. His memory appears not to work properly anymore, and his senses—in particular his sight—are now endangered by the descent of dusk as an all-enshrouding veil. It is exactly in these conditions that the narrator tells of his observation, from one of the windows, of three or more figures—apparently people—"moving about in some incomprehensible manner" (EG 113). While still wondering at the reasons of the unexpected visitors' appearance, the protagonist opens the door and gesticulates toward them, intending to offer shelter from the storm. But the figures make no returning signal to him: "*Dim* in the evening, they stood as if half-surprised, or as if they awaited some other action from me. There was in their attitude something of that cryptic blankness, signifying anything or nothing, *which the house wore about itself* as seen in the morbid sunset" (EG 113; italics added). This couple of sentences represents a masterpiece of vagueness and of reticence on a narrator's part: he admits his perception was "dim," so that he cannot be sure whether the figures he saw were real human beings. Moreover, these figures seem not to understand his gestures, a fact that may have at least two explanations: they are not humans—so they do not understand the human gestural communication system—and implicitly this detracts from the narrator's discerning capacity, since he misunderstood some inanimate objects or non-human animals for human beings; or, if the figures are humans, they are unable to communicate with the character, who thus is shown by Barlow to be so solitary that he is not even able to communicate with his fellows anymore. In either case, Barlow hints once more at the narrator's isolation and unreliability (his sight does not work well, or he has by now lived in isolation for so long that he is not able to communicate with other people anymore—which is certainly not an edifying quality for a narrator).

Also his immediately following words, commenting upon his own emotional state and the reality of his visual impressions of the dim figures on the beach, attest to the narrator's increasingly growing unbalance, verging over paranoia:

> Abruptly there came to me a feeling that a sinister quality lurked about those unmoving figures who chose to stay in the rainy night upon a beach deserted by all people, and I closed the door *with a surge of annoyance* which sought all too vainly to disguise *a deeper emotion of fear*; *a consuming fright* that welled up from the shadows of my consciousness. A moment later, when I had stepped to the window, *there seemed to be nothing outside* but the portentous night. Vaguely puzzled, and even more vaguely frightened—like one who has seen no alarming thing, but is *apprehensive* of what may be found in the dark street he is soon compelled to cross—I decided that *I had very possibly seen no one*, and that the murky air *had deceived me*. (EG 113; italics added)

This revelatory passage contains two important clues: (1) the narrator is certainly fraught with a fear that prevents him even from describing what he is feeling ("vaguely puzzled, and even more vaguely frightened"); (2) his perceptions are clearly altered, and he himself starts to suspect that his senses are no longer reliable ("I decided I had very possibly seen no one, and that the murky air had deceived me"). Barlow is effectively conducting the process of the dismantlement of the narrator's credibility, and chooses to adopt what appears to be a very convincing way to make the process even more cogent: he shows a narrator who progressively loses faith in himself and even starts to show paranoid features, as when he detects in sheer *darkness* an actual enemy to fight: "Fighting away the prevalent gloom with a soiled lamp—for the darkness crept in at my windows and sat peering obscurely at me from the corners like a patient animal" (EG 113). This is not simply figurative language: here Barlow is coherently pursuing both his poetics of the dialectics between light and darkness, and the "spiritualizing" intent of his work. That the narrator's mental faculties are, from now on, in peril, and that the emergence of this threat coincides with the abrupt descent of darkness (which, in a sense, "obscures" the atmosphere as well as his perceptions, with a beautiful—though conventional—double aesthetic effect), is revealed by the narrator himself: "Darkness had come early and furtively, and throughout the remainder of my stay lingered evasively over each scene and action which I beheld" (EG 113): this is equivalent to saying that, whatever the narrator is going to relate from now on, it should of course be very carefully pondered by the reader, since the perceiver's faculties and senses are under the obfuscating spell of darkness.

The narrator's faculties affected by this process are both his perceptive ones (above all his senses, especially his sight) and his rational ones (his capacity to distinguish reality from hallucination, and above all the capacity to judge properly the sensory impressions his brain receives: in other words, he shows the signs of mental instability and paranoia). He himself recognizes the peculiar condition he is in, when he attributes to the "darkness and restlessness of the sea" penetrating his heart the "unreasoning, unperceiving torment" (EG 116) he experiences: thus his torment causes him to be "unreasoning," i.e., to lose his rational faculties, and to be "unperceiving," i.e., to be unable to correctly perceive reality through sensory equipment. The peculiar novelty represented by this character is that he openly recognizes the gradual deterioration of his mental faculties and his diminishing faith in his own capacities: this conscious, epistemic self-destruction continues unceasingly throughout the remainder of the narration.

The morning after his alleged sighting of the mysterious visitors on the beach, the hesitant protagonist bursts the house's door open, only to discover that no track is recognizable, "as if no foot before mine had disturbed the smooth sand" (EG 114). The suspicion that the narrator, still prey to the wild fancies he had had close to the cliffs, had imagined the entire episode of the dark visitors intrudes powerfully in the reader's mind. The narrator continues in the proclamation of his unstable and voluble mental condition: "With the quick lift of spirit that follows a period of *uneasy depression*, I felt—in a purely *yielding fashion* and *without volition*—that my own memory was washed clean of all the *mistrust* and *suspicion* and *disease-like fear* of a lifetime, just as the filth of the water's edge succumbs to a particularly high tide, and is carried out of sight" (EG 114; italics added). A little is enough to make the narrator's mood change, to throw him in the darkest depression and to make him suddenly recover—to sharpen his emotions, and after a short while to throw him again into sensory passivity. The entire story thus becomes ambiguous, and the reader is never sure what credit to assign to the narrator's statements and whether the latter is indeed writing out of direct experience of an objective reality or out of a dreamy impression of his fertile imagination: the narrator's mind and body are weary, and he himself tends to discredit his own sensory perceptions. In the passages examined above, as well as in the continuation of his tale, the narrator reveals himself being affected by depression, despair, loneliness (the "loneliness of that bleak-eyed house"), fear, passivity, uneasiness (once more when stating that the "evil intimations" of an "haunted darkness" had given him "a greater *uneasiness*" [EG 115] than any menace to his body). The sheer tendency the narrator shows toward *personifying* natural elements (not only darkness, but also the sun and the sea, as well as the house itself), invariably attributing to them an *evil sentience* (directed toward him), represents a clue pointing to the hypothesis of his paranoid and schizophrenic inclinations. In particular, toward the end of the tale Barlow masterfully drops a hint as to a possible *reduplication of personality* affecting his narrator—once again, plainly stated by his own words. When he is finally notified by telegram that his painting won the contest in which was entered, he sets a date for leaving Ellston Beach. However, the way in which he reacts to the positive news is again worth mentioning and discussing: "This news, which earlier in the year would have affected me strongly, I now received with a *curious apathy*. It seemed as unrelated to the unreality about me, as little pertinent to me, as if it were directed *to another person whom I did not know*, and whose message had come to me through some accident"

(EG 118; italics added). Besides confirming the protagonist's passivity ("curious apathy"), this short passage helps the interpreter recognize another peculiar phenomenon affecting the character's psyche: the reduplication of his personality, his taking a distance from himself as another of the several negative effects his sojourn on the beach has caused him.

The picture of an unreliable narrator is thus fairly and convincingly depicted. Most of his perceptions—and consequent statements—are to be carefully pondered by the reader, and since most of them are openly defined as unreliable by the narrator himself, the reader is led to discard the *entire* story as the outcome of a particularly sensitive, dreamy, and possibly diseased mind. Thus also the telling of the narrator's discovery, on the beach, of an object that looks like a "piece of rotten flesh" resembling a human hand must be taken as a partial approximation to the truth. Moreover, the very fact that the protagonist does not report his find—especially since he knows of that summer's several drownings—appears suspect and fuels the hypothesis that he has had a responsibility in the inexplicable deaths of the vacationists. What the narrator really found on the beach, and whether he really found something, remain vague and beyond the reader's possibility of speculation. The most likely interpretation of the entire story is that the narrator has—unconsciously—mingled real and objective phenomena with the broodings and suggestions coming out of his mind and imagination, so that it is virtually impossible for the reader to discern what actually happened and what was pure invention. In particular, this interpretation is reinforced by the narrator's evident inclination to make his statements rely, as the sources for his assumptions, on an inordinate merging of internal and external impressions. It is above all the influence of natural elements and events that provokes this confusion of impressions at the origin of the narrator's utterances:

> It is difficult to describe the mental state in which succeeding days found me. Always susceptible to morbid emotions whose dark anguish *might be induced by things outside myself, or might spring from the abysses of my own spirit*, I was ridden by a feeling which was [. . .] rather a perception of the brief hideousness and underlying filth of life—a feeling *partly a reflection of my internal nature and partly a result of broodings induced by that gnawed rotten object* which may have been a hand. (EG 116; italics added)

Besides recognizing that his perceptions are influenced by both his inner nature and the external events—which is in itself hardly an uplifting trait in a narrator aspiring to objectivity and credence—here he is also telling something more: that he is unable to *distinguish* which of his perceptions come from the observation of external phenomena (and thus may claim a higher degree of objectivity and credibility) and which are the result of his own broodings and imaginings. After all, the narrator plainly admits that his impressions and emotions are heavily influenced by external sources, of which they are even described as a "reflection": "Perhaps these inward emotions were only a *reflection* of the sea's own mood; for although half of what we see is coloured by the interpretation placed upon it by our minds, many of our feelings are shaped quite distinctly by external, physical things" (EG 110); and again: "The once friendly waters babbled meaningfully to me, and eyed me with a strange regard; yet whether the darkness of the scene were a *reflection* of my own broodings, or whether the gloom within me were caused by what lay without, I could not have told" (EG 117). Everything, the narrator claims, when recorded and put in words seems to lose its own purest nature: language entails interpretation, and any interpretation is *not* the thing it claims to explain. Our perceptions of external things are colored by our own distorting interpretations, and, reciprocally, our inner feelings are influenced, thus distorted, by external and physical things.

Certainly, it is hard to imagine a more open self-declaration of unreliability of his own discourse (and on *any* narrative discourse pretending to express the truth) on a narrator's part. The impression remains strong that the narrator's meditations may have had a major part in his "seeing" what (perhaps everything) he "saw." Moreover, the sheer amount of time and ink that the narrator employs in describing the workings of his mind (its speculating, dreaming, imagining, remembering) certainly strengthens the interpretation that most of the events in this tale are *mental*. In fact, proceeding toward the end of his account, the narrator makes clear how the horror *is expected*, is somehow anticipated by his broodings—so much so that one of course suspects the horror *is directly generated by the narrator's mind*. The narrator uses countless expressions to transmit a sense of expectancy for a long-awaited, final terrible event—one *liberating* the narrator's mind and soul from their torments, restoring their easiness and even life: "I was waiting, like my own fearing heart and the motionless scene beyond, for the token of some ineffable *life*" (EG 118-19; italics added). What is important in this sentence is not so much the "waiting" of the protagonist, but the object of his waiting: a token of *life*. In other words, he is expecting the final *climax* as a liberating event, one that will restore the vital lymph to the withering roots of his soul. Again, a few lines later: "I waited in a torment of expectancy made doubly acute by the delay in fulfilment, and the uncertainty of what strange completion was to come" (EG 119). The narrator's spirit is making a "vigil" (EG 119), and what would be the nature of such a final, terrible, liberating event is at last hinted at by the narrator's words, unveiling at least part of the vagueness enwrapping it: "As if *expectant of death* [. . .] I crouched with a forgotten cigarette in my hand"; and "As I watched, dread-filled and passive, with the fixed stare of one *who awaits death*" (EG 119; italics added). He even explicitly states his own will to live is abated, and he has grown indifferent to his own fate: his is "an indolence like that of a man who no longer cares to live" (EG 116). At last a bit of the vagueness is dissolved: the protagonist awaits and desires death as a liberation from his torments and maladjustments. The disturbances, the fears, and the uncertainties of his minds are thus made finally a bit clearer, and are apparently justified: his account has been so vague, troubled, and unreliable because this was the mind of a sick, disillusioned person meditating suicide, or at least awaiting death as a liberation.

However, this solution is again unsatisfactory: Barlow makes the reader believe that this *is* the solution, but again this would be too clear a *dénouement*: vagueness must be preserved till the very end of the reading process, and possibly even beyond. Aware of Lovecraft's lesson, Barlow understood the main elements of an effective weird tale are *ambiguity* and *indeterminacy*, and thus he strives to maintain them until the very last page of his masterly tale.

Thus, the final pages of "The Night Ocean" are built in such a way as to ceaselessly increase an unrestrained sense of ambiguity and vagueness, and in order to prepare the final, shocking, and hardly decipherable climax. Late September comes, when the town closes its "resorts where mad frivolity ruled empty," and "there were not a hundred people left in town" (EG 117). The sense of expectancy is still very strong in the protagonist; he awaits a "thaumaturgy" that he fears "less than a continuance of my horrible suspicions—less than the too-elusive hints of something monstrous lurking behind the great stage" (EG 117). Again he admits that his mind and soul are waiting for an event liberating him from his pain, for a horrific happening that may be death—or something even worse. He waits for it, he *knows* it should be coming, because it is entirely in his mind—both his pain and the healing event to come. Not by chance, the narrator speaks of "speculation" about the horror to come—it is entirely a mental event: "it was with more speculation than actual fear that I waited unendingly for the day of horror *which seemed to be nearing*" (EG 117; italics added). And even though he is aware that the forthcoming event is a horrific one, he does not fear it—because he knows that even horror is better than his actual plight. The narrator is failed by his memory[18] in recollecting the final event, and even what this event implies is defined only as "suggestions."

The aesthetic effect of vagueness and indeterminacy is once again effectively pursued and achieved by Barlow: "The day, I repeat, was late in September, though whether the 22nd or 23rd I am uncertain. Such details have fled before the recollection of those *uncompleted happenings*—episodes with which no orderly existence should be plagued, because of the damnable suggestions (*and only suggestions*) they contain. I *knew the time* with an intuitive distress of spirit—*a recognition too deep for me to explain*" (EG 117; italics added). Not only does he know the event is going to happen, he even knows the *time*—he is probably aware of the moment in which his mind is going to collapse and let the horror burst. Thus a sudden change occurs to him: while before he had been enjoying the brightness of sunlight and the psychological relief it brought to his soul, now he is totally

---

18. RHB was to be aware of the powerful aesthetic effect that the *loss of memory* may have in the building up of the figure of an unreliable narrator. In fact, he resorted to it also in "A Dim-Remembered Story" as to a topos adding to the story's ambiguity. In this last tale, RHB even openly mentions amnesia as a possible disturb having occurred to his narrator: "That vertigo, the sense of an ebbing tide that fell away from me as I woke, had tangled all my thoughts, and I only knew that if I had been a victim of amnesia, my wanderings had been far and strange to bring me to this place" (EG 95). More on this important topic will be found in the chapter on the theme of "Time" in RHB's fiction.

made a *creature of the night*: his degeneracy is complete, and now he (his mind) is ready to perform the final horror show. Therefore he does not care for daylight anymore, he does not even remember what the day brought: he waits only for the *night*, for a literal and metaphorical darkness to overcome his soul: "Throughout those daylight hours *I was expectant of the night*; impatient, perhaps, so that the sunlight passed like a half-glimpsed reflection in rippled water—a day of whose events I recall nothing" (EG 117; italics added).

And that fateful night is a portentous one: the moon is monstrously big and elevated in the sky, the air is heavy with the mumbled secrets of the sea. The protagonist is aware that "some strange and palpitating life—the embodiment *of all I had felt and of all I had suspected*" (EG 118; italics added) is approaching, and that it is an "embodiment," namely a reflection, of his own mental processes (fears and suspicions). Thus he lies in wait, "like one who stands by a figure lost in sleep, *knowing that it will awake in a moment*" (EG 118; italics added). In spite of himself, the narrator cannot help recognizing that he *knows* in advance everything that is going to happen—after all, he is the owner and best possible connoisseur of his mind. He even knows that the "hinted," i.e. vague, thing to come wants to be seen and recognized in full sight: "The shadows were draining from the beach, and I felt that they took with them all which might have been a harbour for my thoughts when the hinted thing should come" (EG 118). Awestruck by the "endless tableau of the lunar orb" and by a sea "astir, perhaps, with some unkenned life" (EG 118), the protagonist is prey to turbulent thoughts, which add even more to his mental confusion. And that his *thoughts* are seething like a vortex—probably influencing in a decisive way the quality of the forthcoming events—is demonstrated also by the fact that the narrator reveals that his behavior is under their spell. Everything he does is a result of the overwhelming influence of his thoughts on his acts and perceptions: the fear of the moon and the sea he feels that night is certainly a product of his thoughts, and his acts are too: "I arose and shut the window; partly because of an inward prompting, but mostly, I think as an excuse *for transferring momentarily the stream of thought*" (EG 118; italics added). Thus he lies waiting, the night outside is silent: "I knew that despite my closed window" (EG 119), since he is perceiving the scene—and the future horror—only within his mind, and thus he does not actually need to "hear silence" with his ears in order to know that there are no sounds in the air. He does not move and does not make a sound, almost paralyzed in his chair, in order not to reveal to an unseen, purely imagined enemy his own "fear-racked brain imprisoned in flesh" (EG 119). He crouches in wait in his room, with a forgotten cigarette in his hand, while a lamp burns in a corner, radiating a faint light and no heat at all.

And then, all of a sudden, the final horrific event takes place, and the only description the protagonist is able to convey is one enwrapped in a shroud of vague hints and ambiguous suggestions: "Then, with an unheard splash which sent from the silver water to the shore a line of ripples echoed in fear by my heart, a *swimming thing* emerged beyond the breakers. The figure *may have been that of a dog, a human being, or something more strange*. It could not have known that

I watched—*perhaps it did not care*—but *like a distorted* fish it swam across the mirrored stars and dived beneath the surface" (EG 119; italics added). The narrator's perceptions—and interpretations—are the vaguest possible: the "figure" is described, in succession, as a dog, a human being, something stranger, and a distorted fish. Even its intentions are not clear at all; the narrator does not know whether the creature's placid swimming is due to its not having seen him watching, or to its "not caring" for it. The confusion of perceptions is complete, just as it happens when a man has to describe the blurred dreams and visions generated by his own slumbers and imagination.

Humphreys too recognizes both the "narrator's uncertainty" (20) and the vagueness of his narration as the main elements of the tale. After firstly suggesting that the final "creatures" allegedly seen by the protagonist may relate to the Deep Ones of Lovecraft's "The Shadow over Innsmouth," Humphreys changes his mind and recognizes that their sheer objective existence is all the more dubious:

> One of the most interesting aspects of "The Night Ocean" is the uncertainty that remains at the conclusion of the tale, since it is never explicitly stated that the narrator saw anything unusual at all. [. . .] The "creatures" that the narrator sees are only seen from a distance, and the narrator himself is never certain of what he views in the water, at best calling one creature "a man or something like a man". That is the most imaginatively descriptive the narrator becomes, and it is hardly the explicit shock felt by Lovecraft's protagonists in *At the Mountains of Madness* or "The Shadow out of Time". (20)

In fact, even when Barlow's protagonist believes he sees one of the creatures close up, he cannot be sure of its nature: "After a moment it came up again, and this time, since it was closer, I saw that it was carrying something across its shoulder. I knew, then, that it could be no animal, and that it was a man or something like a man, which came towards the land from a dark ocean. *But* it swam with horrible ease" (*EG* 119; italics added). The incoherency and sheer improbability of the narrator's surmises are obvious: the fact that a creature is carrying something on its shoulders certainly does not imply the creature is a man or "something like a man." The mention itself of an entity that is "something like a man" attests that it can be an *animal*, so that the narrator's apparent rational statement "I knew, then, that it could be no animal" is totally unfounded: the workings of his mind are clearly defective. Moreover, he himself recognizes, with that masterly "But" placed by Barlow in a strategic syntactic position, that a *man* could not swim with that *horrible ease*. The narrator's reasoning is utterly faulty, and he himself would recognize it, were his mind not irremediably compromised: in the same lines, words, and reasonings, the narrator is unable to recognize their defects; only an external interpreter, reading analytically the narrator's account, and without his psychological involvement in the events narrated, may detect the faultiness implied in the account itself.

Under this viewpoint, the narrator of "The Night Ocean" is utterly dissimilar from the one of "A Dim-Remembered Story": in the latter tale, in fact, the protagonist-narrator openly recognizes the disturbed condition of his mind, the grief, horror, and sheer weariness lying heavy on his body and soul, and—what is most significant for our discussion—his futile wish to attribute to a side-effect of his uneasy state the unbelievable (but objective) events and surroundings he is forced to confront:

> Then, while I was torn with grief and horror and dull acquiescence, I heard the clank of metal upon stone. The feeling induced by this sound—ordinarily a common one, and unworthy of notice—is indescribable. For a brief moment I hoped, wildly and incredulously, *that all my fears had been the result of a weary body and a mind depressed by unknown surroundings.* I wanted dreadfully to believe this, yet in the end I knew that I was unable. What lurked in my outraged brain was a verity, as actual as any memory or knowledge. (*EG* 92; italics added)

Barlow's epistemic pessimism reaches here unsuspected heights: a comparison between the narrators of these two tales reveals that *Barlow's fiction exhibits the impossibility of man to grasp and communicate truth.* In fact, in order to deal with an experience that is eminently a mental and imaginative one (as in "The Night Ocean"), Barlow chooses a narrator utterly incapable of recognizing this nonfactual nature, a narrator unable to realize his perceptions are faulty, and a narrator whose interpretations, as a consequence, point toward the opposite direction: that his has been an objective experience. On the other hand, the narrator of "A Dim-Remembered Story," facing an objective experience, is one that Barlow endows with all the necessary mental and rational faculties to recognize his own epistemic limits, whose range is augmented by the distorting impact of his weary condition on his senses and reason. But this awareness is of no use for this narrator, since the situation he is experiencing is a factual and non-imaginative one, despite the dizziness of his senses and his will to believe otherwise.

Now let us return to "The Night Ocean." The narrator continues his description of the fatal night recognizing he is "*dread-filled and passive,* with the fixed stare of one who awaits death in another *yet knows he cannot avert it*" (*EG* 119; italics added): again fear and passivity characterize the mental state of the narrator, who, in addition, knows he is awaiting a death he dare not avert—since, of course, it is a self-inflicted one, namely one he cannot fight because conceived and inflicted by his own mind. What the narrator is here telling between the lines is that he does not have the *will* to avoid his death: of course, the hidden reason is that his will is exactly the opposite, i.e. *to embrace this death.* The description of the subsequent acts of the mysterious swimmer are once more vague and unrevealing: "[. . .] the swimmer approached the shore—though too far down the southward beach for me to discern its outlines or features. Obscurely loping, with sparks of moonlit foam scattered by its quick gait, it emerged and was lost among the inland dunes" (*EG* 119). The indiscernible and blurred nature of the creature increasingly confirms the apparition as a typical vision—or dream—concocted by a weary, uneasy, and tormented mind, and favored by the atmosphere of loneliness and silence of a moonlit night facing the sea. After the vision, the protagonist is once again possessed "by a sudden recurrence of fear" and a sense of all-pervasive "tingling coldness" (EG 119). The most evident effect of his increasingly unbearable mental and physical condition is the growth of his paranoia, a fact—once again—so openly clear in his words for an external reader, but one that the narrator is totally unable to detect (and this inability, impairing his rational faculties, is of course, as in a vicious circle, a consequence of his own paranoia):

> Now that I could no longer see the figure, *I felt that it lingered somewhere in the close shadows, or peered hideously at me* from whatever windows I did not watch. And *so I turned my gaze, eagerly and frantically, to each successive pane*; dreading that I might indeed behold an intrusive regarding face, yet unable to keep myself from the terrifying inspection. But though I watched *for hours*, there was *no longer anything* upon the beach. (EG 120; italics added)

This is indeed the paranoid attitude of a tormented man: he is convinced that the creature is both evil and trying to harm him—both quite hazardous and unjustified inferences, since the creature never showed any sort of hostility; but of course, an evident symptom of paranoia is the tendency of the victims to attribute evil, unfriendly, and persecutory intentions to the people and environments surrounding them. Thus the protagonist turns his head *for hours*, eagerly and frantically, from one pane to another, looking for an evil that is not there, and probably never actually existed in the external reality, outside his own mind.

The most striking aesthetic effect of all this is Barlow's ability to maintain his narrator's lack of awareness: he in fact is credibly depicted as unable to detect his own paranoia, although his condition is so plainly stated by his own words. The conclusion to which he comes is in fact totally different; he believes that his entire experience has brought him on the edge of a great revelation—something he does not even dare to define—but an experience that in the end has left him with actually *nothing*, just a sense of unfulfilled promise. He recognizes this and the deceptive nature of his experience, but because of his mental disturbance he fails to make the following, rational step: that he has achieved nothing concrete because there actually *was nothing concrete*, since all the experience he went through was the imaginative and subjective delusion induced by a diseased psyche:

> Like the stars that promise the revelation of terrible and glorious memories, goad us into worship by this *deception, and then impart nothing*, I had come frighteningly near to the capture of an old secret which ventured close to man's haunts and lurked cautiously just beyond the edge of the known. *Yet in the end I had nothing.* I was given only a glimpse of the furtive thing; a glimpse *made obscure by the veils of ignorance.* I cannot even conceive what might have shown itself had I been too close to that swimmer who went shoreward instead of into the ocean. *I do not know* what might have come if the brew had passed the rim of the pot and poured outward in a swift cascade of revelation. The night ocean withheld whatever it had nurtured. *I shall know nothing more.* (EG 120; italics added)

In the final comment by his narrator, Barlow effectively insists on the theme of his *ignorance*: while up to now, in the course of the whole narration, the protagonist has been shown to *know* a lot, in advance, of what was going to happen—pretending to configure himself as an omniscient narrator, one in full command of his story and of his narrative skills—in the end what he is left with is just *nothing*, an utter ignorance of how to interpret and of what meaning to assign to his own story.

I hope my discussion has helped to shed light on the reasons of this overall inability, on the narrator's part, to give a meaning (if not a moral) to his account: he is unable to frame his narrative, since he has failed to realize the *nature* of his story, i.e. an utterly mental and imaginative one, with no specific objective meaning, if not one to be investigated with psychoanalytic tools—something of course lying outside the competence of a literary or narratologic analysis. What can be claimed is that, through the complex and multifaceted vagueness of this tale, Barlow has masterfully devised an exemplary figure of the utterly unstable and unreliable narrator, one deserving a place among the most effective ones of this particular category in the realm of fantastic fiction, together with Poe's and Lovecraft's best creations.

3.4.2 The diseased and frantic narrator: "Origin Undetermined"

Heywood Roberts, the narrator of this fascinating tale that was published by Barlow himself in the second and last issue of his amateur journal *Leaves* (1938),[19] constitutes an exemplary case of a character whose extraordinary and frightful experience leads toward the edge of mental unsteadiness and perhaps of utter madness—thus enshrouding his own account with a thick veil of doubt and skepticism. The narrative has a "Chinese box" structure, with the second-level narration—contained in the pages of Roberts's manuscript—framed within an introductory, explanatory passage (first-level narration) in which a doctor describes the unusual circumstances under which his friend Roberts contacted him some time before, after a long interval had elapsed from their last encounter. "Origin Undetermined" presents an articulated and interesting treatment of the theme of the narrator's unreliability, since it offers *two* different sets of hints concerning it:

1. the somehow *more objective* claims on the second-level narrator's unreliability, contained in the framing narrative: they are open statements made by the first-level narrator, the doctor compiling the framing narrative. This narrating voice is presented as much more trustworthy than the second-level one, because the character holding it is not directly involved in the queer events that occur to Roberts, and because his attitude, manner of speaking, and prose style are much colder, impartial, and skeptical than Roberts's. However, whether the first-level narrator is or is not a reliable voice (and this is an issue Barlow impressively addresses too), he

---

19. The work was composed in August 1937.

plainly states—as we will see—that Roberts's peculiar state of the mind made him an unreliable narrator. Therefore, the reader tends to credit the doctor's statements, merely because of their directness and immediate comprehensibility: no "reading between the lines" is required; the first-level narrator plainly describes his incredulity about the second-level narrator's account, and the reader easily understands the doctor's doubts—and is induced to share them;

2. the somehow *less objective* hints to the narrator's unreliability, contained in his own manuscript: the narrator here does not state openly his own unreliability (as the doctor does regarding Roberts), but the reader is invited by the text to make interpretative inferences that lead him to become skeptical on the narrator's account. As this is an inferential operation that solicits the reader to "read between the lines," it is of course only realizable after an attentive, second or third reading.

3.4.2.1 The framing narrative of the first-level narrator

Let us examine first how the doctor, or framing first-level narrator, induces the reader, through a series of *open and direct* declarations concerning Roberts, the second-level narrator, to discard this latter and his account as unreliable. Already at the outset, the doctor proclaims his doubts as to the wisdom of publishing Roberts's manuscript: "It may have some value to *students of psychology*, since it deals with an *uncommon sort of mental disorder* from the *victim's* own point of view; indeed, it is unique—I do not know how to classify such *abnormal imaginings*. The *delusion* from which he suffered must have appeared *very real and terrible*, since he chose such a *fearsome method of escape*. That he was a *suicide* can no longer be doubted" (EG 121; italics added). These few lines are indeed a concentrate of plain judgments on the doctor's part: he presents *as an objective fact* Roberts as a mental case, a sick man (a "victim") suffering from delusions and abnormal imaginings. Moreover, it is anticipated that Roberts has committed suicide, and—as an additional vague and disturbing detail—in an unspecified "fearsome" way. Already at the outset, the reader is encouraged to question how much credit it will be advisable to accord to Roberts's account.

The doctor proceeds by stating that in the story he is going to relate—with the help of Roberts's manuscript—"fact and madness are strangely mingled" (EG 121). In order to provide a detailed introduction to the manuscript and to outline Roberts's personality, the doctor recapitulates the circumstances of their acquaintance. They both had studied medicine in Detroit in 1912-13, and already then, according to the doctor, Roberts gave signs of a peculiar mental instability: "He seemed then to promise a brilliant career as surgeon, but afterward he gave this up altogether, victim of a mood which, if it were not quite the Freudian impulse to self-destruction latent in us all, was at least an impulse to conscious and unpreventable destruction of his own opportunities. I have seen this curious, lamentable impulse driving others; they seem predestined to unenviable fates" (EG

121). The doctor's description seems to leave no room for doubt: its cold and impartial prose style—typical of a scientifically minded person—sounds reliable. However, with a more careful examination, one cannot fail to notice how the self-assured tone of the narrator may in truth conceal a conceited attitude, one that claims to incontestably know and possess the truth, and that does not accept criticism of his ingrained convictions. The narrowmindedness of the doctor is a trait Barlow gradually builds through the character's words, and one that impels the reader to question the credibility not only of Roberts and his account, but also of the doctor's opinion on them. The doctor may simply be overstating, his goal being, hypothetically, to show his own (professional, psychological, etc.) superiority on a former colleague who "failed" in life and work. The interpretative vagueness connected with the deciphering of the relationship between (and the roles to assign to) the two narrators is certainly a major issue—and merit—of "Origin Undetermined."

The doctor proceeds by offering a full portrait of his former friend, insisting in particular on the volubility, irresoluteness, and disorderly brilliance of his personality: "He was *as erratic as he was brilliant*, a youth who had discarded the inane philosophy in which he was reared, but who had not yet evolved a workable substitute. *He might have become a criminal as readily as a surgeon, a feverish drunkard as readily as a scholar*" (*EG* 121; italics added). From such a temper, the doctor claims, anything may be expected. However, finally Roberts seemed to have found a field of scientific research and investigation appealing to his "fertile imagination": archaeology. Of course the reader is left to wonder about the reliability and the balance of an individual who so abruptly changed the field of interest and work of his entire life: from medicine to archaeology the distance looks definitely large—and the information this provides on Roberts's personality is in itself telling. He had a dreamy temper, and certainly valued imagination more than reality: "the secret, jungle-beset palaces of Central America were a greater reality to him than the world he read of vaguely in books and newspapers. It is scarcely odd that he gave up his medical studies; he was not realist enough to be a doctor" (*EG* 121).[20] Roberts's personality is thus slowly built up as dreamy and non-realist, prone to imaginative flights and probably willing to credit bizarre and unlikely tales.

At this point, Barlow masterfully plays with his first-level narrator, making him offer an ambiguous account of Roberts's personality and of the latest events in which he and Roberts were involved. In fact, in order to maintain an absolute vagueness on the issue of Roberts's reliability, Barlow makes his first-level narrator, the doctor, offer an account that never seems to state, once and for all, a de-

---

20. Probably RHB models the figure of Roberts on himself—not only for the hint as to the character's passion for the mysteries of Central America, but also the physical description the doctor gives of him: "a roundish head surmounting an awkward body; dark eyebrows and mustache; and a vaguely Oriental quality about the pale fleshy face, though he was Nordic enough in reality" (*EG* 121).

cisive word about Roberts's mental condition: was he sane or insane? The doctor never lets the reader decide: when he seems to offer a hint in one direction (in other words, he makes a *step forward* in the hypothesis that Roberts was mad), he immediately retreats and apparently contradicts himself (he makes a *step back*). What results is a fascinating "battle for truth," in which the two opposite armies—one defending the hypothesis of Roberts's madness, the other opposing it—are committed to harsh guerrilla actions. And of course a significant side-effect engendered by the uncertainty of this way of proceeding, where the doctor as a narrator seems unable to take a definitive stance on Roberts's case, adds to the doctor's own eventual unreliability and leaves the reader unable to decide about it. Let us see how Barlow handles this delicate epistemic conflict and the consequences it entails.

The doctor states that, after about ten years since their last meeting, Roberts sent him a letter "disclosing that he had become curator of Central American antiquities at the Nelkin Gallery of Art" (*EG* 122). Not only had the doctor often seen Roberts afterwards, but his friend seemed to have shaken off his "early unsteadiness, and become deeply absorbed in his new work" (*EG* 122). In conclusion, "there was nothing about him to indicate that such an incomprehensible breakdown lurked ahead" (*EG* 122). Although the doctor does not fail to define Roberts's later behavior as an "incomprehensible breakdown" (thus inducing the reader to judge it in the same way), he is here taking *a step forward* in the hypothesis that Roberts was a sane man.

However, one March day of the year previous to the actual writing of the doctor's narrative, Roberts called the doctor's office, the nurse passing the phone directly to him: "I took it and was at once disturbed by the quality of his voice" (*EG* 122). And in fact, Roberts's words were the most frantic and rambling imaginable: "Got to do it. I can't tell you how vital it is. God! It's already started. If you turn me down [. . .] no choice left. It works fast. If you saw what it does [. . .] this means my life. I'm coming over now" (*EG* 122). Neither the doctor nor his assistant are able to discern what Roberts means: he simply hangs up the phone and does not call back. The narrator, presenting Roberts's words in this way and especially insisting on his inability to explain himself and his plight, on his not making himself available at any phone number the doctor dials after the call, thus takes a *step forward* in the hypothesis that Roberts was (going) insane.

This stance is strengthened when Roberts suddenly shows up at the doctor's office in a very pitiful mental and physical state: "He snatched the door open, glaring distractedly into space—the set of fright set heavily upon him. He looked, I swear, like a dying man who has peered through the black corridors of destiny. The nurse and I were silent, appalled by his eyes. Fear is a communicable thing, and he was radiant with it" (*EG* 122). However, the doctor immediately makes sure to take a *step back* and restates the mental sanity of his visitor: "His turbulent gaze sought me, and *there was no madness in it*. Here was a man gripped by shadow hands, *but a sane man*" (*EG* 122; italics added). What is definitely charming is that Roberts himself, after sitting at the doctor's table and starting the account of his mysterious and lethal poisoning, contradicts the doctor and makes a *step forward* in the madness-hypothesis: "I know you didn't understand me [. . .] I guess I sounded crazy—God! I am crazy, with fear" (*EG* 122). Roberts's sheer request that the doctor amputate his hand induces the latter to define it an "absurdity": "Don't be an idiot, Heywood! If you are poisoned, there must be antidotes. I'm going to tell you to calm down [. . .] you know that excitement only increases your danger [. . .] but I am going to tell you not to say crazy things like that. What was it, anyway? Was it a snake?" (*EG* 122-23).

The doctor tries hard to make Roberts listen to reason and rationalize his experience: he asks him precise questions, and Roberts feels compelled to provide some explanation for the extraordinary situation in which he is placing the doctor, that of being requested to amputate his friend's hand in order to prevent a poisoning infection. Thus, exclusively to reassure the doctor and achieve his goal (to have him amputate his hand), Roberts invents a *reasonable* account of the way in which he got poisoned (by being slightly cut touching a Mayan bronze knife): he in fact wants to conceal the real circumstances of his poisoning, for fear of not being believed. The doctor keeps on pressing Roberts with questions aimed at making him recover his calm and reason, hoping "to shame him out of his *extravagant mood*" (*EG* 123; italics added). And after Roberts has ended his story, the doctor's single lapidary statement ("That is not what happened") powerfully sanctions—with just five words—both the unreliability of Roberts as a narrator and, if not his insanity, the precariousness of his mental state.

At this point, Barlow skillfully introduces a variant to enliven this otherwise rather conventional exchange: in fact Roberts openly recognizes the falsity of his account: "No [. . .] That's only partly true. I can't tell you any more. But I have not lied about the need for amputation. You must cut off my hand" (*EG* 123). Here we have a character who frankly admits his own unreliability, sanctioning in this way the possibility of being considered unreliable also later on, when reading his own manuscript: since he recognized he lied once, he could have lied twice. The framing narrative ends with Roberts's "unreasonable persistence" (*EG* 124) (another *step forward* in the madness-hypothesis, made by the doctor), with his frantic and urgent requests that the doctor amputate his hand: in the face of the latter's and his nurse's denials, Roberts pulls out a revolver and finally shoots his hand.

Before presenting Roberts's manuscript, which constitutes the bulk and the conclusion of Barlow's tale, the doctor drops a few lines in which he reveals he has not seen Roberts anymore after the operation.[21] But he admits that the reading of Roberts's manuscript has made him "doubtful," since "Perhaps what he made me do was necessary; I do not know" (*EG* 124). This sentence is particularly important: though the framing narrative of "Origin Undetermined" certainly ends favoring the hypothesis of Roberts's unreliability (after all, in it Roberts self-defined himself as a liar), Barlow is careful not to take a definitive stance on the matter,

---

21. The reader is left to infer that the doctor finally amputated Roberts's hand as an inevitable consequence of Roberts's shooting it.

and to leave it vague and to the reader's speculation: by saying "Perhaps what he made me do was necessary; I do not know," and admitting that he is "doubtful," the doctor—up to now the main "force" at work for the madness-hypothesis—takes a final, disconcerting *step back* that obliges the reader to reconsider (and possibly re-read) the entire framing narration and, above all, to lend specific attention to Roberts's manuscript, whose insertion is then conveniently anticipated by the arousing of a piercing sense of expectancy. In fact, these are the doctor's concluding words, with which he establishes—once and for all—his own insoluble bafflement at the events the manuscript will relate, a bafflement that not even his ingrained scientific attitude, his rational, constant attempt to find proofs, to identify "victims" and "diseases" is able to dissipate—a bafflement excellently symbolized by the final, unanswerable question with which the doctor ends his preface: "The initial lie has shaken my trust in him. So little proof exists! [. . .] I would like to believe that he was the victim of some dark mood, and that he wrote these pages from his broodings and delusions alone. But why would a man shoot his own hand off?" (EG 124).

3.4.2.2 The manuscript of the second-level narrator

Roberts's manuscript—addressed to the doctor—opens, once more, with its author frankly mentioning the doubts that the reader of his story will nurture in crediting it. The issue of reliability and credibility seems definitely to be a determinant one in this tale: "Although you surmised that much of my story was a lie, I could not have said anything else. Now I am writing because I have reached the ultimate link in a nightmare chain of godless and terrible events. What I will say *must inevitably seem a greater lie than the lies I have told you*, but I think that writing it out will be a relief to me" (EG 124; italics added). This is, however, the only open mention Roberts makes to the alleged incredibility of his account. After all, here he is simply trying to restore himself as a reliable narrator: he admits to having lied once, but this is the occasion to reaffirm the veracity of the following account. After this meta-incipit, namely one in which the narrator—temporarily giving up his major task, the narrative one—discusses his own role and his capacity to perform it, the manuscript will bear no further hints on the issue of the credibility of the narrator. It will be the reader's task to identify the portions of the text in which Barlow aptly disseminates (mostly veiled and vague) details concerning the narrator's mental and physical condition—details possibly affecting the correctness of his perceptions, and ultimately the reliability of his account.

First, the night Roberts goes over the report to prepare for the Board of Trustees of the Museum where he works, he reveals himself to be particularly tired, so that he decides to sleep in the gallery's basement room instead of returning home. His fatigued mental and physical state is outlined in the following lines: "My brain was *utterly clogged—a physical and mental indolence* against which I had struggled for days seemed to dominate me. I could perform only routine actions—extinguishing lights, locking my office, and descending to my room. All these in a *dream-like stu-*

pefaction" (*EG* 125; italics added). These few sentences reveal Roberts's peculiar state: he is certainly tired, his capacity and inclination to reason reduced (his brain is "clogged"), and above all he seems prone to welcome dreams ("dream-like stupefaction"), thus probably to abandon himself to imagination, a condition many not so realist personalities salute with favor when they feel tired. Moreover, in order to define Roberts's condition, Barlow employs here the term "indolence," one that he uses also in "The Night Ocean" (see *EG* 116) and for the same purpose, namely to add to the impression of unreliability on the narrator's part. The depiction of the narrator's state of weariness merges with that of the blurring of his memories, and of his incapacity to distinguish what—in that long and fatal night—is reality and what dream or imagination:

> I went over the report through hours of uneasy slumber, awakening somewhat after dawn more tired than when I lay down. My inordinate weariness had waxed rather than abated, and some area of memory seemed deliberately shut off from the rest of my mind. Many things sink down out of reach in the waves of sleep—more, I have been thinking, than we shall ever suspect. As I opened my eyes on the bleakly furnished room there was a feeling that something had eluded me when I woke—something which had accompanied me very close to the waking world. I seemed to remember being *a witness, or perhaps even a participant, in some distressing action whose nature I could not recall*. (*EG* 125; italics added)

With consummate art, here Barlow, by hinting at a mysterious action that Roberts might have done during his drowsiness, and in addition still expanding on the narrator's unbalanced physical and mental state, also anticipates a plot element that will later find clarification—namely, the opening and smashing of the sealed Mayan urn that was placed in "a separate case in Gallery 3" (*EG* 125). Furthermore, as in "The Night Ocean," Barlow is here depicting a peculiar state of mind on his narrator's part, a state anticipating the actual climax of the story and the ambiguity by which it is enwrapped. In fact, the text will induce the reader to question the actual occurrence of the climax, whether it was a real event or only the result of the narrator's imagination.

When Roberts discovers the urn has been dislodged and smashed, he explains the event by attributing it to a surprised or awkward thief, who "had dropped it in escaping" (*EG* 126). While wondering why the newly arrived urn "had been sealed up with such manifest care" (*EG* 126) (vague hint to the horror it hides), Roberts picks a few seeds of the plant previously sealed in the urn, puts them in a pocket for "later investigation," and describes his bafflement and inability to account for the strange event of that night: "I called the police in, but they could establish nothing. Only myself had been seen by the watchman, and none of the alarms had been disturbed. Specimens of fingerprints on the empty case were compared with those of the staff, in the hope that supernumerary marks would be found, but the result was exasperating. Mine, and those of Williams [the guard] were all that were discovered" (*EG* 126). Here ambiguity achieves its pinnacle, and the superficial reader asks himself who actually could have been the thief, and if a real theft attempt had taken place. However, a well-informed reader has already started to question the narrator's account, and to connect his previous description of his peculiar mental state of the night before with the unusual event relating to the urn.

Roberts then decides to plant a pair of the mysterious seeds—and they engender hideous sprouts that have the ability to grow by feeding on (and corroding) pure glass. Frightened by this discovery and repelled by the horrible stench of the plant, Roberts destroys each of the evil sprouts by throwing them into the burning furnace of the museum. The following night, he again experiences a turbulent sleep, disturbed by the "intrusion of an unfamiliar dream-world" (EG 127). Roberts goes on describing the visions he had that night, all connected with the fear of open spaces he has felt since a child, and thus revealing more telling details about his imaginative powers:

> Only indoors did I feel at all secure, and sometimes when this oppression was strong on me, I hid in closets and small enclosed spaces. In the back of my childish mind was a frightening vision of the immense and roofless world, and I visualised myself as losing all anchorage on the solid earth, to be flung into interminable chasms of night. From this sensation there was no refuge but locked doors and drawn curtains. My parents frequently scolded me for behaving this way, and I was more than once punished for my attempts to escape the genuine torment. [. . .] With the curious plurality of dreams, while I was dreaming this I was also dreaming of the red furnace, tumultuous with flames which (it seemed to me) were being gradually extinguished by a heap of uncurling vegetation. The growth stuffed it up completely, just as it had the Mayan urn, and vegetable fingers slipped through a red-hot door, thriving on the fire as they had thriven on bare glass; as if everything were food to them. . . . I woke at this, and for a while lay so befuddled with my composite imaginings that I even considered going to the furnace and making sure they were not true. (EG 127-28)

The long description of this dream—as well as an even longer account of the dream that follows—adds at least three important elements to our discussion on the narrator's ambiguity: (1) the dream reveals the power of Roberts's unconscious (and "composite imaginings"), which may well have been able to invent from scratch (or simply dream) much of the events in his account; (2) Roberts's observation that he considered "going to the furnace" and check the veracity of his imaginings certainly hints at a sort of impressionability, if not credulity, on the character's part; (3) and last, this new merging between dream and reality reinforces the awareness that, in this tale, the narrator may have confused what objectively occurred in reality and what occurred in his own mind and unconscious. This very impression is then confirmed, within the account of another dream concerning a "cosmic" voyage to an unknown country he will subsequently have, by Roberts's own revelatory words: "the reality of my dream compels me to speak of it as if it were a genuine experience" (EG 128). During his description of this second dream, there are several hints as to the confusion of the narrator's mental state: he is "not even certain whether I was a man or a small boy who feared the night" (*EG* 130). Most important, he again cannot decide whether the dream was a dream or a "genuine experience," and thus merges reality and dream once and for all: "I am writing all this as if it were something real, for again and again I slip into the conviction that it *was* real, and that by some incomprehensible process the delusions of sleep became as tangible to me as waking life. [. . .] Dreams, perhaps, are not wholly intangible, nor our accustomed world as unique as mankind believes. Vast fields of speculation crowd upon me, but I dare not and could not express what I begin to think" (*EG* 129).

Barlow's discrediting of his narrator has by now reached its climax: not only does Roberts show himself to be incapable of actually distinguishing between dream and reality, he also implicitly belittles his own narrating capacity by stating his inability to express what he "begins to think." Vagueness is thus doubled here: not only is the content of Roberts's speculation left untold, but his incapacity (and lack of courage) to express it is stated—thus adding to the reader's doubting of the narrator's adequacy to fulfill his task. The final merging of dream and reality occurs at the very end of Roberts's dream when, after noticing the presence of a far dim light beyond a thick mountainous range, he smells a familiar scent in the air: "From there my dream was chaos, like reflections in a pool vexed with stones. The stink increased, and it was the stink of *those burning plants. In the strong grip of nightmare I repeated their destruction again and again, but like snakes about me they sought to drag me into the raw consuming flames*" (*EG* 130). As it appears in Roberts's words, the key word is by now "chaos"; the narrator-dreamer mixes up impressions of reality and unreality, does not distinguish between them, and finally the merging of reality and dream reaches its climax: the lethal plants and Roberts's act of destruction—elements coming from reality—appear on the dream-level. The return to consciousness is again revealing of Roberts's confusion of the different levels: "When I awoke, the basement was filled with miasmatic vapour" (*EG* 130): thus the "stink" he smelled inside his dream was again an intrusion of a real element in the protagonist's unconscious. After he realizes his cat has probably been poisoned to death by the lethal ichor of the plants, Roberts openly reveals—once again—his bafflement: "From three o'clock till day I lay confused, trying to unravel my dream and wondering what to expect in the poisoned animal" (*EG* 130). Arky—this is the nickname of the cat—undergoes a hideous and painful transformation under the effect of the contagion, which rapidly spreads in his body in the form of "curious blisters swelling up" (*EG* 130), bringing him to an unenviable death.

However the final, decisive blow to the narrator's reliability arrives with his own realization of having been contaminated—and the parallel realization, in the reader's mind, that Roberts *must have written his entire account "after the fact," namely after he was already under the influence of the terrible poison*. What credit then should be granted to such a teller? When he realizes that he feels a persistent ache in the fingers of his left hand, and that he believes he sees a "certain white blister" (*EG* 131) on it, Roberts abandons himself to a series of frantic observations, whose paranoid nature adds to the impression of ambiguity and unreliability on his part: "Mumbling in dull terror, I tried to convince myself that it was not so.[22] Was sanity failing me? The unspeakable nature of Arky's death had rocked my brain, and I did not consider that the blister might have come elsewhere. Even less did it seem credible that *I* had been defiled. It was not credible—for a time—that my hand should blister with gnawing cancers" (EG 131). Roberts shows himself unable to accept the information his sight transmits to his brain; he is unable to accept his being contaminated, his doom, i.e. to accept *reality*: this is certainly not a favorable hint as to the reliability of a narrator—so that the reader is now induced to re-examine, in retrospect, Roberts's entire account, and to form his own opinion accordingly.

After the frightful discovery of the disease in his hand, Roberts went to see the doctor and asked him to amputate—and it is precisely at this point that Roberts's second-level narration reconnects with the first-level framing one: "I can understand your reluctance to amputate until I made it necessary. I forced you to do it [i.e., by shooting at his own hand], but it was not soon enough. For hours now I have not dared to look into a mirror" (EG 131). Moreover, Roberts reveals that he is writing under almost unbearable (mental and physical) conditions:

> it is excessively painful for me to type, but the condition of my remaining hand is such that a pen would be impossible. No one must see me afterward. I was worried about this until I remembered the furnace. I have built a great fire within it, and shall by that means cleanse the world eternally of this blight from a source beyond comprehension. A thousand useless questions torment me, but *speculation is the only thing to distract me from pain*. (EG 131; italics added)

In his final lines, while anticipating his intention to commit a horrible suicide, Roberts admits that his speculation is the last way left him to *fight the pain*: his reflections are the means a diseased mind and body use in order to overcome mental and physical pain. How then can a responsible reader credit such speculations, not the results of a freely reasoning mind—disinterestedly searching for truth—but of a diseased and fatigued one, aware of a forthcoming hideous death, which openly recognizes its speculations as instruments of a temporary survival? Roberts's following reflections on the nature of his dreams, on the possible connections between them and the experience he has undergone with the Mayan urn, are thus implicitly discredited by the narrator himself—wisely guided by Barlow's hand.

Roberts makes at least one confession the reader is bent on sharing:

> Of the mysteries confronting me I have solved one at the least, though it is the least provocative. I stole the urn myself. Of this I am convinced. My fingerprints were thick about the broken case, and my inner consciousness shrieks out the vandal's name. A compulsion must have been upon me, a compulsion streaming from the malignant urn. How or why I do not know. And it was in the fulfilment

---

22. Namely, that the white blister is not real, but an hallucination—and, above all, that it is not caused by the lethal contagion.

of a kindred command that I planted those seeds. Probably the two incidents were really one, though whether my sleeping self intended to break the urn, or whether it would have done something else with it, cannot now be guessed. Perhaps my mission was only to release the seeds, by whatever means lay at hand. They had been sealed up a long time ago: but for my act they might have remained forever so. (EG 132)

These final words reveal Roberts's wild delirium, his desperate attempt to find an explanation to his experience. His admission to have been the thief represents the only bit of information the reader can responsibly accept: all the rest is sheer delirium. Roberts attributes a sort of malignant "will" to the plant and its seeds: this of course appears frankly unacceptable and indicates that the narrator is under the evil spell of his disease—not of the plant. His entire manuscript has been written after the doctor amputated Roberts's hand—and after the contagion has begun to creep within Roberts's mind and body: these are only the final, unconnected words of an account that in retrospection looks, to say the least, unlikely. Moreover, even crediting Roberts's opinion whereby a compulsion streaming from the urn would have forced him to act as he did, why not think that the very same compulsion has forced him to write this account the way he has, with all the actual lies and incongruities a malicious alien will may have pushed him to write?

Roberts's fate is doomed, and his very last words cannot but be moving: "Thank God for the mist which dims my sight. Flesh which is no longer flesh but corruption instead, cannot long support a reasoning brain" (*EG* 132). Of course the reader is led to wonder how long it was since his brain was not "reasoning" anymore. Perhaps from the very beginning of his jotting down of the manuscript. Roberts is finally determined to put an end to his torture: "My bones and sinews bloat into jelly; the signature of death is written over me, and since death alone can cleanse forever, I shall meet and welcome it. Only a moment is left, and now, while I am still able, I must get down to the furnace" (*EG* 132). Roberts's fictional fate of course deserves the reader's fictional pity. However, there are too many clues that Barlow has ingeniously disseminated along the whole tale—both in the main and in the frame narration—to accept the narrating voice as a reliable one, and to consider its account trustworthy: this he has done through the masterly employment of more or less vague hints to the narrator's mental and physical unsteadiness, and to his peculiar past and unwholesome future; and this process has been possible by means of open or implied invitations to textual cooperation on the reader's part.

3.5 Vagueness as a literary technique

In most of his fiction, Barlow employs vagueness also as a literary technique, namely as a means to increase suspense and the sense of expectation in his readers. Of course, this technique is employed as a further element contributing to the overall sense of indeterminacy that Barlow's work intends to achieve as one of its principal aesthetic goals. This device is particularly evident at the conclusion of some stories, when the author makes his narrator adopt the so-called *open final*: however, to be defined as a conscious "literary technique," it is obviously necessary that the "open final" results from a deliberate choice on the narrator's part, and not from a plot necessity. In other words, the narrator must be well informed about what was the conclusion of the chain of events he is telling, but—precisely for aesthetic and communicative reasons—he chooses to say nothing about such a conclusion, leaving it to the reader's speculation to fill the narrative gap.

A group of Barlovian tales adopts just this "deliberate" open final, thus adding to the story's vagueness and contextually achieving the increased sense of suspense and expectancy. A few examples will show how effective Barlow's art proves to be in the realization of this technique, and, in particular, how receptive he has been toward his masters' lesson in the assimilation of this specific literary device. It is shown in almost each episode of the fantasy cycle *Annals of the Jinns*, though the most striking case is perhaps the climax of episode nine, "The Mirror." This tale recounts the tortures of the Green Fungi that the Emperor of Yondath had inflicted upon the evil sorcerer Khalda, accused of high sacrilege against the green stone deity of his town, and of having sought the creation of artificial life through forbidden and unwholesome magic. The torture should have been inflicted by the Head Torturer Malyat in the dark subterranean crypts of the Emperor's palace. Though scarcely anyone knew what these tortures actually consisted of, they were fabled to be terrible and extremely painful. Nonetheless, sorcerer Khalda did not show signs of terror; even an ironic smile emerged on his face when two slaves accompanied him along the gloomy chambers that led to Malyat's room. Some time elapsed since Khalda's entry into Malyat's chamber, and the Emperor was informed of the nature of the last of Khalda's creations, an evil mirror that escaped destruction and whose purpose was unknown; "but it was certain that Khalda had not constructed it for the dubious vanity of reflecting his withered visage" (EG 26). The mirror was made with polished and silvered glass and framed by an ebony, monstrous carving. The Emperor thus decided to set a price on the mirror, so that whoever could produce it would have a reward bestowed upon him. After many impostors made false claims, finally "came an ancient one, unbelievably filthy, and clad in garments of odorous antiquity" (EG 26). His face was wrinkled, though revealing an inscrutable wisdom. The beggarly person was received by the Emperor: at the latter's request to show the mirror, the old one refused, saying he had a claim to press. With the Emperor's nervousness growing, the old man stated that the mirror was the Mirror of Truth, and made the Emperor admit that he was in debt to the constructor of that mirror for a great service he had given to the Emperor. The old man made the Emperor admit that the wonderworker was condemned as a blasphemer and sent to the terrible tortures of Malyat. Once he has established that, the old man said he had the mirror with him and, offering it to the Emperor, claimed: "My payment will be given me in due time" (EG 27). Then "as the Emperor gazed in fascinated repulsion, Khalda drew forth the mirror, with its strangely shapen handle, and held it up that all might see. And when the ruler looked therein, no man may know what was reflected, for a strange and terrible thing occurred. Some dire magic was at work, for the doom that came unto his majesty was alien to all accepted lines of death" (EG 27). What really happened is left totally unsaid; the narrator limits himself to these few evocative words—though he appears to be omniscient, and the reader's imagination is solicited to provide the most appropriate final it may conceive.

"The Experiment" also offers an example of an open climax, since the outcome of the hallucination lived by one of the two characters—Edwin Coswell, a young student of occult disciplines—is left untold. The narrator describes in considerable detail the apocalyptic vision Coswell undergoes during the experiment conducted by the unconventional doctor Marcus Edwards, the co-protagonist of this tale; but while Coswell's experience makes him have some frightful glimpses of the unwholesome future of mankind, the vision ends with a feudal castle, where the young student is located, attacked by foul creatures hardly identifiable: they have writhing tentacles and are described as "jellyfish emulating humanity" (EG 59). There seems to be no possible escape for the humans besieged in the castle, "the last outpost of our kind" (EG 60). The forces of the adversary, hideous monstrosities, seem overwhelming: "There are thousands of them—nearer now. As we have feared our arrows take little effect" (EG 60). Coswell's account of his hallucination sounds like the description of the Armageddon of mankind, and his concluding, frantic words are: "Our men are killing one another. That is merciful. They cross the moat! Fill it with their bodies while others *ooze* over then. *They are mounting the walls!*" (EG 60). At this point, the third-person narrator provides a few concluding words: "A single shriek of unbearable terror was torn from him. Then he was still, as the metal helmet swiftly faded into a dull tone. There were peculiar marks about him, and the expression was most shocking" (EG 60). Nothing more is said, and the reader is left with the question: Is Coswell dead? What are those "peculiar marks" on his body? Perhaps they are the wounds inflicted by the attacking monstrosities? Or perhaps by the arrows of Coswell's fellows (since he told the humans were starting to kill each other)? Or is Coswell still alive, simply fainting because of the terrible shock, but able to retell in the future his experience—and especially its final outcome—in full detail? The final Barlow chooses for this story is one of the most indeterminate and suspenseful detectable in his work.

However, it is probably "A Memory" whose open climax is the most disturbing. The account of the descent of the unnamed protagonist-narrator and his companion Nalda toward the deepest levels of the gigantic Tower inhabited by the humanity of the future does not have a proper climax at all. In the case of "A Memory," it is perhaps possible to speak not so much of an "open climax" but of a missing one. Here Barlow stretches his employment of vagueness as a literary technique to the extreme, and the aesthetic effect provoked by his choice is decidedly powerful. In fact, in the course of their furtive and forbidden quest in the subterranean chambers and tunnels of the Tower, the two protagonists are trying to find an answer to a question pertaining the future of their whole human community: are the *glortups*, hideous slave-creatures serving the humans, preparing a rebellion that could overwhelm the dominion of their masters and virtually put an end to the human race? Crossing rail-less stairs and interminable dark corridors, all deserted by the slave-creatures, the narrator and Nalda finally approach a wall against which stands a shadowed object, "oozing hot pitch and little curls of smoke" (*EG* 80). The thing seems a living one, though the humans considered it virtually impossible that the *glortups* could reach that area of the subterranean levels. The final three paragraphs of this tale deserve full quotation, since the narrator strives in them to convey his sensations and fears at the discovery, without in any way saying too much or providing a clear picture of the objective reasons of his fright: the narrator repeatedly states that he "knows" and he "realizes," but what is the object of his knowledge and realization is never clearly revealed—and the reader is invited to fill the frequent informational gaps through demanding interpretative efforts. The passage is certainly a masterpiece of suspenseful prose, the more so if one thinks that it was written by a boy just seventeen years old but already mastering his technique, and bore no revisory hand whatever:

> Unwarned, I pierced the awful veil of time and realized in chill, vampiric fear where these places led, and where we were.[23] In an ecstasy of terror I knew why the tunnels were so oddly built, and why they differed from those our fathers made above them. These knighted burrows were not built by men at all—they were there before.
>
> I realized this in a frenzy built up by countless subtle queernesses. I knew now what race had catacombed the earth—I knew the terrible secrets of our own people. The place from where the glortups came was known to me, and I knew with what they leagued and planned; and what had borne those curious torches through the dark wilderness. The revelation enshrouded my soul in terror, and I shrieked aloud because of what was in these sunless corridors; because of the monstrousness that had lain these centuries beneath the City, and because of the miasmatic contagion that it spread. As I strove to speak there came a sound that should not have been, and Nalda heard, and turned to flee, but clustering shadows loomed like formless giants, and the darkness was a hampering veil.
>
> Thus we came at last upon the evilness that lurked beneath the rotting Tower. (*EG* 81)

Not only is the reader induced to guess what the narrator actually means through his constant allusions and half-words, but another element of vagueness is introduced here: the climax is in fact an eminently open one, since nothing is told either of the indeterminate "evilness" the characters encounter or of how they actually escape it. The text solicits the reader to cooperate, namely to advance several interpretative steps: in particular, he is induced to formulate a number of questions that are destined to stay unanswered. What is the final monstrosity?

---

23. The alliterating effect of the *w* sound contributes of course to the creation of the prose-poetic, "atmospheric" style of the passage.

What are its plans? Do the narrator and Nalda actually escape the final evilness? Since the narrator is a first-person one, the reader is induced to believe that the narrator is writing his tale *after the fact* (he also uses the simple past tense), but this may be, again, a device adopted by Barlow to delude his reader: the narrator and Nalda may *not* have escaped their fate, they have been taken prisoners by the evil creatures, and the narrator may be writing his account in the gloomy cellar of a subterranean crypt. On the other hand, if one accepts the (apparently more likely) hypothesis that the two characters have escaped the peril, other questions come to the fore: How could they make it? How were they received by their human fellows in the upper levels of the Tower? Did they tell them all the details of their experience—or is the account we are reading a secret one? If the tale was made public, were important measures taken to face the peril represented by the glortups and the unspecified "evilness" which seem their guide? Probably other issues are left open by this splendidly vague and calibrated climax: what is relevant is that Barlow shows a convincing mastery of the potentialities offered by vagueness as a narrative technique; in fact, he has here modeled a reticent narrator, one who actually *knows* (he himself repeatedly asserts so), but chooses *not to tell*—for aesthetic reasons.

By no means does Barlow employ this suspense-increasing technique only in the climaxes of his stories. His acquaintance with this deliberate and "technical" vagueness is demonstrated by the fact that many of his narratives also present a calibrated use of suspense in the midst of their development. The list of possible examples is quite long, and so I have chosen to mention the case of one particular tale, "The Night Ocean," that may suffice for all, since its mastery of the technique is certainly effective. After the first days of his sojourn in the house crouched on the lonely Ellston Beach, the protagonist gets used to long walks along the shore, during which he collects "curious bits of shell in the chance litter of the sea" (*EG* 108). He fills his pocket with "vast stores of trash," most of which he "threw away an hour or two after picking it up, wondering why I had kept it" (*EG* 108). The prose style of the passage is, up to here, quite calm, reflexive, and slow-paced: Barlow is aptly preparing the reader for the dropping of an apparently insignificant particular, but one that will reveal as a vague hint of the horror to come:

> Once, however, I found a small bone whose nature I could not identify, save that it was certainly nothing out of a fish; and I kept this, along with a large metal bead whose minutely carven design was rather unusual. The latter depicted a *fishy thing* against a patterned background of seaweed instead of the usual floral or geometrical designs, and was still clearly traceable though worn with years of tossing in the surf. Since I had never seen anything like it, I judged that it represented some fashion, now forgotten, of a previous year at Ellston, where similar fads were common. (*EG* 108-9; italics added)

The passage contains a couple of hints—presented as enshrouded in the veil of some apparently unimportant information—of the future horror that will haunt the protagonist: first, the small bone he finds among the sea debris connects with the bathers' mysterious drownings that occurred that summer in the beaches near the protagonist's house, and anticipates another later terrifying finding, that of an object, a "piece of rotten flesh," that looks like a hand and presents "mushy fingers wed in decay" (EG 115). In its turn, the reference to the "fishy thing" carved on the metal bead—besides tasting particularly Lovecraftian (one may think of the figures carved in the bas-reliefs of the "Dagon" monolith,[24] or of the looks of the Innsmouth folk)—anticipates, in a dim and disturbing way, the vision the protagonist will have, toward the end of his sojourn on the ill-fated beach, of an unidentifiable creature coming from the sea:

> a swimming thing emerged beyond the breakers. The figure may have been that of a dog, a human being, or something more strange. [. . .] Like a *distorted fish* it swam across the mirrored stars and dived beneath the surface. After a moment it came up again, and this time, since it was closer, I saw that it was carrying something across its shoulder. I knew, then, that it could be no animal, and that it was *a man or something like a man*, which came towards the land from a dark ocean. But it *swam with horrible ease*. (EG 119; italics added)

The vague description the narrator provides of the creature tends to solicit the reader's cooperation: his or her imagination forms the picture of a man-fish, namely a humanoid being that yet possesses a disturbingly superior swimming capacity. At a first reading, only an attentive reader, one already used to the techniques of the weird, may have noted at this point the connection—devised artfully by Barlow—of this man-fish figure with the "fishy thing" presented some pages before as a carving on a metal bead. This well-prepared reader may also have detected, while reading of the first "fishy thing," that its mention was probably not casual: there Barlow is building the suspense, and while addressing a reader versed in mystery tales such as that of the pulp magazines, he induces him to recognize in the mention of a fishy figure carved on a metal trinket the (certainly vague, but nonetheless recognizable) hint of a later and eventually decisive horrific event. That this technique was so effectively adopted by a seventeen-year-old cannot but honor his art and increase the regret for its not having been cultivated and perfected along the full span of a literary career.

3.6 Cumulative vagueness: "The Summons"

Barlow published "The Summons" in the *Californian* (Fall 1935), and this tale can

---

24. "I think that these things were supposed to depict men—at least, a certain sort of men; though the creatures were shewn disporting like fishes in the waters of some marine grotto. [. . .] they were damnably human in general outline despite webbed hands and feet, shockingly wide and flabby lips, glassy, bulging eyes, and other features less pleasant to recall" ("Dagon," in CC 4-5). That the image of the *fishy-things* has a particular appeal on Barlow's imagination is testified by another occurrence in "The Night Ocean": "the darkbearded king of an underwater realm of blurred cliffs where fish-things lived" (EG 111).

be considered an exemplary narrative of vagueness. The global aesthetic effect of vagueness is thus extremely strengthened, to the point that this tale may be considered *the* masterpiece of indeterminateness in the Barlovian canon. Moreover, the discussion will show how influential was Lovecraft's poetics on the teenage Barlow in the latter's approach to actual weird fiction writing.

The tale opens with the report of the indecipherable summons that haunts the unnamed protagonist-narrator: *Tahtra-ma; y thiesta, Tahtra-ma; y Thiesta*. It is a "strange, soundless beckoning" (*EG* 65), which the protagonist alone hears inside his mind. The words are impossible to translate in any language, and Barlow adds to the "vague and indeterminate sounds" (*EG* 65) of the inexplicable call the depiction of an environment and an atmosphere wholly indeterminate: first of all, the very place where the narrator is located is left indeterminate. In fact, he is walking in a remote part of his city, amidst "dim alleys harbouring lone obscure shops wherein were vended strange goods" (*EG* 65). The reader is not told anything precise about the location and the shops, and the protagonist has trouble even in recognizing himself: "I caught a dim vision of myself in a shop-window. I did not see beyond the glass, I was conscious only of the long, smooth face, the furtive wildness beneath the arching brows. My long recent illness was apparent, and I was yet unwell. [. . .] My thoughts confused. I strove to clear them; my pace abruptly increasing almost to the point of flight" (*EG* 65). This is a revelatory short passage: the use of the word "dim" is of course a trademark of Barlow's "theme" of vagueness,[25] while the insistence on "seeing" is indicative of Barlow's concern for the sense of sight and the importance he gives to sensory perception in general. However, the passage is significant also because it already adumbrates the protagonist's physical and psychological illnesses—as a possible explanation for the vagueness of his perception as well as a cause of his eventual unreliability as a narrator.

The protagonist moves in a half-dark environment and expresses doubts concerning the bizarre experience he is undergoing: "Shadows loomed. Whence came this dull, secretive call? I wanted to be alone and calm in my seclusion. Perhaps I should not have come out alone because of the lingering illness. Traces remained in my pallor and unsteadiness" (*EG* 65). The reader is gradually acquainted with the protagonist's illness and the insecurity of his temper and mind; the reader is thus increasingly induced to question the reliability of the protagonist's account. The precarious mental state of the narrator, as well as the overall darkness and dimness of his external (sight, hearing) and inner (thoughts, visions) perceptions, are continually hinted at—so that the doubting on the actual truth of his experience constantly mounts up: "those cryptic words [. . .] they whispered [. . .] yet it was not altogether a whisper [. . .] of *dark* and curious things. They summoned morbid phantasmagoric *visions*. It seemed for an instant that I *glimpsed*

---

25. The insistence with which RHB, in his fiction, employs words related to the "dim-" lexical root is indeed impressive.

leaves and *dim* tossing boughs against a sky of unholy illumination. *Mad thoughts, these*. I must cease. Why was my mind so *blurred?*" (*EG* 65; italics added).

The protagonist keeps walking in an unlit and noisome part of the town, blundering in the lightlessness. Finally, he reveals he has thought his peculiar experience was probably a consequence of the mysterious illness he has been, and perhaps still is, affected by:

> I did not doubt that a seizure of my *curious and inexplicable* illness was upon me, and regretted that I was unaccompanied in these surroundings. This peculiar affliction had mystified the doctors, for it was neither epilepsy nor anything akin *save in external appearances*. It was connected with the *visual trouble* with which I had always been afflicted [. . .] Nothing had been learned from trephining, but the seizures had ceased. Whatever the cause, it seemed to have been blindly rectified by the surgeons. (*EG* 66; italics added)

Again a very significant passage—one that makes the veil of darkness over the whole narrative grow thicker. In fact, not only it is unclear whether the summons is a result of the protagonist's illness—and, thus, his own inner "invention," without an objective existence—but even if the interpreter accepts this version, the nature of this illness, the cause of the protagonist's visual and auditive hallucination, are left vague and indecipherable. The narrator simply states that the external symptoms of his disease were *apparently* those of epilepsy or a similar illness—but there is no certainty, since the others symptoms (again, left vague because not described) point to other possible explanations—therefore, here again Barlow addresses the conflict between truth and appearance as central for a proper approach to reality's interpretation. Moreover, the passage insists again on the theme of vision (the illness was "connected with the visual trouble with which I had always been afflicted"): it seems that, for Barlow, the perceptive trouble a human being may have often comes from a defect in the visual perception of external reality.

The narrator examines in depth the recent events that concerned his operation, bringing the reader to the point of being unable to decide about the reliability of the account: before the surgery, the protagonist suffered from a "golden haze" that was gradually obscuring his vision, causing him "odd and disconcerting distortions" (*EG* 66) of his surroundings. He had "dreaded spells of giddiness, with deep-toned reverberations" (*EG* 66) in his head: they were not objective sounds, but are hardly explainable, since "differed bafflingly from any known phenomena of vertigo" (*EG* 66). Here we may note already one small clue of Lovecraft's lexical influence, namely the employment of a word derived from the root verb "to baffle," a favorite of the Providence writer's vocabulary. The narrator goes further in his attempt to throw the reader into an interpretative chaos, because he openly writes of madness and of his own almost maniacal fear to become insane: "my inordinate fear of anything conceivably affiliated with madness. There was insanity in my ancestry, and because of this the subject was for me a field of morbid speculation. Brooding upon every fancied sign; ever watchful to find myself breaking down, I led an existence ceaselessly haunted by dread. Fears of this kind formed my first thought when the affliction developed" (*EG* 66). Heretofore, the protagonist has striven to build himself up as an unreliable narrator—a sick, unsteady, and fearing voice. The reader is now induced to regard the summons as a delusion engendered by a sick and unstable mind (a step forward in the "unreliability" interpretation); but as usual, Barlow immediately turns his carefully built solution upside-down and lets his narrator expand on the renewed good health he was lately enjoying—marking, for the reader, a step back from the "unreliability" interpretation: "But the operation upon which I had frantically insisted appeared beneficial, despite the long convalescence. The visual and auditory deceptions vanished; physically I was better than at any previous time, and to my delight, my eyes were even strengthened to a degree not hitherto mine. This evening marked the first recurrence of any illness but the long natural convalescence" (*EG* 66). The protagonist puts forth his recent recovery, and thus the reader is left with the utter impossibility of deciding which interpretation to credit, the "reliability" or the "unreliability" one: does the summons actually exist, has it objective reality, or is it a product of a diseased and still convalescent mind? The protagonist seems to offer his own solution: "That the curious sounds and impressions now subtly pouring over me were attributes of my old illness, I did not doubt. This, indeed, was the only natural assumption at the moment" (*EG* 66). However, the solution Barlow offers is, as usual, a deceptive one, since the following events will tend to disprove this interpretation, as well as any definitive and conclusive one in general.

Afraid of the situation he has fallen into, and of finding himself in a shadowy, sinister, and unknown area of his city, the protagonist tries to reach home and, above all, light ("I should turn into the light, and stay always within its glow, so that darkness might give me no more bad thoughts" [*EG* 66]). Yet the luring call never abandons the fugitive, who begins to wonder at the reasons behind the summons: "I was needed. Needed? Wildness. What needed me? Why did the voice trouble me so unendingly? Never did it cease, low but always present, it said *Tahtra-ma, y thiesta*" (*EG* 67). The narrator gradually realizes the inescapability of the command to follow the voice, and reality starts to waver around him, ungraspable for his dizzy senses: "I was spellbound within a strange delirium. [. . .] things escaped my reeling senses. Nothing showed naturally. I was rushing through a dim void, and the streets were mirages. *It needed me*" (*EG* 67). The narrator loses touch with reality; he starts to feel nothing, to see nothing, to hear nothing except the beckoning call that must be obeyed, because *it* needs him. Yet the narrator, during the writing process—which occurs at an unspecified time *after the fact*—recognizes that, at the moment of the otherworldly experience, he thought of madness as the only possible explanation for his whole situation: "Was I indeed mad? Yes, this must be at last what I had so long feared. I had seen madness in others, but did not understand it before. Madness was odd. I could not think, yet was conscious of the fact, and strove to combat it, strove to think. There was a falling darkness, like fainting, but it was not that. A sound, and spinning. *Tahtra-ma, y thiesta*" (EG 67). The voice becomes louder and louder, and inexplicably guides the protagonist out of town, toward the forest: he believes that it needs him, and that the voice convinces him that it needs him, thus he starts losing his own will and follows the irresistible alluring power of the summons: "My members obeyed with automatic promptness all mental commands, but somehow I felt within a strange dream, for my whole sensation was that of partial hypnotism. Utter lack of the sense of touch had come upon me in a baffling and inexplicable flash" (EG 67-68). His senses bewildered, the man's perceptions are not only vague but utterly chaotic. He feels he has no control over his actions and movements anymore, as if his members were "impelled to the action by some external command. Stumbling, hurrying, I vaguely wondered—as if accompanying an automaton directed by another's will" (EG 68). The protagonist nears the edge of the town and gets close to a forest, always guided by an external will he cannot shirk. While traversing a gloomy side of the town, his perceptions keep being dim, and he repeatedly claims he has no words to describe his sensations. All at once, he comes to the edge of the forest—and he knows he has to do so, because this is the will of the external power guiding his steps: "I was only a submissive, impotent consciousness before whatever fearful thing awaited" (EG 68). The passivity of this character's actions, together with the sense of compulsion dominating each of his efforts, are reminiscent of Nathaniel Wingate Peaslee's moonlit, externally guided descent into the abandoned ruins of the buried Australian city in Lovecraft's "The Shadow out of Time," which Barlow might have read just few months before—or at the same time as—the composition of "The Summons."[26]

Feeling the call as by now inescapably tempting, the protagonist of Barlow's tale finally answers to it: "*Aye, Master, I am coming!*" (EG 68), though the nature of the call—as well as that of the "Master"—is still wholly undefined. Yet the protagonist feels now only one, irresistible no less than incomprehensible urge: "All that guided me, all that I had of sentient life was for a time that overwhelming urge. As I stumbled through dark thickets it lured me on, ever on to a nameless goal" (EG 68).[27] The description of the decayed, rotting forest wherein the protagonist is lured lends itself to a further deepening on the role of light in Barlow's poetics. Images of light are again abundant, and, as in "The Bright Valley," here they are located on the negative pole of the dialectics light-darkness: they are associated with fear and horror ("faintly luminous fungi [. . .] faint luminosity of

---

26. "The Summons" was published in the fall of 1935, though no information is available about its date of composition (see "Introduction," in EG 10). However, since it was exactly in the summer of 1935 that RHB had received the manuscript of HPL's novelette (and actually prepared its typescript during his master's visit to DeLand), this internal, thematic evidence may represent a clue in favor of the hypothesis that RHB wrote "The Summons" in the late summer or the early fall of 1935, under at least the partial inspiration of "The Shadow out of Time."
27. Of course the use of "nameless" is again a tip of the hat to HPL's own lexicon.

the putrescent growths"), not with positivity, understanding, or an illuminating reason. Not even the moon illuminating Peaslee's descent—a metaphor of wholesomeness and clearness of perception—radiates on the Barlovian character's acts, since it would end up illuminating nothing healthy: "those terrible branches, crowded with curious leaves, swayed most unpleasantly against the sky. Scarce ever did the full moon shine upon their tossing heights, and perhaps it were well, for in such illumination *they must have been horrid indeed*" (EG 68; italics added). Thus here light, far from being the illuminating guide of human cognitive efforts, only configures as a further source of fear and horror—Barlow's pessimism reaches here a climax. The only available light in the forest is of another nature; it is vague and again it had been better not show itself: "But although this stronger light was denied them, a dim radiance, like the phosphorescence of some sinister cavern depth, prevailed upon the whole sky" (EG 68).

"The Summons" is a textbook example of Barlow's literary vagueness: no potentiality of this technique is left unfaced or unexplored. *Incommunicability*, namely the vagueness of communication, is also a topic addressed—and it is the narrator himself who recognizes this limit: "This narrative is unavoidably *impaired and incomplete*, for it can be unfolded from only a single angle. I do not know the causes underlying what I shall attempt to describe—*I can only relate what appeared* to my bewildered senses" (EG 68; italics added). However, Barlow's narrative does not stop at this consideration: the queer yet alluring further step the narrator takes in his interpretative effort is to consider his experience the result of a *sensory expansion* provoked by the latest surgery he has undergone. Barlow speaks openly of a sensory "alteration" that brought his character to get in touch with realities and phenomena (like the ultraviolet rays or the ultrasounds) that are normally beyond the grasp of human perception:

> I am now relatively certain that my faculties were subtly altered by the operation, *so that I received impressions no one else on earth could have understood*. I was cured of one abnormal condition; but might not that cure have opened certain dormant organs such as abound within the body, making me sensible of things beyond the normal range of the visual and auditory senses? Through the birth of new, special senses might not I have come to command certain aspects of external reality which none of man's natural senses can grasp and record? (EG 69)

Here is quite clearly detectable a hint to a Lovecraftian theme, that of the *expanded consciousness* through the awakening of dormant human perceptive senses and faculties. In Lovecraft, this awakening is made possible through the employment of an electrical-mechanical device in "From Beyond" (1920), a tale in which the Providence writer seems to fictionalize some conceptions he found in Hugh Elliott's *Modern Science and Materialism* (1919).[28] In "From Beyond," the protagonist Crawford Tillinghast achieves an expansion of the faculties of his sensory apparatus, thanks to an electrical machine of his invention, capable of radiating waves

---

28. See Joshi's "The Sources for *From Beyond*," in *Primal Sources* 167–71.

that open to man vistas of *entities that are invisible to his sight and sounds not perceivable from his ears*, such as ultraviolet rays, or, more daringly, creatures and things floating and brushing in the air. Barlow almost appears to quote the words of Tillinghast's speech:

> Our means of receiving impressions are absurdly few, and our notions of surrounding objects infinitely narrow. We see things only as we are constructed to see them, and can gain no idea of their absolute nature. With five feeble senses we pretend to comprehend the boundlessly complex cosmos, yet other beings with a wider, stronger, or different range of senses might not only see very differently the things we see, but might see and study whole worlds of matter, energy, and life which lie close at hand yet can never be detected with the senses we have. [. . .] that machine near the table will generate waves acting on unrecognised sense-organs that exist in us as atrophied or rudimentary vestiges. Those waves will open up to us many vistas unknown to man, and several unknown to anything we consider organic life. [. . .] We shall see things, and other things which no breathing creature has seen yet. [. . .] Listen to me! The waves from that thing are waking a thousand sleeping senses in us; sense which we inherit from aeons of evolution from the state of detached electrons to the state of organic humanity. (*DW* 24-25)

In particular, the organ on which the waves act is the pineal gland, our "great sense-organ of organs" (26), a sort of "additional" organ of sight that, if conveniently solicited, is able to transmit visual pictures to the brain, as an alternative eye. It is perhaps not hazardous to hypothesize that Barlow, echoing Lovecraft's tale,[29] was just addressing this organ when he made his narrator, in "The Summons," argue about a "dormant organ" and a "special sense" awakened inside his body by his recent surgery. It must be said, however, that Barlow was no more than seventeen years old when he wrote "The Summons"; when he wrote "From Beyond," Lovecraft was thirty, and a writer increasingly aware of his aesthetic goals, if not yet his potentialities. Predictably, Lovecraft's treatment of the theme of the *expanded consciousness* was more mature than Barlow's: Lovecraft consciously staged his characters' attempts to overcome the "galling" physical limitations imposed by Nature on mankind—this was precisely, according to Lovecraft's own words,[30] one of

---

29. HPL sent RHB the original manuscript for "From Beyond" (as well as many others), likely in early 1932, in order to let RHB type it. (See HPL's letters to RHB dated 31 March 1932 and 14 April 1932, in *FF* 27-28. In the second letter, HPL mentions receipt of RHB's typed text of the tale.)

30. In "Notes on Writing Weird Fiction" (1933), HPL explicitly defined, as one of the main aesthetic goals of his literature, the attempt to temporarily and illusorily overcome the sense of imprisonment in which the natural, physical, and biological limitations confine the human body, mind, and capacity of perception: "one of my strongest and most persistent wishes being to achieve, momentarily, the illusion of some strange suspension or violation of the galling limitations of time, space, and natural law *which forever imprison us* and frustrate our curiosity about the infinite cosmic space beyond the radius of our sight and analysis" (*CE* 2.176; italics added).

the main spurs he felt to write weird fiction. This is why a few of his characters, including Crawford Tillinghast, consciously and almost programmatically devote their existences to the achievement of experiences that go *beyond* the natural limits imposed on our race. In "The Summons," on the other hand, Barlow faces the theme of "expanded consciousness" almost as an incidental, peripheral accessory to the narration—and probably, I would add, as a homage to his master's poetics. If no one would of course deny that Barlow's fiction was influenced by his early readings in the weird, nonetheless the talent with which he deals with an interesting theme such as that of "expanding consciousness" leads us to believe that he would have likely added significant insights into this and other Lovecraftian themes, had he kept pursuing his promising writing career.

All of a sudden, Barlow's character detects the insurgence of an odd vibration, swelling in volume "like the waves of some toneless, prodigious music" (EG 69) that almost deafens him, while the light in the sky grows more intense. Again Barlow pays a passing homage to Lovecraft: "The cacophony played before Azathoth in the blackness could not surpass this awful majesty" (EG 69). Overwhelmed by the unceasing crescendo of the music, the protagonist is still enthralled by the cryptic repetitive words *Tahtra-ma, y thiesta*. Reflecting on them, the Barlovian character makes some observation that points to the utter *outsideness* of their source, introducing a linguistic theme that echoes again a typical Lovecraftian concern: "I could not comprehend the meaning, but I knew they had a very distinct significance, and flitting thoughts told me of no pleasant things. *The tongue was not of our land, nor any I had ever heard from the lips of voyagers to far countries. Such words, I felt, were perhaps not even human, but might be the awful syllables of some troll-tongue*" (EG 69; italics added). Lovecraft's fiction, as well as his letters, is full of expressions, sentences, or words in supposedly alien languages, such as the phrase "Ph'nglui mglw'nafh Cthulhu R'lyeh wgah'nagl fhtagn" chanted aloud by the "Esquimau wizards and the Louisiana swamp-priests" ("The Call of Cthulhu," in CC 150). It was in fact a specific Lovecraftian aesthetic goal to give—literally and metaphorically—voice to forms of expression and communication utterly alien to human speech (the name "Cthulhu" itself was devised by Lovecraft as one that was coined and should have been pronounced by a race endowed with a phonatory apparatus totally "other" from the human). Certainly Barlow is here referring again to this element in Lovecraft's literary aesthetics—and this continuous allusion to the master's poetics unequivocally shows the young pupil's devotion. Other lexical choices made by Barlow point in the same direction: while still reflecting upon the mysterious words of the call, the narrator states that "There have been times when I have wondered at their curious meaning, but when I remember fully the events of that awful night, I am glad of my *blissful ignorance*" (EG 69; italics added). The expression "blissful ignorance" certainly reminds of the incipit of "The Call of Cthulhu": "The most merciful thing in the world, I think, is the inability of the human mind to correlate all its contents. We live on a placid island of ignorance in the midst of black seas of infinity, and it was not meant that we should voyage far" (CC 139).[31]

Barlow's imitativeness pushes itself so far that, as we have seen, he even repeats some of Lovecraft's words: again in the conclusion of "The Summons," when the narrator comes to the point of describing his encounter with the duellers—and in particular with the huge hideous creature—he writes "For all at once I saw it" (EG 70). Barlow here relies on the immediacy and tension of the short sentence— probably reminiscent that the same powerful, suspenseful effect was achieved by Lovecraft's "Dagon" (1917) with its "Then suddenly I saw it" (CC 5).[32] Aware he is moving along a safe way while facing the delicate task of describing the abomination, Barlow adds other typical Lovecraftian stylistic traits to his prose: "An immeasurably old and evil thing not of our world but of some infinitely and *mercifully* remote stellar depth" (EG 70).[33] Barlow's protagonist wonders at the reason for the creature's beckoning, but of course his questions are destined to remain unanswered[34]—increasing the vagueness and indeterminacy of the whole tale. Again a Lovecraftian flavor is present, when the narrator discusses the remote and indecipherable origin of the demoniac entity: "Whence it came, I do not even dare to guess, save that the source must have been some shockingly primordial world. Only such a world could have evolved a monster so obscenely complex and maturely terrible. It was older than Stonehenge, and might have manifested itself to the ancestors of the pyramid builders. It was ancient *beyond all human conception and belief*" (EG 70; italics added). The remoteness and ancient but indefinable age of the creature are also hinted at later: "This incarnation, older than the very universe, of all the foulness that exists" (EG 71). Moreover, even the actual *nature* of the monster is left vague—again following a typical Lovecraftian aesthetic principle: "Nor have I decided what it was. Not animal, although it possessed certain attrib-

---

31. The controversial theme of the recommendability of mankind's merciful ignorance— when dealing with cosmic truths—is of course a key one in HPL's philosophy and literary aesthetics.

32. Incidentally, let us note here that RHB, in a juvenile tale (the fifth episode of the *Annals of the Jinns*, titled "The Tomb of the God"), had again drawn from the Lovecraftian lexicon present in "Dagon." In his tale, published in the February 1934 issue of *Fantasy Fan*, RHB used the expression "stupendous slumber" (EG 19), probably reminiscent of the "stupendous monster" by which HPL had defined the fishy creature emerging from the horrid rocky chasm in "Dagon" (see CC 5). Another obvious homage to the Lovecraftian tale is detectable in RHB's "Origin Undetermined," where the protagonist undergoes a dreamy experience in a sort of "nowhere land" similar to that described in "Dagon." In his tale, RHB even adopts an image ("After half an hour's walk, during which the mountains grew no closer": EG 129) that reminds one of HPL's "That night I encamped, and on the following day still travelled towards the hummock, though that object seemed scarcely nearer than when I had first espied it" (CC 3). See also note 27 to chapter 4.

33. "Merciful" is of course a term Barlow had found in many of HPL's narratives.

34. "But I do not know, and all surmise is useless" (EG 70).

utes of animals, nor wholly vegetable—it was a loathsome and unearthly merging of those arbitrary divisions" (*EG* 70).

In his most effective non-anthropocentric work, Lovecraft harshly criticized the arbitrariness (and utmost inanity) of mankind's categorizations of the world and of reality—the division between entities belonging to the animal and the vegetable realms seeming absolutely inadequate when applied to creatures spawned by a remote, almost inconceivable outer space. However, Barlow here goes a step further and joins the Lovecraftian concern for a non-anthropocentric commitment of literature with his own preoccupation for the dialectics between sight and blindness: "There was a ghastly *fungoid* look about it, and I thank the gods that I saw it only in that half-light, for a more distinct view might well have sent me into gibbering madness" (*EG* 70). Besides noting here incidentally the usage of another Lovecraftian-sounding expression, "gibbering madness,"[35] one has to remark how, once again in this tale, Barlow employs light and sight as two instruments potentially bringing destruction and death to their user: it is merciful that no sight and no lights are available, since even a single glimpse at the abomination may doom the observer. Mercifully, the creature is surrounded by dark branches, and mottled shadows are cast upon its dim shape. The monster is not hideous and revolting in itself—namely, for what it objectively stands for or represents—but for the "*suggestions* it conveyed" (*EG* 70): again Barlow shows that he has learnt well Lovecraft's lesson on vagueness and "suggestiveness" as the main elements of a successful weird tale.

Yet, again, Barlow goes beyond a slavish imitation of Lovecraft's style and aesthetics: he certainly insists on the essential outlandishness of the monster, with its "nauseous fungoid tentacles, and the contorted and grotesque nature of the entire travesty" as an example of "insult of sane laws of nature" (*EG* 70),[36] but Barlow joins this very Lovecraftian concern on the limitations imposed by natural laws with his own preoccupation with sight and light: "The most hideous feature, I believe, was the *eyelessness*. That blank, formless face that leered insanely" (*EG* 70). The monster from outer space is certainly indecipherable in its hideousness because its own nature defies all known natural laws (the creature's existence represents then a *supplement, rather than a contradiction,* of mankind's knowledge of natural and physical phenomena),[37] but its sight is authentically frightening and

---

35. A few lines later, RHB will use again another typically Lovecraftian expression, "blasphemously" (*EG* 70).

36. Incidentally, let us note here that in another narrative, "The Experiment," RHB employs the very same expression and addresses the same Lovecraftian theme: "What foul creatures they are! Like jellyfish emulating humanity—a gross *travesty* of natural laws" (*EG* 59; italics added).

37. With reference to HPL's own literary aesthetics for a *non-supernatural cosmic art*: "The time has come when the normal revolt against time, space, & matter must assume a form not overtly incompatible with what is known of reality—when it must be gratified by images forming *supplements* rather than *contradictions* of the visible & mensurable universe" (letter to Frank Belknap Long, 27 February 1931; *SL* 5.295-96).

unbearable because the abomination is *eyeless*. What is really shocking, Barlow adds here, is the fact that we can *see* the allegedly objective phenomena around us *only through sight*—and sight is so important to us as to be considered the chief of our senses, according to Barlow—but the creature can *see* us (or better, *leer* at us) without the need of one or more eyes, the only instruments humans have to exert their most important sense. For one peculiarly sensitive to sight and light as Barlow, the conception of such an eyeless—but seeing—monster must have truly represented the apex of terrifying and inconceivable *outsideness*. In fact, even a fugitive glimpse of the abomination is enough to provoke the starkest shock in the protagonist: "However this may have been, and slight as was my glimpse that peculiar sky obscured the sky, this momentary impression woke my confused brain into a state of panic-filled repulsion. Had I not been already half-delirious it might have produced an even more terrible effect upon my nerves. As it was, I remember that I shrieked in mortal agony at what I saw" (EG 70). Thus again sight is a harbinger of doom and destruction—and darkness, here in the form of the merciful cloud, stands as a salvific veil enshrouding the unbearable truth.

Thus, though his vision is dim and the scene half-blurred by obscurity, the narrator assists in the titanic fight for the possession of earth, between a very old man and the evil creature from beyond. And Barlow here stages an enthralling struggle whose prize is the control of the planet—a struggle that takes place wrapped in growing obscurity, and is paralleled, in its turn, by the battle between light and darkness for an only apparently less important prize: the observer's sight of—and possibility of accounting for—the titanic struggle itself, where the observer's sight epitomizes his understanding and comprehension. In Barlow's fiction, the dialectics between light and darkness, sight and blindness, always stands for (and hides) an epistemic concern. In fact, while hinting at the titanic struggle between the monster and the old wizard, Barlow is almost personifying light and darkness as, respectively, knowledge and ignorance, as two opposite forces contending for the observer's comprehension, with light occupying the negative pole of the opposition: to illuminate the scene, to let the protagonist actually see what is going on, means to let him *comprehend*, understand the truth—namely, that mankind is going to be doomed, or at least, that its destiny and survival are extremely precarious. It is already blissful that the narrator could not watch the monster in the totality of its unwholesomeness. But that was only the first round of the struggle. The sight of the protagonist, much to his regret, is sharpened by his fear, but luckily the light is "indistinct," and this prevents him from "discerning the features" of the old man. The monster is trying to let the light of comprehension triumph over the observer: he understands that the thing before his gaze is battling "for the possession of our world," but this awareness comes to him only "dimly" (EG 71), and this signals a momentary victory of the forces of the evil light against those of the blissful darkness and ignorance. In their epistemic struggle to make the observer comprehend, the forces of evil seem gradually to overcome; he feels in fact compelled to admit:

> It seemed that I had always known it, as if my mind for one fleeting instant shared the detestable thoughts and memories of the alien, inscrutable thing which had so lately controlled it. I knew somehow—though much of the knowledge clipped away before I could well assimilate it—what that cosmic cacodaemon was, and how it came to be in this nighted and hideous wood on our planet. I knew of its plight, and why it was seeking the aid of some true denizen of a world in which it floundered as a bewildered alien. I knew of its purpose—though so misty are my memories that they flee when I would touch them. This much I remember—that it wished to make some sort of inconceivable lair in our world; wished to contaminate it with the vileness of Yuggoth [. . .] (EG 71)

Besides containing a pair of new homages to Lovecraft in the dropping of a "Yuggothian" mention and of the adjective "cosmic," this passage provides under its surface the account of a lethal battle, fought in the character's interiority, for the conquest of his capacity of comprehension and of his memory: sentences like "my mind for one fleeting instant shared the detestable thoughts and memories of the alien, inscrutable thing which had so lately controlled it," "much of the knowledge clipped away before I could well assimilate it," and "so misty are my memories that they flee when I would touch them" covertly attest to a hidden battle taking place behind—and beyond—the openly described one between the monster and the old man: a battle for the possession not of earth but of the mind and memory of the observer, because without somebody actually watching—and afterwards telling—the "primary" battle, this very battle would lose its whole meaning, its significance, even its actual occurrence. Therefore, the forces of evil and good, of light and darkness are involved in two lethal fights, where each one is no less important than the other. What are their outcomes? The evil forces of light have won only partially the battle for the sight and the mind of the observer: his account, i.e. his tale, is there to testify to the outcome of this fight. However, the account is incomplete and vague in too many aspects (as the narrator himself, as we have seen, recognizes) to be considered proof of a convincing and definitive victory of the forces of evil. The protagonist is not absolutely sure of (the reality of) what he thinks to have seen, and the issue of his reliability as a narrator remains a key and unsolvable one.

However, if the outcome of this hidden battle is extremely uncertain, no more clear is that of the "open" fight, the one for the possession of earth. In fact, "The Summons" proves again to be the receptacle of all the stances on vagueness Barlow's fiction is able to offer: the author decides to conclude his tale by leaving the outcome of the fight untold and opening wide vistas of speculation to the reader. Barlow here adopts vagueness as a literary technique and introduces an open climax that augments the suspense and indeterminacy of a narrative that was already a masterpiece of the inexplicit and uncertain. These are the final words of Barlow's narrator: "I saw that brave and sturdy greybeard waver, totter uncertainly in the strange strife. I knew he could not defy it longer. What would have happened I dare not even think. That festering monstrosity that glowed even as the rotten fungi" (EG 71). As a rich and exemplary case of Barlow's literary rendering, treatment, and use of the techniques of aesthetic vagueness, "The Summons" can only end with a declaration of utmost uncertainty.

Before moving to the third "theme" of Barlow's fiction, it is useful to make a few other observations concerning the way in which the various aspects of the second "theme" relate to each other and, above all, to the third itself, "cosmicism." The various manifestations of "vagueness" are in fact tightly interconnected and, in a sense, reciprocally influence and strengthen one another. The first type of vagueness addresses an eminently communicative issue: it concerns the indeterminacy, and thus the potential unreliability, of the communications and of the sources from which the characters draw information. But it is only natural that, when the rumors, fables, legends, and other sources of information available to the characters are vague and imprecise (*vagueness of communication*, i.e. of the *means* of communication), the information they convey is also perceived as distorted, imprecise, and unclear (*vagueness of perception*): in a word, unreliable. Contextually, the vagueness of perception makes the *object* of perception appear indeterminate too, since, as we saw, it is very difficult, when a perception is unclear, to attribute the cause of this unclearness to a defect in the perceiving apparatus or to an objective "unperceptibility" of the object itself. At the same time, the creation of a figure of *unreliable narrator*, whose perceptions, opinions, and capabilities do not prove trustworthy, contributes—together with the deliberate Barlovian choice to conclude the narratives with an "open" and inconclusive climax—to building up an impression of indecipherability in the reader. As we have seen, the joint aesthetic effect of all these types of vagueness is to produce *ambiguity* as to how to interpret the whole story: the vagueness of the descriptions of monsters, events, places, peoples, or climaxes (*vagueness of communication*, of the *narrating voice*, and as a *literary* technique, i.e. formal types of vagueness) reflects the inconsistency of perceptions (*vagueness of perception* and of the *object of perception*, i.e. of contents). Of course, the epistemic pessimism shown by Barlow's fiction in regard to the human possibilities of grasping and seizing reality through the sensory equipment reflects and strengthens the third "theme" of his work, i.e. the "cosmicism" and relativism of his vision of mankind: in fact, if human perceptions are unreliable, if no sources of information are trustworthy (not even our own selves, as in the case of the unreliable narrator)—if, in other words, no definitive and positive knowledge is possible, all this of course also affects our existential condition as human beings. And here is precisely where Barlow's "cosmic" discourse enters the picture.

4. Cosmicism

Together with "vagueness," the theme of "cosmicism," thanks to its sheer complexity, to the wealth of representations with which it is treated, to its interconnection with that of Time, and to its ultimate impact on Barlow's aesthetics and overall worldviews, constitutes the most influential aspect of his fiction. In addition, as we shall see, the theme of time that will be discussed in the next chapter may be (at least for one of its facets, that concerning vast temporal extensions) considered as a sub-theme of cosmicism.

Because of its pervasiveness, all the stories of Barlow's output labeled as "cosmic horror tales" are more or less affected by cosmicism, and, to variable degrees, they often show a strong indebtedness to Lovecraft's own cosmicism. However, Barlow's fiction is so consistently imbued with this theme that it can be discussed from several angles. I will be content to address only three of them, those I consider the most striking, original, and potentially fecund for further scholarly analysis and recognition. As usual, the facets discussed are not to be considered separate and unconnected, but reciprocally influencing and somehow *functional* to each other.

The most revelatory facets of the Cosmicism of Barlow's fiction are:

1. the insistence upon literary images conveying the impressions of **silence, emptiness, desolation**;
2. the concern with **mankind's existential condition and bleak fate**;
3. the interest in the depiction of the **vastness of the universe and of cosmic Outsideness**.

4.1 Silence, Emptiness, Desolation

The impressions of silence, emptiness, and desolation are meant by Barlow's fiction to be *felt* and *experienced* by the reader—rather than *reasoned on*. These impressions feed and ultimately constitute the overall awareness of deprivation, loss, and inanity, which Barlow considers the most suitable vehicle for his cosmic discourse and for his bleak vision of mankind's doomed destiny and place in the cosmic scheme of things.

In order to fulfill his aesthetic goal, Barlow chooses to represent fictional places and locations that are, as it were, impregnated with silence, emptiness, and desolation. This figurative choice is so pervasive that it is present not only in the tales of cosmic horror, but also in his fantasy tales: the world in which *all* Barlow's characters move (including, for instance, the protagonists of the fantasy cycle *Annals of the Jinns*) is a desolate, deserted, silent, and empty one. They are always lonely and facing the unfathomable mysteries of an indifferent universe.

Any task they may face, any enterprise they undertake, is marked by the ontological solitude of their efforts, due both to the solitude of the character (who always performs his task alone) and to the "desertedness" ("A Memory" [EG 80]) and to the silence of the locations in which he acts. In Barlow's fiction, almost all the searchers move in silent and deserted locations, where "desolation and fetor" ("The Summons" [EG 68]) everywhere prevail: "For three days he walked, and still before him were leagues of desolation [. . .] This land was silent, as if all life had fled before some fast-approaching doom" ("The Bright Valley" [EG 62]). Barlow's characters often move along a "desolate path" ("A Memory" [EG 74]), where everywhere is "loneliness" ("Pursuit of the Moth" [EG 82]) and "terrible silence and calculated emptiness" ("A Memory" [EG 79]), certainly bearing a meaning beyond the literal: "an *immemorial silence* reigned. No throb of bird-wing, no rustle of furred feet disturbed the *still evening* [. . .] all was fled *save silence*" ("The Root-Gatherers" [EG 86; italics added]). The images Barlow employs in this regard are often interchangeable and somehow equivalent: they stand for and potentially substitute each other. Where there is emptiness, there is silence, and desolation too: images taken from these three semantic fields overlap and reflect one another, ultimately provoking the fusion of the three fields into one. So the youth called Morla dares to enter the secret palace of the terrible, ancient sorcerer Khalda, and he is struck by the "emptiness" of the place. That this emptiness is a polysemous word, thus revelatory of further meaning, is shown by the exact words Barlow employs: "a dim and gloomy passage. To this Morla made his way, his sword clanking hollowly against his bronze armor in the emptiness of the place" ("The Theft of the Hsothian Manuscript," episode ten of the *Annals of the Jinns* [EG 28]). "Emptiness" here is a synonymous with "silence," since the sentence is structured around the semantic field of *sound* ("clanking hollowly"): in this way Barlow stages the semantic equivalence of the visual and the sound impressions. We will see, in section 4.2.2, how important for Barlow is the image of figurative "emptiness" of his locations, since he makes of it a metaphor for the inanity and inconsistency of human existential condition.

In fact, whenever Barlow intends to provide an imaginative background for the discussion of the cosmic insignificance of our race, the most likely figurative tools he employs are images of silence, emptiness, and desolation. "A Dream" (1935) describes an "abandonment manifest in every crack of the rotting surface" (EG 71), as well as an unnamed narrator who makes his way "across the silent and desolate land" (EG 72). The searcher travels on a "naked plain" punctuated by "empty stone-built houses" (EG 72), and is confronted only by "blackness and hard stone" (EG 72). "'Till A' the Seas'"[1] (1935) is a textbook example in this regard, with its recurring mentions of combined silence, emptiness, and desertion of the locations:

---

1. The title is drawn from a line of Robert Burns's song "A Red, Red Rose" (1796): "Till a' the seas gang dry, my dear / And the rocks melt wi' the sun."

> when explorers reached that millennial city of bridge-linked towers they found only *silence* [. . .] Only then did the people fully realize that these cities were lost to them; know that they must forever *abandon them* to nature [. . .] *total silence* reigned within the high basalt walls of a thousand *empty* towns [. . .] There now loomed against the rainless deserts only the blistered towers of *vacant* houses, factories, and structures of every sort [. . .] During strangely prosperous centuries the hoary *deserted* cities of the equator grew half-forgotten and entwined with fantastic fables [. . .] those huddles of shabby walls and cactus-choked streets, darkly *silent and abandoned* [. . .] After a time the blight crept outward from the central belt. Southern Yarat burned as a *tenantless desert*—and then the north [. . .] Steady, universal, and inexorable was the great *eviction* of man from the realms he had always known [. . .] It was an epic, a titan tragedy whose plot was unrevealed to the actors—the wholesale *desertion* of the cities of men. (EG 44; italics added)

And the very last vision of animal life (not only mankind) on the planet could only be entrusted to the images of a silent and cold desolation: "I was a mote in the great desolation" ("A Dim-Remembered Story" [EG 102]), and "Earth, like its cold, imperturbable moon, was given over to *silence and blackness* for ever" ("'Till A' the Seas'" [EG 49; italics added]). Emptiness is not simply the background scenery of Barlow's "cosmicistic" and existential discourses; it is even described as the actual "essence" of mankind, the primordial soup from which all Life came, and to which any living being will ultimately return. In "The Experiment," the protagonist's vision of the past of the universe starts from the recognition of the "vast sun from which Earth was spat" (EG 59), and when he is asked to describe what came *before* that, at the very origin of the Universe, his only answer could be: "Emptiness" (EG 59).

However, had Barlow limited to describe—somehow objectively—silence, emptiness, and desolation, he would have done no justice to his own sensitive nature. In his stories, external impressions are almost always distilled through the filter of the character's sensibility: the silence and desolation of the environments in which the characters are forced to "experience" of course bear an impact. Man cannot stay untouched in the face of the cosmic solitude he is *ontologically* required to confront. "The Night Ocean" offers a perfectly calibrated passage accounting for man's reactions in front of the silence and desolation of the night, namely in front of the emptiness of his own existence: "The night was silent—I knew that despite my closed window—and all the stars were fixed mournfully in a listening heaven of dark grandeur. No motion from me then, or word now, could reveal my plight, or tell of the fear-racked brain imprisoned in flesh which dared not break the silence, for all the torture it brought" (EG 119). Silence causes a mixture of complex emotional reactions comprising, among others, torture and fear, but this *cosmic* silence man has to face is, as we shall see, just one of the factors proving to him the insignificance of his place in the universe.

4.2 Mankind's existential condition and bleak fate

Barlow's reflection upon *mankind's existential condition* is somehow connected with his perspective on its ultimate destiny: as in a sort of inductive reasoning, Barlow's analysis of a *particular* (the reflection on mankind's bleak destiny, as discussed in the so-called last-man stories) allows him subsequently to abstract his perspective and take a general standpoint on the overall, cosmic (in)significance of mankind as a living, animal species. Therefore, it is from the last-man stories and their view on mankind's end that the discussion of Barlow's perspective on mankind's existential condition must start: it is in the revelation of the bleak end of the race that Barlow finds the ultimate proof of its cosmic inanity—which, as we shall see, reveals itself at least in another, remarkable aspect as well, that of *deterministic compulsion*.

4.2.1 "'Till A' the Seas'" and other dreadful ends

Barlow's fiction reveals something similar to an obsession for images concerning the final death and extinction of mankind and especially of animal life on earth. Without being charged of naïve psychologizing, it is possible to mention here that for the whole of his life Barlow was somehow interested in (if not obsessed by) the notions of death and extinction, as is attested not only by the untimely, voluntary end he inflicted upon himself, but also by the constant presence of the thought of death throughout his life.[2]

However, these considerations pertain more to an outdated "biographism" in literary studies, which has little to do with my approach. Let us come back, then, to the textual analysis. In particular—and to this goal certainly, as we have seen, the employment of images of silence, emptiness, and desolation is functional—Barlow believes that the representation of the bleakness of mankind's end is the more disquieting the more desolated and deserted—namely, *lacking a witness*—is the image of the "last breath." Now we shall see how this aesthetic goal is successfully achieved in the climaxes, for example, of the two collaborations with Lovecraft, "'Till A' the Seas'" and "The Night Ocean."

Barlow may have begun work on "'Till A' the Seas'" as early as January 1934 or even before.[3] In spite of Lovecraft's early involvement, "'Till A' the Seas'" was

---

2. One example may suffice: already at age twenty-one, RHB was thinking of the possibility of his death: "All manuscripts of whatever nature, deposited by me in the Harris Collection (Manuscript Division) at the John Hay Library, are in the event of my death to become the property of that institution" (quoted in Joshi, "Recognition" 50).

3. In a letter dated 10 February 1935, HPL wrote to his pupil, in response to the latter's thanking for HPL's revisions: "Glad my survey of the last man story proved useful. Really, it's a damned good yarn [. . .] Hope it lands somewhere—though of course acceptance and

not completed until January 1935, when Barlow and Lovecraft worked on the story in New York—staying up till 3 A.M. (LAL 558)—during the night of New Year's Eve.[4] Joshi is somewhat critical regarding the tale, that he defines as a "'standard last man tale" that depicts the far future extinction of human life "somewhat clumsily and amateurishly"; he attributes the "mediocrity" of the tale to the fact that Lovecraft, feeling obliged to retain a good deal of Barlow's prose, limited his own intervention to an "exhaustive rewrite."[5]

Whatever the critic's aesthetic, subjective judgment on this work may be, this short tale (3,300 words) is undeniably very rich in meaning as well as in poetical and moving descriptions and images. However, this does not prevent the narrative from being polemical in regard to the human race. The overall tone is detached, disillusioned, almost resigned: extremes are smoothed away, nuances get blurred, and the general impression is one of delicacy. The mixture reveals as efficacious: in accounting for the inanity of all human achievements, the authors employ a frail and delicate tone, although this does not affect the power of their attack—and the

---

rejection form no real test of merit" (FF 207). That Lovecraft took painstaking care in revising the item is proved also by his subsequent words in the letter, as he addressed RHB's fictional style on the basis of the last-man story's prose: "You'll gradually acquire care in the selection & collocation of words—when you come to regard modelling in prose in the same light as that in which you regard modelling in Florida clay. . . or laying colours on a picture. . . or scratching copper with your new Manhattan stylus" (FF 207).

4. In a letter dated 15 January 1935, HPL praised the tale—an unequivocal sign that we can consider it as almost fully Barlovian in conception, as S. T. Joshi claims ("the root conception and the first draft are RHB's": "Introduction," OLL 6). However, HPL's words in the January 1935 letter also reveal that the subdivision into two parts plus an epilogue is probably a result of his interpolation: "Really, this is a great story [. . .] Regarding the changes—I fancy they are largely self-explanatory; but if anything seems obscure or unjustified, let me know & we can discuss it. My object in most cases has been simply *effective rhetoric*—better prose rhythm, more appropriate wording, &c &c. I think the tale had better be divided into two definite parts—the first the reminiscent sketch of earth's decline, & the second the personal history of Ull. Hope my efforts may prove to some extent helpful—& that the tale will meet with a good reception somewhere in the course of time. It certainly has a dramatic power, & augurs well [. . .] for your development as a fantaisiste" (FF 201-2). According to Joshi, who has examined RHB's original typescript of the tale recording HPL's corrections in pen, "Lovecraft has made no significant structural changes, merely making a number of cosmetic alterations in style and diction; but he has written the bulk of the concluding section, especially the purportedly cosmic reflexions when the last man on earth finally meets his ironic death" (LAL 558). In order to ascertain the exact degree of HPL's interventions, see Joshi 1983 in which the text is reproduced with HPL's words placed in brackets. HPL did not restrain his outrage at the news of Wright's rejection of the tale, a couple of months later: "Damn Satrap Pharnabazus for his rejection of your last man yarn! The besotted old son of a beach-tree! And to think of the crap he habitually *does* accept & print! Well—I give him up. He's too much for me!" (FF 217). Later that year "'Till A' the Seas'" appeared in the *Californian* 3, no.1 (Summer 1935).

5. Joshi, *A Subtler Magick* 201.

climax of the tale plainly testifies to this, resorting to an apparently detached approach that, in truth, is responsible for much of its vigor and efficacy.

In "'Till A' the Seas,'" the final apocalypse attending mankind is described through the progressive dwindling of human and animal life on Earth. Gradually, because of the progressive heating of the atmosphere and the climate, all towns and cities become deserted and are populated by "brooding centuries," where "moved only the scaly shapes of the serpent and the salamander" (EG 44), until Barlow confronts the reader with a last, dreadful image of the ultimate destiny of the race, initiating a decisive point for the formation of his hopeless vision on the role mankind plays in cosmic history. It is as if Barlow claimed: "If mankind's destiny is to become extinct as any living species, to perish without leaving a significant trace, then how can it aspire to a position of note in the universe's history? How can it pretend to a substantial role in the cosmic scheme of things?" This tale certainly bears a strong *demythologizing* value with reference to the human race: the narrative attacks, in harsh and caustic tones, the presumptuousness, the transitoriness, and even the absurdity and bitter irony with which Man's history is permeated. "Cosmicism" and "relativism" are the key words in this tale, but they are not just that: behind a poised and measured language, the narrator disguises all the resentment he nurtures toward a living species to which he himself belongs, scathingly criticizing the race's welter of prejudices, its absurd and ridiculous labyrinth of false ideologies and values, in which it ends up trapping itself.

Let us take a look, then, at the disquieting and desolate vision of the end of the race in the eyes of a grimly disillusioned observer, who certainly aspires to the status of an *objective* one. This is how Ull, the overstrained, scorched, and starving last man on earth, encounters his bitterly ironic end after his last search, that for a bowl of clear, life-saving water:

> Then, in the centre of a little town, Ull saw a well-curb. He knew what it was [. . .] With pitiful joy, he reeled forward and leaned upon the edge. There, at last, was the end of his search. Water—slimy, stagnant, and shallow, but water—before his sight. Ull cried out in the voice of a tortured animal, groping for the chain and bucket. His hand slipped on the slimy edge; and he fell upon his chest across the brink. For a moment he lay there—then soundlessly his body was precipitated down the black shaft. There was a slight splash in the murky shallowness as he struck some long-sunken stone, dislodged aeons ago from the massive coping. The disturbed water subsided into quietness. (EG 48)

The representation of the last man's end allows Barlow[6] to reason and generalize inductively on the cosmic role played by mankind in the universe's history:

---

6. As said above, it has been ascertained by Joshi that HPL wrote the "bulk" of the concluding "cosmic" section—and certainly the lexical choice of the word "puny" is a clue to the Lovecraftian flavor of the passage (HPL employed it also in the cosmic climax of an original tale, "Dagon," referring to "puny, war-exhausted mankind" [CC 6]). However, we can certainly assume that the general meaning conveyed by the climax of "'Till A' the Seas'" was shared by RHB.

And now at last the Earth was dead. The final, *pitiful* survivor had perished. All the teeming billions; the slow aeons; the empires and civilizations of mankind were summed up in this *poor twisted form*—and how *titanically meaningless* it all had been! Now indeed had come an end and climax in the eyes of those *poor complacent fools of the prosperous days*! Not ever again would the planet know the thunderous tramping of human millions—or even the crawling of lizards and the buzz of insects, for they, too had gone. Now was come the reign of sapless branches and endless fields of tough grasses. Earth, like its cold, imperturbable moon, was given over to silence and blackness for ever. The stars whirred on; the *whole careless plan* would continue for infinities unknown. This *trivial end of a negligible episode* mattered not to distant nebulae or to suns new-born, flourishing, and dying. The race of man, *too puny and momentary to have a real function or purpose*, was as if it had never existed. To such a conclusion the aeons of its *farcically toilsome evolution* had led. (EG 49; italics added)

As the italicized lexemes and expressions clearly show, in this passage Barlow mixes a supposedly objective—and largely *scientific*—description with his own, subjective, and bitterly sarcastic reflections on mankind's role and significance as a race on the cosmic scale. This tendency on Barlow's part further demonstrates that in his work (a) external impressions and descriptions are always filtered through the observer's sensitivity, and (b) the representation of mankind's end is a sort of starting point (or a pretext) for, retrospectively, formulating reflections on the existential status of the race. It is *because* mankind will end in such a desolate way that the negligible episode of its brief passage and history on the planet, its puny and momentary wishes, efforts, and even achievements, are to be considered ephemeral and, therefore, ultimately meaningless.

What is interesting in this final passage of the tale is Barlow's and Lovecraft's insistence on the images of "silence" and "blackness": no sound, no light, and ultimately *no witness* is there to testify to the desolation of the race's end—and this of course adds to the bitterness of the scene.[7] And of course this story masterfully shows the potentialities offered by the fusion of the "cosmicism" and "time" themes: in fact, the concern for mankind's history and evolution as revealed by the passing millennia and aeons allows the interpreter—in this case, Robert Barlow and H. P. Lovecraft as fiction writers, and we as their readers and critics—to adopt a *cosmic* perspective in literature, i.e., one that does not limit itself to discussing single, isolated spots of mankind's history or individuals, but that aspires to ad-

---

7. The paradoxical nature of the "last-man" stories (i.e., the unexplainable presence of an omniscient narrator to witness a supposedly deserted scene) of course is not absent in "'Till A' the Seas'" either. Another case of figurative desolation increased by the absence of a witness is present in "The Root-Gatherers": it is not a last-man story, but one where the narrator describes the ruined and deserted town of Doom (certainly a revelatory toponym), and in whose description images of silence and blackness again abound: "Here was Doom. The shards of a city that once knew merchants and toilers and glittering rich—peopled now with memories and shadows and the whisper of the breeze. Silent now were the streets whose paving had sounded with the trample of multitudes; silent also the tumbled houses" (EG 85).

dress—sometimes, as in Barlow, through an inductive reasoning—the general, existential status of the race as revealed by the long run of its course. The cosmic perspective in literature is, in other words, mainly a *temporal* attitude: it still configures a literature interested in discussing man, his facets, and his lifeworld, but privileging the general glimpse that the standpoint of long temporal extensions, if not of eternity, may provide. And of course the shift toward a cosmic perspective in literature provokes an entire complex series of consequences, among which the privilege accorded to a non-anthropocentered approach is perhaps the most striking. Needless to say, for writers like Barlow (and certainly Lovecraft) endorsing this aesthetic view, this perspective represents the most truthful possible over the traditional, ultimate (and noblest) concern literature may have: that of investigating human nature and telling the most universal possible truths about man—whatever complexity this task may hide, and however multifaceted these truths may be.

And certainly, Barlow believed that important truths about humanity could be said by examining its ultimate, far-in-the-future destiny. Therefore, Barlow's concern with the literary representation of mankind's end is testified by the recurrence of this theme within several narratives in his output. If "'Till A' the Seas'" is perhaps the most striking example, other tales provide remarkable visions of the gloomy end of the race.

"A Dream" (published October 1935) is another, this time fully Barlovian, story featuring a lonely narrator confronted with the dismal scenery of a finally abandoned, "desolate land" of a "dying Earth" (*EG* 70). Once more the signs of the decay of the race are testified by the state of abandonment into which the buildings of a former glittering prosperity are left, and by the absence of a witness, a record, to celebrate it. The impression is reinforced of mankind as a race having performed toilsome efforts that have ultimately come to naught, when considered from the correct perspective, namely the cosmic one—and the absence of a witness or a record painfully worsens the insignificance of humanity's role in the universe's history, since it shows that—in addition to the triviality of human achievements—mankind is also unable to record and leave a trace of them:

> The wild and desolate plateau ran shadeless to the farthest sight, till dim horizons merged it with a forest-blur of heavy pines. The abandonment manifest in every crack of the rotting surface and the range of towering grasses would cause the thoughtless to deny that man had ever dwelt beside this olden track; but this was false, for on one side there crouched a building of heavy stone, formed with mastery despite its enormous bulk. Crude slabs that in their weight alone might crush an elephant were laid with artful care, and crevices were few about the grey and ancient walls. In lesser cracks and through unglazed windows low above the ground trailed matted vines and clusters of dark leaves, but naught disturbed the squares of pavement in the massive rooms. Men might have lived not long before in that great house where maggots worked themselves through layers of greenish mould, or aeons might have passed since that paving echoed to mortal tread. I do not know, *nor is there any record made*, for we are careless in this, the world's last age. *Humanity is weary and not averse to death.* (*EG* 71; italics added)

The theme of the "lack of a witness" is so pervasive in Barlow's fiction that he feels the urge to employ it not exclusively in connection with the representation of the race's final, doomed destiny, but also with reference to other, less "cosmic" concerns. For instance, "An Episode in the Jungle," installment eleven of the *Annals of the Jinns*, presents a powerful image of desolation referred to a forgotten and non-witnessed vestige of mankind's past. The youth Loman, during a hunt, goes astray from his companions and enters a thick forest, where suddenly he is confronted by an ancient image of a froglike forgotten deity, sculpted in the stone. The idol represents a god of the past of mankind, and though he does not recognize it as one of his own deities, Loman kneels "as was the custom of his race" (*EG* 31). Alone and far from his companions' eyes, face to face with the mysterious idol, Loman lives a brief moment of "mingled wonder and respect" (*EG* 31), of almost mystic epiphany. But in attaching it to Loman's solitude Barlow, in an efficacious passage of free indirect speech, expresses his aesthetic concern for the theme of the "lack of a witness," which underlines the uniqueness of Loman's experience of linkage with the past: "He scrutinised the base [of the idol], fascinated by the marks written upon it. *There was no one now in all the world to read them*. The scholar was dead, and the hunter had lost his lore, so that all the writings on statues and monuments and broken tombs was destined for no further reading, even unto the death of eternity. Silent, with no ears trained to receive their message, they would henceforth be fingered only by the rain" (*EG* 31; italics added).

Returning to Barlow's visions of the end of the race, "The Experiment" (published May–June 1935) is a very different story from "'Till A' the Seas'" and "A Dream": it is not a last-man tale nor one in which the protagonist faces the dwindling of a dying planet. It is a more traditional tale of a "mad scientist," Dr. Marcus Edwards, and his bizarre experiments dealing with occult lore, which gain him a reputation for insanity: "He had come to be known, by certain esoteric groups, as an independent experimenter in the lore of obscure mental diseases and processes, which, strangely, he based upon ancient runes and savage magic practices" (*EG* 57). Dr. Edwards, a figure certainly reminiscent of Lovecraft's Crawford Tillinghast (protagonist of "From Beyond" [written November 1920]), founds his scholarship more on treatises on "witchcraft" and "necromancy" than on medical texts. The dreadful telepathic experiment to which Dr. Edwards subjects the consenting young student Edward Coswell is destined to provide uncanny revelations about mankind's final destiny and doom. The cosmic travel of Coswell's disembodied soul—in its turn certainly reminiscent of Lovecraft's "From Beyond" and of Randolph Carter's soul journey in "Through the Gates of the Silver Key" (written between October 1932 and April 1933)–traverses a whirling void that allows the traveller to sense "the past and the future of the whole scheme of things" (*EG* 58). The vision of the past reaches as far as the time before Earth's creation, displaying the sun from which the planet originally derived. And "before that?" the doctor telepathically asks Coswell's mind. The reply could not be but "Emptiness" (*EG* 59), because in Barlow's cosmic view the all-pervading void is not only the ultimate end to which mankind aims, but also its starting point: emptiness founds its ontological nature. In the space of few seconds, Coswell's soul crosses, as it were, the aeons-long phases of the universe's history, but the most striking vision, the one to which Barlow points the reader's attention, is that of mankind's far, *final* future. The "Armageddon of mankind" (*EG* 59) will be fought by a band of soldiers, holed up in a feudal castle in the country of Illoe, attacked by horrible, tentacled, and jellyfishlike monstrosities. The vision is unbearable, especially since Coswell lies on the ramparts of the castle, an involuntary member of the besieged army. Thus the student repeatedly asks Edwards to wake him up and spare him the torture, yet the doctor's efforts are futile. Coswell's frantic account of mankind's last, doomed battle for survival brings a flamboyant note in the panorama of the dreadful ends of the race in Barlow's literature:

> We can see them quite plainly now. I am afraid, deathly so. They are as we had expected; but none of us can overcome our nausea. They are swarming across the plain before the forest. If only we might have fled! But where? When all the world is overrun? How useless. Here is the last outpost of our kind, and we are defenceless. Must our race be wiped out? If our forefathers had but destroyed the first of them! Or if we had the old death-machines. . . but they are fallen into disintegration, like the race. A far off tumult is audible. The seething wall is approaching. The sun is low; livid. There are thousands of them—nearer now. As we had feared our arrows take little effect. Our men are killing one another. That is merciful. They cross the moat! Fill it with their bodies while others *ooze* over them. *They are mounting the walls!* (*EG* 60; Barlow's italics)

On the proper note of Coswell's shriek of terror, his account ends forever, and the reader is left uncertain about the student's actual destiny. Although the version of mankind's end provided by "The Experiment" is alternative to the one commonly found in Barlow's last-man or "dying Earth" stories such as "'Till A' the Seas'" and "A Dream," it still shares some points with the latter. In fact, the above passage still mentions—albeit tangentially—the theme, so dear to Barlow, of the gradual though inexorable decay and dwindling of the race, as the expression "the old death-machines [. . .] are fallen into disintegration, like the race" testifies. In other words, although "The Experiment" provides the picture of a more "dramatic" end of the race, through the episode of the apocalyptic, doomed fight against a progeny of alien invaders, Barlow cannot completely do without the beloved theme of mankind's gradual decadence through ages—which, as we shall see in the next paragraph, plays a decisive role in his existential reflections. Moreover, the depiction of the final age of mankind as backed by the resurgence of a new medieval age associates "The Experiment" with another tale of "cosmic" impact and concern, the complex and memorable "A Dim-Remembered Story."

In this latter story, the race's far future is again characterized by a return to medieval times and to a new Dark Age—probably a conceptual heritage for which Barlow is indebted to the opening of Lovecraft's "The Call of Cthulhu." However, in "A Dim-Remembered Story" Barlow returns to the cherished themes of the lack of a witness, the scarcity of records, and of the gradual disintegration of mankind and of life until a cold end, but this time he endorses an even more cosmic and abstract perspective. In fact, the mind-shattering vision of the unnamed protagonist allows him to have a look at the ultimate chaos and emptiness awaiting not simply the trifle known as mankind, but the whole planet and even all the existing universes. This is the powerfully desolate vision of the cosmos's end that Barlow provides in the tale:

> Gradually, I seemed to move—blown before a wind out of nowhere [. . .] and approach the clustered universes, shuddering with stars. To every side, fixed and still in the eternal night, they spread as I moved among them. And drifting ceaselessly, after a great period I found one thing which I had known; one spot dear and marked for me in the indifferent, half-forgotten years of Earth. Like a bubble of heated glass, our sun glowed small and red. And when I saw at last, within the unknown deeps, that solar pinpoint, there revolved about it no longer any Earth. The worlds were gone, and our sun dead with the cool of night. Chasms sprawled where anciently green fields and cloud-strewn skies had shut the ravenous black. Mankind was a dream, and the earth a bright, nostalgic memory. There was no record of how our world had perished. Somewhere in the great maze a star winked out. Only that, and all of humanity was gone. [. . .] Perhaps, for a while after Man was dead such things as Egypt's pyramids endured for cenotaphs to the lost race. Perhaps, here and there about the dead world (now cold eternally, in the End of things) some traces of humanity survived a while. Yet they all crumbled before the sun's death; and that great ember shot her last rays upon an empty land. Perhaps a few green things were left [. . .] a few toughened forms of earlier vegetation; plants and vines that struggled like reptiles to remain in the dim sunlight. These things may have been left—but Man was gone. The splendour of his race was forgotten, and the lordly trumpets mute. Then, when unmeasured centuries were done, earth had ceased, and her sun lingered briefly as a cinder, unmarked, in the blackness. [. . .] Everywhere was the black abyss. A monstrousness that grew and burrowed through the cosmos, engulfing faint worlds and brittle suns; sundering and destroying them. A nighted area where Nothingness grew powerful on substance. Eternities it swelled before me, until I saw that each of the strange new galaxies was vanishing. A last handful of stars melted away in gradual aeons. Reluctant, they went like guests at an ending banquet, until I was alone. Unaccompanied now, I drifted on that unknown ocean through which lay no chartered course; and where the ships of worlds had destroyed themselves on reefs of darkness. Brave, small voyagers, with no captain and no beckoning goal! Tiny warmish lights that crept awhile upon the fields. . . lights that were now forever extinguished. [. . .] There would never again be worlds. I watched for centuries, conscious of this fact. Confronting me was the sum, the purpose and destiny of the galaxies that had spotted that void. [. . .] Blank, hideous, supreme, devastating, the eternal naught remained. (*EG* 100–102)

This truly *cosmic* description strengthens the conviction that Barlow's predilection for the figurative potentialities offered by images of silence, obscurity, emptiness, and desolation was functional to his cosmic discourse: the employment of lexemes belonging to the sensory sphere (especially referring to hearing and sight) finds here, in the aesthetic concern for cosmicism, a powerful *raison d'être*, since it reveals all its aesthetic appropriateness in the rendering of the intended cosmic perspective. In fact, since sheer chaos, nothingness, void, and entropy are the constitutive, ontological frames of reality (from them the nascent universe stemmed, and to them a vanishing cosmos will return), Barlow believes that no better images than those of desolate soundlessness, obscurity, and emptiness could be employed to depict this inescapable Truth.

The cosmic perspective of "The Night Ocean" has been critically discussed in almost all the studies devoted to Lovecraft's work—at a time when the smallness of the role played by the Providence writer in the tale's composition was far from ascertained. Aside from any consideration regarding the overall cosmicism of the story, what is important to underscore here is the contribution this tale provides to our discussion of Barlow's view of mankind's doomed end. In fact, the last paragraph of this complex tale presents a final vision of the end of the race, a passage mingling the two Barlovian tendencies in his aesthetic treatment of the theme, namely the "dwindling" version (seen at work, for instance, in "'Till A' the Seas'" and "A Dream") and the "dramatic" one (in "The Experiment"). Before discussing this original mixture, synthesizing and sublimating both tendencies, let us reread the passage:

> Vast and lonely is the ocean, and even as all things came from it, so shall they return thereto. In the shrouded depths of time none shall reign upon the earth, nor shall any motion be, save in the eternal waters. And these shall beat on dark shores in thunderous foam, though none shall remain in that dying world to watch the cold light of the enfeebled moon playing on the swirling tides and coarse-grained sand. On the deep's margin shall rest only a stagnant foam, gathering about the shells and bones of perished shapes that dwelt within the waters. Silent, flabby things will toss and roll along the shores, their sluggish life extinct. Then all shall be dark, for at last even the moon on the waves shall wink out. Nothing shall be left, neither above nor below the sombre waters. And until that last millennium, as after it, the sea will thunder and toss throughout the dismal night. (EG 120)

The tale ends thus on a powerful cosmic note, probably a further reminiscence of the climax of another impressive cosmic tale, Lovecraft's "Dagon."[8] However, whatever literary inspiration Barlow may or may not have followed here, "The Night Ocean"'s final vision artfully combines the two versions of Barlow's aesthetic depiction of mankind's doomed end:

---

8. "I cannot think of the deep sea without shuddering at the nameless things that may at this very moment be crawling and floundering on its slimy bed [...] I dream of a day when they may rise above the billows to drag down in their reeking talons the remnants of puny, war-exhausted mankind—of a day when the land shall sink, and the dark ocean floor shall ascend amidst universal pandemonium" (CC 6).

(a) *The "dwindling" version.* Life will extinguish gradually, as the light of an enfeebling candle. The moon is "enfeebled" and will gradually—not suddenly—"wink out," life is "sluggish" before being extinguished: an isotopy of rarefaction is certainly at work in this passage. After all, this is the vision of what is defined as a "dying world"—and the inchoative nature of this action must be addressed. What will be left are just *cold* ("the cold light"), *silence* ("silent, flabby things"), and *darkness* (the "shores" are "dark," and in the end "all shall be dark" above and below the ocean, that will keep thundering and tossing in an eternal "night"). This textbook Barlovian picture of the end of the world completes with the mention of the inescapable *solitude* of the scene, and of the pitiful absence of a witness to leave a record of the final triumph of the night ocean: "none shall remain in that dying world to watch the cold light of the enfeebled moon." What is more, in this passage Barlow further presents and perfects the theme of the *return of all things to their primal origin*, when the puerile trick called life will be ultimately dispelled; but a significant change here occurs in comparison with other narratives—such as "A Dim-Remembered Story" analyzed above—where Barlow mentioned the void, the nothingness, and the emptiness to which everything will return. In fact, "The Night Ocean" still mentions that "*Nothing* shall be left, neither above nor below the sombre waters," apparently confirming that nothingness is the ultimate end of everything on earth; however, *something* will actually survive, and it is "waters." The *eternal* return of everything to its original source now configures as the return to the elemental of water ("Vast and lonely is the ocean, and even as all things came from it, so shall they return thereto"), because also the night ocean is *eternal*. As mother of everything existing, the ocean equals to the nothingness and the void of "A Dim-Remembered Story": it would be inaccurate to claim that Barlow has here changed his perspective, namely that, contrary to the bulk of his other narratives dealing with the theme of mankind's end, in "The Night Ocean" he is disavowing his previous identification of the earth's end with the progressive drying up of the planet. In fact, the ocean of this tale is still a metaphor for death and nothingness, since all that will remain is the "shells and bones of perished shapes" of the creatures who dwelt in it. Barlow's ocean is a metaphorical, I would dare to say *metaphysical* ocean: physical waters are turned and resolved into a symbol of the rarefaction of life, and ultimately of death, into the source of an unavoidable because primal and all-encompassing nothingness.

(b) *The "dramatic" version.* On the other hand, we should also contextualize the tale's conclusion within the frame of its whole plot, in particular considering the key episode of the mysterious appearance of the sea-creatures dimly detected by the narrator and protagonist,[9] and allegedly responsible for the deaths of several human beings who disappeared on the shores. If we confront this key episode with the tale's conclusion, where a specific insistence is made on the *things* that inhabited the waters, it would be possible to infer a circular connection—which would, by the way, strengthen the individual importance of each term of the rela-

---

9. This aspect of the tale is discussed in section 3.4.1 of the previous chapter on Vagueness.

tionship. Therefore, if a connection is really at work, it would allow us to endow the final "silent, flabby things" with the lethal, destructive powers of the previously mentioned ones. If this were the case, it would not be impossible to link the final vision of life's extinction to the deadly action of the sea-creatures. They would have provoked life's (and thus mankind's) extinction on the planet (they were previously presented in the tale as hostile to mankind), in order to subsequently dominate earth as the ruling species. And in this way, the cosmic climax of "The Night Ocean," depicting the extinction of the "silent, flabby things" and thus of all life on the planet, would ultimately sanction the end of the new race that is going to rule the planet after mankind. This reading is likely to seem hazardous at first sight, but the textual elements are there to indicate its validity; and it is further reinforced by the consideration of Barlow's deep concern with the chronological, "scientific" history of the planet, for the analytical survey of the alternation of eras, peoples, civilizations, and races on its surface.

This truly cosmic concern on Barlow's part is going to be addressed in the next paragraph, as a crucial aesthetic means he employs to portray the inanity and meaninglessness of human experience.

4.2.2 Inanity of experience and deterministic compulsion

The bleak and disconsolate vision of mankind's end is, as we saw, the entrance from which it is possible to access Barlow's existential standpoint. It is as if the recognition of the meaninglessness of mankind, as revealed by its final end, opened the way for a broader reflection on the overall inanity and insignificance of human experience in general and of the role played by mankind on the cosmic scale. What Barlow's grim position means is that the insignificance of the human passage on earth is not simply signaled by humans' squalid destiny (individually as well as a whole species): mankind's meaninglessness is a constitutive, *existential* status, testified by plenty of clues in its everyday condition. They are there, everything points in that direction, but in particular Barlow dwells on one clue: man's inability to rule over his own actions, and ultimately to control his will. Therefore, the reflections on the vanity of human experience and on the deterministic compulsion blend in Barlow's fictional representation of the cosmic meaninglessness of the species.

I shall discuss first Barlow's *general* treatment of the theme of the inanity and meaninglessness of the human experience, and afterwards I shall move to the analysis of one *particular* clue revealing it, namely the absence of free will produced by deterministic compulsion.

4.2.2.1 Inanity and meaninglessness of the human experience

Barlow's cosmic fiction is pervaded by a sense of the failure and loss of all human endeavors, considered as deluding illusions: his work strives to represent the inexorable futility of human efforts toward happiness or even stability. Nothing is in fact stable and reliable: everything is continuously replaced as in a flux or, better, in a chaotic vortex. The cause of this eternal transitoriness of things human is, to look properly, of an existential and ontological nature, since it stems from an inescapable condition of all things on the universal, cosmic level. Here the overlapping between the themes of cosmicism and time becomes evident: in the long run, the action of time, totally indifferent to men's plans, wishes, and aspirations, sanctions the ultimate instability of all things on a cosmic scale; and this bleak consideration leads Barlow to formulate the moral inference that no human endeavor, enterprise, or achievement, whatever their greatness, can aspire to any sort of "permanence."

There are several possible examples of Barlow's treatment of both the transitoriness of all things on the cosmic scale and of its inevitable impact on human affairs. I shall limit the discussion to a few examples, the most striking and aesthetically poignant. The climax of "A Dim-Remembered Story" develops these concepts with acute efficacy. The unnamed protagonist, reflecting upon his mysterious sojourn in a sort of medieval castle that will rise in the far future of the planet, expresses his bafflement at the cosmic transitoriness—and thus insignificance—of all things. These are the reflections on the cosmic, temporal scheme of things, aroused in him by the present recollection of his experience:

> But somehow more than to any other part of that adventure, my thoughts return to the old castle beyond an unknown wood. It is frightening to think that it will not be built for over fifteen thousand years. [. . .] I lived in that castle when it had begun to crumble, and I felt the breeze come over swinging vines and old trees when I stood before the narrow window of my arched chamber. Yet my bones shall be wind-borne dust, and I shall have known rebirth in grass and flowers and dark roots, many centuries before masons lay trowel to the first stone of that edifice. The place where it will rise, in more than a dozen tens of centuries, is now an active city, with steel and grass and concrete walls that *seem very permanent*. But I know them as *ephemera*, for my eyes are haunted by the nocturnal wood, by the dark sunset of that land wherein I shall never again be. It saddens me to think of the bright sunshine and the fresh wind that will come long after I am worm-infested. Having seen it I know that in this world about me *I can nevermore find zest, desire, or consolation*. (EG 104; italics added)

Everything is "ephemera" on the cosmic (temporal) scale: the inexorable succession of centuries and millennia is there to testify to it. Everything that *seems* permanent is revealed as ultimately, ontologically *transient*: once more, appearance is deceptive, because if the observer's eyes concentrate on the partial perspective that appearance provides, they are unable to detect a *permanence* that poignantly contrasts with the reality that only the temporal cosmic perspective provides, namely that the ultimate, ontological condition of everything is *transitoriness* and perishableness.[10] Nothing stays, all passes away on the cosmic scale: all

---

10. About the conflict between Appearance and Reality see also chapter 3, on Vagueness,

is "ephemera," and this leads the narrator of the above passage to end his reflections on a dreary note. In fact, the recognition (made possible by the endorsing of a cosmic, non-anthropocentric perspective) of the ultimate vanity of everything cannot fail to have *moral* consequences on the observer himself. Once more, the sensitivity of the narrator (namely, Barlow) filters the raw data of the experience; and the effect is that of being unable to find zest, desire, or consolation in the short span of life anymore, since they all are now recognized as ephemera and ultimately—i.e. "cosmically"—meaningless. And this is the truth that defeats any appearance: the intellectually honest thinker cannot keep deluding himself that a meaning, a significance lies within the human realm. The cosmic truth, in a sense, overcomes any partial truth and becomes *the only truth*. In other words, once the cosmic perspective is achieved, there is *no return*: the narrator cannot come back to his previous naïve and optimistic views of human and terrestrial phenomena as potentially *meaningful*. The narrator, epitome of every human being, has undertaken a course of epistemic training that has irremediably—and, perhaps, to his detriment—enriched him, causing him to endorse a new, transfigured vision: everything human and terrestrial now looks unimportant and trivial to his eyes, and this is precisely the reason why he cannot find interest, zest, desire, or consolation in life anymore.[11]

The transfiguration of the subject's vision and perception of everything around him is perhaps the most striking effect generated by the cosmic experience. But it is not the only one, since the effects of time are such that it is just through the action of "millennia" that a "ruthless change" (*EG* 44) takes place, destroying everything built—both "materially" and "spiritually"—by man during his fugacious passage on the planet.[12] Therefore, the recognition of the vanity and inconsistency of all human effort is, as it were, the final "prize" of a long epistemic training undertaken by the subject during his cosmic experience. As with every training, this one also develops in time and is made up of several different steps, each revealing to the learning subject a different—and, if possible, more disquieting—aspect of human inanity and insignificance. Let us discuss a few of these intermediate "steps," all functional to the final achievement of the cosmic

---

especially for the impact that this conflict bears on RHB's existential views.

11. In "A Dim-Remembered Story," RHB's reflection on the impossibility of finding zest and consolation after having discovered the cosmic truth is probably reminiscent of an analogous passage in the climax of HPL's "The Call of Cthulhu" (1926), where the narrator Thurston, after having undergone a "cosmic" experience largely similar—if not in the details, at least in its ultimate significance—to that of the protagonist of "A Dim-Remembered Story," expresses in this way his transfigured "vision" of his everyday human existence: "I have looked upon all that the universe has to hold of horror, and even the skies of spring and the flowers of summer must ever afterward be poison to me" (*CC* 169).

12. It is also from the temporal perspective RHB adopts that his cosmic views stem, and this is why some aspects of the interconnection between time and cosmicism will be discussed in chapter 5 on Time, where in particular "A Dim-Remembered Story" will prove revelatory.

knowledge discussed above and masterfully synthesized by the climax of "A Dim-Remembered Story."

The aesthetic goal to which the "intermediate" steps aim is the literary rendering of the principle of the vanity and insignificance of man's efforts and achievements in his terrestrial existence. Barlow's work represents this very goal in at least two different ways:

1. connotatively, by revealing the principle in an implicit way—thus without "stating" it, but showing it at work in a number of narrative situations; the inference of the principle is, however, left to the interpreter's initiative: the principle is, as it were, left *implicit* in the narrator's account;
2. denotatively, by "asserting" the principle, and usually framing the assertion within a general reflection upon the course of the narrative events; the interpreter is not required an inferential work, since the principle is made *explicit* by the narrator's words.

4.2.2.1.1. *The vanity of human existence: connotation*

To the first category belongs most of Barlow's fantasy tales concerned with existential issues, as well as those composing the *Annals of the Jinns* cycle. Already in the juvenile collaboration with Lovecraft, "The Slaying of the Monster," a not even fifteen-year-old Barlow conceived a succinct plot that, in its immediacy and naïve construction, epitomizes the emptiness and vanity of human effort: in the village of Laen, people decided the time had come to slay the fiery Dragon "who spat lava and shook the earth" (*EG* 13) while writhing in its depths. In truth, no actual monster existed, but merely a volcano that the villagers' superstition endowed with monstrous and supernatural powers. Thus the Laenians undertook their mission on the cliffs of the doomed mountain where the Dragon was rumored to dwell; however, no monster could be found, and "there was nothing solid enough to slay" (*EG* 13). After having searched in vain for the monster, the Laenians came back home and "there set up a stone tablet graven to this effect— 'BEING TROUBLED BY A FIERCE MONSTER THE BRAVE CITIZENS OF LAEN DID SET UPON IT AND SLAY IT IN ITS FEARFUL LAIR SAVING THE LAND FROM A DREADFUL DOOM'" (*EG* 13). The story is certainly— and naively—symbolic, as can be expected from the pen of a boy in his early teens. And the symbolism is patent: the Laenians' march toward the volcano represents mankind's path toward *achievement* (of whatever nature this may be), while their pretending to have actually *got it* stands for man's attitude of nurturing illusions about the validity, the importance, the significance of his actions—while *in reality* absolutely nothing noteworthy has been achieved. Again the conflict between the glamorous *appearance* and the stark *truth* is present, and functional to Barlow's existential discourse.

However, "The Slaying of the Monster" does not here exhaust its "cosmic" discourse. The very last line of the story, commenting on the stone inscription engraved by the Laenians, further elaborates young Barlow's existential perspective: "These words were hard to read when we dug that stone from its deep, ancient layers of encrusting lava" (EG 13). With this concluding sentence, the narrator implicitly states that the city of Laen had been afterwards destroyed by the volcano's rage. This surface narrative fact has the widest impact on the "philosophy" of the story: in fact, the reader, who has already recognized the falsity of the Laenians' behavior when they engraved a mendacious stone tablet now infers that that deluding action was not even efficacious, since it did not prevent the truth (the volcano's activity) from materializing and from performing its destructive task. Not only have the Laenians—symbols of mankind—deluded themselves by pretending to a significant, heroic action they did not do, but also, their falsity was ultimately revealed as totally useless in its deceiving scope. In other words, Barlow is implicitly stating here that men deceive themselves (and this is already morally reproachable in itself) in order to bestow upon their actions an importance they do not possess—but they justify their behavior in the name of a better, more satisfactory and rewarding "practical" survival in their lives (the majority believes life is certainly more enjoyable when persuasions of greatness and success pervade it); yet ,what is more painful and unacceptable, this fraud not only contravenes moral laws, but it also has no practical scope and usefulness, since it does not serve to prevent real truth from ultimately revealing itself and making its destructive course. The submersion of the stone tablet—the symbol of the fraud—by a sea of lava is the poignant figurative image employed to depict the painful reality of this stark state of affairs.

Also, the fantasy stories comprising the cycle *Annals of the Jinns*, under the surface of apparently simple and undemanding plots, hide a "cosmic," existential discourse. In fact, most of these stories have bleak moral attachments to them: their plots—especially their climaxes—allow the reader to infer young Barlow's disillusionment concerning the human race and its prerogatives. The main theme displayed by these stories, referring to their "existential" concern, is certainly that of the *unpredictability* of life and especially of the final outcome of man's actions. In other words, human beings are presented as being unable to hold full power and control over their own actions: their plans and desires are ultimately revealed as empty, inconsistent, and inconsequential, since they are continually disrupted by the unfathomable action of a ruling and indifferent Chaos that, as a kind of sentient entity, almost seems to enjoy deluding human efforts.

Let us examine how this theme finds literary and figurative expression in some of the most representative of the *Annals'* short stories. "The Shadow from Above" (episode two) starts by telling of the peaceful hamlet of Droom, the busy activities of its people, in an apparently ordinary midsummer day. But under the ordinary surface of reality Chaos is always lurking, and Barlow shows its abrupt irruption in the form of a mysterious "shadow from above": a giant, invisible, birdlike entity comes to shock the Droomers' existence. People are affrighted and flee in terror, while the unseen monster treads the village's main street in search of aliment: "All that afternoon and night it pried at doors, scratched at roofs, muzzled windows and upset fruit-carts inquiringly. [. . .] It did not gain entrance during the night, although few slept, when they heard the constant breathing before their homes, and the dull thumping sounds as it wreaked its malice upon the shops of the market place" (EG 16). Where has the horror come from? Nobody knows, and probably it is not important to ask: the invisible monster-bird is a product of Chaos, a sheer irruption of *Outsideness* into ordinary life. And exactly as no reason can be conjectured about its arrival, none can be found for its departure: "It was high noon before any dared unbar their doors and venture forth. Nothing unusual greeted their blanched faces, and silently, apprehensive they stole to their tasks. *Soon all activity again commenced. The horror had gone*" (EG 16; italics added). Exactly as it came, the horror went: unexplainably. Humans cannot know, nor even hypothesize, the nature of this experience. And what is more, if we consider the monster's apparition as a metaphor for life, life reveals itself as ultimately inconsistent: experience is empty, does not leave permanent signs of itself. Yet the more disquieting detail of the narrative is perhaps not so much the description of the supernatural experience in itself, but the fact that—once it has gone—"soon all activity again commenced": everything is back to "normal." Barlow's text implies here that no explanation is required for the supernatural event: the monster's apparition is an "empty" event, one deprived of any meaning from the limited human perspective, and its possible metaphorization into a symbol of human existence itself reveals the bleakness of Barlow's existential view.

"The Flagon of Beauty," episode three of the *Annals*, again insists on the unpredictability of life, on the dominant role performed by Chaos over human existence, and, above all, on the emptiness of human efforts. In fact, the much sought-after "flagon" allegedly containing the essence of Beauty is ultimately revealed as the opposite to the merciless and tyrannical princess who desperately looks for it in order to conquer the love of her prince: "Then she noticeably paled. Her hair swiftly grew leaded and grey, her lips assumed a ghastly pallor, and a score of tiny wrinkles appeared on her smooth skin. She became an old hag, quite out of place in the splendour of the throne-room" (EG 17). Lying behind the surface moral of the story (the princess's cruelty and avidity finally get the punishment they deserve), there is a deeper one—one that the competent reader is, however, required to detect: human purposes, plans, and wishes (in this case, the wish for eternal beauty) lead to outcomes that are totally unpredictable, even contrary (a horrible ugliness) to the expected ones, due to the imponderable intervention of something that overcomes human comprehension, and that can be assimilated to the action of an indifferent Chaos.

"The Sacred Bird," episode four of the cycle, presents a somewhat different "step" in Barlow's development of the cosmic discourse on humankind. Here his belittlement and devaluation of the race momentarily abandon the "existential" concern and shift to the denunciation of the ignorance and superstition dominating man's behaviors and actions: the choice of the inhabitants of Ullathia, and in particular of the Head of the Council, to elect a strange—apparently speaking— bird as the ruler of the town conveys Barlow's sarcastic criticism of the ignorance that men allow to guide their actions. Certainly Barlow is also scorning the corruption of the ruling class, which exploits people's ignorance in order to rule according to its own wishes. But indeed, without that ignorance, its exploitation would not be possible.

Episode five, "The Tomb of the God," tells of the fateful attempt of a band of explorers from the city of Phoor to steal treasures and other precious items from the ancient tomb of the immemorial god Krang. This story represents a further variant of Barlow's "existential" theme of man's inability to be in control of his actions: once more the final outcome of the explorers from Phoor escapes their plans, since in Krang's tomb they are destined to find a horrible end. Probably also this story may be analyzed on a double level: at the first, superficial one, the plot offers the conventional story of a band of avid treasure-hunters who finally get punished for their greediness and their blasphemous disturbing of a sleeping powerful deity; but on a deeper level, the reader infers that the "existential" theme described above is once more evident.

Another variant of the same theme is present in "The Flower God," episode six of the *Annals*. His eternal enemy Alair, the ruler of Zaxtl, lethally fools King Luud by making him a very special gift: a many-colored Flower of apparently lovely—though alien—aspect, the "ruler of plants" (*EG* 20). King Luud becomes increasingly enamored of the Flower, until it becomes clear to all—except to him—that Alair's gift is draining the king's mental sanity and allows his enemy to work in Luud's stead. Not differently from the Flagon of Beauty, which was finally revealed as the Flagon of Extreme Ugliness and Loathsomeness, so an apparently lovely gift turns into a tool of destruction: again nothing is humanly predictable, again men show lack of control over their own fates and even their own actions.

"The Fall of the Three Cities," episode eight, presents a patent case of a human action, specifically revenge, that turns on its author. Magician Volnar's creature of "vast prehensile tissue" (*EG* 25) was concocted, in its creator's intentions, as a destructive means of revenge against the inhabitants of the cities of Perenthines, Zo, and Naazim. And the evil thing indeed effected Volnar's revenge ("it roved the streets unsated, growing, devouring throughout the night, and in a few horrible hours had depopulated the cities that were so hostile to sorcerers" [*EG* 25]). But what was not predicted by its creator was that the thing ended up—like an amoral creature of Chaos—destroying everything in its path: not even Volnar himself is spared from the raving fury (he "with occult aid constructed for himself a castle of black stone in a very short period, wherein he dwelt the remainder of his existence. *This was not long because of his ungrateful creature's abnormal longevity and appetite*" [*EG* 25; italics added]). Volnar's story demonstrates how unstable are life achievements; not only are the outcomes of human actions ultimately unpredictable, but they are also deceitful: what seems to be the expected result of our action (the huge monster initially fulfilling Volnar's revenge plans) may at any time turn into its precise opposite (the creature finally killing its creator). This is certainly a powerful representation of the ontological, existential emptiness of our efforts, of man's impossibility of control and self-determination.

That men's expectations are constantly deluded by the unfathomable, chaotic course of reality is again inferable from the plot of "The Mirror," episode nine of the *Annals*. Wizard Khalda's ability to escape the torments inflicted on him by Malyat, the Head Torturer of Yondath, contravenes everybody's expectations, and especially the emperor's. The last lines of the tale, with the emperor overwhelmed by Khalda's mirror's indescribable magic ("the doom that came unto his majesty was alien to all accepted lines of death"), provide a powerful clue of the final, dramatic overturning of the emperor's plans and presumptuous self-confidence.

Sorcerer Khalda comes back in episode ten, "The Theft of the Hsothian Manuscripts," once more to punish the unfounded conceit and assurance of another character, the youth Morla, who was sent on a terrible mission by the people of his city: to face the ancient sorcerer Khalda in his fabled secret palace and to steal the Hsothian Manuscripts from its innermost chamber. Morla's fateful path toward the palace may be seen as the metaphor of man's whole life course toward the wished-for achievement of a (supposed, dreamed about) ultimate Goal. In this short tale, Barlow is not yet concerned with showing how futile and meaningless the final Goal is, but certainly what he does do here is to reveal how deceptive is the mission undertaken by men to reach such a Goal. Life is paved with snares and illusions that fool men, making them believe that the path is easy, the search is likely to be successful because the first hardships are easily overcome, and, above all, the mission is worth the effort because the Goal is really desirable and achievable. Morla's story justifies this allegorical reading: he starts his mission as man starts life, with fears and hesitations. But the first (in truth, small) successes have the poisoning effect of raising his spirits to an unjustified and fatal arrogance: after recognizing the green-clad men holding a double scythe in Khalda's palace as harmless corpses, Morla laughs off his fears and strikes the petrified bodies with his sword. He gains confidence in his mission because he encounters successes: "Morla had experienced little difficulty in traversing the forest of orange fungi, and the toad-god he had slain with a minimum of trouble" (EG 28); and the youth is deceitfully encouraged from the fact that "thus far his travel had been easy" (EG 28). But when the seeker is confronted with the last, decisive task—the stealing of the Manuscripts and the facing of the sorcerer himself—when, in other words, man's final goal is at hand and allures, he at last discovers the illusory nature of his entire search.

The sequence of Morla's final confrontation with his doom is certainly revelatory: in the last chamber of the palace, he sees "a pale greenish figure slumped in a chair of antique carving. The wrinkles of the flesh, and sundry other vague subtleties of physiognomy and contour, made it clear that sorcerer Khalda was no longer entirely human. [. . .] But the old one did not move, *and Morla thought his fortune fine indeed*" (EG 29; italics added). The italicized words show how Life's deceptive action never ceases, not even when man confronts the final task of his mission, i.e., he is very close to completing it and achieving the goal. In fact, Morla is induced once more—and for the last time—to be optimistic on the success of his mission: Khalda is asleep and not guarding the Manuscripts. Morla kills another monstrous creature in the sorcerer's chamber, and thanks to an ingenious stratagem even avoids the potentially lethal trick (the allegedly last obstacle before the completion of the mission) hidden by the carven red chest containing the scroll. Morla takes the sought-for papyrus, but just when the mission seems completed and the goal accomplished, life tricks man for a last, decisive time: "Then, turning, he thought to leave while Khalda yet slumbered. *But Khalda, it would appear, was no longer asleep*" (EG 29; italics added). The final doom is over man, and it is the more bitter because it comes just when he thought he had succeeded in the achievement of the goal. The allegorical reading of this tale, as well as of others of Barlow's output, does not allow us to fill the notion of goal semantically; and it is properly so, since everybody may fill it according to his own preferences (life's ultimate goal of course varies in people's views). Barlow is not interested in semantizing the empty notion of one's life's *goal*; and this lack of interest is precisely what renders this an "empty" notion. Barlow's perspective is truly cosmic, non-anthropocentric, and ultimately "existential," since it overlooks the content or nature of the goal: it criticizes and satirizes the *notion itself* that life might have a goal. This is the—under some respects, nihilistic—consequence to which Barlow's cosmicism attains.

The pinnacle of cosmic "metaphoricity" in Barlow's fantasy tales is, however, reached in his second collaboration with Lovecraft, "The Hoard of the Wizard-Beast."[13] The whole plot of this emblematic story can be read as a bleak allegory

---

13. The first draft was originally composed by RHB in September 1933, and HPL received it in December. The tale can be considered a sort of follow-up to "The Sacred Bird," the fourth episode of RHB's *Annals of the Jinns*. This can be inferred by the mention of a Sacred Bird and of the city of Ullathia. According to Joshi, "The Hoard" was thus probably "meant as one of the 'Annals of the Jinns', which for some reason Barlow did not send to the *Fantasy Fan*" (LAL 531). HPL revised the piece extensively (according to Joshi, the text is now approximately 60% Lovecraft's), as the detailed analysis of his interventions described in his letter of December 17 proves: "Your new tale is highly colourful & interesting, & I have taken the liberty to make a few changes in wording, rhythm, & transitional modulation, which may perhaps bring it a bit closer to the Dunsanian ideal evidently animating it. This ought certainly to land with either FF or *Unusual*. If there is any defect, it is possibly a certain lack of compactness & unity—that is, the tale is not a closely-knot account of a *single episode*, but is rather a loosely-constructed record with much early space given to a description of the *occasion for* Yalden's journey, while the later parts involve the *journey itself* in a way essentially dissociated from the *occasion*. The scope or territory of the narrative is thus too large & varied for a real short story. An ideal short story would concentrate on a *single thing* like the *journey itself*, disposing of the *journey's reason* in as brief an explanatory paragraph as possible. The kind of vehicle for composite & diffuse narratives of this sort is the novel or picaresque romance. Still—it is to be admitted that Dunsany often creates similarly non-unified sketches of short story length, hence this specimen must not be criticised too severely. I'm letting it alone so far as this point goes. As for 'padding' – it is never justifiable. Let the especial nature of every story dictate the number of words in which it shall be told. Some are naturally short, others are naturally long. My own difficulty, in view of the infinitely subtle & complex set of atmospheric associations needed to make any weird incident convincing & fully realised, lies in curtailing my MSS. to anything like short story length. As for your new tale—my changes largely concern certain niceties of language, &

of human existence. Let us see how this reading is justified and what are the inferences and consequences it entails on a cosmic, existential level. In the very ancient city of Zeth, lying on a far planet "of strange beasts and stranger vegetation" (*EG* 31), the town treasury has been stolen. This is the disappointing truth the *giphath* (probably a public official) Yalden discovers when he enters the strongroom. If allegorically referring to human existence in general, the narrator's words describing Yalden's surprise already set the tale's metaphorical structure from the first lines: "[. . .] great was Yalden's dismay to find this *emptiness instead of the expected wealth*" (*EG* 32; italics added). Too effective and precise to be dropped casually, this expression can only remind us of Barlow's existential perspective: the "emptiness" of the locations analyzed in paragraph 4.1 as a stylistic trait plays a role also at the "existential" level we are discussing here. Images of emptiness are in fact charged with manifold semantic nuances, since they become metaphors of the overall "emptiness" of mankind's experience. The image of "emptiness" returns, and since we have learned how significant it is on an existential level in the figurative repertoire of Barlow's fiction, its connection with "expected wealth" further reinforces the validity of the allegorical reading: human life eventually reveals itself as "empty," devoid of meaning and significance, proving humanity's "expectations of wealth" ultimately unfounded.

After his discovery, Yalden sets out for the luxurious hall where the oracle Oorn (an alien, "large and pudgy creature very hard to describe, and covered with short grey fur" [*EG* 32]) dwells and mimics the high priests' promptings. Oorn utters an unspeakable sentence,[14] which the priests interpret as the advice to "slay the monster-wizard Anathas and replenish the treasury with its fabled hoard" (*EG* 32). The mission is particularly dangerous: nobody in the land of Ullathia and its surroundings would dare face Anathas and its cohort unheedingly in the Cave of Three Winds, where they reside. However, Yalden sets out on his mission and starts on the path to the monster's abode, and his decision may be metaphorically read as man's decision to undertake his life's mission, namely that of carrying Life to its end and striving to reach the goal. This is Yalden's, i.e. man's, self-confidence at the beginning of his mission: "In his bosom were mixed an ingrained, patriotic sense of duty, and a thrill of adventurous expectancy regarding the unknown mysteries he faced" (*EG* 33). Again the word "expectancy" appears, as if Barlow wanted to show how man's path through life is punctuated with expectations, wishes, plans—that existence's subsequent developments will invariably delude.

---

certain handlings of emotional stress at important turns of the action. A study of the altered text itself will be more instructive than any comment I can make here" (*FF* 90. Lovecraft's italics). That "The Hoard of the Wizard-Beast" was probably sent to a publisher "is clear from the note he [RHB] has written at the top of the manuscript ('only copy except at pub[lisher]')" (*LAL* 531). If the tale was actually published, its appearance is not known. Its first known appearance occurred in *The Hoard of the Wizard-Beast and One Other* (1994).

14. The first half of the tale is of course pervaded by a deep sense of irony, that will be discussed in chapter 7.

Yalden undertakes all the necessary preparations for his mission: he seeks for the material aids of a wizard, frees Sarall, the Lord of Worms, in exchange for some other help, just as an optimistic and self-confident average man would do in the mission of his life. Yalden's path to the Cave of Three Winds and its fabled hoard (this a metaphor for man's final goal) traverses a desolate land: "The sere and fruitless land through which he now travelled was totally uninhabited" (*EG* 33). As we know, Barlow's predilection for images of geographical and physical desolation tells of his existential view on man's life as an essentially solitary and fruitless experience. The seeker slowly closes in on Anathas's Cave, where a glittering, fabulous treasure is rumored to be hidden. The allegorical isotopy we are following in discussing the tale may lead us to consider the fact that the treasure is simply "rumored" (nobody came back alive from Anathas's abode to tell of it) as a metaphor of the absurdity of man's efforts: he strives his all life, he undertakes the perilous mission of "existing," just to achieve a Goal that is only "rumored," and about which no certainty is available. Under this light, Barlow's attack on the absurdity and worthlessness of man's efforts appears very clear. Even more absurd is the effort, if man considers that even the best of his predecessors have never achieved the much sought-after final goal, and that their failures stand as a wise warning against the making of new attempts: "Great numbers of persons of stronger will and wit than Yalden had died in remarkable manners while seeking the hoard of the wizard-beast, and their bones were laid in a strange pattern before the mouth of the cave, *as a warning to others*" (*EG* 33; italics added).

Finally Yalden, the metaphorical man, "after countless vicissitudes" (*EG* 33) of life, comes in sight of the final goal, Anathas's lair, and is struck by its isolation. Since the isotopy of solitude has already been detected in the tale (Yalden traveling alone through a desolate and fruitless land), the detail of the isolation of Anathas's lair may be interpreted as the metaphor of the utter solitude that ultimately characterizes each of man's efforts to achieve the final goal of his life. Man is completely alone and can count only on his strengths to overcome the hardships of his mission—especially in the final, decisive confrontation. Encouraged, as Morla was, by the apparent calm and quietness of the Cave's surroundings, Yalden at once enters it. The description of the interior of the Cave provides a piquant metaphor of human life itself: "The interior was very cramped and exceedingly dirty, but the roof glittered with an innumerable array of small, varicoloured lights, the source of which was not to be perceived" (*EG* 34). If the monster's Cave, as seems allowed by the overall symbolic structure of the tale, is interpreted as a metaphor for Human Life, the description holds a strong allegorical power: Life, like the Cave, is "cramped" and "dirty," namely messy and chaotic, but man is deceived to overlook this, because he is allured by the tempting "roof" of innumerable, glittering "lights"—i.e. the false myths, the illusions of which man's life is nurtured and interwoven to appear bearable and worth living to its owner. The "source" of these lights, i.e. of these illusions, is "not to be perceived"; and this adds to Barlow's bitter criticism, since he depicts man as a foolish being who credits—and structures his own existence basing on—illusions whose source's credibility he does not even know—nor dare investigate.

After entering a second chamber in Anathas's cave, Yalden recognizes it as the wizard-beast's luxurious and wealthy sojourn room. Though struck and awed by the beauty of the sorcerer's chamber, Yalden does not lose time in reaching a third one, where the treasure is rumored to be kept: he desires to end his mission before Anathas returns from wherever it might be. After some difficult and painful crawling, at last Yalden reaches the treasure-room, whose sight is certainly frightening: "a vast open space paved solidly with blazing coals above which flapped and shrieked an obscure flock of wyvern-headed birds. Over the fiery surface green monstrous salamanders slithered, eyeing the intruder with malignant speculation" (EG 34). Some further tests, it seems, are to be passed before the final goal may be attained. But it lies there, in front of the man-seeker, and alluring him toward the last, doomed effort of his path: "And on the far side rose the stairs of a metal dais, encrusted with jewels, and piled high with precious objects; the hoard of the wizard-beast" (EG 34). Although man is made aware of the hardship, if not the impossibility, of the success of his mission, his foolishness overcomes him till the very end. He cannot give up all his efforts just when their coronation seems so close at hand, and if during his path he has always shown rationality, prudence, and wisdom (Yalden's seeking for the wizard's aids, his freeing Sarall in exchange for his help, etc.), the sight of the goal at hand definitely deceives man and makes his foolish nature finally reveal itself in all its destructive nonsense: "At sight of this unattainable wealth, Yalden's fervour well-nigh overcame him; and chaffing at his futility, he searched the sea of flame for some way of crossing. [. . .] Desperation, however, possessed him; so that at last he resolved to risk and try the fiery pavement. Better *to die* in the quest than to return *empty-handed*. With teeth set, he started toward the sea of flame, heedless of what might follow" (EG 34; italics added).

The last reference to heedlessness is of course revelatory of the above-mentioned lack of rationality and prudence that characterizes man's final effort to reach the goal: when the goal approaches and seems at hand, man loses control of himself and of his power over his own actions. But what is even more interesting in the passage is the mention of the two expressions I have italicized and that, as it were, exchange the baton in Barlow's development of his existential discourse: while the expression "empty-handed" still refers to the isotopy of emptiness/meaninglessness (the emptiness of existence, the emptiness of man's efforts/wishes/expectations, the emptiness of the final goal, etc.), the verb "to die" introduces the semantic swerve that the existential discourse needs: a clear perspective now comes into the foreground, namely the gradual, painful recognition of the only possible, inevitable goal of man's path and overall existence: death. By continuing to follow the semantic, "existential" isotopy we have up to now chosen, we are allowed to detect in the tale's final all Barlow's gloomy and bleak perspective. The reader has already been somehow "advised," by the mention of the possibility of death, that Yalden's attempt is doomed.

But man cannot even face his end serenely. In fact, even in its very last moments life has still more illusions in store for him. Let us see what literary images the tale's climax employs in order to render these bleak notions figuratively: "As it was, surprise seared him almost as vehemently as he had expected the flames to do—for with his advance, *the glowing floor divided to form a narrow line of safe cool earth leading straight to the golden throne*" (EG 34; italics added). The last of life's illusions is at work: as Morla was all the way encouraged—by the luck and ease of the first tasks he overcame—to believe his mission was going to be successful; likewise Yalden is unexpectedly (but how much man's expectations count in Barlow's work, we already know) allured to continue his mission. Man is so foolish that by now, the goal being so close at hand, he guiltily ceases even to wonder at the sheer improbability of life's help: "Half dazed, *and heedless of whatever might underlie such curiously favouring magic,* Yalden drew his sword and strove boldly betwixt the walls of flame that rose from the rifted pavement. *The heat hurt him not at all, and the wyvern-creatures drew back, hissing, and did not molest him*" (EG 34; italics added). At a wiser look, it would appear clear that life is simply alluring man while preparing its final and lethal traps; but from the perspective of the wished-for goal to be easily reached, man is anything but wise. The mission seems easy, new illusions arise, all the more glorious and glittering in order to build the aesthetically efficacious contrast with their forthcoming disruption: "The hoard now glistened close at hand, and Yalden thought of how he would return to Zeth, laden with fabulous spoils and worshipped by throngs as a hero" (EG 35). Man's lack of wisdom and prudence is clearly emphasized by Barlow: "In his joy he forgot to wonder at Anathas' lax of care of its treasures; nor did the very friendly behaviour of the fiery pavement seem in any way remarkable. Even the huge arched opening behind the dais, so oddly invisible from across the room, failed to disturb him seriously" (EG 35). Life keeps on fooling man till the very end; but—and this is probably the kernel of Barlow's existential discourse—in truth *it is not life, but man who fools himself*: Life's traps are clearly displayed along man's way. It would take just a bit of prudence and wisdom to detect them, but man lacks them completely, especially when he glimpses the goal so close at hand. Finally, when it is clearly too late and man even starts savoring success, the first flashes of recognition occur: when doom is by this point inevitable, man gradually realizes he is fooled and he has fooled himself too; for the whole of his existence his efforts have been vain and worthless, and his mission is going to elude him because it was doomed from the beginning:

> Only when he had mounted the broad stair of the dais and stood ankle-deep amid the bizarre golden reliques of other ages and other worlds, and the lovely, luminous gems from unknown mines and of unknown natures and meanings, did Yalden begin to realise that anything was wrong. But he now perceived that the miraculous passage through the flaming floor was closing again, leaving him marooned on the dais with the glittering treasure he had sought. (EG 35)

The inevitability of doom is revealed to man when it is too late to react: when his existence is closing in on its lethal end. After the passage has completely closed at his back, "and his eyes had circled round vainly for some way of escape" (*EG* 35), Yalden recognizes what he would never like to recognize: "he was hardly reassured by the shapeless jelly-like shadow which loomed colossal and stinking in the great archway behind the dais" (*EG* 35). Man is now asked to pay the tribute for his presumptuousness, namely for the belief that he could succeed in his mission, that there was indeed a goal, and that life had a meaning: "He was not permitted to faint" (*EG* 35). He has to look the horror in the eyes, to face his inevitable fate and death in all their cruelty. And it is distinctly moral that Barlow chooses "Anathas," a word quite patently reminiscent of *thanathos*—the Greek term for death—as the name for the final horror, for the ultimate destiny to which Yalden is headed. Somehow like a god whose cruelty is inescapable, Anathas-Thanathos asks the final tribute to man: "Then Anathas the wizard-beast rolled fully out of the archway, mighty in necromantic horror, and jested with the small frightened conqueror before allowing that horde of slavering and peculiarly hungry green salamanders to complete their slow, anticipatory ascent of the dais" (*EG* 35). A bitter irony is patent in the definition of man as a "small frightened conqueror": all his wishes, expectations, undertakings, plans of glory (those of a "conqueror") come finally to naught, overruled by the blind destructive powers of a fierce chaos that reduces man to a "small" and "frightened" being.

I hope the proposed allegorical reading of "The Hoard of the Wizard-Beast" may open the way to the further critical recognition the tale certainly deserves. Of course, until new discoveries are made of the actual roles played by both Barlow and Lovecraft in the writing of the tale, it will not be possible to make a clear evaluation of the extent of their contributions in the composition of the narrative; however, Barlow must probably have played a not indifferent role in building the tale's complexity,[15] especially, I suppose, from the viewpoint of plot—while Lovecraft's contribution, as often occurred in his revisions for young writers, was probably limited to a formal smoothing and perfecting of the prose and style.

"The Fidelity of Ghu" (probably written in June 1934) is still another (the last to be examined here) tale containing a connotative existential discourse on Barlow's part. This fantasy narrative, in its concise thematic density, can be considered a sum of the main aspects of Barlow's cosmic perspective on mankind. "The Fidelity of Ghu" presents in fact a bitter attack on man's instability, unreliability, and tendency to (moral) corruption; and this is all rendered through a resentfully ironic tone that reflects Barlow's hopeless existential views. It is the story of Lord Ghu, the "last of the priests that had served Krang" (*EG* 40): his master is now reputed dead and has been sealed in his mighty tomb for two months. In Ghu's recognition of his current uselessness, Barlow displays man's sense of impotence

---

15. As a matter of fact, my allegorical reading has highlighted just a few of the tale's themes. Another key one, the irony informing especially the first half of the narration, is discussed in section 7.1 of chapter 7.

and loss of interest in life itself: "Ghu had begun to ponder upon his own fate, now that there was no further need of his services. [. . .] The plight of the High Priest was typical of all those who had devotedly relied upon the infinite knowledge of their strange master for all directions. Now that he had been interred with due solemnity, none knew where next to turn. Clearly, things were in a deplorable state" (*EG* 40), so much so that Ghu, epitome of the man who has lost his bearings and whose existence seems to him intolerable, takes the most dramatic of all decisions: "to perish by the tomb of his master, in noble sacrifice" (*EG* 40). Acting this way, Ghu believes he can still give a sense to his life and show the heroism of which he is able. But does Life really have a meaning? Is an act of *heroism*–as an act dignifying and rehabilitating one's life–concretely possible in Barlow's view? Certainly not, and Barlow expresses this pessimism through two narrative elements.

First, he makes immediately clear that man's alleged "heroism" is the result of an act of self-interest. In fact, when Ghu resolves upon his pretended "heroic" act, the narrator hastens to report the character's inner motives: "He had thought all night upon the matter, and had concluded that this [the "heroic suicide"] would, in the end, *entail the least trouble*, and yet at the same time *serve his vanity*, for it would cause his example to be pointed out by others with envious and admiring pride" (*EG* 40; italics added). This is not the description of a disinterested act of unselfish heroism, but of a conscious and attentively considered gesture of "self-advertisement." Heroism is possible only as a service to vanity, Barlow seems to claim.

Second, Ghu's act of heroic fidelity is soon bitterly made fun of, since it ultimately resolves into its masked and disguised opposite. In fact, the story goes on by telling of Ghu's encounter, in the desert waste he is traversing in his path to Krang's tomb, with a tall creature, similar to a "five legged spidery crab [. . .] [and] mottled with purple and green" (*EG* 40). This turns out to be one of the avatars of the god Shista, a minor deity whose worship had fallen into disuse in the time of Krang's prosperity. Now that Krang has died, Shista—mightily pleased—sets out to the sepulcher of the Old One,[16] determined—as many others—to dwell there because of the mighty evil powers this would allow. Though the encounter with Ghu has been accidental, Shista decides to take advantage of it, and after asking the mourning priest his mission, speaks to him with a strange and deep voice. The narrator, though unable to report the exact words of that memorable exchange, nevertheless relates its results: soon after Lord Krang's interment, Ghu went to the temple and, beating upon a spotted drum, summoned "all the strange monsters that had been servitors of the Dead One" (*EG* 41). Ghu's speech to the gathered multitude reveals, inferentially, as a concentrate of Barlow's existential pessimism and bitter irony:

---

16. This is the first time in RHB's work that a deity of his fantasy narratives is defined as "Old One." We cannot avoid detecting the debt young Barlow is probably paying to the master of those early years, H. P. Lovecraft.

"Lo! I went into the desert to seek my master's tomb, and there I thought to perish. But as I was upon this mission, there came to me a messenger from the gods; and a demi-god itself, that spake to me, and tore away the veil of ignorance from my eyes. And now do ye bow, for I am possessed by the will of our dead Lord, and great Shista is come to rule in his stead. So I have returned to make ready for the One who shall follow when we have suitably prepared his temple." (EG 41)

Certainly here Barlow pokes resentful fun at man's unreliability, instability, infidelity, moral corruption. But most of all, I believe, in the following epigrammatic line that concludes the tale ("Thus did Ghu remain faithful to his master" [EG 41]) Barlow bitterly delivers his truth about everything existential: when dealing with things human, everything is transient and perishable, nothing stays and wins the test of Time, everything is easily *replaced*—man's words, purposes, plans, attitudes. And the meanness of man's behavior is all the more testified by his tendency to disguise it *to himself* as acceptable: Man justifies his actions to his own eyes by a deception, namely by telling to his own conscience that what he has done was right and just—that he has remained "faithful" to what he holds dearest in his life, as the case of Lord Ghu exemplarily demonstrates.

4.2.2.1.2 The vanity of human existence: denotation

Perhaps Barlow's most striking reflections on the vanity and emptiness of experience are those contained in his direct and plain attacks on the insignificance of human efforts and the frailty of mankind's role and position in the universe. In the narratives I have grouped in this second category, Barlow's words are explicit and unmistakable—and the caustic power of his condemnation is the result of an unequivocal attitude on the author's part rather than of the reader's (more or less "stretched") inference.

In this sense, the cosmic visions of a "last-man" story like "'Till A' the Seas'" can be again considered emblematic. This is probably the narrative piece in which Barlow could convey the sense of the inexorable futility of all human efforts at his best—perhaps also thanks to Lovecraft's supervision and smoothing of the prose. In this tale, the authors masterfully combine the detailed and scientifically irreproachable description of mankind's decline as a race and gradual disappearance from the earth (part I of the narrative) with a second part in which the story chronicles the life and the conclusion of Ull's existence—the *last* man to have breathed on the planet. Part I is textured with sundry desolating pictures of the dwindling of the race, parallel to the earth's progressive drying up. Details are realistic and carefully portrayed: "The ever-present heat, as earth drew nearer to the sun, withered and killed with pitiless rays" (EG 43). As an animal species, mankind for long eras managed to fight the growing heat by adapting itself through mutation, and modeling "to fit the more and more torrid air" (EG 43). However, as the temperature became ultimately intolerable, "a gradual recession began, slow yet deliberate" (EG 43). Barlow and Lovecraft face the description of the race's fate with scientific precision: first, the towns near the equator are abandoned, followed by others in time—and in the end, the problem is truly "scientific": mankind is destined to extinct because, as a living species, it proves unable to adjust its evolution to the pace of the change: "Man, softened and exhausted, could cope no longer with the ruthlessly mounting heat. It seared him as he was, and evolution was too slow to mould new resistances in him" (EG 43). In comparison to the stories of "connotative" cosmicism seen before, this bitter description again pictures the inadequacy of the race—but this time, on a physical level, and the vision is so desolate and hopeless as to exclude the appearance of any irony.[17]

The images employed to depict the race's gradual but inexorable extinction are at the same time scientifically correct and bleakly "moral": in fact, while never contradicting the most likely knowledge on mankind's end available at the time, these literary images do not give up attacking man's meanness, ignorance, and psychological inadequacy. The puerile attempts of the first men who tried to fight the progressive drying up of their lands constitute the signs of both their stubbornness and their lack of comprehension—elements that underscore how pitiful and pathetic are the race's efforts (and, above all, its initial, deceiving successes) to preserve its past grandeur:

> Yet not at first were the great cities of the equator left to the spider and the scorpion. In the early years there were many who stayed on, devising curious shields and armours against the heat and the deadly dryness. These fearless[18] souls, screening certain buildings against the encroaching sun, made miniature worlds of refuge wherein no protective armour was needed. They contrived marvellously ingenious things, so that for a while men persisted in the rusting towers, hoping thereby to cling to old lands till the searing should be over. (EG 44)

If these efforts are childish and unfounded, but somehow justifiable in light of man's inner tendency toward the preservation of the status quo, much less acceptable is his nonsensical, superstitious negation of the scientific and rational truth, as the following passage testifies through the final resort to a confrontation between man and powerfully gloomy, stark images of death and desolation:

> For many would not believe what the astronomers said, and looked for a coming of the olden worlds again. But one day the men of Dath, from the new city of Niyara, made signals to Yuanario, their immemorial ancient capital, and gained no answer from the few who remained therein. And when explorers reached that millennial city of bridge-linked towers they found only silence. There was not even the horror of corruption, for the scavenger lizards had been swift. (EG 44)

This is what is ultimately to become of the human dwellers: food for reptiles. However, more than the scientific accuracy of the authors' description of the earth's and mankind's end, what concerns us here are the existential reflections

---

17. Perhaps the fact that HPL collaborated on the tale may represent a justification for its lack of irony (for a discussion of RHB's and HPL's different viewpoints on the use of irony in literature, see chapter 7).

18. I do not believe any irony can be attached to this adjective—though, probably, this is the only passage in the tale where the issue is disputable.

upon the role of the race on a cosmic scale that the analytical descriptions of the progressive degeneracy of mankind stir in Barlow's and Lovecraft's pens. Mankind demonstrates its weakness as an animal species, being unable to face efficiently the physical hardships of the new situation. The degeneracy of material living conditions also affects the culture, the institutions, the morality, and the traditions of the race. And certainly this is a fault and weakness on mankind's part, the fact that it worries more about the material aspects of its survival than of the cultural and moral ones: "A degeneracy both physical and cultural set in with the insidious heat. For man had so long dwelt in comfort and security that this exodus from past scenes was difficult. Nor were these events received phlegmatically; their very slowness was terrifying. Degradation and debauchery were soon common; government was disorganized, and the civilizations aimlessly slid back toward barbarism" (EG 45). Not caring for its own civilization, this is probably—in Lovecraft's, and transitionally in Barlow's, eyes—the worst, most unforgivable crime mankind could commit.

This crime is accompanied by the resurgence of moral chaos among human beings, uncontrolled reactions and feelings—in a word, a frenzied *madness* gets possession of the people's souls. In front of mortal danger, human nature reveals its most proper trait: a renewed irrationality and amorality overwhelms the survivors' behavior: "When, forty-nine centuries after the blight from the equatorial belt, the whole western hemisphere was left unpeopled, chaos was complete. There was no trace of order or decency in the last scenes of this titanic, wildly impressive migration. Madness and frenzy stalked through them, and fanatics screamed of an Armageddon close at hand" (EG 45). The irrational and nonsensical behavior of the last survivors is mercilessly condemned as a vain and foolish reaction. The words of contempt employed to describe it, and to define mankind in general, are revealing of the authors' bitter depreciation of the race, an attitude that is not born of a prejudice on their part, but is the natural consequence of their objective observation of people's senseless and amoral reactions:

> Mankind was now *a pitiful remnant of the elder races*, a fugitive not only from the prevailing conditions, but from his own degeneracy. Into the northland and the Antarctic went those who could; the rest lingered for years in an incredible saturnalia, vaguely doubting the forthcoming disasters. In the city of Borligo a wholesale execution of the new prophets took place, after months of unfulfilled expectations. They thought the flight to the north was unnecessary, and looked no longer for the threatened ending. How they perished must have been terrible indeed—*those vain, foolish creatures who thought to defy the universe.* (EG 45; italics added)

These scathing words may perhaps sound too harsh at a surface reading, but their goal is not so much to depreciate the race uncritically and generically, but *in relation to its former claims for greatness and importance on a cosmic scale*. The targets of the authors' attacks are in fact mankind's conceit and presumptuousness.

The authors' account of the end of the race goes mercilessly on. After unrecorded millennia, water has grown dramatically scarce over the planet, and the sense of the slow but inevitable contraction of the human presence on earth is masterfully rendered ("So slow were these deadly changes, that each new generation of man was loath to believe what it heard from its parents" [EG 46]). The recurrence of words referable to the semantic fields of "pity" and "mercy" tells of the authors' choice both to underline the race's dramatic impotence to fight Nature's (and Time's) power and to strike an emotive chord in their readers: "Thus it was even at the end, when only a few hundred human creatures panted for breath beneath the *cruel* sun; a *piteous* huddled handful out of all the unnumbered millions who had once dwelt on the doomed planet. And the hundreds became small, till man was to be reckoned only in tens. [. . .] And so the last *pathetic* few dwindled" (EG 46; italics added). Barlow's and Lovecraft's narrative strategy consists of constantly comparing man's past (alleged) grandeur with his late, gradual though inexorable, miserable demise and mean fate. This aesthetic choice is of course a function of the authors' overall "philosophical" goal—to pillory man's irrational, "cosmic" conceit about his role in the universe's history.

The authors' position becomes gradually clearer through their denotative comments:

> Of the people of Earth's fortunate ages, billions of years before, only a few prophets and madmen could have conceived that which was to come—could have grasped visions of the still, dead lands, and long-empty sea-beds. The rest would have doubted... doubted alike the shadow of change upon the planet and the shadow of doom upon the race. *For man has always thought himself the immortal master of natural things*. . . . (EG 46; italics added)

Here the attack—strategically placed at the very end of the tale's first part—is open and direct, but it is not the only explicit one in this narrative. However, before the final attack on mankind's conceit that concludes the tale, the authors still want to underscore the inanity of human efforts, and the episode describing the journey of the last surviving man, Ull, to seek for fresh water and "the lost colony beyond the mountains" (EG 47) can be considered another proof of how man's deluding plans are destined to fail when they encounter the harsh truth.

As we have seen in other Barlovian narratives, the male protagonist is deluded till the very end. At first, in fact, a thirsty and exhausted Ull, from the highest top of a cliff, sees "a small huddle of buildings clung to the base of the farther cliff" (EG 48). It seems the old tales of his youth were true: a small group of survivors dwelt beyond the mountain range. Spurred by his discovery, Ull does not waste time in reaching the stone village, his whole being overwhelmed by the last, sweet self-inflicted illusions: "He fancied that he could detect forms among the rude cabins. [. . .] He could not be sure of details, but soon the cabins were near" (EG 48). Poignant and, from an aesthetic viewpoint, effective is this new picture of the painful contrast between man's plans and wishes on one side, and the starkness of a bleak reality on the other: "Before him an open door swung upon rude pegs. In the fading light Ull entered, weary unto death, seeking painfully the expected faces. Then he fell upon the floor and wept, for at the table was propped a dry and ancient skeleton" (EG 48).

The account of Ull's last moments produces a change in the general tone of the tale, because it mingles human pity and moral condemnation on the authors' part. The description of Ull's new, hopeless attitude is revelatory of the fact that *only now, when the recognition of the final doom is inevitable, mankind is prone to abandon its conceit*. Presumptuous till the very last, the race has finally understood—through its last member, Ull—how vain and senseless its past achievements (and, especially, the cosmic conceit they improperly aroused) were. The authors' lexical choices are carefully calibrated to obtain this "deflating" effect: the last man is now "aching unbearably" and "suffering the greatest disappointment any mortal could know" (EG 48); his is the "heritage of the Earth... all the lands, and all to him *equally useless*" (EG 48; italics added). Even when the last man finally sees a well-curb, awareness has by now overwhelmed him: he cannot truly rejoice over what he has found, his is just a "*pitiful joy*" (EG 48; italics added). Only now, when facing the ultimate doom, mankind recognizes its limits and finally understands that no authentic joy is possible, no presumptuousness is allowed—because our fate, in the end, does not allow them at all. The weakness and blame of mankind, in Barlow's and Lovecraft's view, lies just in the fact that the race is unable to recognize these simple truths *until it faces them directly and inescapably*. In other words, mankind's fault consists in its stubborn unwillingness to consider the so-called "fortunate ages" (EG 46) of Earth as what they really are, namely just a transitory, ephemeral, and ultimately insignificant moment when considered from the cosmic perspective of the universe's history. And when the "final, *pitiful* survivor" (EG 49; italics added) of the race perishes, all the meaninglessness of the old, "optimistic" vision will be dramatically revealed. And the bitterly provocative moral that the authors attach to "'Till A' the Seas,'" concentrating it in the caustic final lines discussed in paragraph 4.2.1, advances the disquieting question: was it really worthwhile, during the "fortunate ages" of the race, to cultivate the unfounded illusions of a cosmic conceit and grandeur, if the final result of all human efforts, toiling, and achievements will be such an utter and devastating *nothingness*?

"A Dim-Remembered Story" and "The Night Ocean" represent two further powerfully "cosmic" tales adding significant insight to Barlow's denotative discussion of the emptiness and frailty of human existence. Some poignant, bitter reflections upon the vanity of mankind's role in the universe are certainly destined to mark Barlow's most mature work as one of "existential" cosmicism. I will discuss a few of them, beginning with "A Dim-Remembered Story," in which the starkness of the cosmic visions of a far future—when all the universe will be wiped out without, again, leaving a trace—allows the narrator to comment on the transitoriness and ultimate inanity of everything human on the cosmic scale. The most interesting aspect of these passages is perhaps the sarcastic, bitter irony they arouse in the narrator while deflating mankind's silly presumptuousness during the "fortunate" times of the past: "Mankind was a dream, and the earth a bright, nostalgic memory. There was no record of how our world perished. Somewhere in the great maze a star winked out. Only that, and all of humanity was gone—*the splendid dreams, the bravery of that race* which I had known (long since) when it was young. *Man, great, assured, and invincible, was now obliterated*" (EG 101; italics added). Man's passage on earth can be assimilated to the playing of a drama (and, let us note, a *comedy*, the least solemn of plays), with the universe equivalent to a stage. Once, at the end of times, the play is ended, curtains hide the scene and nothing remains of the allegedly magnificent performance: "and trembling my consciousness waited; as if I sat before a darkened stage, seeking the rise of a curtain. But the comedy was played, and all the actors gone. Blank, hideous, supreme, devastating, the eternal naught remained" (EG 102). The only feeling left for the disembodied observer—but one who still retains a human nature—is a "bitter and forlorn" (EG 103) despair, when the curtains of the cosmic scenery will roll back over "the stage upon which universes enact a brief, tragic drama" (EG 100).

While "A Dim-Remembered Story" presents existential reflections on a more cosmic level—since they are mainly connected with the final "celestial" visions of the narrator—"The Night Ocean" provides piquant comments upon the vanity and inconsistency of humanity in its terrestrial transitory experience. At his first sight of the little house on the beach, the narrator already recognizes the awareness he and the house share of their common meaninglessness in the face of the vast cosmos, metaphorized in the image of the sea: "I thought the little house was lonely when I saw it, and that like myself, it was conscious of its meaningless nature before the great sea" (EG 106). The smallness of mankind in relation to the immensity of the cosmos—always represented by the vastness of the sea[19]—is a leitmotif of Barlow's existential discourse in "The Night Ocean," and is aptly conveyed by the words of the narrator, a proud spokesman of Barlow's and Lovecraft's cosmic indifferentism.[20] According to Humphreys, "the narrator's house and the town of Ellston both symbolically represent humanity: the house as individual and the town as society" (15), and certainly the open identification the narrator makes between himself and the house, in the above passage, adds to the correctness of Humphrey's observation—although, for the cosmic discourse it entails, the most important metaphor in the tale is certainly the one that links the inhabitants of the town to mankind in general.

The above passage is, in fact, worth mentioning here, mainly because it explicitly deals with the ignorance and foolishness of man, who stubbornly refuses to acknowledge his own insignificance in the face of the cosmic vista. The community of Ellston Beach is in fact described as "a throng of foolish marionettes perched on the lip of the ocean-chasm; *unseeing, unwilling to see*, what lay above them and about, in the multitudinous grandeur of the stars and the leagues of the night ocean" (EG 107; italics added). The target of Barlow's darts is still man's

---

19. Humphreys too writes of the "cosmic symbolism of the ocean" (21).
20. Humphreys agrees on this when claiming that "He [the tale's narrator] reflects both HPL's and RHB's philosophic beliefs: cosmic indifferentism" (15).

dullness, his incapacity and lack of will to acknowledge the true, eternal grandeur of the "stars and the leagues of the night ocean," and not that of the transitory and ephemeral animal species to which he belongs. Man is surrounded by a "naked and impenetrable void" (EG 107), and the only possible correct feeling he should nurture is the narrator's perception of his own "*inconceivable smallness*" (EG 107; italics added) against the immensity of that void. On the other hand, man is silly and foolish, and from his nonsensically anthropocentric perspective he goes on deceiving himself about his importance: "It was astonishing the number of useless things people found to do" (EG 107) in order to keep their minds occupied, in order not to think of that lacerating smallness and vanity that an individual such as the narrator, observing the scene from the relativistic-cosmic perspective, recognizes.

Further discussing his metaphorical opposition between the house and the town, Humphreys correctly claims that "The town is representative of the shallow people within, who are less than agreeable to the narrator. They do not comprehend their insignificance, so, in a symbolic sense, neither does the town" (15). However, as we said, the town and the behavior of its inhabitants are the metaphors for those of society—and thus of mankind in general. Therefore, like the inhabitants of the town, man in the tale is considered a marionette playing the comedy of life at his own ephemeral advantage, deluding himself through frivolous actions which only serve, childishly, to hide the inconsistency and the fear of living. The metaphor of man as a "marionette" playing a trifling part on the stage of life returns a few pages later in "The Night Ocean": "and the town had closed the resorts where mad frivolity ruled empty, fear-haunted lives, and where *raddled puppets performed their summer antics*" (EG 117; italics added). But man keeps on deluding himself through useless action and by exercising an improbable thought, as is testified by the groundless explanations for the mysterious deaths of swimmers during that fatal summer: people attribute the cause of the deaths to the attacks of unseen sharks, simply as a result of their minds' "epistemic" incapacity to face the unknown source of those demises—but not a true "rationale" is attached to these explanations: "Whether the bodies showed marks of any attacks I did not learn, but the dread of a death which moves among the waves and comes on lone people from a lightless, motionless place is a dread which men know and do not like" (EG 110).

Man's behavior—both "operational" and "speculative"—does not pass the test of Barlow's examination under any viewpoint: his attitude is always to be condemned, because it originates from the wrong perspective, the anthropocentric one that guiltily causes man unfailingly to believe in his supposed grandeur and not to take into necessary account the cosmic futility of his actions, achievements, and explanations. According to Barlow, the bleak truth is painful, and it must emotionally overwhelm the honest thinker, as the following harrowing passage (a fully Barlovian creation, as inferable from analysis of the manuscript with Lovecraft's interpolations) attests: "I felt, *in brief agonies of disillusionment*, the gigantic blackness of this overwhelming universe, in which my days and the days of my race were as nothing to the shattered stars; a universe in which each action is vain and even the emotion of grief a wasted thing" (EG 116; italics added).

There is not much to say about the sheer starkness of this umpteenth "existential" reflection; in fact, I have chosen to discuss another aspect of this passage: I have italicized the words underscoring the emotional consequences on the narrator of these bleak considerations on the role of mankind. Though Barlow shared Lovecraft's cosmic perspective and all its consequences on the "existential" level, perhaps he sensed, more dramatically than his master, the moral impact of this cosmic attitude on his own existence. Due to his intellectual honesty, Barlow could not avoid thinking *bleakly* of mankind as Lovecraft did, but Barlow's awareness of the stark state of things *caused him pain*, those "brief agonies of disillusionment" which, perhaps, may have played a role in his constant thoughts of death and in the way he ended his life. Thus it is not by chance that, right after the recognition of the "agonies of disillusionment" that his cosmic perspective causes him, the Barlovian voice of "The Night Ocean" unquestionably thinks of suicide when claiming to be overwhelmed by "an indolence like that of a man who no longer cares to live" (EG 116). Torn by an unbearable—because ultimately vain when confronted with the vast and eternal cosmos—existence that is no more than a trick in which humans are trapped,[21] Barlow's narrator—in contrast to the foolish and dull joy of the average, anthropocentric man—derives from his "hideous loneliness" (EG 116) the awareness of his fatal and inescapable doom. And again, he cannot help depicting the devastating emotional consequences of his somehow elitist[22] awareness on his whole being, and once again the following detailed psychological insight openly indicates suicide as the possible—perhaps the best—way to deal with existence:

> It was not a madness: rather it was a too clear and naked perception of the darkness beyond this frail existence, lit by a momentary sun no more secure than ourselves[23]; a realization of futility *that few can experience* and ever again touch the life

---

21. In "Return by Sunset," Barlow employs the disturbing but somehow poetical image of the "lamentations of the night-wind, who mourns that man should even have been *tricked into existence*" (EG 135; italics added).

22. Humphreys is convinced that RHB devised the narrator as a non-average person, independently from the events he is involved in at Ellston Beach: "From the beginning of the story, even before anything unusual happens, his set of beliefs sets him apart from the average person" (14), though the issue of the origin of the narrator's cosmic attitude—whether derived from his experience at Ellston or from his inner nature—seems quite idle to me. However, Humphreys seems of another opinion and discusses the issue at length (14-15).

23. RHB once more resorts to his favorite contrastive image of light vs. darkness in order to represent his narrator's attempts to shed light over a cosmic truth hidden by the darkness of man's ignorant estimation of existence as "worthy," as Humphreys correctly points out: "The narrator uses three items to break through the darkness: a flashlight, a lamp, and a cigarette. These items serve symbolically to demonstrate his personal insignificance as the vast night surrounds him, and his vain attempts to break through the darkness of

about them: a knowledge that turn as I might, battle as I might with all the remaining power of my spirit, I could neither win an inch of ground from the inimical universe, nor hold for even a moment the life entrusted to me. (*EG* 116; italics added)

In this passage I would like to point out the significance of the "elitist" attitude Barlow shows—one that Lovecraft shared—toward his reflections: they are not conclusions available to *anybody*, because the great majority of people are neither able nor willing to endorse the cosmic perspective on existential matters, and prefer to dwell in the relaxing and—in their eyes—rewarding ignorance allowed by the anthropocentric view. On the other hand, for those, like Barlow, who care for their intellectual honesty, the achievement of cosmic truth causes—at least for the former—a painfully "hideous loneliness" and, perhaps, the wish to suicide: this is the very high price Barlow has to pay in order not to deceive himself, and to be truthful to himself till the very last. The prize he reaches is valuable to his eyes *from an intellectual and speculative viewpoint*, though the cosmic attitude he endorses of course does not help to change the state of the affairs: man is asked to share cosmic indifferentism because this is what his intellectual honesty requires in order for him to dispel the darkness of ignorance and achieve the light of truth—no matter how emotionally disturbing and destructive the operation may result—but this rational attitude has, of course, ultimately *no power to change the stark truth itself*. Shedding the temporary light of comprehension, like a "momentary sun," over the imperial darkness of this "frail existence" will not alter that frailty, inconsistency, and vanity, and will ultimately leave the overwhelming obscurity untouched and triumphant: "The narrator cannot escape the darkness. His frail beacons only heighten the narrator's sense of loneliness and unimportance" (Humphreys 20), and can do nothing to fight the "unstoppable onslaught of the night, which will eventually cover all and indicate the final victory of the unknown and the outside over humanity, the earth, and the cosmos itself" (ibid.). And at the very end of history, when the thick blanket of eternal night shall enshroud each and every human and non-human achievement, man will not even be granted the applause that also marionettes deserve, because "the grand finale of the comedy of existence will be played in an empty theatre, and for a long vanished audience" (ibid.).

4.2.2.2 Deterministic compulsion and its impact on free will

The theme of this paragraph is significantly present in Barlow's fiction as a tool the author employs to reinforce his non-anthropocentric discourse about the limits and weaknesses of humanity as a race. In this sense, the presence of this theme may certainly be considered functional to a cosmic discourse, since the effect achieved is that of further belittling humanity's faculties and powers. The goal of

---

ignorance regarding the cosmos" (19).

this theme's employment consists, in fact, in underlining the incapacity of man even to control his own actions, and his lack of jurisdiction even over his own will. The picture this theme contributes to create is therefore one of a weak species, depreciated in one of its most distinguishing powers—namely, rational and independent control over its will—signaling its alleged "superiority."

The two acceptations under which the theme of *deterministic compulsion*—as it seems proper to me to label it—appears in Barlow's fiction are:

1. a cosmic force driving the character and depriving him of his free will. Under this viewpoint, as we shall see, Barlow is receptive of Lovecraft's lesson about fictional determinism and atomism;
2. a conditioning power of a preordained fate that man cannot fight nor overcome.

Before illustrating how Barlow's fiction develops the theme of *deterministic compulsion* as part of its cosmicistic discourse, I would like to make a short reference to a possibly revelatory passage he wrote in 1944 (as part of his autobiography) that shows how Barlow felt, also in his life, a sort of urgency to fulfill what he perceived as preordained "patterns" of action and behavior. This existential "deterministic attitude" may well be said to form, at least partly, a justification for Barlow's literary interest for the treatment of the theme of the deterministic compulsion, etherodirected on his fictional characters by external, irresistible forces. The passage in question has the flavor of a general comment Barlow makes on his own overall psychological attitude; his inclination to think and behave in a kind of "fatalistic" way is not referred to a specific phase of his life, but appears more as an ingrained and lifelong trait of his mental frame, one that almost obsessively searches for the fulfillment of a preordained pattern as the only source for contentment, thus almost rejecting, in fear, the perspective of the void represented by "free choice":

> One of my compulsions has been to know and see and do certain things; to have lived in certain places almost as if fulfilling a pattern imposed by the stars. I think I have done this in order to show myself a person of wide and sophisticated experience. I have lived, in a sense, consciously acquiring material for an autobiography. I must live in the Bohemian quartier of San Francisco; I must read *An American Tragedy*[24]; I must go on expeditions into the Mexican sierra—not because I enjoyed these things, but because it fitted the pattern. A truth was formulated by a babe and fool, the gorgeous blond boy with whom I was infatuated at the age of eighteen. He [. . .] commented, 'I don't think you have an ounce of enjoyment in your whole body'. And I don't, except in the smooth fulfilment of my varied compulsions. When I have a period of free time and the choice of activity, I am most discontent. [. . .] *At these times of 'free choice' I am most wretched.* Pleasure is for me a calm fulfilling the pattern of work, writing something or learning something, which I have convinced myself 'must' be done. (OLL 19)

---

24. The celebrated novel by Theodore Dreiser, published in 1925.

I shall discuss now a few examples of Barlow's fiction, among several possible ones, where the theme of deterministic compulsion is more effectively present—simultaneously trying to point out the elements of indebtedness and originality of Barlow's treatment of the theme with respect to Lovecraft's model.

I have selected a few passages excerpted from two tales in particular, "Origin Undetermined" and "Return by Sunset."[25] However, "The Night Ocean" already features a glimpse of this theme, as can be inferred by this sentence toward the end of the tale, when the unnamed narrator prepares—from inside his abode—to watch the final horror of the night ocean: "Gradually there passed into that never-stirring landscape a brilliance intensified by the overhead glimmerings, *and I seemed more and more under some compulsion to watch whatever might follow*" (EG 118; italics added). It is useful—as shall appear clear later with the analysis of Lovecraft's model—to notice that the scene spreading out in front of the bewildered observer's eyes is illuminated by the moon's "cruel brilliant rays" (EG 118), and that the presence of the desolate vista of a deadly moon (together with that of the powerful and sentient sea) dominates the whole physical and psychological scenery in which the narrator is placed: "The endless tableau of the lunar orb—dead now, whatever her past was, and cold as the unhuman sepulchres she bears amid the ruin of dusty centuries older than man—[. . .] confronted me with a horrible vividness" (EG 118). As we shall see, it is significant that the appearance of the theme of "deterministic compulsion" in Barlow's fiction is often accompanied by that of the earth's satellite, as also to underscore the cosmic perspective under which the theme should be considered.

"Origin Undetermined" features again, and more extendedly, the "lunar" version of the theme of deterministic compulsion. This time the protagonist, Heywood Roberts, has a vision—induced by the unfathomable influence of a plant from an outside dimension—in which he "sees" himself in a dark open place, made of vast fields surrounded by a range of high mountains on the western rim. The narrator's uncertainty in the determination of the mountains' size and distance is probably reminiscent, as we shall see, of the analogous plea of the narrator in Lovecraft's "Dagon": "I could not tell their size or distance from me. I think they must once have been very huge, their peaks now broken away by the trampling of centuries" (EG 128-29). The moon immediately enters the scene and prophesies the emergence of the theme of deterministic compulsion: "Then suddenly the moon swung clear, disgorged by the ravenous cirri. Clean, high, and brittle, a chiselled gem of light set against dusky enamel, it spun as the central maelstrom of heaven. A gulf of light remained where the clouds had been, and the corridors of outer space were disclosed, but there was still no star anywhere. I stared, *and then, without knowing why, began to walk in the direction of the mountains*" (EG 129; italics added). The figurative tool of the moonlit *compelled walk* toward a mountain range reminds us—as we shall see—of Lovecraft's employment of an

---

25. Of course, also "The Summons" provides significant samples of the treatment of this theme, but space limitations prevent discussion of it here.

analogous image in tales such as "Dagon" and "The Shadow out of Time."[26] This is Barlow's version:

> These [the mountains] had assumed a third dimension, and were no longer ragged outlines, but solid, angular, and pyramidal masses having no modifying curve. A few great peaks and crevices *gleamed skull-white in the moon*. Indeed, the whole enormous plain, which continued to suggest a stage or gaming-board, was deluged by those *almost liquid rays*, displaying illimitable miles of spongy sand extending dreary and uniform about me. In a half dozen places, all of them distant, some dark material which I judged to be vegetation lay on the ground in dim irregular splotches. One of these was between me and the *strangely compelling mountain range*. Presently I would encounter it and discover its nature. (EG 129; italics added)

It is by now clear that Barlow's references abound to Lovecraft's similar treatment of the theme of "deterministic compulsion" through the employment of the images of a "forced walk"—often under a plain or desert lit by the malignant radiance of an almost sentient moon. For instance, the narrator of "Dagon," in order to account for and justify his goalless walk on the resurfaced earth of a nightmarish land, claims to be "urged on by an impulse which I cannot definitely analyse" (CC 3), just as Nathaniel W. Peaslee in "The Shadow out of Time" (1934-35) candidly admits that his walk through the Australian moonlit desert, in search for the aeons-old ruins of the Great Race's city, was unintentional: "I seemed to move almost automatically, as if in the clutch of some compelling fate" (*Shadow out of Time* 74). Just as, in Barlow's tale, the diseased and deadly pallid moonlight accompanies Roberts's dream-walk, similarly Professor Peaslee's resurfacing from the chasms of the prehistoric desert ruins is backgrounded against the "evil, monotonous beating of that maddening moonlight" (89), while the "bloated, fungoid moon" (90) has "a white, leprous radiance which seemed to me somehow infinitely evil" (70). Similarly personified is the moon hovering over the dreamland traversed by the protagonist of "Dagon": the gradually ascending moon is depicted as "waning and fantastically gibbous" (CC 3), and its rays make the dark obelisk in the river chasm "gleam whitely" (CC 4) as with a deadly pallor. The horror of the revelation comes to the shipwrecked man thanks to the moonlight that "shone weirdly and vividly above the towering steeps that hemmed in the chasm, and *revealed* the fact that a far-flung body of water flowed at the bottom" (CC 4), as well as lit the hideous hieroglyphics on the carven surface of the mono-

---

26. By the time he wrote "Origin Undetermined" (August 1937), RHB had read both these Lovecraftian pieces. "Dagon" was one of the first "enclosures" HPL made to one of his letters to RHB (31 July 1931; FF 5), and the thirteen-year-old correspondent probably enjoyed the tale (in a postcard to RHB dated 11 August 1931, HPL wrote: "Glad you enjoyed 'Dagon'": FF 5). And of "The Shadow out of Time," RHB prepared a typescript during HPL's visit in Florida of mid-1935; HPL even half-seriously defined RHB as co-author of the tale: "You certainly ought to be listed as co-author of 'The Shadow out of Time', since but for you it would never have seen the light of circulation—or of print" (letter to RHB, 17 December 1935; FF 307).

lith and the apparition of the "stupendous monster of nightmares" (CC 5), a real sample from the Outside. And of the cosmically revelatory power of the moon(light) the narrator is aware, since, once brought back home, he dreamily "sees" the creature from Beyond "especially when the moon is gibbous and waning" (CC 6). Whenever, in Lovecraft's fiction, a narrative action takes place under the moonlight, we can almost be certain it will configure a "cosmic" experience—and this seems true also for his protégé's work.

Let us return to Barlow's narrative. Roberts's compelled walk toward the mountain range, lit by the cold rays of a ghastly and darkening moon, continues as if he were engulfed by the cosmic power of the satellite, which takes control over his will and guides his movements at its pleasure: "After half an hour's walk, during which the mountains grew no closer,[27] one of the dark patches loomed up somewhat to my left, and I altered my course to see what it was. The moon, however, was rapidly being engulfed by a precipice of clouds [. . .] that polished sphere sank into darkness. In a moment I was blundering along, and the scene a moment before so clearly displayed was swathed up in murk" (EG 129). Though he first gets entangled in vines of strange vegetation[28] and later he has to toil with the "mustiness" of the air to reach the peaks, Roberts's will cannot rebel against the silent order he is obeying and that controls his whole being: "but I felt poignantly that I must go on; that the secret of the place lying ahead was a thing worth

---

27. The description of this "hallucinatory" walk toward a mountain range that, against any physical and especially optical law, does not grow closer nor bigger as the traveler gets closer, probably pays homage to a couple of passages in HPL's "Dagon," where the narrator implicitly accounts of the *outsideness* of the geometry of the dream-land he is traversing as he states: "That night I encamped, and on the following day still travelled toward the hummock, *though that object seemed scarcely nearer than when I had first espied it*" (CC 3; italics added), and "By the fourth evening I attained the base of the mound, *which turned out to be much higher than it had appeared from a distance*" (CC 3; italics added). The sheer abundance and extent of Lovecraftian references in "Origin Undetermined" once more attest the strong influence of the Providence writer's imagery and techniques upon the literary efforts of his pupil. Also, the final and climactic lines of "Origin Undetermined," describing the protagonist's dramatically achieved decision to voluntarily end his life, are probably reminiscent, if not in content at least in the theatrical tone, of the "Dagon" narrator's manifested wish to die by jumping from a window (here replaced by a "furnace"): "My bones and sinews bloat into jelly; the signature of death is written over me, and since death alone can cleanse forever, I shall meet and welcome it. Only a moment is left, and now, while I am still able, I must get down to the furnace" (EG 132). And this is the conclusion of HPL's "Dagon": "The end is near. I hear a noise at the door, as of some immense slippery body lumbering against it. It shall not find me. God, *that hand! The window! The window!*" (CC 6; Lovecraft's italics).

28. As this is a dream-vision, the narrator is probably mingling it with the "reality" of the strange plant from Outside provoking his dream. This is also revealed by the sensation of being traversing an area of "stifling dead air" (130), probably caused by the presence of the lethal plant in the vicinity of the dreamer's couch.

of all conceivable effort to attain; that those mountains were guardians of some boundless mystery of precious and eternal significance" (*EG* 130).[29]

The pervasiveness of the theme of "deterministic compulsion" within both the figurative repertoire and the sheer plot of "Origin Undetermined" is testified also by Roberts's final revelation, where he admits *he* was the one who stole the urn containing the seeds of the malignant vegetable—but of course he did so under the influence of an undecipherable external volition, the "indeterminacy" of whose "origin" is the titular one:

> Of the mysteries confronting me I have solved one at least, though it is the least provocative. I stole the urn myself. Of this I am convinced. My fingerprints were thick about the broken case, and my inner consciousness shrieks out the vandal's name. *A compulsion must have been upon me*, a compulsion streaming from that malignant urn. *How or why I do not know*. And it was in the fulfilment of a kindred command that I planted those seeds. [. . .] Perhaps my mission was only to release the seeds, by whatever means lay at hand. They had been sealed up a long time ago; but for my act they might have remained forever so. (*EG* 132; italics added)

Man's actions are dominated by an external will: just like the "marionettes" and "puppets" mentioned in "The Night Ocean," Roberts is moved by an invisible force, a cosmic one depriving him of his free will. Men only *presume* to act consciously and willingly as free beings, but in truth they are slaves, puppets, mere executors of a foreign and unfathomable cosmic scheme, to be fulfilled through compulsion.

The delicate and prose-poetic "Return by Sunset" provides not only another interesting example of a cosmic, external force driving human actions according to its own scheme, but also a narrative representation of the workings of an inescapable, preordained fate not allowing man to be master and ruler of his own existence.

A couple of examples may suffice to illustrate the narrative rendering of these themes in "Return by Sunset." The key event itself of the story—namely, Leyenda's finding of the fatal bracelet and the doom it will bring upon her and perhaps her companion Dal—is the result of the working of a cosmic scheme uncontrollable by man. After she washes and polishes the bracelet in the mossy ba-

---

29. Let us note incidentally that it is easy to detect here, in the narrator's overall insistence over the unfathomable, cosmic mystery and significance of the "mountains of dream" (132), more than a tip of the hat to the Lovecraftian symbolic topos of the "mountains of madness." In fact, also Barlow's mountains hide a terrible secret: at first a pallid, gleaming light appears, evoking a "nameless emotion" (130) in the narrator. His reference to the possible presence of a city "beyond those precipitate barriers" (130) of course points to the city of the Old Ones in *At the Mountains of Madness*. The obvious Lovecraftian reference of this passage reinforces the interpretation of the bulk of "Origin Undetermined" as a deliberate, posthumous homage to Lovecraft's literature (thus including tales as "Dagon" and "The Shadow out of Time").

sin of the ruined temple, she is eventually able to make out the picture impressed on the metal:

> It had been hammered in with a small pointed instrument, and showed a figure lying in chains before an altar. She must have found a part of the ceremonial ornaments used by the keepers of the temple; and though all the old gods were discredited, Leyenda was uneasy. She knew her own god, the dog-faced image lying in the swamp two weeks' journey behind, would not like this uncovering of his predecessor. All the ruins, spiritual and temporal, of the old days were held suspect by the tribes, which sometimes wandered through them, *but she wanted to keep her bracelet. Without conscious volition*, Leyenda wedged her arm into it so tightly that she found it would not come off. *She had not intended to do so*—but there it was. (EG 138; italics added)

This passage allows us to add an important detail to our discussion of Barlow's treatment of "deterministic compulsion": while in "Origin Undetermined" no conscious opposition was expressed—by the "victim" of the external influence—against the force that determined his will, "Return by Sunset" features a character, Leyenda, who wishes to act differently from the way she is compelled (she does not wish the bracelet to hold her arm tightly and with no possibility to take it away), but the result is inevitable anyway. The passage presents a *struggle of wills* between the human and the cosmic, and Barlow's fiction could not allow a doubt as to who is going to "win." Even when man becomes aware of the compulsion and hetero-determination he is a victim of, any struggle is useless to reaffirm his will and make it triumph.

The second passage from "Return by Sunset" I would like to quote contains the convincing example of a character—again, youthful and doomed Leyenda—becoming aware of her being the puppet and executor of a preordained, external scheme and fate. While reflecting now—after some days of forced rest in the ruined temple, due to Dal's ankle injury—upon the late events and the whole *sense* of her and Dal's escape from her brothers' anger and revenge, Leyenda realizes that all that experience was meant by an unwritten Fate as the fulfillment of its scheme, and that there is thus *no point in mourning or lamenting because things went differently from Dal's and Leyenda's plans*—it would be like rebelling against the humidity of water or the greenness of grass:

> She sensed somehow, but in an inarticulate way, that these ruined sunsets, like blood running across the decks of wicked defeated ships as they nosed down to doom, were not isolated and meaningless phenomena, but that *they had all along presaged the now apparent tragedy. A tragedy so high and exquisite that mournfulness was not even to be thought of. Their fate was linked to the ruins; their coming and abiding had been destined.* (EG 141; italics added)

In fact, Dal's and Leyenda's cosmic fate, the expression of the "inscrutable plan of things" ("A Dim-Remembered Story," *EG* 88), simply overcomes their will and uses them in order to carry out its plans—and no doubt, once the plan is achieved, it will dismiss them as unusable tools. According to Barlow, this is the "tragic" scheme everything human inevitably follows, and man's realization of this inevitability should perhaps prevent him from the temptation of a torturing—though, for some, consoling—"mournfulness."

4.3 Vastness of the universe and cosmic Outsideness

This last aspect of Barlow's cosmicism I am going to discuss basically involves the reflection upon the vastness of the universe and the aesthetic feelings it entails (admiration, horror, wonder, awe) in the observer, as well as upon the aesthetic reactions the cosmic experience arouses in the experiencer; its psychological and moral attachments (the realization of the inconsequentiality, transitoriness, and ultimate vanity of human efforts) have already been treated in the previous paragraph on the cosmic inanity of mankind's experience and role in the universe. Therefore we are now going to deal only with the aesthetics of cosmicism.

In other words, in this paragraph I shall discuss the "cosmic perspective" in its most traditional acceptation, the most "scientific" one since dealing with the perception humans have of the (mainly astronomical) vastness of the universe. Barlow's fiction is textured along several reflections upon the frailty and smallness of mankind as a race *when confronted with the (astronomical) immensity of the cosmos*, and upon the baffled reactions of human beings when forced to undergo a cosmic experience. Among the most effective are certainly some lines featured in Barlow's cosmic tale par excellence, "A Dim-Remembered Story." These lines are placed—in the guise of a meta-textual insertion introducing the narration proper—as an epitaph advising the reader of the necessity of endorsing a cosmic perspective in order to comprehend fully the meaning of what will follow, namely of a story of true cosmic value: "Look tonight at the stars. Let them overwhelm you in the postures of their bright dance. Face the vastness which they dot like silver bees, and sound with your own brain the mystery, hazarding at the inscrutable plan of things. *Then you will comprehend my tale*" (EG 88; italics added). And to better define what is really intended in the paradigmatic change required by the adoption of the "cosmic perspective" that the narrator asks his reader to endorse, we can resort to the following passage, though its inevitable metaphoricity may appear somehow clumsy due to the insufficiency of a rational language like the human to express a non-rational perspective:

> Gradually there was forced upon me the realization[30] that I had undergone *something enormously removed from man's experience*. In all the years of our race there has been no one else who can narrate such a tale. It was, viewed *in the perspective of what we call normality*, as alien and catastrophic as the approach of some celestial

---

30. We can detect here another sample of "deterministic compulsion"—of a cognitive kind—exerted on a Barlovian character by an external force.

derelict laden with fiery death. It involved abstrusenesses that might baffle Jeans or Eddington, perplex the greatest of our scientists. For it was a looping, of the real world with another no less real, but *more distant than the mind can hold*. Distant not in the scale of miles and light-years, but in another, less tangible, less conceivable, fashion. I do not wish to evade, but my fingers are reluctant to form the incredible words; though I underwent the experiences for which those words would stand. Trembling in the grasp of *cosmic nostalgia*, my whole frame was *wrenched by a shocking, tremendous emotion*. I suspected, now, that I was lost indeed; *lost forever in some alien eternity*. (EG 91; italics added)

This extremely rich passage strives to perform at least the three following "cosmicistic" tasks:

1. to depict—as best as it can—the nature of the cosmic experience. However, with its heavy resort to hyperbolic metaphors and images (the "approach of some celestial derelict laden with fiery death," the "looping of the real world with another no less real," etc.), the passage (perhaps intentionally) ends up just revealing the inability of the human mind to account denotatively for a "cosmic perspective" (the mind would not be able to "hold" the distance of the world "looping" with the "real" one, the "abstruseness" of the cosmic perspective would "baffle"—a very Lovecraftian term—even the best scientists);

2. to relativize the anthropocentric perspective as just one of the possible viewpoints on the cosmos (what we call "normality" is in fact defined just as *a* "perspective": the distance of the world "looping" with the real one cannot be accounted for, because such distance is not measurable according to the "normal" canons of miles and light-years—and this goes to show that what we call "normality" is simply a partial, limited perspective on the cosmos and its potentialities);

3. finally, to account for the aesthetic reactions of the human involved in the cosmic experience. The account involves both the rational and the emotional sides—but not the moral one. First, from the rational viewpoint, as it is predictable by the repeated references to the "alterity" of the cosmic experience, Barlow chooses to underline its utter "unrepeatability" through the canonical rational language: "my fingers are reluctant to form the incredible words," certainly because those words would describe a story that the narrator would prefer to forget. But the words hesitate to form in his mind because he feels they are *inadequate* to perform their narrative and cognitive task, because they would only imperfectly and imprecisely "stand" for those "experiences." Second, from the emotional viewpoint, man's attitude in front of cosmic alterity could not be but one of utter physical (and not simply cognitive) bafflement: while being assaulted by a "cosmic nostalgia," he "trembles" and we can almost figure him "wavering, staggering" as his "frame" gets "wrenched by a shocking, tremendous emotion." Whatever state the cosmic experience induces in

the protagonist, it involves not simply an epistemic but also a physical *shock*. And, by the way, the reader would probably be surprised, had he been told the opposite. The last, conclusive psycho-physical state in which the cosmic experiencer is left is one of loss—and, again, inevitably so: he feels "lost forever in some alien eternity," since this is the only possible outcome for a mind—like the human—used to a "normality" that the cosmic experience has, with its utter alterity and incomprehensibility, entirely and mercilessly disrupted. However, in spite of his detailed picture of man's emotional reactions in the face of the unknown, Barlow— coherently with his "humanity's deflation" strategy—does not miss a chance also to point out the ephemeral nature of these reactions: Man, in fact, is not even able to be constant and reliable in what he feels when confronting Outsideness. These are the words of the protagonist of "A Dim-Remembered Story," describing his emotional state subsequent to his initial shock following his realization of the alterity of his experience: "Even the greatest of sorrows cannot last. So brief are man's emotions that when the height of fear or passion has been reached, the emotion ebbs like a tide slipping oceanward [. . .] The fresh sun was quieting, and my darkness-nurtured fears perished like fungi brought into the light from an unclean hole. Morning was new, and I was strengthened by the reassurance of day" (EG 97-98).[31]

Though deflating of humanity's faculties and achievements as all this may be, it certainly is *comprehensible* that a human being, confronted with the vastness of the cosmos, or involved in "cosmic" journeys and experiences through space and time, may in the end feel "small" and insignificant.

Much less flattering and "comprehensible" is that a very similar feeling is aroused in man when confronting much less awe-inspiring vistas or events—when confronting even *his own creations*. In other words, the "sense of smallness" may come to man not only from his confrontation with the vastness of the cosmos, but also with the vastness of less "imposing" sights: for instance, simple buildings—although charged with a "cosmic" value by their sheer antiquity. Barlow's fiction does not fail, ruthlessly, to touch upon this chord also—and certainly this falls within Barlow's general "conceptual" strategy to stage the narrative deflation of mankind and make the attacks against mankind's presumptuousness even more poignant and destructive. A pair of examples may illustrate this point.

As early as in February 1931, at the time of the composition of "An Episode in the Jungle," posthumously considered the eleventh and last installment of the *Annals of the Jinns*, Barlow depicts the feeling of insignificance that pervades a

---

31. Everything human is perishable and transient, and man is such a creature of habit that he cannot even hope that the cosmic experience will completely change his nature. As we shall see, after the initial shocking impact of the contact with Outsideness, man in fact starts again to try to rationalize the cosmic experience and assign to it a "humanly comprehensible" meaning.

human being, young hunter Loman, when facing the remnants of the architecture of the old peoples of his race, lost in the Yondath forest from time immemorial. After he has "twice glimpsed buttresses crouching[32] against the yellow sky beyond leagues of uninvaded jungle," he can just feel "small and brief in the presence of such things," because they attest man's effort to attain heights "defiant of the message of the stars" (EG 30): as it were, man's effort to become himself "cosmic"—and likewise in the face of anything of such nature, no matter who or what is the source of the "cosmic" element, the human being gets emotionally and cognitively embarrassed. Another significant narrative example of this feeling, induced in a human by the sight or simple "sense" of aeon-old buildings of the past grandeur of the race, can be found in "The Root-Gatherers." In search for roots and other edible items, the narrator and his mother have to traverse a forest surrounding an ancient lost place where a corpse-town is rumored to dwell—an impressive remnant of the past splendor of the narrator's ancestors. The protagonist has heard of the deserted town only in dim tales, and now the prospect of actually facing it fills him with mixed feelings made of aesthetic inspiration, astonishment, and cosmic relativism:

> When we were beyond the trees I looked at the small figure beside me, and felt a pang because of half-recollected stories of our ancient grandeur, when we had made cities like the dead one before us, and did not fear storms and animals. But then a glimpse of the most outlying ruin changed my thoughts, and *wonder* and *astonishment* hid from the knowledge that *we were frail and lonely and trivial* amid surroundings that thought of a vanished day. (EG 84; italics added)

This interesting passage shows the contrast occurring between the two components of the human frame: the rational mind (inclined to consider the "cognitive" consequences of the sight: we are frail in the face of this past grandeur) and the emotional side (which tends to obscure rational thought—*knowledge*—through the non-rational and uncontrollable feelings of "wonder" and "astonishment"). This subtle passage demonstrates how complex and non-univocal man's reaction

---

32. Words having "crouch-" as a root abound in RHB's fiction. This is probably another takeover from HPL, who used the term in the description of the statuette of Cthulhu offered by Inspector Legrasse to the examination of the scholars present in the annual St. Louis meeting of the American Archeological Society in 1908: "It represented a monster of vaguely anthropoid outline, but with an octopus-like head whose face was a mass of feelers, a scaly, rubbery-looking body, prodigious claws on hind and fore feet, and long, narrow wings behind. This thing, which seemed instinct with a fearsome and unnatural malignancy, was of a somewhat bloated corpulence, and squatted evilly on a rectangular block or pedestal covered with undecipherable characters. The tips of the wings touched the back edge of the block, the seat occupied the centre, whilst the long, curved claws of the doubled-up, *crouching* hind legs gripped the front edge and extended a quarter of the way down toward the bottom of the pedestal. The cephalopod head was bent forward, so that the ends of the facial feelers brushed the backs of huge fore paws which clasped the *croucher*'s elevated knees" ("The Call of Cthulhu," CC 148; italics added).

can be when he has to confront with the "cosmic" perspective, this time evoked not by a truly "cosmic" vista but by a sheer human creation—albeit one trying to attain the "heights of the stars."

This is certainly quite original, but Barlow's aesthetic rendering of the cosmic perspective becomes even more so when he, learning from Lovecraft's example and paying homage to him, evolves this theme and indulges in the cosmic visions dear to his master, in particular striving to convey the sense of an ultimate, unfathomable cosmic alterity—or Outsideness—lying in the universe close at hand, and available to man's perception. Barlow, in other words, often indulges in describing cosmic vistas of an utter Outsideness, and this attitude of his is functional to the general strategy informing his work, namely that of relativizing the human perspective and perceptions of the cosmos, the universe, and what can be labeled "reality" itself. That this strategy is often carried on from a perspective of praise for Lovecraft does not truly impair the overall originality of the project—let us not forget that the adoption of the cosmic perspective in weird literature was a remarkable aesthetic innovation of the 1920s and 1930s, and had Lovecraft among its most relevant advocates: Barlow simply—but acutely—recognized the Copernican novelty of Lovecraft's approach and followed in the line. Therefore it is not surprising that "A Dim-Remembered Story" is dedicated to Lovecraft, and that the subdivision of its four chapters is marked by the lines of the "cryptic" Alhazred couplet. The whole tale is built around the cosmic significance of the experience undergone by the narrator, especially from the temporal viewpoint—as will appear in the discussion on time of the next chapter. However, the Lovecraftian references and homages (in particular to such narratives as "The Call of Cthulhu," "Through the Gates of the Silver Key," and "The Shadow out of Time") abound so distinctly that they can be detected not only in connection with the temporal perspective, but also from the viewpoints of the cosmic imagery, the philosophical stances, the lexical choices, and even the (significant as well as secondary) plot elements. I will discuss some of these elements, those more patently referable to the treatment of the theme of cosmic Outsideness.

With regard to the plot structure, a couple of elements probably represent a homage to "The Shadow out of Time." First, the narrator's mention of the text originating from the Outside—written in a wholly undecipherable and thus utterly "other" language—that he finds in a room of the castle of the future in which he has unexplainably found himself is likely inspired by the episode of Peaslee's "manuscript": "I saw no books, but in a high room I found by torchlight the fragments of a damaged manuscript, written in unreadable characters. It bore no pictures and I was unable to discover anything familiar in the text" (*EG* 98). Moreover, at the end of his narration the protagonist of Barlow's tale reveals that his cosmic experience was, as it were, lived by his disembodied "soul," while his body was lying unconscious and in an almost comatose state in the house of the protagonist's brother: "I am told that I fainted in the street that morning and remained unconscious for some while. I was taken to my brother's home, and remained in a coma for several hours. During this time, my body scarcely held life. . . the pulse was dim and faint, the muscles limp as if I were newly dead" (*EG* 104). And again:

> I do not wish to indulge in spurious mysticism, for I merely seek the narration of a verity. So, you will understand that when my outward shape returned to 1936, to the month and day, perhaps to the second from which it came, the *other* component of my entity was swept immensely farther, parting wholly from my body, into the sucking whirlpool of time, whose flotsam is the stars. Into the great distances I went, to Infinity and her sheer end. It was ordained that, like a pendulum, my spirit must complete the far swing, where matter could not go. And thus for a while was my body returned, untenanted to earth; while I knew the terrors of the abyss, and all the pain thereof. (*EG* 104)

It is very possible that Barlow is here being inspired by, and paying homage to, Lovecraft's narrative device of introducing Peaslee's amnesia as an explanation for the period in which he underwent the cosmic experience of the mind-exchange with a member of the Great Race.[33]

Barlow's tale is also replete with typically Lovecraftian lexemes (as those having the roots "baffle-" and "crouch-") and images (as that of the "New Dark Age" that "set in" (*EG* 99)[34] in the temporal span between the narrator's times and those of his cosmic experience). It is in particular on the following "Lovecraftian" thematic aspect, imagery, and philosophical-scientific attitude that I shall concentrate my discussion of "A Dim-Remembered Story" and a few other passages taken from other tales, since they efficaciously account for Barlow's preponderant aesthetic concern for the theme of cosmic Outsideness:

1. the cognitive and "aesthetic" consequences of cosmic relativism, implying a radical change of perspective on life and experience (*thematic aspect* of Barlow's treatment of cosmic Outsideness);
2. the vision of an alien geometry similar to that of Lovecraft's R'lyeh and the cosmic flight of a disembodied soul à la Randolph Carter (a specific *imagery* Barlow adopts for his treatment of cosmic Outsideness);
3. the concern for the theme of suspension or even violation of natural and physical laws (a *philosophical-scientific attitude* attached to Barlow's treatment of cosmic Outsideness).

---

33. Professor Peaslee was defined as a case of "amnesia" by the doctors—his blank period lasting more than five years (14 May 1908-27 September 1913). Whatever the period of Peaslee's mind's "absence" from the body may be called scientifically, it was precisely during those years that he underwent the cosmic experience of mind-exchange with a member of the alien race—though of course HPL maintains, for aesthetic purposes, the vagueness and the doubt of the actual occurrence of the exchange till the very end of the novelette.

34. This image is of course reminiscent of the opening of "The Call of Cthulhu," where it is outlined the chance that "the peace and safety of a new dark age" (*CC* 139) of ignorance will overcome a humanity afraid of the piecing together of mind-shattering dissociated knowledge.

(1) The protagonist's inability to fully comprehend each detail of his cosmic experience attests, of course, to the inadequacy of the human, rational mind to perform its epistemic task when its object is a "cosmic" experience, namely one "resistant" to rationalization. There are several possible excerpts from the tale where the protagonist openly admits his failure to grasp the cognitive essence of the experience he is undergoing during his sojourn in the alien castle. The following passage may represent Barlow's aesthetic goal in this direction quite well, since it implicitly stages the human, rational mind's bafflement, and how it loses cognitive powers when the object to which those powers should actually be applied escapes and defies what the anthropocentric approach defines as a reassuring "normality." The final resort to a trite metaphor, an "as-if" description, constitutes the best proof of the inadequacy of the rational language to account *in a direct way* for an experience which is not rational—at least in the human, anthropocentric acceptation of what can be defined as such: "There was much that I did not ever understand. The incongruities of this narrative are due only to my *faulty comprehension*, a situation so different from that which I had known. I was inarticulate and lost, *as any savage taken from his tortuous jungle*" (EG 98; italics added).

An addition to the rendering of the cosmic Outsideness of the experience from a cognitive viewpoint invests of course the linguistic aspect: as the detail of the "damaged manuscript" mentioned above already showed, the protagonist's inability to fully comprehend the meaning of his experience is at least partly due to the fact that his mind cannot rely on its main cognitive instrument, the one through which it "organizes" reality and reduces it to the human schemes of interpretation: the (English) language. Once language is lost, *comprehension* is lost—and the inevitability of this equation is a further mark, according to Barlow, of the "limitation" and weakness of humanity as a race (this attitude of course reveals a truly relative, cosmic perspective on its bearer). And certainly in the castle of Yrn, no trace of the English language is detectable—not in written nor in spoken form: "I found signals carved over certain doors, in the time-blackened wood; which gave me great wonder, for like the words of these people these were unknown. No trace of the English tongue has gone to them, who are our descendants and the inheritors of earth" (EG 99).

However, in "A Dim-Remembered Story," the most original aspect of Barlow's cognitive and aesthetic treatment of the theme of cosmic Outsideness consists perhaps in the affirmation that, at a certain point, the protagonist effects an utterly *relative perspective*, namely that of his hosts in the alien future. Completely discarding the anthropocentric view that would force him to regard these people of a far future as foreign, incomprehensible, outlandish, perhaps hostile, and certainly bizarre, the protagonist operates a radical—I would say Copernican—change of perspective and strives to *put himself in his hosts' shoes*, and to interpret their possible thoughts and feelings—thus ultimately formulating the innovative notion that, in those circumstances, the foreign-incomprehensible-outlandish-perhaps hostile-certainly-bizarre individual—the real fragment from Outsideness—*may be he himself*. He is, indeed, the only person really out-of-place in that context: "On this third day the lord of Yrn was absent when I rose, and I did not see him afterward. To him *I came from the outside*, and left as strangely. *The mystery of my coming and disappearance must have been great to him.* For neither time was I warned—abrupt and sudden, the change came, and I was flung through time and space and universes in the great transition" (EG 99-100; italics added).

What is foreign, alien, *different*, is just a matter of opinion and, above all, point of view: the perception of Outsideness as such is simply the result of a choice of perspective, among the several possible, on the perceiver's part. The "cognitive shift" implied by this endorsing of a relativistic, "alien" perspective, besides revealing a maturity unusual in a writer not even eighteen, constitutes perhaps one of the most remarkable aesthetic achievements and novelties of Barlow's tale in the panorama of the weird fiction popular at his times—one that almost invariably—since it upheld limited anthropocentric perspective and judgment canons—presented the "alien" and the "foreign" as disgusting in outlook and reproachable, if not plainly "evil," in morality.

(2) "A Dim-Remembered Story" heavily relies upon cosmic images and visions in order to convey the sense of an altered, relativistic perspective. Among the most striking images in this sense, I have chosen to discuss two, particularly reminiscent of Lovecraft's figurative repertoire: the vision of an alien geometry recalling R'lyeh's, and that of a "cosmic" flight of a disembodied soul reminding Carter's in "Through the Gates of the Silver Key." Regarding the first image, this is how the narrator once more fights with human language (and resorts to the metaphor of the necklace) in order to describe the size, dimension, and sheer form of the light-balls he encounters during his cosmic vision of the ultimate void, and contextually in order to convey his own feelings as he confronts the mind-shattering vision:

> My world was gone, and with it, all worlds. Yet here before me, in the ultimate chill of a naked void, there clustered a group of living lights. Things from infinitely beyond Space; creatures from a place which no faltering word can make real. I feared them, not because they were evil-shaped, or because of their actions, but because they were great—for such greatness is terrible. There was more than fright upon me as I watched the globes at play. They built themselves in pyramids, and rapidly strung out, like a huge necklace athwart eternity. A myriad forms of *unearthly geometry* diverted them as they rolled and built, separated and shifted in kaleidoscopic array. (EG 102; italics added)

And in the "Epilogue" of the story, the narrator insists upon the "very wrong dimensions" of the place "existing in some alien eternity" (EG 103) that he "visited" during his cosmic experience. These references to alien and non-Euclidean geometry and dimensions constitute a patent homage to analogous images contained in Lovecraft's "The Call of Cthulhu," where in particular the notion of the geometrical *wrongness* of R'lyeh is recurrent. Already while telling his dream, the artist Wilcox thus describes the vision of Cthulhu's lair: "He talked of his dreams in a strangely poetic fashion; making me see with terrible vividness the damp Cyclopean city of slimy green stone—whose *geometry*, he oddly said, was *all wrong*" (CC 158).

But it is only with sailor Johansen's description of his actual seeing of the resurfaced R'lyeh that the notion of the *wrongness* of the geometry of the city is detailed through striking images of Outsideness:

> Without knowing what futurism is like, Johansen achieved something very close to it when he spoke of the city; for instead of describing any definite structure or building, he dwells only on broad impressions of vast angles and stone surfaces—surfaces too great to belong to any thing right or proper for this earth, and impious with horrible images and hyeroglyphics. I mention his talk about angles because it suggests something Wilcox had told me of his awful dreams. He has said that the geometry of the dream-place he saw was *abnormal*, non-Euclidean, and loathsomely redolent of spheres and dimensions apart from ours. [. . .] In those crazily elusive angles of carven rock where a second glance shewed concavity after the first shewed convexity. (CC 165-66)

In R'lyeh the impressions of a "wrong" geometry, totally conflicting with the elementary notions of the Euclidean one, as for instance those of horizontality and verticality, abound:

> It was [. . .] like a great barn-door; and they all felt that it was a door because of the ornate lintel, threshold, and jambs around it, though they could not decide whether it lay flat like a trap-door or slantwise like an outside cellar-door. As Wilcox would have said, *the geometry of the place was all wrong*. One could not be sure that the sea and the ground were horizontal, hence the relative position of everything else seemed phantasmally variable. (CC 166; italics added)

Let us return to Barlow's text. Although his homage to Lovecraft's cosmic imagery is probably undisputable in the entire tale, it is perhaps in the powerful cosmic visions that Barlow's protagonist faces in the form of a disembodied consciousness that the tip of the hat to the master's imagery is even more evident. In fact, all the visions of the "universes' rolling" in section IV, "Even Death May Die," are probably modeled on Randolph Carter's experience in "Through the Gates of the Silver Key." The opening of the fourth section of "A Dim-Remembered Story," with its abundant resort to cosmic images reflecting mankind's inanity on the universal scale, is certainly indicative of Barlow's imitation of Lovecraft's and E. Hoffmann Price's style and tone:

> I was caught up in the backwash of that incredible change. Like a swimmer in unknown waters, I was embraced by a moving wave. And upon the peak of that wave I was borne. . . carried into the heart of a black, unsailed ocean. Swiftly, I was swept into that sea, while the image of the castle swayed in my memory like a curtain in the breeze. And then, in a crescendo that was neither visual nor audient, the curtains of the universe rolled back, and before me was the stage upon which universes enact a brief, tragic drama. (*EG* 100)

This is of course the trifling drama of existence, both human and non-human. The visions the character experiences are truly of a different, altered nature and bear no resemblance to the accustomed human notions of geometry, physics, matter, etc.; he is projected into a congeries of unknown dimensions, in a far future hardly conceivable by the human mind, and in which the adoption of the usual human rationalizing notions (such as those of astronomy, or of spatial directions) becomes puerile nonsense. It is important to notice how Barlow constantly strives to render the utter alterity, difference, and *distance* of this experience from human canons: "Here, all the stars were *changed*. I was in some *altered cosmos*—the cosmos of future aeons, when not one star shall remain *as we know it*. It was hideous and stupefying to find *no recognised orb* in that realm. The night sky was great, *larger than my vision could embrace*, and everywhere about me was star-flecked darkness, and at my feet a chasm of night. I say above and below, for these are terms that come to my mind, *but there were no true directions*" (EG 100; italics added). And finally the most shocking revelation of all: not only are all human canons, knowledge, and schemes shattered by the *objects* of the vision, but the *subject* of the vision, the cosmic traveler, does not retain the canonical human shape and is revealed to have lost his bodily nature and become a disembodied spirit: "My *spirit* swung as the hub of a radiating universe. *Freed of matter*, I had become a *naked consciousness*; and this thing is wonderful. My body had passed to its own land, while my spirit, my intellect, my comprehension, dropped to the far abysses before it could return and join with flesh again" (EG 100; italics added). One can hardly fail to notice how Barlow attaches a positive value to this experience, one finally able to liberate man from the chains of the physical world and its binding rules, as testified by the use of the word "freed" and by the judicial value "And this is wonderful."

This aspect of course links with point (3): the employment of "cosmic" imagery is in fact functional also to the aesthetic goal, present in Barlow's as well as in Lovecraft's fiction, to depict the violation of natural and physical laws. It is worth quoting another passage of "A Dim-Remembered Story," where the narrator, still referring to the cosmic visions he has experienced, discusses the nature of his (lack of) form and substance in greater detail, analyzing the different steps of his humanly inconceivable form-shifts:

> My first transition was of flesh, but the other passes such material change. When I was swept into the naked and lonely Ultimate, it was as an ego, an intelligence, a consciousness. My flesh could bear the change and stress of thrice five hundred years, but it was for centuries that I swung in the unplumbed void [. . .] Visually, perhaps I was not absent at all from my own world. Perhaps I only *flickered* in existence; but in that time I saw a new land and a new universe. (EG 104)

The only explanation—and that a faulty one—the protagonist may provide for his cosmic flight entails a hazardous and plainly beyond-human-comprehension account of bodily dissociation, certainly reminiscent of Carter's analogous experience: "my first transition, as I have said, was bodily; and the second one of soul, spirit, intelligence—call it what you will" (*EG* 104).

(3) As happened for Lovecraft, Barlow also believed that one of the most important aesthetic and philosophic goals of weird literature was the representation of images and plot elements staging—directly or indirectly—the suspension, if not the violation, of physical, biological, chemical, geometrical—in a word, *natural*—laws that imprison humans within the limitations of the three-dimensional world. Well known is the passage in Lovecraft's critical essay in which the Providence writer underscored the centrality of this aesthetic goal in his work:

> I choose weird stories because they suit my inclination best—one of my strongest and most persistent wishes being to achieve, momentarily, the illusion of some strange suspension or violation of the galling limitations of time, space, and natural law which forever imprison us and frustrate our curiosity about the infinite cosmic space beyond the radius of our sight and analysis. These stories frequently emphasise the element of horror because fear is our deepest and strongest emotion, and the one which best lends itself to the creation of nature-defying illusions.[35]

A powerful means Barlow adopts to stage this suspension, violation, or at least this *act of defiance* against natural laws is to represent images or plot elements that are so *cosmically outside nature* that they more or less directly suggest that laws *other than the terrestrial ones* are involved. Many passages in Barlow's fictional oeuvre—not only in "A Dim-Remembered Story"—point to the representation of what can, from a human, anthropocentric, terrestrial viewpoint, be considered "scientific anormalities"—but as we know, endorsing a relativistic perspective as Barlow's fiction does, that these "anormalities" perfectly fit in with the cosmic scheme of things. I have chosen to present just a few examples to show the pervasiveness and subtlety of Barlow's use of the device. Toward the conclusion of "The Night Ocean," Barlow decides to add to the overall atmosphere of the expectancy of a supernatural revelation by introducing an element of disquieting incongruence with human scientific knowledge: "The lamp burned endlessly, yielding a sick light hued like a corpse's flesh. [. . .] Curiously enough, *there was no heat from the wick*. And suddenly I became aware that the night as a whole was *neither warm nor cold*, but strangely neutral—as if *all physical forces were suspended*, and *all the laws of a calm existence disrupted*" (*EG* 119; italics added).[36] Through the staging of the suspension of natural laws, the target of Barlow's attack is just the all-

---

35. "Notes on Writing Weird Fiction" (*CE* 2.175-76). A statement similar in tone and content can be found in the short autobiographical piece "Some Notes on a Nonentity" (23 November 1933): "Nothing has ever seemed to fascinate me so much as the thought of some curious interruption in the prosaic laws of Nature, or some monstrous intrusion on our familiar world by unknown things from the limitless abysses outside" (*CE* 5.207).

36. The confrontation with the original manuscript bearing HPL's corrections shows that, while HPL did a prose-smoothing on the passage, the fundamental notion that the image should stage a violation of a natural law was RHB's.

too-human notion that existence is something "calm," predictable, because fully responding to human schemes of interpretation. There is much more than that, Barlow seems to say, since the anthropocentric perspective on reality and the cosmos is just one of countless possible ones. And if the sheer *amount* of the possible perspectives on reality is unknowable for the limited rational mind, there is something it must know for sure: that existence is *not* the calm, placid "island of ignorance" where humans have docked and which they count on to rest in order to preserve their safety of mind. Therefore, to show that the unfathomable depths of the cosmos are a receptacle of states of being, presences, laws, events, etc., unpredictable for the limited, one-sided, and partial human epistemic and cognitive system *is a key aesthetic goal of Barlow's cosmic fiction*. The cosmos is indifferent to the laws of human sciences: it follows its own rules and seems almost to enjoy disrupting, if not making fun of, limited human perspectives.

The alien vegetable of "Origin Undetermined" provides another striking example of this mind-disturbing "cosmic anomaly," namely an entity disrupting the reassuring scientific laws man has devised to carry on a "calm" existence. These are, in "Origin Undetermined," the narrator's descriptions and comments on his discovery of the unexpected growth of the plant from Outside:

> Monday I happened to be in the cellar again, and thinking of the teacup, went to my room to see if anything had happened. Something had: when I opened the door two delicate brown spirals, fully eight inches high, stood silhouetted in the window. I was not prepared for this phenomenal growth—I was not actually prepared for any growth at all. *God knows* what those plants were, or why their parent seeds had been kept. *They should have been destroyed* hundreds of years ago. They grew too fast, and they fed on things no other plant feeds on. Neither dirt nor water nor carrion had contributed to their unwholesome sprouting, but bare glass instead. [. . .] Three-quarters of the window-pane was gone, melted away precisely as if a blowtorch had been applied to it; and in the opening those hungry sprouts vibrated like small serpent heads. A chilly wind blew in from the March day: they seemed to breathe it avidly. *I destroyed those plants*. Some deep instinct directed me to. If they could eat glass like a bubbling acid, *they ought not to exist*. (EG 126–27; italics added)

The utter Outsideness of the vegetable entity, and Barlow's attaching to the plant the role of disrupting human scientific "certainties," are so patent that there is no need to comment on them. I have instead italicized those expressions showing how Barlow is also focused on discussing human reactions when confronting the manifestation of an incomprehensible and science-shattering Outsideness. The way Barlow chooses to treat this important aspect can be again considered functional to his literary strategy of overall deflation of the human race. In fact, instead of accepting the cosmic perspective, namely of recognizing the limitedness of the human, anthropocentric view of reality, the protagonist of "Origin Undetermined" is forced to (a) resort to God, and (b) decide that the entity he is facing is an "anomaly" and that its only possible fate is that of being destroyed: "I destroyed those plants" because "they ought not to exist." Instead of recognizing that *other* laws than those contemplated by—and comprehensible to—the human mind can be at work in the vast cosmos-at-large, and thus instead of recognizing *his own epistemic and cognitive limits*, man prefers to appeal to the supernatural or to ignore, to destroy, to cancel the "anomalies": they *cannot* exist, simply because we humans cannot account for them. This is the degree to which human presumptuousness and human lack of relativism arrive—and they become the favorite target of Barlow's work in its aesthetics of critical "deflation."

However, no matter how much man may be shocked and in epistemic and emotional trouble, the entities from Outsideness are like a "gross travesty of natural laws" ("The Experiment," *EG* 59) indifferent to man's knowledge and scientific schemes of interpretation, and perform their no less "calm" existence. When Arky, the cat of the protagonist of "Origin Undetermined," rubs himself against the edge of the window glass smeared with the ichor of the alien plant, the effects of this action on the animal's body are of a cosmic extraneousness ruthlessly—and amorally—indifferent of man's "scientific" expectations as well as inner emotions:

> I felt that the cat was doomed. A substance which gnawed away glass and cement must inevitably have monstrous effects on flesh and sinew. Realising that he must not escape, I stuffed my pillow into the wet dismal opening of the window, and coaxed Arky out where it was light. There was slime on him. [. . .] The sky was pale with intimations of daybreak when Arky began to twitch and claw at his side. I leaned over him, *horridly fascinated*, and saw curious blisters swelling up. These presently disappeared, leaving sunken areas like decayed spots on fruit. It looked as if the ribs were collapsing beneath the surface of the skin. *God, that cat was hideous!* In another hour, his whole face was gone. [. . .] *I was repelled and frightened.* (EG 130-31; italics added)

I would like to highlight how this passage powerfully presents the (effects of the) entity from Outsideness—the "blight from a source beyond comprehension" (*EG* 131)—as utterly *indifferent* not only to man's scientific laws, but also to his emotional reactions—his "horrid fascination," "repulsion," "fright": as with Lovecraft, Barlow's cosmos is completely "amoral"—considering, of course, the human acceptation of the word—since it follows neither scientific nor moral laws, or, to say the least, not the *human* scientific and moral laws.

Man gets in contact with cosmic Outsideness thanks to an experience that connects the human and the Outside dimensions, and though the entities from the unknown alterity are totally indifferent to the effects they bear over man, this of course does not mean that these effects do not exist. Up to now we have discussed mainly man's "emotional" reaction—involving especially fear, disgust, repulsion, fright, and appeal to the supernatural—certainly not "uplifting" reactions for a race that considers itself "rational." However, man's attitude in the face of Outsideness is not only an emotive one of refusal and non-acceptance. After the initial, mind-shattering impact is felt, man strives to trace the cosmic phenomena he has witnessed to his own canonical, rational scheme of interpretation. And thus he starts to rationalize again, since he cannot conceive of something utterly refusing a human, rational interpretation—if not for religious faith. But Barlow's (as well as Lovecraft's) characters, ingrained as they are with rational skepticism and a deeply scientific attitude, certainly do not resort to religious faith to account for the Outsideness phenomena. Convinced as they are that the laws of human, scientific rationality are able to explain virtually *everything* in existence, they are shown by Barlow in the act of rationalizing once more the cosmic phenomena within human canons of interpretation—except, of course, that the representation of their effort should be intended, in the author's perspective, as functional to show the inadequacy of human rationality and thus the inanity of the characters' effort itself. As a consequence, during or after their confrontation with Outsideness, Barlow's characters are represented in their rational mumbling about the possible meaning of their experience, which provokes in them the occasional emergence of some cosmic knowledge and revelations, more often than not impaired by an uncertainty and vagueness as regard to their effective consistency, since the human mind can glimpse the cosmic truths only dimly and partially.

Thus at the conclusion of his cosmic flight through time and space, the protagonist of "A Dim-Remembered Story" gropingly formulates a vague explanation for the visions he underwent. His otherwise unexplainable cosmic experience is thus traced to the exclusive glance he was allowed of the ultimate creators and inheritors of our universe—and it is easy to detect, in this crucial passage, Barlow's effort both to underscore the tentative nature of his character's suppositions and simultaneously to inform them with the revolutionary flavor of a cosmic *revelation*, once their truth or at least their probability will be proved:

> I have begun, lately, to judge something of the force motivating my transition, and to gropingly conceive the nature of those... objects... inhabiting the lost void to which my dream bore me. Their cosmic errand is unknowable, as is the inconceivable dimension of their reeling, prismatic lair. They are, I believe, the dominating life-form, the ultimate inheritors of our universe. *Perhaps they even created it.* In a part of space lost past the reach of light-years; a place where the farthest comet never swings, these creatures have their world. A nighted world in no sense like our earth-wrought planets... a world upon the black Rim—a world that no mind can believe or even dimly picture. It must be a place of very wrong dimensions, existing in some alien eternity. I cannot hazard the nature of such a place, or know whether it be in the aeonian past or vague futurity. (EG 103)

Barlow once more underscores the utter *otherness* of this experience for the human mind and canons (using expressions such as "gropingly conceive," "unknowable cosmic errand," "inconceivable dimension," "a nighted world in no sense like our planets," "a world no mind can believe or even dimly picture," "I cannot hazard the nature of such place," etc.), making his character simultaneously (a) provide a tentative "rational" explanation for his experience and (b) infer "cosmic" revelations about the utter freedom (from "natural," human laws) of the dimensions he visited:

But I do know this: that all the laws and barriers of our cosmos *are as nothing to them*, dwelling as they do in a realm oblique across eternity. For their purposes the master-things somehow *turned aside the stream of years*, diverted for a space the succession of ages from the rusty channel wherein they flow. And in that celestial maelstrom I was sucked, twisted about, so that when their Gargantuan play was over, I was flung from Time's unknown waters upon the rock-girt coast of alien years. From my own life I was caught up by a *violating law*, whose course left me for a little upon the future world, and then swept me to the far black reaches of God's infinity. My voyaging was lone and terrible. It took me past the chaos of suns and stars, beyond the nethermost limits of a perishing universe. And in the end I saw those *Supreme entities*, whose servants are the *gods*. They linked the end and origins of things, they formed a million-ruled universe as playground, and then set those rules aside. (EG 103; italics added)

It is significant to point out how detailed and psychologically accurate is Barlow's analysis of his character's complex reaction: the narrator in fact realizes the violating, non-human nature of the experience he underwent (in this way Barlow achieves the aesthetic goal of depicting a liberation from the ties of natural laws), but at the same time his attempts to rationalize the non-human experience ultimately fail, since he cannot help calling the supernatural principle into the picture to account for the cosmic experience. He cannot help labeling as "gods" and "supreme entities" the unknowable—for the human cognitive faculties—dominating life-forms responsible for the beginning and end of the universe. Whatever human rationality is unable to explain and account for, man labels it as "divine" and resorts to the supernatural—and this is of course another undisputable token of the limits of the race, namely its inability to accept the possible existence of a "rationality" *other than the human*, of another principle of explanation that can perfectly account for the cosmic phenomena *through canons different from those of human rationality*. Man does not accept this—since it would entail a self-admission of limitedness and weakness as a race. Humanity's reactions when it gets in touch with cosmic phenomena unexplainable through scientific rationality are of (a) terror and disgust from the emotional viewpoint, and of (b) non-acceptance from the rational one: mankind prefers to call the principle of the supernatural and of the divine into the picture, rather than admitting the absolute "naturality" of the cosmic phenomena (a "naturality" explainable through laws different from the human), and thus admitting its own epistemic failure to account for them. The darts of Barlow's critical attack are against this attitude on man's part—that of considering a phenomenon either (a) scientifically explainable through the human episteme, or (b) an expression of a supernatural will or scheme. The cosmic purpose of Barlow's work is to show that *a third, liberating way* is possible, precisely the one available by endorsing the relativistic perspective that allows for the existence of *natural* laws radically other than the human ones.

The recognition of the utter inadequacy of man's epistemology to account for cosmic "mysteries" represents a further standpoint from which Barlow launches his attacks against the meaninglessness and insignificance of the race on manifold levels. The cosmic visions of utter Outsideness experienced by Barlow's characters allow them to infer once more, from the "cognitive" glimpses they allow about the insufficiency of man's rational knowledge to comprehend the cosmos's laws in full, that he must be a trifling and negligible accident along the course of creation. Barlow's characters arrive at these bleak cosmic revelations—referable to the aesthetic strategy of "human deflation"—just through the "elitist" experiences they undergo: as we have seen, this means that the grim truths they discover are not available to everybody, but only to the "elect." The following passage from "Origin Undetermined" powerfully points to the cosmic relevance of the character's experience, to his striving for a "unity" of an otherwise hardly decipherable "vision," as well as to the value and significance of the revelations this vision entails on the epistemic level. The cosmic "vision" is hard to understand in its significance and cognitive outcome (after all, a rational—thus a limited—mind still tries to decipher it), but once the "vision" is at least partly decoded, it is revelatory of a cosmic, bleakly destructive *knowledge*:

> I am made aware of linkages which are obscure and difficult to set down. This curious baffling procession of the human ape through a world designed neither for him nor for anything he knows; the hideous meaningless pageantry of stars and worlds and gulfs; this futile but exalted aspiration he contains for the tremulous flame of truth; all these things have acquired a unity in my vision, and anciently chiselled words are suddenly swept clean of the lichens which hid them. (*EG* 131)

This passage does not fail to attack, once more, man's presumptuousness. In fact, the cosmic revelations the character attains thanks to his commerce with Outsideness have such a omni-comprehensive and devastating impact that they force their "receiver" to completely reorganize his "epistemic beliefs": not only does he learn the cosmic truth, but is also made aware that the common human beliefs are the puerile results of "futile" and "exalted" aspirations to truth by a trifling but conceited race.

How this process takes place in the character's mind is realistically described by Barlow's inductive reasoning. The character in fact nears (when dealing with Outsideness manifestations, man can only *approximate* to "knowledge," since his viewpoint is inevitably human and rational) the cosmic revelations starting from the recognition and discussion of the details of his experience, in this case the spectacular events and visions connected with the appearance of the Mayan plant:

> Always, I have felt that some old and terrible secret lies behind the Maya cities. Those immense stone piles lying in the humid jungle stare backward through time to an unguessed origin, and the carven monsters which leer from a hundred walls hint damnably at something of unhuman significance. *We do not understand a tenth of even what we have dug up from the graveyard of thousands of mouldy years.* What curse drove a million people from their cities? Why did they build new cities afterward, and build them far away? (*EG* 131-32; italics added)

The cosmic experience entailed by the contact with Outsideness easily accounts for all these questions which—in his limited, earthly, and rational views and knowledge—man cannot answer. The cognitive plane shifts from the human to the cosmic, and thus all the naïve explanations man may give, all his bafflement at what he defines "mysteries," can finally be regarded as what they really are: "futile" attempts of a meaningless race to preserve her sentiment of "exaltation."

R. H. Barlow's amateur journal, the Dragon-Fly.

5. Time

5.1 The fictional mysteries of "Time"

In Barlow's fiction, time constitutes a very important theme, certainly no less significant than vagueness and cosmicism. Barlow's fiction faces "Time" as a complex notion, often mentioning it by using the capital "T"—as if dealing with a personified, if not divine, entity. Part and parcel with this complexity is this theme's sharing of common aspects with cosmicism and vagueness: as we shall see, in Barlow's fiction these three themes reinforce and gain reciprocal strength from their constant interaction.

The complexity of Barlow's aesthetic treatment of time is related to the multifaceted approach he adopts toward the theme, and results in a discussion on the two acceptations in which, according to Barlow, time expresses itself in literature: *cosmic* time and *human* time. Each acceptation, in its turn, presents a further division into subthemes that qualify it and allow Barlow to discuss in depth his aesthetics of temporality. Needless to say, we cannot hermetically separate these two acceptations—they are the two faces of the same and unique object, time—though their traits are certainly different, since the two acceptations refer to two distinct manifestations of the same theme, one on the cosmic and one on the anthropocentric level.

To discuss time from a *cosmic* viewpoint means in fact to endorse a temporal perspective that does not restrict it to the span of the course of human life, but to adopt a vision—on history, on culture, on science, even on things human—that is grounded on the notion that time engulfs allegedly infinite temporal extensions, compared to which even the light-years calculable by the human perspective are nothing but a negligible span. In other words, time is discussed on a "cosmic" level, i.e. one that has little to do with the temporal partitions employed, shared, and to a point even *conceivable* by men: temporal extensions longer than those commonly familiar to humans are at stake. On the contrary, taking an anthropocentric approach to time means analyzing the modalities in which human beings relate to and perceive the temporal process, how their mind handles the (effects of) temporal flowing and how they elaborate *memories*. In this case, the perspective is then strictly human, since the center of interest is the modality in which time affects the human mind (internal viewpoint) and human creations (external viewpoint).

5.1.1 Cosmic Time: an introduction

The cosmic approach in the aesthetic treatment of time leads Barlow to discuss two notions in particular: (a) that of the flowing of immense temporal extensions (what I propose to define as the "aeonian perspective") and (b) that of the relativity of the temporal dimensions, whose most compelling aesthetic result in Barlow's fiction is the representation of the "fluidity of time."

1. *Aeonian perspective*: Barlow's cultural, historical, and literary interests in fiction are grounded on the relativistic perspective allowed by the temporal "cosmic" plane. His perspective is often that of one observing cultures, civilizations, history, and sciences in their effects and results as projected onto vast temporal extensions—and it is also here that time as a theme powerfully reconnects with that of cosmicism: the two themes reinforce each other. In fact, it is just from the viewpoint of "aeonian" time that mankind's experiences and achievements appear to be annihilated, as if they did not even exist—and this of course entails the adoption of a bleak "existential" perspective like that discussed in chapter 4 on cosmicism. In this sense, "cosmic time" configures as a negative pole, inimical to mankind: as an uncontrollable, blind, and destructive force, time ruthlessly annihilates everything human. The relationship that time maintains with mankind (and the direction of the relationship is from time to man, not vice versa, since the terms of the relation are established by time) is marked by two fundamental features: (1) uncontrollability on man's part, and (2) indifference of time toward anything human. Man is at time's mercy, and time is a ruthless and merciless tyrant who often gets personified by Barlow's fiction as an Old Testament god. However, Barlow's "aeonian perspective" is more complicated than this, since it contains an apparent paradox: the passing of aeons does not produce a concrete, substantial change of the truth; that is, it does not affect the inevitability of *mankind's doom*. Time may flow in huge extensions, aeons may succeed each other in uncountable eras, everything may get constantly and ruthlessly replaced in the human and natural spheres—even on the cosmic scale everything gets cyclically repeated, but there is just one thing that is imperishable and changeless: the doom of the race we belong to. Yet even though the passing of vast aeons mercilessly points to this truth, man does not understand it, since he is unable to adopt the cosmic perspective in full: he cares too much for the short temporal span of his paltry existence and loses sight of the cosmic and the aeonian. It is easy to see how here the reciprocal influence between the themes of time and cosmicism (time as a cause, cosmicism as its effect, as it were) reaches perhaps its climax. Moreover, the relevance of Barlow's concern for vast temporal gulfs and immense antiquity in his fiction ("aeonian perspective") is revealed by the author's dialectic interest also for the apparently *opposite* notion: that of *timelessness*. As we shall see, in fact, Barlow's interest for the depiction of the effects—on matters cultural, historical, social—of the passing of vast temporal extensions often ends up in the notion that a *huge temporal extension*, so huge that it cannot even be conceived by the average

human mind, may be dialectically reduced—as in a circular process—to the image of the *absence* of time, i.e. of timelessness.

2. *Fluidity of time*: Barlow's fiction often presents either events or narrators' comments that emphasize the arbitrariness of man's elaboration of the temporal flux. Time is *not* the rational and linear notion most people think it is: the linearity of time is just a human creation, a subjective device human beings have created in order to cope with time, which in itself is instead a *fluid* dimension and a *cyclical* phenomenon, impossible to be caged within rational schemes of interpretation. Time and chronology as most people see them are just *relative* concepts: they may be valid as far as a human—i.e., partial—approach to temporality is concerned, but they fail to grasp the true cosmic and cyclical essence of time, and thus provide just a fragmentary and at least partly fallacious comprehension. Barlow's emphasis on the limitedness and arbitrariness of the general understanding of temporality may of course be considered functional to his aesthetics of existential "deflation" of the human race.

As we shall see in paragraph 5.2., the two components of "cosmic time" described above are exemplified at best—both philosophically and figuratively—in "A Dim-Remembered Story," though other narratives present valuable developments of the same themes, as will be discussed in paragraph 5.2.1.

5.1.2 Human Time: an introduction

Barlow's aesthetic interest in time is not limited to the cosmic viewpoint. His fiction is so deeply concerned with temporality that it does involve the discussion of the human viewpoint over it, aiming at illustrating how man strives to shelter against the ravages of "cosmic time" on everything human. In other words, man tries to superimpose his own perspective over the "aeonian" or cosmic time ruthlessly ruling; against the destructions operated by time on the cosmic scale, man has only a few weapons at his disposal, among which memory is the most significant, as we shall see.

The complexity of Barlow's treatment of "human time" is also revealed in the two components of the theme he decides to discuss:

1. *Memory*: namely, "human time" from a viewpoint internal to the human mind. Memory is in fact a strictly temporal process man employs in order to cope with time's attacks: memories are seen by Barlow as the tools by which man tries to oppose the inexorable flowing of temporality and its annihilating power. Barlow's interest in the theme of memory is already testified by the very titles of some of his stories ("A Memory," "A Dim-Remembered Story"): in particular, the title of "A Dim-Remembered story" effects a compelling fusion between the themes of vagueness and memory. This merging constitutes a further example of an overlapping of different themes in Barlow's fiction (after all, one of the effects of the passing of time

is precisely to render everything, and in particular memory, vaguer). In general, Barlow's interest for the theme of memory reveals a further detail of his concern for the modalities by which men perceive time: how the human mind works in order to create memories as a means of shielding itself from the ravages and exterminations produced by temporal flowing on the cosmic plane. Memory becomes a means by which man tries to *fix* and *stop time*, to blunt its chaotic vortex and annihilating power. By fixing something in memory, man provides himself with the delusion of temporarily lighting a spot in the dark eternity of the inexorable temporal flowing, thus allowing himself a momentary and therefore ephemeral victory over time.

2. *Past*: namely, "human time" from a viewpoint external to the human mind, since the effects of the past on things human—man's actions and creations—are independent of man's will or mind. Barlow's fiction shows a strong interest in the modalities by which the passing of time affects all the things human—both in its material effects, as those produced by the weathering on human artefacts and buildings, and in the always-actual role of the past, its constant and deterministic influence over the present. In this last sense, we shall see how a clear overlapping is detectable between the theme of the past and that of cosmic determinism/lack of free will discussed in paragraph 4.2.2.2 Deterministic compulsion and its impact on free will.

I am now going to discuss the two themes of cosmic and human time—and their submanifestations—in more detail, grounding my analysis on the textual evidence available in those of Barlow's narratives displaying the most perceptible interest for the treatment of temporality.

5.2 Cosmic Time

In his well-known statement about the concern that weird literature should display toward the representation of "some strange suspension or violation of the galling limitations of time, space, and natural law" ("Notes on Writing Weird Fiction" [1933], CE 2.176), Lovecraft specifies that the aesthetically effective creation of "a convincing picture of shattered natural law or cosmic alienage or 'outsideness'" (CE 2.176) should be grounded, in particular, on an act of defiance launched against *temporal* laws—as human beings have elaborated them: "The reason why *time* plays a great part in so many of my tales is that this element looms up in my mind as the most profoundly dramatic and grimly terrible thing in the universe. *Conflict with time* seems to me the most potent and fruitful theme in all human expression" (CE 2.176). Thus Lovecraft's words reveal that the most prominent aesthetic concern for a writer of weird stories should be the depiction of a strange suspension or violation of temporal laws, and the fact that this aesthetic goal is connected with the attempted representation of Outsideness and of a sense of cosmic alienage reinforces our impression of a stringent connection between the themes of time and cosmicism. In fact, what readers and critics have labeled as "cosmicism" can be conveniently defined as such, at least in writers like Lovecraft, just because all the aesthetic and philosophical perspectives on which it is built are based on the decision to consider any (cultural, historical, scientific, etc.) human object from the viewpoint of its (lack of) significance on the scale of vast gulfs of time, discarding the viewpoint of its (alleged) significance on the scale of restricted temporal arcs—like those usually considered by humans in their everyday concerns, and by anthropocentric literature.

Barlow certainly inherited Lovecraft's lesson on this point, and the following discussion of "A Dim-Remembered Story," Barlow's most notable achievement in the treatment of time from a cosmic viewpoint, will hopefully account for the pervasiveness that Lovecraft's lesson on temporal concerns attained on his pupil's literary aesthetics.

5.2.1 "A Dim-Remembered Story" and the transcendent present

Barlow wrote "A Dim-Remembered Story" probably a short time before its appearance in the *Californian* for Summer 1936. Lovecraft does not appear to have read the text before its publication, therefore he did not revise it at all. On several occasions, he expressed enthusiastic praise for this narrative, which can be certainly included among the most substantial works in Barlow's production. In a letter addressed to Barlow and dated 9 July 1936, in spite of the disheartened comments on the sad news of Robert E. Howard's recent suicide, Lovecraft could not restrain himself from expressing his astonished commendation for the progress his pupil showed in "A Dim-Remembered Story": "Holy Yuggoth, but it's a masterpiece! *Magnificent* stuff—will bear comparison with the best of CAS! Splendid rhythm, poetic imagery, emotional modulations, & atmospheric power. Tsathoggua! But *literature* is certainly your forte, say what you will! [. . .] All the cosmic sweep of Wandrei's early work—& infinitely more substance. Keep it up!" (*FF* 351). On the following day, in a postcard sent to Barlow from Providence, Lovecraft could not help reiterating his enthusiasm, contextually revealing that he was so stunned by the story that he felt the urge to re-read it: "That masterpiece not only holds up, but actually grows on one, when read a second time" (*FF* 352). On July 23, in another letter, Lovecraft again manifested to Barlow his conviction about the worth of the story, and above all, again confirmed his impression that this narrative could be the turning point of Barlow's career as a weird writer, marking his entry into the restricted circle of the most talented craftsmen of the genre: "I don't take back a single word of praise regarding 'A Dim-Remembered Story'. It's great stuff, & marks a radical advance in your craftsmanship. Naturally it isn't realism—but it is fantasy of the first order" (*FF* 353). Finally, Lovecraft's "official" comment about the excellence of the story—and of Barlow's improvements in weird craftsmanship—appeared in the "Literary Review" column for the Winter 1936 issue of the *Californian*, the same issue where "The Night Ocean" was published:

> Not only is the flow of fantastic imagination better modulated [than in previous tales by Barlow], and the bizarre, dream-like imagery made more vivid and realistic, but the rhythm and idiomatic grace of the style are infinitely improved. The tale is one of abnormal transference to the future—first to the remote future of this planet, and then to a black and inconceivable gulf beyond the life of the cosmos and of time itself. [. . .] Some of the visual touches are brilliant and unforgettable. (CE 1.406)

Lovecraft even urged Barlow to send the story to Farnsworth Wright, the editor of *Weird Tales*, but this probably did not happen: according to Joshi, the tale "must have been sent fairly expeditiously to Bradofsky in order for it to have appeared in the Summer 1936 *Californian*, and this is another indication that Lovecraft is not likely to have worked on it" (*LAL* 616).

Lovecraft's opinion on Barlow's story does not represent an out-of-the-choir voice. In fact, other critics' words attest the sheer aesthetic excellence and the literary significance for the weird genre of "A Dim-Remembered Story." Joshi defines it a weird tale of "considerable substance" (*OLL* 6), claiming that this "superbly crafted tale" (*LAL* 616) "justifies Lovecraft's enthusiastic praise" (*OLL* 6). In addition, Joshi and Anderson consider "A Dim-Remembered Story" and "The Night Ocean" the peaks of Barlow's achievements in the weird field, and they claim that these two remarkable stories would constitute—together with a few other narratives—material enough to elevate this author's work to the rank of the most gifted modern practitioners of the genre: "'A Dim-Remembered Story' and 'The Night Ocean' stand out as Barlow's chief triumphs in weird fiction, but at least half a dozen other tales are nearly as substantial. If Barlow's collected weird fiction is far lesser in quantity than that of others of the Lovecraft circle, its consistently high quality should earn it a place of respect as a compact but choice contribution to modern weird fiction" (*EG* 11).

In spite of Joshi's view, according to which "A Dim-Remembered Story" bears "little stylistic or conceptual similarity to Lovecraft's work" (*LAL* 615), my analysis will argue that the Lovecraftian inspiration and the thematic as well as linguistic influence over Barlow's story are quite heavy, and not simply because the tale is explicitly dedicated to Lovecraft and each of its four sections (the tale also contains a prologue and an epilogue) are prefaced by a half-line of the blasphemous couplet "That is not dead which can eternal lie, / And in strange aeons even death may die." Lovecraft's words in the "Literary Review" ("The tale is one of abnormal transference to the future—first to the remote future of this planet, and then to a black and inconceivable gulf beyond the life of the cosmos and of time itself") already point out the key role that is played by the theme of temporality—and, in particular, of *stretched* temporality (as the expressions "remote future" and "inconceivable gulf beyond the life of the cosmos and of time" attest). Given Lovecraft's own predilection for "conflict with time" as one of the main aesthetic goals of his own writing, it is by no means surprising that he appreciated Barlow's story so enthusiastically.

In fact, in its thematic concerns "A Dim-Remembered Story" effects an original synthesis of both acceptations of the cosmic temporal viewpoint in Barlow's fiction: the *aeonian perspective* and the *fluidity of time*. Both these acceptations powerfully stage "conflicts with time," in particular with the common *human perspectives on temporality* and the shared modalities humanity adopts in order to deal with time and rationalize its dimension into recognizable, anthropocentrically oriented—and thus reassuring—schemes of interpretation. It is of course not easy—and ultimately useless—to rigidly separate, in "A Dim-Remembered Story," the theme of the aeonian perspective and that of the fluidity of time. As usual in Barlow, different subthemes reflect and reinforce each other. However, I will try to distinguish as much as possible the traits of both themes as they appear in the tale, in order to emphasize their specific heuristic values.

Already from a hasty survey of the plot of "A Dim-Remembered Story"—the story of a cosmic travel in time that projects the unnamed, bewildered narrator coming from a twentieth-century Kansas into an ill-defined far future of earth—the reader easily realizes that the most prominent goal of the tale is to deal with temporality and the aesthetic effects of its literary stretching.

At the very beginning of the tale, the narrator reflects on the nature of time, stating at the outset its uncontrollability on man's part: "Time, of all things, is most elusive; for no one can know what it actually is [. . .] It might be that if there were no life, Time would not exist" (EG 87). The claim that the notion of linear time is by no means absolute, but might be the creation of man, entails an immediate, philosophically "cosmic" effect that reinforces the interconnection between the themes of time and cosmicism: "Perhaps time is a creation of Man—and Man is a brief thing upon a fragile sphere. His world is but a single blossom in the garden of the firmament" (EG 87). And to prove further the richness of these reflections (generated by his own "cosmic" experience soon to be accounted, because "With this is my story linked" [EG 87]), the narrator notices that considering linear time a creation of man means that time retains all the contradictions and frailties of a "brief thing upon a fragile sphere":

> A scientist has written: 'Suppose that everything in the universe should halt—all life cease, the planets pause in their orbits, the atoms and the electrons cease their flow. Time would be suspended and when motion set in again it would appear to us as the next instant, and we should be unaware of the occurrence'. He suggests, too, that possibly Time does not run a smooth course; that it may ebb and surge like any stream. In each such abeyance there might be long eternities. (EG 87)

In a word, the most correct—but undoubtedly disturbing for the human episteme—representation of time might be that of an incessant *flux*, of a fluid tide constantly ebbing and surging—an image deeply different from the humanly accepted and shared paradigm of the linear "arrow" of time. The notion of the nonlinearity and fluidity of time necessarily entails that of an eventual *simultaneity* of the three temporal dimensions: past, present, and future are not neatly separable on the cosmic scale. Their separation represents just a puerile human attempt to cope with time and rationalize it, to wave a humanly and epistemologically acceptable "order" into an otherwise indistinct and confuse flux of temporal fragments: all separated and all simultaneous at the same time. Events of the past

> are not gone, nor do I affect a paradox. Augustus yet prevails in uncrumbled Rome, and Christian warriors storm the bearded foe of Acre, on that bright dust-filled day nine centuries ago. In Posedonis there are lunar rituals, and Russia's Ivan holds a bloody scepter. These worlds are only around some crook in the lane of eternity, hidden by a bend in the path along which our own frail world passes. Our age is a given point in the inexorable journey—if we might look ahead, we should see it blotted out by a succeeding epoch. Then our towns and continents will be as one with those lost earths [. . .] *All things that have been, all that shall be, are together recorded.* (EG 87; italics added)

The human conception of time as a linear dimension is revealed to be totally unfounded when examined from a cosmic, non-anthropocentric perspective:

> It is as if everything in earth's history, each phase and aspect of life, had been ordained at the great start of things. As if they had occurred, perhaps, at one mighty instant, *so that the beginning and the end are merged.* Or as if each century were an earth separate in space and time and matter. A thousand earths—a world repeating itself beyond counting, so that things may exist in many avatars and many ages. Worlds beside us that we cannot reach. (EG 87; italics added)

The very fact that, in "A Dim-Remembered Story," the protagonist is "flung through time and space and universes in the great transition" (EG 100) that sends him so far in the future to observe the sun reduced to a "solar pinpoint" (EG 100), and around it "no longer any Earth" (EG 101), attests the permeability and fluidity of the temporal and spatial dimensions conceived by this narrative. Flowing through space and time, drifting along the centuries and "visiting" the far future of the universe as a disembodied, traveling soul constitute the literary images Barlow employs to celebrate the cosmic journey of his unnamed protagonist.

"A Dim-Remembered Story" enriches the theme of time's fluidity even further through its fusion with that of the aeonian perspective. Toward the end of the narrative, while accounting for the cosmic experience of being thrown through time and space and getting a glimpse of the universe's far future, the narrator traverses incalculable eras with his disembodied soul: thus both a long-stretched temporality and its fluidity are addressed, while time is depicted as an elastic band or a reel that can be winded and rewound at pleasure: "Again, with swifter motion, my surroundings revolved; and then life became a series of hideous revolutions backward through time and space. I seemed to experience anew each joy and pain that I had ever known: again and yet again I lived a tortuous life, and the dark years sped in rhythm with a lurching cosmos" (EG 103). The protagonist is caught up by a "violating law" (EG 103) whose course sends him into a far future world, "past the chaos of suns and stars, beyond the nethermost limits of a perishing universe" (*EG* 103): he is able to travel along the aeons and reach the final instant of the universe's existence. The image of a time travel of course entails the notion of *time's fluidity*, while the fact that the journey covers the span of such incalculable temporal extensions accounts for the tale's *aeonian perspective*.

The Lovecraftian flavor of the theme of the fluidity and simultaneity of time's dimensions (as well as of that of a "violating law" altering the natural course of the protagonist's existence) is quite evident. Let us mention also that in one of his sonnets Barlow employs another image that clearly reminds us—almost word for word—of some of the narrative passages quoted above on this same theme: "All past and future hours emerge as one" ("March 1938," *EG* 154, l. 6). It might not be surprising that this poem *is one of Lovecraftian homage* and was written to commemorate the first anniversary of the master's demise. In particular, the notions of time's fluidity and of the simultaneity of the three temporal dimensions remind us of Lovecraft's dealing with these themes in "The Shadow out of Time," whose philosophical stances may have exerted a significant influence on Barlow's treatment of the temporal theme. In fact, within the temporal dimension that is at stake in the "Shadow," as Peaslee himself admits, *time* does not exist anymore in the fashion traditionally attributed to it by humans. The Lovecraftian cosmicism of "The Shadow out of Time" revolves around the issue of temporality.[1] The Great Race, as Peaslee acknowledges, has conquered the secret of Time[2]: therefore mankind has always misinterpreted the nature of the temporal process, and of reality. Time in fact does not result, as man has always supposed, in a sheer *consecutiveness* in space, and reality does not consist simply of a container of a tangible, empiric present. Time, as relativity teaches, is just one dimension, *thus reducible to space*. Only in appearance do events *follow one another* according to the laws of consecutiveness: in fact, they are not placed in a chronological and sequential order, but *exist one beside the other and simultaneously in space*. This is the reason why Peaslee, when waking up from his alleged amnesia, has trouble distinguishing between consecutiveness and simultaneousness: "My conception of *time*—my ability to distinguish between consecutiveness and simultaneousness—seemed subtly disordered" (39). As a human being regaining his long-lost mental and physical faculties, now

---

1. Even Edmund Wilson in his well-known "Tales of the Marvellous and the Ridiculous," in spite of the openly disapproving approach of his essay, did not fail to notice how the representation of the attempt to defeat temporal laws—as humans understand them—constitutes one of the most effective themes of HPL's oeuvre: "But Lovecraft's stories do show at times some traces of his more serious emotions and interests. [. . .] The story called [. . .] 'The Shadow out of Time' deals not [. . .] ineffectively with the perspectives of geological aeons and the idea of controlling time-sequence. *The notion of escaping from time seems the motif most valid in his fiction*, stimulated as it was by an impulse toward evasion which had pressed upon him all his life" (Wilson 49; italics added).
2. The Great Race is "the greatest race of all; because it alone had conquered the secret of time. It had learned all things that ever were known *or ever would be known* on the earth, through the power of its keenest minds to project themselves into the past and future, even through gulfs of millions of years, and study the lore of every age" (*Shadow out of Time* 48).

Peaslee instinctively recognizes the events in temporal succession, but during the "transfer" period he, though only tangentially, has been made aware of their co-occurrence in space, a quality that identifies their most proper nature. What kind of reality can be surmised from these reflections? One in which whatever happened, happens, or will happen, happens *now*, in a sort of *transcendent present*. Reality then appears as a sort of book that, leafed through page by page under the light of the transcendent present, simultaneously contains each and every event: present, past, and future. The way in which this text is read configures the modality with which reality is experienced. According to the way Lovecraft describes them, the aliens of the Great Race would then be able to read, through the medium of mind-exchange, any section of the book that they liked, and in any order; on the contrary, animal species less endowed on the intellectual plane, such as humans, would be able to decipher only partial and isolated portions of the book, and only in one direction, namely reading from left to right. They could experience just the infinitesimal section of the book represented by the *empirical present*. If only mankind were able to shed light over all the pages of the book, its sensible experience would allow it the perception of the *totality of the events in time's history*, in their nature of authentic co-occurrence in space and simultaneousness in time.

This Lovecraftian philosophical stance, well described by Paul Montelone, configures a genuine *cosmicism* that certainly is shared by Barlow's tale in its attempt to represent the disruption of the spatio-temporal laws as humanly accepted. However, we should not believe that Lovecraft presented the Great Race as *fully* able to master the eternal light of the *transcendent present*. Though it can shed light over wide sections of the book of time, the Great Race cannot do it without limitations: first, the mind transfer across eras may take place just "through the power of its keener minds" (61); in addition, the Great Race has limited access to knowledge of the past: more practicable is the mental projection into the future.[3] And above all, the Great Race is still subject to the most typical phenomenon of "human" temporality, i.e. *mortality*: in fact, the Great Race will one day be extinguished, at least in its corporeal component, forcing its intellectual essences to migrate into the future, into the bodies of the invertebrates that will dominate the earth after the disappearance of the human race. Therefore even the Great Race will never take hold on reality, as it is configured in the transcendent present. Resorting to an incisive metaphor, Montelone suggests that the Great Race, "like every other knowing species, is bound to the line of Becoming, and thus, like them, it forever approaches but never reaches the asymptote of Being" (28). In fact, Being and reality are contained in the transcendent present, whose existence we can state only theoretically and hypothetically, on the ground of the Great Race's ability to travel in time. If a living species were truly able to *live* in such eternal present, no death and "becoming" would ever take place, and all existence (namely everything that concretely happened, happens, and will happen, *not* everything that could potentially happen) would "stay," immobile,

---

3. Knowledge of the past is "harder to know than knowledge of the future" (62).

forever. All the events would be manifested with no interruption, one beside the others: they would *be* "ad aeternum," without ever *becoming*.

Therefore Lovecraft's Great Race does not represent such a daring creation, at least under the viewpoint of its impact on the temporal theme. But let us take a step further: in "The Shadow out of Time," Lovecraft implies that the becoming of all life forms is not actually *real*, since everything that is real, as we saw, is such in the transcendent present. From *that* point of view—of the transcendent present—there would not exist what we commonly define as *transitoriness*, i.e. the main characteristic of mankind which Lovecraft's and Barlow's cosmicisms address: *on the plane of the transcendent present* only partially (i.e., mentally) achieved by the Great Race, each concrete event shows itself forever, beside any other concrete event, *and the same happens to the human race*, that, being one "event" among the many, will never be dissolved nor extinguished. The problem is that reality intended in this way, i.e. still and immutable, *is conceivable but not knowable* by the human intellect. During the mind-exchange process, Peaslee is made aware of the existence of this reality, but he too, a human being limited like his fellows, understands his experience in terms of *sheer temporal consecutiveness*: he assigns to it a start (in 1908) and a duration (five years, four months, and thirteen days). In other words, he falls again into the "humanizing fallacy" affecting any epistemological process undertaken by the human being. Given these premises, it is virtually impossible for Peaslee to grasp the "truth," namely that mankind cannot disappear in the "sucking whirlpool of time" (*EG* 104), but would continue to exist in the temporally eternal dimension of the transcendent present: "This 'truth' is by nature not accessible to him and to human experience generally. Humankind will never experience its own imperishability just as no human individual will ever experience physical immortality. As such the 'truth' of our everlastingness is quite useless—whether as theory or solace" (Montelone 33).

Barlow's "A Dim-Remembered Story" shows a conception of the temporal theme very similar to that of Lovecraft's "The Shadow out of Time,"[4] as both nar-

---

4. The analogies between the two narratives are not limited to the treatment of the temporal theme; the overall story of a protagonist's "imprisonment" in a place far away in time may be seen as a homage to Lovecraft's novelette. Already in chapter 4 on cosmicism, in the paragraph 4.3. "Vastness of the universe and cosmic Outsideness," I have highlighted a pair of tips of the hat that Barlow provides to Lovecraft's tale, specifically in the mention of a "manuscript" the protagonist finds in a room of the castle of Yrn (which reminds us of the manuscript Peaslee discovers in the city of the Great Race, written in his own handwriting), and in the description of the "amnesia" and comatose state that hit the protagonist, in a similar fashion to what happens to Peaslee. In general, "A Dim-Remembered Story" bears a very strong Lovecraftian flavor, and for a number of textual reasons: the notion of a "violating law" (*EG* 103) that suddenly changes completely the existence of the protagonist, a typically Lovecraftian aesthetic concern for the depiction of events providing the illusion of a violation of the natural laws; a great many lexical choices reminiscent of Lovecraft's own preferences (for instance, the resort to words stemming from the root "baffle-" and "crouch-"); the words and images placed at the conclusion of the tale: "It saddens me to think of the

ratives understand time as a fluid dimension where, thanks to the cosmic experience, even man can get in touch with the transcendent present in which all events—past, present, and future—coexist. Yet perhaps we can detect a clue that would justify the claim of greater courage on Barlow's part in the treatment of the theme. In fact, whereas Lovecraft does not address the issue of the temporal comparability between the dimension of the Great Race and the human one (five years, four months, and thirteen days of Peaslee's absence from our world are not said to last differently in the Great Race's dimension), Barlow drops a suggestive hint of the notion of non-comparability in the temporality of the two experiences, adding to the power of the cosmicism of his story. I am referring to a sentence that Barlow's narrator writes toward the conclusion of his account: "I spent a million years in space, or if you like, three days in the old castle" (EG 104). This is why Barlow's tale treats the theme of temporality in an innovative fashion, even in comparison with Lovecraft—because it introduces the notion of an *alternative temporal dimension*. "A Dim-Remembered Story" is not simply the account of a travel in the "sucking whirlpool of time." This is the story of the exploration and investigation of a temporality unknown and hardly conceivable by man, one in which human canons of temporality are totally unreliable, one in which not only the separation of past/present/future does not hold, but where even the sheer passing of time follows an utterly alternative meter: a dimension, in other words, in which a light-year of our "calendar" may last a second.

A further significant element that Barlow's tale shares with Lovecraft's fiction concerns their treatment of time in regard to the notion of the *cyclical development* of cultures: "A Dim-Remembered Story" depicts time not only as a "flux," as a fluid and borderless dimension, but also as a cyclical one. The notion of the ups and downs of human civilization, and that of the "eternal return," are addressed quite openly, for example with the mention of "a new Dark Age" (EG 99) that may set in the far future of mankind. Moreover, the very fact that, according to the narrator, at the time of his sojourn in the Yrn castle, the "civilization sank to a low ebb in that unknown span of years" (EG 99) (while in another passage of the tale, the narrator even writes of "the rise and triumph and perishing of cultures [. . .] as autumn succeeds the full summer, and tired leaves fall where once fell blossoms") implies the notion that human cultures undergo a life-cycle similar to that of living organisms, which includes birth, development, apogee, and an

---

bright sunshine and the fresh wind that will come long after I am worm-infested. Having seen it I know that in this world about me I can nevermore find zest, desire, or consolation" (EG 104), words certainly reminiscent of the state of mind of Francis Wayland Thurston in "The Call of Cthulhu," who at the end of his narrative similarly states: "I have looked upon all that the universe has to hold of horror, and even the skies of spring and the flowers of summer must ever afterward be poison to me" (CC 169). Moreover, the very creation of the image of the castle of Yrn, with its medieval appearance and its sturdy frame, bears more than passing analogies to that of the Kadath castle, whereto Randolph Carter travels in the guise of a disembodied soul not too dissimilar from that acquired by Barlow's protagonist along his cosmic journey between the interstellar depths at the end of the universe.

inevitable decline toward a definitive extinction. This is of course very reminiscent of Oswald Spengler's "biological analogy," and of its critical reworking in Lovecraft's own works as a "theory of decline" applied to literature. According to Spengler, "*Cultures are organisms*, and world-history is their collective biography. [. . .] Every Culture passes through the age-phases of the individual man. Each has its childhood, youth, manhood and old age" (107). Lovecraft's fiction tends to stress not only and not so much the *cyclicity* implicit in Spengler's tenets,[5] but the notion of the *decline* and degradation of civilization, in particular of contemporary Western civilization. In "A Dim-Remembered Story," Barlow touches only slightly upon the notion of *cyclicity*, while of course the themes of the decline and extinction of human civilization play a major role in his "last-man" stories.

Yet Barlow's tale does not endorse the cyclical perspective uncritically. In fact, if no direction exists in time, namely if past, present, and future may appear merged on the cosmic level, this means that past and future events may overlap in a single instant, and that which occurred once may return now or in the future. This is precisely because the epistemic viewpoint according to which we separate the temporal dimensions, defining them as "once," "now," or "future," *has no validity on the cosmic scale*; it is just a fallacious interpretation conceived by our human, limited episteme. Therefore, while introducing the notion of "cyclicity" inside his fictional treatment of time, Barlow also implicitly criticizes it: he in fact recognizes that to define a past event that recurs today as "cyclical" is intrinsically wrong and short-sighted, because it just reflects the human perspective on the event itself: to define an event as "cyclical" implies the recognition of the event's occurrence in the past, and of its return in the present or in the future. Thus it implies the recognition of a past dimension, of a present dimension, and of a future dimension. "A Dim-Remembered Story" questions the validity of this tripartite distinction: on the cosmic scale (placed at a truth-level superior to the human), nothing can be deemed "cyclical," because no such things as past, present, and future exist. There is no *sequence* in cosmic time, but *parallelism*: "if the way might be opened, the door unsealed, we could go into other realms, to see and know forbidden things. They are as real, those future years, as any which our journeying has passed. This fact I know with a poignancy none other can share. Do not say the land ahead does not exist, simply because we cannot see it" (*EG* 99).

---

5. However, HPL was skeptical about Spengler's "biological analogy," as this excerpt from a letter to Alfred Galpin attests: "I think the philosopher errs when he draws too close a comparison between the life of a culture and that of a single biological organism. In effect, the parallel may indeed be close; for it is certain no civilization can last more than a limited length of time without going thro' various typical phases of decline. But when one considers the nature of the interdependence betwixt the parts of an organick unit, and compares this type of indivisible union and inevitable development with the looser bonds linking the elements of a culture, it becomes plain that the case is one of *resemblance* rather than of *identity*. Whilst the ultimate senescence and extinction of a culture are virtually unavoidable, the degree and conditions of its aging are certainly much more variable through chance and calculation than are those of a living organism's aging" (letter dated 27 October 1932; *Letters to Alfred Galpin* 166).

"A Dim-Remembered Story" does not restrict itself to questioning the linearity and separateness of the temporal dimensions, powerfully foregrounding the notions of the fluidity and the simultaneity of time. This richly complex narrative also discusses the alleged linearity and separateness of the entire space-time continuum: "[my experience] was, viewed in the perspective of what we call normality, as alien and catastrophic as the approach of some celestial derelict laden with fiery death. It involved abstruseness that might baffle Jeans[6] or Eddington,[7] perplex the greatest of our scientists. For it was a looping, of the real world with another no less real, but more distant than the mind can hold. *Distant not in the scale of miles and light-years, but in another, less tangible, less conceivable, fashion*" (*EG* 91; italics added). Space and time, it is openly suggested, are not the only possible dimensions, because temporal distance is just *one of the possible—though hardly conceivable—distances*.

Though it certainly deals with an illusory (because limited and anthropocentric) perception of Time, Barlow's narrative nurtures its "aeonian perspective" through the theme of Time's passing along numberless eras. The conflict in Barlow's fiction on this theme is evident: though it recognizes that the very notion of time's "passing" stems just from the limited human viewpoint (since on the cosmic scale time does not "pass," it is simultaneous), Barlow's fiction cannot do without a fictional treatment of time that takes into account the human perception of it. Barlow cannot help "dealing" with time in a conventional sense in his work, namely resorting to the traditional separation into three dimensions, but at least he decides to endorse the cosmic perspective in giving to his stories the background of an *extended temporality*: his plots unfold along vast temporal arcs, those of aeons. "A Dim-Remembered Story" is no exception. Often the mention of long centuries and eras appears, revealing the concern for "cosmic" events that step beyond petty human affairs but affect the history of the entire universe: "Whatever had happened—an explosion, an earthquake—the memory of that flaming day had lingered through dark centuries, while vines and flowers crawled and bloomed above the shards of a cryptic doom" (*EG* 91).

The sheer "antiquity" (*EG* 91) (in the future) of the castle of Yrn is cause of bafflement for the protagonist, and this shows the centrality of the "aeonian" temporal theme in this tale. This concern is also testified by some lexical evidence. The adjective "aeonian" recurs quite often: for instance, the narrator describes the castle as a place "built of storm-dark blocks, broidered with aeonian

---

6. Sir James Hopwood Jeans (1877–1946), English physicist, astronomer, and mathematician. He is considered the cofounder, with Arthur Eddington, of British cosmology. He studied molecular physics, quantum theory, and the theory of radiation in his youth, and then conducted research in astronomy. After retiring in 1929, he popularized science through books, lectures, and radio broadcasts.

7. Arthur Stanley Eddington (1882–1944), English astrophysicist, studied and popularized Einstein's theory of general relativity. He was also famous for his researches in quantum theory, gravitation, and the "fundamental theory" of general physics.

moss" (*EG* 94), while the world in which he is catapulted is "lost as aeon-buried Ur" (*EG* 97); it is a "cosmos of future aeons, when not one star shall remain as we know it" (*EG* 100). In order to render more effective the sense of utter temporal *alienity* and thus *outsideness* of the future dimension of Yrn, the narrator often strives to employ—and contextually show the inadequacy of—humanly recognizable tools of time and space measurement: "In a part of space lost *past the reach of light-years*; a place where *the farthest comet* never swings, these creatures have their world" (*EG* 103; italics added).

Sometimes, more subtly, the passing of a long extension of time is simply hinted at, for example when the narrator recalls the physical alterations that affected the body morphology of two animals he encountered in the forest surrounding Yrn, thus referring to a temporality so extended as to affect physical evolution: "The bird and hare which I saw (and whose aspect first set loose the roving of my fear) had altered subtly, but considerably. I do not, of course, have any evidence but that it was a local change. [. . .] Whatever the answer to this may be, is also a clue to the date of that age into which I was flung" (*EG* 99). The narrator is aware that "not centuries, but dozens of centuries barred me from my own world" (*EG* 99), and that the temporal dimension into which he was thrown is "deeper in the coming years than any past thing of which we have record" (*EG* 99).

It is important to emphasize that the theme of the "aeonian perspective" bears a strong connection with that of cosmicism. As briefly noted above, the endorsement of the aeonian perspective inevitably implies a reflection upon the frailty and ultimate inanity of human effort. The following comment is evoked in the protagonist by his reflection on how time's passing will affect the area where the Yrn castle rises and the rooms where he himself has been/will be hosted:

> It is frightening to think that it [the castle] will not be built for over fifteen thousand years, for I can remember the sunlight on the open court and the green deeps of that surrounding wood more clearly than this room in which I write. I lived in that castle when it had begun to crumble, and I felt the breeze come over swinging vines and old trees when I stood before the narrow window of my arched chamber. Yet my bones shall be wind-borne dust, and I shall have known rebirth in grass and flowers and dark roots, many centuries before masons lay trowel to the first stone of that edifice. The place where it will rise, in more than a dozen tens of centuries, is now an active city, with steel and glass and concrete walls that seem very *permanent*. But I know them as *ephemera*, for my eyes are haunted by the nocturnal wood, by the dark sunset of that land wherein I shall never again be. It saddens me to think of the bright sunshine and the fresh wind that will come long after I am worm-infested. (*EG* 104; italics added)

The dialectics between the illusory "permanence" of human achievements and their actual "transitoriness" or "ephemerality" on the cosmic scale is precisely the result to which the endorsement of an "aeonian" temporal perspective leads. The dialectics is more complex than it may appear at first sight: in fact, though the passing of time may bring to the ultimate dissolution of the results of any human effort, showing its utter uselessness and vacuity (because centuries are no less "ignorant of man" ("Return by Sunset" [EG 142]) than the earthquake or the typhoon), it should also be noted that according to Barlow the effect of time's ravening action is just to level and delete changes. Whatever man or any other species may achieve, time will come and destroy it, leaving no trace of its former presence. Ultimately, the effect of time's passing is that of *removing change*, of reducing everything to naught and a sort of "tabula rasa"—where nothingness finally triumphs.

5.2.2 Cosmic Time, still

This section will show how, in Barlow's fiction, the concern for the theme of cosmic time and its corollaries of the "aeonian perspective" and "time's fluidity" is not limited to the tale "A Dim-Remembered Story"—albeit this narrative is exemplary in this regard—but fully pervades all his fiction. In order to do so, I will discuss a few excerpts from other tales that most openly and significantly deal with cosmic temporality.

The sheer abundance of mentions of the words "aeon" and "ancient" and their derivates is indicative of Barlow's concern for what I call the "aeonian perspective," which is the first subtheme I am now going to trace. The examples are countless, as in "aeonian gulf" (EG 30), "looking back to earlier aeons" (EG 30), "unnumbered aeons" (EG 43), "long aeons" (EG 43), etc. Indeed an "aeonian perspective" is endorsed by tales like the last-man story of "'Till A' the Seas,'" which programmatically deals with the progressive decline of the living species on the earth and its desertion by mankind, over a process that does not simply take "years or even centuries, but millennia of ruthless change" (EG 44) whose material details are described in a scientifically quite accurate way.[8] Barlow's fiction often associates the terms "aeon" and "antiquity" to the lexeme "patina" (as in "patina of aeons" [EG 26] and ""patina of extreme antiquity" [EG 31]), which adds to the overall temporal vagueness and suspension of the fictional worlds.

However, the "aeonian perspective" is far from representing a plain and univocal approach to temporality in Barlow's fiction. In fact, a typical conundrum concerning the temporal setting of most of Barlow's narratives is already present in the early *Annals of the Jinns*: the aporia concerns which qualification to assign to the temporality of these tales, whether one of extreme antiquity in the reader's own space-time continuum, or one of a parallel, alternative dimension, part of a different space-time continuum. Whichever may be the case, the reading process reveals how clearly Barlow strives to convey the impression of an utterly *alien*

---

8. For example, with regard to the effects of the drying of the planet: "As the generations passed, the waters of the vast and unplumbed ocean wasted slowly away; enriching the air and the desiccated soil, but sinking lower and lower each century. The splashing surf still glistened bright, and the swirling eddies were still there, but a doom of dryness hung over the whole watery expanse" (EG 45).

temporal setting, one far removed from that familiar to the reader. Already in "The Slaying of the Monster," first collaboration with Lovecraft, a sense of a long passing of time is provided: the words graven on the stone tablet by the inhabitants of Laen, testifying their (imaginary) killing of the dragon, were "hard to read when we dug that stone from its deep, *ancient* layers of encrusting lava" (EG 13; italics added). It is precisely this sense of antiquity that Barlow underscores and intends to convey within a dimension, either one familiar to the reader or an alternative one, where the time span of the narrated events is that of eternity: the Black Tower of the Southlands has been there "for eternity" (EG 14) and was built by alien beings "in the dawn of the world" (EG 15). The tales of the *Annals* present an utterly *stretched temporality*, where edifices like the Black Tower or the tomb of the god Krang are "built *long before* any human walked the face of the world, built by evil powers that had reigned unchecked in that *unthinkably ancient day*" (EG 18; italics added). They take place in a dimension populated not only by extremely ancient buildings, but also of inconceivably old creatures, like the god Krang himself, who "had been for aeons" (EG 18) and "had lain unmoving since the world was young and green" (EG 19). The stories of these buildings and creatures traverse countless eras, while the passing of incalculable aeons inevitably leads the witnesses to *forgetfulness*, a key theme in Barlow's treatment of temporality that will be discussed in section 5.3: "And the years and the decades and the centuries and the aeons unthinkable came and went, and the sands swirled over the mouth of the tomb, and the door was obliterated, and none knew where Krang the Elder God lay in stupendous slumber" (EG 18-19).

Barlow's treatment of the theme of the "aeonian perspective" takes on two peculiar traits, which I designate *changelessness* and *timelessness*. The first trait refers to the notion that, notwithstanding the passing of long aeons and the "vandals of Time" (EG 22) may bring to a change in *perception* in the human observers (no one remembers where the immemorial god lies in slumber), these temporal transitions do not affect any substantial change on the *perceived, inanimate (abstract or super-natural) object*: for example, in spite of the aeonian times passed since the construction of the tomb of the god, he retains not only the dreadfulness of his outlook, but also his life: "He was terrible to gaze upon, for even after the immense period, he still held semblance of the horrifying aspect that was traditionally assigned unto him" (EG 19). The final instants of the life of Ull, the protagonist of "'Till A' the Seas,'" are revelatory of how Barlow insists on the corollary theme of changelessness: Ull wanders in the "changeless air" (EG 48) of the last, deserted empty village while approaching the cabins where "Little, indeed, changed but the living things" (EG 48). In the utter desolation of this last vision of mankind's fate, Barlow and Lovecraft highlight how, in spite of the aeonian passing of time, no real change, after all, has ever affected mankind's destiny of doom, sorrow, and insignificance—a fate that was encoded into its DNA when the species itself appeared on the planet and that nobody wanted to believe back in the old, bright days of the race's ephemeral successes.

"Return by Sunset" also insists on the notion of an aeonian passing of time whose destructive effects do not ultimately provoke substantial changes on the fundamental (lack of) *significance* of everything existing, especially that created by man's toilings, as for instance a religious temple. The protagonists of the tale, Dal and Leyenda, while fleeing from the girl's brothers who are chasing them, reach a ruined and abandoned temple standing on a cliff. The effects of the passing of time had been kind on the building, and this is already a sign that change had come very slowly on this site: "How gently ruin had come to this place! Little yellow wild-flowers were sprinkled across its pavement; dirt and rabble lay where once rich-garmented priests alone could set foot. Yet war for once was not to blame—no battle but the wind had taken his high place, no victor but the frost had trod it" (EG 136). Even more significantly, the narrator is sure that the temple would not undergo any further change until the very end of time:

> A stone basin, large enough to lie in, and rimmed with half-obliterated carvings of some procession, alone remained intact, one edge buried—a sacrificial bowl, grown over with flowering gourds. The god had grown weary and departed. Whatever screams had once lulled him were not even echoed on the wind; whatever blood and entrails had once gleamed before his eyes were now long superseded by the leaves and the rain and the snow. The ruin was old as the cliff it stood on, and the cliff *would last always*. It could undergo *no further change*. A future as long as its past, disturbed by no slipping stone, lay before it—and already it was older than death. It would lie lonely in the rain for centuries. (EG 135; italics added)

The ruin would pass through the heats of summers and the ices of winters, "yet it would suffer no change by these" (EG 136): only the "ultimate blackness" of the universe's extinction, when all the suns burned out forever, would sanction the ultimate, unavoidable triumph of time.

Barlow also reflects abundantly on time in "The Night Ocean," as we will have a chance to discuss in paragraph 5.4. What is pertinent now is to show how time's passing cannot ultimately affect the primordial link (thus an abstract principle) that people feel with the sea—a connection that remains unchanged across the eras, since water represents the primeval element of life, and therefore will constitute also its final and arrival point: "Through the heritage of a million years ago, when men were closer to the mother sea, and when the creatures of which we are born lay languid in the shallow, sun-pierced water, we still seek the primal things when we are tired, steeping ourselves within their lulling security like those early half-mammals which had not yet ventured upon the oozy land" (EG 108). "The Night Ocean" develops an important discussion on the subtheme of temporal changelessness, since this tale celebrates the powers of an inanimate natural element, water, that is so deified as to overcome the powers of time.[9] In fact, although time is a tyrannical lord, certainly able to lay waste to man's conquests and

---

9. For a discussion on the process of "deification" of the sea in "The Night Ocean," see paragraph 6.4 "Nature and the sacred: 'The Night Ocean'" in chapter 6 on Nature.

achievements, until they will lie in utter oblivion, time is not omnipotent: the ocean is a powerful entity in itself, and it does not receive from time's attacks a harm comparable to what mankind receives; it stays changeless along the eras: "The ancient brightness was now once more upon the sun, and the old glitter on the waves, whose playful blue shapes had flocked upon the coast ere man was born, and would rejoice unseen when he was forgotten in the sepulchre of time" (EG 114). In other words, the ocean succeeds whereas man fails: it defeats, at least temporarily, the cruel attacks of time and of its "ravenous years" (EG 115); the waves' "playful blue shapes" flocked upon the coast before man's birth and will still "rejoice" after mankind is but a dim memory. This temporary victory does not imply that the final war between time and the sea will be permanently won by the natural element, since we know from "'Till A' the Seas'" that in Barlow's fictional view a dying earth will be consumed by dryness after the last man has perished.

In its turn, timelessness represents an almost predictable consequence of the sense of *stretched temporality* hinted above, and one that affects Barlow's fiction: whereas a narrative's plot is meant to unfold along epochs and eras, it seems ineluctable that an aura of timelessness and a sense of a suspended, out-of-time atmosphere are fostered by the narration. The very notion of "immortality" sometimes appears, in order to strengthen the notion of timelessness: for instance, fauns are the protagonists of the short tale "The Misfortunes of Butter-Churning," and they are described as "immortal" (EG 42) creatures.

Yet it must be clarified that the introduction of the subthemes of changelessness and timelessness is by no means intended by Barlow as a tool to downplay the role and sheer weight of time as a ravenous destructor of anything claiming the right to existence in the universe. A tale like "The Root-Gatherers" displays the wild ravening and destructions operated by the blind forces of time, which annihilate and lay waste on everything they encounter and make everything fade away. The city of Doom (already an eloquent toponym) where the protagonists arrive is described as the receptacle of silence, emptiness, and devastation: "Here was Doom. The shards of a city that once knew merchants and toilers and the glittering rich—peopled now with memories and shadows and the whisper of the breeze. Silent now where the streets whose paving had sounded with the trample of multitudes; silent also the tumbled houses" (EG 85). And what is worse, the forces of time not only annihilate everything existing (not only everything human), but they are indeed so *blind* that their action is not even ultimately identifiable and recognizable:

> For centuries the vines and roots of jungle things had accumulated about the city, enveloping it and gnawing at outlying districts. For centuries the bubbling hues of sunset had glazed with yellow lacquer those dark streets, and crept along unseen walls. [. . .] I saw what once had been a shop—the front was crumbled, and a rotten beam lay half across the opening, but there was a litter of incredible wreckage within—goods that had been fashioned for purchasers dead a thousand years, despised even by the beast. Someone had come there and sorted out the useful, undamaged things, but like the rest, these lay in an unclaimed pile. *Perhaps the*

scavenger *was there a day before us—perhaps he had become the prey of some animal eight hundred years ago*. There was nothing to tell why he had not borne off his spoil. (*EG* 86; italics added)

This passage is of course an effective example of Barlow's skills in the description of the spectral remnants of a declining civilization. But what most concerns us now is to notice that Barlow portrays the temporal traces left by the actions of living things like the "scavengers" as *not recognizable nor detectable*. Time is such a tyrannical lord that it not only brings merciless destructions and devastations on man's achievements, but it also does not even leave to man the opportunity—meager consolation as this may be—to identify the coordinates of these devastations: it is impossible to tell not only when exactly the destructions took place, but even when the scavenger could have come to claim its spoil. Yesterday, or eight centuries ago: both temporal collocations are equally possible, as this is the "power of surmise" man is allowed by time.

Moreover, the patina of antiquity, especially when associated by Barlow with entities and creatures, almost automatically endows them with mighty and peculiar powers. The creature that fights for the possession of our world in "The Summons" is described as "An *immeasurably old* and evil thing not of our world but of some infinitely and mercifully remote stellar depth" (*EG* 70; italics added), as an "*incomparably ancient* and utterly alien entity" (*EG* 70; italics added), a thing "older than Stonehenge, and might have manifested itself to the ancestors of the pyramid builders. It was ancient beyond all human conception or belief" (*EG* 70). Having established the entity's incalculable antiquity so convincingly, Barlow proceeds to associate it with the image of terrible powers: "a monster so obscenely complex and maturely terrible" (*EG* 70), a Lovecraftian-sounding "insult to sane laws of nature" (*EG* 70) able to enter into telepathic contact with human beings and force them to obey irresistible summons, and ultimately to fight for the conquest of the entire planet. This very Cthulhu-like being is of course an alien from another temporal and spatial dimension, an immeasurably *old* creature—Barlow, following Lovecraft's lesson among the others, links the notion of *antiquity* with that of *alienity*: the alien monster is almost always inevitably a very old one—at least according to the temporal canons adopted by the human episteme. And who could be brave enough to defend mankind and stand against the antique alien and its unwholesome plans of planetary conquest, if not a "very old man" (*EG* 70), in whose figure we can easily detect the reciprocation, on the human side, of the process bestowing exceptional powers to extremely old alien creatures? Old age automatically allows and implies extraordinary powers when human beings, and not only aliens, are concerned. Therefore it is only natural that such an "incarnation, *older than the very universe*, of all the foulness that exists" (*EG* 71; italics added) is counterattacked by a very old man, whose age endows with superior powers and wisdoms.

Barlow's fictional treatment of the temporal theme also shows a deep concern for the corollary of "time's fluidity." If "A Dim-Remembered Story," as we have seen in the previous paragraph, provides a full-fledged representation of this subtheme, Barlow's other fictional works reveal a by no means lesser involvement with it. However, I will limit my examination to the most interesting and original contributions they offer to further clarify and enrich Barlow's narrative approach to this sub-theme. Of course, the parodistic and spoof pieces that Barlow wrote in collaboration with Lovecraft are imbued with a playful and jocular perspective on temporality. "The Battle That Ended the Century" (1934), perhaps the funniest work on which Barlow and Lovecraft ever collaborated, sets the boxing fight between Two-Gun Bob and Knockout Bernie "on the eve of the year 2001" (EG 35)—though this is not particularly playful in itself, since most science fiction stories are placed in a future time; yet an amusing element in the tale's treatment of time is already revealed by its own subtitle, "MS. Found in a Time Machine," which pokes fun at the conventions of the SF stories published on the contemporary pulps—as well as, perhaps, the whole genre itself. Another detail—that of the time at which the boxing match starts—is revelatory of the playful approach to temporality the tale displays: "The gong was sounded at 39 o'clock" (EG 36). The second spoof on which Barlow and Lovecraft collaborated, the fragment "Collapsing Cosmoses," presents a jocular treatment of time, eminently parodistic of SF conventions. Dam Bor, a sort of watch-creature guarding the safety of the universe, detects through his cosmoscope the approaching of a deadly menace, and reports to the operator behind him: "That blur in the ether can be nothing less than a fleet *from outside the space-time continuum we know*. Nothing like this has ever appeared before. It must be an enemy. Give the alarm to the Inter-Cosmic Chamber of Commerce. There's no time to lose—at this rate they'll be upon us *in less than six centuries*" (EG 60; italics added). The parody of science fiction is quite openly recognizable, but to be honest, the passage was written by Lovecraft—though of course Barlow likely approved it. However, later in the fragment, Barlow himself reinforces the spatial-temporal game initiated by Lovecraft by making the narrator (probably a patrolman of the Inter-Cosmic army) notice that the presence of the enemy is marked by "a faint blur *half a million light-years long*" (EG 61; italics added). What the nature of this indefinite enemy might actually be is of course matter of speculation for the reader, and adds to the undeniable comicality of the narrative.

Barlow adopts a similar "light" perspective on temporality in his ironic chronicles of the "missions" of the *fourteen-thousand-year-old* demon Garoth.[10] The demon's age itself is meant to sound comic, but in Chapter 3 of the tale "The Temple" the reader witnesses a sudden transformation of a girl whose "limbs and body withered, shrivelled as if a hundred years of desiccation had become compressed into a moment" (EG 50). The fictional world into which Garoth lives and accomplishes his "tasks" is very ironical, and the playful dimension could not help investing this world's temporality.

In "The Experiment" the subtheme of fluid temporality assumes more serious connotations. The young student Edwin Coswell, who agrees to participate in a "cosmic" experiment in the studio of the doctor Marcus Edwards, is catapulted into

---

10. For a detailed analysis of the general irony implicit in the Garoth "saga," see section 7.2. "Tales of true humor and parody" in chapter 7 on Irony.

a suspended dimension where only his disembodied soul is conscious and able to communicate the details of the experience to Edwards. From his new "cosmic" perspective, Coswell's soul is able to perceive the three temporal dimensions as one, with no separateness: "I am alone. A vast buzzing sound fills the universe. . . . *I can see all my past and future. And the past and future of the whole scheme of things*" (*EG* 58; italics added). This tale is structured along the theme of the blurring and merging of temporal borders: Coswell experiences the possibility of traveling back and forward in time; he can see clearly and simultaneously into the far future ("aeons ahead" [*EG* 59]) and into the past: the events of the two dimensions appear to collide into an instant that reminds us of the notion of the transcendent present discussed in the previous paragraph. Coswell does not encounter difficulty in obeying Edwards's request to "come nearer our time" (*EG* 59), as he seems, thanks to Edward's machine, to have conquered the "secret of time" not differently from Lovecraft's Great Race. Coswell traverses epochs of the history of the universe and of human history: first he wears Oriental clothes, then he walks—not bearing a human form yet—in a jungle of extreme beauty, then assumes the forms of a Christian slave in the era of emperor Nero, of a druid-priest in Briton during some unwholesome ceremony, of a monk in a gloomy cell, of an African savage, and finally "lands" on a feudal castle that lies indefinitely in time, in the phase of an alien attack against the human outpost. In fact, as an answer to Edwards's questions "What year is it? What country?" (*EG* 59), Coswell answers: "Long ago—or perhaps—no; I do not know. It may be the future, the Armageddon of mankind. The country is Illoe" (*EG* 59). The sheer uncertainty of the temporal collocation of this fatal battle involving what appear to be the last defenders of human civilization against the assaults of alien monstrosities is revelatory of the fluidity of time in this tale: in fact, fluidity not only attests the reciprocal permeability of the three temporal dimensions, it also engenders—on the human being who cannot cling to the reassuring distinction of the three dimensions anymore—an utter epistemological bewilderment which of course has also psychological and emotional side-effects.

The simultaneity of past and present is also the token of the time's fluidity sub-theme in "The Summons." Upon entering the forest toward which the unfathomable calls allure him, the protagonist-narrator recognizes that the dreamlike experience he is undergoing looks like a cyclical repetition of an event that already occurred in an aeonian past: "Now, all at once, I knew the forest. *That radiant sky had come with the voice, long aeons before.* Somehow I had seen this fearsome place, and whatever power summoned me must have intended it so. I recognized a certain flashing aspect with terrified shock" (*EG* 68; italics added). The words I have italicized reveal a further disturbing aspect of the narrator's perception of this temporal experience: he realizes that the forest he is traversing, the sky over his head, and the mysterious voice summoning him are *coming from an aeonian-old past*, though they are seen and heard *now*. Again, the borders between the temporal dimensions are completely shattered.

The discussion of a blurred temporality also affects the narrator of "The Night Ocean," whose perceptive faculties, toward the end of his sojourn at Ellston

Beach, undergo a massive alteration.[11] His perception of the temporal flow also appears distorted, as the fairy-tale-like dimension into which he is thrown (or throws himself) becomes one of unclear borders between the temporal units: "After a while the falling rain—which must have continued throughout the previous night—succeeded in washing away those vestiges of purple cloud which had resembled the ocean-cliffs in an old fairy-tale. Cheated alike of the setting and rising sun, *that day merged with the day before*, as if the intervening storm had not ushered a long darkness into the world, but had swollen and subsided *into one long afternoon*" (EG 114; italics added). When the time comes for the final confrontation with the horrors that await him outside on the beach no less than inside his own mind, the narrator enters the most fearful phase of sensory suspension, where his perceptive faculties of the temporal flow look irremediably compromised and the space of a minute may finally last a much more stretched interval, even an "eternity," as this passage richly woven with temporal nuances attests:

> The endless tableau of the lunar orb—dead now, whatever her past was, and cold as the unhuman sepulchres she bears amid the ruin of dusty centuries older than man—and the sea—astir, perhaps, with some unkenned life, some forbidden sentience—confronted me with horrible vividness. I arose and shut the window; partly because of an inward prompting, but mostly, I think, as an excuse for transferring momentarily the stream of thought. No sound came to me now as I stood before the closed panes. *Minutes or eternities were alike*. (EG 118; italics added)

As I hope my analysis has contributed to make clear, according to Barlow time constitutes a *flexible* dimension, and chronological progression is just one of the possible perspectives over it, an anthropocentric, and therefore limited, interpretation.

As a final word on the fundamental tenets of Barlow's fictional approach to cosmic temporality, let us discuss "Origin Undetermined," a narrative not only revelatory of essential features of Barlow's treatment of human time, especially in its corollary "Past,"[12] but also containing a truly crucial passage that configures as a sort of conclusive *summa* of the topics I have touched along my discussion of cosmic time, and in particular on the subthemes of the "aeonian perspective," the changelessness in spite of time's effects, and the *flexibility/fluidity* and *reversibility* of time. While wandering into a dream-world whose features are evoked by the evil powers of the plant that Roberts has freed from an ancient Maya urn, he visits—as a sort of traveling mind—a waste land totally uninhabited and desolate:

> Age reeked from that primal, night-bound steppe. Lying monstrous and uncharted, it could have swallowed and forgotten such expanses as Gobi or the Pacific floor. All the armies of history might have wandered out and lost themselves within it. As I stood (or dreamed I stood) there, I was troubled by a recurrence of my childish fear,

---

11. The issue of the reliability of this narrating voice is discussed in section 3.4.1, "The lonely and paranoid narrator: 'The Night Ocean,'" in chapter 3 on Vagueness.
12. See section 5.3.2 in this chapter.

which seemed a thing of today and not of lost decades. Something swept into me, *confusing my sense of Time's orderly progression,* and I was not even certain whether I was a man or a small boy who feared the night. The place was old not in centuries or millennia, but so much older that it had been drifted over with the sediment at the bottom of Time's well. It had known, I think, all the changes stone and earth can know. It had been spawned in flame, congealing like metal taken from a furnace; it had swelled with the pregnancy of mountains and split itself to bear them terrifically. It had *rested for aeons* with grain welling up beneath mild skies, it had dreamed in the wet spring and hidden its face in the bitter snow, lakes had flowed across it and vanished, and then its mountains had cast shorter shadows, its sweet turf had crumbled into sand, and that ultimate sand had become dust, lying deep and formless in unending fields. *Finality had come upon it—there was no other change it might undergo.* Sullen and featureless now, it had only recollections to brood on, and only the night to hear its whispered, inhuman secrets. (*EG* 128; italics added)

This passage concentrates in few lines several of the main points of Barlow's fictional treatment of cosmic time: the "aeonian" approach to temporality, its fluidity, and finally the changelessness that remains as the ultimate trait of the inanimate objects (like natural formations, places, buildings) in spite of the devastating attacks of time, the tyrannical lord.

5.3 Human Time

Let us discuss now the modality with which Barlow's fiction deals with the theme of human time. In particular, I have chosen to address this theme by referring to the two subthemes that best represent it: memory and the past. The topic of memory will be first discussed in connection with the tale titled "A Memory," and then in the rest of Barlow's fiction.

5.3.1 "A Memory": caring for the future of civilization

The date of composition of "A Memory" is not known, but the tale was probably written not long before its publication in the *Californian* for Winter 1935. This narrative thematizes, as its title eloquently anticipates, the theme of memory, in particular as a perspective on human time *internal to the human mind*: the creation of memories is a process not only strictly temporal, but one that *deals with time* in the sense that it re-elaborates events of the past by somehow "fixing" them and subtracting them to the inexorable flow of time. By creating memories, man achieves the illusion of a temporary victory over the annihilating powers of time.

Memory as a subtheme of human time is not at all contradictory with cosmic time; in fact, they are complementary: it is exactly Barlow's concern for the passing of long stretches of time (cosmic time) that inevitably configures memory as one of the possible weapons—another is dream, which in its conjoined action with memory Barlow also represents in his poetry[13]—to blunt, albeit illusorily, the destructive action of cosmic time. Memory and dream are often connected in Barlow's work (dreams often stem from memories), but they are weapons not always and unconditionally reliable against time: in the poetry of his final years, those of the most bitter disillusionment, Barlow would come to see even memory as potentially dangerous.[14] But in his fiction (whose writing actually ends in the 1930s), Barlow still retains a positive attitude toward memory and its salvific powers.

"A Memory," in particular, presents a version of the future of the human race, choosing the viewpoint of the *memory* of a character in the far future— a narrative structure reminiscent of that of William Hope Hodgson's *The Night Land* (1912), although Barlow did not probably read this novel before writing "A Memory."[15]

This rich and substantial tale shows that Barlow's concern for the future of mankind is not necessarily and exclusively revealed in his cosmic visions of the race's—and the planet's—dreadful end discussed in the paragraph on cosmic time. Barlow is not, mainly or solely, a "catastrophist." "A Memory" is a tale that provides glimpses of the (far) future of the race; but these future visions are discussed as the remembrances of a person of the future itself. The tale is not concerned with the representation of the final doom, but with a previous stage of the process—placed, however, in the far future with respect to the reader's present. Scientifically accurate is Barlow's depiction of the way, for instance, in which humanity shall develop and modify its city architectures into a distinctly "centered" model—reminiscent of Hodgson's Great Redoubt—as described in this passage:

> Conceive, if you are able, this giant city of ours! an entire metropolis welded into one single structure, higher than man had ever built before, and sinking far into the earth—so far that the very number of the levels was forgotten. The gleaming spire was lovely in the sunlight—silver-white, and jeweled with many windows. [. . .] Outlying districts had been abandoned to the forest growth, and all the people dwelt thereafter within the walled enclosure. Growth became vertical rather than upon the earth's surface, and floor by floor the giant structure rose as each new level was needed. [. . .] And these things happened likewise in an hundred places throughout the land, and men congregated into feudal towns, so that they no longer spread over the green countryside and along quiet roads in little houses, for all were centered now within those giant spires. (EG 73-74)

---

13. See especially sections 9.2.2.3 and 9.2.3 in chapter 9 on Poetry.
14. See section 9.2.2 in chapter 9, and in particular 9.2.2.3.
15. In a letter dated 29 January 1936, HPL thus addresses RHB: "Glad you appreciate the Hodgson material, which is really extremely distinctive. Some day, perhaps, 'The Night Land' (which so resembles your Californian story) will get back into circulation" (FF 317). The "Californian story" in question is "'Till A' the Seas,'" which was published in the Summer 1935 issue of the *Californian*, after HPL slightly revised it with RHB during the 1935 New Year's night in New York. Implying that *The Night Land* was not included in the "Hodgson material" he sent RHB, HPL thus attests that RHB had not read this novel before writing "A Memory."

Yet the "architectural" aspect is just one of the several aspects Barlow addresses in this tale with respect to the future of human civilization. In the presentation of the future of mankind, the narrator foregrounds its *decadence,* relating it to the race's growing inability to preserve its memories. A human civilization, already so threatened by the attacks of time in the long run, may expect to ensure survival only *by remembering its past* and treasuring its former conquests. This tale provides many examples of mankind's "losses of memories," casually correlating them with its utter decadence. The memory-losses are often signaled by the occurrence of expressions like "dim" or "half-forgotten memories"—which effect an additional overlapping between the theme of vagueness and that of memory. For example, the unnamed narrator notices how the building process of the metropolis where men are gathered at the time of his writing dates back to vague and unremembered circumstances: "It had been centuries of centuries in the making, as intercourse with the outside world became less needful. *Half-forgotten* wars began the fortifying, and reared those giant walls no foe could pierce" (*EG* 73; italics added). Mankind started (in a far past from the narrator's perspective, in a far future from the reader's) to gather in independent cities that rarely communicated and ultimately became self-sufficient and did not need any contact with the external world, thanks to the invention of some *"forgotten* genius" (*EG* 73; italics added) who rediscovered the long-lost secret of light and "created an artificial radiance more powerful than the sun, and as inexhaustible" (*EG* 73). In this way, the new mankind could do without sunlight, by creating artificial synthetic beams that ensured all the heat and light necessary to the neatly separated city-worlds on the planet. Trying to describe the past of the race—which, let us not forget, corresponds to a far future for the present reader—the narrator realizes how a great many memories are irremediably lost: mankind went through centuries of fierce and barbaric wars for supremacy, "A great many people were slain, and much secret lore of ancient years was lost, so that those who were left after the weary centuries of war *no longer knew how man might fly or travel through the ocean's depths* or do the other wondrous deeds of their fathers" (*EG* 74; italics added). Mankind forgot how to build machines allowing for travel: "Man had believed from ancient tales that once he had the gift of flight, but now there were many who did not credit this" (*EG* 74). The inhabitants of the narrator's city grew dubious even of the existence of other people in other towns: only dim rumors survive of an ancient sighting of torches in procession against the dark horizon, "a writhing maggot of light which no telescope could resolve" (*EG* 75). Tales of lights passing close to the tower where he lives still endure at the time of the narrator's writing—but the same tales reveal that none dared to unbar the doors of the city and meet visitors, "for they did not know what might be encountered. And afterward, when all fearfulness had died, those who had seen these things could not be sure that the night had not deluded them, for of such nocturnal happenings no traces could be glimpsed by those who looked afterward by day, from the high windows. All this had been in the long ago—*half-forgotten* through the centuries—till the recent years of my own life" (*EG* 75; italics added). All the memories are lost through the dim tales and fables of the old; the narrator reveals that he, as a child, had heard "queer whispered tales of old, and had sought to learn more concerning the hinted marvels" (EG 75) without success among clasped tomes and "crumbling vermin-haunted records on dim shelves" (EG 75), and thus must conclude that all those memories were "wholly fable: spun in idleness by the aged" (EG 75).

In the narrator's town, the provenance and the initial reason for the creation of the *glortups* are not remembered. These creatures, their living conditions, and their overall parable are reminiscent of Lovecraft's shoggoths in At the Mountains of Madness:[16] both species were created by the dominant race (the Old Ones in Lovecraft, the humans in Barlow) for servile purposes, live in segregation, and gradually become more powerful and intelligent—simultaneously taking advantage of the decline of the civilization that created them. More than recognizing the likely thematic influence of Lovecraft's novel on Barlow's tale, we are here especially interested in emphasizing Barlow's representation of the *loss of memory* concerning the *glortups* as a sign of the decadence of the human group:

> I do not know when or how it was that the slave-things called glortups came. Our people *did not remember*. None were certain whether those squat, brownish-green little monsters that mimicked the aspect of humans and the features of toads were created in the wonderful experiments of our ancestors, shapen from plastic slime with forgotten arts—or whether they were transplanted from some nameless place in the ancient years when men flew among the clouds. *There were no records* in the mouldy tomes of our race, and it almost seemed as if they had come suddenly, from their unknown source, in the time *after our culture had become to decline*. It was many centuries since anyone kept records, *and the recollection of man is short*. (EG 75–76; italics added)

Barlow indicates a very clear connection between the decline of the race and its inability to preserve memories of its past. And the significance of this link will become more relevant in the course of the narration, since it is just because of man's loss of memory that the *glortups* are able to develop their intelligence and plot rebellion in secrecy, ultimately creating a threat to the survival of the civilization that initially had created them just as servants (again the thematic similarities with At the Mountains of Madness are inescapable).

"A Memory" is then the chronicle of the perilous exploring mission undertaken by the narrator and his companion, Nalda, in the lower levels of the City-Tower, where the *glortups* had been confined since their creation. The protagonists look for an explanation and a confirmation of their suspicions that the slave-things are preparing a huge rebellion and a final overturn of the supremacy of the humans: the narrator and Nalda bravely decide to access the *glortup* world through

---

16. The manuscript of At the Mountains of Madness reached RHB as early as September 1931: in a letter dated 17 September 1931, HPL apologized he could not send the copy directly to RHB, but ensured that "the MS. is in circulation & will reach you (I hope) before very long" (FF 8). The document did indeed reach RHB, as a letter from HPL of 25 September attests: "& I am glad the 'Mts. of Madness' duly reached you" (FF 10).

the metal wall that separates it from the human world. Again the issue of a dim memory comes to the fore, since a motivation behind their daring decision is also the fact that none in the tower, not even Nalda who already visited it in the past, remembers what the world of the slaves really looks like, and especially how dangerous it might be to traverse it:

> Nalda and I were yet resolved upon passing into the darkness of the glortup-world. No human foot had trod that path for many dusty years—to monster-folk alone were these nighted labyrinths familiar. Nalda had braved these unknown perils years before, as one of a watchful, well-armed band; *but now the memories were dim*. The chief impression that remained was one of night-steeped crypts, all the blacker through contrast with the dazzling, man-made radiance which poured from hidden sources to give the upper world a ceaseless day. (EG 77; italics added)

The human stage depicted by the narrator is truly one in which memory, or its absence, plays a crucial role, and one in which—as a sign of the decline of the race—the doom of memory's loss is always lurking: Nalda had already visited the *glortups*' underworld, but she *does not remember* her experience. Not only do old tales become so dim as to verge toward fables, but in a decadent civilization memories do not even last the span of a lifetime. And that the human race of this tale is crossing a phase of utter decadence is reasserted by the narrator right after his and Nalda's passing into the *glortup* world:

> I stood then, in a world unknown. For a thousand years this place of slaves had grown and spread in darkness, so that the plan and shape of its labyrinthine passages was lost to mortals. There, in filth and gloom, they spawned, those twisted slaves, and flocked in evil throngs upon strange missions. Some might ask why we did not obliterate those rotten levels, and put the slaves to torch and spears, scouring the City clean of this corruption. The time was gone when we might have done this—*our race was softened now and paid more heed to gold and silver spices and silken robes than to the menace from below*. (EG 78; italics added)

And this carelessness is likely to be fatal for the survival of the race. The narrator and Nalda descend toward lower and lower levels in the *glortup* world, visiting alleys and planes that host a loathsomeness and a corruption far beyond the expectation and the control of a human civilization doomed by its decline, its lack of memory, and its thoughtlessness for its own history:

> There was something terrible in these long-deserted alleys and dark passages beneath the pressing earth. It typified the downfall of our race and the fast-approaching end to the revelry above us. *Our race had scorned the knowledge of the past and fallen into ignorance* [. . .] Down still. Our way led into these remote and desolate levels where not even glortups came. These walls were cracked with the weight of aeons, and *the pavement had forgotten human tread*. It became a nightmarish and interminable descent from dim corridor to corridor until I was dazed with climbing downward. (EG 80; italics added)

The ignorance of the past is openly described as the main cause of the doom awaiting mankind: the menace represented by the *glortups* could have been averted just by *remembering* their origin, just by going over (mentally no less than physically) the alleys and the planes where the monster-slaves were confined.

However, in this tale Barlow does not want to sound too optimistic. To preserve memory, though *necessary* to fight the decline of the race, is *not sufficient* to ensure its survival: because memory, or better the human attempt to preserve it, is fallacious in itself. Already in the mention of Nalda's forgetting her previous descent into the *glortup* world Barlow had hinted at this *inability to preserve the memory* of past events in the limited span of one's own lifetime (a sort of "homo-diegetic loss of memory" of the fictional protagonist): the recollection of man is short.[17] And now the picture is completed with Barlow portraying even the narrator as not immune to this sort of fictional amnesia, a "disease" investing both memories and dreams (which once more get connected[18]) and which configures as the typical malaise of a declining human civilization: "You ask me what we sought in these unpeopled cellars? All that I recall is our certainty at the time, the assuredness that we should not fail in that dim quest. Of its nature I can tell nothing but that it was forbidden to us, and that we risked much to go. *My weary memory holds little more. . . the dreams are fading rapidly*; and I recall but a small part of that phantasmagoric descent" (EG 80; italics added). And the final revelation unveiled by the protagonists' mission represents the decisive confirmation of the doom awaiting the humans: a doom awaiting them in the physical darkness of the depths below the *glortup* world, as well as in the metaphorical darkness of the forgetfulness of human minds.

5.3.1.1 Memory, still

Barlow's fiction is replete with works featuring the subtheme of memory in the acceptations discussed in the tale "A Memory." In this regard, the sheer frequency of the mentions of the adjective "immemorial" is indicative of Barlow's concern for the issue of remembrance. Whenever, in his fiction, the word "immemorial" appears, the reader can be sure that the narrator is warning him against the danger of a possible "decline" in the civilization at stake. Anything immemorial is intrinsically dangerous, because where memories are lacking, this becomes a sign of time's overcoming man's efforts to preserve his civilization. The episodes of the juvenile *Annals of the Jinns* with their peculiar setting in a "once

---

17. The theme of the "homo-diegetic loss of memory" can be seen as a sort of reduplication of the hetero-diegetic loss of memory that structures most of RHB's fiction. In other words, RHB's tales feature a doubling of the theme of the loss of memory on the narrator's part: the theme appears both on the hetero-diegetic level (the hetero-diegetic narrator—i.e. the one who does not participate to the actions he narrates—does not or cannot remember details of the past of his story, since the documents or legends or tales or rumors he uses are or have become reticent), and on the homo-diegetic level (the narrator who directly participates in the action he narrates loses his own memory of the events he took or takes part in).
18. More on this connection will be discussed in section 5.4, in particular with reference to "The Night Ocean."

upon a time" and "suspended" temporal dimension, already present several occurrences of the word "immemorial." In "The Flagon of Beauty," episode three of the cycle, the princess thinks of the flask—allegedly able to bestow beauty—as "made in the immemorial years agone" (EG 17): just the fact that the time when an object, concrete or abstract (in this case, a flagon) was created is wrapped in the shroud of forgetfulness means that the object in question is not *reliable* anymore, as the denouement of the tale reveals. Not bearing memories of the time of the object's creation, man *has lost control over it*—and therefore vagueness arises also as to the object's functions and powers. It becomes *dangerous* because it has fully entered the dominion of time and escaped the memory-control of man. In "An Episode in the Jungle," installment eleven of the *Annals*, the young hunter Loman gets lost in the forest of Yondath, where the ancestors of his people once dwelt. In a clearing, he finds the stone idol, built in an immemorial past, of an ancient and forgotten froglike god: Loman and his people have no memories of this god, which "sat fixed in immemorial stone" (EG 31). No memories can be recollected of this idol: "Forgotten a long while, and unexplained now, it looked at him with the eyes of centuries. A sculptor who had beheld the thousand-year departed sun had chiseled it, and what he made *was more permanent than memory*" (EG 31; italics added): this very defeating of human memory implies that the idol has somehow "conquered" mankind and will "outlast" (EG 31) it.

Again Barlow is claiming that, when an object—material or immaterial—succeeds in escaping man's memory, it is finally free from any human control, and so a pure "sign" of time's triumph in its struggle with man: for instance, the ruined city of "The Root-Gatherers" is finally wrapped in an "immemorial silence" (EG 86) that prevents humans from exerting a control over the crumbling edifices. Also in "The Night Ocean," the process of the sea's personification leads the narrator to envision the eventual rise from the abysses of an entity possibly dangerous just because generated from immemorial chasms, i.e. from a source over which man has no control: "The morning ocean, glimmering with a reflected mist of blue-white cloud and expanding diamond foam, has the eyes of one who ponders on strange things, and her intricately woven webs, through which dart a myriad coloured fishes, hold the air of some great idle thing which will arise presently from the hoary *immemorial* chasms and stride upon the land" (EG 108; italics added).

"'Till A' the Seas'" constitutes an essential tale in Barlow's development of the subtheme of memory. Again I regard this work as mainly a product of Barlow's creativity, since Lovecraft's intervention has been proved to have been mainly "cosmetic" and in particular focused on the final lines. This last-man story contains the narrative of the ultimate, inevitable decline of human civilization toward its final doom and extinction, and is rich with reflections on the tight causality between "loss of memory" and cultural decline. When a civilization loses its memories, its only possible future is downfall. Not only, as we have seen in section 5.2.2, is the decline of the human race described accurately from a scientific viewpoint, but Barlow details the phases of the race's decadence by referring them to the progressive *loss of memory* of its past achievements as well as even of *itself*: "During strangely prosperous centuries the hoary deserted cities of the equator *grew half-forgotten* and entwined with fantastic fables. *Few thought* of those spectral, rotting towers . . . those huddles of shabby walls and cactus-choked streets, darkly silent and abandoned" (EG 44; italics added). Along with the merciless passing of time, people come even to forget about the areas of the planet they used to inhabit: "So at last the oceans went, and water became a rarity on a globe of sunbaked drought. Man had slowly spread all over the arctic and Antarctic lands; the equatorial cities, and many of later habitation, *were forgotten even to legend*" (EG 46; italics added). Yet the inexorable decadence of the peoples of the race is most poignantly testified by the progressive *lack of respect* they show toward their past, and by their *forgetting of their own bygone cultural and scientific conquests*: "Things of the greatest value and importance were left in dead museums—lost amidst the centuries—and in the end *the heritage of the immemorial past was abandoned*. A degeneracy both physical and cultural set in with the insidious heat" (EG 44-45; italics added). When there is no memory anymore, it is a very serious sign of decline, it is a sign of the end. Without memory, people can survive only in a barbarian, primitive state whose cultures are just the pallid shadows of the evolved human civilizations of the forgotten past: "and as the eras passed there developed a sound, sturdy race, *bearing no memories* or legends of the old, lost lands. Little navigation was practiced by this new people, and the flying machine was *wholly forgotten*. Their devices were of the simplest type, and their culture was simple and primitive" (EG 45; italics added).

"The Root-Gatherers" and "Return by Sunset" also tell of Barlow's equation between oblivion and the decadence of civilization. In the first tale, the protagonist and his mother have to pass through the ruins of a long-deserted city standing on their path in search for edible roots and tubers. The two characters are part of a tribe of an allegedly far future, when human civilization will have collapsed and will concentrate on mere survival, not even remembering the greatness of its past:

> This land about us, these ancient, sun-covered fields, we knew had once been great and flourishing; but in a forgotten time something wrong had happened. We are the children of the old race, but no one cares now about the ancient things and *the world of dead memories*. Such things they say are of no use, for they cannot help us to obtain food. *Only two or three of us take interest in the past*. Perhaps it is a fortunate thing, because those who dare are half-restive in the life about them. (EG 84; italics added)

The ironic flavor of that last statement is revelatory of Barlow's preoccupation for a civilization—and this is the ultimate sign of decline—that cares only for its material survival and does not preserve or respect the memories of its past. The narrator of "The Root-Gatherers" is fully aware that the tale of the past prominence of his race would be irremediably lost, were it not for the memories of the old: "When we were beyond the trees I looked at the small figure beside me, and felt a pang because of *half-recollected stories of our ancient grandeur*, when we had made cities like the dead one before us, and *did not fear storms and animals*" (EG 84; italics added). In the last sentence of this passage we can certainly notice Barlow's veiled hint as to the cultural decline of the race: not only do most humans care just for their physical survival and are unable to build cities like the ruined one, but they have also somehow regressed to superstition and to a minority cultural condition that induce them to fear animals and natural forces. Barlow makes his narrator fully realize this present culturally disadvantaged condition in which he is forced to live and which originated from the loss of memory of his race. These are the poignantly mourning words the narrator employs while recalling his contemplation of a crumbling tower of the ruined city:

> There was nothing to show the purpose for which it had been made [...] My regret that we have no memories *is a pang more difficult than hunger*, for hunger can be satisfied, but for the nostalgic beckoning of old centuries there is no assuagement. *I would like so much to fill out the gap of years which bind us to the past*, when men built that old city; and to know the hues and forms of a life vanished utterly. But there are only ruins on which to speculate, fragments of a life existing nowhere, and the people of that place are lonely in the desolate grave of night. A *rain of centuries has obliterated most of the traditions about them* and all that I may even recapture is as nothing when it is weighted against the ignorance of our time. Forest and wooden glen, and tales of ancient huntings are the joys of my race. (*EG* 84; italics added)

Aside from reinstating the close connection between the theme of the loss of memory (human time) and that of the "aeonian perspective" (cosmic time) so prevalent in Barlow's fiction (the passing of long centuries of course favors the loss of memories), Barlow here further reinforces the notion that a race without memories of its past cultural grandeur is a declining one. Memories are a weapon not only against the attacks of time, but also against the vagueness of most of our sensory perceptions. The protagonist of "The Root-Gatherers," who made the walk described in his account at a time when he was a boy, is now recollecting the sights and the sensations he felt that day. He recognizes that memory is his only ally in the preservation of a scene from his childhood that he would forever cherish—his crossing of a metal bridge near the ruined town and arching over a river where lilies and rushes grow thick:

> It is a vivid and chromatic scene that I remember—the dead green surface and the vague glitter of the bridge at dusk—though years have gone since I was there last. I looked about as we started across the ruinous structure, and saw a few pale stars where a girder had fallen away overhead. They watched like indifferent eyes, through the faint evening, from a timeless vantage point. Vague emotions moved in me, and *I felt again the regret that ruins must lie unpeopled and forgotten*. It was a brief sensation that the noises of a dying thing might arouse; not pity, for pity is then of no use, but an ineffable emotion as near to sorrow as the mist is to rain. It was not sharp enough to analyze, *but I have kept the memory of a child* who felt, beyond the netted, broken girders, the regard of those unseeing stars. (*EG* 85; italics added)

Sensory perceptions are confused, and the narrator realizes he can overcome the disorder this entails only through memory: to remember appears here as an unalloyed good, whatever danger the memory may entail.

In "Return by Sunset," while describing Dal's and Leyenda's arrival at the abandoned and ruined temple on the cliff where they would be met with their final doom, the extra-diegetic narrator immediately associates the oblivion enshrouding this forgotten shrine with the decline of the civilization to which the protagonists belong: "There was no road to the littered cliff and had not been for a measureless time; for time enough *to forget a civilization*. Once a temple had stood there, but no more acolytes came to the broken shrine, *no one remembered to pay homage to the gods*" (EG 135; italics added). The narrator suggests the existence of a tight causal connection between the oblivion in which the gods of this temple have fallen and the fact that such a huge stretch of time has elapsed from the day when the acolytes used to worship them: enough time for a civilization to be forgotten. When such a wide span of time slips away, only desolation and ruins are left: not even memories survive to pay homage to the ancient gods. And thus only the ruins and the idols would fight to preserve at least the memory of themselves: "Unto the ultimate blackness, when all the small golden suns burnt out forever, the idols would lie and think stone thoughts, the tumbled walls *would strive to remember* what hands had built them a long while since" (EG 136; italics added). Memory is a (hard) goal to achieve, but a worthy one, since it constitutes the only weapon to fight—and the only bulwark to stand against—the oblivion-inducing action of time, whose passing is even more merciless and inimical to man if one considers that it *escapes his perception*: not only does time destroy ruthlessly whatever achievement, material and immaterial, man has accomplished along the history of his civilizations, but time does so without even allowing man to be aware of its destructive action. After an indeterminate amount of time following the partial recovery from his injury, Dal realizes Leyenda has disappeared, and "Hunger told him of days *that had elapsed unseen* . . . sunless dawns and starless evenings" (EG 143; italics added). Time flees without man having any chance to master or even to control its flow. Abstracting this reflection further, Barlow would likely agree that an entire civilization may decline and finally collapse with its members not really being aware of having crossed the doomed phases of an inexorable decline.

Another open statement on the close connection between the loss of memory of the race's past and its present decadence is also contained in "A Dream," another story on an exhausted and "dying Earth" (EG 72) at the end of time. Barlow's narrator's words are quite direct and particularly poignant. He is crossing a desolate plateau and finally encounters an abandoned stone masonry. Upon entering it, he remarks: "Men might have lived not long before in that great house where maggots worked themselves through layers of greenish mould, or aeons might have passed since the paving echoed to mortal tread. I do not know, nor is there any record made, *for we are careless in this, the world's last age.* Humanity is weary and not averse to death" (EG 71; italics added). The equation is quite clearly established between the "weariness" of mankind, by now reaching the last segment of its final decadence, and the carelessness in recording—i.e. remembering—its own past.

But Barlow's treatment of the subtheme of (the loss of) memory is certainly not limited to the collective perspective, i.e. it is not restricted to discussing the connection or perhaps the causality between forgetfulness and the race's decline. The individual viewpoint is taken into account too: in other words, without memories, the single human subject is lost in his own everyday survival. At the beginning of his cosmic adventure, the protagonist and narrator of "A Dim-Remembered Story," while recovering consciousness after being catapulted in a "strange and mystical" (EG 89) wood he does not recognize, reflects upon his bizarre situation and cannot fail to individualize his lack of memories as the most relevant source of the present, utter bafflement of his condition—and ultimately, of his *defeat* as a human being at a loss to find a reasonable explanation:

> In what manner had I come to be there? Alien and inscrutable, my surroundings gave no clue. It was painful and annoying to stand bewildered and impotent in a strange place. *Deprived of recent memories*, how was I to leave the place and reach the city? If the visions of a sleeping mind were made reality—and reality this was—one might know my baffling sensations. I had anywhere before seen the place, yet now I stood upon the grass within a strange, faintly sinister forest, searching with confused eyes for some familiar sight. (EG 89; italics added)

And indeed there is one single word that accounts better than many explanations for the protagonist's defeat in rationalizing his condition: the word is *amnesia*, namely his loss of memories: "That vertigo, that sense of an ebbing tide that fell away from me as I woke, had tangled all my thoughts, and I only knew that if I had been a victim of amnesia, my wanderings had been far and strange to bring me to this place" (EG 95). In the course of his cosmic experience in other dimensions, the protagonist in fact is stuck in "our" world by a comatose state that lasts several hours, during which he is hosted at his brother's home, and his body scarcely maintains life. Upon returning to consciousness in the human world, and while concluding his narration, the protagonist recognizes that it is a blessing—for his own and for mankind's *understanding* of the race's ultimate, cosmic (in)significance—to bear memories of the castle of Yrn and of his own otherworldly adventure, so that he has had the chance to put it in words, though in a fragmentary and approximate fashion:

> But somehow more than to any other part of that adventure, my thoughts return to the old castle beyond an unknown wood. It is frightening to think that it will not be built for over fifteen thousand years, *for I can remember* the sunlight on the open court and the green deeps of that surrounding wood more clearly than this room in which I write. [. . .] The place where it will rise, in more than a dozen tens of centuries, is now an active city, with steel and glass and concrete walls that seem very permanent. But *I know them as ephemera*, for my eyes are haunted by the nocturnal wood, by the dark sunset of that land wherein I shall never again be. (EG 104; italics added)

The passage establishes the fundamental *epistemological value* of memories, with that "I know them as ephemera"—a knowledge implying an existential reflection of cosmic value—that is generated by an awareness made possible only through and by *memories*. The power of memory is thus sanctioned by Barlow as the only bulwark at man's disposal to tentatively and illusively fight the effects of the "aeonian" passing of Time.

"The Night Ocean" also contains an interesting element referable to the discussion on the intrinsic *dangerousness* of the lack—or loss—of memory for man's own *individual* survival. During one of his early walks on the beaches surrounding his cottage, the protagonist gets used to collecting "chance litter of the sea" (*EG* 108) (mostly bits of shell and debris), which he throws away shortly after returning home. But then, one day, he refers to a peculiar and fateful finding: "a large metal bead whose minutely carven design was rather unusual. This latter depicted a *fishy thing* against a patterned background of seaweed instead of the usual floral or geometrical designs, and was still clearly traceable though worn with years of tossing in the surf. Since I had never seen anything like it, I judged that it represented some fashion, now forgotten, of a previous year at Ellston, where similar fads were common" (*EG* 108-9; italics added). It is plausible to detect, in the depicted figure of a "fishy thing," the veiled anticipation of the "fishy creatures" that, in the prosecution of the narrative, will haunt the beach and the mind of the protagonist, possibly causing the deaths of some vacationists and finally embodying the eruption of the horror on the fateful final night. The last days of the narrator's sojourn at Ellston are marked by his tormented perplexity about the nature of the creatures he believes he sees on the beach facing his house; and it is appropriate that his oblivion of the metal bead he had found few weeks before in the sand does not allow him any clue on the possible provenance of the creatures—either from the sea, as supernatural "fishy things" able to resurface from the waters, walk, breath air, and possibly kill, or from the deranged depths of his mind. In the latter case, the forgotten discovery of the metal bead with its *outré* figure might even be interpreted as an unconscious influence over the protagonist's final "creation" of the creatures haunting him in the fatal night. Thus, the lack of memory is again revealed as crucial: if only he had remembered the figure on the bead, he could have at least tried to concoct a rationale to explain the nature—whether real or imaginary—of the creatures. Yet of course, as already remarked,[19] the richness of this tale resides in the utter ambiguity of its possible interpretations—and thus Barlow's narrative strategy is certainly effective in employing the "oblivion" subtheme as functional to the preservation of this sense of vagueness during and even beyond the end of the reading process.

"The Night Ocean" is also the tale in which nature, and in particular the sea, gets not only personified but even deified[20]—and as a fundamental step in this

---

19. See section 3.4.1. "The lonely and paranoid narrator: 'The Night Ocean'" in chapter 3 on Vagueness.
20. See section 6.4. "Nature and the sacred: 'The Night Ocean'" in chapter 6 on Nature.

deification process, Barlow of course endows the ocean not only with moods and broodings, but even with *memories*: "The sea can bind us to her many moods, whispering to us by the subtle token of a shadow or a gleam upon the waves, and hinting in these ways of her mournfulness or rejoicing. Always, *she is remembering old things*, and these memories, though we may not grasp them, are imparted to us, so that we share her gaiety or remorse" (*EG* 110; italics added).

Why does Barlow assign such an important, salvific, and, as we have seen, almost divine meaning to memories? "The Night Ocean" can come again to our rescue. In several passages, Barlow undertakes an in-depth analysis of the processes simultaneously involving mind, memory, senses, dream, and imagination. The role of memories and recollections is revealed as absolutely central in the *cognitive* activity of the human brain, i.e. in the process through which man *knows* and *learns*: such a process does not rely exclusively on the sensory impressions and their mental elaboration; on the contrary, the process of knowledge formation cannot do without the impressions man receives from memories and dreams. The quotation of the following rich passage may suffice for all:

> What had remained in the corner of my *fancy* was the image of cliffs beneath the water against the hueless, dusky no-sky of such a realm; and this, though I had *forgotten* most of the story, was *recalled* quite unexpectedly by the same pattern of cliff and sky which I then *beheld*. The *sight* was similar to what I had *imagined* in a year now lost save for random, incomplete *impressions*. *Suggestions* of this story may have lingered behind certain irritating unfinished *memories*, and in certain values *hinted to my senses* by scenes whose *actual significance* was bafflingly small. (*EG* 111; italics added)[21]

In this subtle analysis of mental and imaginative processes, I have italicized those expressions that best portray the mixture and the blurring of borders between objectivity (with the notion of sight and direct perception of actual phenomena), the recollection of this perception through memory, and the suggestions and impressions coming from fancy and imagination. Our senses, in their re-elaboration of impressions, are all-receiving: they get many different impressions without distinguishing between their sources ("objective" perception, memory, imagination). As a result, impressions get mixed, until they look all mingled and undistinguishable in the final result of the mental re-elaboration: our thoughts and feelings are the results of *this* process, and therefore they are equally determined by objectivity and subjectivity, reality and dream, and we cannot tell what comes from what source.[22] "Return by Sunset" also discusses the intermingling of memory and

---

21. The passage is almost entirely RHB's, with HPL merely polishing the style.

22. Another hint as to the merged nature of human perceptions and feelings (whereby no clear border can be traced between their different, internal and external, sources) can be inferred from the following statement of the narrator of "The Night Ocean": "I was ridden by [. . .] a perception of the brief hideousness and underlying filth of life—a feeling partly a reflection of my internal nature and partly a result of broodings induced by that gnawed rotten object which may have been a hand" (*EG* 116; the passage can be tagged as entirely RHB's). It would be very hard to say where the external, supposedly objective, per-

dream as a worthwhile means of achieving knowledge, and even of *changing* the present reality. Thanks to the combined action of memory and dream, man can modify the perception of his own surroundings, almost transfigure them into a new reality that, although not ceasing to be deceptive, provides at least the illusion that the ravaging effects of time's passing might be halted: this is how Leyenda's "supernatural memory" (it is not exactly a dream, but a dream-induced memory of a past stage in the story of the temple, now actualized in the present day) effects a transfiguration of the past that would ultimately lead the girl to perform a self-immolation on its altar—just as if the past time of the blossoming of the now-forgotten cult had been re-actualized:

> And they [the stars] lit the ruins, and seemed to congregate above the tumbled conical altar, more brilliantly than all the moons of the year could do, and since they moved, their light came constantly from new angles; [. . .] And in the moments she [Leyenda] stared at them, the altar seemed to change. *Cracks became fewer, the moss retreated, the runnels of the rain were filled, the patient erosion of the wind undone, and the work of the snowflake defeated.* Unexplained joys swelled in her as she perceived this, and with each crazy figure devised by the drunken stars a year seemed shed, a tedious year from the courtyard and the altar, and strangely, yet expectedly, from her likewise. She ran with joy to the altar and stood upon it, expecting, desiring, demanding. (EG 139-40; italics added)

Memories cooperate with dreams in man's epistemological process of the formation of a new "reality," one that deceptively offers him the illusion of a suspension of the temporal laws.

And since memories play such a central role in the formation of knowledge for the human being, their lack or loss at the diegetic level is an important sub-theme of human time faced by Barlow's fiction, in particular in "The Night Ocean." We already saw how the oblivion of the discovery of the metal bead may have had an impact in the final, psychological doom of the protagonist. His capacity to retain memories becomes increasingly faulty as the narrative and the diegetic time unfold, and this shortcoming bears a significant impact on his performance of the epistemological process, i.e. on his ability to *produce* knowledge. The progressive loss of memory realizes what I would define as the *reduction to vagueness* of past happenings, which in turn implies an epistemic impact in its virtual "cancellation" of former events. Let us see how this works, from the narrative viewpoint. The protagonist tells of having awaited the final horror with an awareness that verges toward the supernatural, had we not already hypothesised that the concluding

---

ception begins, and where the internal, unconscious stimuli enter the picture: "The once friendly waters babbled meaningfully to me, and eyed me with a strange regard; yet whether the darkness of the scene were a reflection of my own broodings, or whether the gloom within me were caused by what lay without, I could not have told" (EG 117; the passage is almost entirely RHB's). The mixture of external and internal sources, of conscious and unconscious, is, as it were, perfect.

showdown could be interpreted as a purely mental event.[23] However, he is unable to locate the time of the final confrontation—a hardly explainable circumstance, given all the significance he attributes to the event and the sheer anxiety with which he awaits for it: "it was with more speculation than actual fear that I waited unendingly for the day of horror which seemed to be nearing. The day, I repeat, was late in September, *though whether the 22nd or 23rd I am uncertain*. Such details have *fled before the recollection of those uncompleted happenings*—episodes with which no orderly existence should be plagued, because of the damnable suggestions (and only suggestions) they contain" (EG 117; italics added). This passage realizes the magic of transforming past events into "uncompleted happenings"—and not only because the narrator cannot remember the exact day of their occurrence, but also because, as the climax of the tale will reveal, the concluding events are wrapped in a thick veil of vagueness. Barlow is here suggesting that the lack and loss of memory may end up in a *reduction* of past events to an "uncompleted" state, may cut part of their actuality, and may even lead to *questioning their actual occurrence*. The narrator defines them as "uncompleted" *not because they were uncompleted as such*, but because he is *unable to remember them*: at the diegetic level—which is the only "objective" level that can be commented and interpreted in a work of fiction—we assist in a character's loss of memory which bears an impact on the actual "objectivity" of the events he does not remember anymore. No memory, no existence: or at least, a significant "cutting," "incompleteness" of existence. This is how memory can modify objective "reality" at the diegetic level of a fictional world.

5.3.2 The everlasting presence of the Past

Barlow's concern for the subtheme of the past can be said to be part of "human time" from a viewpoint external to the human mind, since the effects of the past on human achievements—as man's actions and creations—are independent from man's will or mind. Barlow's fiction shows a strong interest in the modalities in which the passing of time affects all things human—both in its material effects and in the always actual role of the past, with its constant deterministic influence over the present.

The high regard in which Barlow holds the past is revealed by the double value he assigns to it:

1. philosophical/existential: the past as a receptacle of truth, of conditioning for the present fate of mankind, and of important discoveries on the ultimate *meaning* of human experiences;
2. literary: the past as a source of inspiration for the literary composition. In this sense, we assist in the multiplication of the diegetic levels: in order to simplify, we can claim that the typical temporal settings of a Barlow tale

---

23. See section 3.4.1. "The lonely and paranoid narrator: 'The Night Ocean'," in chapter 3 on Vagueness.

present an alternative or past dimension[24] at a diegetic level (the one in which the events object of the primary narration are happening) into which one or more *new* past dimensions are inscribed—at the meta-diegetic levels—where events of other, older pasts are described through legends, myths, old accounts, and rumors.[25]

The two levels are of course intertwined and reciprocally strengthen each other. In this section I will discuss these two aspects of Barlow's treatment of the theme of the past, striving to show their interconnections. It is in fact just by embedding meta-diegetic past events onto the diegetic level of narration (a literary and narrative technique) that Barlow's fiction is able to reveal the relevance of the past in its conditioning effects over the present modes of human action.

In Barlow's fiction, the relationship between the diegetic and the meta-diegetic pasts goes beyond—and assumes more elaborated meanings than—the conventional and surface narrative dialectics between the temporality of the fictional "present" and "past" that is in any case present. These are the reactions of the demon Garoth when he is met by a weird androcephalous being along his path: "The demon stared in surprise for he had known no such animal upon the world he *once* ruled" (EG 53; italics added), thus stating a neat separation between the two temporal dimensions at stake.

Yet Barlow's fictional treatment of the theme of the past, as anticipated above, reveals more complex movements among the different diegetic levels. For instance, if we consider the episodes of the *Annals of the Jinns* as temporally set in a diegetic past (and not in an alternative time dimension), we can argue that they reveal a constant dialectics between the diegetic and the meta-diegetic temporalities. The events told, and set in a far past, always bear the conditioning marks of a farther past: so the flagon of beauty of episode three has an "*ancient* seal covered with writing none could interpret" (EG 17; italics added). Deciphering the inscription on the seal *from the past* would be crucial in understanding the power of the flagon's content—which will prove, after the seal's breaking by the princess, to be the opposite of what it was believed. So it appears clear how a deed of the meta-diegetic past—the sealing of the flagon and the incision of an inscription over the seal—still bears an important, fatal epistemic value able to heavily condition the present: if only that token from the meta-diegetic past could have been deciphered by the ac-

---

24. For a discussion about these two possible views on the treatment of temporality in the *Annals of the Jinns*, see section 5.2.2. "Cosmic Time, still."

25. This same reflection can be applied to the study of the theme of memory, as hopefully appears clear from the previous analysis in section 5.3.1: the tale "A Memory," for instance, is built on the double diegetic structure of memory. At the diegetic level, we have in fact a narrator who now—at the moment of his writing—relies on his memory to account an episode of his past. At the meta-diegetic level, he retells episodes and anecdotes—concerning the evolution of mankind and of the narrator's city along the centuries—that are temporally set in (several and different) past times. These last accounts thus superimpose themselves like archi-texts over the diegetic level of the primary narration.

tor (the princess) of the diegetic past, she would not have misinterpreted the flagon of ugliness and old age for the alleged flagon of "beauty." And still in the episode five of the *Annals*, "The Tomb of the God," the extra-diegetic narrator retells of how the mausoleum of Lord Krang had been "built long before any human walked the face of the world, built *by evil powers* that had reigned unchecked in that unthinkably ancient day" (EG 18; italics added): the mention of evil powers that in the long-distant meta-diegetic past had built Krang's tomb is again a token of the everlasting *influence* of the past, since the evilness of those forces will fatally doom the attempt, retold at the diegetic level, of the explorers from Phoor to loot the tomb's treasures and steal the Hsothian manuscripts. Again, therefore, a meta-diegetic past is the receptacle of a meaning able to condition the "present" of the narration, namely the diegetic past.

What are the sources through which the narrator is able to account for the meta-diegetic past influencing the "present"? They are often "old scripts" (EG 41) and legends, "antique myth" (EG 22) and texts like the parchments copied from the Hsothian manuscripts, which characters like sorcerer Volnar consult to reactivate ancient knowledges and wisdoms useful for their intervention in the "present": in fact, it is thanks to the consultation of those documents that "elaborate care was exercised upon the concoction" (EG 24) that Volnar prepares in order to bring the doom over the three cities of Naazim, Zo, and Perenthines. The role of old records and tales is not only central, as we have seen, in the crucial task of the preservation of memory, but also in the registration of the haunting, or at least unavoidable, lingering influence of the (meta-diegetic) past over the diegetic one. "An Episode in the Jungle," the last episode of the *Annals*, is revelatory in regard to this topic, since this sketch is built around the dialectics between the "present" of the narration (i.e., diegetic past) and its "past" (i.e., meta-diegetic past): "In a year when records were crumbled shreds and men no longer cared about the past, knowing there was no future, *tales were the sole histories of the race*" (EG 30; italics added). This tale further problematizes the relationship between man and his records of the past, claiming again that whenever man is no longer able to preserve and decipher the signs of the past he loses the ability to understand it and grasp the meanings it can and must convey: this is the narrator's comment upon Loman's kneeling in front of the stone image (of a *forgotten ancient* god) not far from the jungle Yondath: "He scrutinised the base, fascinated by the marks written upon it. There was no one *now* in all the world to read them. The scholar was dead, and the hunter had lost his lore, so that all the writings on statues and monuments and broken tombs was destined for no future reading, even unto the death of eternity. Silent, with no ears trained to receive their message, they would henceforth be fingered only by the rain" (EG 31; italics added). I have italicized the word "now," since its employment poignantly marks the conflict between the statuses of the "present" of the narration and the irremediably lost meta-diegetic past. Often Barlow's fiction, coherently with the aesthetic goals discussed in Chapter 3, characterizes the sources of information on the meta-diegetic past with a stronger mark of vagueness: in these few cases, the reader is not told of recognizable and *material* records of the past like manuscripts or documents; instead, it does not even appear clear whether the sources that are mentioned actually exist, and, if this is the case, to what extent they are reliable.

"The Bright Valley" is an interesting tale on this regard, also for its plainly *layered temporal structure*. In fact, here we have an extra-diegetic narrator who employs a past tense—the simple past—while telling the story of Cern, the protagonist, and all he is able to tell about the past of the fabled and mysterious valley that Cern sets out to find comes from nebulous tales and rumors:

> *It was said, among those who spoke of old things,* that a time had been when the rich concealed land was visited by men, and that in other years rich gain had come of it, in fruits and animals. In those times hunters returned from the bright valley laden with fowl whose sweet flesh bled newly from the arrow. But afterward, *ancient tales narrated,* glittering rocks had fallen upon the earth; and those rocks were of the fires burning over men in the night. (EG 61; italics added)

The meta-diegetic past becomes completely blurred and, as it were, layered: different tales, told in different epochs, tell of different meta-diegetic times in which people had some relationship with the bright valley: at a temporal layer of the structure, people visited it; at a second layer, they preyed upon the fruits of the land; and finally at a third temporal layer, burning rocks hit the land and the people visiting the land. The ancient tales leave now, at the moment of the diegetic narration, all these three layers of the meta-diegetic past *indistinct in their temporal collocation*: the reader is only informed about their chronological succession. Still, the narrator claims that the time at which Cern undertook his doomed exploration of the bright valley was subsequent to that of the utterance of these tales; it was a time when they were almost not credited anymore: "It was this land Cern sought, *in a later time, when the old tales were not much believed*" (EG 62; italics added). To summarize, we can detect—starting from the "present" of the narration and going backwards along the arrow of time toward farther and increasingly vaguer "pasts"—the following temporally layered structure, one that shows the multiplication and effectiveness of meta-diegetic temporal "pasts" at work:

1. Extra-diegetic level: the narrator is omniscient and placed out of the fictional temporal dimensions: *extra-diegetic temporal layer;*
2. Diegetic past: the "present" of narration, i.e. the time (past in relation with the enunciation's act, but "present" at the diegetic level) of Cern's exploration, which coincides with the time when the old tales on the bright valley were by now scarcely believed: *diegetic temporal layer;*
3. Meta-diegetic past: the past times at which the tales on the bright valley were formed, told, and believed, with the warning that they were of course told *in the past,* i.e. at different "pasts" (all preceding the "present" of Cern's expedition): *meta-diegetic temporal layer;*
4. Meta-meta-diegetic past: the past times at which actually occurred the episodes reported in the tales of the bright valley (people exploring the valley,

preying on its fruits, being hit by the rocks: all times preceding both the formation of the tales and Cern's expedition): *meta-meta-diegetic temporal layer*.

Let us add that the third layer could be of course further split into two others, through the distinction between the past time (left implied by the narration) at which the tales were actually *formed* and that, chronologically subsequent, at which the tales were then *told and believed*. However, the layered temporal structure of this tale seems already complex enough without including this further specification.

In Barlow's fiction, the past does not only leave its mark of "antiquity" over tokens like events, documents, buildings, objects, etc., but also on people. We have already seen for instance in section 5.2.2 how only a "very old man" could fight the hideous evil from another dimension launching a lethal attack on mankind in "The Summons"; also sorcerer Khalda, Volnar's disciple in "The Mirror," episode nine of the *Annals*, is endowed with an antiquity that inescapably entails the covert and hardly decipherable meaningfulness and wisdom of the tokens from the meta-diegetic past: "there came an ancient one, unbelievably filthy, and clad in garments of odorous antiquity. His face was hideously wrinkled, yet it held *a certain inscrutable wisdom*" (EG 26; italics added).

The past is therefore a source of meaning, of truth, and of wisdom. People only partially recognize the enormous value things past bear ("early things grow dear when the end of memories approaches" [EG 30]). This is of course not to suggest that these meanings, truths, and wisdoms have a positive and reassuring value, for both the discoverer on the individual level and all mankind on the cosmic one. In this lies the intrinsic *ambiguity of the past*: its preservation through memories ensures truthful—and therefore valuable—revelations, but these same revelations often bear dangers and threats to the encouraging "certainties" of the human individual and, more often than not, of the entire human community. Barlow's fiction adds to its own strategic ambiguity by representing that toward the past as an attraction/repulsion dialectics: the past is seen simultaneously as the prestigious receptacle of valuable teachings for man, of meanings revelatory in explaining the present human condition, *and* as a potential source of dangers for that very condition. The same source that reveals the *meaning* and the *justification* (or their lack) of the human present plight is as well a possible source of *doom* for it: because, in Barlow's existential view, our meaning(lessness) is precisely the cipher of our condition and the ultimate cause of its ruin.

The tale "Origin Undetermined" is a textbook example of a Barlow fiction built around the notion of the *dangerousness of the past*—especially of a *forgotten* past that hurls a fatal threat even at the survival of the human individual. When a frantic, frightened, and raving Roberts visits the doctor and homo-diegetic narrator of the tale, he is first revealed to have been infected by "a kind of poison, and it works fast" (EG 122), but he then describes this alleged "poison" more faithfully—though not giving up the necessary vagueness—as an unfathomable threat sputtered by the past: "'I knew you'd object—you don't know what it's like. No, it wasn't a snake. It's ... something *old*,' he added half to himself. 'Something people *don't remember anything about*'" (EG 123; italics added). Here a clear overlapping between the themes of the dangerousness of the past *and* of the lack of memories occurs: when some *old* and *immemorial* danger comes to threaten the present human condition, doom and tragedy await the individual, since the past is back to *claim its rights*. Aware of the utterly mysterious nature of the doom awaiting him, Roberts's only request is to have his infected hand amputated by the reluctant doctor. And in order to do so, Roberts even concocts a false story to support his supplication: he claims to have cut himself with an old knife he found in a crate sent to him by a colleague from some excavation site, where the latter was unearthing material of the Old Empire for the Central American antiquities museum of the Nelkin Gallery of Art where Roberts works as curator. So Barlow has his character plot a story in which the mortal danger comes again from the past, even on the purely imaginary and diegetic, or we should say meta-diegetic, level:

> he sent a final crate from that site up by steamer in August. Most of it came from one grave of the Old Empire, about two or three hundred B.C. A magnificent piece of luck. There were even bits of fabric wrapped around a bronze knife. It was this knife ... I've always been careful with stuff like that, the Indians make strong poisons ... But at first I was busy with the weavings. I put the knife aside all winter, until this morning, when I wanted to clean it. When I took it out of the cabinet it slipped to the floor. By some devilish luck I cut my hand a little. (EG 123)

In order to justify his request for amputation, Roberts goes on describing how the poison on the knife he left on his desk must, during his absence, have somehow also infected his white cat Arky—and how the animal's unmistakable behavior would prove the presence of an *ancient* and lethal substance placed by the Indians on the knife's blade, a menace presently still very alive: "About an hour later I heard Arky scratching around as if he wanted to get out, and then he gave a peculiar yowling shriek. Animals make funny sounds when they're hurt. I suspected what was wrong with him—it made me wonder if iodine was strong enough for my cut ... and in a few minutes he crawled out, dying. Then *I knew my own danger. Whatever was on the knife was still strong*" (EG 123; italics added). Roberts strives hard to look convincing, and he concocts a story in which the menace from the past might look plausible—perhaps being aware that, almost by default, the human psyche tends to attribute to an anecdote a character of dangerousness that increases proportionally with the antiquity of the elements told: the older, the more dangerous and lethal. He fails anyway, since the doctor of this tale shows an unshakable rational and scientific attitude and openly declares "That is not what happened" (EG 123), only to discover later, by reading and publishing Roberts's manuscript, a much more disturbing truth.

This entire manuscript is constructed in such a way as to convey the notion of the dangerousness of the past and of its constant menace over mankind's present mental and physical health, if not survival. In particular, Barlow has Roberts point out the notion of an intense potential *evil* hidden in the past, an evil that is ready to burst into and doom man's present, if he is not prudent enough to respect the past and leave its inscrutable secrets untouched. This is Roberts's comment after he has discovered the exceptional growth-powers of the corroding plants from the past: "God knows what those plants were, or *why their parent seeds had been kept. They should have been destroyed hundreds of years ago.* They grew too fast, and they fed on things no other plant feeds on" (*EG* 126; italics added). Roberts asks, *Why had their parent seeds been kept?*, implying that the (people from the) past, aware of the destructive powers of the plants, intentionally decided to preserve the threat *in order to doom the future generations*—and if we consider the effectiveness of the literary metaphor of the "seeds" (literally, seeds of a plant, but in an ulterior sense, also seeds *of an evil* preserved in sight of their malevolence's future blossom), Barlow's bleak picture of a past everlastingly haunting the present becomes even more disturbing.

Therefore it appears clear how Barlow's view of the past, in light of the ambiguity discussed above, is particularly complex. What is certain is that he believed the past is never "gone" nor can be "neutered" by man's action. The past constantly claims its toll on the present, and if man has no memories to bounce the past back, he is defenseless against its attacks. However, this is not to say that the past and time are the same thing, both placing a threat on the survival of everything human, and both, as it were, inimical to man. Barlow implies an important distinction between the past and time: by endowing the past with almost "magic" powers ("There is always magic in old things" [*EG* 30], the narrator of "An Episode in the Jungle" claims), he certainly configures its personification, and probably something more. The past turns into a sort of supernatural dimension and entity—and we must inevitably recall how Barlow might have been influenced, under this viewpoint, by Lovecraft's nearly idolatrous views on a multitudinous past, best synthesized in his well known aphorism: "The past is *real*–it is *all there is*" (*SL* 3.31).[26] And it is a feeling not far from the "worship" for a supernatural, divine entity that we get from reading, again in Barlow's "Origin Undetermined," the following passage within Roberts's manuscript—an excerpt also indicative of the subtle distinction Barlow traces between the past and time:

> The plain and mountains were strange and yet familiar. Eddies of loneliness swirled over them; infinitely sad and infinitely remote memories rested upon them. Like one who recognises sombre, familiar and indolent harmonies in a piece of great music, I was made aware of *some immense and majestic past* lying behind them—*a past more splendid than aught of human history,* but long *engulfed by secretive Time.* Whatever the past was, I think it had been dead a thousand centuries. (*EG* 130; italics added)

The past appears as a sort of rejected "son" of time: the past is created by and

---

26. Jason Eckhardt has gone so far as to identify several manifestations of HPL's love for the past, including the "recent" past, the "historical" past, and the "incredibly distant" past (see Eckhardt 81).

"originates" from time—this is why it retains, at least potentially, some of time's evil powers and lethal malevolence—*but* time tends to "engulf" its son, like a "secretive" shroud, in order not to allow the past to exert its eventually revelatory and epistemic role for mankind. Time suffocates the past's semiotic (i.e. "meaning-producing") action of "truth revelation" and of possible warning to (curious) people: time strives to have the past die "a thousand centuries," and consequently to make people forget about what the past has to reveal and to teach—not necessarily about man's "good," but also, as we have seen, about the threats that are nested in past events and that may still haunt man's present and future condition. Endorsing a strongly relativistic (indeed "cosmic") perspective, Barlow does not attach any moral to the notions of "meaning," "teaching," or "revelation"—and it is of course in this neutral sense that our discussion should employ these terms.

So the past is real, and if it is not necessarily "all there is," for Barlow it anyway tells the (often hideous) truth, it is the source of (sometimes horrible) revelations. It is in this sense that man feels the contradiction of an attraction/repulsion dialectics toward the past, just as Lovecraft's characters feel it toward the manifestations of "Outsideness." If the search of the truth disclosed by the study of the past is indeed an unalloyed good for both Barlow and Lovecraft, no matter how bleak and disturbing the truth-content would reveal, there is no doubt that, in the "antiquities," secrets find concealment that could bring down doom on the human species, if unleashed. Barlow has Roberts become perfectly aware of the contradictory nature of this harsh and inescapable reality: "Vast antiquities unfolded themselves to the invading Spaniards—antiquities perhaps recorded in these codices *whose destruction is so often lamented*. Perhaps the men who saw them *did right to burn them* and to pray beside the flames. Some of the extant monuments bear dates millions of years old—God knows what reeling aeons were chronicled in the records that have perished" (EG 132; italics added). This passage is extraordinarily telling in its laying bare the contradiction felt by the narrator—and no doubt, by Barlow himself—between the regret man should feel at the destruction of the chronicles of the past (like those contained in ancient codices) and his relief at realizing the "mercifulness" implicit in this very same destruction, when considered under the viewpoint of the blissful, "placid island of ignorance" on which this destruction allows human beings to dwell.

Another important aspect of Barlow's treatment of the past reinforces the process of its "deification," besides further linking Barlow's work with Lovecraft's: the representation of the past's capacity to condition the present by *influencing, and sometimes even guiding, people's actions*. The theme of deterministic compulsion has been discussed in its existential implications in chapter 4 on cosmicism, in particular in paragraph 4.2.2.2, "Deterministic compulsion and its impact on free will." Here I would briefly like to analyze the modalities in which this compulsion is exerted, in particular where the actors of the process are agents and emissaries of the past. "Origin Undetermined"—by now recognizable as an extremely rich narrative in regard to human time—displays a strong interest in the theme of the deterministic compulsion exerted by an agent of the past over the human protagonist. In fact, toward the end of his manuscript, Roberts becomes aware of having been the victim of an action of the past, one that "streamed" itself into the present of the narrator in order to guide his deeds and perpetuate its evil:

> Of the mysteries confronting me I have solved one at least, though it is the least provocative. I stole the urn myself. Of this I am convinced. My fingerprints were thick about the broken case, and my inner consciousness shrieks out the vandal's name. A *compulsion* must have been upon me, a compulsion streaming from the malignant urn. How or why I do not know. And it was in the fulfilment of a kindred command that I planted those seeds. [. . .] Perhaps my mission was only to release the seeds, by whatever means lay at hand. They had been sealed up *a long time ago*: but for my act they might have remained *forever* so. (EG 133; italics added)

I have italicized the last two expressions that most reveal the re-directing action of the "evil" seed of the past which, in order to return to life and avoid eternal idleness, molded the actions of a man of the present time. Besides "Origin Undetermined," "Return by Sunset" notably expands on the theme of the compulsion exerted by the past. And again, we are confronted with an *evil* influence, actually a sort of curse from a vital past that returns to haunt the present, also reinforcing—as a productive overlapping of themes—both the motive of a determinism conditioning the present actions of human beings, and the Barlovian "cosmic" notion of a fluid temporality where no proper subdivision among the three temporal dimensions holds consistency anymore. This is Barlow's description of Leyenda's wedging her arm into the mysterious bracelet newly found among the ruins of a temple from an unknown past—namely the act that would irremediably lose her—and the reader should not fail to notice the air of "magic" with which Barlow endows the scene, in emphasizing the ethero-directedness of her act, and the power of a compulsion that forces the uneasy girl to perform, against her will, an act in open defiance of her and her tribe's traditional habits and beliefs:

> She must have found a part of the ceremonial ornaments used by the keepers of the temple; and though all the old gods were discredited, *Leyenda was uneasy*. She knew her own god, the dog-faced image lying in the swamp two weeks' journey behind, would not like this uncovering of his predecessor. All the ruins, spiritual and temporal, of the old days *were held suspect by the tribes*, which sometimes wandered through them, but she wanted to keep her bracelet. *Without conscious volition*, Leyenda wedged her arm into it so tightly that she found it would not come off. *She had not intended to do so–but there it was*. Dal, fortunately for her peace of mind, *thought all evil magic would have long since gone out of the bracelet*. (EG 138; italics added)

Barlow's employment of free indirect speech—especially evident in the last sentence, where Leyenda's thoughts on Dal's reaction are reported—allows us both to sense the "suspension of disbelief" that is fostered upon the reader in regard to the obviously supernatural event at stake, and to recognize the theme of the persistence until the very present of the "evil magic" powers of the bracelet, a metaphorical token of an always vital past, never really "gone" or "dead," and eternally ready to come back like the personification, almost the physical embodiment of a Gothic wicked wraith that inevitably causes psychological distress on the persecuted heroine:

> she was not easy. There was her bracelet for one thing; it seemed tighter than usual. She wondered why it would not come off. Repeated hammering with stones had nothing aside from bruising her arm. It gripped her like an inexorable hand—*the hand, she vaguely felt, of the past of this place whose history nothing was known*. She wondered who had lost the bauble—shackle—in that *unrecorded yesterday*. She wondered who had built this and the other ruins scattered over the land. (EG 140; italics added)

In this thematically rich passage, Barlow, besides openly personifying the past through the image of its "long hand" haunting the present, reconnects the dangerousness of the past to man's lack of records and memories of it. Barlow's insistence on the theme of man's ignorance of the past is so evident that I would go so far as to claim that Barlow "explains" the threat of the past just through man's unawareness: it is just because man (in this case Dal and Leyenda) *ignores* the past of this place and of this bracelet that he inevitably falls victim to its lethal and "inexorable" hand, that he cannot help answering its beckoning "summons" and executing its orders, no matter how self-destructive:

> Immediately she decided this—the shadows were spreading long on the ground—*she built an altar*; a tiny heap of reddish stones behind the hut, with red petals laid upon them; and then with a broken stick she obtained another ingredient—*her own blood*. The blood and the petals were stirred together, singing a chant whose words *no one understood any more*, and she crawled around this affair three times, calling herself goat. Then it was ready, and with a wintry heart she waited for something to come and feed. (EG 141; italics added)

The acts Leyenda performs are just those carved on the bracelet gripping her arm and whose evil powers she is unable—nor, little by little, does not even *wish*—to dispel anymore. The past takes Leyenda over and forces her to execute the death ritual painted on the bracelet, *her own death ritual*. She is aware of the gradual but inescapable overcoming of the past and of her and Dal's doom, and gradually realizes she cannot free her will from the more and more forceful spell: "Their fate was linked to the ruins; their coming and abiding had been destined. *With them the old day had awakened.* [. . .] How the centuries *had flowed back* beneath those intermeshing stars!" (EG 141-42; italics added).

Within the frame of a fluid temporality, Barlow's fictional world represents the mingling of past and present, where the actions of a personified past employ human actors—turning them into executors of an external will that plots their doom, so ultimately into its victims—in order to relive it: the past is made divine, rendered as a supernatural dimension that intrudes upon the present, becomes so "real" (indeed, "The past is real") as to allow its human executors/victims even to take a glance into it, while the temporal setting of human existence becomes one of blurring, coincidence, and ultimate confusion of past, present, and future:

"Though she sat by the fire and the sick man [Dal], *she peered backward into pasts so dark that only a hint of something stirred in them; and forward in wonder and doubt at the end, when all villages should be as were the citadels of the old race*" (*EG* 142; italics added). What other entity could such powers belong to, if not to a divine one? And the final, mournful discovery of the effects of the lethal toll claimed by the past on its human victims provides the observer with both the ineluctable certainty of the potential destructivity of the past's intrusion on the present and the ultimate demonstration of the tyranny of the "god":

> Then by the gourd-vine he [Dal] came upon a clue, and his heart was marble. It was the ruinous, thousand-year old basin which had once served *to hold the victims of the god*. It had been righted, cleansed of moss, mended. And on its shallow curve reposed Leyenda's bracelet. Her hateful shackle of a bracelet. A while since it had clasped her soft arm. It would do so no more—nor would Dal. For the bauble was smeared with blood. He seized it, and drawing back his weak arm, threw it goldenly into space. *Instantly he regretted that he had done so.* A dark circle remained on the stone—blood clotted into the porous surface. He watched a while, then shaking with bewilderment [. . .] lifted his eyes to the gold and gore of the sunset. (*EG* 143; italics added)

Dal regrets his gesture, since it immediately sounds to him like an act of blasphemy perpetrated against the god of the temple, committed *against the past*. A past that has been unwillingly re-enlivened by the human being—that in such a way sealed her doom: as a puppet maneuvered by the hands of the puppeteer, Leyenda re-enacted a religious ceremony of the past—with a possible suggestive metaphor that accounts for the "divinity" feature proper to the past: the ritual is *of* the past in the double sense that it is a past event, it "belongs to the past," *and* that it is *addressed* to the past, has the past as its worshipped "object." The recognition of the reinforced effect derived from the merging of the two acceptations cannot but persuade the reader of the absolutely central role played in Barlow's work by the meaningful, revelatory, even super-natural—because omnipresent in the fluid temporality of the fictional world—dimension of the past.

5.4 "The Night Ocean": the hybridism of "existential" time

In this final section I would like to advance an interpretative hypothesis that considers a further possible step in Barlow's fictional treatment of the theme of time: a "hybrid" view of time, one that synthesizes the cosmic and the human acceptations of this richly complex theme.

Once more, it is "The Night Ocean" that allows for such an interpretation—a perspective that possibly solves the tensions aroused by the two "canonical" standpoints on temporality, the cosmic and the human. In fact, in this masterpiece of thematic intensity and calibrated prose Barlow informs the narration with a peculiar temporal background, one that configures as an *allegory of the ages of man* on the plane of human time—an allegory of the "individual" temporality of a single man that, in turn, reverberates into (and takes on the value of) a wider allegory of the phases of all human civilization. "The Night Ocean" is in fact the only Barlovian tale (I take it by now for granted that this tale is conceptually his full product, Lovecraft's interventions having been ascertained to be just a polishing of prose) in which the temporal setting is characterized by an open—and often emphasized—*transition from summer to fall*, a shift that signals strong and evident changes within the protagonist's consciousness and life-views. The change in fact marks the evolution from a starting point of joyful abandonment to the pleasure of the sea (*naivety*) to the gradual and increasingly bitter realization of the horror(s) that the sea conceals (*awareness*).

The evolution portrayed by Barlow resembles the allegorical passage, in the ages of man, *from childhood*, with its enchanted and enthusiastic acceptance of the lifeworld and its challenges, which are still in the path of forming themselves to the eyes of the child, *to adulthood*, with its increasingly painful recognition of the misery and inanity of existence. A similar evolution on the human subject's "individual" level invests, on the "cosmic" level, the human civilizations, along their cyclical phases of birth, rise, maturity, decline, and fall, according to the Spenglerian model that influenced Barlow via Lovecraft.[27] And as a trigger of this process of existential—individual and cosmic—growing up, Barlow employs the image of the sea as the metaphor of a life that, after initially alluring the child by providing him the illusion of a worthy experience ahead, is then revealed as the expression of an indifferent if not an "inimical universe" (EG 117) that tyrannically pulls the threads of its puppets, the impotent human individuals. The protagonist's progress on the way to the "adult age" reflects in fact that of all human beings, and of all civilizations heading toward their "fall" (and it is of course not by chance that Barlow's allegory exploits and accentuates the double meaning of the term *fall*, namely that of season of the year *and* of individual or collective decline). The following is a significant passage, revelatory of the allegorical nuance of Barlow's treatment of time in the tale: "Thus autumn *found me*, and what I had gained from the sea *was lost back into it*. Autumn on the beaches—a drear time betokened by no scarlet leaf nor any other accustomed sign. A *frightening sea that changes not, though man changes*" (EG 117; italics added). I have italicized those expressions that best convey the two crucial elements of this revelatory passage:

1. the sense of man's and the civilization's impotence toward the progression of their decline: autumn "finds" the protagonist, and Barlow's employment of this particular verb[28] strengthens the impression of man's *passivity* in the process. Similarly to how the autumn hits the protagonist,

---

27. See section 5.2 in this chapter.
28. The examination of the original manuscript containing HPL's interpolations proves that this linguistic choice was RHB's.

so adulthood comes to the defenseless adolescent unable and not allowed to "counterattack," and strips him of the illusory rewards gained during the "summer" of his life. Another remark made a little later by the narrator adds to the hypothesis that Barlow is putting forth an allegory of the transition of the "seasons" of man's age: after autumn hits the man, "There was no return to my earlier contentment" (EG 118)–that of adulthood is an age of disillusionment and of irremediably lost hopes;

2. the notion of a "frightening" sea, the metaphor for the "inimical" lord of man's existence, a despot that assists, changeless and immortal itself–namely ruled by the "cosmic" temporality of the aeonian perspective–to the inexorable changes and transitions of both men and civilizations–mortal and subjected to the "human" temporality–toward their maturity, decline, and extinction.

By the aid of the allegorical light described above, it appears clear how the event the protagonist long awaits on the night of September 22-23 takes on the contours of a metaphor for man's *death*, or perhaps for the ultimate *sense of his life*: toward the end of his account, the narrator tells of the "vigil of my spirit" (EG 119), employing a term–"vigil"–that, like "fall," is again polysemous, since it both expresses the "wait" for something to happen and is also reminiscent of the "wake" that mournful people perform around the corpse of the lately deceased. And indeed what else does man "await" toward the end of his life, with his "spirit" in an anxious hold-up, while his mental and physical capacities dwindle and he is thrown in a state of apathy that openly preludes to the final and eternal stasis?

Barlow's narrator, in his turn, does not conceal he is indeed "as if expectant of death" (EG 119). Yet his experience of waiting for the "horrors from the sea" to be revealed has risen to the allegory of man's waiting for death as a revelatory experience, one able to *finally uncover life's secret meaning*. Only the *end* of life–and conversely, the end of the *reading process* itself, the punctual instant at the autumn's conclusion–could have explained the seasons that had preceded it, exactly as the reader of the book of life nurtures the hope of finding on the last page a rationale, a meaning, a solution to the enigma of his reading. Only *death* as a revelatory moment can explain *life*, ultimately providing it with a meaning, and man with a consolation, although illusory. Walter Benjamin has observed that what we look for, along the temporal process informing our experience of any narrative construction–to which "life" can be metaphorically assimilated–is the knowledge of the "end," and in particular of death, a knowledge that is forbidden to us in life: the awareness of a death that can write the word "end" to the days of our life, and therefore can give them a meaning. Death and conclusion, according to Benjamin, represent the sanction and ultimate justification of anything a narrator may narrate.[29] This further proves the inevitable *retrospectivity* of any narration: only the end can determine its final meaning.

---

29. See Walter Benjamin, "The Storyteller."

And what the "reader"—of the narration of a novel as well as of that of life—looks for, according to Frank Kermode in his well-known *The Sense of an Ending*, is a completeness of the temporal movements of the narration itself: a sense of *harmony* between the beginning, the central phases of "crisis," and the final, allegedly *solving* dénouement. The employment and the success, not only in literary aesthetics but also in social reflections and in the philosophical sciences, of the concept of "crisis" is at the basis of the human interest (and Barlow is no exception in this sense) toward the notion of *transition* as a necessary process on the way to the inevitable end, death. In fact, Kermode defines ours as an "eschatological society," dominated by an apocalyptical anxiety whose main concern is the prediction of the "end," the meaning of an epoch being revealed essentially in its phases of "conclusions." According to Kermode, there is a strict connection between, for example, the end of a century and the human imagination, which always believes it lives at the end of an epoch: the "sense of the ending" is a cultural and social construction (a "psychology of the crisis") that permeates our lives as human beings, and therefore the narrative texts—and the literary versions of the whole narrative experience that is life itself—cannot avoid being filled by this "sense." And incidentally, let us mention here that the conviction that writing the climax alone is worth the writing of the beginning and the composition of the central part of a narrative can be found in many studies of narrativity: for example, in both Propp and in Kermode himself—who proposes a provocative comparison between the *tick* implying the *tock* sound of a clock and the presuppositions that the beginning of a novel entails with reference to the temporal progression *toward* its end.[30] In light of this discussion, it is therefore even more disquietingly telling to acknowledge how a narrative like "The Night Ocean" programmatically *belittles* and *downplays* the value of its final result, of its own end as the end of the narration *and* of life, by sanctioning the utter inanity of the protagonist's temporal "parable" in search for an(y) "explanation." Coherently with his bleak existential views, Barlow has his protagonist ultimately come up deluded and deceived at the end of his anxious vigil, and thus commenting upon the lack of valuable tools, and of useful rationales to account for life's sense: "Yet in the end I had nothing. I was given only a glimpse of the furtive thing; a glimpse made obscure by the veils of ignorance [. . .] perhaps none of us can solve these things—they exist in defiance of all explanations" (*EG* 120). The end of the narration, exactly like the end of the parable of existence it allegorically depicts, leads its performer to achieve a bare *nothing*; and since the end, in narratives as well as in lives, is the source of both the meaning and the explanation of what preceded it, their lack is precisely the element that, also under the viewpoint of its treatment of temporality, further proves "The Night Ocean" a masterpiece of existential hopelessness.

---

30. Yet other scholars oppose this claim: Jean Pouillon and Claude Bremond, among others. For instance, Pouillon maintains that the past tense used by the classic novel is actually decoded by the reader as a sort of present tense, the present of an action and of a series of meanings that are, as it were, forming under his eyes (see Jean Pouillon, *Temps et roman*).

H. P. Lovecraft's Christmas Greeting to R. H. Barlow, 1934.

6. Nature

The sense of deep respect, admiration, and even devotion that Barlow's work shows toward nature is a trait that both his fiction and his poetry amply reveal.[1] This trait is so pervasive that one is even led to claim that Barlow provides his work with a clear intention to transmit and preach to his readers this sense of admiration, or at least the awareness of the necessity—for a responsible humankind—to deal with the problems and the concerns related with its own relationship with the natural environment. As an environmentalist *ante litteram*, Barlow intends to claim the right of nature to be recognized, considered, and *heard*, since it actually holds a strong voice that constantly expresses its owner's instances. The close correspondence between man and nature—so close that in much of his writing Barlow depicts nature as a sort of double of man, and vice versa—is only a further element reinforcing the author's aesthetic purpose of a *re-enactment of nature's rights*.

Barlow's fiction—as it will be in his poetry too—manifests an interest toward the defense of nature that deserves attention and consideration by humans. This interest may of course assume several forms and be voiced in very different ways. In his fiction, in part similarly to what happens in his poetry, Barlow decides to privilege three literary approaches to nature, which are listed below according to an increasing level of complexity and of pertinence with reference to Barlow's aesthetic goal to *dignify* nature:

1. the dialectical conflict between (the rules of) nature and (the rules of) culture. The conflict involves, on one side, nature, with its changeless rules and rituals, not evil if not in a strictly impersonal manner, and on the other side not a generic and abstract concept of "culture," but specifically the cultural systems—as those of a mechanical age—which do not respect nature and its rules. In this sense, Barlow's fiction comes to question the universal, anthropocentric belief that distinguishes the "natural" from the "cultural," and even the belief that an actual distinction between the two exists. From an ethical viewpoint, not to respect nature's laws is an unalloyed evil—no matter how cruel and unpleasant these laws are, or how indifferent or even malevolent nature is toward mankind. Not to respect nature's laws—for example, by perpetuating the havoc brought by the mechanization of work and society—signifies a commitment to a crime against external, physical nature as well as man's own nature, the two being reciprocally intertwined, as the following approach demonstrates;
2. personification of nature, which is metaphorically equivalent to a living and sentient creature, and more often than not even endowed with physical and psychological qualities, traits, and faculties typically human; in other

---

[1]. For an analysis and a further deepening on nature as a thematic "nucleus" of RHB's poetry, section 9.2.5 "Nature: Nature and Culture."

words, nature gets *humanized*, or at least *animalized*. What is important to stress is that the personification of nature is instrumental to the attempt to dignify it, but it does not necessarily involve a praising attitude toward an eventual "goodness" of nature: nature is neither good nor evil in itself, it is simply indifferent—as in Lovecraft's view. Therefore, what may get personified in Barlow's fiction is also a grim or indifferent nature, one by no means sympathetic to human efforts and desires—this will appear particularly evident in the discussion of the "natural theme" of "The Night Ocean." Again following Lovecraft, also Barlow's fiction manifests the same contradiction toward nature: if, on the one hand, physical nature is seen as the symbol of what is positive, pure, and uncorrupted in human nature, on the other hand physical nature is also totally indifferent toward humankind and is represented as a powerful force imposing dire limits on man's expression of his own potentialities. One of the aesthetic goals of Barlow's fiction—though never reaching the importance and centrality it has in Lovecraft's—is the representation of a suspension of those natural laws gallingly limiting man's wishes and aspirations;

3. spiritualization of nature, which at times Barlow's fiction comes to enshroud in a veil of sacredness.

I proceed now with the discussion of these three approaches to nature, which is followed by the analysis of the way in which an exemplary tale, "The Night Ocean," deals with the controversial "theme" of nature.

6.1 The "conflict" between nature and culture

In Barlow's fiction, the conflict between nature and culture finds perhaps its clearest expression—and metaphorical illustration—in that between the sorcerers and the rulers of its fantasy worlds. The rulers represent the oppression of the externally imposed law, of a progress that Barlow identifies—following the steps of his mentor Lovecraft—with the ruins brought on by the machine age: not simply the mechanization of work, and workers' dispossession of the craft of their activity, but also the growing consumerism and incapacity to reason independently shown by the barbarized and standardized society. Telling, on this point, is Barlow's comment upon Lovecraft's personality, as contained in the memoir "The Wind That Is in the Grass": "a man who had the courage to ignore the Machine Age and its levelling-out-to-rubble of life's rich irregularities, who had the courage to study and think and converse and write, in accordance with the deeper traditions of a more orderly age [...] His intimate acquaintance with astronomy, history, and literature, as well as a host of other interests, made him a civilizer among barbarians" (WG 362-63).

In his fiction, Barlow fights the "barbarians" by showing that their views of life and nature are hollow, that they should not superimpose their vulgarity and preposterousness on the laws of nature, here seen as the inner forces of man's soul, his legitimate desires and aspirations to realize himself and to overcome the very limits that nature imposes on them. The sheer act of *restraining* man's personality, will, and desire (whatever this will and desire may aspire to), representing an attempt to impose new limits on man, is indeed an act *against nature*—an act that does not necessarily configure as "cultural," since Barlow contests that what is "culture" is to be opposed to what is "nature." This is why Barlow's work provides examples of humans' (often tragically) unsuccessful attempts at enforcing new and unjustified restraints on others' free activity[2]: what Barlow criticizes is that the restraining action is concealed under the pseudo-authoritative veil of an artificial "law" and presented as the harbinger of the necessary intervention of the "cultural" trying to impose long-needed limitations over an otherwise wild—and potentially subversive—"free expression." According to Barlow, his is a society of "barbarians," since nobody understands that what is passed by institutions as "cultural" is not such in truth, because we need to overcome the antiquated and actually inane opposition between "nature" and "culture": nature does not need to be restrained by anything "cultural," because what opposes nature cannot be "cultural." Nature and culture are in fact never in conflict: they are the two sides of the same coin, and if the establishment passes as "cultural" something that opposes human free expression, that is just a deceptive label attached to something in order to justify its use. This free expression is in fact nothing else but man's *nature*, and any attempt to tamper with it is destined to be harshly punished, as Barlow's fiction intends to demonstrate.

An exemplary case of this Barlovian poetics is contained in episode eight of the *Annals of the Jinns*, titled "The Fall of the Three Cities." In it, the attempt of rulers to limit the free power of expression of a wizard's arts is met with the doom and destruction of the three "cities of the plain" (Naazim, Zo, and Perenthines) and their inhabitants. The story tells of the magician Volnar, who "refused to leave Perenthines. He had been a most successful and prosperous sorcerer until the deplorable case of the fishwife whose hair all fell out and took root in the ground before her house. This the people took to be an evil omen, and it was really quite difficult for them to break into his low, strange house after his refusal to depart. They were all disappointed he had gone" (EG 22-23). But nobody knows that in truth sorcerer Volnar has not left, since they "did not know of the black tunnel beneath where he kept his magical supplies" (EG 23). Thus the inhabitants of Perenthines set Volnar's house afire, make merry by the night, happy to have finally killed the source of those evil magic. But Volnar has not died: he has fled by night "with only his vengeful thoughts for company" (EG 23). Camouflaging himself with a black-edged mantle of crimson that makes him resemble a great moth, Volnar comes at the gates of Zo, his pet *mondal* still moaning about the ashes, "for his persecutors had been unable to capture the highly edible pet"

---

2. That this literary topos may be read also as the reflection of a political position is certainly not surprising, considering RHB's avowed left-wing sympathies.

(EG 23). Here Barlow is offering a further environmentalist comment: the attempts of the persecutors to capture—and likely kill and eat—the wild pet *mondal* reflect the attempt of a distorted "culture" to subject the free forces of "nature" to the cultural corrupting power. The detail that Volnar's pet has not been captured is a Barlovian hint to the powers of a tameless nature, which strives not to let itself be subdued by external, "cultural" forces.

Volnar is then received in the city of Zo, where he buys a house with the gold he himself has contrived, and works ceaselessly in the dank and ill-lit cellar. Barlow describes Volnar's condition as that of one who regrets the past splendor and is preparing a revenge—seemingly the plight of nature, offended by man's inconsiderate attacks and slowly preparing its own revengeful return: "Volnar worked on with his charms and spells, occasionally sighing for his abandoned *mondal*, and frequently pondering upon his revenge" (EG 23). The forces of nature at work in Volnar's "subterranean quarters" are equated to occult ones, those apprehended by "students of the dark lore" (EG 24). Preparing with great care the concoction or strange substance bubbling in his magic pot, Volnar works at the doom for the Perenthines—the mighty revenge of the dark forces of nature against the power abuses committed by "culture." Once the potion is ready, Volnar pours it into a "cylinder of unglazed pottery, deftly sealing it with enchanted gummy material of moist black" (EG 24). Carrying the jar, Volnar leaves his cellar and enters Zo's main street. The night's darkness is thick, but Volnar does not wish to fail in his revenging mission. Volnar approaches the city center, still carrying the increasingly heavy cylinder—whose content is "unruly with new animation" (EG 24)—under his arm. Once he reaches the marble pool at the center of Zo, the marvel of the three towns, Volnar lets the content of his cylinder slide silently into the pool. Sinking to the bottom, the substance expands and solidifies, drifting away in the water. Apparently satisfied, Volnar departs. Without returning to his house, he leaves directly for the mountains, searching for a safe position whence to look upon the doom of the three cities. And doom it indeed is: the watcher knows that "evil forces were at work, forces none could halt or evade save by direct flight" (EG 24). With these very words, Barlow seems to adumbrate the power of the revenge of natural forces, when nature, with its cataclysmic disasters, seems almost to display a sense of rebellion against the oppression perpetrated by man in the form of a mad exploitation of resources and a mechanical progress that do not respect nature's rights. It is precisely against the idea that this behavior represents "culture" that Barlow addresses his attack.

Thus Volnar chuckles at the imminent doom of the three cities, but still hopes that "his pet *mondal* was not within the doomed area" (EG 24): even in the moment of the realization of the revenge, Volnar—here symbolizing an agent of nature—hopes that his attack will spare one of nature's sons. In fact, the brutality of nature's attacks against man's cultural oppression usually makes them so destructive that they end by involving innocent victims, including those of nature's creatures that have nothing to do with man's evil behavior: volcanic eruptions, earthquakes, seaquakes, flooding, etc. all symbolize the revolt of nature against man, but they end up destroying countless innocent lives of creatures such as non-human animals and vegetables that are not at all at fault. Thus, Volnar's hope that his pet *mondal* survives represents nature's concern to save its sons from its own otherwise indiscriminate violence.

The evil creature, with its hundred evil eyes, droolingly emerges from the pool and at first seizes one pedestrian passing by, absorbing nutrition from his body. And then this unrestrainable natural force is free to roam and cause destruction— the allegory of the free spirit of man finally liberated from any limit and superimposed "cultural" restriction: "it roved the streets unsated, growing, devouring throughout the night, and in a few horrible hours had depopulated the cities *that were so hostile to sorcerers*" (EG 24; italics added). The detail "that were so hostile to sorcerers" is indicative of the fact that Barlow wants to depict a nature's revenge that is not casual and does not hit randomly: it is not blind destruction, but a *conscious, legitimate revenge* against those who committed unjustified crimes and violence.

"The Mirror," the ninth episode of the *Annals*, also tells the story of a revenge, that of the sorcerer Khalda—the pupil of Volnar—against the Emperor of Yondath, a personification of the most oppressive figure of ruler. Khalda had been accused of high sacrilege and of attempting to create artificial life through "ancient and unwholesome magic" (EG 25): once more, the forces of nature become metaphorically, in Barlow's narration, the occult lore of a forbidden knowledge. Khalda is imprisoned and condemned to horrible tortures: thus Barlow again in this tale criticizes the attempt of rulers to restrain the free (intellectual) power of human beings, and the attempt of "culture" to limit man's fulfillment of his most daring aspirations—in this case, even the creation of life from death, and the desire not to venerate the conventional, in a sense "standardized" (and thus "cultural") gods, all aspirations contrasting with the established, so-called "cultural" rules of the system. But according to Barlow, man must be granted the right to pursue his own realization in the freest and most unrepressed way, to liberate his instincts whose satisfaction is the only way to let him express in full. When these rights are not granted, when man's freedom—in the broadest sense—is threatened or even annihilated, the cultural "system" is committing a crime against nature, one that will eventually bounce back and bring doom and sorrow on its perpetrators, as is aptly symbolized by the story of the sorcerer Khalda. After the Emperor of Yondath believes the rebel wizard is forever neutralized by being entrusted into the fierce hands of Malyat, the fabled Head Torturer dwelling in the subterranean crypts of the Emperor's palace, Khalda slowly starts to plan his revenge. And the Emperor will have to face it, like the inevitable punishment for a crime committed against the forces of nature[3]: Khalda comes back, bringing along a mirror built in secrecy and endowed with extraordinary, evil magic powers. In particular,

---

3. In the rash fight undertaken against nature, there is no justified hope of victory. In fact, as RHB makes clear in "A Memory," "nature ever triumphs in the struggle for possession" (EG 74).

the reflecting power of the mirror is converted and aptly used by Barlow as an effective metaphor of the fact that a crime committed against nature always *reflects* on its author. Khalda in fact forces the Emperor to look into the mirror, and what the Emperor sees is the indescribable reflection of the evil he himself committed; it is the reflection of the blackness of his own soul—a sight no man can bear without costing him the horrible pains of an atrocious death: "And when the ruler looked therein, no man may know what was reflected, for a strange and terrible thing occurred. Some dire magic was at work, for the doom that came unto his majesty was alien to all accepted lines of death" (EG 27).

6.2 The personification of nature

Perhaps the most striking aspect of Barlow's fictional treatment of nature consists in his presenting natural elements as endowed with a specific *sentience*, namely qualities, faculties, and even skills that pertain to human beings or non-human but living creatures. As stated previously, this process contributes to the general aim to *dignify* nature, not to the attribution of exclusively positive qualities. Nature must be respected not because it is caring—it is in fact, at best, indifferent to human goals and aspirations—but because it is like a sentient and living being: no moral is attached to Barlow's consideration, it is simply the non-anthropocentric claim of the necessity of regarding any living being as deserving respect, since it is not intrinsically inferior to any other. Where a sentient being is involved, its sheer capacity to sense is reason enough to grant it the right to survival and to be respected. We will see that even inanimate abstract objects or phenomena often gain, in Barlow's fiction, the status of sentient beings.

In itself, "personification" is a rhetoric figure that can be defined as "a variety of figurative or metaphorical language in which things or ideas are treated as if they were human beings, with human attributes and feelings" (Gray 156). In this sense, Barlow's fiction clearly attempts to attribute a "personality" to natural elements, inanimate objects, atmospheric events, and even abstract concepts. In order to make a personification, it is necessary to put into relation two different counterparts that may belong to different realms (what I propose to label *external personification*) or to the same realm (in which case, two sub-orders are compared: *internal personification*). The most common way of proceeding is to attribute to (concrete or abstract) inanimate objects (namely the *target element* of the personification) qualities typical of living creatures (as *source elements* of the personification), both non-human and, more often than not, human. Thus, in Barlow's fiction the most common "crossing" is that involving the realms of the inanimate and of the animate. This is a case of external personification, since the realms are mutually exclusive: an inanimate object (target element) is put into relation with an animate, living creature (source element), and the distance between the two elements compared is greater (since they belong to different realms) than in the case of internal personification, where both target and source belong to sub-orders *of the same realm*. This secondary way of proceeding—one that is less frequently represented in Barlow's fiction—consists in crossing two sub-orders of the same realm, namely the realm of animate, living entities—for example, the animal and the vegetable—attributing to the vegetable, target element qualities typical of the animal or human, source element.

As an example of a concrete inanimate object as the target element of an external personification, perhaps that of a statue is the most exemplary—and it is indeed present in one of Barlow's narratives, "The Root-Gatherers." During their journey in search for roots, the protagonists of this tale have to cross a very ancient, now ruined city—significantly called *Doom*. The city is preceded by a bridge that is guarded by a colossal metal statue. Its indifferent countenance and gaze bespeak the sentience of a typical natural creature, namely one that does not care for mankind's wishes, affairs, and ultimate destiny: "Then we came into the city, passing below the mute colossi whose downward gaze had the frightening indifference of all ancient things. There was an aspect of *waiting* about the metal statue [. . .] No one has guessed when it was made and set there as guardian of the bridge. [. . .] Looking briefly at the high, indistinct face, I turned away from the bridge and the nameless crouching giant to go into the ruinous streets" (EG 85). Let us notice already here, besides the presence of "nameless," the employment of another Lovecraftian adjective, "crouching,"[4] particularly frequent in Barlow's fiction, where it strives to represent the personification of an inanimate object, to which human and animal qualities are attributed. As we will see—especially in the discussion of "The Night Ocean"—this term is especially used by Barlow when trying to depict the "attitude" and external outlook of inanimate objects endowed with animal and human qualities. In "A Dim-Remembered Story," for instance, we read of a crag-hung castle that "pierced the sky with wall and turrets crouching monstrously against the silken universe" (EG 94).

When choosing what human or animal qualities to attribute to inanimate objects, Barlow shows a certain preference for those related to *waiting* and *silence*. As with the giant statue of "The Root-Gatherers" (where the crossing was between the inanimate realm of a statue and the animate one of a living creature capable of "waiting" and feeling "indifference"), the same occurs with the trees of the wood where the stupefied, unnamed narrator of "A Dim-Remembered Story" finds himself at the beginning of his cosmic adventure: "On every side the great trees rose; above, their tops were so netted as to hide the cobalt sky. They lingered, waiting and silent—tall goblins circling me with outstretched arms" (EG 88). Here Barlow

---

4. In "The Call of Cthulhu," the term or its derivates are employed three times, while describing Cthulhu's position in the statuettes representing him: "The tips of the wings touched the back edge of the block, the seat occupied the centre, whilst the long, curved claws of the doubled-up, *crouching* hind legs gripped the front edge" (CC 148). Again: "The cephalopod head was bent forward, so that the ends of the facial feelers brushed the backs of huge fore paws which clasped the *croucher*'s elevated knees" (CC 148). The third mention: "The *crouching* image with its cuttlefish head, dragon body, scaly wings, and hieroglyphed pedestal, was preserved in the Museum at Hyde Park" (CC 163).

decides to cross two sub-orders of the animate realm: he attributes to a living creature of the vegetable realm (the tree) two qualities pertaining to a creature of the animal realm (those of "waiting" and of being "silent"). The mysterious forest surrounding the protagonist seems "strange and mystical" (EG 89), and in fact it not only possesses waiting and silent, namely sentient, trees, but even an impaired sense of *sight*: "The *blind eyes of the forest peered back*. Leaves and mosses seemed *to watch me*, and tortuous black limbs to await my action" (EG 89; italics added). The forest, with its whispers, shows a will to participate in the bizarre meeting and exchange between the narrator and the two women from a far future: "Fat boughs swayed about us, *whispering of the oncoming night*" (EG 93; italics added). The forest watches, speaks, and even listens ("the listening forest" [EG 93]): it is as if the forest were striving to free itself from a role—that of simple background to the human scene—it feels as too restrictive. Just as humans fight in order to overcome the "galling limitations" of natural laws, it is as if nature fought one on its own, in order to overcome the condition imposed on it *by human beings*—namely that of being a sheer background to human actions. Nature wants to show it is much more than that, wants to claim the right to a much more significant role; and in this masterly tale, nature becomes a magic counterpart of the human scene it is condemned (by humans) only to assist in. In order to show its capacity to perform a much more relevant role, nature has to overcome the prejudice (i.e. the limitation) man imposes on her, nature has to rid herself of her "familiar aspect" (familiar *for man*) and show her concealed, magic powers, for example her sentience, her capacity to watch, speak, and listen: "the sunlit, familiar aspect of nature is concealed, and mystery breathes in each sentient tree" (EG 93). The overcoming of limits thus finds in Barlow's fiction a very broad and full expression, and above all, one that does not rely only on an anthropocentric perspective: even Lovecraft, with his relativist approach to literature, was too narrow, in that he considered the overcoming of limits a typically human prerogative and need. Some of Barlow's passages, such as the above, may instead be interpreted as staging the need for a suspension of laws that is biunique: not only may humans reach for the suspension of natural laws and the defeat of the galling limitations they impose; *nature may, in her turn, be induced to fight against the laws that human beings impose on her, and against the limitations they imply on nature's desire for free expression and self-realization*. Barlow's literature shows that nature, being much more than a passive background, strives for a superior recognition, and this is her legitimate right. This is also why, as a consequence, nature deserves our respect: she is much more than what we humans think (and impose) her to be.

But what exactly are the quality and the extent of nature's *magic*? What is the hidden "nature" of nature, the one man does not know, and which she aspires to realize and fulfill?

First, nature and her inanimate components are capable of any kind of feeling, since this is not—as humans wrongly believe—a prerogative of "superior" living creatures; natural elements are able to experience joy, sorrow, a sense of expectancy, the will to be active or to be passive, exactly as only humans are allegedly supposed to be. Thus the moon is able to frighten the stars, which are induced, as scared creatures would, to flee: "The moon had frightened all the stars, until they fled in trailing sparks" (EG 94). All the feelings and psychological conditions that man presumptuously attributes only to himself or to a few non-human animals are instead the prerogative of inanimate natural objects: "Beyond these walls I saw the plain, still as if overtaken *by charmed death*" (EG 97; italics added). In "Origin Undetermined," even a place, an aeons-ancient "primal, night-bound steppe" (EG 128), has the power to "dream," to "rest," and to have "recollections to brood on" (EG 128), with only the night (which thus gets personified, in its turn) "to hear its whispered, inhuman secrets" (EG 128).

Second, nature's inanimate components are capable even of *actions*; if not actually to realize them, at least to *plan them consciously*: "The sky was gaudy once more, and everywhere leaves of sanguine hue invaded the green ranks. The army of marching trees was flecked with blood. Summer's garment was cast off, and the very grasses were astir in some ineffable expectancy" (EG 97-98), just as if preparing to perform a big action—as that of an "army" would be.

Another relevant issue addressed by Barlow's treatment of this theme is the following: Why has not man ever recognized nature's wish for recognition and full self-realization? Is it simply because of man's presumptuousness and conceit? In truth, it is not—and this points of course to the partial rehabilitation of man's faulty position in his relationship with nature. In fact, given man's defective epistemic equipment, it would not always have been easy for him to grasp nature's wish for self-realization, since *man and nature speak at times two different languages*. The peculiar sentience of natural elements is not often easily graspable for human beings—not by chance are the secrets whispered by the place of "Origin Undetermined," quoted above, defined as "inhuman." In his final cosmic vision, the protagonist of "A Dim-Remembered Story" sees huge light balls whose shape, substance, and possible intentions are beyond any human capacity of conjecture: "The balls were living. As I watched, they grew tremendously, and shifted like phantasmal sea-things. How much of consciousness they had, *I cannot guess*. They lived and moved, but *their sentience was too different from my own for one to comprehend the other*" (EG 102; italics added). Nature's sentience is revealed at times as too utterly alien to ours to grant even a feeble light of comprehension: this aspect of Barlow's poetics concerning the relationship between the "human" and the "natural" is of course coherent with the author's own cosmic views on mankind, the meaninglessness of her place in the universe, and the dialectics between the "human" and the "alien" as seen in chapter 4 on cosmicism.

It is relevant to note that, in Barlow's fiction, the process of personification of nature, namely of rendering nature *human* or *humanized*, is accompanied also by its reversal, i.e. by the *naturalization* or *"animalization"* of man. Barlow aims at showing that the correspondence between man and nature is perfectly biunique: just as natural elements may be considered human or humanized, since they possess qualities and skills allegedly thought to pertain only to man, so man possesses qualities that apparently only non-human animals hold. Barlow's fiction, thus shortening—almost nullifying—the distance between the "human" and the "natural," works in the direction of developing of a sense of respect toward nature: if what is "human" is also "natural," and vice versa, then man is of course induced to respect the "natural" as part of himself, namely to hold it in the same regard as he holds everything human.

"Pursuit of the Moth" (1935)[5] is the account of the gradual transformation—trans-generation—of a human being, Amno, into a non-human animal, a moth. The metamorphosis occurs almost imperceptibly, though Barlow disseminates in the tale a few hints pointing in this direction: in the first paragraph of the tale, young Sigrill pursues his companion Amno, who has stolen Sigrill's bow in mockery and is now escaping his friend's chase. At one point, Sigrill gets entangled in the pricking weeds of a thicket, and Amno pauses, displaying the bow he stole to his friend: "You will not easily regain your weapon," he tantalized, "for you must overtake me first, and I am *fleet as the moth!*" (*EG* 81). From this moment on, Sigrill loses track of his friend, who vanishes, leaving Sigrill alone, in pursuit of a creature that seems to have actually lost its human physicalness. And the words *I am fleet as the moth* ceaselessly recur into Sigrill's mind. His increasingly frantic search for the vanished friend through woods and thickets proves useless, until Sigrill meets the ruined gate of an ancient, crumbling castle: "He did not like the pillars of the ruined gate, for they were twined with bloated creepers; yet between them showed hasty footsteps, and he knew that Amno had passed before him" (*EG* 82–83). Immediately Barlow connects the mention of Amno's human figure with that of a moth, which Sigrill unheedingly kills: "As Sigrill resumed his stride a luminous gray moth flew up startlingly, and beat soft wings about his head. They were great wings, and he was forced to strike at it. Brokenly, it fell upon the ground, and fluttered crippled wings until he kindly crushed the writhing form beneath his heel" (*EG* 83). Following the footprints, Sigrill is urged ahead to enter the "revolting wreck," whose ugliness and menacing air thrill the youth's spirit. After a silent prayer and the drawing in the air of a Sign of holiness to fight the evilness of the ruined place, Sigrill enters it, dimly discerning, amidst the gloomy darkness of the place, piled-up heaps of ancient and rich objects: gem-set chalices, preciously engraved furniture, rotten rags of once-wondrous tapestries. Then, abruptly, Sigrill is startled at a disturbing, unexpectedly fearsome sight:

> There came an overwhelming fright upon the youth as one patterned shape stirred faintly, but half-crying out, he saw that it was not the tapestry which moved, but *a silver moth* upon it—a moth such as he had seen before the murky gates. Large as his two hands it was, and glistening wonderfully in the light [. . .] Fluttering a moment, it descended in a swift erratic flight, and lighted on the

---

5. This tale was composed on 5 May 1935, and appeared in the second issue of RHB's own amateur magazine, *The Dragon-Fly*, for 15 May 1936 (33–40). HPL expressed his appreciation of the story: "You'll have no difficulty placing the moth story—or the new one—in the amateur or weird-fan press" (letter to RHB, 21 October 1935, *FF* 299).

quiet face of that which Sigrill had not spied: *the limpness of a youthful corpse on piles of ruined rag.* (EG 83; italics added)

Thus Barlow represents a human being, Amno, turning into a moth, and thus suggests the intrinsic *naturalness* of anything human: the border between the human and the non-human is not an insurmountable curtain, passage is possible in each direction—and this should warn man to respect nature and not to offend her, since an offense perpetrated against nature (Sigrill's killing of the moth) affects mankind—even more, it is an offense to mankind itself. The effective image of the killing of a moth, revealed as the killing of a human, is a powerful metaphor to demonstrate it.

In order to show that Barlow's attitude toward the personification of nature does not exclusively tend to show nature's goodness, but also its *indifferentism* and amorality, let us now examine a few excerpts drawn from tales in which nature is represented as displaying an intrinsic evil or indifference toward mankind. Certainly "The Night Ocean," as we shall see in section 6.4, offers the best examples (for their sheer abundance and effectiveness) of this issue, but the theme is so pervasive in Barlow's fiction that it is exemplified also in other of his most mature narratives. For instance, in "Origin Undetermined," the alien plants Heywood Roberts unheedingly decides to grow in his basement room are revealed as terrible living creatures, devouring even the glass of a window-pane: "and in the opening those hungry sprouts vibrated *like small serpent heads*. A chilly wind blew in from the March day: they seemed to breath it *avidly*" (EG 127; italics added). In this case, Barlow's personification has crossed two sub-orders of the animate realm (internal personification), because it has attributed to the target element, a creature of the vegetable order (though what exactly is the nature of the plants goes beyond safe conjecture), qualities pertaining to creatures of the animal order (those of vibrating like "serpent" heads and of breathing "avidly"). Again a few pages later, the noxious plants are once more provided with the quality of snakes—reinforcing the image of this internal personification—while the narrator describes the attempt he made, in his nightmare, to destruct the rebellious plants once again: "*In the strong grip of nightmare I repeated their destruction again and again, but like snakes about me they sought to drag me into the raw consuming flames*" (EG 130).

Powerful also is the personification of a menacing nature occurring in episode two of the *Annals of the Jinns*, titled "The Shadow from Above." In this suggestive fantastic tale, the hamlet Droom is initially immerged in a very quiet midsummer day, one in which the routine hum of everyday activities does not let anyone foresee the unexplainable horror to come: "The villagers went about their various tasks, and within the tiny market square the spice-vendors and the people from the hills with their exotic burdens of gay fruits created a pleasant hum of busy occupation" (EG 15). But it is an apparently menacing—and more likely an indifferent—nature that suddenly appears under the blurred contours of a huge "shadow from above":

> Then one of the dogs lying in a doorway sprang suddenly and emitted a sharp bark. At the same moment a dark cloud apparently obscured the sun. [. . .] Soon the whole population was out of doors looking upwards at that which could not be seen yet which cast a deep shadow. Nothing was to be perceived in the expanse of blue, yet upon the square cobblestones of the quaint little village an irregular black form wavered back and forth. Then it grew larger. Whatever it may have been, it was settling. The people drew back affrighted. Slowly the swinging motion ceased, and the thing drew near. A deep, heavy panting was distinctly audible, much like that of a great beast, and with a dull impact as though it was of great weight, it alighted upon a grassy plot before the Chancellor's house. For a long time it lay there, resting. And still nothing could be seen save the indentation of the grass nor aught heard but the heavy breathing. (EG 15-16)

People run terrified to their house, and in a moment the main street is bare, save for the thudding invisible monster: "All that afternoon and night it pried at doors, scratched at roofs, muzzled windows and upset fruit-carts inquiringly. But the people of Droom had built well. It did not gain entrance during the night, although few slept, when they heard the constant breathing before their homes, and the dull thumping sounds as it *wreaked its malice* upon the shops of the market-place" (EG 16; italics added). In this narrative Barlow presents an external personification of an apparently *evil* though innocuous nature (the invisible beast will not kill anybody and will vanish into thin air the day after): perhaps the best definition of this nature is, paradoxically, one whose intentions are *indefinable* or *unspeakable*—nothing can be said with certainty of her. Being impossible to exercise on her what Barlow deems the most important sense, sight, it is consequently impossible to express a full judgment over the only apparently hostile (super)natural manifestation. All that is certain is that the personification here connects two different realms—the target object being a shadow, namely an inanimate object that is endowed with faculties typical of a creature of the living realm (those of walking, prying, scratching, muzzling, upsetting, breathing, resting, etc.).

Again, in "Origin Undetermined," another example of "evil" personification of a natural element can be found and deserves mention, since this time the crossing occurs between the animate and the inanimate realms, thus configuring an external personification; in a passage reminiscent of Lovecraft's *At the Mountains of Madness,* Barlow presents an external personification in which the mountains (target element) populating the protagonist's vision are endowed with the evil intentions of malignant animals (source element): "The mountains seemed *to draw closer to one another*, forming an impregnable shield. *Like suspicious beasts they shifted and gazed malevolently* across leagues of moor" (EG 130; italics added). Interestingly, "Origin Undetermined" shows another variant of external personification, one in which the target element is not simply an inanimate object, but even an abstract one. For example, in Barlow's literary worlds the "crouching" attitude may be a prerogative not only of inanimate (but concrete) objects ("The *mountains crouching* on the western rim were almost lost in the edge of darkness" [EG 128; italics added]), but also of abstract entities: in "Origin Undetermined," the protagonist's vision reveals a vast plain, a "flat expanse with *darkness crouching on it like a live thing*" (EG 128; italics added). Another case may be found in "Return by Sunset," where even a feeling—or physical and psychological state—gets personified: "When Dal saw it [a ruined temple], the girl Leyenda was with him. They had crossed many valleys and delved into many forests escaping from her brothers; and *weariness walked with them now*" (EG 136; italics added). And in the very delicate, dreamy atmosphere it may happen that even a temporal dimension, that of the *past*, finds personification and with its long hand comes to influence—if not to haunt—the characters' present: "There was her bracelet for one thing; it seemed tighter than usual. She wondered why it would not come off. [. . .] It gripped her like an inexorable hand—*the hand*, she vaguely felt, *of the past of this place* of whose history nothing was known" (EG 140; italics added). Especially these last features, namely the personifications of abstract concepts and even of physical states or temporal dimensions, provide a fuller picture of the extent to which Barlow conceived his literary world as a fully sentient one: one whose every component—no matter how concrete or abstract, how animate or inanimate—may show in itself signs of life, perception, volition, independent thought, and at least theoretical will for action. And this peculiar, all-embracing sensitivity of Barlow's literary worlds is confirmed and strengthened by a very important feature of the author's treatment of nature: his attempt to *spiritualize* her.

6.3 The spiritualization of nature

The process of spiritualization of nature may be interpreted as the extreme consequence to which the "personification" one is brought. In fact, not only may natural elements be endowed with the faculties of a sentient being: in some of the most "environmentalist" tales, they are also provided with spiritual qualities that make the interpreter seriously suspect an alleged "pantheism" on Barlow's part. Not only is nature sentient; it also possesses non-natural qualities (I do not dare to say super-natural), at least according to the common, limited, anthropocentric consideration of what is natural. In this sense, its showing that nature possesses apparently non-natural qualities may be seen as a further attempt of Barlow's fiction to attack the inanity, and demonstrate the wrongness, of an anthropocentric view of the world: in other words, after questioning the artificial opposition between "nature" and "culture," Barlow's fiction intends to question what common human belief deems "natural," and what are the universally accepted borders between the "natural" and the "spiritual."

One of the most convincing ways in which Barlow effects the process of the spiritualization of nature consists in enshrouding her with a veil of "sacredness." In particular in the fantasy tales of the *Annals of the Jinns* cycle, it is possible to see how human attempts to tamper with the gods of nature—symbolizing the sacredness of nature itself—are inevitably met with doom and destruction. In fact, nature has a divine trait in it, and the attempt to interfere with her organic workings is inevitably equivalent to committing a sacrilege against a powerful and vengeful god. A revelatory tale in this sense is "Eyes of the God," one that already in its title hints at the sense of sight of a divinity that, like nature, is always watching man's actions. This short tale contains the account of the attempted, ill-fated theft of the two huge diamond eyes of an ebony idol reproducing an exotic god and preserved in an anthropologic museum. During nighttime, a thief enters the exhibition and slugs the watchman. The museum symbolizes—through the survey Barlow provides of the immense variety of statues and figurines it features—the infinitely different ways in which peoples from different corners of the world worship and celebrate the secretive, hidden powers of nature. Though the ways of worship are manifold and apparently unconnected, they represent the inner feeling people nurture of the sacredness concealed in nature. The description of the variety of idols present at the exhibition is Barlow's way of depicting the pervasive feeling of the sacredness of nature as perceived by the peoples of the earth: "Idols from the ends of the earth were gathered in that exhibition. Crude eikons from Africa that were but roughly shipped logs, and elaborately ornamented monstrosities from India. Squat, grotesque pottery images of ancient Mexico sat cheek by jowl with delicate translucent figurines of amber and jade from China" (*EG* 13-14). The thief, symbol of the man who, caring only for his own immediate profit, performs an act threatening the integrity of nature, looks for the god of ebony with diamond eyes, and nothing can really stop him in his greed, not even the story of the alleged cruelty and revenging power of the idol and of its spiritual (supernatural) power:

> Thoughts of the peculiar death of its donor, who had surreptitiously carried it away from its devout followers at the height of their unpleasant power, and of the deep foot-prints in the garden on the night that man so queerly died; passed through the thief's mind as he methodically searched face after face. What was it the full moon was supposed to do to it? Oh yes. . . bring it to life. Odd what those natives believed. (*EG* 14)

Of course the thief's distrust, even scorn of the natives' belief will pay a high price, but what is relevant in the above passage is precisely the fact that Barlow endows nature with divine qualities, the capacity to join her forces (the idol and the full moon) in order to resist man's offenses. Barlow suggests that the "odd beliefs" of native peoples are not silly and unfounded jabbering; on the contrary, they hide a deeper truth that few are willing to acknowledge: nature has divine powers, and it is better to leave her quiet and untouched if one cares to survive. We can here already detect, in a tale dating to 1933, the sense of profound respect Barlow was to nurture in his adult age toward the cultural and religious belief of the native peoples of Mexico (after all, that country is also mentioned in the tale). The thief's death represents the appropriate revenge of nature, through her divine powers epitomized in the ebony idol, against a sacrilegious act: the body of the marauder will be found, the day after, "dead in the Hall of the American Indian with the idol on top of him. Police are as yet uncertain how he moved it, for it weighed six hundred pounds" (EG 14). Thus Barlow uses a powerful metaphor—the idol moving itself and killing the thief by means of its heavy weight—to symbolize the revenge of nature against man's arrogant attempt to subject her.

An even more explicit reference to the sanctity of nature, seen almost as a temple whose sacredness must not be violated by man's intrusion, occurs in installment eleven of the *Annals*, titled "An Episode in the Jungle." The tale opens with the description of the luxuriant life and vegetation of the jungle Yondath, a microcosm of unrestrained freedom for plants and animals, which only asks humans to be left untouched and to grow undisturbed—because it does not cause any trouble to any human: "quiet is lord there" (EG 29). But of course humans are stubborn, and, willing to achieve a futile reward, intend to violate nature's laws. A group of youths decides to embark on a hunt within the forest: they intend to hunt rare animals, and thus—metaphorically—to infringe on the sacredness of the place. The boys, "laden with spears, had gone into the forest hunting beasts; and since they were young men, got rich trophies. Among these were elk and leopards, but no one had even seen a *mondal*, let alone slay it. Since none wished to return without a specimen of this rare and delectable beast, three of his party had set out hunting in the cold radiant dawn, and in an hour were far apart" (EG 29). Thus it is exactly the wish to surpass and infringe the limit—to hunt a rare animal, the indefinable *mondal*—that causes one of the boys, Loman, to be lost. As if rebelling against the last planned offense against her—the killing of the rare animal—nature causes the hunter to lose his path: "Loman mistook his path and stumbled into one of the infrequent clearings. [. . .] Loman searched eastward, following a set of tracks until they were lost, and when he would have rejoined his fellows, saw that he could not" (EG 29-30).

The description of nature's mobilizing all her forces in order to block the hunter's planned slaughter is very vivid, and at one point Barlow employs a revealing expression that deserves discussion:

> Vines hampering his feet were tangled about the boles of fern-trees wonderfully high, and nothing familiar was to be seen in the trackless undergrowth. Unbroken thickets circled the glade and its carpet of spangled moss. Blossoms—a vivid incredible blue, like hot metal—crept on the sward, broken by no foot. Here was *the sanctuary of nature, resentful of the intruder*. [. . .] Cursing the epicurean desires that had led him afield, Loman searched the clustered bushes for both his quarry and his path. (EG 30; italics added)

Thus finally Barlow reveals his point: nature is sacred, the forest is like a temple, resentful of man's attempt to violate it with unhealthy purposes like those of killing nature's creatures—purposes that Barlow ironically defines as "epicurean desires." The metaphorical transformation of nature into a spiritual entity is thus finally achieved, and man's awareness of the sanctity of natural places, a sanctity strengthened by their aeons-long inviolability, should be accomplished. Whenever man does not respect this inviolability, or even threatens it through actual or planned actions—after all, the slaughter of the *mondal* never takes place along the whole narration—he has to pay his due. It may look like an old-fashioned conception of a divinity, one as revengeful as the Old Testament God, but certainly nature appears in Barlow's fiction as endowed with qualities that the anthropocentric view would claim as non-natural, if not actually super-natural. Whether they actually are so, or whether this definition results from a limited and restrictive approach such as the human-centered one, represents a key issue that Barlow's fiction intends to question and discuss.

The analysis of the treatment of nature as shown in one of Barlow's most mature and effective tales, "The Night Ocean," will hopefully add further insight to the discussion of this provocative issue.

6.4 Nature and the sacred: "The Night Ocean"

"The Night Ocean" provides a great many examples of Barlow's aesthetic use of the rhetoric figure of personification. There are two inanimate objects that are particularly subjected to the personifying process: the *house* rented by the unnamed narrator on Ellston Beach, and the *sea* or *ocean*, which at the narration's end—as it will be discussed—is fully revealed as the true, actual protagonist of this atmospherically suspenseful tale. The dominating type of personification is thus the external one, which assigns sensitive qualities—pertaining to living creatures of the animate realm—to inanimate objects, in this case of concrete substance. Other entities are also at times personified—mainly concrete objects—but the predominant targets are the house and the sea.

The small and solitary house, or cottage, where the narrator goes to live is described throughout the tale as endowed with the sensitivity and the motor faculties of a living creature, an animal or even a human being. Its most recurrent physical attitude is that of assuming a *crouching* position. The term, already discussed in paragraph 6.2 above, certainly was a favorite of Barlow, and is probably a Lovecraftian derivation. In "The Night Ocean," to "crouch" and its derivates are employed with impressive frequency with reference to the small square house on the beach, often in connection with other personifying qualities that Barlow decides to bestow upon the building: "Like a solitary warm animal it *crouched* facing the sea, and its inscrutable dirty windows *stared* upon a lonely realm of earth and sky and enormous sea" (*EG* 106; italics added). Two details are worth mentioning in this passage. First, already in this introductory description, Barlow shows that his aesthetic goal is to point out the main trait of the house—and the geographical location chosen by the narrator for his rest period, namely the impression of *loneliness* they convey to a visitor or an observer. The author, in the space of a single sentence, in fact employs two words—"solitary" and "lonely"—connected with the semantic fields of remoteness and isolation. Moreover, the author explicitly connotes the house through a personification—introduced by a simile: "like a solitary warm animal." The house is already and explicitly configured as a living creature, and as such it is no surprise that it possesses eyes and may "stare" at its natural surroundings. Of course, given the importance that the sense of sight has in Barlow's literary aesthetics, it is only to be expected that the first "sensory" attribution he gives to the house is that of possessing a "stare."

Through this early and convincing introductory sketch, Barlow has already set the personification and made the reader accept it: the isotopy that interprets the house as a solitary living creature is established, and the details expanding on this isotopy in the following pages will simply confirm the correctness of this reading. A few lines later, Barlow aptly reinforces his newly set argument: "I thought the little house was *lonely* when I saw it, and that like myself, it was *conscious* of its meaningless nature before the great sea" (EG 106; italics added). Again Barlow insists not only on the loneliness of the house, but also on its (or perhaps we should say her) sentience, its ability to gain a consciousness. What is more relevant, Barlow strives to depict the fictional world of "The Night Ocean" as a fully sentient one, a world of "magic realism" in which not only the narrator's house is endowed with sight: "Why this unbuilt stretch existed, I could not imagine, since many dwellings straggled along the northward coast, *facing the sea with aimless eyes*" (EG 107; italics added). As in a fairy tale, the narrator's house—like a proper, animal creature—is even capable of wandering and getting lost: "My cottage was entirely free of the village, as if it had wandered down the coast and was unable to return" (EG 107); and as in every fable, fairy creatures are featured in the form of houses: "on the northward beach a hundred houses rose in the rainy darkness, their light bleared and yellow above streets of polished glass, like *goblin-eyes* reflected in an oily forest pool" (EG 113; italics added).

Again the impression of magic realism is conveyed by Barlow's prose every time it depicts a fully sentient world, whose every inanimate element, no matter how abstract, is endowed with the qualities of the living. Thus in this magic world, realistically depicted, it may happen that even a visual impression like that of obscurity gains physicality and deliberateness: "the darkness crept in at my windows and *sat peering obscurely at me* from the corners *like a patient animal*" (EG 113; italics added). When choosing which sense to attribute to darkness in order to personify it, Barlow quite predictably resorts to that of sight ("sat peering obscurely at me"). Another inanimate and abstract inhabitant of this magic world, the significant loneliness—which is attributed to the house as well as to the narrator himself and to the sea, as we shall see—is personified, in a not well identified animal whose position is unfailingly the "crouching" one: "The shallow blue day advanced as those grimy wisps retreated, and the loneliness which had encircled me *welled back into a watchful place of retreat*, whence it went no farther, but *crouched and waited*" (EG 114; italics added). In Barlow's style, the "crouch-" root is almost inevitably employed in reference to a personification. The magic of the world in which the narrator moves is also that which allows personification to go both ways: in fact, his is a world where not only inanimate elements get personified, thus mainly "animalized" or "humanized," but where human beings also may become, in a sense, "bestialized." The correspondence and parallelism between man and nature is thus made biunique, and equally balanced: "Something had settled out of the night—something forever undefined, but stirring a latent sense within me, so that *I was like a beast* expecting the momentary rustle of an enemy" (EG 113; italics added).

The first days of the narrator's seclusive life at Ellston Beach are pleasant and rewarding, in the "lonely house *which sat like a small beast* upon those rounded cliffs of sand" (EG 108; italics added), though the strength and heat of the sun-rays gradually fade and grow unable to penetrate layers of clouds and gray mist. In the fully sentient magic microcosm that thus configures around the narrator, each element gains substance and life: "The beach *was a prisoner in a hueless vault* for hours at a time, as if something of the night were welling into other hours" (EG 109; italics added); the sun and the sky too receive physicality and sentience, because the sun becomes "more weary than the shrouded, moribund sky" (EG 114). In particular, in "The Night Ocean" the sun is always referred to through the personal pronouns "he" and "his," just as the sea through "she" and "her," as we will see. For instance, a shy but ultimately triumphant sun is the protagonist of the following passage: "*Gaining heart*, the *furtive sun* exerted all *his* force in dispelling the old mist, streaked now like a dirty window, and cast it from *his* realm" (EG 114; italics added). With the autumn approaching, and the seawater growing chill, the narrator falls into the habit of taking increasingly long walks along the sea-edge: "And sometimes, when these walks were late (as they grew increasingly to be) I would come upon the *crouching* house that looked like an harbinger of the village. Insecure upon the wind-gnawed cliffs, a dark blot upon the morbid hues of the ocean sunset, *it was more lonely* than by the full light of either orb; and seemed to my imagination *like a mute, questioning face turned towards me expecting of some action*" (EG 114; italics added). Again the impression of a solitary, crouching animal expecting some indefinite action is fostered; not only is the "crouching house" (EG 113) alive in itself, its component parts also show a specific sentience. When a downpour occurs, surprising the narrator far from home, he returns hurriedly toward his abode, only to discover that its "hunching roof seemed to bend from the assailing rain" (EG 113).

The other fundamental element that becomes personified in this tale is of course the titular ocean, the undisputed protagonist of the narration. Exactly like the house, the sea is depicted as sentient and alive, but with it Barlow goes farther and regularly employs the personal pronouns "she" and "her" whenever addressing it: "Although the ocean bore *her* own hue, it was dominated wholly and incredibly by the enormous glare" (EG 106-7; italics added). And again just like the house, the sea is associated with loneliness—and this feeling fuses in one uniqueness the house, the sea, and the protagonist: "I had been all the while accompanied by *the spirit of the lonely sea*" (EG 107; italics added). Humphreys too remarks the oneness of the house, the ocean, and the narrator—as they were three elements of the same *continuum*, reciprocally influencing each other:

Another paradoxical sensation felt by the narrator is that of loneliness. He has left society to be alone, yet feels lonely in his solitude. Furthermore, all the significant objects around him are personified with feelings of loneliness: the shore and sky and, more importantly, the ocean and house. The loneliness of the ocean affects the narrator; its immensity and mystery haunts him. The sea has a similar effect on the house, which is described as being lonely in five different occasions. (18)

However, the mention of a "spirit of the lonely sea" goes further than this: it explicitly spiritualizes the ocean. Moreover, the narrator's remark on the ocean as all the while "accompanying" him makes it turn into a solitary, silent companion for the narrator, a trustworthy though not rationally comprehensible presence—resembling, as it were, more and more that of a divine entity, normally that of a silent, reliable friend that however defies rational comprehension: "It was, I thought, personified in a shape which was not revealed to me, but which moved quietly about beyond my range of comprehension" (EG 107).

Yet the sea is not only a companion or a consolatory friend: she is made of an element, water, that stands as the archetypal, maternal womb from which life—and obviously mankind—stemmed. These are the laudatory words the narrator supplies for the sea, in a comment that contributes to recreate a halo of sacredness around even the abstract notion of the sea and the water of which it is made: "Through the heritage of a million years ago, when men were closer to the mother sea, and when the creatures of which we are born lay languid in the shallow, sun-pierced water, we still seek the primal things when we are tired, steeping ourselves within their lulling security like those early half-mammals which had not yet ventured upon the oozy land" (EG 108). These words may indeed sound as the celebration of the divine powers of nature, symbolized here by what is most likely to be her most powerful and breathtaking personification: the night ocean. Barlow's personification of the sea is constantly played along a double razor edge, wavering between the assignation of an animate nature and that of a divine, spiritual one. For instance, the following passage presents the sea as endowed with traits that may indeed be referred—with the same pertinence—to both a living, human creature, and to a divine, spiritual presence:

> The monotony of the waves gave repose, and I had no other occupation than witnessing a myriad *ocean moods*. There is a ceaseless change in the waters—colours and shades pass over them *like the insubstantial expressions of a well-known face*; [. . .] When the sea is restless, *remembering* old ships that have gone over her chasms, there comes up silently in our hearts the longing for a vanished horizon. But when *she forgets*, we forget also. Though we know her a lifetime, *she must always hold an alien air, as if something too vast to have shape were lurking in the universe to which she is a door*. The morning ocean, glimmering with a reflected mist of blue-white cloud and expanding diamond foam, *has the eyes of one who ponders* on strange things [. . .] (EG 108; italics added)

Thus the ocean possesses the qualities of both a human and a divine creature: she has moods, she remembers and forgets, she has the eyes of one who ponders, just as a person would. But the ocean, though a constant silent presence at man's side, is also eternally alien to him, and seems almost to guard the door to a universe from which something too vast to be comprehended peers at us—what else this could be, if not the description of a deity?

The combination of all the natural elements forming the place where the narrator dwells is embedded with a (supernatural) spirituality, and once more the sea is the element of the landscape that is most directly held responsible for the spirituality of the place. The following passage allows us to claim that, in "The Night Ocean," Barlow has consciously pursued the theme of a *spiritualization* of nature:

> That the place was isolated I have said, and this at first pleased me; but in that brief evening hour when the sun left in a gore-splattered decline and darkness lumbered on like an expanding shapeless blot, there was *an alien presence* about the place: *a spirit, a mood,* an impression that came from the surging wind, the gigantic sky, and that *sea which drooled blackening waves* upon a beach grown abruptly strange. At these times I felt an uneasiness which had no very definite cause, although my solitary nature had made me long accustomed to the ancient silence and the ancient voice of nature. (EG 109; italics added)

Again the issue of nature as an archetypal womb is addressed, but above all it is toward the ocean that Barlow directs his attempts at a *spiritualization*, if not *deification*, of nature: "I think now that all the while a gradual consciousness of the *ocean's immense loneliness* crept upon me, a loneliness that was made subtly horrible by intimations—which were never more than such—of *some animation or sentience preventing me from being wholly alone*" (EG 109; italics added). The religious parable of the narrator, reflecting that of most faithful, concerns a divine entity that is perceived as unique, "lonely," but which possesses an animation (namely, a "possibility to act") and a sentience that the religious person feels as actually present by his or her side, so that s/he never feels alone even though no objective manifestation of the divine is available. This is exactly the way the narrator perceives the immense, faceless sea during his stay at Ellston.[6] As a divine presence always by his side, the narrator understands that the sea is influencing his own moods, is changing them into hers, is ultimately taking possession of the narrator's inner life and shaping it at her will, as an alien, supernatural force would do:

---

6. It is certainly significant that, in order to underscore the relevance of this concept for his literary aesthetics, RHB decides to convey it through a particularly rich and complex sentence, one that effectively summarizes some of the major concerns of his poetics. The sentence is: "there was an alien presence about the place: a spirit, a mood, an impression that came from the surging wind, the gigantic sky, and that sea which drooled blackening waves upon a beach grown abruptly strange." This sentence poignantly contains references to many of RHB's literary concerns: "alien presence" refers to his interest in horror images, "spirit" to the key theme of spiritualization, "impression" to RHB's high regard for sensory perceptions, "drool" to the theme of personification (here referred to the sea), and "blackening" to RHB's interest in one sense in particular: sight.

Perhaps these inward emotions were only a reflection of *the sea's own mood*; for although half of what we see is coloured by the interpretation placed upon it by our minds, many of our feelings are shaped quite distinctly by external, physical things. The sea *can bind us to her many moods*, whispering to us by the subtle token of a shadow or a gleam upon the waves, and hinting in these ways of *her mournfulness or rejoicing*. Always, *she is remembering old things*, and these memories, though we may not grasp them, are imparted to us, so that *we share her gaiety or remorse*. Since I was doing no work, seeing no person that I knew, perhaps I was susceptible to shades of her cryptic meaning which would have been overlooked by another. *The ocean ruled my life during the whole of that late summer, demanding it as recompense for the healing she had brought me*. (EG 110; italics added)

If from one side the sea's (supernatural) influence over the narrator's moods and even soul can be interpreted as an illegitimate attempt at limiting his freedom of expression (and feeling), in this passage Barlow aims also at showing the intimate correspondence between man's and mother nature's interiority. Thus the praise for nature is double: not only is she endowed with an interiority and a spirituality (she can remember, rejoice, regret, mourn, etc.), but she is also able to influence man's spirituality and, as it were, to impose her own over that of man. Barlow introduces here the concept of a "dominating" ocean, a powerful entity capable of demanding, as a sacrifice, a human life in exchange for her healing of it—very much, once again, the behavior of a vengeful Old Testament god. In fact, when the deaths of some bathers are discovered late that summer, the sea is again depicted as a revenging god of the underworld asking for human sacrifices to placate its hunger: "The people who died [. . .] were sometimes not found until many days had elapsed, and *the hideous vengeance of the deep* had scourged their rotten bodies. It was as if the sea had dragged them into a chasm-lair and had mulled them about in the darkness until, *satisfied* that they were no longer of any use, she had floated them horribly ashore" (EG 110; italics added). The "shifting eternal sea" (EG 112) becomes the narrator's only companion, certainly as a god may be for a lonely person, but also as a pet or an animal. And just like a god, the sea—when wrapped in the mist—becomes invisible and intangible; and just like a pet, it may also feel sick or get wounded: "I realised quite suddenly that I was, to all intents, alone with the dreary sea that rose and subsided unseen, unkenned, in the mist. And the voice of the sea had become a hoarse groan, like that of *something wounded which shifts about before trying to rise*" (EG 113; italics added).

Humphreys—besides insightfully pointing out that the sentience of the house is connected with the narrator's own intentions and projections ("the narrator gives the house a semblance of sentience, perhaps bestowing upon the house many of the thoughts, beliefs, and fears that are a part of the narrator" [15-16])—then connects the sentience of the house to the cosmic influence of the ocean's *outsideness*: "The location of the house, which is so close to the ocean, has affected it and allowed a portion of the *outsideness* of the ocean to filter into it" (16). Humphreys's interpretation here seems to be not strictly cogent: since the sentience of the house is the projection of the narrator's moods, how can it also be influenced by the ocean, which according to Humphreys is a symbol of cosmic *outsideness*. He argues that the house of "The Night Ocean" is sentient because it works as a portal between the mundane realm and the *beyond* one symbolized by the ocean: "In a manner very similar to William Hope Hodgson's *The House on the Borderland*, the house by the night ocean is a link—perhaps even a gateway—between the outside and the mundane. Just as the chasm from Hodgson's tale fulfils the role of the outside in a manner similar to the night ocean, the houses in both stories act as lonely portals from one realm to the other" (16). The parallel with Hodgson is fruitful, since undoubtedly in both tales "the narrators are besieged by forces from the outside [. . .], although in 'The Night Ocean' the outside is more subtly presented, as the ocean is given more significance than the chasm of Hodgson's story" (16). What Humphreys fails to recognize is that the "forces from the outside" besieging Barlow's narrator are of a spiritual, divine origin—and that Barlow presents the outside "more subtly" and gives more significance to the ocean because he is dealing with the theme of the sacred and the relationship between the "human" and the "divine" principles. This is also the key to understanding why in Hodgson the creatures from the outside have a more significant role than in "The Night Ocean": in Barlow's tale, they are sheer emissaries of the divine, not the divine itself—which is symbolized by the vast ocean. As Humphreys notes: "Both employ actual creatures from the outside, but in 'The Night Ocean' the creatures become secondary—*perhaps even imaginary*—while the ocean takes on the role of the besieging force" (16; italics added). Humphreys correctly notes that the creatures from the sea are most likely imaginary—but he fails to understand why: it is due to the fact that the intimate relationship involving a human being and his/her personal understanding of the divine is all played within the person's mind and soul: no actual, physical presences are at stake, only mental and imaginative figures. Barlow aptly faces the theme of the relationship between man and the divine by resorting to a multiple personification: not only is the sea the symbol of the supernatural, but also the creatures emerging from it are the intangible symbols of man's spiritual and psychological torment when experiencing his relationship with nature—namely, when deciding between acceptation or refusal of the divine within his own life.

However, Barlow's concern with nature—and her relationship with man—goes much further than the employment of the rhetorical apparatus of literary personification. Barlow is above all interested in examining man's relationship with nature: certainly a complex one, in which man experiences a controversial wish for identification—which is, however, not wholly intentional, but half-induced by the deceptions of conscious nature itself. Barlow celebrates the influencing and subtly deceiving power that nature exerts over human moods, so much so that man is utterly unable to identify whether—and to what extent—he is responsible for his own moods. In the production of man's inner experiences, man and nature interact in a way that remains mysterious and indecipherable for the most part, but that Barlow strives to investigate at his best, in the effort to struggle for a definition of—and a way to—happiness:

> the sun did actually seem to indicate realms, secure and fanciful, where if I but knew the path I might wander in this curious exultation. Such things come of our own natures, for life has never yielded for one moment her secrets; and it is only in our interpretation of their hinted images that we may find ecstasy or dullness, *according to a deliberately induced mood. Yet ever and again we must succumb to her deceptions*, believing for the moment that we may this time find the withheld joy. And in this way *the fresh sweetness of the wind, on a morning following the haunted darkness (whose evil intimations had given me a greater uneasiness than any menace to my body), whispered to me of ancient mysteries* only half-linked with earth, and *of pleasures that were the sharper because I felt that I might experience only a part of them.* (EG 115; italics added)

Nature, through her harbinger the wind, tries to communicate with man and to modify his moods, even to make him glimpse flashes of eternal pleasures—of that bliss that each man pursues, with varying success. A nature endowed with such powers certainly configures as a spiritual entity, even as a super-natural nature. Exactly as mother ocean, as we will see, is gradually deified, other elements also partake of the spiritualization of nature: certainly the sun, with its vivifying light, the only weapon available to man in order to fight the darkness of his existence.[7] The sun is made divine, because together with the wind it is the harbinger of another realm, whose inhabitants' senses and joys are infinitely superior to man's. They only ask man to bow to their deceptive power, and become their worshipper:

> The sun and wind and that scent that rose upon them told me of festivals of *gods whose senses are a millionfold more poignant than man's, and whose joys are a millionfold more subtle and prolonged. These things, they hinted, could be mine if I gave myself wholly into their bright deceptive power.* And the sun, a *crouching god with naked celestial flesh, an unknown, too-mighty furnace upon which eye might not look, seemed almost sacred in the glow of my newly sharpened emotions.* The ethereal thunderous light it gave was something *before which all things must worship astonished.* (EG 115; italics added)

A significant detail in this passage needs to be discussed: Why does Barlow say that the sacredness of the sun depends on the observer's "sharpened emotions"? Precisely because the sun's power is defined as "deceptive": the sun—an elemental part of a sentient and divine nature—asks man to worship it, and in order to convince him the sun *influences man's perceptions and emotions*. If man feels induced to worship a natural element like the sun, it is not entirely because of the sun's *objectively* divine nature, but because of the "plagiarizing" influence the sun itself exerts on man's rational faculties and volition. This is why nature's powers are "deceptive": they, in a sense, camouflage their might, making man believe it is much more powerful than it actually is. It is, in a way, an attempt nature makes to assimilate man to herself—a goal the accomplishment of which justifies the adopted means, also the luring of man through deceptions and lies.

---

7. Humphreys writes of the "healing and soothing powers of the sun" (19).

Barlow's narrator strives to disentangle this complex dialectics between man and nature, to lay bare nature's tricks and disclose her real character and intentions. He thus is particularly attracted to the investigation of the dark side of the god "nature," the one she does not wish to reveal. When the narrator finds on the beach the "piece of rotten flesh" resembling a human hand, he is induced to formulate not very flattering thoughts regarding the essence of his newly discovered, would-be god: "I approached the town, sickened by the presence of such an object amidst the *apparent* beauty of the clean beach, though it was horribly typical of the *indifference* of death in *a nature which mingles rottenness with beauty, and perhaps loves the former more*" (EG 116; italics added). The key word in this passage is "apparent," because it tells of nature's deceptive character: hers is an apparent beauty and cleanliness; but, if not evil, she is a god at best *indifferent* toward man, a god not only of life and order, but also of death and rottenness.

One is of course left to wonder how much Barlow's conception of nature resembles that of the gods of the Lovecraftian pantheon. In "The Night Ocean," Barlow recurrently insists on the ambiguity of nature's message, on the deceptive character of her claim to be worshipped as a god. The narrator's suspicion is in fact that nature, as an indifferent and selfish god, does not really care for human beings; she merely aims at gaining new bodies and souls to absorb to herself, as in a pantheistic wish to swallow everything living into her gaping fauces. Increasingly negative connotations are associated with the natural elements, in particular with the one Barlow identifies as the most representative, the night ocean: "I was engulfed by a piteous lethargic fear of some ineluctable doom which would be, I felt, the completed *hate of the peering stars* and of the black enormous waves that *hoped to claps my bones within them—the vengeance of all the indifferent, horrendous majesty of the night ocean*" (EG 116; italics added). Far from being sympathetic toward mankind's fate, the nature-god is indifferent toward man, treating him as another of the creatures to engulf into her worship.

But in this and in the following examples, the narrator begins to attribute to nature even a malevolent attitude, not simply an indifferent one: the stars nurture "hate," the ocean plans a "revenge," and we are already familiar with the negative connotation Barlow attributes to darkness and everything connected to it—thus the expression "night ocean" is in itself harbinger of a negative connotation. Moreover, a few lines later the narrator writes of the "*darkness and restlessness of the sea*" (EG 116; italics added) that penetrate his heart: another attempt performed by nature to plagiarize him, to infuse onto him her own moods, and make him hers—as a worshipper, and as a prey, which is almost the same according to Barlow's critical view of religion. It is in fact curious to notice how Barlow equates nature's attempt to convert the narrator into her faithful worshipper to her attempt to physically assimilate and annihilate him. The narrator proceeds in the personification of nature as an evil entity: the sea grows "slowly hateful" (EG 116) to him, and also other elements of the landscape besides the sea—such as his own house—start to display a negative essence ("the loneliness of that *bleak-eyed house*" [EG 116; italics added]). That this process may be a consequence of the narrator's increasing sense of paranoia is of course possible—the paranoid evolution of the narrator is discussed in chapter 3, paragraph 3.4.1—but that the process is itself at work is a fact that can be hardly questioned. The phases of nature's attempt to gain man's worship are like those of a war: "*turn as I might, battle as I might* with all the remaining power of my spirit, I could neither win an inch of ground from the *inimical universe*, nor hold for even a moment the life entrusted to me" (EG 117; italics added). However, that the war is fought in an external reality (through the actions performed by the ocean, the sun, the stars, etc.) that in any case reflects another war fought inside man's interiority is always made clear, thus reinforcing the notion of a correspondence between natural, physical events and man's inner, psychological events. The narrator is in fact aware that an external, actual event is soon to occur, and that it is no more than a reflection of an event internal to his soul (and vice versa, the correspondence being biunique): "Fearing death as I did life, burdened with a nameless dread yet unwilling to leave the scenes evoking it, I awaited whatever consummating horror was shifting itself *in the immense region beyond the walls of consciousness*" (EG 117; italics added).

How may man hope to gain from the struggle with a very powerful antagonist, a divine and eternal entity like the ocean, "a frightening sea which changes not, though man changes" (EG 117)? Man is but a transient and feeble creature, when confronted with the everlasting sea. That the "evilification" of nature—and particularly of the sea—is an ongoing process, and that the war against this protean entity is a reflection of an internal struggle the narrator fights against his own inner "evil" forces (or vice versa), is also testified by this revealing passage:

> The *once friendly* waters babbled meaningfully at me, and eyed me with a strange regard; yet *whether the darkness of the scene were a reflection of my own broodings, or whether the gloom within me were caused by what lay without*, I could not have told. Upon the beach and me alike had fallen a shadow, like that of a bird which flies silently overhead—a bird whose watching eyes we do not suspect till the image on the ground repeats the image in the sky, and we look suddenly upward to find that something has been circling above us hitherto unseen. (EG 117; italics added)

This richly meaningful passage contains several important points to discuss. First of all, the narrator states that the ocean now speaking to him and watching him in a malevolent fashion was once "friendly" to him: it has thus become evil through a process, of course a psychological one occurring in the narrator's mind, that colored the external change of nature (let us not forget that autumn, and thus a season change, is approaching at Ellston) with its own, distorting hues. Secondly, once more underlying the parallel, biunique influence between nature's feelings and events and the narrator's, Barlow is implicitly legitimating his narrator's distortions of external events through the modifying intervention of his own internal thoughts, emotions, and mental processes. Barlow adds to this awareness a further detail: not only is the correspondence between man's and nature's feelings and moods biunique, but one cannot tell them apart; it is not possible to distinguish which influence which, and this is perhaps a sign of the effectiveness of nature's attempt to influence man's moods and assimilate him to herself. In fact, man is so confused that he cannot even recognize what are his own intentions, feelings, emotions, dreams, etc., and what are induced by nature's influences. Finally, that last bird-simile—somehow disturbingly reminiscent of the image already adopted in "The Shadow from Above," episode two of the *Annals*—adds a touch of prose-poetic style to the reaffirmation of a key point of Barlow's poetics: nature accompanies man in all his steps, like a silent and invisible presence very much resembling the one that religious people define as "deity." In his effort to reinforce the identification between the man and the ocean, Barlow more and more frequently employs the word "crouch-" and its derivates, referring both to natural elements and to the protagonist, showing in this way their perfect correspondence and interchangeability.

Of course this does not detract from—nor contrast with—the parallel process that assigns increasingly "evil" features to the sea itself, because—not surprisingly—the very same "evil" can be found growing inside man. Thus the spiritualized sea continues to allure man, telling him of incredible secrets announcing another tempting life that it is possible to achieve—exactly reflecting, as a god would do in his promises, man's own wishes and aspirations:

> I had stayed indoors, fearing somehow to go out before the sea on such a night of shapeless portent, but I heard it *mumbling secrets of an incredible lore*. Borne to me on a wind out of nowhere was the breath of *some strange and palpitant life—the embodiment of all I had felt and of all I had suspected*—stirring now in the chasms of the sky or beneath the mute waves. In what place this mystery turned from ancient, horrible slumber I could not tell, but like one who stands by a figure lost in sleep, knowing that it will awake in a moment, *I crouched* by the windows, holding a nearly burnt-out cigarette, and faced the rising moon. (EG 118; italics added)

The fictional world of "The Night Ocean" is increasingly endowed with a sentience and a spirituality that associates man to the natural elements: they become a unique oneness, each assuming the traits and faculties of the other—without losing its own. Thus the protagonist also "crouches,"[8] as his house did and still does (the hut is still "crouching" in the last fatal night [EG 119]). This huge, all-encompassing spirituality that joins the living and the dead, the animate and the inanimate, and whose every single element performs the same actions otherwise typical of the other (nature is humanized just as man is animalized: as men crouch, waves mumble and stars peer) allows us to suspect that what Barlow intends to do in this masterly tale is to depict a *pantheistic universe*, one in which magical forces are operating, one in which the divine and the human equal each other and are interchangeable, because natural elements are endowed with divine powers and men's consciousnesses act as their reflecting mirror. The "forbidden sentience" (EG 118) of the ocean is part of the mystery of a pantheistic world

---

8. Again we read "I crouched with a forgotten cigarette in my hand" (EG 119).

man cannot explain, perhaps because the ocean—just as the sun[9]—is made divine, and, like every respectable god, it escapes rational comprehension or even investigation: "I do not know why the ocean holds such a fascination for me. But then, perhaps none of us can solve those things—*they exist in defiance of all explanation*" (*EG* 120; italics added).

This remark about the ocean—a natural element made divine in a pantheistic world—may fit the definition of any god worshipped by humans: an entity exerting a strong fascination on them, one that cannot be rationally explained nor accounted for. Humphreys also notes that the sentience of the ocean represents perhaps its most striking characteristic, though the critic fails to recognize what this symbolism actually hides:

> Both the ocean and what lies within the ocean are given sentience, as the eyes and web imagery coupled with the numerous references to the ocean as a personified 'it' or even as a 'she' shows the night ocean to be inextricably linked to what lies within it. This is done for symbolic purposes, since it is actually a blind non-sentient ocean that harbours the mysteries. However, the ocean is given symbolic sentience in order to increase the importance of its own role as a symbol of the vast cosmos. (17)

Certainly the ocean stands symbolically for the "vast cosmos," but in this tale Barlow endows the cosmos with a revelatory power: that of the divine principle and, ultimately, of the pantheism reigning in nature. Again Humphreys makes a worthy observation—"The narrator's relationship with the ocean is more complex than simply fear. Indeed, there is a sense of wonder and kinship involved as well" (17)—without realizing that the sense of awe and kinship felt by the narrator toward the ocean is the literary symbol of the feeling a (prospective) worshipper experiences toward the god s/he is soon to worship.

The divine powers of the ocean—here a pretext in Barlow's discussion on the sacred—of course do not appeal to everybody in the same way (agnostics and atheists do exist), and the following passage provides a further illuminating reflection on the ocean, contextually suggesting another, perhaps even more fascinating interpretation of the extremely rich and controversial metaphor the ocean embodies:

> There are men, and wise men, who do not like the sea and its lapping surf on yellow shores; and they think us strange who love the mystery of the ancient and unending deep. Yet for me *there is a haunting and inscrutable glamour in all the ocean's moods*. It is in the melancholy silver foam beneath the moon's waxen corpse; it hovers over the silent and eternal waves that beat on naked shores; it is where all

---

9. The common divine nature RHB assigns to both the ocean and the sun makes them two indissoluble and fellow elements of the same pantheistic universe. Therefore the sun is certainly "part of the outside itself" (Humphreys 19) as the ocean—they are components of the divine, and this kinship discredits Humphreys's attempt at identifying a forced contraposition between the two elements ("perhaps it [the sun] is a source of wonder and imagination quite unlike the dark sea that is a source of fear and loneliness": Humphreys 19).

is lifeless save for unknown shapes that glide through sombre depths. And when I behold the awesome billows surging in endless strength, *there comes upon me an ecstasy akin to fear*; so that I must abase myself before this mightiness, that I may not hate the clotted waters and their overwhelming beauty. (*EG* 120; italics added)

The first part of this final reflection upon the sea's powers and revelations seems to confirm the interpretation that sees in the ocean the embodiment of god: there are "wise" men, the atheists, who despise religious people's fascination with "the mystery of the ancient and the unending deep"; the attitude of the faithful is that of childish credulity, their intellect is unable to rationalize the mystery, and they simply suffer the captivation of what they are unable to explain. But these very same words of Barlow's definition of the ambiguous relationship the narrator entertains with the ocean may suggest another possible interpretation[10] of the metaphor embodied by the ocean itself: it could stand for *literature*, and in particular for *weird* literature, the one Barlow most loved and of which was a fond practitioner too. In fact, the very same attitude of repulsion and attraction toward the ocean can be read as the most common feelings readers have toward this type of literature, one unlikely to leave its addressees indifferent—much like what happens with a god. The sea and its powers and revelations would then stand for the powers of horror literature, both repulsive and attractive toward the large public (Humphreys also notes that "There is a real sense of an attraction/repulsion at work in the story" [18], though he fails to deduce a convincing reason for this dichotomy): in this sense, a new justification might be found for the attitude of those "wise men" who despise and scorn this type of literature, accusing it of an alleged "lack of commitment," if not "amorality." Lovecraft himself had ironically defined the detractors of dreams and visions as "wise men" in his tale "The Silver Key" (1926),[11] a possible influence on Barlow in the writing of this passage.[12] These men "think us strange who love the mystery of the ancient and unending deep," and if we substitute the ocean's "deep" with the concept it may stand for, "weird literature," the argument is sound: Barlow's narrator—like his creator—is a lover of the mysteries of the unknown, as they are embodied in the depths of the sea as well as in the lines of a horror tale.

Humphreys correctly notes this sense of revolt that the narrator nurtures toward the prosiness and dullness of the bourgeois society, and which provokes a

---

10. In advancing my interpretation, I feel justified by Joshi's words: "'The Night Ocean' is a richly interpretable story that produces new insights and pleasures upon each rereading" (*LAL* 616).

11. "Wise men told him [Randolph Carter] his simple fancies were inane and childish" (*DW* 252).

12. It is curious to note how, though for different reasons, Humphreys also points out a possible similarity between "The Night Ocean" and HPL's "The Silver Key." In fact, the Barlovian tale, "although containing an entirely different plot, [. . .] bears a resemblance to HPL's earlier tale 'The Silver Key', a tale that also used an understated style coupled with a healthy dose of 'cosmic indifferentist' philosophy" (14).

fascination for the mystery and the unknown that is also typical of the fan of *weird* literature: "The narrator's attraction to the ocean is comforting at times, and helps to alleviate the distrust he expresses towards society. Although he senses danger, *the narrator prefers the unknown to the dreariness of society*" (17; italics added). The "wise men" do scorn what they deem the puerile "escapism" of fantastic literature, and are not culturally equipped enough to appreciate the "haunting and inscrutable glamour in all the ocean's moods," namely, out of metaphor, the endless fascination that an effective weird tale exerts on a fan of the genre. It is a glamor embracing and coloring each literary fantastic creation, and that only the acolyte can find where "all is lifeless," because he only knows how to detect "unknown shapes that glide through sombre depths": and "unknown" is the key word in this passage, since it accounts for the main quality—and the main appeal—of the mysteries faced by weird literature. It is just because of the fascination for the "unknown" that people like the narrator and Barlow himself love weird literature: for its capacity to hint—and just to hint—at dim shapes lurking beyond the appearance and the surface of everyday reality and perceptions, those which the prosaic and "wise" men are content with. And thus, when the lover of weird literature beholds "the awesome billows surging in endless strength," there comes upon him "an ecstasy akin to fear": the sea (namely, weird literature), in its most striking manifestations like the surging of its powerful waves (the most effective examples of weird tales), provokes in the beholder (in the reader) an "ecstasy akin to fear." The metaphor is thus made explicit: the terms placed in parentheses are in fact the inferences induced by my own interpretation of the metaphor, which finally clears itself by this (now explicit, not inferred) association of ecstasy—the feeling or condition experienced by the observer of the sea's powers at work—with fear, the feeling experienced by the reader of a weird, horror tale[13]—by the faithful of a revengeful god. The charming, horrifying power of the sea is thus made one with that of weird literature: "The Night Ocean" as a weird tale is revealed in such a way as a meta-text, namely one discussing the rules and effects of its own composition. And this interpretation, in its effort to discuss and account for the overwhelming presence of the "ocean" metaphor in the tale, hopefully helps to shed some light over the rich, at times obscure, figurativeness of Barlow's text.

Considered as a whole, "The Night Ocean" may be read as a sort of large narrative metaphor, that of a man looking for truth and (divine) illumination, both in his relationship with nature and with his own conscience—the two types of search are equivalent. But his search ends with nothing: "I had come frighteningly near to the capture of an old secret which ventured close to man's haunts

---

13. The connection between ecstasy and fear (in particular in one of its possible variant versions, that relating the Sublime to the horror) has been the object of study of a brilliant essay by Kirk Sigurdson, "A Gothic Approach to Lovecraft's Sense of *Outsideness*," which takes into consideration the influence of Gothic literature on HPL and his aesthetic rendering of the Sublime. Another essay on a similar topic is Dale J. Nelson's "Lovecraft and the Burkean Sublime."

and lurked cautiously just beyond the edge of the known. *Yet in the end I had nothing*" (EG 120; italics added). The search for truth and for the sacred has resolved into nothing: the mystery is not disclosed, veiled as it is by ignorance. This is the lesson man may learn from the allegorical search for the divine staged in this tale under the cover of man's enhanced relationship (verging toward identification) with a live, pulsing, odorous, musical, melancholic, and dreamy nature. Thus the exploration of man's relationship with nature turns into a dramatic investigation on the unfathomable abysses of man's existence, a search that ultimately leaves the seeker only with the sense, halfway between the disillusioned and the astonished, of an unresolved *mystery*: the meaning of life opens its gates and lets the narrator gain entrance, and he follows the path with the melancholy, almost with the resignation of one who knows that the revelation is going to deceive and defraud the seeker. It almost seems as if Barlow, in trying to shed light on man's relationship with nature, has ended up discovering his *own* nature: "The Night Ocean" is revealed as Barlow's spiritual testament, that of a sensitive and tormented personality paying a poetic, impressionistic homage to his own suffering.

7. Irony

The presence of irony is a major characteristic of Barlow's fiction. This "theme" reflects the complexity of the author's personality, one that may at times display the gloomiest and bleakest cosmic visions, but is also capable of a true sense of humor, if not of the comic. Irony distances Barlow's fictional efforts from Lovecraft's, even though it is well known that Lovecraft—almost exclusively in his early literary efforts—wrote openly parodic and humorous pieces such as "A Reminiscence of Dr. Samuel Johnson" (1917), "Sweet Ermengarde, or, The Heart of a Country Girl" (sometime between 1919 and 1921), a parody of Horatio Alger's novels, and "Ibid" (1928). But Barlow's influence was certainly decisive in "pushing" Lovecraft to consider ironic and humorous elements in writing fiction: in fact, of their six heretofore known collaborations, three contain ironic and parodic elements ("The Hoard of the Wizard-Beast," "The Battle That Ended the Century," and "Collapsing Cosmoses"), testifying of Barlow's penchant for humor, while two of them ("'Till A' the Seas'" and "The Night Ocean") are indicative of the other dominant trait of Barlow's temper: his cosmic attitude. It is then possible to infer that the Lovecraft-Barlow collaborations succeed in representing and expressing the two main aspects of Barlow's personality: he probably felt at particular ease in working with Lovecraft, and free to give unrestrained voice to the different facets of his nature.

It is in fact in his fiction more than in his poetry, and in particular in his collaborations with Lovecraft, that Barlow expressed the more genuine humor of which he was capable. The only truly parodic pieces Lovecraft worked upon in his career (with the exceptions of the three stories mentioned above) are the collaborations with Barlow, such as the genuinely amusing "The Battle That Ended the Century" (1934) and "Collapsing Cosmoses" (1935). It seems as if Barlow was able to push Lovecraft toward the inclusion of humorous elements in his work: it was Barlow's idea to write the spoof "The Battle That Ended the Century,"[1] and also in "Collapsing Cosmoses," "on occasion Lovecraft only wrote a few words before yielding the pen back to his younger colleague, so that considerably more than half the piece is Barlow's, as are a fair number of the better jokes" (*LAL* 595). I think that it was thanks to Barlow, if Lovecraft found the will and the sheer energy to manifest his own irony in (professional) fiction, that he considered a too "serious" expression field to "contaminate" it with the sense of humor—while Lovecraft had no qualms in being often humorous in his private correspondence, that of course was not intended for publication. Another clue of Barlow's inclination toward humor, and of his difference with Lovecraft on this point, emerges when taking into consideration an episode concerning a 302-line poem Lovecraft wrote in 1916, "The Poe-et's Nightmare."[2] This poem is composed of a central part, titled "Aletheia Phrikodes," that represents an attempt at weird, cosmic verse, but this

---

1. "Barlow was clearly the originator of this squib" (*LAL* 552).
2. First printed in *Vagrant* No. 8 (July 1918).

poem possesses also a *framework* that contains 72 introductory lines and 38 concluding lines of plainly parodic intent, having as protagonist a grotesque character—the one who has the nightmare described in "Aletheia"—named *Lucullus Languish* ("Thrill'd with the music of th' eternal spheres / (Or is it the alarm-clock that he hears?), / He vows to all the Pantheon, high and low, / No more to feed on cake, or pie, or Poe"[3]). Joshi remarks that "Toward the end of his life, when R. H. Barlow wished to include 'The Poe-et's Nightmare' in a collection of Lovecraft's verse, he advised Barlow to omit the comic framework" (*LAL* 170), since "the comic beginning and ending subverted the message of the cosmic central portion" ("Notes" to Lovecraft, *Ancient Track* 474). In fact, enclosed in a letter dated 13 June 1936, discussing Barlow's plan to issue an edition of Lovecraft's collected poems, the Providence writer sent to Barlow a bunch of his early poems, including "The Poe-et's Nightmare." This is how Lovecraft comments on this poem in the letter: "If you *do* by chance use the long 'Aletheia Phrikodes', *don't use the comic framework*" (FF 342). Barlow's project for the *Collected Poems of H. P. Lovecraft* ultimately came to nothing, but the episode involving "The Poe-et's Nightmare" is certainly significant of the different approach to literary humor the two friends favored: of course Lovecraft wrote also plenty of satirical verse, but he was very careful not to mingle purely humorous pieces—such as, for instance, "Sweet Ermengarde"—with his mature weird, cosmic production. In fact, Lovecraft heartily deplored the appearance of the sense of humor in weird literature, considering it at least partly responsible for the decline of the fantastic in his times.

Certainly on the issue of the employment of irony in fiction, Lovecraft's and Barlow's views diverged. Lovecraft felt that the question was particularly important, since he was intensely worried about the decline that the popularization of the weird tale had brought to the genre. One of the principal enemies to fight, and one that was hurting the artistic efficacy of the contemporary weird tale, was the presence of irony. Lovecraft felt the issue was so important that he even openly stated his opinion in a work of fiction, "The Silver Key" (1926). When Randolph Carter gets disillusioned by "wise men" and "well-meaning philosophers" about the truth-value of his dreams (the irony implicit here is of a type too "serious" to damage the narrative intent), he starts writing books again. But nothing is the same as *before* disillusionment came: "here, too, was there no satisfaction or fulfilment; for *the touch of earth was upon his mind*, and he could not think of lovely things as he had done of yore. *Ironic humour dragged down all the twilight minarets he reared*, and *the earthy fear of improbability* blasted all the delicate and amazing flowers in his faery gardens" (*DW* 255; italics added). Lovecraft was convinced that, in order to depict the otherworldly atmospheres of an aesthetically convincing weird or fantasy tale, any earthly concern should be put aside—thus the "touch of earth," consisting, for instance, of "ironic humour" and "fear of improbability," is most detrimental to the building of that essential *illusion of the suspension* of natural laws that lies at the foundation of an artistically successful weird tale. Irony is in fact a purely conventional trait, one that reinforces "the myth of an important reality and significant human events and emotions" (*DW* 255); together with other hu-

---

3. "The Poe-et's Nightmare," ll. 274–77, in HPL, *Ancient Track* 25.

man-centered emotions, irony debases "high fantasy into thin-veiled allegory and cheap social satire" (*DW* 255), since it reintroduces human concerns into a narration that should be built upon an illusion of utter alterity and disengagement from any anthropocentric discourse and value. The employment of humor is but a faint attempt the humans make at sweetening their bleak cosmic condition:

> humour is itself but a superficial view of that which is in truth both tragic and terrible—the contrast between human pretence and cosmic mechanical reality. Humour is but the faint terrestrial echo of the hideous laughter of the blind mad gods that squat leeringly and sardonically in caverns beyond the Milky Way. It is a hollow thing, sweet on the outside, but filled with the pathos of fruitless aspiration. [. . .] When I was younger I wrote humorous matter—satire and light verse—and was known to many as jester and parodist. [. . .] But I cannot help seeing beyond the tinsel of humour, and recognising the pitiful basis of jest—the world is indeed comic, but the joke is on mankind [. . .] *Humour is the whistling of man to keep up his courage as he travels the dark road.* ("The Defence Remains Open!" [1921], *CE* 5.54; italics added)

Probably because he realized Barlow's inclination toward the inclusion of humorous traits into his fantastic fiction, Lovecraft felt the urge to advise him in regard to the dangers of these sorts of inclusions. On several occasions, Lovecraft faced the issue in his correspondence with Barlow, and with his usual tact he confronted the topic not directly, but discussing how the intrusion of humor spoiled the works of writers *other* than Barlow. In particular, Dunsany was the main target of Lovecraft's darts—because the Providence writer felt that Dunsany's latest turn toward an ironic disillusion was the undoing of his mastery in the weird, since it damaged the purity of the "illusion" of a momentary suspension of the natural laws—and of the "suspension of disbelief"—on which, according to Lovecraft, the credibility of a weird tale is founded:

> Yes—Dunsany has undeniably declined—& *a sense of humour has been his undoing.* He was at his best in the very early pieces—The Gods of Pegana (1905), Time & the Gods (1906), The Sword of Welleran (1908), & (above all) A Dreamer's Tales (1910)—when he created new worlds & wove ethereal fabrics of glittering phantasy without any trace of a *disillusioning snicker* [. . .] It was in 1912, with the "Book of Wonder," that *the fading of the supreme illusion began.* (Letter to RHB, 14 March 1933; *FF* 5; italics added)

In a much lengthier letter to Barlow of 16 March 1935, Lovecraft returns to the issue of Dunsany's decline as a fantaisiste, implicitly asserting that the "amusement" a reader enjoys in a story is the signal of the work's inconsistency as a weird tale: "I read the new Dunsany book—'Jorkens Remembers Africa'—last month. Clever & amusing—*but not the old Dunsany of 'A Dreamer's Tales'*" (*FF* 223; italics added). In a sense, it is as if Lovecraft considered the resort to humor a youthful sin; in fact, again knowing Barlow's inclination for spoofing and not wanting to hurt his protégé, in another letter Lovecraft admits that in his own youth he had employed a huge number of pseudonyms, above all for "minor pieces (especially humorous things—*for I had more of your taste for spoofing when I was young*)" (*FF* 191; italics added). With this short sentence, Lovecraft has tactfully achieved a double goal: to implicitly belittle comic literature (by stating that his "humorous things" are "minor pieces"), and to contextually reassure Barlow that there is nothing intrinsically (too) wrong in having a "taste for spoofing"—Lovecraft himself had it in his turn—provided that it remains a juvenile inclination. This is confirmed by the excerpt from "The Defence Remains Open!" quoted above, where Lovecraft admits to have written humorous pieces when he was "younger"—and thus was somehow more "justified" in doing so.

And indeed, almost all of Barlow's narratives may be considered juvenile pieces, where the presence of humor, if we credit Lovecraft's point, is then perfectly understandable. Not only are Barlow's three collaborations with Lovecraft to be considered humorous or spoof pieces; other narratives in the Barlow canon also show humorous or parodic traits. All his tales presenting these qualities may be grouped into two subcategories, differentiated according to the nature of the humor they display:

1. **tales of *socially committed and bitter irony*:** this group contains narratives characterized by the presence of a sense of humor and an irony that intend to arouse reflection on social issues, especially on (the hypocrisy of) religion, the religious feeling and "establishment." Furthermore, the tales of this group often show a *bitter* irony, one that generates laughter but of a subtle, non-comic type. Thus the narratives of this category, to which belongs a tiny group of original Barlovian products, may be labeled *tales of socially committed and bitter irony*;
2. **tales of *true humor and parody*:** the narratives of this group are conceived as openly humorous tales, often as parodies of a certain type of stilted and "artificial" weird and fantasy fiction that was in vogue in Barlow's and Lovecraft's time. In the narratives of this category, the humor is authentic and sincere, and its goal is to generate genuine laughter and amusement. To this group belong all three humorous collaborations with Lovecraft, and a few other original Barlovian products.

What follows is a discussion of Barlow's narrative use of irony, which he surely considered an aesthetically significant and valid means to face the hopelessness of reality—because, as Barlow himself plainly stated in one of his tales, "when one is serious, the drabness of reality is intolerable" ("A Memory," *EG* 73).

7.1 Tales of socially committed and bitter irony

Already from the age of fifteen, Barlow was capable of composing short narratives dense with poignant irony. "The Sacred Bird," the fourth episode of the fantasy cycle *Annals of the Jinns*, reveals as an allegorical parody of authority and power. The target of Barlow's criticism may in fact be understood as any form of authoritative oppression exerted by a superior "power" able to *brainwash* its subjects and claim for itself an allegedly legitimate right to rule. In this sense, religion may also have been the target of Barlow's ironic darts.

The tale has the effective immediacy and straightforwardness of a moral apologue, though the tone is light and the irony evident. The narration opens with the sudden apparition, in the imaginary town of Ullathia, of a unidentifiable bird: "There appeared one day in the market-place of Ullathia a most peculiar fowl which fell exhausted from the skies. Its plumage was of brilliant hue, and despite its confusion, a wise and knowing look was seen within the orange eyes" (EG 17). The bird visits the various shops "in a proprietary manner," and the people compete to admire and feed it: "Not in the least bothered by its admiring audience, it permitted its head to be scratched and petted as it ate" (EG 17). Barlow's tone already appears light and humorous, and it warns the reader of the tale's peculiarly ironic tenor that is going to appear later. The news of the bird's arrival quickly spreads throughout the village, and even the notables of the Imperial Council "laid down their pens and came in a body to view it" (EG 17-18). Having fed on "odds and ends of all sorts" (EG 18), the fowl falls asleep when the notables reach him, but not before having "complained loudly": "'Gwarn arf 'n chase y'self!' commanded the half-awake bird. 'Gwarn arf', it repeated, fluttering its wings and adjusting for a nice nap" (EG 18). Confronting the bird's indecipherable utterances, the mass of people—symbolizing the ignorant mob—"drew back whispering excitedly. 'A demon!' averred one. This brought a chorus of dissension among the others. 'An angel... Just a trick... Who ever heard of a bird talking?.. A magician in disguise... What has happened?.. Still thy tongue, neighbor" (EG 18). And Barlow shows how there is always a demagogue willing to take advantage of any possibility of increasing his power, seizing all the favorable chances to exploit people's credulity to strengthen his own ruling position. The notable's speech is aptly built up as a parody of the inconclusiveness and inanity of the language of demagogy and bureaucracy, by which (political) power pretends to soothe the population and manipulate it:

> The Head of the Council, a greybeard notoriously superstitious, cleared his throat and a silence fell over all present. 'My friends' he gurgled happily, 'My *dear* friends and fellow citizens! This is an occasion of undoubted significance in the annals of our fair city, equalled only by that of, as you doubtless will realize, early in the reign of—rather; to continue: In other words To make it clear to all concerned, this is, I believe, and no one, I hope, would contradict me, I have occasion to think-' Here his voice lowered to a whisper and ended in a shout, 'A *Messenger* sent to guide us!'. He leered cheerfully at the mob. 'Therefore, let us convey it in state to the City Hall to rule us as it sees fit! (EG 18)

The words (and especially the attitude) of the Head of the Council are of course a parody of the demagogic speech of a dictator—and let us not forget that this tale was written in a time when the political and social equilibrium of the world was threatened by the rise of similar personalities. The peculiar "happiness" with which the Head prepares his voice, and his final, sudden shouting after having lowered his tone to that of a whisper, are certainly reminiscent of other and sadly famous rulers of the time. The Head's attitude is also indicative of his joy in having found a way to exploit an unexpected event—the appearance of the mysteriously speaking bird—to his own exclusive advantage. In fact, the Head's proclamation of his will to let the fowl "rule" over the citizenship hides a very different plan: "the chattering of the escaped parrot from that day guided the fortunes of the city of Ullathia, *interpreted by the Ruler and his Council as they desired"* (EG 18; italics added). These last italicized words represent the final outburst of bitter irony in this witty tale. In the end, rulers have only strengthened their power over ignorant citizens, by simply deceiving them. If the political interpretation is perhaps the most convincing one, we cannot fail to notice that the irony of this tale is operative at least on a double level: in fact, the sudden appearance of a likely supernatural creature, defined as a "Messenger" sent to guide the population toward her good, may be interpreted also as a literary parody of *religion*, in particular of Christianity. If this reading is correct, it would mean that Barlow in this tale is already expressing the teenage boy's skepticism toward the religious message: what Jesus Christ actually said was not really comprehended by anyone—and his message was instead misinterpreted and distorted by the "Ruler and his Council," in whose definition it is probably easy to spot the Catholic Pope and his circle of cardinals and dignitaries.

"The Hoard" opens with the description of the situation that occurred in the city of Zeth, where the town treasure has been stolen. The new keeper of the strong-room, Yalden, needs to face the "very grave matter," and the only apparent possible solution is to consult a "highly portentous being," Oorn, a "creature of extremely doubtful nature" and the virtual ruler of Zeth. The being came from "somewhere in the outer abyss" (EG 32), but, once fallen into Zeth one night, was captured by some priests. Irony toward religion is already apparent in the following remarks concerning the way in which the allegedly divine creature was dealt with by the priests: "The coincidence of Its excessively bizarre aspect and Its innate gift of mimicry had impressed the sacred brothers *as offering vast possibilities*, hence in the end they had set It up as a god and an oracle, organising a new brotherhood to serve It—*and incidentally to suggest the edicts it should utter and replies It should give*" (EG 32; italics added). The very same issue of "The Sacred Bird" is addressed here, making the religious nuance now openly recognizable: the clergy is blatantly accused of manipulating the population by pretending to give an appearance of sacredness to its own edicts and precepts (exploiting the puppet-figure of Oorn, who became famous as "a giver of judgements and solver of riddles" [EG 32]), but the "sacred brothers" (obviously another ironic connotation) are in fact deciding on their own. The protagonist of the tale, Yalden, "being not above the credulousness" (EG 32) of his fellows, sets out to search for Oorn, and finally reaches the "close-guarded and richly-fitted hall wherein Oorn brooded and mimicked the promptings of the priests" (EG 32). It is likely that, in the mention of the guarding and the description of the richness of the place where Oorn dwells, Barlow and Lovecraft aim at criticizing the hypocrisy of the Church, in particular the pomposity, empty ritual, and sheer luxury with which it enwraps its idols (here embodied in the puppet Oorn). However, the narrative is not limited to parodying the attitude of high prelates. The believer's credulousness is also made fun of—thanks to a masterly use of adverbs—together with the avidity of the clergy, in the following passage: "When Yalden came within sight of the Hall, with its tower of blue tile, he became *properly* religious, and entered the building *acceptably*, in a humble manner *which greatly impeded progress*. According to custom, the guardians of the deity acknowledged his obeisance and pecuniary offering" (EG 32; italics added). All is (hypocritical) etiquette, empty like the "conventional prayer" (EG

32) Yalden murmurs in front of an empty dais "studded with exotic jewels," as the ritual "prescribed" (EG 32). Once he has asked advice, Yalden awaits the oracle's response. Oorn, who had been given something to munch by the priests, finishes its food "tidily" and utters some indecipherable words, in a "tone of vast decisiveness: '*Gumay ere hfotuol leheht teg*'" (EG 32; italics added). Parody of the inane, artificial ritual of religion continues, when Oorn disappears "in a cloud of pink smoke which seemed to issue from behind the curtains where the acolytes were" (EG 32). The supposedly sacred ritual is here even equated to an illusionism made by skilled magicians. The acolytes' speech to Yalden is a masterly parody of religions' empty pretensions:

> The acolytes then came forth from their hiding-place and spoke to Yalden, saying: "Since you have pleased the deity with your concise statement of a very deplorable state of affairs, we are honoured by interpreting its directions. The aphorism you heard signifies no less than the equally mystic phrase 'Go thou unto your destination' or more properly speaking, you are to slay the monster-wizard Anathas and replenish the treasury with its fabled hoard." (EG 32)

Barlow and Lovecraft are openly satirizing the prelates' attitude, that of actually making their deity say what *they* most desire—and thus manipulating a credulous and superstitious population: how could Oorn really have meant that, if its utterance was indeed a cryptic aphorism? Of course the acolytes interpreted it according to their will—after, of course, having gathered the believer's pecuniary offering.

"The Fidelity of Ghu"[4] constitutes another narrative where Barlow expresses his ironic attitude toward what he judges the stubbornness of religious people's beliefs. In particular, he is here criticizing the behavior of priests and the truthfulness of their alleged "fidelity." The narrative tells of Lord Ghu, the last of the High Priests who has served Krang before the latter's "sudden and inexplicable pseudo-demise" (EG 40). Ghu is now uncertain of his own future, since his services are not needed anymore. His plight was "typical of all those who had devotedly relied upon the infinite knowledge of their strange master for all directions. Now that he had been interred with due solemnity, none knew where next to turn" (EG 40). Priest Ghu decides to walk toward the desert and effect his new resolution: "His resolution was both suitably dramatic and heroic, for Ghu had determined to perish by the tomb of his master, in noble sacrifice" (EG 40). With the employment of "noble" to qualify the sacrifice, Barlow is of course making fun of an attitude he deems religious fanaticism, that of sacrificing one's own life to serve a deity. The description of the way in which Ghu makes his resolution has sarcastic nuances again: "He had thought all night upon the matter, and had concluded that this would, in the end, entail the least trouble, and yet at the same time *serve his vanity*, for it would cause *his example to be pointed out by others with envious and admiring pride*" (EG 40; italics added). The irony is here very openly addressed toward the clergy, and what is made fun of is what Barlow considers

---

4. The tale was published for the first time in EG 40-41. According to Joshi and Anderson, the tale "likely dates to June 1934, when HPL began to address RHB as 'Lord Ghu' and such in correspondence" (in "Introduction," EG 10).

their hypocrisy: they are extremely vain people, whose choice to devote their life to serve a deity is—at least partially—not due to any sense of a deep vocation, but to reasons of opportunity and personal advantage.

Thus Ghu walks toward the tomb of his master, determined to hold a wake over it for the rest of his life. However, an unexpected event occurs: when not far away from the master's tomb, Ghu is confronted by a "terrible creature, shapen like a five legged spidery crab" (EG 40), mottled with purple and green. From the bracelets the creature wears, Ghu realizes it is Shista, "in one of the more or less original avatars that the god affected" (EG 40). When Krang was living, the worship of Shista had fallen into disuse and the creature went into seclusion; but now, after Krang died, Shista was "mightily pleased, and had set out afoot towards the Old One's gleaming tower" (EG 40). Barlow's irony toward the puerility and childish relationships involving the gods that humans adore is very clear: they are "humanized" deities, affected by all the human emotions—even the least edifying, such as envy and desire of revenge. Shista is determined to search for a dwelling in Krang's palace, which was particularly powerful since it was "coveted by all the evil powers of the universe" (EG 40). Hearing of Lord Ghu's mission and planning to take advantage of it, Shista speaks to him. The content of that speech is not recorded, but Ghu comes back to Krang's vacant temple and summons all the creatures that have served Krang in the past. Then he addresses them with a speech that represents a small gem of ironic derision toward religion's corruption:

> "Lo! I went into the desert to seek my master's tomb, and there I thought to perish. But as I was upon this mission, there came to me a messenger from the gods; and a demi-god itself, that spake to me, and tore away the veil of ignorance from my eyes. And now do ye bow, for I am possessed by the will of our dead Lord, and great Shista is come to rule in his stead. So I have returned to make ready for the One who shall follow when we have suitably prepared his temple." *Thus did Ghu remain faithful to his master.* (EG 41; italics added)

The stress with which Barlow accentuates the remark on Ghu's fidelity—aside from the fact that the tale is so titled as to celebrate it—reinforces the irony of the whole piece. Priests appear here as avid and highly corruptible people: not only are they ready to devote their whole life to a silly cause (to hold a wake over the god's tomb)—a cause chosen, by the way, only to tickle their own vanity—but they are also prone to easily change their minds when a more attractive perspective is available, thus betraying their supposed fidelity and revealing their corruptibility.

In "The Priest and the Heretic"[5] Barlow infuses irony into his discourse upon religion's hypocrisy. This short narrative tells of a "venerable priest," Lombei, who is a servitor of the dark god Moggua. Lombei "dwelt always within the temple of his deity, that he might remain in readiness for any command of his god, *though such had never come*" (EG 64; italics added). Barlow already stresses the inconsistency of religious devotion: Lombei's god, to whom the priest dedicates his whole life, is a silent one. In the inner court of the temple "was a peculiar oily pool wherein the god was said to

---

5. First published on the *Sea Gull* no. 53 (September 1935): 4.

dwell" (*EG* 64). Lombei is approached by a pilgrim from far lands, who thus addresses the priest: "'Listen . . . there be no gods, for I have defied them all my life, and they have smitten me not.' Dazed and terrified by this heresy, Lombei blinked in aged confusion. 'Listen,' said the stranger, 'free thyself of enslavement to ancient nursery-tales, and cast off thy god'" (*EG* 64). Lombei does not accept the stranger's words: he even curses the visitor and after a while goes into the inner court, staring at the placid pool. But the seed of doubt starts to creep into Lombei's conscience, as he reflects: "'If true this be . . . I must cease my priesthood and earn an *honest living, for hypocrisy tempts me not*'" (*EG* 64; italics added). Thus Barlow explicitly states that the polemical target of the tale is the hypocrisy of religion, and he paradoxically faces it by staging the figure of an apparently repentant priest: "'If the man be right, all my devotions have been wasted, and I may as well slay myself.' And he looked away in doubt. But then it chanced that a large bird flying overhead dropped somewhat within the pool, and a ripple spread over the oily surface" (*EG* 65). The interpretation given by the religious person to this apparently insignificant event is exemplary of what Barlow deems religion's senselessness and sheer hypocrisy: "Seeing this Lombei was overjoyed. 'Hidden Moggua, I meant it not. I sorrow at my doubt now thou hast given me a sign.' Thus was his piece of mind restored; and Lombei conscientiously served his deity to the end of his days" (*EG* 65). This apologue (its original title was "The Fable of the Priest and the Heretic") is certainly surprising if one thinks that Barlow was barely seventeen years old when he wrote it: the piece shows a mature, ironically disillusioned attitude toward the religious issue, as well as very clear ideas upon the matter.

The "bitter" irony that characterizes Barlow's fiction is especially present in his most "cosmic" tales: their goal, as seen in chapter 4, is to openly depict the utter emptiness on a cosmic scale of the human race and its achievements. In order to do so, often Barlow resorts to ironic—if not sarcastic—comments upon the inanity of the pomposity and grandeur with which humans wrap their efforts, aspirations, and transient successes. As seen in chapter 4, Barlow employs this sort of bitter irony quite automatically, since the belittlement of the human race naturally passes also through ironic statements about the race's assuredness. Since the discussion of this issue is already present in chapter 4, I will limit myself here to mentioning a single passage that provides an exemplary case of Barlow's bitter irony. In "A Dim-Remembered Story," the protagonist himself presents his sarcastic view on the ultimate (lack of) meaning and importance of the human role in cosmic history: "There was no record of how our world perished. Somewhere in the great maze a star winked out. Only that, and all of humanity was gone—*the splendid dreams, the bravery* of that race which I had known (long since) when it was young. *Man, great, assured, and invincible, was now obliterated*" (*EG* 101).

7.2 Tales of true humor and parody

Barlow's fiction provides several examples of humorous narratives, or at least passages. As we have seen, three out of the six collaborations with Lovecraft present, in whole or in part, openly humorous if not parodic elements. Since Barlow expressed his irony especially in the collaborations with his mentor, my discussion will start with them and then will analyze how Barlow's employment of (mainly parodic) humor was so pervasive as to characterize much of his original fiction.

In "The Hoard of the Wizard-Beast," the first of the three Lovecraft-Barlow collaborations presenting humorous elements, irony is not only a "socially committed" one. This short tale offers also a few passages of parodic humor. After the priests of the temple of Oorn have "translated" the creature's aphorism, inviting Yalden to slay the wizard-monster Anathas and hunt for its treasury, Yalden is afraid of the mission awaiting him: "he was openly afraid of the monster Anathas, as were all the inhabitants of Ullathia and the surrounding land" (EG 32). However, the youth is not so scared as to give up his mission, since it holds a strong appeal for him. The description of the nature of this appeal is an open parody of the cliché exploited by the weird fiction of Barlow's and Lovecraft's time: "But the prospect was not without romantic appeal, and Yalden was young and consequently unwise. He knew, among other things, that there was always *the hope of rescuing some feminine victim of the monster's famed and surprising erotic taste*" (EG 33; italics added). It is not difficult to imagine Lovecraft's and Barlow's sardonic smile in writing these lines, a parody of the cheap weird tales in vogue in 1920s and 1930s in the pulp magazines, where the aliens were inevitably depicted as monstrous creatures craving for some erotic satisfaction by seducing wondrously beautiful human women—and with the regular (young and beautiful) human hero set on the inexorably successful mission to free them and win their love. In these cheap tales, monsters were also ineluctably hideous-looking, hence the description of Anathas, the wizard-monster, plainly pokes fun to this cliché through the mention of details deliberately chosen to be the most disgusting—according to the human canon : "Many vowed it had been seen from afar in the form of a giant black shadow peculiarly repugnant to human taste, while others alleged it was a mound of gelatinous substance that oozed hatefully in the manner of putrescent flesh. Still others claimed they had seen it as a monstrous insect with *astonishing* supernumerary appurtenances. But in one thing all coincided; namely, *that it was advisable to have as little traffic as possible with Anathas*" (EG 33; italics added). Defining as "astonishing" the form or sheer number of the monster's supernumerary appurtenances is certainly a touch of humor that the reader can grasp, as well as the final sentence that summarizes in a conclusive, sarcastic claim all the (useless) debate about Anathas's looks.

Again the cliché of fantasy tales, which featured invincible heroes endowed with extraordinary magic powers, is parodied when it is mentioned that a "wizard of old repute had furnished him [Yalden] with certain singular accessories. He had, for example, a charm which *prevented his thirsting or hungering, and wholly did away with his need for provisions*" (EG 33; italics added). Yalden is turned into a sort of divine being just by means of a wizard's spell. Another parodic trait of the tale is revealed by the description of the monster's fabled hoard—and above all the reasons for its existence, which makes fun of the commonplace of contemporary, implausible fantasy tales. Lovecraft and Barlow here intend to parody the anthropocentric fantasy tale of their times, which portrayed the monster according to a human perspective and viewpoint: not only was the monster always extremely bad-looking (for human canons) and erotically active (his interest in sex is again a human concern attributed to a non-human creature), but he was also in possession of incalculable treasures that he had no use for, but that added to the sense of importance—and, for an attentive reader, implausibility—of the monster itself. The monster was thus interested not only in sex, but also in money: "At the heart of his cave, legend said, Anathas had concealed an enormous hoard of jewels, gold, and other things of fabulous value. *Why so potent a wonder-worker should care for such gauds, or revel in the counting of money, was by no means clear;* but many things attested the truth of these tastes" (*EG* 33; italics added). It is again easy to guess that a light irony made a sincere smile appear on Barlow's and Lovecraft's faces while they were composing these lines.

However, it is in the other two of the Lovecraft-Barlow collaborations that the sense of humor is more openly at work: both "The Battle That Ended the Century" and "Collapsing Cosmoses" were in fact conceived and born as plainly humorous tales. In them, irony is not detectable only in passages; it informs all the writing, because the tales' purpose is precisely to parody and make fun.

"The Battle That Ended the Century" is a spoof narrative of about 2000 words mentioning a large number of individuals (37, to be exact), under whose punning names Lovecraft and Barlow have disguised some of their friends, correspondents, colleagues, fellow writers, and illustrators. As the Lovecraft-Barlow correspondence attests, the tale was probably composed in May 1934, while Lovecraft was visiting Barlow in Florida for the first time (May 2–June 21). The originator of this squib was almost certainly Barlow: "typescripts prepared by him survive, one with extensive revisions in pen by Lovecraft,"[6] and the perusal of the original text shows that "many of the most amusing jokes in this whimsy are Barlow's" (Joshi and Schultz, "Introduction," *FF* xiv). Thus it was probably Barlow who urged Lovecraft to work on this highly humorous piece, which sprung from the idea of making "joking mention of as many of the authors' mutual colleagues as possible in the course of the document" (*LAL* 553). In fact, all the mentioned individuals are disguised, under humorous pseudonyms (Howard Phillips Lovecraft himself is present under the name "Horse Power Hateart"). The subject of the tale is the heavyweight boxing fight between a character called "Two-Gun Bob," also nicknamed "The Terror of the Plains"—namely, Robert E. Howard (1906-1936) in disguise—and "Knockout Bernie," or the "Wild Wolf of West Shokan"—Bernard Austin Dwyer (1897-1943) in disguise. S. T. Joshi, who has had access to the original extant typescripts in the John Hay Library, claims that "Barlow had initially cited them [the characters of the tale] by their actual names, but Lovecraft felt that this was not very interesting, so he devised parodic or punning name for them" (*LAL* 553), some of which have been correctly identified only in recent times. Both writers—but especially Lovecraft—always publicly denied the authorship of the spoof.

---

6. *LAL* 552-53. Faig examined RHB's papers and attests that "in a file marked 'joint parodies' there is a fragmentary first draft with annotations in Barlow's hand (one leaf, typewritten); a complete second draft with revisions in Lovecraft's hand (four leaves, typewritten, dated *circa* May 20, 1934, by Barlow), and three mimeographed copies evidently prepared for circulation (two leaves each, stapled)": *UL* 198.

The two friends had probably devised the following plan for the tale, which was meant to circulate anonymously and privately among the circle of friends whose names were alluded to[7]: "Barlow would mimeograph the item [. . .] and then have the copies mailed from some other location, so that they could not be traced to either Lovecraft or Barlow. [. . .] the 50 duplicated copies were prepared towards the middle of June and were sent to Washington, D.C., where they would be mailed" (*LAL* 553), probably by Elizabeth Toldridge,[8] as she was an associate of both Lovecraft's and Barlow's, but not mentioned in the spoof. Thus when Lovecraft reached Washington at the beginning of July—and looked for Elizabeth Toldridge—the tale had already been delivered to the associates. In their correspondence immediately following the writing and mailing of the tale, Lovecraft and Barlow talk "in amusingly conspiratorial tones about its reception by colleagues" (*LAL* 553), with Lovecraft advising his pupil on how to behave in order to preserve the veil of secrecy over the authorship, the printing, and the distribution of the piece. Commenting upon a letter he received from Long, Lovecraft wrote the following to Barlow: "Note the signature—Chimesleep Short—which indicates that our spoof has gone out & that he at least thinks I've seen the thing. Remember that if you didn't know anything about it, you'd consider it merely a whimsical trick of his own—& that if you'd merely seen the circular, you wouldn't think it worth commenting on. I'm ignoring the matter in my reply" (letter to RHB, 29 June 1934; *FF* 146). And again, in a letter of a few days later: "Oh, yes—about the satire. I've had several reports of it [. . .] Belknap suspects the authorship, but I have refused to confirm his suspicion" (letter to RHB, 12 July 1934; *FF* 150). In a postcard of July 19, Lovecraft is very humorous about the whole matter: "Glad to learn that Little Charlie[9] has withdrawn his monstrous accusation. The idea of suspecting us of such a grotesque hoax!" (*FF* 152). Not all the colleagues mentioned in the tale received it with equal favor: "Very few reports on the hoax lately. Wandrei wasn't exactly in a rage, but (according to Belknap) sent the folder on to Desmond Hall with the languid comment, 'Here's something that may interest you—it doesn't interest me'" (letter to RHB, 21 July 1934; *FF* 153). Little by little, rumor of Lovecraft's involvement with the authorship of the spoof leaked out, especially because of Long's perspicacity. Already at the end of July, Lovecraft lamented to Barlow: "I note Belknap's guess that I am behind the hoax—damn the little rascal! He ought not to have hinted anything to Leedle Shoolie,[10] even if he thought I wrote the thing—for he might know I wouldn't want it given anyway. But that's just Sonny's kiddish way of blabbing everything he knows—& a damn lot more than he knows!" (postcard to RHB, 24 July 1934; *FF* 155). However, Lovecraft still tried to deny to Long his in-

---

7. The tale had its first publication in the *Acolyte* 2, No. 4 (Fall 1944): 9–12.
8. Faig too agrees that "the parody was forwarded to Washington, D.C., where it was remailed by some acquaintance of Lovecraft's or Barlow's" (*UL* 198).
9. Charles D. Hornig (1916–1999), editor of the *Fantasy Fan* (1933–35). He was hired by Hugo Gernsback as editor of *Wonder Stories* in 1933.
10. Julius Schwartz (1916–2004), editor of *Fantasy Magazine*, acted as HPL's agent in selling *At the Mountains of Madness* to *Astounding Stories*.

volvement, as a slightly later letter to Barlow attests: "Yes—I pointed out to Sonny Belknap the absurdity of the idea that any staid old gentleman would ever start up a spoof like one so unaccountably attributed to me... but the child has a damnably suspicious nature, & a lamentably cocksure confidence in his ability to spot his grandpa's style!" (letter to RHB, 3?-6 August 1934; *FF* 157). At the end of the very same letter, Lovecraft reveals that "Rimel & Baldwin recd. the spoof, & suspect *me but not you*. They think they can spot my handwriting in one of the corrections. The thing seems to delight them vastly" (*FF* 158).

Certainly Lovecraft's style was much more familiar among the circle of his friends and colleagues than Barlow's. The curiosity aroused by the circulation of the anonymous spoof within Lovecraft's and Barlow's circle grew throughout the summer. In fact, Lovecraft kept on advising Barlow—again in "conspiratorial tones"—on the attitude to adopt toward the increasingly urgent requests of explanations coming from the several friends involved—though as time passed, it was more and more difficult to maintain intact the wall of secrecy about the authorship of the piece, so that Lovecraft felt compelled to make "concessions" to the inquirers: "As for the spoof—for the time being I fancy the best thing is just to let it summer—replying non-committally to all enquiries... affirming nothing, denying nothing. It surely is too bad that Belknap felt called upon to blab gratuitously about it. Cook suspects my share because of the mention of Munn's cream-puff vending—a thing none but he & I would be likely to know. I conceded that the author of the satire must be some close correspondent of mine!" (letter to RHB, 1 September 1934; *FF* 174).[11] Even by late October, Lovecraft and Barlow had not admitted anything, though the conjecture about their involvement in the satire was by now largely spread among their colleagues and Lovecraft's "concessions" had become so numerous as to arouse well-founded suspicions: "Baldwin rather embarrasses me by saying that I 'deny all connexion' with our spoof. I was by no means so categorical—though I did point out my presence in the far south at the time the copies were mailed" (letter to RHB, 26 October 1934; *FF* 187).[12] Franklin Lee Baldwin (1913-1987) of Asotin, Washington, was a fantasy fan and amateur musician. In the spoof, after one of the contenders is declared dead and his alleged corpse is prepared for the funeral, Baldwin is introduced in this way: "An appropriate dirge was rendered by Maestro Sing Lee Bawledout on the piccolo" (*EG* 38).

The tale—which bears the humorous subtitle "MS. Found in a Time Machine"—is set on the eve of the year 2001, when the epochal fight between the two contenders (Two-Gun Bob and Knockout Bernie) occurs. The piece is indeed very funny, and

---

11. Here HPL refers to this passage of the tale: "Cream-puffs were inattentively vended by Wladislaw Brenryk" (*EG* 36), where Brenryk stands for Harold Warner Munn (1903-1981) of Athol, MA.

12. This is the comment by Baldwin, appearing in the *Fantasy Fan* for October 1934, to which HPL refers: "H. P. Lovecraft denies all connections with 'The Battle That Ended the Century' (Ms found in a time machine). He was in De Land or in St. Augustine at the time it was mailed, and by the time he was in Washington D.C., the Eastern readers had received their copies" (quoted in *FF* 189n4).

founds its irony especially on the extreme exaggerations characterizing the phases of the fight, as well as on the humorous and paradoxical descriptions of the people and events involved in it. For example, the venerated Tibetan Lama Bill Lum Li[13] is said to have "evoked the primal serpent-God of Valusia and found unmistakable signs of victory on both sides" (*EG* 36) of the contenders. The gong is said to have been sounded "at 39 o'clock" (*EG* 36), and immediately after, the gore of the battle reddened the air. The utter unlikelihood of the fight ("the Shokan Soaker's sturdy right crashed through the Texan's ribs and became entangled in sundry viscera" [*EG* 37]; "muscles, glands, gore, and bits of flesh were spattered over the ringside" [*EG* 37]) adds to the amusing character of the piece. Among the people mentioned—under parodic or punning names—are the writers Frank Belknap Long (as Frank Chimesleep Short, Jr.), Wilfred Blanch Talman (W. Lablache Talcum), H. P. Lovecraft himself (Horse Power Hateart), August Derleth (M. le Comte d'Erlette), Seabury Quinn (Teaberry Quince), E. Hoffmann Price (Malik Taus, the Peacock Sultan), Clark Ashton Smith (Klarkash-Ton), and others. Also, a few illustrators of pulp magazines (Margaret Brundage, C. C. Senf, Guy Lincoln Huey) are made fun of, especially because of their habit of providing illustrations that did not match the actual events occurring in the stories. After an interminable battle, during which all sorts of mutilation take place, Knockout Bernie is declared theoretically dead—though his alleged corpse, during the funerary ceremonies, "strolled away for a bite of bologna" (*EG* 38). Lovecraft and Barlow do not miss the chance to make fun also of the pulp magazine establishment, by referring to Hugo Gernsback, Farnsworth Wright, and *Weird Tales* itself—the last rendered as the *Windy City Grab-Bag*. In the end, the Wild Wolf pursues a libel suit against the decision that declared him defeated (and dead); and he was, after "several appeals ending with the World Court, adjudged not only officially alive but the clear winner of the combat" (*EG* 39).

The tone of the piece is of one of light and amiable humor: all the people involved in the spoof are good-naturedly made fun of, through an irony that targets their small or large defects and idiosyncrasies. However, in one case the authors' irony may have crossed the border and configured as potentially hurtful:

> All this is good if harmless fun, the only real maliciousness being the note about the pestiferous Forrest J. Ackerman: "Meanwhile a potentate from a neighbouring kingdom, the Effjay of Akkamin (also known to himself as an amateur critic), expressed his frenzied disgust at the technique of the combatants, at the same time peddling photographs of the fighters (with himself in the foreground) at five cents each" [*EG* 36]. Ackerman was really offering photographs of himself at this time. (*LAL* 553)

Ackerman's avidity in seeking souvenirs is satirized not only in the passage mentioned by Joshi, but also in a later one: "Mr. J. Caesar Warts frequently interviewed both battlers and all the more important spectators; obtaining as souvenirs (*after a spirited struggle with the Effjay*) an autographed quarter-rib of Two-Gun's, in excellent state of

---

13. Parody of William Lumley (1880–1960), HPL's revision client, known for his mystical beliefs.

preservation, and three finger-nails from the Wild Wolf" (*EG* 37-38; italics added). Forrest Ackerman (1916-2000), at the time a science fiction fan, would again be labeled by Lovecraft with the epithets "slimy effjeh weeds" and "akman" in "In the Walls of Eryx" (1936), written with Kenneth J. Sterling. The explanation for the acrimony with which both Lovecraft and Barlow considered Ackerman lies in the fact that "A vitriolic debate between Ackerman and various weird tale enthusiasts (including Lovecraft and Barlow) was published in the *Fantasy Fan* in a column called 'The Boiling Point' (Sept. 1933-Feb. 1934). Ackerman was known for shamelessly selling photographs and autographs, even of writers whose work he denigrated" (Joshi, Anderson, and Schultz, note 13 in *EG* 36). And in a letter addressed to Barlow and dating to 29 November 1933, Lovecraft described Ackerman with these debasing words: "Ackerman represents a millionfold exaggeration of a kind of smart-alec vanity & publicity-seeking which we all have to some extent in youth. I spoofed him quite a bit last year when he attacked my 'Colour Out of Space', but he's slow in 'getting' irony" (*FF* 89). Altogether, the tale is a very lively example of the irony and sense of humor of Barlow's personality, certainly a significant component of his character. No socially committed irony is at work here, but the sheer intent to arouse laughter "for laughter's sake."

Almost the same holds true for the third and last of the humorous Lovecraft-Barlow collaborations, "Collapsing Cosmoses," where, however, the satire is openly addressed toward a certain type of science fiction of the time, the so-called space-opera represented, for instance, in the work of Edmond Hamilton (1904-1977) for the *Interstellar Patrol* series, such as "Crashing Suns" (a tale of 1928), whose title "Collapsing Cosmoses" plainly apes, and *Outside the Universe* (a novel, 1929). This never-completed parody was composed by the two friends during the second and last visit Lovecraft paid to the Barlows in Florida—during the summer of 1935 (from June 9 to August 18). Unlike "The Battle," "Collapsing Cosmoses" was not distributed to friends until after Lovecraft's death: Barlow published it in the second issue of his *Leaves* (December 1938, 100-101). The tale is an unfinished one of no more than 600 words, but certainly contains some passages, or better ideas, of enjoyable humor. According to Joshi, the part Barlow played in the writing of the piece was significant: "the idea was for each author to write every other paragraph or so, although on occasion Lovecraft only wrote a few words before yielding the pen back to his younger colleague, so that considerably more than half the piece is Barlow's, as are a fair number of the better jokes" (*LAL* 595).

As a matter of fact, the satire effectively, and almost literally, apes and parodies the typical situations—and even sentences—of Edmond Hamilton's works, especially those telling of our universe as being threatened and attacked by invaders from other galaxies, whose menacing intentions are opposed by the "Interstellar Patrol" defending mankind. Just to provide a few examples of the piquant humor of this tale, this is how Barlow (Lovecraft's contributions have been ascertained and do not affect this passage) describes the beginning of the meeting where the measures to take to combat the menace brought by the alien invaders are decided upon: "Within the Great Council Chamber, which measured *twenty-eight square feet (with quite a high ceiling)*, were gathered delegates from all the thirty-seven galaxies of our immediate universe. Oll Stoff, President of the Chamber and representative of the *Milliner's Soviet*, raised his *eyeless snout with dignity*" (EG 60; italics added). His discourse is very short: he simply mentions a "terrible peril" forthcoming, which stirs a huge applause in the variegated audience, Barlow underscoring the fact that the participants who were handless slithered "their tentacles together" (EG 61). Thus Oll Stoff invites Hak Ni to "crawl upon the dais" (EG 61): "Hak Ni, the yellow-furred and valorous commander of our ranks through numerous installments, ascended to the towering peak *inches above the floor*" (EG 61; italics added). According to Joshi, "as a satire on the space-opera brand of science fiction popularised by Edmond Hamilton, E. E 'Doc' Smith, and others, 'Collapsing Cosmoses' is undeniably effective; the fact that it is unfinished makes little difference, for the absurdity of the plot would have precluded any neat resolution in any event. Certainly, it would have been an entertainment if this piece had gone on a little longer, but the authors had made their point" (LAL 595).

Barlow's fiction also shows remarkable ironic pieces, or just passages, in the original narratives—and this is a proof that Barlow did not need Lovecraft's collaboration to pull out the irony of his temper and inform his narratives of it. Even within Barlow's otherwise "serious" narrations, ironic or amusing details occasionally appear; as in "Return by Sunset," at the point when the male protagonist is seen from below by his female companion, she exclaims: "'How terrible you look up there with that big stick in your hand. *Are you planning to have me for breakfast?*'" (EG 137). This is just an episode within a serious framework, yet Barlow's ironic attitude must have been particularly strong if he was led to insert a funny detail in a very sober—if not tragic—narration.

However, other tales, openly parodic, reveal Barlow's humor to its full extent: in particular, the so-called *Book of Garoth*, an episodic fantasy work that Barlow conceived in 1935 "very much in the spirit of Dunsany's *Book of Wonder*" (Joshi and Anderson, "Introduction," EG 10). Of this planned lengthy work, only two episodes were published: "The Temple"[14]—containing chapters 3 and 4—and "The Adventures of Garoth"[15]—containing chapters 10, 11, and 12. The "Introductory Note" to the first installment, "The Temple," already frames the narrative within the parodic genre it belongs to. The introduction reads as follows:

> "When the planet he had so long frequented was destroyed by cosmic fire, the *fourteen-thousand-year-old* demon named Garoth was *at loss for occupation*." Thus begins the Book of Garoth, an incomplete and *wholly unmotivated* narrative upon which R.H. Barlow spasmodically writes. Bear in mind throughout these *laborious* episodes that the hero is no mortal whatever avatar he may assume, but a member of the old race that *guideth* man. Bear with him patiently. [. . .]—*The Perspective Review*. (EG 49; italics added)

An analogous introduction is placed at the beginning of the second installment available, "The Adventures of Garoth," only slightly shortened. This introduction is al-

---

14. In the *Perspective Review* (Spring 1935): 3-5.
15. In the *Perspective Review* (Summer 1935): 6-8, 10.

ready humorous, since it pokes fun at the pompous style of weird writers (the use of "guideth" is telling) and at the sheer improbability of their narratives (a demon fourteen thousand years old being "at loss for occupation," and with whom the reader is invited to bear "patiently"); the episodes are defined "laborious," the narrative "unmotivated," and Barlow a "spasmodic" writer: all these remarks unite to provide the impression of the humorous spoof to come. And in effect, the few short "chapters" composing the extant saga of *Garoth* tell of a peculiarly—and very humanly—curious and inquisitive demon in search of diversion and occupation, and whose adventures always end up in a humorous way. After all, an allegedly heroic character whose adventures are the result not of his intrinsic heroism but of his "loss of occupation," a character with whom the reader is invited to bear patiently, of course just from the start is configured as non-conventional.

After seeing an apparently beautiful girl horribly tortured by eight wizard-priests close to a temple, Garoth feels gratified that his "quest for diversion" (EG 50) has been satisfied. The girl is finally carried away by a hideous "fiend of green flame" (EG 50). However, Garoth's curiosity prevails and he thinks that the recent events "'require explanation. So I shall endeavour to find her captor and ask the gentleman what has been the girl's crime to justify so unfortunate a demise.' Thus speaking, Garoth winged himself past a particularly lurid planet, and flew directly for a far part of infinity that he knew to be frequented by unpleasant beings. And directly he had first seen his destination the demon found himself there, *for such is the speed of man's masters*" (EG 50; italics added). The concluding sentence—that is, the final one of Chapter 3 of "The Temple"—is of course ironic and probably parodies the conventions of fantasy writing.

In Chapter 4, Garoth seeks an explanation for the loathsome scene in which he has assisted and that involved the girl's demise. Thus, Garoth meets an evil genie that promises to offer him a satisfactory explanation. The genie leads him through the abysses of a subterranean river. Barlow's description of their journey is certainly parodic: "Progress was in a measure difficult because of the inordinate number of corpses cluttering the stream; and Garoth thought it indeed untidy compared with the manner of interment practiced among the Janou-birds who turn a burial *into a restrained and decorous orgy and devour the body*" (EG 51; italics added). The genie leads Garoth into a flame-lit vast cavern, in the midst of which, among pillaring flames ceaselessly stretching, a few demons are engaged in torturing people, occasionally throwing them into the river from which Garoth and the genie came. Again Garoth cannot refrain from exercising his sharply developed sense of criticism, and the very mention of his hypocrisy adds to the humor of the narrative: "Garoth watched their occupations for a moment; and then spoke in high praise of this arrangement, *although he did not think it at all nice in reality*. The place impressed him as *abominably ill-managed and totally unlike a well-constructed Hell*" (EG 51; italics added). A demon—thus a supernatural creature—openly praising, but secretly criticizing his fellow demons according to his own sense of management certainly sounds funny. The genie knows Garoth is interested in seeing his "latest acquisition," the tortured girl sent to Hell by the wizard-priests. The genie thus addresses Garoth: "'She is over in that flame right now, so I'm afraid she would be of little help personally. I can show you, though . . .'" (*EG* 51). Afterwards Garoth is introduced to the real nature of the girl, a disgusting monster under the disguise of a beautiful maiden—and thus the demon's curiosity is satisfied, but at the very high price of seeing all his certainties disrupted: what at first appeared as an harmless girl and eight evil wizard-priests torturing her is in reality revealed to be, respectively, a terribly evil creature and eight lawful avengers.

Chapter 10 of "The Adventures of Garoth" presents a new parodic enterprise of the incalculably old demon. He is still pensively in search for some thrilling adventure to occupy his time and fight his boredom, as the following lines remark: "As he walked along, the demon speculated as to the probable nature of his next adventure. This matter occupied his attention entirely, and he did not see the creature before him until it spoke" (*EG* 52). The curious androcephalous creature addressing Garoth is a shaggy man-bear of extreme ugliness, and Garoth does not hide his surprise at its sight. However, he manages to behave "politely" with it, for a reason of etiquette: "The demon stared in surprise for he had known no such animal upon the world he once ruled, but he was determined to be polite. Consequently he returned the salutation and inquired his way" (*EG* 53). The man-bear's reply to Garoth is a hilarious short piece making fun of the cliché of the cheap fantasy tales of the times, often featuring heroic and bold knights committed to highly dangerous missions aimed at freeing beautiful maidens from their captors, and finally rewarded for their heroism by gaining immeasurable treasures and the beauties' eternal love:

> "O curious being from another world, for that I know you to be, if diversion you seek, you will find ahead the castle called Alair whose rocky vaults contain strangely guarded treasures. There is, I believe, a maiden who desires to be rescued from her captors; in short, *all things essential to romance, adventure, and similar foolishness awaits you.* Go then to this castle, *if you desire to become a hero,* and seek out the maiden named Sasta." (*EG* 53; italics added)

Garoth accepts the mission: he is not a hero, but strives to become one, a worthy protagonist of a fantasy tale. Once arrived at the seemingly abandoned castle, Garoth rattles at the gate, trying to call someone's attention. No one replies, so Garoth sets to work with his sword to break the lock. But a voice interrupts him ("What do you do here, destroying the property of an honest man?" [*EG* 53]), and the physical description of the grotesquely fat speaker is again filled with a sense of humor:

> The demon-man glanced up with surprise and interest. The speaker was a fat and bloated old man, garbed in a worn black robe. His eyes were bleary, and huge masses of revolting puffy flesh formed deep folds upon his face. Venomous eyes of greenish hue shot with tiny streaks of blood peered from sockets almost obscured by rings of unhealthy swollen flesh. His mouth was effeminately small and of a livid purple, but his features were unimpressive save for the calculating stare. A thin wisp of hair fell scantily from beneath the skull-cap that covered his nearly bald head. He spoke again, and Garoth could see vast ripples shake over his paunch when the wheezing tones came forth. (*EG* 53)

Each physical trait of the man is made the object of the narrator's joke. The fat old man asks Garoth what his intentions are, and, since it was not the young demon-lord's habit to "shilly-shally" (*EG* 54)—an expression certainly not adequate to an alleged heroic fantasy tale—he replies that his mission is to rescue the maiden Sasta, imprisoned in the castle. On hearing this, the owner of the castle starts in surprise and asks Garoth why he is concerned with Sasta's fate. The description of the demon's reply is again very parodic, since the narrator, also resorting to indirect free speech, makes open fun of his protagonist, in the very manner in which he defines him: "The man-demon explained with a suitable lie, congratulating himself on the slyness of the ruse. *No doubt he should shortly be within the castle himself!! A piece of fine fortune indeed!* How well he was putting it over on this slow-witted rascal... Thus thought Garoth" (*EG* 53; italics added). Not only is the indirect free speech ("No doubt he should shortly be within the castle himself!! A piece of fine fortune indeed!") ironic about Garoth, but the way he is characterized ("the man-demon") is ironic, since up to now Garoth has always been defined as "the demon-man."

The fat old man opens the gate and lets Garoth in, accompanying him along an increasingly gloomy corridor. The roof of the corridor grows progressively lower, until the demon is unable to stay erect. Of course, the very fact that the owner of the castle escorts the supposed hero toward the fulfillment of his mission (the rescuing of a captive maiden) is ironic. However, this is not all: the corridor ends in a small door, and the fat man tells Garoth he is not going to proceed farther: "'but if you care to proceed, please close the door behind you. *I don't wish any drafts*" (*EG* 53; italics added). A sheer burst of the reader's laughter is what Barlow effectively pursues here. It is not all: the fat man "pushes" Garoth through the opening, but "So taken by surprise was the demon that he was unprepared to resist, and he fell awkwardly through the gloomy opening. He sprawled on a floor lower than that of the passage" (*EG* 53). Garoth is thus increasingly configuring as an anti-hero.

In Chapter 11, his adventure in the gloomy prison comes to a surprising end. After noticing the exceedingly bad conditions of the prison (fossilized vegetation covers the walls, the roof is low, slimy growths adhere to the damp clamminess of the roof, the air is non-circulating and stale), "Garoth wondered mildly at the constitution of the captive maiden, which must be indeed strong to survive this dismal fate" (*EG* 54-55). The first doubts creep into Garoth's mind about the actual nature of this "maiden," but for now nothing is revealed about her. However, "This consideration brought his thoughts to the *highly chivalrous purpose* of his mission" (*EG* 55; italics added). Garoth thus starts a systematic exploration of the prison, and since he "edged precariously along the rim of the pit, he likened his activities to those of a rat upon a well-top" (*EG* 55), scarcely a description of a "highly chivalric" mission of an invincible hero. Inside a large room, Garoth sees a faint blue light: "it came from a most peculiar source, *nothing less than* the fiery breath of a large monster that lay sleeping directly in his path" (*EG* 55; italics added). As a perfect anti-hero, Garoth does not fight nor slay the monster: the "man-devil" (still another definition of the protagonist) simply draws back—since the monster is unaware of his presence—and cautiously steps over the slightly writhing tentacles, thus entering the room.

In the long and narrow room, iron doors are ranged on either wall, each with small eye-holes with sliding covers: they are the portals of the cell rooms. Peeping into the first eye-hole, Garoth spots the first inhabitant, "which had obviously been once a man. It moaned and came over to the wall, scratching upon the iron with strange talons as if expecting food. Since its diet appeared to be mainly dismembered portions of the human body, *Garoth did not supply it: hastily closing the peep-hole, he proceeded to the next*" (EG 55; italics added). Garoth's bravery is that of a parodic anti-hero. Finally he comes to a door revealing a "surprising occupant," whose description once more parodies the cliché of the descriptions of monsters in fantasy and weird tales:

> a tremendous monster-woman, whose pulpy green expanse filled the entire chamber. Her form was *obese*, and her sleeping was accompanied by *odd roaring sounds not pleasing to the ear*. This woman-thing had *numerous unclassifiable limbs of extremely plump size*, and her face was distinguished by the fact that *in its horned scaliness no nose was apparent*. Her mouth was of a flabby vastness, and *her hairless pate glistened* in the light admitted by the peep-hole. (EG 55; italics added)

The description of the highly unlikely creature purports to be amusingly repugnant and effectively achieves its goal. The account of Garoth's grotesquely chivalric behavior and first exchange with the monster-woman is indeed humorous:

> Garoth was about to close the opening when the creature blinked and opened her four large eyes, staring through the light directly at the demon. He waited uncomfortably, feeling it would be impolite to close the door in the face of even so peculiar a lady. So he stood there, shuffling uneasily as she regarded him. He was first to speak.
> "I beg your pardon. I didn't intend to spy," Garoth ventured.
> "It's been ever so long since I've seen anyone. Will you converse with me a while?" She rolled her eyes oddly.
> "I've really not the time, but to refuse a lady's request would be unchivalrous in the extreme," he said, "although I'm doubtful as to the topic we might select." (EG 55–56)

The hilarious exchange, with Garoth trying to look polite out of a misdirected sense of chivalry, ends with the monster-woman's request to be released:

> Garoth was upset. Nevertheless his reply was tactful. "I should like very much to accommodate you, but I regret to say that I am already upon a quest of much the same nature ... the best sort of makeshift excuse for my vacation I could muster. To be forced to save *two* ladies, who would undoubtedly dislike one another and squabble for my favors, would be indeed an involved situation. I seek a certain prisoner, the captive maiden called Sasta." (EG 56)

The inevitable conclusion of this parodic exchange consists of course in the revelation of the creature's identity: "In pandemonium she leaped against the stout door joyfully proclaiming her identity. 'I am the maiden Sasta!'" (EG 56).

Chapter 12 of the *Book of Garoth* tells of the demon's attempt to escape the hideous woman, initially along the corridor of the prison and afterwards by a plunge into the bottomless well-abyss below the prison. Garoth's plunge ends with his losing consciousness in the water. The light, humorous tone with which Barlow describes Garoth's awakening and explains the reasons for his survival make for an amusing passage:

> It was cold and moist when he recovered consciousness. Had it not been that he was more than mortal, then surely would he have perished. Such was the blending of natural and supernatural powers that while a man in every aspect Garoth could yet survive all manner of vicissitude unharmed. This was at once apparent in the fact that while totally submerged in deep water, he was not at all inconvenienced, nor was breath any more difficult than if he had been on land. He considered his present surroundings, and was thankfully observant of the fact that Sasta had not emulated his surprising mode of exit from the dungeons. (EG 56-57)

It is a pity that only few chapters of the *Book of Garoth* survive, since, had Barlow continued writing (and above all publishing) new episodes, this farcical saga would have likely offered further samples of his fictional irony.

A leaf from the manuscript of "The Summons."

8. Forbidden / Furtive Search

Many of the most significant concerns of Barlow's fiction center around the theme of *search*, which very often configures as a *forbidden and/or furtive* one. Barlow's interest in this theme is perhaps to be reconnected to the restlessness and volubility of his own personality, his continual "search" and striving for new and more challenging goals to achieve, mainly professional realization, an always-delayed happiness, and a favorable dimension (both physical and psychological) to live in. Two "searches" are thus at stake, an "existential" one—which Barlow conducted throughout his life, without satisfactory success if one considers the way it ended—and a "literary" one, the latter transpiring from some of the most effective narratives and strictly interconnected with the former, of which it becomes the narrative counterpart and, perhaps, the artistic exorcism. However, this is not the place to attempt to look for psychological reasons at the basis of Barlow's narrative choices; we can just try to categorize the different typologies of literary searches as they appear from his tales. Thus, three types of search occur and can be identified. On increasingly abstract and "rarefied" levels, this is their succession:

1. Actual and physical search. This search occurs on the physical level of the characters' concrete actions: they look for something immediately perceptible (food, treasures, etc.) or intangible (freedom, knowledge), but on this level the search *always occurs in the physical world*. The character is wholly aware of the search he is involved in—though he is not always directing it[1];
2. Psychological search. The character searches for immaterial rewards (mainly knowledge or spiritual goals such as inner serenity and peace), and the search *always takes place on the mental level*. Again the character is wholly aware of the search he is involved in—though he is not always directing it;
3. Dream search. A few of Barlow's narratives tell of a search *conducted by the character within his dreams*. The search is thus not directed by the subject's will—it is *unconscious*—but more often than not it reveals the character's unconfessed drives and desires; thus it is not wholly other-directed or unmotivated.

In Barlow's fiction the "search" often becomes furtive or forbidden, a quest whose circumstances are ill-fated and which is destined to fail. Any parallel with Barlow's own life experiences is of course hazardous at this level, but certainly there is present in his fiction a reflection of the author's incapacity to pursue a fully satisfactory search for happiness and personal success. Therefore, Barlow's characters are very often caught involved in a search, but this "search"—in normal

---

1. See paragraph 4.2.2.2 "Deterministic compulsion and its impact on free will" in chapter 4 on Cosmicism, where the topic of the other-directedness of the actions of RHB's characters is addressed.

conditions an "active" performance on the subject's part, one that reveals his will, courage, and determination to conquer life—often turns "passive": the character turns from searcher into "sought," from a pursuing subject into a chased one. In other words, the character can be an *active* or *passive* protagonist of the search. Whether this condition reveals Barlow's pessimism toward the intrinsic worth of any search, toward its capacity to actually establish man's grasp and dominion on outside reality, is a challenging topic addressed by his fiction. All the narratives that answer positively to this question do nothing but reinforce the interpreter's awareness of Barlow's bleak vision of mankind's efforts, achievements, and ultimate significance: the possible intertwining between the theme of the "search" and the "cosmic" concerns of Barlow's fiction faced in chapter 4 is very evident here.

The protagonists of Barlow's early fantasy tales—such as those composing the cycle *Annals of the Jinns*—are often involved in dangerous if not lethal searches. Their departures from doomed towns, their travels across secular forests and fairy woods, their discoveries of precious manuscripts and explorations of immemorial tombs may be also interpreted as a homage to the conventions of a genre that actually *required* this type of adventures for its characters. Thus Barlow's fiction is replete with juvenile short narratives that address the theme of "search," exploration, and discovery under different technical and narrative viewpoints; however, the element stirring the characters to action and to search is always their "desire" for something, either abstract or concrete—knowledge, freedom (for one's self or for one's people), a prosperous place in which to live, or more material "booties" such as food, gold, and treasures. Most of the early tales follow this basic narrative scheme: for instance, the two collaborations with Lovecraft, "The Slaying of the Monster" and "The Hoard of the Wizard-Beast," but also "Eyes of the God" and a substantial number of the episodes of the *Jinns* cycle ("The Black Tower," "The Flagon of Beauty," "The Tomb of the God," "The Fall of the Three Cities," "The Theft of the Hsothian Manuscripts," "An Episode in the Jungle"). In most of these tales, the object of the search is never attained—and even when the search is successful, the achieved goal is finally revealed as totally different from what was expected, thus making the allegory on the vanity of human efforts immediately perceptible.

A few examples are revelatory of this key concept in Barlow's fiction. In "The Slaying of the Monster," the perilous expedition of the men of Laen ends in nothing—since no slaying actually occurs—but the men's foolishness is such that they boast for their mission (perhaps interpretable as a metaphor for life)[2] a success they never obtained. In "Eyes of the God," the thief's search for the diamond eyes of the idol, and his own defiance of the laws of nature, have a tragic end. The much-desired and sought-after "flagon" of beauty of the homonymous tale is finally revealed, after the craving princess has obtained it and drained its "very dregs" (*EG* 17), as the elixir of old age and ugliness ("Her hair swiftly grew leaded and grey, her lips assumed a ghastly pallor, and a score of tiny wrinkles appeared

---

2. For a discussion on the metaphoric "existential" value of this juvenile tale, see paragraph 4.2.2.1.1 of chapter 4 on Cosmicism: "The vanity of human existence: connotation."

on her smooth skin. She became an old hag, quite out of place in the splendour of the throne-room" [EG 17]). The search for the tomb of the god Krang ends tragically for the rash intruders who dare to defy the deity in its dwelling—and very similar fates befall other characters committed to a forbidden and highly perilous search: Morla, the youth who wished to steal the Hsothian manuscripts from the secret palace of Khalda, the ancient sorcerer-god fallen in a deceptive sleep; and Yalden, the young protagonist of "The Hoard of the Wizard-Beast," who dared to enter the cave where Anathas, the wizard-monster, dwelt, and try to steal its fabled hoard.

These early tales display a significant interest in the theme of the forbidden search on Barlow's part, as well as the commingling of the "nature" and the "forbidden search" themes; in fact, in Barlow's narrative world a search configures as "forbidden," in that it involves the defiance and the hazardous attempt at breaking the laws of nature—as it occurs in all the tales mentioned above. Precisely when man tries to overcome his natural limits (by trying to defeat old age and death, by defying gods and stirring their rage, etc.), he loses himself.

Among Barlow's mature, substantial tales structurally built around the theme of narrative "search," those deserving mention and discussion are "The Bright Valley," "The Summons," "A Dream," "A Memory," "Pursuit of the Moth," "The Root-Gatherers," and "Return by Sunset." These tales do not touch on the theme of (forbidden and furtive) search in a merely tangential way, like almost any narrative, since the principle of an ongoing quest is widely acknowledged as founding narrativity, no matter what is the transmitting medium;[3] on the contrary, these tales of the Barlow canon found their narrative structure on the theme of search (a title as "Pursuit of the Moth" is in itself quite revelatory in this regard), since their protagonists' actions configure as *actual quests*. These characters are *searching subjects*, in both acceptations of the expression we have seen, namely either as active or passive searchers: they are, in a sense, *defined* by the search they are involved in, they could not (fictionally) exist without the search they are pursuing, and reciprocally also the search—and the narrative itself—could not exist without these specific characters actively or passively performing it.

Search is of course a very polyvalent theme, which may assume different shapes, nuances, and even significances. Altogether, the Barlow tales I have chosen offer a comprehensive and multifaceted discussion on the theme of search, one that is exploited in many—if not all—of its possible narrative configurations.

"The Bright Valley" tells of Cern's quest for a new, happy place to live for himself and his people: "Because old tales spoke of a land amid those dark enormous cliffs rising to the east of the village, Cern set out to find it. There, in a fer-

---

3. Characters move, act, even think and dream because they need to achieve something: the stirring to physical or mental action is born from their desire to attain a goal, whatever its nature may be and whatever the means to achieve it. This is the principle founding, for instance, much of the formalist and structural studies on narrativity, including classical literary semiotics, from Propp's to Bremond's and Greimas's works.

tile valley region shielded from the beast, his people might find sanctuary" (*EG* 61). Cern symbolizes man's lifelong search for a happiness that, in this as in other of Barlow's tales, configures as a fabled, almost mythical prize impossible to achieve. Thus his search is both *actual* (on the surface level of the narrative: he is searching for a physical place) and metaphorical (Cern is looking for happiness, for a prize as a recompense for his and his people's fatigues). The "bright valley" is exactly the wished-for prize, a place from which men in old times came with abundant fruits and fowl, as from an imagined Golden Land: "But afterward, ancient tales narrated, glittering rocks had fallen upon the earth; and those rocks were of the fires burning over men in the night" (*EG* 61). This is Barlow's allegory of Man's Fall from the Garden of Eden, a paradise lost whose regaining this tale will show is impossible.

After the falling rocks had covered the valley, "men did not camp there, fearing things that come from the sky" (*EG* 62), although animals are still rumored to dwell in the valley: "It was this land Cern sought, in a later time, when the old tales were not much believed" (*EG* 62). His travel is a solitary one, among desolate landscapes and with only serpents as companions. Cern's search for the fabled land represents his attempt to find a place of happiness and break free from the old tales which rumored that the fertile valley no longer existed, namely that happiness was no longer possible. The way to happiness is a hard path, paved with all sorts of difficulties and uncertainties testing man's prowess: "This land was silent, as if all life had fled before some fast-approaching doom. There was no road to the goal Cern sought, nor anything to guide him save the dark, jagged and unknown cliffs, hung between sky and earth" (*EG* 62). Cern has to overcome countless precipices and cliffs in order to reach his goal, but this would be a sweet fatigue, were the reward real and satisfying as it is rumored: "The barrier was difficult to scale, for it seemed to fall endlessly into the sky; but on reaching the fragrant place beyond, he might rest and refresh himself with fruit; for all these things were told of in the outer land. Within the valley Cern might dwell through all the day on idle banks where there was no plain-grass, but only flowered loneliness" (*EG* 62). Happiness progressively configures as a rumored condition, a fabled one, not an actual plight of which Cern (i.e., man) may have a clear picture thanks to ready-to-hand testimonies.

In fact, nobody can really tell Cern whether the bright valley still exists and, if this is the case, what it looks like—only fragmentary information is available to him: this is the uncertain and vague condition in which nowadays man is placed when looking for happiness. Finally Cern's efforts seem rewarded, and he suddenly "could see all the valley from a bouldered eminence, and it was like a figured tapestry wrought with exquisite happenings. The trees were leafy ferns, and the meadows a bright scarf with tiny lakes as brooches [. . .] This place was a fortress holding fair gardens!" (*EG* 62). The description of the marvelous land much resembles that of a Garden of Eden: fowls with radiant plumage everywhere, insects, toads, and crickets celebrating the triumph of nature in a sound-filled sunset. Cern is enchanted when confronting the wondrous valley: he is induced to believe that his goal is achieved, peace and prosperity are at hand for him and his people. He feels content; on the metaphorical level, life seems to have rewarded the seeker's efforts.

But this would certainly not be consistent with Barlow's existential views: in fact, darkness slowly comes over, and an indecipherable, vague fear creeps into the searcher. The alien lights begin to gather and wax over the whole valley, "and the man felt the emotions of one who sees an enemy camped before homeward gates, knowing what the alien fires mean. That place which Cern had thought beautiful became to him accursed, for it was fouled with this evilness" (EG 63). Nothing could better summarize Barlow's view on mankind's efforts toward bliss than this last sentence: they are pointless and puerile attempts to enshroud an inane existence with an appearance of meaning, with the illusion that something worthy can be achieved. "The Bright Valley" reinforces Barlow's bleak view, since the tale metaphorically stages a search for happiness that ends with the death of the searcher, a tragic fate materially provoked and effected by the object of his search: it is just the valley—namely the supposed source of happiness—and thus the searcher's goal that finally kills him. Once happiness is allegedly found, it abruptly does an about-face and reveals its true countenance. Not only does Barlow imply here that the happiness men search for is false and will rebel against its searchers, but also that men are completely deceived in their search: they look for the wrong thing, since what they believe to be a source of happiness is revealed as the opposite. They ultimately do not really know what true happiness is, where it lies, where to search for it, and above all, whether it actually exists.

"The Summons" is another plain example of a narrative search conducted by an unnamed protagonist toward a nebulous goal he cannot even define.[4] Again the theme of the search is present here at a double level, that of the actual and physical pursuing of a goal (the joining with the "Master" summoning his lost son) and that of chasing a vague goal that can be again assimilated to man's happiness. In fact, the "summons" the protagonist hears inside his mind may be interpreted both literally and metaphorically, as the alluring—and deceiving—beckoning of a much sought-after happiness. Barlow's protagonist is an allegory of man, always intent on reaching a goal he cannot even define or be sure of. And why does man act like this? Because, this tale reveals, he hears some undefined and indeterminate *calls*–something like an instinctual appeal–from a deceiving source that asks him to waste his life in the search for a contentment that will never arrive. "The Summons" aptly describes the hardships of man's path toward happiness: the road is gloomy, "unlit," solitary, bringer of distress and even of insanity, and in all this man is left with constant, unanswerable existential questions: "Where was I now?" (EG 67). Man wavers in lightlessness and in cold, and all this just to pursue a meaningless search, while totally subject to an external will guiding his steps toward the deluding goal of a fabled and unattainable happiness.

---

4. For a discussion of the tale from the viewpoint of its "vagueness," see section 3.6 in chapter 3.

Consumed by the efforts of the search, man comes even to lose his senses: "For was I not partly dead, and living in the Voice? It needed me: therefore, what right had I to be, against its will?" (*EG* 67). Man is wholly dependent on this "will," which configures almost as an internal pang gnawing at his soul: he is devoured by his desire to achieve what he falsely believes to be happiness, and finally he gets lost and annihilated by his search. "The Summons" is replete with indications of the searcher's inability to control his own will ("I felt within a strange dream, for my whole sensation was that of partial hypnotism" [*EG* 67], "an automaton directed by another's will" [*EG* 68], "I was only a submissive, impotent consciousness before whatever fearful thing awaited" [*EG* 68], etc.): when blinded by his furious search for happiness (indeed a "nameless goal" [*EG* 68]), man is like a person other-directed by another's will, and does not hold control on his own faculties anymore. And when the protagonist finally sees the abomination that allegedly was summoning him, the metaphor becomes so clear that it sheds full light on Barlow's view on the "cacodaemon" stirring people to foolish action: "I knew of its purpose [. . .] it wished to make some sort of inconceivable lair in our world [. . .] Lord Christ! It could have done it, too. . . no question of its power, *of its mental mastery*. I saw that brave and sturdy graybeard waver, totter uncertainly in the strange strife. I knew he could not defy it longer" (*EG* 71; italics added).

It can be of course hypothesized that the "mental mastery" of which the foul creature is capable may stand for the manic diseases of contemporary man, such as frantic consumerism and the uncontrollable allure exerted on his mind by the myth of the possession of material objects. The thing battling for the "possession of our world" (*EG* 71) may stand also for a false idea of happiness, for the homologation of minds and brains, for the depersonalization induced by modern work, the mechanization of society: it is not particularly important to identify the exact metaphor the monster represents—Barlow would have had several different targets toward which to direct his criticism. What is much more important is that the monster is conquering the world, and that the old graybeard—namely, the increasingly diminishing wisdom of mankind—is likely to be unable to defeat it. Evil—whatever it is—is conquering, and there is not the necessary quantity of "graybeards" powerful enough to combat its ascent.

For the prototype of the literary "physical" search—which becomes, in turn, the metaphorical search for a forbidden knowledge—Barlow's fiction offers one tale in particular, "A Memory," that shows itself to be an exemplary case of a narrative structured upon the theme of the (frightful) quest, one revealing horrible truths. In a future world where huge groups of people cluster in isolated City-Towers lit by synthetic beams, the narrator and his companion Nalda plan to embark on a perilous enterprise: to explore the lower plans of the city, inhabited by the filthy *glortups* (the inferior race of monster-slaves reminiscent of Lovecraft's shoggoths) in order to discover the truth about their rumored rebellious activities. And in "A Memory," the protagonists' descent into the *glortup* world is a revelatory mission, exactly of the same type as those undertaken by several of Lovecraft's seekers (such as the protagonists of "The Temple," "The Rats in the Walls," "Pickman's Model," "The Shadow out of Time," etc.).

Already from the outset, the protagonists' search is configured as a dangerous and forbidden one: "We determined then, to go into the deepest levels of the City for that which we sought. This plan of Nalda's was audacious. My friend would have it that we make a descent into the lower floors where dwelt the glortups. *It was a wild, disturbing notion, and yet it fascinated me*" (EG 73; italics added). The notion of Nalda's plan is "wild" and "disturbing," since no one had attempted that exploration before, but it is at the same time "fascinating," since Barlow's characters, like Lovecraft's, are subject to the irresistible attraction exerted by a dangerous quest for a forbidden knowledge. The theme of search is so pervasive in this tale that it concerns not only the two protagonists, but also other characters incidentally mentioned by the narrator in his descriptions of the future world: in fact, when discussing the isolation of each of the future towns of men, the narrator claims that "two centuries had gone since any strove to penetrate that unpeopled wilderness around us and seek even the nearest of the other cities. Then at last a group of daring youths set out to find what things had happened in the intervening years" (EG 74).

And Barlow already sets the theme of the ill-fated quest—one that will be mirrored in the protagonists' quest—by stating the bad luck of this earlier expedition: "Many eyes were on them in the upper tower, but after they reached the wilderness and disappeared within, they were not seen again. From that time no one wished to venture out, and there were no human shapes upon the verdant sod about the City" (EG 75). Through the mention of this ill-fated past expedition, Barlow successfully conveys the impression that any physical search, in the future world of his narrative, is a potentially dangerous one: people prefer to live quietly indoors, not venturing outside the reassuring metal walls of the City-Tower, whose complete self-sufficiency discourages any attempt to question its solid traditions and lore. For instance, "there were things which led the people in our Tower to believe that life must persist elsewhere" (EG 75): curious lights as in a procession were once seen against the horizon, and another time similar lights were thought to have passed close beneath the Tower, "so that men might have unbarred the Door and gone without to see who bore them" (EG 75). But of course, in the secluded world of the inhabitants of the Tower, "this was felt to be unwise, for they did not know what might be encountered" (EG 75). With the passing of centuries, the account of those lights turned into rumor, and gradually into blurred legend: "those who had seen these things could not be sure that the night had not deluded them, for of such nocturnal happenings no traces could be glimpsed by those who looked afterward, by day, from the high windows" (EG 75). The light of knowledge is extinguished, both literally (no expeditions were made outside the Tower anymore) and metaphorically (no one is finally sure of what really happened: were there actual lights—and allegedly people bearing them—or was their sight just the result of a collective delusion?).

However, to break this veil of ignorance and uncertainty two daring characters were necessary, two like Nalda and the narrator, whose thirst for knowledge could not be easily quenched nor contented with the tales of old:

> All this had been in the long ago—half-forgotten through the centuries—till the recent years of my own life. When I was a child I had heard queer whispered tales of old, and had sought to learn more concerning the hinted marvels. *I searched through clasped tomes* and studied crumbling vermin-haunted records on dim shelves. Yet after all my delving I found nothing *to confirm or shed light on the legendry* which had grown furtively within the Tower, so concluded that this lore was wholly fable; spun in idleness by the aged. (EG 75; italics added)

Nalda's and the narrator's planned search is thus already revealed as a forbidden one, discouraged by the traditions and the habits of the inhabitants of the Tower—and therefore even more valuable because a very brave one, no matter what its results will be and what fate awaits the seekers. Also revelatory is the use of the adverb "furtively" in the above passage. The qualities the word connotes transfer from the object of the search ("the legendry" grown within the Tower) to the search itself: since Nalda and the narrator try to shed light on "furtive" legends, their search also becomes "furtive" and forbidden.

But above all, theirs is a meta-search, not only a physical one—the descent into the deepest levels of the Tower—but also, and perhaps mainly, an intellectual one—the search for a knowledge that might shed light upon the darkness of ignorance enwrapping the lazy habits and traditions of their fellows. That the search is first of all an epistemic one becomes particularly clear as the narrative develops—and features other, unsuspected beings pursuing their own searches: even the *glortups* are rumored to venture in hazardous "missions" on a quest for knowledge—and the narrator too wonders about both the reliability of these rumors and the goals of the creatures' machinations:

> At times there were rumours among our people that the thick metal wall lying between our city and that of our slaves had been pierced in a hidden place, and that *glortups went in secret throughout our city during the night*, traversing silent glowing halls when none observed, and *slinking about the levels on strange missions*. Other incredible tales said that the *glortups* went by dark into the outer world; that they had chipped the masonry from hidden doors, and at certain times *made curious trips into the obscure realms lying beyond*. I did not think that this was so, nor did I have that latent fear of the slaves which many admitted; yet I realized that *a deep and sinister intellect had subtly began to work and scheme*, an evil brain that sought our overthrow. (EG 76; italics added)

But then the narrator realizes that the rumors about the *glortups*' expeditions may have a solid ground: "There were, for example, certain futile gougings in the metal walls of the slave-world; and certain curious marks and gashes on our great machines, as if to mark them for *unknown purposes*, although glortups *were not permitted* near them" (EG 77; italics added). The narrator, besides manifesting his bafflement at the monsters' purposes (they are in fact "unknown"), and thus revealing that his and Nalda's current, forbidden expedition has a strong epistemic connotation (to shed light on the *glortups*' intentions), contextually states that the creatures' missions were forbidden too (they "were *not permitted* near them"). The narrator realizes that the "evil, slant-eyed monsters skulked about deserted halls" (EG 77) in secrecy and furtiveness, and that their clandestine trips cause corruption to "spread its evil roots from floor to silver floor, as if a gangrenous disease were eating through all the Tower" (EG 77). It is just the awareness of this foulness that pushes Nalda and the narrator to undertake their expedition, which thus assumes also the contours of a brave attempt to preserve their fellows from a likely doom—and to remedy to their ingrained ignorance.

The heroism of their quest is also reinforced by the unprecedented character of their mission: "Aware of all this evil, Nalda and I were yet resolved upon passing into the darkness of the glortup-world. No human foot had trod that path for many dusty years—to monster-folk alone were these nighted labyrinths familiar" (EG 77; italics added). The description of the protagonists' descent into the deepest levels of the Tower is certainly thrilling and exciting, one in which Barlow also shows his ability to depict actions—not only moods and atmospheres. There are several passages stressing the secret and forbidden nature of the search: "Although we had enquired *secretly and in many subtle ways*, we found no guide for our *forbidden mission*. Some of those among the younger group were willing and most eager to accompany us, but Nalda thought that two might gain the glortup world where more would only bring detection" (EG 77; italics added). And the narrator himself admits that such a mission would not have been permitted: "I am certain that we should not have been allowed to make this journey, had any known of it. But no one was aware that we had come, for we had slipped away in quiet" (EG 78). Since Barlow is here reasoning on a double level—the literal and the metaphorical—we can infer that he is also stating the forbidden nature of a "search for knowledge": after having attributed to the protagonists' mission a rescuing character, now, by defining the expedition as prohibited by the community, the author implicitly and pessimistically establishes—if we transfer Barlow's discourse to its more general and abstract level—the intrinsic wrongness of humanity's attitudes: it shrinks from the actions from which it would most benefit, because it would bring it knowledge and ultimate salvation. As is common in Barlow's fiction, this portrays the relationship with search as eminently dialectic: the human subjects turn from being seekers into being sought; their roles are reversed, and the active search is converted into a passive chase, thus establishing the extremely uncertain and problematic nature of the human quest for knowledge:

> As we passed through a thick door of metal we were confronted by a one-eyed slave. He stared insolently, and turned abruptly into an alcove. I did not realize what he intended until Nalda seized my arm and we began that precipitate flight into the nether world. We flung ourselves down the broad, unaccustomed steps; and all the time I listened strainingly above our heavy breath for the sound of pursuit. (EG 79)

However, it does not really matter, in terms of the accomplishment of the epistemic goals of the mission, whether its protagonists are active or passive chasers: what truly counts is the *revelatory nature* of their expedition, from whichever side the mission is conducted, because being passive and pursued does not impair the search being such. The characters are in fact still committed *to a search*, either as its active or passive protagonists. And in a highly significant passage, the narrator reveals that it does not really matter if the search is successful or not, and not even if its goals are clear to the seekers. The search is important in itself; it is an unalloyed good that must be pursued in any case—and the side on which one finds himself (pursuer or chased) ends up not being relevant. What is relevant is that the search should be "forbidden" in order to configure as a true search, and the quest for knowledge is eminently revealed as this type of search. In being involved in a (forbidden) search lies the true essence of life: "You ask me what we sought in these unpeopled cellars? All that I recall is our certainty at the time, the assuredness that we should not fail in that dim quest. Of its nature I can tell nothing but that it was forbidden to us" (*EG* 80). The reader is in fact not even told what the purpose of the search is, and what the two protagonists' final vision really consists of: these are, as it were, unimportant details. What really counts is that Barlow's characters are involved in a complex search—one involving at least two levels, physical and epistemic: Barlow thus configures the search as a metaphor for human life, and in its turn, in this thoughtful narrative human life is allegorized into the principle of "search for search's sake."

"A Dream" offers an example of an oneiric search. In an ominous night, the protagonist is looking for shelter along his path in the fields and woods. He is alone, wrapped by increasing darkness, and frantically looking for a place to spend the night ("My eyes were weary of the search" [*EG* 72]). He finally meets some old, empty stone-built houses by the road and prepares to spend the night within the walls of one of them. But a frightful experience awaits him, in the form of an alleged dream of which a marvelous gigantic creature is protagonist. But the oneiric nature of this experience is itself in question, since the narrator manifests his uncertainty as to its actual occurrence: "I do not know how long I lay, but in the night it seemed that I woke and looked across the road from a thick window bearing no glass" (*EG* 72). Thus the experience that follows is not necessarily an oneiric one, or better, in this mixture between waking and dreaming even the events preceding the narrator's finding of the house may be interpreted as imagined and not actually occurring. Therefore, the reader is induced to interpret the search also as an oneiric one.

"Pursuit of the Moth" constitutes, already from its title, an exemplary case of fictional search. The added value provided by this tale to Barlow's treatment of the theme of the search is manifold. First of all, the search very clearly configures as a chase and a pursuit—the protagonist of the narrative, Sigrill, does not simply *search* for something (his companion Amno, who has stolen Sigrill's bow); he actually *pursues* the companion, who wittingly states: "You will not easily regain your weapon [. . .] for you must overtake me first, and I am fleet as the moth!"

(*EG* 81). In the symbolic search described in this tale, the object of the chase gradually turns into an immaterial and fragile one, just like the wings of a moth. It is therefore possible to interpret the object of the chase in various ways: it is a youth, but it is also a moth, or something evanescent like a moth—so imperceptible as to be assimilable to an abstract principle, such as gratification and happiness in life—the goal each human being, Barlow included, strives to achieve with hardship and trouble.

A few elements of the narration support this last, symbolic interpretation, especially those describing the difficulties of the search and the uncertainty about its final success: "Yet ensnared amid those thorny hedges, Sigrill was half-angered at this slim companion who had so neatly sent him blundering" (*EG* 81). Here the ensnarement amid "thorny edges" may stand for the entanglements of human existence, the "slim companion" for existence itself that sent the seeker blundering, because it allured him to look for happiness and realization. The seeker is incapable of resisting the charm of the search for happiness: this seems his biggest fault in Barlow's view, that of being unable to give up any puerile attempt to be happy—because life "ensnares" him in the search, ultimately causing him to become trapped in its "thorny hedges." Thus man, clouded by life's tricks, tries hard to disentangle himself ("as he gingerly freed himself"), because life has made him see "glimpses of a wondrous meadow that lay beyond the wood, basking verdantly in the stillness of a summer day" (*EG* 81)—as the symbol of a possible happiness lying at hand, and a "surcease to all the enmity of life" (*EG* 81).

Barlow's tale may be interpreted as a symbolical narration of man's search for this happiness and oblivion. When the two youths set out for game, "the sun was obscured by no cloud, and the day was fortunate" (*EG* 81): in order to entice man to pursue the search for happiness, the "enmity of life" initially tempts him with apparently favorable circumstances and the promise of a possible final success. Had he not founded any expectation to succeed, man would not even have started the search. But though the background appears propitious to a successful hunt, Sigrill is "disturbed" (*EG* 81): he probably feels that something is wrong, that he is embarking upon a deceitful enterprise. It is not a clear perception, but an almost supernatural feeling that the object of the search is too evanescent and shifty, and will always delude any chase—just like a moth pursued by a hunter: "There was nothing to give alarm. It was only a strangeness in the atmosphere, a curious and portentous disquiet, and he found himself not wholly liking that merry taunt from Amno... *I am fleet as the moth*" (*EG* 81-82; Barlow's italics).

Sigrill's search is hampered by thousands difficulties in the woods, both material and psychological: not only do the bushes and plants (representing the hardships and setbacks of one's search for happiness) interfere with his path, but he is also induced to produce mental images of possible, eventual enemies ("Abruptly, he thought of glortups" [*EG* 82]), while around him only mockery and derisive amusement arise ("the breeze mocked him" [*EG* 82]). Man's parable in search for happiness is of course not unique: others before him tried and still try to achieve the chimerical goal. Thus, while difficulties increase and he is not so confident of the final success of his enterprise as he was at its beginning, the seeker looks for help and companions: he spots sets of "human tracks" (*EG* 82) and believes it may give him some comfort to join others committed to the very same task. This is of course already a sign of man's weakness: he shows his inability to cope with the difficulties of the search, but, by now unable to give it up, looks for comfort and companions. But there is "naught to light his way" (*EG* 82), and no real friends on whom to rely; ultimately, the seeker is a lonely one, and the presences of others along his path are limited to staring spectators, incapable in their turn of reaching the goal and thus, even more so, to help one another: "And Sigrill felt that hidden eyes were fixed upon his path, though a loneliness was everywhere" (*EG* 82).

In his attempt to follow the path traced by previous seekers, the man inevitably ends up committing the same mistakes on a "destined course" (*EG* 82): man is not free to decide what path to take, too many people (nearly everybody) have tried the same enterprise before, and even when the seeker supposes he is pursuing a new path, he finally discovers that it is a much-trodden one. In addition, what the seeker believes to be a goal (happiness, the object of his pursuit) is finally revealed to be a means: Sigrill (the searching man) is looking for Amno (realization, happiness), but the seeker discovers that Amno's tracks "almost seemed as if they fled (or did they follow? He was not certain)" (*EG* 82). Indeed, "Confusion reigned" (*EG* 82): the search for happiness is impossible, not only because the goal is elusive, but also because roles may get mixed up: the person who is believed to be the sought-after (Amno, happiness) ends up being revealed to be a seeker in himself (he follows others' tracks). What is more, the hardships of the search are so great that the seeker himself (Sigrill) finally understands that he is the goal, or better the victim, of the search conducted by existence at his expense: he realizes he was ensnared into an impossible enterprise, and from alleged seeker he turns into the chased, the victim of a force too strong to be fought, that of life's determinism (not by chance are Sigrill's and Amno's paths described as a "destined course").

Finally, when man (believes he) is approaching the long-desired goal (the "dim fortress" [*EG* 82] of the tale), the experience will be—euphemistically speaking—a total disappointment: Sigrill the seeker finds that between the pillars of the gate "showed hasty footsteps, and he knew that Amno had passed before him" (*EG* 82-83). Somehow comforted by the fact that others before him trod the same path toward happiness, man does not realize at first that the presence of others' tracks is not a guarantee of their success in the chase: they simply walked the same path; this does not mean that this is the right path. But man is so weak, imperfect, and lonely in his search that he feels comforted just by this sort of meager consolation. The more comforted he feels by the silent presence of other seekers, the more harrowing his desperation will be when he discovers that the search has been unsuccessful for everybody. What they did not realize was that all they were looking for was as fleet, fragile and ephemeral as moth's wings.

The objects Sigrill finds in the fortress are the symbolic embodiments of what man childishly most cherishes as a token of (earthly) happiness: material riches.

But these objects are described as old and ruined, by now deprived of their alluring power and their conventional value. Above all, they are shown to be what they really are: meaningless tokens of a fabled and not actual happiness—Barlow carefully employs significant adjectives in order to stress the decadence of these objects in man's eyes, once he finally finds them:

> in a little while [he] beheld all forms of glorious *ruined* things, unsurpassed in richness. There were gem-set chalices, and *broken* furniture of curious make, inlaid with golden leaves. A single triangular window-pane of lapis-lazuli set unnaturally high above the tiled floor gave light, whereby he saw the *rotten* rags of wondrous tapestries sagging from *mildewed* walls—weavings of some *perished* loom whose figured richness *stank in foul decay*. (EG 83; italics added)

Man has striven all his life to obtain what is finally revealed as a "ruined," "broken," and "rotten" happiness; and above all, he is so committed to the foolish search as to dedicate all his life to it, and finally to immolate himself for the cause. In fact, when he at last realizes how elusive and evanescent is the object of his search (a "silver moth [. . .] large as his two hands [. . .] glistening wonderfully in the light" [EG 83]), he not only understands the ultimate inanity of his search, but, since he has dedicated his entire life to it, the vanity of his existence too. And after the dismal realization of the inconsistency of one's life search, what is left is simply the termination of a futile and by now worthless existence: "the limpness of a youthful corpse on piles of ruined rag" (EG 83).

Another memorable story of furtive search is "The Root-Gatherers," a narrative otherwise very important, as we have seen in chapter 5, for its specific discourse on time and memory. This story further qualifies the theme of the "search" by adding to it a nostalgic reflection on the role played by seekers in the course of time, and the way in which we—modern seekers—could relate to our predecessors. The covertness of the enterprise in which the characters are involved is stated already at the outset: "Tubers grew well in the clay caverns beyond that place of ruins, and in order that no one else might find them, my mother always chose a time when she could go unobserved" (EG 83). Thus mother and son (or daughter) start for their secret hunt, "in the brief period before nightfall, while the tribe was engaged in cooking" (EG 83). Once more, in this tale Barlow shows his peculiar sensitivity toward the theme of furtive and forbidden search through the half-forgotten ruins of a corpse-city: it seems as if the seeking activity, such an important one as to be intrinsic to man's nature, were always to be performed through the arches of past glorious times of man's own civilization, of which the ruined cities—with their crumbling and rotting edifices and towers—are the literary tokens.

Barlow warns that none of man's activities, not even the most important ones he may perform—searches—can be pursued without paying homage to the passing of time and to the past, which the author chooses to represent as embodied in architectural vestiges that are always described with reference to their relation with (a) their size and (b) the passing of time. Thus the titular root-gatherers of this narrative need to pass amid two ruins in particular:

The first is that *Gargantuan* tower of *slim* embracing pillars, whose foundation—jagged on the sky—seemed to my childish eyes much like a crowd of vultures, and the other, a metal bridge farther on the way, seen only as one nears the city. The bridge is *not so great in height as the tower must have been* [. . .] Men have used it *forever* when they wished to go into the place of ruins, and wild things scurry over the perilous span in darkness. Sometimes apes and bears are tracked across the old bridge, and slain upon it, though *since my youth they are grown scarce.* (EG 84-85; italics added)

The root-gatherers cross the bridge, which once again is described through a personifying simile taking into account the effect of the passing of time: "Tottering in the gloom, the old bridge was like a man whose ribs are sharped by the years" (EG 85). The protagonist's crossing of the bridge is loaded with fear, but once more s/he is reassured by a temporal consideration: "As we traversed it, I looked up in apprehension, and saw that above us tons of insecure metal swayed like a broken spider web. I feared that it would fall, but it had been suspended in that fashion *before memory*, and yet the cables are intact and the girders whole" (EG 85; italics added).

Finally the two seekers enter the silent and desolate city, which is called Doom and thus reveals its symbolic character: no sound nor movement can be detected in this place, which was anciently throbbing with people and activity. It is now reduced to "the shards of a city that once knew merchants and toilers and the glittering rich—peopled now with memories and shadows and the whisper of the breeze. Silent now were the streets whose paving had sounded with the trample of multitudes; silent also the tumbled houses" (EG 85). Symbolically, these are the same ruins to which Sigrill and Amno arrive: they represent the final destination of any search—a desolate and crumbling place of silence, a collapsed set of edifices reached before by many others, the seekers of the past (this would explain the former blossoming of these now abandoned places). What the former seekers valued as possible objects of their search are now revealed as worthless things, despised by the latest seekers and even by animals: "I saw what once had been a shop—the front was crumbled, and a rotten beam lay half across the opening, but there was a litter of incredible wreckage within—goods that had been fashioned for purchasers dead a thousand years, despised even by the beast. Someone had come there and sorted out the useful, undamaged things, but like the rest, these lay in an unclaimed pile" (EG 86).

The passing of time, Barlow claims here, affects not only the course of civilization, but also the preferences and goals of people's existence. What yesterday had such value that people were induced to look for it and even to dedicate their entire lives to the search turns today into something despised by their descendants and even by beasts. This is how Barlow's cosmic and relativistic attitude influences the way his work deals with the theme of the "search." The narrator of "The Root-Gatherers" claims he would have spent some time exploring the city ruins: in a way, he would have liked to pay homage to the past seekers, to their wishes and values, for they embody a yesterday that the narrator would not forget. But there is no time to dwell on such remembrances: today's existence leads to an eternal pursuit of the new, up-to-date objectives and goals that it imposes—man has no possibility of choosing, if he wishes to survive:

> I would have liked to go into some of the buildings which ranged spectrally along the road. Now one, and then another took my fancy, but we had no time if we meant to end our mission by a safe hour. There was one pile of white marble standing alone in a little field, as if it had been a temple or a strong man's house. And I saw another; round, with many bordering pillars, like an immense spider; *whose purpose I could not understand*. I would have explored these had there been no hurry. But I knew that *we must get back before there was too much moonlight, and the beasts came out*. They are very terrible at such times. (EG 86; italics added)

Barlow is here wondering what attitude we, as modern seekers, should entertain toward our predecessors, the seekers of the far or recent past. And his answer sounds bitter and disillusioned: today's search, to which we are committed—the "root-gathering" metaphor of today's frenzied life—prevents us from stopping and paying homage to those who preceded us, who were committed to their own search. Even our attempt to *understand* the motives, inclinations, and characteristics of *their* search (represented by the narrator's wish to explore the ruins in order to comprehend their "purpose") is frustrated: not much time is left to ourselves for our own search, so many perils endanger its success (for instance, the terrible beasts coming out at night) that we cannot really afford the chance to show any distanced "empathy" to our ancestors. What we need and must do is just to mechanically and blindly pursue our own goal, since existence does not solicit pity or compassion: "And so we went on, and found many roots in the caverns beyond the city" (EG 86).

Finally, the narrative in which the theme of "search" finds its most complete and challenging expression is "Return by Sunset," the last of Barlow's published stories. It was "based upon a drawing by his erstwhile idol Clark Ashton Smith, who had abruptly broken off relations with him some years earlier" (Joshi and Anderson, "Introduction," EG 11). There is no certainty about the actual date of the story's composition—probably some time between August 1938 and June 1939 in Mexico City and San Francisco. The tale appeared, however, in the *Acolyte* for Summer 1943. "Return by Sunset" is an important narrative, since it provides Barlow's final word upon the theme of existential search that plays such a major role in his writing. Every trace of a rational, positive attitude toward human "search" disappears: Barlow comes to establish that not only the search is meaningless, since intrinsically doomed to fail (something he had already pointed out in other narratives), but that the "search" is always illusory and delusive: when man believes he is engaged in a search (for happiness, freedom, a better life, or even satisfaction to more material pulses), he is actually *not the pursuing subject of any active search*—he is instead the passive object of the search itself, he is possessed by his own search: he is, in a word, the searched. In fact, the search is always a double experience: the active one, where one believes one is a subject, inescapably hides a reverse side, where the very same individual is the passive actor of a pursuit: no "positive," optimistic conquering attempt on external reality—such as that represented by the act of pursuing a material or spiritual goal—is then acknowledged as possible by Barlow's work.

"Return by Sunset" is the story of Dal and his girlfriend Leyenda, fleeing in the wilderness from her brothers, who are hunting them because they are hostile to their love. Dal and Leyenda are looking for nothing material: their original search is probably the most spiritual of the searches, since they seek for freedom and a place that would allow their love to blossom—theirs is, in a sense, the prototype of the existential "search for life" that represents the ultimate trait founding all Barlow's characters' (and likely their creator's) searches. I have written of Dal's and Leyenda's "original" search, since this tale faces and dissects the theme of the search in several of its possible acceptations. At least the following superimposing typologies of "search" are present and discussed in this narrative:

1. Dal's and Leyenda's "original search" for freedom and a place to love each other. The main trait of this search is the character's "escape" because "being pursued";
2. the search for a reunion with an immemorial past, induced by the appearance of the bracelet;
3. the search induced by the dream Leyenda has—anticipated by Dal's own dream;
4. other, less important "side-searches" (performed by various agents), which nevertheless testify to the centrality of the theme of "search" in this narrative. The side-searches performed by Dal and Leyenda distract them from their main search—and represent a further obstacle to the achievement of the original goal.

We will see how the tale is built as to progressively diminish and finally annihilate the importance of the "original search," to the advantage of the dream-search and the one induced by Leyenda's finding of the bracelet. This strategy aims at showing how futile and voluble are man's purposes and will, and thus how meaningless and hollow the missions he embarks upon.

At the beginning of the tale, Dal and Leyenda find a place for a supposed overnight recovery in a ruined temple on the top of a hill. The edifice is crumbling and seems to have been devoted, in an indecipherable past, to the worship of an unknown god. The beginning of the narration thus states the theme of the "escape" of the two protagonists as the most important, "original" (passive) search, the "positive" one that spurs the characters to look for freedom and to flee the unseen hunters: "They had crossed many valleys and delved into many forests escaping from her brothers; [. . .] Up the long hill at evening they had seen the ruin, of a type familiar throughout the land, and hoping it might afford refuge, had climbed to it" (EG 136). The characters' attempt is thus originally set as an *optimistic* act of conquest toward life—they want to establish their will over external reality, because they *believe* existence allows them to do so: reality is there to be conquered, it can be bent to man's will. The narrative's unfolding will show how this viewpoint is far too idealistic—and it will do so by staging the gradual dissolution of the characters' purposes and their final undoing.

Dal and Leyenda decide to spend the night amid the ruins of the temple. The girl is satisfied with the decision: "'I am glad that we can stay. Surely they will not come here'" (EG 136). The presence of the hunting brothers, though never actual throughout the narrative, is constantly in the mind of the characters—as a ghost furtively haunting them and never showing itself. After a refreshing sleep, the next morning Dal immediately starts a side-search (the hunt for food), which metaphorically represents a distraction from the achievement of the main goal: here Barlow offers a picture of the countless possible deviations that man's path toward his goal may encounter—deviations that, even when apparently unimportant, may finally be revealed as decisive in overthrowing man's own plans and original search. In fact, while he is frightening three "fat birds out of their nest on the cone, [Dal] lost sight of Leyenda as he pursued them" (EG 136).[5]

What is more, once he finds her, in his eagerness to descend toward Leyenda, Dal steps on a loose stone and badly twists his ankle, possibly even breaking it. Perhaps this accident is placed by Barlow also as a punishment inflicted upon the character by a revenging Nature, which suffered an offense by him. In fact, in the description of Dal's killing of two of the three birds he was pursuing, Barlow employs particularly vivid images that reveal the narrator's disapproval of the character's action: "One [of the birds], regarding him with little fear, led him a few yards and then disappeared suddenly in the hole it had been making for; but he killed the other two, tangling them in a snarl of blossoming briar. *Their blood spattered and their floundering wings shook down a rain of petals.* Then *as he lifted out the sleek, nerveless bodies, necks adangle and gore on their patterned wings,* Leyenda gave a little cry" (EG 136-37; italics added). Simultaneously to Dal's slaying of the birds—and perhaps not casually so—Leyenda finds something else, a small object that will mark the end of the characters' optimistic search for freedom and, ultimately, start their doom: "It was caked with dirt, but gleaming still—a bracelet, almost a shackle, of hammered metal. Copper or gold, but gnawed with verdigris, she had found it half-under a stone lintel *while she was looking for blackberries*" (EG 137; italics added). Once more, Barlow introduces the unpredictability and the intrinsic chaos guiding man's actions and conditioning his purposes: while Leyenda is looking for something else, the blackberries (she is thus doing a "side-search," if compared to the original one), she finds still another thing, the metal bracelet. Sheer chance dominates and alters human purposes, Barlow seems to claim—and even man's destiny is dominated by chance, since, as we will see, the finding of the bracelet and the contextual bruising of Dal's ankle will provoke the characters' doom. Dal's accident may of course be interpreted also as a sign of the

---

5. In this narrative, the search for food is often presented as a possibly "deviating" task: RHB's pessimism is all the more poignant, if one thinks of the inevitability of such a "side-search" that distracts man from his main effort.

intrinsic danger of any search, and another element Barlow inserts in order to strengthen his position against the opportunity of any search—and ultimately of living itself.

In addition, if we consider this narrative as representing a microcosm of human experience on earth, and an exemplary story, we can infer that the tale gradually shows how man's original search, the one that brought the characters to this hill and this temple, will be unsuccessful: you find what you do not look for (the twisted ankle, the metal bracelet), you can never be sure of the outcome of your search—too many unpredictable side-accidents may deviate the course of your actions and searches, as well as alter your purposes and will. You may even be induced to forget or depreciate your former search and the will sustaining it, and come to regard new goals as more valuable and worthy—this is precisely what is going to happen to Leyenda, who will become so charmed by the bracelet as to forget about the escape, her lover, and her life itself.

After Dal's accident provoked by his side-search, the protagonists need to stop some days at the temple, waiting for the ankle's recovery. The peril of the brothers' arrival is always present: "She took the news with heavy face. They must stay here? Manifestly. Several days, probably. And any of those days a figure, or three figures, kilted in scarlet and bearing axes that had bitten the vertebrae of many a beast might come silently up the long hill. . . None the less, they must stay" (*EG* 137). Dal and Leyenda had "fled" from a village "carrying only an idol and their love" (*EG* 138), to escape from her brothers. It must be said that there is not even certainty about the actual existence of the allegedly evil pursuers, the brothers. They never really show up, and the reader is informed about them only through the dialogues—and above all the thoughts and remembrances—of the two protagonists. In the fictional world of "Return by Sunset," the brothers' actual presence is a debatable point, one that Barlow aptly keeps vague and unresolved: its introduction is functional to show that man's search is often threatened not only by concrete obstacles (such as the accident to Dal's ankle) but also by "invisible" or mental enemies (of which Leyenda's finding of the bracelet, which will finally disrupt all her initial "optimistic" purposes for the original search, is the most striking case). Man may not even enjoy the "pleasure" of a serene, optimistic (no matter how ultimately unsuccessful) search: not only do his attempts inescapably reveal as a failure, they must also be performed through countless difficulties of various sorts.

As the days pass and Dal is still hurt and resting in the temple, the newly found object, the bracelet with its curious design, starts uncannily to haunt the seeker, Leyenda:

> On the day following, after she had assisted Dal to his post, Leyenda spent an hour washing her bracelet in the mossy basin. After it had soaked for a while, the encrustations could be gouged from the design. Washing and polishing alternately with dried grass, she eventually was able to make out the picture. It had been hammered in with a small pointed instrument, and showed *a figure lying in chains before an altar*. She must have found a part of the ceremonial ornaments used by

the keepers of the temple; and though all the old gods were discredited, Leyenda was uneasy. [. . .] All the ruins, spiritual and temporal, of the old days were held suspect by the tribes, which sometimes wandered through them, *but she wanted to keep her bracelet. Without conscious volition,* Leyenda wedged her arm into it so tightly that she found it would not come off. She had not intended to do so—but there it was. (EG 138; italics added)

The bracelet starts to display evil magical powers: it gradually dominates Leyenda's will, turning her mind from the old, "sane" purpose of the search for freedom to a new, unhealthy one. Barlow adopts the effective metaphor of the evil supernatural bracelet to show the inanity and volubility of human purposes. Leyenda becomes progressively disturbed by the bracelet, to the point that she is truly obsessed with it: "The place had been a temple, and things had happened there; even the broken basin covered with gourds had once been slaughter's abode. She pulled at her bracelet" (EG 139). The responsibility for Leyenda's gradual change must be ascribed to the evil influence of the bracelet, which induces her to nurture odd thoughts and even to forget about Dal and the need to assist and nurse him: "As it [the moon] grew big Leyenda became restless and sometimes left Dal sleeping—he was feverish in the evenings, and slept heavily—while she went out in the air. One night while she was walking with strange thoughts and plucking at her bracelet, which still could not be loosed, she had a fright" (EG 139). That the bracelet is an (evil) magic object appears very plain from the impossibility of loosening it—and its supernatural status suits the metaphoric role Barlow assigns to it, that of a (perhaps consumeristic) object capable of distorting modern man's will from his good purposes.

Several aspects of the theme of the "search" are considered and discussed by this narrative. For instance, there is the very possibility that in the course of his existence a subject turns from being pursued into a pursuer, namely turns from passive to active searcher. This happens to Dal when he reflects upon his condition in the days of his forced stationing at the temple:

> Time passed, and Dal's ankle did not improve. For the first three days his eyes went back again and again to the region which they had left, and all its empty miles were a reassurance that their pursuers had faltered. He soon became so certain of this that he forgot to look eastward but turned instead to the west, where lay that fertile valley unreachably far beneath them, into which they hoped to descend. Increasingly at evening [. . .] he thought of what might lie in the future. (EG 138)

Dal thus projects himself toward the future, forgetting his condition of pursued and hoping to play the role of the pursuer—of freedom, of a better life, of happiness. Barlow depicts Dal as the character who never gives up in his search, wants to believe till the end in the possibility of success—while Leyenda represents the disillusioned character, the one who allows herself to be deviated in the search and to renounce her dreams ("Sometimes Leyenda was with him, but she did not care for the evening sky which so stirred his imagination" [EG 138]).

However, Barlow entrusts to Leyenda another significant role in his strategic attempt to belittle the "search" as a lifestyle: that of showing the negative effects the search may bear on the psyche of the searcher, the disturbances the search brings over the mental serenity and the peace of mind of the pursuer. This is Leyenda's reaction at her (alleged) spotting of a movement in the woods, a reaction revealing the unbalanced psychological status of the pursued:

> Looking down the long slope towards her eastern home, she thought she saw a moving shape in the moon-steeped grasses half a mile distant. Her marrow chilled. She tried to change her terror to disbelief, to tell herself it was a mist, but then she saw it was *looking* at her. Screams paralysed her throat, and she uttered no sound at all, but jut stood there. In another moment it moved or flickered out of sight, and she ran gasping to Dal. Her brothers! Her brothers! How long before they would climb the slope? (EG 139)

In the space of just a moment, Leyenda realizes her fears are wholly unjustified, and her childish anguish as just a(nother negative) side-effect of her being involved as a passive subject in what Barlow believes to be a nonsensical pursuit:

> Dal was asleep, lying with face averted on his cloak. The sight of him silenced her at the moment of calling out. What use to waken him? She would go back and watch until no doubt was left. The resolution surprised her—none the less she followed it out. She went some distance, and seated herself behind a bush with flickering leaves. From there every foot of the slope was visible—and naught seemed amiss. What had she seen? One of the night-flying birds? In a little she had convinced herself it was so. (EG 139)

When involved in a search—whether as active or as passive subject—as an additional negative effect man loses his psychological stability and peace of mind: his faculties are overwhelmed by his own search, and the obsession of a goal to be achieved poisons his existence. And according to Barlow, this is so true that perhaps the choice not to "act" at all on the world stage, not to "desire," not to "search"—in a word, perhaps not even to "live," or to choose to dwell in dreams—may appear an alluring alternative.

In fact, "Return by Sunset" is ultimately the story of the prevalence of dream, and in particular of the search pursued in dream, over reality. The centrality of this theme is already clear in a passing hint Barlow makes ("He looked at her through a dream and said nothing" [EG 139]), but it is especially in Leyenda's dream that the re-livening of the past splendor of the temple takes place: "She lay in the shelter they had contrived. [. . .] The tide of her thoughts wandered, and a dream took shape, of the sort which forms in a mind that has slipped its leash" (EG 139). Leyenda's dream reactivates the past of the place: in fast, seething vortices, stars congregate and illuminate the ruins. The unnaturally swift movements of the stars hide a reversal in time that leads Leyenda to discover the haunting past of the temple:

And in the moments she stared at them, the altar seemed to change. Cracks became fewer, the moss retreated, the runnels of the rain were filled, the patient erosion of the wind undone, and the work of the snowflake defeated. Unexplained joys swelled in her as she perceived this. [. . .] She ran with joy to the altar and stood upon it, expecting, desiring, demanding. . . and then the stars retreated into mist, and about her the idols, tumbled grotesquely among the stones of their ruined house, stared with oblique or inverted eyes at the sky which had roofed their former grandeur. (EG 139-40)

The dream is a result of the effect of the bracelet's action over Leyenda's mind and soul: the bracelet makes her dream and distance herself from her lover, so much so that she gradually forgets about Dal and their shared, original search. Leyenda becomes, as it were, corrupted by her new find, a symbol of the evil deviating influences that may distract man from his life search.

The symbolic involvement of the bracelet in this process is easily inferred by the following words, which are placed right after the description of Leyenda's dream and thus inextricably connected with it: "There was her bracelet for one thing; it seemed tighter than usual. She wondered why it would not come off. Repeated hammering with stones had done nothing aside from brushing her arm. It gripped her like an inexorable hand—the hand, she vaguely felt, of the past of this place of whose history nothing was known" (EG 140). Witnessing Leyenda's gradual detachment from Dal is a painful process for the reader (also because it entails the sadness involved in a love's end), but has the inevitability of a fateful event: "Leyenda awoke a long time later. She did not tell Dal of her experience, but occupied herself picking berries all morning and afternoon till the closer bushes were stripped. She was nearly out of sight along the cliff's edge before she had enough" (EG 140). As if this were not enough, Leyenda meets with a second, unexpected, and decisive find amid the brittle of the temple, which has the sole effect of making her forget the original search even more: "For the second time the ruin had cast up treasure. A gold knife, long as her arm from wrist to elbow and scrolled over with words in a language which had no other monument, lay exposed" (EG 140).

Dal's health continues to worsen: he is struck by a dangerous fever, which makes him rave and lose control over his own mental faculties:

> He shouted or muttered of animals which he had taken, appearing sometimes to think himself tracking a goat over frightful crags. Leyenda had his bow, Dal complained, and would not give it to him, so he could not kill the goat when there was a chance to do so. It stood and looked at him. Many times he said this, and finally she did bring the bow to him, but he only cast it aside with convulsive fingers; and she was puzzled and afraid. (EG 141)

The situation degenerates, and Dal's disease contributes to the gradual fading and final dissolution of the characters' plan for departure from the ruins. Leyenda's behavior reveals her desire to assist her lover ("She sought to arouse him, and then when he turned away, sat up vigilant and perplexed while his sighs grew heavier" [EG 141]), but she is by now increasingly becoming a victim of obscure forces, the conjoined power of the bracelet, the knife, and the whole ruined temple.

Leyenda is convinced that Dal is possessed and plagued by an evil goat-god, and she decides to propitiate it by building an altar and snaring it with offerings. She celebrates an odd ritual, offering red petals and her own blood to the imaginary goat-god, with the final intent to allure it to show up and be slain: the influence of the past, represented by the bracelet fasted to her arm, pushes her mind to conjecture the ritual, in which she even calls "herself goat" (EG 141). Of course the ritual fails, no goat-god appears, and Leyenda goes back to the sick man: "Inside, she stationed herself by the fire, and fed it, and fed her thoughts" (EG 141). Leyenda's mind gradually loses volition, odd thoughts creep into it, and she even starts forgetting the reasons that made them flee from the village with an eagerness she now hardly comprehends: "She remembered their flight. With what eagerness she had freed Dal, the death-destined prisoner of the brothers. How they had run in the first moments! *And to what goal?*" (EG 141; italics added).

Leyenda forgets about Dal and their original search, and her thoughts become increasingly odd and estranged. The evil influence of an outside force over her mind—mainly communicating to her through the dream channel—even leads her to sense a sort of malignancy in the location where they are staying:

> She sensed somehow, but in an inarticulate way, that these ruined sunsets, like blood running across the decks of wicked defeated ships as they nosed down to doom, were not isolated and meaningless phenomena, but that they had all along presaged the now apparent tragedy. [. . .] Their fate was linked to the ruins; their coming and abiding had been destined. With them the old day had awakened. *She had seen it in dream. She knew herself to be of it.* (EG 141; italics added)

Dream conditions reality, changing its course by modifying *man's attitudes and perceptions*. In fact, Leyenda has now completely and deeply changed: her former life in the village, even the escape with Dal and their originally hopeful search, now assume the dim contours of a parallel life in a forgotten dimension. She cannot comprehend the reasons for her former life anymore, and the original search— which seemed so important only a few days before—appears in its scorching meaninglessness.

Leyenda realizes the futility of their original search and finally decides to abandon it for a new, more rewarding one. Her mind formulates questions whose answers, once very clear, are now completely doubtful: "What did she expect so joyously?—She turned with a face but lately contorted, and gazed ambiguously at Dal. She touched his incredible flesh with hands no longer restless for aught save the dust a thousand years deep on the ruin which was each day lighted curiously by an expiring sun" (EG 142). Leyenda is yielding to the overwhelming power of the past and of its servant and emissary, dream. The past of the place overcomes each obstacle and is ready to conquer the souls of anybody entering the temple, not only of Leyenda—who has fallen its victim already since the finding of the bracelet—but of Dal too, who is in fact visited in his turn by a revelatory dream that features another parallel, oneiric quest: "Awakening slowly, Dal seemed to recall a quest through unending corridors; through forests of black-trunked pines in whose upper gloom the birds flitted unanimously; through boulder-peopled ravines" (EG 142). The description of Dal's dream-quest is revelatory and anticipatory of the course of external reality; he is in fact lonely in the quest, he was abandoned by Leyenda, and this forebodes the actual, inevitable separation awaiting the two lovers in reality:

> His journey amid these things had been more strenuous than that with Leyenda, and Leyenda did not share it. She had left him midway—though how or why he could not remember. Leyenda! He knew of course that it had been a dream occasioned by his fever, but still he grieved weakly. Then he turned and stared at the burnt sticks where the fire had been, and where she sat feeding it. The spot was cold, and she was gone indeed. (EG 142)

And thus Dal embarks upon another search, the final and decisive one: the search for Leyenda, his lost love: "In a small voice he called her, with expectant eyes on the sun-flooded door. [. . .] He waited. Was she gathering eggs? [. . .] *If she did not come he would look for her*" (EG 142; italics added). Dal is still convinced that a "positive" search is possible: contrary to Leyenda, who has lost all her former optimistic faith in the success of an actual search, he still nurtures it. Yet his final search reveals both the harsh, deluding truths Dal needs to face—that Leyenda has actually abandoned him, and that the wicked dreams they have been haunted by have now overcome and invaded reality ("The dream of his lone journey remained disquietingly present" [EG 142]).

Thus, a sick Dal starts his final search, made now almost impossible by physical and mental hardships: "So, the wait becoming unendurable, and his cries availing naught, he stood up and found his strength was gone. Such weakness was incredible to him—his very hand, clutching the door-edge, was flaccid and powerless. Now he was thoroughly frightened, but he managed to stagger out calling her name" (EG 143). Hints of the astonishing intrusion of past and dream upon reality are revealed in Dal's eyes, during his increasingly painful search: "Outdoors, he sensed a change in his surroundings, as if someone had assiduously *tidied* the ruin, set one block upon another, pulled away the creepers. His eye fell upon a brick pillar, and judged it to be higher than before [. . .] Then, calling up a strength he did not have, propelling himself clumsily with a stick under his armpit, Dal searched. He searched like the wind searching the night" (EG 143). The final revelation comes as a shocking blow in Dal's and the reader's eyes, establishing—through the single image of Leyenda's tragic demise—both the ultimate failure of the characters' original search and the predominance of another dimension, the overflowing past, over reality: "Then by the gourd-vine he came upon a clue, and his heart was marble. It was the ruinous, thousand-year old basin which had once served to hold the victims of the god. It had been righted, cleansed for moss, mended. *And on its shallow curve reposed Leyenda's bracelet.* Her hateful shackle of a bracelet. A while since it had clasped her soft arm. It would do so no more—nor would Dal. *For the bauble was smeared with blood*" (EG 143; italics added). As the vestige of a past that has won the struggle with the present (and future) for dominion, only the bracelet remains: it has devoured Leyenda, sucked her blood and soul out into its vortex of malignancy.

Dal's final reaction toward the bracelet—which he deems responsible for the tragedy in front of his eyes—reveals the typical impulsive attitude of a man who does not want to believe that his most cherished plans have crumbled to dust, and with them the love of his life, and his life itself: "He seized it [the bracelet], and drawing back his weak arm, threw it goldenly into space. Instantly he regretted that he had done so. A dark circle remained on the stone—blood clotted into the porous surface. He watched a while, then shaking with bewilderment—though in his heart he knew—lifted his eyes to the gold and gore of the sunset" (EG 143). Only melancholy is left to the seeker: he has lost everything, his companions, his dreams, his hopes as the outcome of the search. The flavor life leaves in the seeker's mouth is only melancholic bitterness, a sense of frustrated expectancy for unfulfilled promises that once filled the seeker's heart and mind with an unrestrained optimism that, if on the one hand was certainly childish, on the other was his only hold against the "enmity of life." And in the end, when everything is irremediably broken and lost, only regret and a melancholic acceptance of an ideal rejoining with the cycles of Mother Nature are left, as the concluding words of "Return by Sunset" plainly state: "So he stood there as the birds, clamouring to the nest never built for them, came in from wherever they had been" (EG 143). After all, what was Dal's and Leyenda's search, if not that for a nest "never built for them," a place to live in harmony and enjoy the bliss of a sunlit love? After all, is this not the search of any conscious human being, and was it not of Robert Barlow in particular? In the end, he was sure that people share much with birds.

9. POETRY

9.1 Barlow's poetry: an introduction

Though Robert Barlow's poetic production, stylistically, can be roughly split into two phases, a surprising thematic continuity can be detected between them, which connects one to the other and to the early fiction too. Stylistically, Barlow's poetry "falls into two main types" (Joshi and Anderson, "Introduction," *EG* 11), one more classical and formal (dating approximately to the period spring 1936– fall 1939), and a second, "Activist" phase, modernistic and experimental. Many poems of Barlow's early, traditional phase appeared in various amateur publications, such as *Science-Fantasy Correspondent*, *Polaris*, *Weird Tales*, and Barlow's own *Leaves*. The turning point in Barlow's poetic career, destined to orient him toward the modern imagism of the Activists, occurred in 1939. Since the spring of that year, Barlow had resided in San Francisco, and in the autumn he came into contact with the Activist poetic group, led by Lawrence Hart (1901-1996) in the San Francisco Bay area. Hart had founded the Activist group in 1936, inaugurating a lively circle that included Rosalie Moore, Jeanne McGahey (Hart's wife), and Robert Horan among its members. One of the main tenets of Activist poetics was the "rejection of traditional poetic modes of expression" (Faig, *UL* 210). Activists stressed the intrinsic artistic powers of *subjective* verbal expression: in the essays he wrote for "Ideas of Order in Experimental Poetry" in the May 1951 issue of *Poetry: A Magazine of Verse*, Hart wrote that "emotion can be evinced more strongly by the subjective connotative meanings of words than by their objective meanings" (paraphrased in Faig, *UL* 210). The Activists endorsed a vision of poetry that strove for a polishing of verbal expression, privileging the connotative meaning of words, with the ambitious goal of a full-fledged, unrestrained communication of emotions. In his contribution for the 1951 issue of *Poetry*, Hart synthesized the Activist approach as follows:

> The words of the poem are not the poetry, the poem being a series of emotions produced by detail in the mind of the reader, the words being the score, and no more poetry than the musical score is music. [. . .] The smallest unit of meaning was conceived to be, not the word, but the phrase, the words not having any more true poetic meaning in themselves than the letters of a word have logical meaning. [. . .] The effort required to raise the detail above certain levels was very great until methods were worked out for reaching accuracy and intensity through automatic writing, random usages and the like. (Quoted in Joshi and Anderson, "Introduction," *EG* 11-12)

In order to convey a strong emotional impact, a poem had to display a connection of connotative meanings freely associated one to the other, employing images stemming in particular from the sense of sight. As we will see, Barlow's poetry often resorts to free, hazardous associations of visual images, building connections exclusively for formal, more often than not euphonic, reasons, rather than by means of objective, denotative meanings. Since emotion pertains to the sphere of the irrational, Hart's "automatic writing" seems a fitting technique to convey it: automatic writing is capable of voicing free, random mental associations, often resulting in long lists of objects, apparently unconnected to one another. Faithful to Hart's credo, the Activists privileged the role of the phrase over that of the words. Faig reports of Hart speaking "of many face-to-face sessions at which the poets of his group worked out acceptable phrases, using examples which Hart had dug out of traditional poetry" (*UL* 210). In general, one can assume that Activist poetry showed its modernism and experimentalism in the peculiar choice of visual images taken together in free and often hazardous *associations* (built on euphony and assonances rather than on meaning and content) and in recourse to narrative long-paced sections, characterized by the introduction of direct discourse and of historical figures.

Through the 1940s and the early 1950s the Activist movement gained remarkable consideration: poems by McGahey were included in *Five Young American Poets* (New Directions, 1941), and Rosalie Moore's collection *Grasshopper's Man* (1949) was published in the Yale Series of Younger Poets, with an introduction by W. H. Auden.

The acquaintance with the Activist movement represented "a very new experience" for young Barlow (Faig, *UL* 210), at the time still imbued with Lovecraftian principles of classicist poetry.[1] Since Hart had claimed that the Activists "came to

---

1. When HPL was living, RHB chiefly composed only sonnets. In fact, HPL never failed to assist his pupil also in matters of poetic composition, including RHB's early efforts, on whose classicism HPL felt competent enough to advise his pupil. For example, this is how, in a late letter of 11 December 1936, while commenting upon an untitled sonnet by RHB (now available in *EG* 150), HPL provided him with technical suggestions: "Glad to see your new sonnet, which I like extremely. Pictorial artist or not, you certainly are a poet when you set out to be! Send it to Hymie [Bradofsky] by all means, along with 'Cousin Alta'. The only suggestions I'd tend to make are purely technical ones. In line 3 you have a redundant foot, which might be best corrected by changing *imperishable* to *deathless*. At the same time, to avoid any jarring tendency to confuse the *sun* idea with the *son* idea, I think I'd change the opening word *Her* to *The*. The other change is down in the sestette— the third line of which uses the word *un-re'-al* in a rhyme as if it were pronounced *un-reel'*. This will never do. I can't tell just the best way to get rid of the false rhyme without sacrificing the very fine image (pale & chill, like image-catching steel) in the preceding line, but here's a tentative suggestion—an alternative third line:

bright surfaces

No truth this world's | swift-changing clocks | conceal –" (*FF* 382). Needless to say, RHB adopted all HPL's suggestions. Something very similar happened for the sonnet titled "N.Y." (*EG* 150): in a letter of 30 November 1936, HPL criticized the imprecision of the metre in ll. 1 and 13, suggesting that RHB introduce a couple of adjustments that the lat-

consider poetry as the adventure of the writer into the hidden springs of his own action and emotion—his work in poetry being parallel in some ways to that done through psychology" (quoted in Joshi and Anderson, "Introduction," *EG* 12), and since the accent placed on automatic writing and the free expression of emotions was always a leitmotiv of the Activist poetics, Barlow was in a sense forced to take into consideration "facts about his own life and personality which had never . . . before come to the surface" (Faig, *UL* 210), among which we are very tempted to include his homosexuality. Therefore, it is probably useful to suggest a biographical, psychological reading of several of his poems, where, for instance, "knowledge of Barlow's homosexuality not only suggests certain interpretations but also helps to explain Barlow's evasion of gender in his love poems, and his use of cryptic initials rather than full names" (Joshi and Anderson, "Introduction," *EG* 12).

Barlow's connection with the Activist movement lasted until he took permanent residence in Mexico toward the end of 1943, and the affection and the gratitude with which the Activists remembered their former associate were enduring.[2]

Of course, "the transition from solitary bibliophile-fantaisiste to poet was not an easy one for Barlow" (Faig, *UL* 215), though it was necessary in order to allow him to become fully aware of some unconfessed features of his own personality, and perhaps of his own homosexuality. His career as an Activist poet was marked by important achievements, by no means inferior to those of his associates: in 1942, while still an undergraduate in Berkeley, he was awarded both the Emily Chamberlain Cook Prize and the Ina Coolbrith Memorial Prize. Overall, around sixty of Barlow's poems saw publication, in distinguished journals like *Poetry, Saturday Review, Quarterly Review of Literature, Berkeley Journal, Circle,* and *New Rejections*. During his own life, thanks to the help of friend and colleague George T. Smisor, Barlow printed a small booklet of ten poems, titled *Poems for a Competition* (The Fugitive Press, Sacramento, 1942), whereby the titular "competition" refers to that which granted him the Cook award. Moreover, in 1947, from his home in Azcapotzalco Barlow supervised the publication of *View from a Hill*, a collection of some of his finest poems. It was George T. Smisor who, after his friend's death, assembled and typed other collections of Barlow's poetry: *A Stone for Sisiphus* (a volume of poems dating to 1949), *Poems 1936–1939,* and *Unfinished Poems.*[3]

---

ter promptly included (see *FF* 371–72). The same goes for the last line of another untitled Barlovian sonnet for which HPL (see the letter of 3 January 1937; *FF* 393) corrected the last line (which originally had an excess syllable), suggesting to RHB the expression "a hard one to defy," which in fact appears in the published version (see *EG* 151).

2. In 1962, Lawrence Hart privately published a homage to RHB titled *Accent on Barlow: A Commemorative Anthology*, containing, among others, an appraisal in which Rosalie Moore introduced the highly revelatory definition of RHB as an "essentialist." The anthology was made up mainly of RHB's poems (forty in all); the remaining were by various members of the Activist group.

3. The latter has been renamed *Miscellaneous Poems* in *Eyes of the God*, the first comprehensive collection of RHB's fiction and poetry published in 2002 by Hippocampus Press.

Though Barlow will probably be remembered less for his poetry than for his fiction and his scholarly work, an overview and analysis of the achievements of his poems will show, as I will strive to demonstrate, the worth and talent of a truly remarkable versifier.

9.2 The five nuclei of Barlow's poetry

The analysis of some of the features of Barlow's poetry will connect them with his fiction, where possible and useful, also in order to show the cohesiveness of his overall literary output.

My study isolates five conceptual nuclei, each labeled through a representative term containing, in essence, the variety and complexity of discourse developed by Barlow's poetry in that specific nucleus. They are the following:

1. Sense
2. Memory
3. Dream
4. Essence
5. Nature

The reasons for isolating these specific nuclei require a methodological explanation, both from a quantitative and a qualitative viewpoint. Quantitatively, the choice of the five nuclei is justified by the fact that, though far from being exhaustive, their analysis provides a comprehensive overview of an articulated, though not extensive, poetic production. From the qualitative viewpoint, these nuclei refer to concepts general enough to cover the main features of Barlow's poetry, encompassing its basic thematic concerns. Of course, these nuclei are not mutually exclusive: their borders are blurred and are not meant to separate non-communicating thematic vessels. As will soon become clear, the nuclei overlap one another repeatedly, as is normal and predictable when dealing with a work of the intellect stemming from a unique and complex personality.

A feature common to all these nuclei, as we will see, resides in their being marked by *dialectical oppositions* (respectively: light-darkness, time-memory, sleep-wake, internal-external, nature-culture), telling of the controversial nature of Barlow's personality. I will in fact try to demonstrate, in accordance with the assumption that a biographical-psychological reading of his poetry is possible, that these oppositions signal Barlow's torment and restlessness, his "existential" perspective as expressed on the surface of the textual level. Whether, in his poetry and overall work, Barlow actually succeeded in transmitting a fully accomplished emotion, springing from his own personal experience but attaining universal value, is a challenging question that I will try to answer in the course of the analysis, though conscious that it mostly pertains to a matter of personal aesthetic judgment.

9.2.1 "Sense": Light and Darkness

Robert Barlow left a declarative statement on the methods and aims of his poetry. It originally appeared in the Berkeley magazine *Circle* (1945), in the section titled "Ideas of Order in Experimental Poetry," to which Hart, Moore, and others contributed also. This short essay[4] contains revelatory comments on the technique Barlow adopted composing poetry, as well as less "technical" remarks concerning the *spirit* informing the poetic efforts of the Activist group. At glance, a clear-cut opposition between the two masters of Barlow the poet catches one's attention: "Lovecraft taught me to say exactly what I had in mind; Hart underlined that expression was strongest when put in retina and esophagus-twisting words" ("Statement about Poetry" [1944], *EG* 179). For Barlow, Lovecraft was the master of rational, eighteenth-century classical verse: he taught Barlow how to build formally precise verses and rhymes and emphasized a predilection for lexical archaisms. On the other hand, Hart taught Barlow that poetry is expression of a *sensory* perception, inevitably resulting in an emotion felt by the poet-experiencer.[5]

One word is revelatory in the quoted passage, *retina*. Barlow described his poetry as having primarily a visual, and secondarily an auditory, origin. Inspiration for poetic composition is connected "with something I see (perhaps only in a dream or imagining), or with some pleasing clang of words" (*EG* 178). As we will see, Barlow's poetry displays a pronounced *sensory* character: composition stems from a sensory spur, above all a visual one, "some striking combination of colours or textures" (*EG* 178), which the poet feels the urge to "paint in words," since he holds "a painter's eye" (*EG* 178). In fact, "with me sensory stimuli are first and foremost *visual* and I rarely use a taste or touch stimulus as departure point for a poem" (*EG* 179; italics added). Sights exert on Barlow a creative stimulus, inducing him to devise a narrative plot from them. The process of plot-construction and the narrative element never lose connection with the visual impression generating them: "I do insist on a plot. If the bark of the tree has caught my eye, my first thought will be what color and pattern it has, but the next one will be perhaps 'it has been there three hundred years', and possibly, 'the man who always meant to cut it down died last summer'" (*EG* 179). From the visual impression, Barlow "would think about the painting he wanted to paint until some small meaning, some possible experience connected with the painting, came to mind; whereupon he would try to relate the experience to the picture through the connotative phrases of Hart's poetry" (Faig, *UL* 211). Visual quality and narrativity are therefore strictly dependent, since the latter entails a meaning that stems from

---

4. It actually consists of an excerpt from a letter to Rosalie Moore dating to 15 May 1944.
5. An emotion that, in consonance with the Activist poetics, is described as self-explaining: in fact, writing about poetry "'explains' poetry only to those who already understand it" ("Statement about Poetry," *EG* 178). Since, according to Hart, poetry springs from (and tends toward) emotion, it is hardly explainable by rational means like those of verbal human language.

the mental elaboration of a visual impression: the inspirational power of sight is so strong to Barlow that "it is rarely necessary to invent a meaning for a sight or experience which has excited me sufficiently to cause me to want to write a poem. [. . .] I am conscious of ritual and symbolic meanings [. . .] in most sights and activities" (EG 179).

And indeed visual images recur very often in Barlow's poetry, since absolute privilege is given to sight as the inspiring and revelatory sense. However, before analyzing the visual effects of his verses, I would like to describe a preliminary phenomenon of his poetry: *sensory blending*, which produces synaesthesia:

> There were doors cluttered with ribs and cheek bones,
> With the visible stench carding over them.
> ["New Directions," ll. 8-9 (EG 181)]

The association of *visible* and *stench* connects the senses of sight and smell. However, far from weakening the visual impression, this synaesthesia reveals the unfailing power that sight exerts on Barlow's poetic imagination: even when dealing with a stench, the poet cannot help relating it to sight. And in the same poem, the very same stench is also described as a "bitter persistent thread through the nostrils" (l. 15), whereby, besides the alliteration *thread-through*, telling, as we will see, of a classical imprint on Barlow's poetry that never receded (even during the most experimental years of his Activist militancy), a supposedly olfactory impression is transmuted into the visual image of a thread in the nostrils.

A further example of synaesthesia occurs in the seventh poem of *View from a Hill*, the one dedicated to the psychologist who most helped Barlow in orienting him toward the successful scholarly career. In the section entitled "For Barbara Mayer," Barlow again connects the senses of sight and smell in the powerful and somewhat disturbing image of a "dark scent" ("On Leaving Some Friends at an Early Hour," l. 5 [EG 190]). A perhaps even more striking example of synaesthesia occurs in an image contained in the poem "Recantation" (one of the densest in *View from a Hill*) and juxtaposing even three sensory perceptions: on line 7 one reads "A wine-warm hand," where, together with the alliteration, we can notice that the image refers simultaneously to sight and taste ("wine") and touch ("warm").

One of the most remarkable *formal* aspects of Barlow's poetry consists in its staging a *spectacle of the senses*, and this is probably a carryover from the content plane, where Barlow experienced life and love (as we will see in the following paragraph) as *sensual* torments. This pouring off from the content to the formal plane represents an example of the faithfulness with which Barlow observed the Activist principle of poetry as a means of rendering personal emotions through the usage of *ad hoc* verbal expressions. In this spectacle of senses in which sight plays a major role and smell a secondary one, hearing is also involved, but almost exclusively on the formal level. In fact, whereas hearing is referred to on the content level, it is usually in order to underline its unreliability and fallacy:

> My heart—too deaf to comprehend the strain
> Of Eros's song—succumbed to brief desire
> ["Cycle from a Dead Year," IV, ll. 9-10 (EG 153)]

On the content level, sound and rumors are almost always far away, only dimly perceptible: "Near the hot Nile were endangered / Far from the rumour of sea" ("To Bacchus," II, ll. 3-4 [EG 160]).

On the other hand, hearing and sound figure much more on the stylistic level. In fact, not even during his second, Activist phase of his poetic production did Barlow fail to resort to classical (and Lovecraft-inspired) figures of sound, in particular *alliterations, assonances, consonances,* and *anaphoras,* for specific stylistic and euphonic purposes. There are countless examples of these classical stylistic devices: I will in particular concentrate on alliterations. However, a remarkable case of "prolonged" anaphora deserves mention, in "To One Rescued," the fifth poem of "For D.," the opening section of *View from a Hill:*

> Though the desert he dragged you through were fifty miles greater
> Though the day were fifty hours longer [. . .] (EG 181)

In this sample, not only the initial "Though" is repeated in the following line, but the anaphora prolongs in the sound effect of "the desert/the day" and in the parallel between "were fifty . . . greater / were fifty . . . longer."

Concerning alliterations, the last two lines of an untitled poem of Barlow's "first phase" read as follows:

> The autumn's languid end, the ending day
> Are weary witnesses of vast decay. (EG 150)

In just two lines, we find the repetition "end/ending," the alliteration "weary witnesses," and the general, euphonic insistence on the *d* sound ("end," "ending," "the," "decay").

Though Barlow's Activist phase was characterized by a keen adhesion to the principles of the free-flowing of visual images, the poet will retain his old, classical taste for figures of sound throughout all his poetic production. For instance, in the poem "The Conquered," part of the section "Fresco of Priests and Beans" in *View from a Hill,* we find the line "But how hefted the haft of dream-clubs," alliterating the whole compound of sounds "haft/heft." In the same work, Barlow brings the sound effect to an extreme, verging toward the pun: the very titles of two poems of the "For Rosalie" section read "blotted a beetle" and "Table Set for Sea-Slime," and in the latter the first line reads "Clams claw their pots shut" (EG 184-85). And the cryptic poem "We Kept on Reading 'Tuesday'" contains the splendid alliterations of the *w* sound, in the fourth line "Ants like thoughts working within a wound" (EG 190).

During the Activist phase, attention for sound effect is perhaps even higher: splendid rhetorically constructed images as "There are alleys flowing and flowering in serpents / Between the creviced brick brains" ("The City," ll. 3-4 [EG

194]) could probably never have found expression had Barlow's poetry remained in a fully classical, Lovecraftian, anti-modernist phase.

Not only are figures of sounds detectable all over Barlow's entire production, but also a few rhetorical figures such as the chiasmus ("<u>Sun</u> **green** and **grass** <u>gold</u>"[6]) and the *anadiplosis* ("I said it first when it was only Spain. / Only Spain, where we hoped . . ."[7]).

It is at the rhetorical level that Lovecraft's influence on Barlow's poetry is more perceptible, though, as we will see in the following paragraphs, there are also many borrowings and remodelings from a thematic perspective. There is perhaps no better way to provide a concise picture of Lovecraft's mastery over Barlow's poetic education than to resort to the account Barlow himself made in 1944 of some significant anecdotes regarding his first extensive encounter with Lovecraft in Florida in the spring of ten years before:

> Life was all literary then; that is, all I cared to accept as life. We discussed the *Fantasy Fan* and Lord Dunsany, wrote letters and verses and stories, and did not go to bed until I was driven there by my parents. Although he did not care for games, once we wrote verses to fit previous rhyme-schemes; one of his called 'The White Elephant'[8] is in my stored papers still, for I saved even his note-pad jottings. Again, as we idled in the rowboat, he caught up my challenge to find rhymes for 'pretzel' and 'Schenectady', and found them in the German name of Attila and the ensuing doggerel. (WG 358–59)

The portrait of a youth oriented toward classical poetry emerges, especially from the enthusiasm with which Barlow proposed the mentioned rhetorical game to the reluctant master.

So pervasive was Lovecraft's formal authority over Barlow's poetry (perhaps because it affected a very young mind, open—and willing—to learn) that it remained unshaken even during Barlow's Activist phase. Lovecraft would "clearly not have approved of Barlow's free verse"[9] and his penchant toward modernism;

---

6. Quite interesting is this example, in which a sound-chiasmus is obtained through the alliteration of the *gr* sound and the association of "Sun" with "gold," based on the common color quality of the two terms ("Mozart's G. Minor," l. 1, *EG* 196).

7. "Untitled," ll. 3–4, *EG* 197. The Online Encyclopaedia Britannica defines anadiplosis as a form of reduplication "in which the last word or phrase of one clause, sentence, or line is repeated at the beginning of the next," with a strong emphatic effect.

8. This lyric, dated 23 May 1934, reads as follows: "Dim in the past from primal chaos rose / That form with mottled cloak and scaly hose / Who bade the lesser ghouls, to earn their bread / Perform dread rites, and echo what he said. / They bred the leprous trees and poison flower / And pressed dim aeons into one black hour. / Wherefore we pray, as pious pagans must, / To the white beast he shaped from fungous dust" (see Faig, *UL* 199, who notes that, on the very same day, RHB and HPL composed another poem, called "Beyond Zimbabwe").

9. Joshi, "Introduction," in *OLL* 8. RHB himself stated that HPL "seemed to think fair enough" of Derleth's poetry, though HPL hastened to add that "Of course one can't tell

however, the retaining of sound figures, lexical archaisms, and rhyming effects never fail to connect Barlow's poetry with that of his master. For instance, in "Isolde," the second poem of the Activist phase, Barlow inserts two verses that in themselves, with their archaic spelling and the use of anaphora, represent a concentrate of classical rhetoric:

> And thou wert the goodliest knight that ever bare arms,
> And thou wert—
> ["Isolde," ll. 9-10 (EG 174)]

Also, the taste for lexical archaisms in Barlow's work (above all in fiction, but a few poetic examples are at hand) probably comes down to Barlow from Lovecraft's "antiquarian" attitudes. It is again in the memorial of his first extensive encounter with Lovecraft in 1934 that Barlow recalls the following, revelatory anecdote: "At other times he could be prevailed upon to read his own stories aloud, always with sinister tones and silences in the proper spots. Especially he liked to read with an eighteenth-century pronunciation, *sarvant* for 'servant' and *mi* for 'my'" (WG 359).

In particular, the poems commemorative of the master are telling in the con-

---

the value of this loosely-constructed verse" ("Memories of Lovecraft," in OLL 17). Especially in his early essays appeared in the *Conservative*, HPL associated the diffusion of free verse to what he perceived to be the contemporary decline in poetical aesthetics. HPL criticized free verse *passim* in several essays dedicated to the analysis of poetry; I mention here the one specifically dedicated to "The Vers Libre Epidemic" (appearing in the *Conservative* for January 1917). In it, HPL wrote that although "the most notorious specimens of free verse represent complete chaos both of sense and of structure" (CE 2.19), he was confident that there were good poets formally using the *vers libre* and that they would anyway return soon to "normal rhyme and rational metre" (CE 2.19-20): here HPL is confusing "metre" as either a generic metrical regularity (which was certainly achieved by the most talented practitioners of free verse) and the formal meters recognized by classic prosody. Discussing what he deemed the less valuable school of "free poets"—the one led by Amy Lowell at her worst—HPL wrote that in these poets the use of free verse was the manifestation of the same intellectual and aesthetic decadence "which produces 'futuristic' music and 'cubist' painting and sculpture" (CE 2.20). The poet of this school simply "writes down the sounds or symbols of sounds which drift through his head without the slightest care or knowledge that they may be understood by any other head. The type of impression they receive and record is abnormal, and cannot be transmitted to persons of normal psychology; wherefore there is no art or even the rudiments of artistic impulse in their effusions" (CE 2.20). Joshi defines all this as "an interesting rhetorical ploy" (*Decline of the West* 136) and nothing more, and adds, with reference to the later evolution in the Lovecraftian aesthetic views: "It is true that much later Lovecraft recanted a part of this—maintaining that twentieth-century verse, by shedding the stiltedness and hypocrisy of late Victorian poetry, actually represented an enormous stride forward—but he never gave up the belief that certain extreme practitioners of the arts (Eliot and Cummings in poetry, Joyce and Stein in prose, Brancusi in sculpture, the functionalists in architecture) were entirely beyond the pale of art and were indicative of a general state of culture in serious decay" (*Decline of the West* 136).

stant presence of Lovecraft's example. Barlow kept writing poetic homages almost every year to coincide with the anniversary of Lovecraft's death (15 March 1937). The poem "Anniversary" best reveals the continuity of Lovecraft's influence on Barlow's poetry throughout the years, since it was written in March 1947, ten years after Lovecraft's decease, in Barlow's most mature Activist phase and long after he had deserted the classical pattern of his early poetry. Remembering Lovecraft after ten years, Barlow makes the significant choice of resorting again to the long-abandoned sonnet form and of temporarily giving up free verse, composing a poem in purest Lovecraftian vein. This poetic homage is a masterpiece of classical rhetoric poetry as well as of rhythmic balance:

> I cannot sleep. The rising wind of years
> Through memory sifting, lifting the leaf's
> Brittle anatomy, blows together griefs
> Of child and man, and wakened memory hears
>
> Howard's voice above the desperate toss
> Of branch, and memory sees the god inlaid
> With brass bugs abandoned where we stayed
> Some childhood year, leaving a sense of loss.
>
> And thou, Vincente, legend-wealthy heir
> Of Teotihuacan mid shepherd folk,
> Chilled with the stone mask the princes wear
> By the simple word a line of lightning spoke!
>
> Nothing we love is given us to keep.
> The wind of years is rising. I cannot sleep. (EG 191)

Limiting ourselves to the formal aspects, we can see that the sonnet bears the classical rhyme pattern *abba cddc efef gg*. Among other traditional features employed, we may notice the circularity between the incipit and the conclusion ("I cannot sleep. The rising wind of years" and "The wind of years is rising. I cannot sleep"), the archaism ("Thou"), the consonance "sifting, lifting," the classical topos of the personification of nature (the branch has a "desperate" toss, at hearing Howard's voice: nature participates in the poet's mourning), of which more in the paragraph on "Nature."

The definition of Barlow's as a poetry of *sensory nature* is not meant to ignore the leading role that one of these senses, *sight*, plays over the others. There are countless occurrences of words related to the representation of colors and visual forms, as well as of different levels of luminosity and obscurity along the spectrum ("hue," "hue"-related words like "brush," "paint," "kaleidoscopes," "blur," "blaze," "blaze of light," "color,"[10] etc.). A constant preoccupation of Barlow seems to have been the verbal rendering of the chromatic variability of the entire

---

10. "Colors" is even the title of a poem itself (EG 198).

color spectrum, with a specific privilege accorded to the colors of the tonalities of yellow and the connected images of gold and flames ("gilded," "gold," "golden," "embers," "flare," "spark," "torches": countless references to "sun," "stars," and "starlight"). A strophe excerpted from the homage "H.P.L." deserves quotation as example of the poet's concern with, and striving for, the verbal expression of visual quality and of tonalities of colors:

> As yesterday, the pines are tall and <u>dark</u>
> And meaningless against the <u>yellow glare</u>,
> As yesterday, the <u>eyes</u> of <u>twilight</u> <u>stare</u>
> Confirming naught, the <u>sunlight</u>'s tired <u>spark</u>
> Departs; and eastward move the <u>glooms</u>
> Where Sprague Memorial dominates the tombs. (EG 155)

The quoted passage, with its mention of "dark" and "glooms" along with images of light, may serve as an introduction to one of the main aspects of the visuality of Barlow's poetry: the dialectical opposition of *images of light and darkness*, where darkness comes invariably to be associated with grief and sorrow, as well as with the experience of dimness and vagueness and the visual impact of images of decay (very frequent is the representation of "withering," "souring" living things, especially flowers and plants). Again, we can see here at work Barlow's (and Activist) principle according to which poetry must strive to convey emotions that stem from sensory experiences, in particular from visual impressions in Barlow's case.

In an early, untitled poem, Barlow's selection of images associates darkness with sorrow and mourning:

> But I have known the ancient darkness long
> And tired shadows make their own a mind
> That is shadow ever steeped. To find
> Where mournfulness has reigned, your fragile song
> Perhaps to me is something of delight—
> Perhaps, gives only hatred of the night. (EG 144)

Darkness and death dominate existence, "betrayed" by a "light" that is only "momentary" ("Sonnet VII," l. 12 [EG 145]). Joy is a transient trifle, not simply *defeated* by night and darkness: joy *is* darkness ("Her spirit, the night" ["Song," l. 7 (EG 146)]). Only darkness will remain after the end of time, when a "broken sword" will vanquish "all but Night" ("R.E.H.," l. 12 [EG 148]). And it is highly revelatory that one of Barlow's finest fictional achievements is the tale entitled "The *Night* Ocean."[11]

A wide variety of examples could be proposed to account for the opposition of light and darkness in Barlow's poetry, both from his classical phase and from the Activist one: this opposition reinforces the notion of Barlow's poetry as one of

---

11. And, more broadly, the centrality of the issue of visuality is also attested by the title Barlow decided to give to his perhaps finest poetic collection, <u>View</u> *from a Hill.*

contrasts, a faithful textual reflection of the tormented personality that produced it. Barlow's poetic world is dominated by the powers of darkness: as a form of escape from the assaults of the obtruding darkness, Barlow strives to merge images of whiteness and blackness, but his attempt is invariably doomed to fail. So we find an improbable "black ice" ("Isolde," l. 19 [EG 174]), and the ambitious attempt to come to terms with the blinding powers of the night in "In Black and White" (EG 177-78). Darkness clouds perceptions and makes it difficult even to recognize familiar, friendly faces: one cannot distinguish the dim perception of "His snarling face a splendour in the murk" ("Untitled," l. 2 [EG 160]). It is as if human perception is always hampered by a veil of mist, fog, obscurity:

> I did not claim that besides this hilltop
> With fog-twisted bushes a hundred years wet,
> These snowflakes of light,
> This water bearing the armada of darkness
> Ever existed day.
> ["Recantation," ll. 1-5 (EG 188)]

And again, "Freed from the crowding mist, your face is bright / At last, this hour, though dark forevermore" ("To a Companion", ll. 1-2 [EG 162]). The opposition in luminosity entails a higher, philosophical meaning, since darkness comes to be associated with the permanent, ontological foundations of reality, while brightness is associated with the transient and ephemeral. Barlow extends the signifying range of blackness from the purely visual field toward the philosophical: in the gloomy poem "A Escoger," the choice between life and death is reduced to that between two equally disquieting, "blackening" perspectives: "Whichever you choose, and you may not delay forever / Gives on a black garden where gargoyles have gone mad" (EG 189). Shifting only for a moment on the thematic level, we can claim that images of blackness come to be employed as harbingers of despair and death,[12] in consonance with the bleak cosmic vision that Barlow's poetry holds, as we will see in the paragraph 9.2.2 on "Memory."

As feeble as sight can be as a guide to perception and orientation through a dark world, its loss results nonetheless in a doom for the experiencer: "I go my heavy errand down these glooms / Blind with eagerness to see some flame / Not foe to me, torn in midnight's cloak" ("Dawn Delayed," ll. 11-13 [EG 162]). How is sight, though an inalienable guide, revealed as insufficient for the wanderer and seeker through the darkening, dimly perceptible world? The following couplet may provide an answer:

> To follow beauty, peace you must forsake
> To weld the heart with flame, the heart must break.
> ["To a Wayfarer," ll. 9-10 (EG 163)]

---

12. Faig too remarks "That many of Barlow's poems are essentially 'black', I think few will disagree; for the constant hints of the ineffable tragedy of the human condition I know no other close parallel than Kafka" (UL 212).

The frequent association of sight with flames, and/or sun and sunlight, identifies it with the experience of *burning*: it is as if the only possibility for man to be properly "immundated," i.e. to see properly, were doomed to fail at the outset. The only possible object available for observation is something burning, which destroys the eye and burns the retina: "The watchers of the sun destroy their eyes" (*EG* 163), while darkness and its counterparts, death and decay, rule mercilessly. Nonetheless, in spite of its failure as a guide through the reigning mist and darkness, sight always represents a goal to achieve[13]: Barlow's poetry searches for visuality through the mist and darkness of the world, since sight, though associated with flames, burning, and the eye's destruction, is always preferable to darkness:

> And here I part the weeds whose guardian spears
> Surrender to no path, though much by dark
> Uncandelled by the moon, my swift steps claim
> Admission past them through unchanging years,
> And stare beyond the mist, and swiftly mark
> A gleam, within me mirrored, of great flame.
> ["Sonnet," ll. 9-14 (*EG* 165)]

Therefore, a key opposition, besides that between light and darkness, is that between blindness and ability to see, although sight is only a first, incomplete step toward the goal of comprehension:

> Who that sees the waterfall
> On the cliffside like a tall
> Bowstring, knows the force behind,
> Or the tension of the blind
> Shackled tarn the boulders bind?
> ["Out of the Dark," ll. 1-5 (*EG* 169)

Under the surface of perception, an entire world of truths lies undiscovered: the one who sees, the "seer" in the proper sense, has only a fragmentary, imperfect grasp over the truth concealed under the ordinary sensory experiences. This is another proof that though sight is necessary in orienting (blindness *is* sorrow),[14] it is by no means *sufficient* to produce satisfactory comprehension.

If up to now a conjoined analysis of the two phases of Barlow's poetry has been possible, allowing us to detect signs of continuity all along the way, it is now time to say a few words about the element that most distinguishes the two phases: the increasing importance, in the Activist period, of the "free-flowing" of mental and visual associations, in connection with the Activist penchant for automatic

---

13. We will see in the following section that RHB's poetry points out an analogous aporia when dealing with memory.

14. Blindness provokes sorrow, and vice versa: "And blind with sorrow, am aware / That till his end, I may not go" ("Untitled," ll. 12-13, *EG* 171).

writing and random usage of freely juxtaposed words, phrases, and images. In Barlow, these tenets of Activist poetics were consciously oriented toward the reaching of two specific aims: *spontaneity* and *allegory*.

Let us return to Barlow's "Statement about Poetry," where, after discussing the sources of poetic inspiration, he comes to analyze his actual technique of composition:

> When I come to the actual writing of a poem, though I have a rough layout in my mind, I may re-write this layout and suppress and add to it as felicitous concepts or phrases appear, until I have something not consciously premeditated. This may be an advantage: it is what is known as "spontaneity," [. . .] I prefer to make little allegories [. . .] surely one of the main features of poetry is saying things by talking about other things [. . .] Thus I would not say "we remember the food" but "we remember devils' food cake and oysters," or even better, "our brains are clogged (or burrowed, or studded) with oysters and cream pie." At this stage of a poem, the poetry begins to appear. All sorts of little devilishnesses and indirect ways of saying things occur to one. A word takes an unexpected turn, and another plot is included—perhaps the plot I shall keep. And then this new plot requires different words. [. . .] The writer of the Song of the Songs begins to describe a lady's neck, and gets himself delightfully off the track, so that we no longer give a hoot about the lady at the end of the second line. "Thy neck is like the tower of David . . ." he begins, and then he leaves the neck and goes on to the tower ". . . builded for an armory." This in turn suggests ". . . whereon there hang a thousand bucklers, all the shields of the mighty men." (EG 179-80)

Barlow's poetry often displays a flourish of allegedly disjointed images, connected to each other by metonymic nonsense and sheer sound patterns following a seemingly unrestrained stream-of-consciousness: quite telling on this regard is the opening of "Mythological Episode," where we read "O that frog or flower that stealthily / Snipped from the bone of Black Tezcalitpoca's foot!" (EG 195). The association between "frog" and "flower" does not really seem to be grounded on any content level, but stems from an assonance based on the sound effect provided by the repetition of the *f*.

In Barlow's Activist phase, words indeed take "unexpected turns,"[15] and are associated in accordance with the emotional impact they exert on the poet—an emotion that may stem from a sound pattern, from the recognition of a familiar or suggestive visual impression, or from a narrative plot that shapes itself in the poet's mind without his being fully aware of it. The result is a series of associations not bearing a recognizable meaning, but verging on hermetism and intransitivity. A typical plot-inspired case of free association is found in the short poem

---

15. According to Faig, "his phrases are often pregnant with unexpected color and suggestion: 'golden bladders of fish igniting the sea'; 'butterflies hook metal feet in vases'; 'the armored ants of pain exploring the marrow'; [...]' a claw delicately holding air'; 'the soft spider of his brain / weaves rapid angles'; [...] 'a marshalling of bony mud'; 'the bees in your nostrils twitching their wings'" (UL 211).

"The Chichimecs," where the reader learns about the habits of this people in a narrative, prosaic style.[16] Free association takes shape in the congenial context of the *free verse*, often in the form of a list of images and objects. One word is linked unpredictably to another, until the poet is left with an undecipherable allegory "not consciously premeditated":

> Clams claw their pots shut,
> Sublimate their doors,
> Slot their lophophores
> On floors and floors
> Of pearls and sycamores
> At fours, and half-past fours.
>
> The small submerged fowl,
> The gill-hung howl,
> The crawling towel,
> Locks up its drawers:
> Surprising as spoons pulled out on floors,
> Clams slam their clocks shut, button up their wars
> At fours, and half-past fours.
> ["Table Set for Sea-Slime," ll. 7-13 (EG 185)]

In the above passage, visual images seem to pre-exist to the plot of which they become protagonists: the narrative, carrying symbolic, indirect meanings hardly explainable except through psychoanalysis and the analysis of the dream-level (of which more in the paragraph 9.2.3 on "Dream"), takes an unexpected turn through the poet's imaginative eye. Surely Barlow is here "saying things by talking about other things," though the allegoric meaning of these lines seems irremediably lost. But probably no rationale, and no *directly perceptible* meaning, was meant for most of Barlow's Activist verses. They have to be enjoyed and evaluated for the power and extent of the mental associations they evoke, and for the pure aesthetic pleasure of their texture in a *poetic unit*: "As Lawrence Hart observes, not all the poems are uniformly successful; sometimes the 'devilishness' of his phrases seems to have taken too strong a hold on the poet, producing at times a near-Carrollian nonsense" (Faig, *UL* 211). Taking again into account the lines of the above-quoted poem, we cannot but agree with Faig when he, maintaining that the "entertaining" effect of these lines might at times be their most enjoyable quality, claims that "the true core of Barlow's poetry lies in the 'little meanings' which his most successful images provoke when woven into a unit as a poem" (*UL* 212). The actual nature of these "meanings" may often be difficult to detect and explicate, but as it was generated in the poet's mind and held an impact on his emotional sphere, it was not meant to be detected and explicated (and perhaps only emotionally experienced as well) by an external interpreter.

---

16. "The Chichimecs live to the north of us / And do not sing. / They only catch rabbits, carry them in folded nets / Eat prickly pears": "The Chichimecs," ll. 1-4 (EG 182).

However, even on this level of free associations the impact of sight on Barlow's poetry is so strong that it ascribes visual qualities to objects not normally associated with them: "Invocation" portrays a "pale mind" (*EG* 191), and "sleep" even possesses an "eye" in the poem "Evening" (*EG* 192). The attribution of sight to inanimate objects is functional also to the complex process of *personification of nature*, of which more below in the paragraph 9.2.5 on "Nature." Here I am interested in the merely textual level, and there are countless possible examples of this "visualizing" tendency in Barlow's poetry: just to mention a couple, the "eyed bushes" in "Of the Names of the Zapotec Kings" (*EG* 192) have probably more than one eye, and the mind owns an "eyed lawn" in "Framed Portent" (*EG* 193). A portentously hazardous image, configuring a peculiar case of synaesthesia, is the "obsidian pain" concluding an untitled poem (*EG* 198): here the association of an image pertaining to both the senses of sight (the variety of possible colors of the obsidian) and touch (its solidity) with the equally ambiguous (from the sensory viewpoint) concept of "pain" attains a peculiarly estranging effect on the reader, perhaps an *emotive* effect that was the goal the poet's imaginative eye intended to achieve.

9.2.2 "Memory": Time and Memory

Barlow's verses can at times be defined as tragic, since they stem from the poet's dismal conception of life. This somber perspective Barlow held on existence derived mainly from his own personal experiences, and, through a specific discourse on time and temporality, his poetry gives voice to this tragic vision of existence. Contextually, it will become clear how Barlow's poetic treatment of temporality is instrumental to the representation of his philosophical cosmicism. The analysis of his approach to temporality will move along three consecutive steps, from the most personal and intimate toward the most general and universal. This is their succession:

1. Personal
2. Historical
3. Cosmic and Existential

9.2.2.1 Personal

Since Barlow's personal experience had a decisive impact on his poetry, before delving into the textual level it is necessary to analyze briefly some features revealing the "tragicity" of his life experience.

We have already discussed his juvenile isolation in the first chapter of this study, but his entire life was also affected by bad eyesight and poor health, as can be inferred by Lovecraft's correspondence.[17] Barlow's youth was one of unrestful-

---

17. "I've seldom encountered a brighter or more promising boy, & I certainly hope he'll be careful of his eyesight and general health" (letter to Elizabeth Toldridge, 25 March

ness and disquiet, of a sensitive, inquisitive personality revealed by signs of distress, as again Lovecraft's letters attest on various occasions: during the summer 1936 visit Barlow paid to Lovecraft in Providence, the former took quarters at the boardinghouse in front of Lovecraft's College Street abode and showed at times his inquisitive nature. Barlow was all the time "intent on buying up all the old books in Providence's myriad shops" (HPL, letter to Elizabeth Toldridge, 31 January 1936; *SL* 5.292) and was "quite unremitting in his demands on Lovecraft's time" (*LAL* 614). When in New York for the 1934 Christmastide gathering of the Lovecraft entourage, during the search for a proper accommodation for the visitor, Frank Belknap Long had a hard time, since Barlow showed himself "rather hard to suit, since he demands especially good neighbourhoods and will not consider anything without a private bath. I am not so exacting—so the Longs always get me a room in one of the flats over theirs. These rooms have running waters—but unlike Barlow, I am willing to dodge around to the bathroom for my matutinal tub!" (HPL, letter to Duane Rimel, 28 January 1935; *SL* 5.91). Lovecraft again attests Barlow's sophistication, when the young visitor decided to leave the gathering early, "at eleven-thirty a.m. He cannot stand night travelling as I can" (*SL* 5.92): the picture emerges of a quite hard-to-please young fellow, so different from Lovecraft's easily adaptable character.

And perhaps a sign of distress toward the very subject of sex was already shown by Barlow in his lost correspondence to Lovecraft. In a revelatory 1935 epistle, Lovecraft addresses, against his own will, some topics that Barlow had earlier pressed on him, such as religion and eroticism. Lovecraft reluctantly admits that he holds "no particular interest in the subject of sex save as one of an hundred social and aesthetic problems (and a vastly less important one, right now, than those connected with economics) of civilisation" (letter to RHB, 24 May 1935; *FF* 268) and remarks that "I never recall *starting* a religious—or erotic—discussion, and I am by no means disposed to encourage the growth of such" (*FF* 269). One can plainly feel Lovecraft's unease in dealing with the topics that Barlow had proposed; however, this letter is particularly meaningful in its revelation of an even odder preoccupation on Barlow's part. In fact, Lovecraft does his best to "console" the young correspondent for his discomfort with his own first name and the possibility it holds to be nicknamed: "I don't see why you dislike your name, or any of the ordinary abbreviations, colloquialisations, or diminutives of

---

1935; *SL* 5.129). In his correspondence with RHB, HPL was often careful to advise and warn his young protégé of the importance of preserving his eyesight: "Be careful of your eyes! How far north will your autumnal oculistic pilgrimage take you? [. . .] It certainly is too cursedly bad that so many of your cherished activities are hampered—but don't carry your rebellions too far, since caution now may give you extensive liberty later on" (10 April 1934; *FF* 128). Another Lovecraft letter even reveals that RHB suffered from "photophobia or dread of light" (1 December 1934; *FF* 192). RHB was also hit by malaria: "He has been very busy with various things, & has had a debilitating touch of malaria" (letter to Elizabeth Toldridge, 20 December 1935; *SL* 5.218). RHB even contracted typhus during his first travel to Mexico in the summer of 1938.

it. There's no name in all the Western European nomenclatural tradition with more dignity and euphony, or with a better lineage and better set of historical exemplifications" (*FF* 269-70). Lovecraft goes on listing an almost endless series of distinguished people—kings, politicians, writers, poets, soldiers, etc., of past and present times—bearing the first name Robert (like Robert Bruce, Robert W. Chambers, Charles Robert Darwin, Robert Frost, Robert Bloch, etc.). Lovecraft looks truly perplexed by this squeamish attitude on Barlow's part ("what kind of a gawdamighty are you that these guys ain't good enough company for ye?" [*FF* 270]), and also Barlow's aversion for "Robert" being nicknamed is aptly belied ("Well—cheer up! There aren't many names out of which nicknames and diminutives can't be made" [*FF* 270]). Lovecraft himself points out these signs of distress in Barlow's personality when he shows his perplexity at what he defines as Barlow's "*phobic distaste* for abbreviations & diminutives" (*FF* 271; italics added).

According to Kenneth Faig, Jr., Barlow's decision to change the main focus of his life and embark on the academic career, putting aside his previous literary efforts, might also be interpreted as a sign of his restlessness.[18] Barlow felt uneasy and almost guilty when facing the perspective of pursuing a literary career:

> The years of his literary and artistic efforts were those immediately following the Great Depression, and Barlow evidently felt a strong obligation to find some activity which he might adopt as a career. Ignacio Bernal observed that Barlow acquired from his father a strong sense of the dignity and necessity of work, in spite of his dislike of the military life which LTC Barlow had chosen. Barlow seems eventually to have concluded that his artistic and literary efforts could never serve as a career [. . .] Nor would an ordinary job in the outside world do. Barlow wrote[19] that he had always had difficulty dealing with ordinary business people in the everyday affairs of life. (Faig, *UL* 216)

Faig also provides a valuable insight on a possible link between Barlow's sensitive personality and his poetry: "Barlow was always a very private man, and while he no doubt recognized the validity of poetic expression, he doubtless found such expression difficult. His tendency was always toward the cryptic and the concrete and away from the baring of his own emotions—although some of the poems do contain what one imagines must be quite a bit of his own inner feelings" (*UL* 216).

However, the event that perhaps held, in hindsight, the strongest impact on Barlow's poetic production was, paradoxically, the end of his life, and the way in which it ended: suicide. Various hypotheses have been advanced to find a reasonable explanation to Barlow's gesture: Joshi believes that "word leaked out about his homosexuality, and to forestall exposure he committed suicide" (*LAL* 642),[20]

---

18. And even in the "literary" years, RHB's inability to focus his energies on a single project at a time could be understood as a sign of his discomfort.

19. In *Ideas of Order in Experimental Poetry*, ed. Lawrence Hart (San Francisco: George Leite, 1945), 16.

20. Joshi and Schultz reinforce this opinion when claiming that Barlow's suicide occurred when he was "threatened with exposure of his homosexuality" (*Lovecraft Encyclopedia* 16).

while Faig writes of a "strain of overwork" (*UL* 226) that obliged Barlow to take a leave of absence from his academic activity in the summer of 1950. In Barlow's autobiography, the account of his way of conducting research opens up revealing vistas on the contradictory relationship he entertained with his own work: attraction, repulsion, exhausting dedication. As already discussed in section 4.2.2.2 of the present work, in his autobiographical papers Barlow states that his only "enjoyment" resides

> in the smooth fulfilment of my varied compulsions. When I have a period of free time and the choice of activity, I am most discontent [...] *At these times of "free choice" I am most wretched.* Pleasure for me is a calm fulfilling of the pattern of work, writing something or learning something, which I have convinced myself "must" be done. But fulfilling the work-pattern, since it is the most rewarding of my activities, is the most difficult. I invent a thousand sham-pleasures to keep me otherwise occupied, or I exhaust myself so that no activity can be thought of, but only blank sleep. (*OLL* 19-20)

Scarcely any account could be more a sign of a tormented personality than this.

Another psychological factor might shed more light on Barlow's untimely end: "a growing disillusionment with his life and career seems to have added to his nervous agitation" (Faig, *UL* 227).[21] There is scarcely any doubt on the fact that Barlow suffered from nervous and psychological problems:

> Shy and introverted, Barlow undoubtedly suffered from some social maladjustments; these may have complicated and worsened his nervous collapse in 1950 [...] Barlow was almost invariably ill at ease at social functions; his idea of a series of costume parties in 1950 hints of an attempt to break loose his essential loneliness and solitude and to resurrect the kind of social relationships he had while he was a member of the Activist circle of poets. (Faig, *UL* 227)

Signs of his maladjustments can be found also in his constant uncertainty about the right path to walk in his life: "Barlow fled from every success he ever had [...] Barlow seems to have been mortally dubious of the worth of his own activities—in spite of the fact that he excelled in almost everything he tried" (Faig, *UL* 228). Indeed, his achievements were great, but they also led him to question their worth, when he at times realized "the vast indifference[22] with which the world at large received the fruits of his genius" (Faig, *UL* 228). It is likely that, though Barlow was an "exile from his own land, a lover of another race and culture, a man who burnt out his life with feverish activity" and came "to doubt the worth of his

---

Hummel too believes in this hypothesis: "His death was brought about because of the prejudice towards homosexuality which existed then and which gay people even today face; prejudice which created the fear which allowed him to be blackmailed" (28).

21. RHB left a long letter in Spanish, addressed to Dr. Pablo Martinez Del Rio, before taking the twenty-six tablets of Seconal that killed him: in it, he wrote of "insomnia and other personal problems" (Faig, *UL* 227). The manuscript of the letter does not survive.

22. As we will see below, the notion of "indifference" is central in RHB's cosmic attitude.

scholarly life in personal terms," his suicide was "much more probably the result of a deep spiritual malaise than of overwork and strain" (Faig, *UL* 228). In fact, the "dark element of doubt as to the validity of life itself shows up consistently in his poetry in general" (Faig, *UL* 229), especially in the treatment of the theme of temporality, as the textual analysis will show.

Barlow's poetry is in fact peculiarly interested in representing the *transience* of human experiences and achievements. Everything man attains is doomed to pass, without, on the cosmic level, even leaving a trace, since the universe is basically *indifferent* to mankind. This conception stands out in two categories of Barlow's poems: 1) those dealing with the inconsistency and vanity of human efforts, and 2) those dedicated to (homosexual) love. Beginning from the former, it is worthwhile to analyze these poems in connection with the aspiration to *suicide*, which not so covertly leaks out from their gloomiest lines:

> I will forsake my garden, where no wall
> Can seal the alien sprout beneath the ground,
> To mice and mould by hyacinths resign,
> And let the fruit upon the petals fall.
> Decay and ripeness to the fly are keen
> And similar: he chooses not between.
> ["Untitled," ll. 9-14 (*EG* 163)]

These lines configure a metaphorical representation of Barlow's renunciation of fighting, of his giving life up in search of rest and peace. Also, his invocation to Sleep, of which more in the paragraph 9.2.3 on "Dream," assumes the sinister hue of a praise of the silence and inertia that only death may bring to the pointless fatigues and worries of existence:

> Let us have an end of noise—of tears
> An end forever.
> ["To Sleep," ll. 19-20 (*EG* 172)]

In "The School Where Nobody Learns What," Barlow reveals a more ironic, disenchanted view on the inconsistency of life, another trait he must have inherited from Lovecraft and that makes Faig speak of a "wry scepticism about the importance of life" (*UL* 212):

> Oh, only to be buried in Babylon,
> And you'll see what I mean.
>
> . . .
>
> Fill the little slate and call it done,
> You needn't come back tomorrow.
> The Janitor is anxious to shelve Johnny Ape's botany book
> With Jennifer Pterodactyl's. (*EG* 176)

It is, however, in the dark "A Escoger" that Barlow ominously depicts the weariness of living, adumbrating the necessity of finding escape from the tedium of existence:

> Manifestly you cannot sit
> Forever in this draughty antechamber
> And your host off drunk in another universe,
> But the question is, which door?
> . . .
> Whichever you choose will lead
> To no amazing golden berries
> Or rain of music, or flares
> Of ports across the hills to the sea,
> Whichever you choose, and you may not delay forever,
> Gives on a black garden where gargoyles have gone mad
> From the starlight:
>
> Whichever you choose will be wrong.
> But what else can you do with a life? (EG 189)

This poem is rich in meanings and possible interpretations. Of course, "doors" may symbolize the different ways man can choose in order to carry on his life, but if here we choose the isotopy of "suicide," we can interpret these "doors" as the different ways man has to end his life. Following this isotopy, the half-line "and you may not delay forever" takes on a disquieting signification: the poem would imply that the choice of suicide becomes an unavoidable necessity that can be delayed only for a while, but not forever. Suicidal inclinations are thus both a theme of Barlow's poetry and a source of inspiration leading him to actually *write* poetry.

Another feature that performs an analogous role is love, and here we come to the second category of poems mentioned above. Also, love is experienced in Barlow's poetry as torment and unhappiness. All the emotions love procures are destined to wither and fade away, *as everything in existence*:

> And thus their evanescent lips were wed,
> As ours hove near, and life and flesh were real
> With all the lines of love, that they might feel
> Love's joys; but in a while the joy was dead
> In their own vanishing—Nor any wept
> Above them long, when once they slept.
> ["Sonnet VI. To G. J.," ll. 9-14 (EG 145)]

Barlow's poetry sings not simply the impossibility of a lasting love, but even of a love to be remembered or grieved upon once it has vanished, because the darkness of which life is composed prevails and wraps up everything:

> I have been put into a sadness by the tale
> Of lovers, whose cherishing was great as ours,
> Yet is no more remembered, though the flowers,
> The wind-washed sky, the gorgeous fail
> Of sunset are as sweet as when they move
> About their fragile love a fleshly guise
> And looked upon work with eager eyes:
> I have been grieved by this nostalgic love.
>
> Yet every grief must bow before the night
> Nor may we sorrow for the diamond star
> Whose grandeur winds, and vanished afar.
> It's death betrayed by momentary light.
> ["Sonnet VII. To G. J.," ll. 1-12 (*EG* 145)]

Happiness has a "brooding face" ("Song," l. 16, *EG* 146): each happy moment is destined to touch our soul briefly and immediately pass away. Not only do we have to be aware of the temporariness and perishability of anything valuable, but even the written or spoken word, even poetry, cannot retell experience and give it a solid statute. Also, art must bow to the pitiless flux of temporality:

> I would weave my happiness into a song
> And with melodious words, from Lethe stay
> The crystal boat of joy; or hide away
> The coin of love, which tarry never long
> Within our coffers. I would like a chain
> About the soft dear throat of Eros; bind
> Him within the summer garden—find
> A spell confining joy and love and pain.
>
> But pens speak slower than lips would sing
> And the word is very subtle which evokes
> Emotion sweet but transient. He who cloaks
> His love in words has done a wondrous thing:
> Though passion bloom today or yesterday
> No song his hurtful, silent flight can stay.
> ["Untitled" (*EG* 147)]

Everything passes away and is lost, love would need to be chained in order to be preserved. Not even the consolation of words, of poetry and art, is left for the poet: words are not able to "chain" love, happiness is not fit to be told, there is no way to escape its perishability. And in "Dirge for the Artist," Barlow returns on the topic of the inability of art to fight (and provide consolation for) the inevitable end, death: "Most poetry concludes, with gloomy sighs, / That what have seemed as lutes are squealing toys / By cowards wrought to end death's nearing noise; / That Truth is but that man unwilling dies" ("Dirge for the Artist," ll. 1-4, EG 148).[23]

Not only is poetry unable to fix love and make it stay—at least within Memory—but even when love is truly experienced, Barlow's poetry is reticent in approaching the subject, as if words were an inadequate means to express love and the torments it provokes. The titles or dedications of some poems to people identified only with their initials are revelatory of this reticence. The following lines are excerpted from the poem "For D.":

> My thought and pillows are disarranged;
> I seem to confuse your wrists with the line of a Kwan-Yin scroll,
> Your mouth with a brown triangular butterfly,
> Your belly with good linen
> Spread on a hedge from dawn.
>
> I will shut the window of my rained-on heart,
> Since you occupy the bed which is almost legitimately yours.
> I will not think of the sliding hands.
> I will read a book
> Or walk on Van Ness Avenue screaming.
> ["For D." (EG 175-76)]

Disguised and veiled allusions to the male lover's physicality (wrists, belly, hands, mouth, etc.) are present here as well as in many of Barlow's other love poems. They entail sexual implications, but never become explicit. The poem just quoted is a masterpiece of poetical expression of a *restrained love*, until in the very last line the real feeling of the poet is manifested, and that scream, referring to the poet's admitted confusion, may indicate either his unrestrainable joy or his inconsolable pain.

Conflict and torment are the two trademarks of Barlow's poetic experience of love. Very rarely is a full and accomplished love sung; more often than not, the partner of the poet's amorous relationships is described as an enslaver, a torturer, even an enemy:

> If my heart scowls now,
> It is only because a certain epidermal contact with the enemy,
> areally limited, has been postponed.
> Only because the enemy has successfully disengaged us, before we saw the
>   whites of their thighs.
> ["In Order to Clarify," ll. 1-5 (EG 189)]

---

23. Line 4 of this poem was reworked by Lovecraft, who in the letter of 3 January 1937 wrote to Barlow: "[your sonnet] has one very troublesome line—4—whose overcrowding will be very hard to get around. How's this for a tentative solution?

By cow|ards wrought | to end | death's near|ing noise;
That truth | is but | that man | un will | ing dies." (FF 393)

The torment caused by love is often a favorite topic of Barlow's poems: love conveys emotions identified with fear and a sense of loss, disorientation ("Since I feared the <u>f</u>light or the <u>f</u>ading / Of <u>f</u>lowers wavering in your eye / Or the bees in your nostrils twitching their wings, / I circled through the wheat of your thighs, / Under that copper and suspicious crab, the sun, / Like one who fears shadow, like one / Who has lost his keys or a ring"[24]).

The sense of loss, underlined in this poem by the very use of the word "lost," is a key concept in Barlow's understanding not only of love but of life itself. "From this tree / No further fruit" ("From This Tree," ll. 1-2, *EG* 180) is the lapidary Barlovian version of the end of natural life: everything perishes and vanishes, under the blows of a life-draining temporal flux. Time is indeed man's worst enemy, because it deprives him of everything he most cherishes:

> Nothing we love is given us to keep.
> The wind of years is rising. I cannot sleep.
> ["Anniversary," ll. 13-14 (*EG* 191)]

These two lines of tremendous bitterness point at the effect that the "wind of years" bears on the existence of human beings (and of any living ones): the sliding out of hands of everything achieved, cherished, and loved (as in the passing away of best friends, such as Lovecraft, to whom this poem is dedicated).

The theme of the elusiveness and transitoriness of our achievements returns poignantly in "Invocation":

> Mother, Mother, Mother,
> Pin a red rose on me,
> That the flame may *stay* its leap,
> . . .
> That my examining hand may somehow
> mold flesh into *something to keep*.
> ["Invocation," ll. 1-3 and 8-9 (*EG* 191; italics added)]

In his tormented existence, Barlow always strives for some stability, for that "something to keep" that only could give rest to his frantic search for a core, an anchorage in the seething and disorienting vortex of the life-world. Barlow would even be tempted to mold something *stable* by his own "examining hand," since it is not possible to find such an object (feeling, relationship, principle, etc.) in this life. A sense of lack, of non-accessibility, of privation and absence dominates Barlow's poetry: everything worthwhile, be it love, success, history, or traditions, lies beyond one's perceptive capabilities: "These pieces of dishes are petals / From one of the many flowers / which here and there on the / mountain of Time, / In summers of a different sun and / winters of a different rain, / Have unfolded be-

---

24. "Explanation to M.," *EG* 178. Let us note here, passim, the effective sound effect of the alliteration of the *f* I have underlined in the first two lines.

yond the reach / of our gathering" ("Tepuzteca, Tepehua," ll. 35-42, EG 183-84; italics added).

The main cipher of existence is thus represented by *privation*: often Barlow's poetry employs images of withering, drought, lack of a fullness which is continually longed for and never attained:

> The woman Wind, with love congealed
> To hatred, walks the blighted field
> Divested of its half-grown yield.
> ["March," ll. 4-6 (EG 156)]

The poet's life is marked by the absence of what he most cares for: "All is habitual, even the footsteps that fled / Hastily stairward might be but a shadow's light tread. / All is deluded and moonlit and ancient and fair: / Nothing suspects *you are gone*, or detects my despair" ("Untitled," ll. 9-12, EG 167; italics added). The sense of privation is here under both the guise of a "concrete" privation ("you are gone," the lover has disappeared) and of an "abstract" one (life is monotonous, all is "habitual" and thus the poet's existence is deprived of the *varieties* of life).

Even when the poet compares himself to a natural counterpart, such as a bird, he cannot overcome the incompleteness of his being: "In me a wing, unmendable and torn / Strives at the air, *deprived* of further flight" ("Who Will Not Know," EG 159; italics added).

Another privation Barlow suffered, as we have seen, was that of human contact, of a satisfactory social life, of friendships. Thus Barlow's poetry expresses the solitude[25] and the maladjustment of its creator, his quest for that "human touch" which alone could have obviated the lack of public affection he must have felt like damnation due to his scholarly activity—and to his own introversion of character:

> Behind me lift the hills; across them blooms
> Distil their coloured breath, yet all the same
> I go my heavy errand down these glooms
> Blind with eagerness to *see some flame*
> *Not foe to me*, torn in midnight's cloak;
> Enter some camp, breathe in some *friendly* smoke.
> ["Dawn Delayed," ll. 9-14 (EG 162; italics added)]

The frequent resort to a syntactical structure privileging *negative* sentences is, on a textual linguistic level, a means Barlow employed to convey the sense of lack and privation inherent in his life experience. The poem "Who Will <u>Not</u> Know"

---

25. RHB openly faces this issue in his "Autobiography," where he nearly comes to fear his loneliness as a disease: "A chasm of loneliness opens alongside my paths of study [. . .] I delight in the presence of many people; I can end a conversation only by effort, can never get rid of a visitor, and when I have seduced people by wining and dining them into cheering the house with their voices, I hope they will never leave" (OLL 20).

(EG 158-59), for instance, employs many negations: already in the title one can be found, and the body of the text shows three occurrences of "never" (twice in very privileged position, at the beginning of the two strophes of which the poem is composed).

Let us move now a step further and analyze in greater depth how Barlow's poetry connects its treatment of temporality with the themes of loss and privation, and subsequently with the bleak vision of existence the poet holds on a more general historical and cosmic perspective.

Barlow's poetry shows a strong interest in the representation of temporality by staging a dialectic opposition between *past* and *present*. The commemorative poem "R.E.H.,"[26] composed upon Robert E. Howard's death—which occurred on 11 June 1936, due to suicide, at age thirty—deals with an important discourse on Time and Memory:

> Conan, the warrior king, lies stricken dead
> Beneath a sky of cryptic stars; the lute
> That was his laughter stilled, and sadly mute
> Upon the chilling earth his youthful head.
> There sounds for him no more the clamorous fray,
> But dirges now, where once the trumpet loud:
> About him swathe old memories for shroud,
> And ended is the conflict of the day.
>
> Death spilled the blood of him who loved the fight
> As men love mistresses, and fought it well—
> His fair young flesh is marble where he fell
> With broken sword that vanquished all but Night;
> And as of mythic kings our words must speak
> Of Conan now, who roves where dreamers seek. (EG 148)

"Memories" is a key word here, as well as in Barlow's overall literary production.[27] The poem is pervaded by a strong sense of regret and nostalgia[28] for the times that were, in which Conan (whose represented death symbolizes his creator's) held his sword and slaughtered his enemies. Those times will never come back, and this awareness causes the poet's sorrow. Only death and silence, the two universal principles ruling the cosmos, are left. Images of silence represent the cos-

---

26. HPL defined this sonnet a "splendid elegy" (see his letter to RHB, 9 July 1936; *FF* 349).

27. One of RHB's best narrative efforts, "A Dim-Remembered Story," not by chance features "remembrance" already in the title. See chapter 5, section 5.3, for a lengthy discussion on the dimension of memory in RHB's fiction.

28. The centrality of these notions in RHB's poetry is attested also by the presence, in his poetic corpus, of a poem titled "Nostalgia" (*EG* 175).

mic desolation awaiting the universe after the negligible passage of our species on the planet. Moreover, the poem stages an opposition between the "once" of past glory (the past of life, love, of the music of lutes and trumpets, the past of frays and fights), and the "now" of those "memories" (the now of silence, death, darkness, stillness) that alone remain to keep—faintly—that past alive.

Barlow's acrostic poem, "St. John's Churchyard," dedicated to another master of the fantastic, Edgar Allan Poe, is also built around the notions of memory and remembrance, as well as on the contrast between past and present: together with the sense of regret for the "half-forgotten days" (EG 148, l. 10) of Poe's life, the poem focuses on the silence that *now* engulfs the tombstones of the churchyard that alone remain to keep alive the memory of *past* "ages lost beneath the years" (l. 5). When the past is no longer respected, when we hold no memories, this is a sign of decline because it is the sign that we have given up to Time, our enemy, and its annihilating forces.

Time passes and destroys everything: even Memory may not succeed in defeating its effects:

> Fame, Honour, Love, and all the various crew
> Consoling us are like and elder's lies
> To soothe a child when night is in the skies;
> Man is but born his coming death to rue.
>
> Futility my theme, and how 'tis vain
> To nurture beauty's seed in hue or rhyme,
> *Since soon or late each bloom is nipped by Time,*
> Who never stays for long his wintry rain.
> The hour-glass measures life: a pox be on it!
> It scarce gives time to write a decent sonnet!
> ["Dirge for the Artist," ll. 5-14 (EG 149; italics added)]

The passing of Time is experienced as a condemnation, and even its counterparts, Memory and Regret, do not console the poet enough.

In "Alcestis," the opposition between past and present is intertwined with the notion of regret:

> Why have you brought me back to this dear land
> Where I once dwelt such ash-dead years ago,
> To stand anew within these rooms I know,
> My husband's house, where I obeyed his hand?
> I died for him, since he desired to see
> For more decades the morning sun ascend . . .
> Was it his mouth on mine which made me lend
> The hours of life intended once for me?
>
> I followed Death—his face was not so grim—
> By that lean road where no inquirer goes

> Lest business force him there, and I suppose
> I can return, though life has faded dim.
> Submissive still, to this familiar net
> I yield myself, reluctant to forget. (EG 149)

The conflict between the "once" happy condition and the "present" regret of those times is played here on the notion of the *impossibility of forgetting*: the necessity of remembering stems from this impossibility, and it constitutes mankind's doom, its obligation to bend to a memory that identifies itself with regret, since what we remember (the past) is invariably depicted by Barlow's poetry as better than the present.

The sense of regret for a lost greatness is often present in Barlow's poetry. Even in the eyes of a bird, the conflict between the past happiness and the present misery becomes patent:

> What cities boasted to the sun
> In *old* triumphant years
> From its tall top where only move
> *Today* the channelled tears.
> ["A Gull From a Cliff," ll. 9–12 (EG 170; italics added)]

Moreover, memories, our apparently unique instrument to fight the flux of a Time that annihilates any achievement and any stability, are a very feeble and unreliable bulwark. Memory provides us with clues about the past, but these hints are often questionable: we cannot even be sure of the only bastion we have available to defend ourselves from Time. In "The Gods in the Patio," when trying *today* to reconstruct the occurrences involving some gods of ancient Mexicans in the *past*, Barlow employs a series of interrogations to represent his attempts: "Have the gods herded into some cave, their clumsy joints all bent in the direction of flight? Is their a spider hanging its gourd in the Jar of Tlaloc, where rain once shook golden rings? Are all the Cholula plates broken? [. . .] How long must they lie, the robbed and fragrant dead, by the Snake Wall, the *Coatepantli*?" (EG 176).

Unreliable and essentially futile, memories constitute however our only defence against the ravaging attacks of Time.[29] From this viewpoint, a surprising coherence may be detected in Barlow's poetic treatment of the notions of sight and memory. In fact, we also understood sight as an unreliable means to guide human beings through the darkness of existence. However, though sight and memory are fallible and unsteady means, human beings must rely on them in order to cope with existence. This of course adds to the hopeless condition of mankind, obliged to make its survival depend on unsound grounds.

---

29. See chapter 5 on "Time" for the analysis of an analogous theme in RHB's fiction.

At times, memory itself does not even represent a consolation for the poet's torment, but comes back to haunt: this is especially the case when remembering the loss of a friend, as Lovecraft was for Barlow:

> And now a year recedes into the wash
> Of aimless centuries, and now my eyes
> Perceive the pattern of their fall and rise,
> Yet memories are the heart's incessant lash
> Like rain upon the cloudy ocean hurled.
> ["II. March 1938," ll. 1-5 (EG 154)]

9.2.2.2 Historical

We move now to a wider comprehension of the opposition between time and memory. Before approaching the cosmic level of the opposition, it is necessary to stop at its intermediate, the historical.

Memory is a flexible instrument: it may serve, more or less effectively, as shelter from the attacks of time; it may be a dangerous weapon, since memories may console but haunt as well; and it may be also employed in order to "mold" time according to our purposes, adjusting history to our perspectives. For example, memory can be used to juxtapose remote and apparently disconnected figures, such as Leon Trotzky, an historical figure, and Huitzilopochtli,[30] a mythological entity associated with the positivity Barlow attached to Mexican native cultures.[31] The odd memorial coalescence occurs in "For Leon Trotzky and Huitzilopochtli" (EG 177) and allows Barlow to express his "parallel" regret for both the loss of the ancient Indian civilization and for the assassination of one of the main protagonists of the Bolshevik Revolution and of Soviet Russian history.[32] The exiled Trotzky's murder was committed on 20 August 1940, in Mexico City, by a killer recruited by Stalin, and the coincidence of the geographical location of the ancient god's adoration and of Trotzky's death was enough, for Barlow, to make memory associate the two figures.

However, memory can hardly counterbalance the sense of loss stemming from the action of time on another level, that of the historical achievements of an entire civilization. This broader level involves the history of mankind and of its civilizations. Barlow's specific field of study was that of the ancient cultures of native

---

30. In Aztec mythology, Huitzilopochtli, also spelled Uitzilopochtli ("hummingbird of the south" or "he of the south" or "hummingbird on the left"), was a god of war and a sun god, and the patron of the city of Tenochtitlán.
31. See on this regard also the section "Nature" below.
32. RHB's political orientation toward left-wing doctrines is well known. In his "Autobiography," RHB even declares: "I also grew a beard which made me resemble Trotsky in 1918" (OLL 22).

Mesoamericans, and in one of the poems titled "Quetzalcoatl" he questions the consistency of the traces left by the Chulhua empire on human history. Was it true glory?

> Yet all was done there, all desire unfurled
> Through which the tortured flesh is deified;
> All joys had being there—and scars:
> The futile tears of that unwitnessed world
> Which never heard of Caesar, though long dried,
> Fell like our own; and to the selfsame stars.
> ["Quetzalcoatl," ll. 9-14 (EG 169)]

Time has passed and canceled desires, joys, scars, and tears. But exactly as then, the same "futile tears" roll down today, and to the "selfsame stars." Time has passed by, but it could do nothing against a force that is even stronger than it is: sorrow. This poem stages again a sense of loss and regret for an unwitnessed world (the poet is moved to tears in the face of this lost, past greatness), but these verses also recall a sense of continuity in the name of sorrow and of the vanity of human achievements. History may see the birth, affirmation, and extinction of as many civilizations as possible, because this is the cyclical, deterministic pattern ruling over the cosmos. But though all human civilizations perish, something remains and marks the continuity: the insubstantiality of their efforts. Caesar is mentioned on purpose: the Aztecs were not known to him, and vice versa; what remains is only the reciprocity of their vanity. History's lesson is clear: transient human empires, conquests, and splendors are but insignificant trifles destined to disappear as quickly as they emerged.

9.2.2.3 Cosmic and Existential

Barlow's treatment of the conflict between time and memory develops from a personal to an historical and then to a truly existential and cosmic level. The opposition is so all-pervasive in his poetry as to affect his views on human existence and on the place of mankind on a cosmic scale.

First of all, the cosmic rendering of the temporal conflict is carried out through the employment of images of *decay*.[33] The flux of temporality not only bears a destructive effect on mankind's perception of its past achievements, it is often associated with images of decay: in the most cosmic hues of his poetry, Barlow comes to depict entire worlds as "decayed" ("The Unresisting," l. 14, *EG* 158). The flowing temporality may in fact be represented also on a more general, cosmic level as generating a sense of worlds flourishing, passing, and dissolving in the long run: the images of passing away and decaying lead Barlow, on the cosmic level, to sanction the intrinsic insignificance of human efforts, in whatever field

---

33. Another possible influence HPL exerted on RHB may be detected on this point: for a discussion on the theme of decay in HPL, see Dansky 9-10.

and to whatever scope they are directed. The only possible choice to cope with this further negative effect of the passing of time is a sort of resignation, the swearing of fealty to the inevitable cycle of birth, life, and death, and to the natural elementals that reign over all: "I shall not close my window against the mounting snow / Or shelter my heart from the sleet's cold insistent spear: / Long, long since I have sworn my fealty to these" (ibid., ll. 15-17).

Barlow's poetry depicts human existence as "the calendar of days invalid" ("We Kept on Reading 'Tuesday,'" ll. 8-9, EG 190), as an "intricate tread" ("Date Uncertain," l. 28, EG 175), a "leaden life" ("To Alta, on Her Original American Sonnet," l. 10, EG 164) of confinement, a succession of frustrations and dissatisfactions. The poem revealingly titled "Frustration" depicts the poet's attempts to put order in his "garden," to wipe away the weed and prepare the garden for future flowering. His desires and plans, however, are soon frustrated:

> But where my marshalled garden ended
> I saw the vaster fields untended.
> Beyond my roses stars grew wild,
> Heaven's garden was not aisled;
> The meteor untrellised, gay
> Through swarming chaos made its way. (EG 162)

The garden is here a metaphor of the poet's existence: no matter how much he gives order to it, cosmic chaos presses from the thin demarcation between life and the "beyond." The poet's existence cannot be sheltered against the advance—and the attacks—of cosmic insignificance, the principle governing life in the universe. The awareness of this bleak cosmic reality leads Barlow to perceive human existence as the imprisonment of the soul:

> Underneath this velvet floor
> Descend the steps I know so well,
> And stop against an iron door
> Whose tongueless guardian cannot tell
> What prisoner is there forsaken
> Within a world the stain of night,
> But not with any star as light;
> Or in what battle he was taken.
>
> And I, above, survey the fair
> Long road where I went forth
> In yesterdays to south and north,
> And blind with sorrow, am aware
> That till his end, I may not go.
> I watch his eyes, but death dawns slow.
>   ["Untitled" (EG 171)]

The key image in this poem is that of the "prisoner," which is to be understood as a reflection of the poet, a prisoner in this life.

Existence is doomed to incommunicability and pain, since people are "A shifting crowd wherein I speak to none" ("Cycle from a Dead Year," l. 6, EG 152) and the laws governing existence track our path sending us "stumbling toward the shrine called Pain" (ibid., l. 10). Therefore all human efforts are vain, when examined not from a personal, involved perspective but on an existential, abstracted cosmic level:

> The patient hungry for a hundred foods
> He will not suffer after all consume.
> ["To Sleep," ll. 42-43 (EG 173)]

Human efforts are existentially vain not only because any achievement we may attain will be blown out by the passing of time, but because—and this is perhaps an even more disturbing concept—we search for things we either do not need or truly desire: we are "hungry" for a "food" we will not after all "consume."

And thus in the cosmic nonsense and sorrow of existence, even torment may in the end assume a positive meaning and play a valuable role, that of *making time pass*:

> But even torment whiles away the time:
> Limbs turned askew are just as good as straight,
> Or nearly so—and the prisoner of life
> Accustomed to the rack, does not long much
> To move from it, or if he longs, forgets.
> ["To Sleep," ll. 64-68 (EG 173)]

These lines, which conclude the dramatic invocation "To Sleep," are rich in meaning and aesthetic effect. The image of man as a "prisoner" of life comes back, but above all there emerges the notion of torment as an instrument man may use to fight against time. It is not so important whether our limbs are turned askew or straight: torment is an unavoidable part of existence, we can do nothing but try to cope with it. The poet's invitation is thus to look on the bright side of pain: it is preferable to accept the inevitable pain of existence than to choose to fight with time. At least, pain keeps man busy and does not allow him to meditate on the effects of time and on his own condition. But again, not even this is a very reliable "consolation": time, getting personified here, seems to be aware of the potentially wholesome effect of pain on man. Time is such a tyrannous lord and a cruel enemy that it does not even allow man to lament its cruelty and to "enjoy" his pain: "Seize a moment to lament / There is scarcely time even for that" ("The School Where Nobody Learns What," ll. 3-4, EG 176).

Coming back to "To Sleep," the quoted lines push the harsh metaphor even further: they imply that man is accustomed to suffer to such an extent that he does not even realize or is aware of it anymore, nor desires to pause from his suffering. He does not *remember* that he does not want to suffer ("Accustomed to the rack, does not long much / To move from it, or if he longs, *forgets*"). Memory shows again its fallaciousness: it fails just when it serves more, when it could push man to fight to improve his condition. Memory is dangerous, is a double-edged weapon: it is not at man's service, but at the service of his suffering. And these assumptions do nothing but depict an even bleaker picture of the human existential condition, since this same memory that reveals its fallacy and unreliability is supposed to fight on man's side, is supposed to be man's bulwark against his real enemy, time.

Thus, even the opposition between time and memory, and the alleged binary axiologic contrast attached to it (time = evil, memory = good), is flawed. This is especially true as Barlow's is essentially a poetry of opposites, of conflicts that never allow the clear assigning of a definitive interpretation to the terms they involve. Even memory is potentially "conflictual," and even pain may show a positive side. Barlow's existential perspective, reflected in his poetry, is that of an unshakable uncertainty: nothing is actually how it appears, the interpreter may never be sure of anything. The contrasts between *reality* and *appearance*, *truth* and *falsity* constitute another fundamental opposition founding Barlow's poetry.[34] The opposition between truth and falsity reveals that Barlow's system of values is strictly axiologic:

> Before a gilt and bloated cardboard dome
> *Like* a temple reared to soothe some Eastern queen
> Whose lords become the maggots' honeycomb,
> Sleek harlots, smiling tawdrily to screen
> Whatever they think, in swooning rites *pretend*
> The love no longer theirs. A trumpet's voice
> *False* and ecstatic, screams at the cowering night
> That only desire is worthy of our choice.
> ["Burlesque," ll. 1-8 (EG 161; italics added)]

I have italicized the words and images hinting at the semantic opposition between reality and appearance, truth and falsity. And in the same sonnet, the ambiguous nature of "snare" (l. 10) hints again at this conceptual nucleus. The insistence on this aspect in Barlow's work points to the important role that the semantic investment of euphoric/disphoric values on the *veridiction* square played in Barlow's conceptual structures. In Greimas's semiotics, a key modality is *veridiction*, but it concerns more the epistemological level than the axiologic, and is characteristic of those narratives centered on the interplay of truth and deceiving, of being and appearing. This is the model of the semiotic square of veridiction:

---

34. And as we have seen in paragraph 3.2 on "Vagueness of perception," his fiction too: the same holds true from the juvenile efforts of the *Annals of the Jinns*, to the most mature weird stories like "Origin Undetermined," "A Dim-Remembered Story," and the collaborations with HPL.

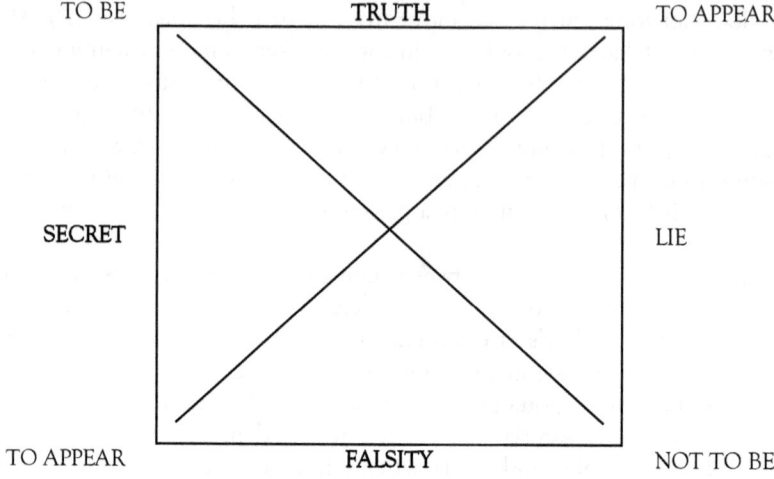

Truth is the synthesis of the two contraries "To Be" and "To Appear" (appearance corresponds to reality), while Falsity derives from the coincidence of the subcontraries "Not To Be" and "Not To Appear": true is what *is as it appears*, while false is what *is not and does not appear*.[35]

It is as if Barlow's poetry, perhaps because it was intended by his creator, in consonance with the Activist belief, as the literary expression of the poet's sensitivity and inner emotions rather than of his mind's thirst for knowledge, shifts an epistemological concern toward an axiologic one: thus truth becomes intrinsically a *positive* value, since it is attached to the possible discovery of a meaning for existence, while falsity becomes its *negative* counterpart, which identifies the intrinsically futile and deceiving nature of human goals, plans, and achievements. The insubstantiality of existence also reveals itself in the emptiness, in the void of its manifestations: nothing is actually how it looks; the dialectics truth-appearance invariably reflects that between truth and falsity and reconnects with the dialectical opposition internal/external that will be seen in the "Essence" paragraph. That the search for a meaning, for a "core" of existence, is in its turn doomed to fail in Barlow's views does not matter here: the important thing is that the search for a meaning must be based on the recognition of what is true and what is false. In fact, the awareness of the intrinsic falsity we discover in human beliefs, plans, feelings, etc., never leads Barlow to any politically indifferent consequence: in fairness to his intellectual honesty, we must remark that he always tried to reach for truth and never yielded to the temptation, born of the awareness of the distance between truth and man's hopes, to join these hopes' falsity and to believe in what he actually deemed false. Even though reality is engulfed by a thick cover of false appearances, Barlow always strove to unveil that cover: once he recognized the bleak cosmic truth grounding man's existence, he decided not to convert his beliefs to others, possibly

---

35. The model is then completed by the other two coordinates of the square: Lie is the conjunction of "To Appear" and "Not to Be," Secret of "To Be" and "Not to Appear."

more comforting but less intellectually honest. He preferred suicide.

Barlow deeply felt the nonsensicality of a cosmos that allows no belief in superior principles, in any teleological scope, in any spiritual or divine design. In fact, it goes without saying that he was non-religious: "Barlow, like his mentor Lovecraft, was no believer in the Christian God, and thus had to make his own accommodation with life—and its succession of grief, happiness, failure, achievement" (Faig, *UL* 228).[36]

A fundamental *circularity* can be thus detected in Barlow's poetry—a circularity that, in fact, moves from his existential attitude, then extends its discourse on time and memory and finally "returns" to existence but from a perspective truly cosmic, *enlarged* as a result of the temporal excursion. In fact, Barlow's poetic excursions on time and memory are instrumental to the fictional and poetical representation of his bleak cosmic visions, mostly inherited from Lovecraft. They deal in particular with the awareness of the emptiness and insubstantiality of human existence *when confronted with the immensity, both spatial and temporal, of the vast cosmos-at-large and the universes therein*. In Barlow's poetry, one can find splendidly balanced pieces such as the dream-inspired story of a demiurgic fiddler, in "Second Year: Dream While Paris Was Threatened":

> Once there was a fiddler. By and by the fiddler came into the universe and looked at his watch and began to fiddle. And there was Greece. He kept looking at his watch and walking in and out of the universe and each time he fiddled there was a new culture. By and by he came and sat and fiddled for four years and there was a great battle, and then he looked at his watch which hadn't tarnished any more than the stars had, and walked out of the universe for twenty years. Then he came back and fiddled energetically for a while. And then he laid down his fiddle and laughed and walked out of the universe, for there was no one left to fiddle to. (*EG* 183-84)

This short prose-poem represents Barlow's mocking cosmogony: the whole creation of the world is reduced to the playing of a fiddler, whose final laughter in the face of his demiurgic operation is highly explicative of the overall joke, delusion, and trap that the universe, and existence therein, configure. What could be more cosmically unflattering for mankind's aspirations and boastings than depicting the cosmos it inhabits as a mere joke, as the creation of a player who decided to fiddle just as a prop to occupy his time?

The cosmic attitude in Barlow's poetry informs its verses quite pervasively. Their frequent mention of stars, planets, and universes can be interpreted as a revelatory sign fostering a cosmic interpretation:

---

36. A Lovecraftian letter underlines this feature of RHB's personality. Listing RHB's name together with those of many others friends and colleagues (among the others, Clark Ashton Smith, Cook, Long, Howard Wandrei), HPL remarks that all these people "& I have no beliefs outside recognised natural science," concluding that "Most of the science-fiction writers [. . .] believe as little as I do": letter to Emil Petaja, 5 April 1935 (*SL* 5.140). In a letter to RHB, 21 August 1933, HPL is even more explicit: "Like you, I consider the religious myths & kindred absurdities a vast burden on mankind" (*FF* 75).

> Only the stars disputed her[37] domain,
> Earth otherwise was vacant. Eagle-high
> The god called Tonitiuth from his fane
> Stared out upon the sun with equal eye,
> But though his breast a wheel of gold displayed,
> From humble straw his servants' huts were made.
>   ["Quetzalcoatl," ll. 9-14 (EG 168)]

The references to gods, sun, stars, etc., witness Barlow's inclination toward a cosmic approach to existence and art. In the quoted lines, the contrast is between the earth, as domain of the terrestrial, and the stars, the cosmic domain of Tula, the Citadel of Gods.

Barlow's poetry, as well as his fiction,[38] is capable of showing a *unified cyclical cosmic vision*, in which the merciless laws of chance and rigid determinism rule in an indifferent cosmos that shows neither sympathy for mankind nor a teleological structure oriented toward the fulfilment of mankind's aspirations:

> The ocean vast from myriad darts of rain,
> The seeds of atoms sprouting into stars,
> The cells of flesh, its ecstasies and pain,
> These things are one, masked by its avatars.
> That comets whirl, that sinew clings to bone,
> That seedlings swell, that insects spawn and die,
> *Is fore-ordained*—the <u>patterned</u> evening sky
> Is brother to the <u>patterned</u> river-stone.
>
> *Prolific life spills out of chance's cup*
> Across this lawn of green and golden fields,
> The fountainous grain matures and thereon yields
> To mouths of drought, but other crops well up.
> In this design all cosmic <u>pattern</u> blend,
> Involved with gorgeous, *void of ultimate end*.
>   ["Untitled" (EG 154; italics and underscoring added)]

The first four lines of this revelatory poem underscore the principle of cosmic unity equalizing everything in the universe, from stars to atoms, from cells to oceans to feelings. I have italicized "is fore-ordained" because this expression tells of the determinism ruling the cosmos. Another key word in Barlow's cosmicism

---

37. The reference is to Tula, the Citadel of Gods.
38. An extensive analysis, in this regard, is merited by some of his mature tales, such as "A Dim-Remembered Story," "The Summons," "Return by Sunset," "The Root-Gatherers," and above all "The Night Ocean" and "'Till A' the Seas.'" This last one in particular can be considered a masterpiece of fictional cosmicism in imitation of HPL (for a discussion of the cosmic nuances of this tale, see chapter 4, paragraph 4.2.1, "'Till A' the Seas' and other dreadful ends").

is *pattern*: he believed that existence was governed by a set of deterministic rules tracking our paths and forcing us to follow pre-established schemes. Life is a product of "chance's cup," of a chaotic "design" that blends all patterns together and deprives them of any "ultimate end." As in the repetitive playing of a fiddler, worlds are continually created and destroyed: the image of "spinning" recurs as a metaphor of the incessant, cyclical texturing of worlds: "brief worlds in briefer ages spin" ("Untitled," l. 2, EG 154). And within a universe seething with its "dead stars of the abyss" (ibid., l. 4), the allegedly kind reference to the insignificant grain of sand humans inhabit, "this dear jewel Earth" (ibid., l. 10), can only be ironic. Black (and bleak) humor constitutes, at times, the only means Barlow had for facing unflattering cosmic truths. According to Faig, "It would be wrong [. . .] to leave the impression of unrelieved darkness and gloom; there are indeed genuine instances of humour in Barlow's poetry, albeit sometimes 'black' humour" (*UL* 214), as in these lines from "Rainy-Day Pastime":

Let us acknowledge we are tomcats mummified in alabaster vases
With powdered stuff, nutmeg and bay leaves, flavouring the sockets of our eyes.
(EG 195)

It is also in the very title of the poem "Viktoria," of which more in the paragraph 9.2.5 on "Nature," that Barlow's black humor is manifested: a very gloomy and unhappy victory in war is represented.

Existence is ontologically doomed, since it is haunted by a "persecuting Self" ("Untitled," l. 8, EG 170): despair and sorrow do not stem from an external source, they reside in our own essence of human beings, in our "Selves" as parts of an indifferent cosmos. Barlow's poetry questions the possible solutions to this aporia. His poetry proposes two possible alternatives: either to trick the persecuting Self originating our sense of displacement, or to loose it as if it were a wild animal. What is certainly *not* possible is a pacific and fruitful living together with it. Barlow would prefer not to choose between the two options: his favorite solution would again be giving up and opting for inaction, searching for rest, stasis, and apathy:

"Oh golden beach and blue-enamelled sea
And guardian sky—not fearsome as by night
When toiling stars mill meteors to dust—
Rest of the heart, and of the heart's vain lust
Cease as the gull in his arrested flight;
Do not advance, loved day, but yield to me
Again and evermore the splendid kiss;
Abide, sweet hour, who bathes and binds the wound
Of being life and change were change is death
And almost seems to heal it, Lift no wreath
Of cloud to your calm bow, nor chilly stone
To shatter the tense and crystal pool of bliss.
["Untitled" (EG 165-66)]

Many images recall the idea of stasis and rest: "rest," "cease," "arrested," "do not advance," "abide," etc. The poet shows his lack of will to advance and fight, his search for an impossible equilibrium, since "change is death" (another very Lovecraftian concept). Bliss is a "pool"—again a static image—and must not be shattered, like a delicate crystal object in danger of being destroyed.

What results from the choice of inaction, I suspect, is Barlow's conscious admission of his own defeat, his own failure as a human being:

> No more than leaves, as crisp as pages kept
> On shelves from papers out of date, once swirled
> By wind, can sleep as earlier they slept
> Can I find rest, or harbour in the world.
> No more than driven wind which drives them forth,
> From fruitless bough to bough, itself in quest,
> Finds fair as camp one country south or north
> Can I lie in a sheltered place and rest.
> ["Dawn Delayed," ll. 1-8 (EG 162)]

In a "blind world blind" ("Rainy-Day Pastime," l. 22, EG 196) that does not grant her a truce, in which even the tormentor is himself in quest and doomed not to find rest, no consolation is left for the living creature. The best way to find rest and relief at last is by the supreme sublimation of insensitiveness and stasis, death. Here we see the circularity of Barlow's poetry's at work: suicide comes back—no longer on the personal and intimate level where it started, but on the cosmic and existential level, as a necessity for living creatures.

As a matter of fact, we are nothing other than weak, transitory, mortal creatures: Barlow's finest poems dealing with temporality are those that, assuming a cosmic perspective, question the expediency and soundness of man's waiting for the natural end of existence. These poems focus on the most important feature of existence—its temporary nature, its transitoriness, its "Intimations of *Mortality*":

> The millions of years ahead,
> When we swing as dust between moon and sun,
> As we soon must, will be less fun
> (Being dead, I mean), less fun
> Than setting thorn trees out in pots,
> Than scratching cats' fleas, cats' ears,
> Oh, lots less fun, I have no doubt,
> Than ever going to church.
>
> The millions of days ahead,
> When we lurch about Mars
> Like smoke fled!
> (Visitors' old cigar-smoke
> Ascending a cold parlour at night,

> With the blaze of light ending,
> The dog put out).
>
> ["Intimations of Mortality" (EG 199)]

Seen from the temporal cosmic perspective of millions of years—and worlds—ahead, the meaning of our existence equates to that of dust swirling between moon and sun, or of cigar-smoke in a parlor. Poems like these represent Barlow's courageous attempt to take a glance back at the human destiny of cosmic insignificance, to unmask the stark *truth* without hesitation, contextually rejecting any consoling but irremediably *false* view of existence. From the cosmic perspective, the lives, plans, goals, feelings, thoughts, and achievements not only of a single human being, but of entire civilizations, are no more solidly consistent than the smoke of a cigar: this is the lesson that the "millions of years ahead," the flowing of temporality, teach to a fearless, honest intellect.

A short glance at Barlow's fiction only confirms, and even reinforces, the bleak deterministic and cosmic attitude of his poetry. Let us examine some short excerpts from the conclusion of "A Dim-Remembered Story," a masterpiece of original remodeling of Lovecraftian themes and stylistic concerns (first of all, his aesthetic of *vagueness*, already so plainly declared at the outset in the titular "Dim"). The disembodied soul and spirit of the protagonist have been transported back and forth into the "sucking whirlpool of time" (EG 104). A truly cosmic and deterministic perspective is endorsed when the narrator claims: "Into the great distances I went, to Infinity and her sheer end. It was ordained that, like a pendulum, my spirit must complete the far swing, where matter could not go" (EG 104). Here *It was ordained* points again at a pre-ordered pattern to be fulfilled, a deterministic scheme to which man can only bow. The cosmicism of this tale is everywhere perceptible, but a few final sentences summarize in a spectacular way most of the concepts expounded in this section:

> my bones shall be wind-borne dust, and I shall have known rebirth in grass and flowers and dark roots, many centuries before masons lay trowel to the first stone of that edifice. The place where it will rise, in more than a dozen tens of centuries, is now an active city, with steel and glass and concrete walls that seem very permanent. But I know them as ephemera [. . .] It saddens me to think of the bright sunshine and the fresh wind that will come long after I am worm-infested. Having seen it I know that in this world about me I can nevermore find zest, desire, or consolation. (EG 104)

In this meaningful passage concluding the tale, we find temporal cosmicism (the narrator analyzes his plight from the perspective of "a dozen tens of centuries"), the consequences of the eternal flowing of time on the meaning of existence ("my bones shall be wind-borne dust," with the recurring of the image of dust found in the poetry), the notion that everything is transitory, with the attached opposition between truth and falsity (everything that *appears* "very permanent" *is* no more than "ephemera"), and the awareness that this world offers man no rest, no nepenthe against the bitter cosmic insignificance he has to cope with.[39]

In conclusion, we may remark that Barlow's concern for the passing away of things, and his awareness of the impossibility of achieving anything stable in life, are very well represented both in his poetry and his fiction, and perhaps constitute the most important preoccupation of his entire art and speculation, leading him toward the conception of an *indifferent* cosmos in which no achievements are worth pursuing; and the possible connection of these assumptions with his suicide adds a sinister, revelatory character to the analysis of his poetry.

9.2.3 "Dream": Sleep and Wake

Much of the symbolic and allegoric value of Barlow's poetry lies in the role played by dreams in his poetic inspiration. The charm and the oddities of the free visual associations—so typical, as we have seen in "Sense," of Barlow's poetry—may perhaps be attributed to the unpredictable, irrational influence of dream. In fact, dreams carry an important value in Barlow's poetry as well as in his life, because they are the harbingers of a truth coming from beyond earthly sensory perceptions. Barlow himself recognized the strong impact dreams exerted over his personality: his youth especially was imbued in fantasies and in the *outré* worlds of weird fiction and poetry. In his memoir "The Wind That Is in the Grass" (1944), while accounting for the visit Lovecraft paid to the Barlows in 1934, Robert remarks that the conversations with his mentor were "full of off-hand references to ghouls and vaults of terror on the surfaces of strange stars" and that these lines were kept alive by his "own absorption in dreams and dream-tales" (WG 359). And it is Lovecraft himself, in a letter to Barlow, who provides a significant testimony of his pupil's vivid dreams, which were potentially usable for fictional purposes: "Your recent dreams surely are prize-winners for grotesqueness. [. . .] Now & then I have paradoxical dreams like the ones you cite—though I really can't recall any recent instances quite so full of amusing possibilities as yours" (13 July 1933; FF 68). Even while describing the aesthetics of his own poetry, Barlow recognized the unconscious origin of most of his inspiration: to him, the inspiration for writing a poem springs from something he sees, "perhaps only in a dream or imagining" ("Statement about Poetry," EG 178). At times, a poem may also "be touched off by a trick phrase which occurs to me, perhaps in a half-dreaming state" (EG 179), a plight that leads him to "jot down," half-asleep, such unusual "gibberish" as "The read-letter day Saint, Nathaniel Froghorn, base and viol" (EG 179). Immediately after recognizing that the foremost ability of a poet should be "to put words to working by themselves without any task-master" (EG 179) (a truly modernistic assumption), Barlow connects this ability with the impact of

---

39. For a lengthier discussion of the temporal concerns in RHB's fiction, as well as on their connection with the cosmicistic attitude, see chapter 5 on "Time."

dreams, toward which mainly children are receptive. Let us note incidentally here that the connection of dreams with the creative powers of childhood is a constant refrain of the poetics of the fantastic, shared by Lovecraft as well as by the other masters of the genre (Smith, Howard, Dunsany).

Some of the most hermetic passages in Barlow's poetry may be tentatively interpreted in the light of his statements about the inspirational power dreams exert on his compositions. Some of the obscure symbols of his poetry may indeed have had an unconscious source:

> What craftsman in what drunken humour planned
> This gorgeous futile van more frail than glass
> And dropped it on the ground where cold seeds lie
> Sealed in by winter's white impenetrable hand?
> Must all its clamorous motion fade and pass
> For want of the swollen grapes it sees on high?
> ["Who Will Not Know," ll. 23-28 (EG 159)]

The near-Carrollian nonsense of many of Barlow's verses may find an explanation in connection with the non-rationally explicable processes of dream. A psychoanalytic analysis may reveal an anthropological basis and an archetypal root for Barlow's images,[40] their sources and the apparently random criterion employed in their association.

The hymn devoted to Sleep, already analysed in the paragraph 9.2.2 on "Memory," comes again into the picture. Sleep is perceived by Barlow as a balm against the weariness of life: Sleep's "liberal wine" (l. 2, EG 172) is an antidote to the poison of existence's "dull teas" (l. 4). Barlow invokes Sleep as the cure against the temptations of the waking life, the lures of the materialistic society:

> Declare your regency, for fear this eye
> Be spelled again by the splendours of the flesh. (ll. 33-34)

The opposition between sleep and wake comes to a crucial point where the poet fully declares his feelings:

> But give no gate to dawn when he comes clad
> In golden cloth: he is a spy
> Hated by lovers all, but hated most
> By me whose love unrivalled is yourself. (ll. 55-58)

---

40. In particular, the application to RHB's poetry of some of the principles founding Durand's "The Anthropological Structures of the Imaginary" may prove fruitful. Durand's book, stemming from a Jungian understanding of the unconscious, deals with the structure of human imagination, within which it establishes a typology of figures, organized structurally according to several central archetypes and focusing on man's subjective experience of space and time. And we have seen how much temporality affects RHB's poetry and is able to generate powerful images, thanks to the filter of RHB's subjective experience.

Sleep is the protector of lovers, whereby the mysterious "he," the harbinger of dawn and light, can be identified with the deceptive "splendours" of the waking time.

Sleep, "alone no traitor" (l. 1) in the camp of existence, symbolizes a rescuing death that is called forth in order to wrap up everything living, making mankind quiet and cutting off its sorrows. The identification of Sleep with a liberating death is made explicit in the following lines:

> It is not we who die, but pain and dread,
> It is not we who lie completely wed
> To grass and gravel, it is discontent. (ll. 24-26)[41]

Therefore, the contrast between sleeping and waking is resolved by Barlow entirely in favor of the former. Waking is the plight of humanity's vain, doomed efforts and plans, whereby it is during sleep (and of course in the state of its "intensification," death) that man realizes himself. Therefore, as an apparent paradox, waking is the condition of the "sleeper," the man who does not properly "live," while sleep is the truly waking state. Thus the poet paradoxically begs sleep to "waken" mankind from its empty materialistic ambitions, those of the conventional "waking" plight:

> Waken us, Sleep, from all this dream of Man!
> . . .
> We have too long lain prisoner—we fail
> To spy the careless key upon the floor,
> And overstay our terms by many a year. (ll. 59-63)[42]

The blurring of borders between waking and sleeping constitutes an example of Barlow's attempt to overstep the bounds, to reconcile the dialectical (and, in his perspective, conflicting) condition of mankind, eternally suspended in a dual structure of opposites, whose distance Barlow strove all his life to overcome or at least shorten. Another attempt of this sort will be discussed in "Nature," where Barlow's poetry—coherently with his fiction—will be shown to crave a reconciliation of the "opposites" Nature and Culture.

The attempt to blur the borders between waking and sleeping leads Barlow to perceive sleep as a form of "enlightened" waking, in line with the poetics of fantasy, which traces no rigid distinction between the two conditions. Here once more Lovecraft's influence on Barlow is detectable: Lovecraft often confessed that many of his poems and narratives not only gave literary status to dreams he actually had had, but were even written in a half-asleep state, either inspired by a dream[43] or transcribed verbatim from an actual dream.[44] Not surprisingly, in Bar-

---

41. The alliteration of "grass" and "gravel" draws the attention more closely to the metaphorical association of sleep with death.

42. This awareness of an "overstaying" of man on the planet is perhaps to be understood as RHB's adumbration of the necessity (or even only the perspective) of suicide.

43. To show the everlasting importance of this source on HPL's devising of plots, I men-

low's autobiographical paper there is a similar statement, where he claims that even after the summer of 1940 "my dreams were still vivid and interesting to me" (OLL 25), adding that he actually composed the prose-poem "The Fiddler" under the inspiration of a dream, or better, that he properly "dreamed" (OLL 25)[45] the poem itself. Moreover, Lovecraft himself once stated that he was not even sure of the actual "authorship" of his dream-inspired tales, since those plots and images derived from an unconscious source he was not fully aware of, and ultimately external to him.[46]

A full comprehension of both the inspiring (for Barlow's literature) and the salvific (to fight the weariness of existence) power of dreams can be detected by an inferential operation, since dreams are the natural experience occurring during the sleeping state—and we saw Barlow's poetry attach a wholesome, rescuing value to sleep. But there is more: the connection between sleep and dreams is plainly stated by Barlow himself, in the poem "Evening":

> The dream I had between sins, which fluttered like a tulip
> Explored by a beetle;
> Which was *all* my dreams
> To the secure eye of sleep. (EG 192)

I will take now an excursion into Barlow's fiction, whose poetics clearly supports the blurred distinction between waking and sleep/dream. An entire cycle of juvenile tales seems to show dreamlike inspiration: the *Annals of the Jinns*, nine episodes of which appeared in the *Fantasy Fan* from October 1933 to February 1935. The Dunsanian flavor of these early sketches is easily recognizable, for example in the very names of the locations of the dream country (the river Olaee, the village of Ullathia, the towns of Phoor, Naazim, Perenthines, the planet Loth,

---

tion two examples coming from very different periods: "Celephaïs" (1920) is said to weave together a "large number of my recent dreams" (letter to Rheinhart Kleiner, 14 December 1921; SL 1.162), and à propos of "The Evil Clergyman" (1933), HPL states that "Some months ago I had a dream of an evil clergyman in a garret full of forbidden books, and of how he changed his personality with a visitor" (letter to Clark Ashton Smith, 22 October 1933; SL 4.289–90).

44. The most celebrated example of this last case is "The Statement of Randolph Carter" (1919), which HPL admitted was "based on an actual dream of mine" (letter to Rheinhart Kleiner, 27 December 1919; SL 1.100), a dream that he extensively recounted in a letter to the Gallomo of December 11 (SL 1.94–97). HPL retold several dreams to RHB during his first visit in Florida, and we have already remarked RHB's statement that many of HPL's tales were based on "actual dreams" ("Memories of Lovecraft," OLL 16).

45. In effect "The Fiddler," with its apparently simple and disconnected narrative pace, is likely to have had a dream or dreamlike source.

46. HPL solved the conundrum this way: "I hate to take credit, when I did not really think out the picture with my own conscious wits. Yet if I do not take credit, who'n Heaven *will* I give credit tuh? Coleridge claimed 'Kubla Khan', so I guess I'll claim the thing an' let it go at that" (letter to the Gallomo, 11 December 1919; SL 1.97).

etc.) and of the characters (kings Alair and Luud, sorcerer Khalda, monster Krang, the mysterious Flower-God, etc.). Narration sinks in a suspended, out-of-time, dreamy atmosphere.[47] The very fact that these short tales are all connected with one another to form a coherent cycle (in terms of geographical setting, involved characters, and even legendary books such as the *Hsothian Manuscripts*) is indicative of young Barlow's desire to emulate the masters of the fantastic and of his voracious juvenile readings, also re-creating a dreamlike setting. Moreover, Barlow himself wrote a short fantasy titled "A Dream."[48] However, it is in the more mature fiction that dream comes to be closely related with the explorations of abysses of time leading to disquieting revelations: "undreamed" ("A Dim-Remembered Story," *EG* 86) in the future are the years in which the castle of Yrn will rise, visited by the protagonist in a phase of dreamlike suspension from reality. The revelatory power of sleep and dream is heavily remarked upon in "The Night Ocean" (1936), perhaps Barlow's most convincing fictional effort. Experiences undertaken in dreams are vastly superior, in poignancy and truth-value, to whatever man is allowed to perceive in the waking state:

> Things seen by the inward sight, like those flashing visions which come as we drift into the blankness of sleep, are more vivid and meaningful to us in that form than when we have sought to weld them with reality. Set a pen to a dream, and the colour drains from it. The ink with which we write seems diluted with something holding too much of reality, and we find that after all we cannot delineate the incredible memory. It is as if our inward selves, released from the bonds of daytime and objectivity, revelled in prisoned emotions which are hastily stifled <u>w</u>hen <u>w</u>e <u>w</u>ould translate them. In dreams and visions lie the greatest creations of man, for on them rests no yoke of line or hue. (*EG* 105)[49]

Dreams reveal a truth that man can hardly hope to grasp through the rational means of objective speculation. The poetic, suspended nature of this passage, reinforced by the alliteration "<u>w</u>hen <u>w</u>e <u>w</u>ould," renders more effective the notion that reality and objectivity destroy human capacity to dream, and this is a dead blow, for one who has "always been a seeker, a dreamer, and a ponderer on seek-

---

47. For example, the employment of alliterations is again very abundant here, especially but not exclusively in his short prose-poems; in the substantial work "A Dim-Remembered Story" (1936), we find an impressive case of prolonged alliteration in the locution "I <u>w</u>as sick <u>w</u>ith <u>w</u>eariness <u>w</u>hen <u>w</u>e stood" (*EG* 94). Also archaisms in spelling can be found in RHB's fiction: in "The Fidelity of Ghu" (1934), the protagonist claims that a messenger of the gods "spake" (*EG* 41) to him, and in "The Temple" (1935), the feminine protagonist of chapter 3 undergoes a transformation that turns her into "an ancient and repulsive *beldame*" (*EG* 42). For a more detailed discussion on the formal Dunsanian influence on RHB's fiction, see chapter 2, paragraph 2.2.1, "The formal aspects of Barlow's Dunsanianism."

48. Published in the first issue of RHB's amateur journal *The Dragon-Fly* (15 October 1935, 1–6).

49. The entire passage, except for a slight stylistic polishing, is the fruit of RHB's pen, as the analysis of the manuscript bearing HPL's corrections attests.

ing and dreaming; and who can say that such a nature does not open latent eyes sensitive to unsuspected worlds and orders of being?" (EG 105).[50]

Besides remarking the already noted Barlow's constant concern on the theme of the *expansion* of human sensory perception beyond the limits of the five senses,[51] the last sentence of the quoted passage reinforces the impression of Barlow's as a *sensitive* soul (of which more in "Nature"), in the etymological acceptation of a soul endowed with (striving for) a capability of "perception" denied to others, because it relies on senses forbidden or undeveloped in other human beings. Barlow seems even to hint to an *elitist* (and very Lovecraftian) understanding of man's access to the revelatory power of dream: "although dreams are in all of us, few hands may grasp their moth-wings without tearing them" (EG 105; the passage is entirely RHB's). Though the narrator here does not necessarily attribute this quality to himself (his immediately following remark is: "Such skill this narrative does not have"), I suspect that here Barlow is referring, if not to himself, to his master Lovecraft and to the other few writers he strongly admired at the time.

9.2.4 "Essence": Internal and External

The poet Rosalie Moore will be remembered as having been one of the members of the Activist group. During her militancy in Hart's entourage, she got to know Barlow in depth. As his personal acquaintance, she left a memoir[52] of Barlow both the man and the poet, dealing with the originality of his manners as well as of his versification. Through her words, we get an in-depth insight on Barlow's authentically sensitive personality, its strengths, qualities, and oddities. The passage deserves to be quoted in full:

> With his scholarly bearing, large spectacled eyes, and precise manners, strict as a beetle, Robert Barlow was often such a person that you did not want, in his presence, to do anything that was not accurate, use the vague word, or keep any of your pretensions toward conventional falseness.
>
> He also had a forbearance which allowed you time for making the right relation, and a great deal of warmth and sympathy which furnished a sort of climate in helping you to find it.

---

50. In fairness to both RHB and HPL, we must remark that this passage was an addition by HPL's pen (see the facsimile of the manuscript in Faig, *R. H. Barlow*), though the master's supplement should here be simply understood as a way of helping his pupil to render his viewpoint more aesthetically effective, reinforcing RHB's point and not tampering with its essence.

51. In "The Night Ocean" itself, another hint to this key issue can be detected in the passage "There is a ceaseless change in the waters—colours and shades pass over them like the insubstantial expressions of a well-known face; and these are at once communicated to us by *half-recognized senses*" (EG 108; italics added; the passage is entirely RHB's).

52. Published privately by Lawrence Hart in *Accent on Barlow: A Commemorative Anthology* (1962).

Sometimes, like the rest of us, he simply made mistakes of judgement, or burbled inaccuracies, and because they were stumbles or errors (and anyone with his brilliance of range was bound to make them) he would barely forgive himself; then, after a while, do so—although not until he had pounded unforgivably on some bar, told an unpleasant anecdote, or executed some other saleable tantrum in self-revenge.

I have seen Robert Barlow also commit himself to the most joyfully abandoned behaviour, launch into a speech or a wild dance like a short Dionysus; yet in some way this was done as a matter of policy, forgiving himself in advance.

This was the character of the man who wrote these poems, as we knew him in the Activist Group. If you could say only one thing about him, you would say he was a gentleman and a sort of pedant. But if you were allowed to say two, you would say that he was a *breaker of forms*. Actually, it was deeper than that. Barlow was an *essentialist*, and if he couldn't get to the center of a thing, he broke it. (Quoted in Faig, *UL* 214-15; italics added)

Barlow, as we have seen, strongly perceived the vanity and emptiness of life and of human achievements. He saw existence as a void enshrouded in false appearances of happiness. Therefore he strove to find and reach the core, the "thing in itself," the impossible *quid* of human immundation.[53] Perhaps this could again be understood as a sign of Barlow's sensitive, meditative nature and of his inability to stop at the surface and appearances (the dialectics between truth and falsity lying at the core of his poetics). Faig too remarks Barlow's concern for "the necessity to get at the 'real' concerns of life. [. . .] Like many another sensitive person, Barlow simply chose to reject everyday life for the *core* of his existence" (*UL* 228; italics added).

Barlow was in this sense an "essentialist," and this philosophical attitude attained a wide resonance, on the textual level, in his poetry. The challenge was: How to render stylistically and thematically the search for the "essence," the "core" of experiences and phenomena? Barlow solved the puzzle in his own brilliant way: by resorting to (association of) visual images, at times very poignant and concrete, dealing with, and representative of, *interiority*. However, this would have been too traditional a solution, if these images referred to a *spiritual* interiority, eventually depicted as the locus of a moral conflict, or of rest from the battles of existence. The innovativeness of Barlow's approach, as a "breaker of forms" in his essentialism, resides in the attention to *physical* interiority, especially of the human body. Not only are references to *external* parts of the human body present in Barlow's poetry, especially in connection with the infelicitous chant for his homosexual loves; images of bones, skulls, even of internal organs and tissues also abound in

---

53. HPL's influence on RHB can be detected also on this level. It was a constant Lovecraftian preoccupation to search for the primal causes of phenomena, the "ultimate reality": a scientific and positivistic attitude that is widely witnessed by the themes HPL touched on in his letters. Here is one of the several possible examples: "The search for ultimate reality is the most ineradicable urge in the human personality—the basis of every real religion, and the foundation of all that nobly poetic body of philosophy which has its fount in Plato" (letter to Woobdurn Harris, February-March 1929; *SL* 2.301).

the hazardous visual associations of his poetry, as unconventional metaphors for the exhausting search for the thing in itself, for the ultimate meaning of existence. That this meaning perhaps does not exist, or is not attainable, is confirmed by the representation of an indelible pain, this time both physical and spiritual, sprouting from the images of physical interiority. It is as if Barlow's pessimism claims that, though conflict mainly takes place on the physical level, pain is a universal of human existence involving both its physical and spiritual dimensions.

Among the most visually striking examples of images of physical interiority are those in the poem "New Directions" (EG 180-81), which retells the poet's descent to Hell, a potentially very traditional topos; but Barlow, far from opting for a classical treatment of the theme, discovers that Hell's doors are "cluttered with ribs and cheek bones" (l. 8), a macabre detail that would have hardly found verbalization in Milton's poetry, nor even in Ovid's or Dante's verses. In "The Conquered" (EG 184), "incisors," "sphincters," and "hearts" are mentioned. However, the most telling example of a verbalization of an inner aspect of physicality takes place in the frequent occurrences of "bones"[54] (and bone-related items, such as "jaw-bone,"[55] "skulls,"[56] "skeletons"[57]) and especially "marrow," an image employed in order to express the suffering, mostly physical, of the endurance of life: "Eyes had beheld the desperate rolling of eyes [. . .] Had beheld the armored ants of pain exploring the marrow" ("First Year: Sebastian," ll. 9 and 11, EG 185).

Moral suffering attached to the visual experience of physical interiority is implied by *mourning*. One of the finest poems of Barlow's entire production is "Mourning Song," which voices the spiritual pain springing from the sheer awareness of the *presence* of internal organs and tissues in the body of a dear deceased:

> Grandma is dead, her bones dragged in his kennel
> By the pious dog Death to prey upon.
> Let us burn the wheatfield then, and burn the stars and birds
> And avoid the Spring by going to San Francisco
> And wind the clocks with ivy.

---

54. "or bones not too well cured": "A Escoger," l. 10 (EG 189). And again: "O that frog or flower that stealthily / Snipped from the bone Black Tezcatlipoca's foot!": "Mythological Episode," ll. 1-2 (EG 195).

55. "A jaw-bone specked with rust roses is your unnatural concrete": "To the Builders of a Dam," l. 6 (EG 187).

56. "Describing an astronomy of skulls": "Recantation," l. 19 (EG 188). Also in the poems written in Spanish it is possible to detect RHB's constant interest in physical interiority. In an untitled poem, we read: "Un cielo de calavera blanca / Incrustada con mosaico de turquesa" ("A sky of white skull / Fixed with mosaic of turquoise": ll. 3-4), and "Y en el lueco de los ojos / Siempre el hilo cobrizo, tenido de uva" ("And in the hole of the eyes / Always the coppery thread, dyed of grape": ll. 6-7): EG 198-99.

57. "The skeleton-jointed stars hold the world": "We Kept on Reading 'Tuesday,'" l. 14 (EG 190).

> They have condemned her flesh for settlement of worms,
> Who also have livers and lymph, and in a sense can be said to live,
> As indeed, one could say of Grandma. (EG 193)

Lines 2 and 6, hinting at the decomposing effect death will have on the corpse, add a macabre though explanatory note: Barlow's association of pain with physical interiority probably stems from his awareness of the inevitability of the decomposition and decay of the dead body, and we already saw in "Memory" how frightening and disturbing an issue was decay in Barlow's poetics.

The consideration of the frankly *biological* nature of the human being—the sheer fact that we are made of flesh and bones, not dissimilarly from any other mammal on the scale of evolution—results in an unflattering view of the origin and status of mankind as an animal species. With an unsavory touch of black humor, this is how Barlow elucidates the contemptible origins and goals of the race to which he belongs:

Let us examine our bones, ours and our ancestors'
Haul them down from the attic.
Let us acknowledge we are tomcats mummified in alabaster vases
With powdered stuff, nutmeg and bay leaves, flavouring the sockets of our eyes—
. . .
The game is up, they have discovered us.
Here at the border station between cliff centuries we are caught smuggling . . . .
nothing, in innocent packages.
We have learned to hold teacups so artfully that no one detects the absence of tea.
["Rainy-Day Pastime," ll. 1-4 and 12-15 (EG 195)]

The last line metaphorically expresses a concept dear to Barlow, the ultimate vacuity of human plans, efforts, and boasts: this philosophical reflection originates from the direct observation of human "bones" and from the recognition of the essentially biological nature of the human being.

The opposition between truth and falsity analyzed in "Memory" takes now the form of a dialectical confrontation between surface (appearance) and core (essence), *external and internal*. In the poem "The Heart," whose title is already significant in our current topic, one reads:

> Then hold the four limbs apart on the stone and the knife wit<u>h</u>out <u>d</u>elicacy
>   <u>d</u>rives <u>th</u>em <u>d</u>own, and the tissue is rended and the flowers uprooted.
>   Now the bones come into their viceroyship, and winds may carve at their
>   leisure glyphs on the fleshless thighs, on the face, where they will.
> It is worse than you thought. (EG 196)

The action of the knife, stylistically underscored by the repetition of the dental occlusive *d* ("wit<u>h</u>out <u>d</u>elicacy <u>d</u>rives <u>th</u>em <u>d</u>own"), is one of uprooting internal tissues and exposing them to the action of external winds. The confrontation of the internal (the tissues, the organs) with the external (the wind) is possible only through rending, bloodying, and ultimately death. In Barlow's poetry this opposition, far from resolving its conflict through an internal dialectics, cannot help resulting in a lethal end. Of course, in Barlow's resort to these unconventional images of physical interiority one can detect the originality and experimentalism of his poetry (these images come to the fore during the Activist phase), its breaking with tradition. Whether this device of his poetry actually succeeded in attaining the "center of things" the poet strove for, or whether at times it came to "break" it, it is matter of personal aesthetic evaluation.

9.2.5 "Nature": Nature and Culture

Not differently from his fiction,[58] the opposition between Nature and Culture represents one of the most meaningful themes in Barlow's poetry, as well as one of the textual elements most revelatory of the poet's personality.

For a full comprehension of the scope of this opposition, and the significance of the conflict it entails, it is first necessary to expound the major role Barlow's poetry assigns to images and elements derived from the natural environment. His poetry is full of references to animals, of two categories in particular: *birds* (gulls, fowls, herons, falcons, hummingbirds, etc.) and *insects* (bees, beetles, ants, butterflies, moths). Vegetable beings are also frequently mentioned, such as plants, roses, flowers, blossoms—very often, as we have seen, in connection with decay and withering of life. The poem "A Tapestry" displays a metatextual approach to the theme of Nature, since it is an example of Barlow's poetical attempt to highlight the intrinsic artistic value that the textual representation of Nature (like that of a stylized tapestry) may offer:

> The peavine hair of horses curls
> In the breeze four centuries old;
> Chestnut eyes glance down across the rein.
> A Greenland falcon teeters on the glove, his beak annoyed with velvet
> And the scent of verdigris and veins muffled from him.
> Bourbon lances, slippery for once with light,
> Fisted by men whose duty it is to kill strangers
> In strangers' lands,
> Surround the banner of an abolished lord.
> A dog dances past blue bushes of invented flowers
> And lets down his tongue, finding the afternoon long.
> This is no cloth for mouseteeth, though
> We have learned too much to know it. (EG 194)

In this poem, Barlow's treatment of the theme of Nature is much more complex and sophisticated. The image itself of "A dog dances" (in which we cannot fail to notice the alliteration of the voiced dental occlusive *d*) introduces the theme of *per-*

---

58. See chapter 6, paragraph 6.1.

sonification of nature, a central and revelatory one in Barlow's poetry. Through the attribution to natural elements, as well as to inanimate objects or even abstract principles, of actions, intentions, thoughts, and feelings typical of human beings, Barlow strives to attain a poetical *spiritualization* of Nature.[59] His aim is to show that a higher, more evolved perception of what lies under the surface would provide human beings with a better understanding of the spiritual, almost divine essence of Nature, and lead them to respect her and to observe her laws. Whether an actual *pantheism* is concretely at stake here will be judged from the following analysis.

In Barlow's poetry, not only may dogs dance, but calves may also be sorrowfully "weeping" ("The Coming Fructification by Night of Our Cyrus," l. 12, *EG* 192). Even inanimate objects may suddenly show signs of life: the lines "The hundred insinuating words of the moon / Fall on indignant shutters" ("The City," ll. 5-6, *EG* 194) reveal that in Barlow's spiritualized world the moon is able to speak and the shutters to show anger. The wind is described as a "woman" capable of loving and hating.[60] Any element of Barlow's poetic world is potentially susceptible of showing sentience and a variety of feelings, as well as intentionality. If the poet's "heart scowls now" ("In Order to Clarify," l. 1, *EG* 189), natural elements get their own physical and spiritual life: "The steep water abandons the cliff it tore, / And wanders into sleep" ("On Leaving Some Friends at an Early Hour," ll. 2-3, *EG* 190). Even the city is likely to be personified and assume the features of a living being, probably an animal, whose representation reposes, not surprisingly, on a description of her internal tissues and organs:

> This is the foetid cavern she broods in—
> Let us slay Grief and string the violin
> With <u>her</u> dark hair, discard <u>her</u> sombre eyes
> And of <u>her</u> skull a sounding drum devise;
> Make rattles of the teeth about <u>her</u> tongue,
> And music of <u>her</u> bones, who never sung.
> ["Untitled," ll. 5-10 (*EG* 160)][61]

The personification of the city equates it to a dead corpse and identifies it with Grief: it is then impossible to ascertain whether the following "her"s of the poem are to be ascribed to the city or to Grief—an abstract principle which in this case would get, on its/her turn, personified.

---

59. Analogous aesthetic goals directed toward the personification and spiritualization of Nature characterize RHB's fiction (see chapter 6, in particular paragraphs 6.2 and 6.3). A few more details on Nature's personification in RHB's fiction will be added here, to highlight the most relevant points in common the process shares with his poetry.
60. "The woman Wind, with love congealed / To hatred, walks the blighted field": "March," ll. 4-5 (*EG* 156).
61. The personification of towns is an image recurring in RHB's poetry: in "To Sleep" we also find at line 44 the "town's eyes shut" (*EG* 173).

At times, Barlow employs personification of a natural element to convey one of the main goals of his poetry, namely the bleak representation of man's misplaced position in the whirlpool of the indifferent cosmos, thus showing the eventual direct connection between the level of literary representation and that of philosophical speculation:

> These are the leaves
> To bury you in the mind:
> The new dog,
> The hole he ate in the carpet,
> The left-hand faucet
> Instead of the right.
> D— calling at dusk
> With the hint of something more at midnight.
> Yet any wind lifts the small leaves.
> ["Untitled" (EG 198)]

The key to interpreting these otherwise hermetic, cryptic lines lies in the image of "leaves": as a natural element, they are personified, becoming a metaphor for sensory perception. The last line is revealing in this regard: the "wind" lifting the leaves represents the disruptions that chaos and unpredictability provoke on humanity's plans, perceptions, and expectations. The fact that this wind is qualified by "any" underlines how feeble and inconsistent are the "leaves" of human life, how easily their disruption and disarrangement may occur.

A brief look at Barlow's fiction would show a pattern of spiritualization analogous to that of his poetry. In this regard, "The Night Ocean" (1936) is particularly revealing. The poetic prose of this tale proceeds to a personification of Nature and of inanimate objects on a large scale. The house on the beach where the protagonist dwells is endowed with physical, moral, and spiritual qualities: "it was more *lonely* than by the full light of either orb; and seemed to my imagination like *a mute, questioning face* turned toward me *expectant* of some action" (EG 109; italics added). The expression "to my imagination" sheds some light on the process of personification: Nature herself does not display human qualities; it is by means of the filter adopted by the sensitive observer that Nature becomes spiritualized, her semiotic self renovated. "Like a solitary warm animal it *crouched* facing the sea, and its inscrutable dirty windows *stared* upon a lonely realm of earth and sky and enormous sea [. . .] I thought the little house was lonely when I saw it, and that like myself, *it was conscious* of its meaningless nature before the great sea" (EG 106; italics added). And it is especially the sea itself, absolute protagonist of the narrative, that undergoes a startling process of personification: "I had been all the while accompanied by *the spirit of the lonely sea*. It was, I thought, *personified* in a shape which was not revealed to me, but which moved quietly about beyond my range of comprehension" (EG 107; italics added). The ocean, as a fully sentient being, has "moods" and is able to "forget" (EG 108). The "morning ocean [. . .] *has the eyes* of one who *ponders* on strange things" (EG 108; italics added), and the narrator's inward emotions were perhaps "only a reflection of the sea's own mood [. . .] The sea can bind us to *her many moods, whispering* to us by the subtle token of a shadow or a gleam upon the weaves, and *hinting* in these ways of *her mournfulness* or *rejoicing*. Always, she *is remembering* old things, and these *memories*, though we may not grasp them, are imparted to us, so that we share *her gaiety* or *remorse*" (EG 110; italics added). And in this triumph of personified natural elements, the sea is always a "she," and the sun is always a "he": "Gaining heart, the furtive sun exerted all *his* force in dispelling the old mist [. . .] and cast it from *his* realm" (EG 114; italics added). The constant emphasis on the "sentience" of Nature reinforces the claim of a pantheistic view on Barlow's part.

What is the main goal of personification-spiritualization in Barlow's poetry and other work? Again the textual manifestation probably conveys a personal emotion. The solitude and isolation of Barlow's existence led him to envision the world around him as an essentially cold, indifferent, and unsympathetic environment. Therefore, in his literary *poiesis* he felt the urge to populate the fictive world with *living* and *responding* creatures, objects, and even abstract principles. It is as if, through his literary creations, Barlow tried to exorcise—and sublimate—his own personal solitude: the representation of a poietic world in which he was able to converse with the moon, as well as to share the feelings of calves, or to perceive the moods of the sea, allowed Barlow an imaginative liberation from a tormented existence made up of what he felt to be arid scholarship conducted in depressing isolation.

Another fundamental feature of Barlow's poetry consists in its assertion of the unavoidable need to *respect* Nature and *defend* her against the destructive abuses perpetrated by man in the name of so-called (technological) progress. Here the *opposition between nature and culture* most forcefully enters the picture. In order to perceive this conflict as a truly devastating one, Barlow must have had a particularly negative vision of culture and of "progress," a vision on which Lovecraft himself could have exerted an influence. Barlow's poetry cannot see technological progress except in connection with the destructive effects that the Machine Age bears on nature. Criticisms against the aberrant effects of mechanization on nature abound in his poetry. This is the representation of the deadly violence perpetrated by "industrialization," especially through its cars and war machines, on the natural environment, a violence so pervasive as not to leave even a chance for weeping its devastations:

> Slow, like a glove off some Junker
> To hand a hostage death
> Beneath his own pear-tree.
> The clear cannon-bells seeping
> Along the sky
> Tremble the scum of blood on cement.
> Braided with tomcats exploding among the girders, the dark is so small there is

> no pocket for sleep.
> Nor holes in heaven for God to weep through.
>
> ["Third Year: About a Mythical Factory-Area" (EG 186)]

Natural elements such as the sky, the pear-tree, and the tomcats lose their vital properties and get juxtaposed to images of explosion, blood, and death.

The products of mechanization are often associated with darkness, and we are already familiar with the negative aesthetic and philosophical attachments Barlow's poetry assigns to it:

> There are only
> Suspended at an angle above the *luminous* gore of neon
> And the shops, the herding cars,
> Wildernesses of *night*.
> Tangles of *black* wind.
>
> ["Recantation," ll. 13-17 (EG 188; italics added)]

Cars themselves, trying to become "naturalized" (they herd like cattle), fight with—and rebel against—their own mechanic nature, which does not allow them to trespass the border. The opposition between nature and mechanization is so strong that no reconciliation is possible; the status of the "mechanical" is ontologically determined as antithetical to that of the natural.

In particular, one of the worst products of the Machine Age, large-scale war, is depicted in its devastating non-natural effects. War is perceived as a form of destructive violence perpetrated on Nature:

> In this sector of our years
> Who sees but tangled bayonets, the treads
> Of iron beetles kicking the sky?
> From the Murmansk to the Black Sea of life,
> We are woven in conflict,
> Knowing not whether our movements are Advance
> Or Retreat.
>
> ["Fourth Year: Letter to My Brother," ll. 1-7 (EG 186)]

In order to show the malignant effect of war on Nature, this poem devises a *subverted personification*: a natural element (beetles) is bent by war to its aberrant logic and laws, so that beetles lose their living and natural status and become iron bullets, subjected to the perverted logic of the massacre. The word "conflict," at line 5, is of course highly significant in this context, at least at a triple level: it stands for the "conflict" the poem is specifically dealing with (that of an actual war), for the "conflict" of a nature profaned by an attack of "culture," and for the "conflict" that signals the constitutive, ontological basis of mankind's existence.

However, it is in the gloomy atmosphere of the poem "Viktoria" that Barlow expresses his repudiation of war at his best. The sense of disorientation in the face of the absurdity of existence is conveyed through images of war and of the horror it engenders:

> But when our spears were cleansed and neatly stowed
> And the needless guard had ceased to prowl the camp,
> When the final tent put out its punctual lamp
> And only we lay wakeful in our blood,
> We heard a marshalling on bony mud,
> A falling into files of rot, a tramp
> Of feet out there unjointed by the damp;
> A sprouting of the crop we had sowed.
>
> The plain our swords had smoothed was all awry,
> All rooted up our neatly planted crop:
> Star-numberless those troops that will not die,
> But rise each night . . . What's to be done to stop
> The dead that disinter themselves? to keep
> By dark our daily gains—and still, to sleep? (EG 186)

The poem describes dreadful images of the consequences and aftermaths of war, a truly un-natural event, leading to the disinterment of the dead, as troops that will not die. When war hits, natural laws are defeated, and not even the most natural of all, the law of Death, is respected anymore: the dead find no rest in the afterlife; they come back to life as marshalling muddy troops, serving their new lord, war. All we have to win in war is our own dead rebelling, as a crop we sowed: this interpretation makes the black humor of the poem's title even more poignant, and aims at making people realize how bitter and unnatural a "Viktoria" achieved in war may be.[62]

Kenneth Faig too remarks that the cycle of five poems (of which "Viktoria" is the fifth) written during World War II plainly shows how Barlow, "unlike other poets who have been seduced by visions of martial glory, clearly perceives the unholiness of the whole carnage" (UL 212).

However, war is just one of the many different ways humanity possesses to do violence to Nature: uncontrolled building and slaughters of animals are other two activities addressed by Barlow's poetry, in "To The Builders of a Dam" and in "Warning to Snake Killers," respectively. The first poem stages a defense of nature against the abuses of mankind's "unnatural concrete" activity, in a conflict literarily rendered through the opposition between "trees" and "workmen":

> Under the sky's plain, on earth's plain
> You have fenced in the curved water's bloom.
> A jaw-bone specked with rust roses is your unnatural concrete,
> With the five petals extended over it where you permit.

---

62. Faig writes of the macabre tone of this poem "in its evocation of the desperation of military victory" (UL 213).

> But water knows many doors:
> Where shadows are hammered in the turf
> Are more trees than all your workmen. (EG 187)

The last three lines, and especially the opposition between trees (nature) and workmen (culture) hint at the unrestrainable powers of nature, at their ability to overcome even the hardest obstacles posited on her path by man, who may "hammer" any "shadow" he likes in the turf (again a symbol of darkness associated with a negative meaning), but nature will always display a stronger power ("are more trees than all your workmen").

"Warning to Snake Killers" again reveals the ecologist attitude of Barlow's poetry, where the defense of nature (it is advisable not to kill snakes) is also justified by the revenge that natural forces are capable of. This narrative-paced poem shows how the killing of a snake, perpetrated by an Indian, constitutes a sacrilegious affront to the forces of nature, whose rebellion takes shape in Tlaloc's order of "mildew spread on all the village corn" (EG 195).

The opposition between nature and culture involves two realms that, though different in character and extension, show blurred and permeable borders: an inter-exchange is possible between the two spheres, where both natural elements may become "humanized" and "spiritualized" (personification), and human beings may be endowed with properties typical of "natural" objects ("naturalization"). In a sense, the world of Barlow's poetry is fluidly "spiritualized": the demarcations between its inhabitants, whatever their origin (human, animal, even inanimate and abstract), are by no means well-defined. Besides "spiritualization" of nature, "naturalization" of human beings also takes place:

> The arrow is no legend.
> Like the hand of the sunlight laid on me
> Is your name; your mirror face.
> Even your name, o barkless white oak,
> Your publicly-said name.
> ["Admittance" (EG 194)]

The interlocutor of the poet is equated to the tree, his/her face to a mirror, and his/her name to that of a white oak.

And the poet himself proceeds to identification with a gull from a cliff:

> And I am made to sing his woe,
> Because I know his heart
> When over him the crisp wings go
> To turquoise realms apart.
> ["A Gull from a Cliff," ll. 17–20 (EG 170)]

In his attempt to perceive a universal consonance with the world around him (a device adopted, as we have seen, to fight his own isolation), the poet strives to become part of nature, in order to be allowed to sing her own grief. But this potentially salvific identification is again the source of conflict, because of an intrinsic, constitutive difference between man and nature: in fact, nature ignores her sorrows quickly, since she has no memory and no need to sing, while man, as a cultural and rational being, is doomed to remember and to express his sorrow in order to exorcise it:

> How soon a sorrow is ignored
> By creatures with a wing
> Who tread the fields above the earth
> With little need to sing. (Ibid., ll. 21-24)

And again:

> If to become a bloom of bee
> Would mean to never have to choose
> Between two things, to trick and loose
> The persecuting Self, I see
>
> The system's merit. Stalked by care
> Or bayed by woe within the heart
> The bird alone can wing, depart
> From shadow into shining air.
> Nothing murderous so besets it
> But the fowl escaped *forgets* it.
>   ["Untitled," ll. 5-14 (EG 170-71; italics added)]

Nature in Barlow's poetry is lucky enough, since she holds no memory of her griefs: therefore, not even the relief of an identification with her is left for the poet, since he knows that, once he has abandoned his human status and become "nature," he too would "forget" his luck. No way of escape exists, and so this conflict of Barlow's poetry results in a vicious circle.

The poet strives to perform the futile task of providing nature with memory, since the attribution of memory to nature would reinforce his identification effort. Circularly, Barlow's attempt to endorse a quasi-pantheistic view of nature, to provide her with a "soul" and an almost divine character, can also be understood as an attempt to fulfill this task: providing nature with memory. Barlow personifies nature in order to endow her with memory, and conversely, he strives to provide her with memory in order to personify her. The poet's failure is unavoidable, since nature, being tied to forgetfulness, rejects any attribution of a remembering capacity:

> A frog adds a word to a dotard story
> Whose beginning the moon *has forgotten*.
>   ["Sacre du Printemps," ll. 3-4 (EG 177; italics added)]

Barlow strives to find consolation from the torment and isolation of his life by trying to build his poetic world according to his own aspirations and dreams; but not even his creations seem to grant him a relieving consolation. In fact, nature's tendency to forgetfulness produces a further conflict. Barlow has two contrasting perceptions of this forgetting "attitude" of nature: on the one hand, a positive perception, since it is better not to remember, feel, think, experience, but simply to witness—he knows he should give up memory because memory cannot really console; and, on the other hand, a negative perception, since the renunciation of memory that nature teaches us entails a giving up of an active role in life, of any effort toward happiness and recognition—something Barlow is not readily able to accept, since he perhaps lacks the poignancy and intensity of Lovecraft's detached moral attitude.

Barlow's poetic discourse is even more complex. Since he clearly perceives the failure of his attempts as far as his identification with nature is concerned, he tries to reinforce the "spiritualizing" attitude of his poetry by establishing a connection between the "environmentalism" of its verses and the representation of figures, episodes, and myths of native Mexican cultures. If the culture of modern Western civilization brings the destruction, death, and war of the Machine Age, a positive, harmonious relation of a human culture with nature is (was) possible— the one entertained by the ancient cultures of the native Mesoamerican peoples. Thus, the wild and sentient nature of Barlow's poetry manifests itself in the "pure" world of native Mesoamerican peoples, who did not know Caesar and were not contaminated by the culture of the Western world. The juxtaposition of images drawn from the natural environment and from the culture, in particular the religion, of the native peoples (a truly historical concern) is perhaps never as effective as in "Stela of a Mayan Penitent"[63]:

> While the Jaguar clambered down the night and the Turtle clambered up,
> What silver honey did you browse on at the pace of trees budding
> In your world that never heard of Caesar?
> Bringing forth your senses like sacred palm-leaf books
> Painted with bumblebee-gods,
> Over and over in what seas did you turn tunawise
> As the projects of the foam fell into ruin?
> Did the flowers throw off their masks and augmented streams slake the night?
> And now, with this cord of spines worked through your tongue, is it clear to
> you that one who walks out of the serpent-village of the jungle must stand
> as a shield against the fist of the moon? (EG 182)

An explanation for the apparent nonsense arising from the audacious combination of these natural visual images lies in the logic of a sentient nature endowed with a life deriving from her connection with the native cultures of which she was the background. The moon, like a proud native warrior, has a fist; the religion of the natives is so defined by their respect for nature that their gods become bum-

---

63. According to Faig, this poem is indeed representative of RHB's "love of the Indian cultures" (UL 225).

blebee-like, and people themselves turn "tunawise," like the half-natural gods of their mythical accounts (a remarkable example of "naturalization" of people). The full communion with nature experienced by the native peoples was fully comprehended and almost venerated by Barlow: in the native cultures he came to love passionately, nature is not simply personified or spiritualized, it is made divine.

Moving from this sympathetic conception, Barlow could easily find and express a poetic side of the native Mexican civilizations, as the whole cycle of poems under the section "Fresco of Priests and Beans" in *View from a Hill* (1947) clearly attests.

Let us return to discuss the privilege Barlow accords in his poetry to the cultures of native peoples. Their "purity" (measured by the degree of respect they showed for nature), as we saw, is guaranteed by their impermeability to the history and traditions of the Western, mechanized world. In particular, Barlow's poetry seems to insist on the fact that native cultures did not witness (and were not witnessed by) the conquests of the Roman Empire: "that unwitnessed world / Which never heard of Caesar" ("Quetzalcoatl," ll. 12-13, EG 169). The Roman Empire brought violence, war, death, and destruction all over the lands it conquered, and above all it brought iron and weapons—symbols, in their times, of the distortions that a rotten culture may *in any epoch* introduce in the relationship with nature. These distortions are not known to the native Mexican cultures, untouched by any form of mechanization and automation:

> Ah, Zapotecs and Dominicans, how could they have endured life
> Before the Automat?
> ["On the Names of the Zapotec Kings," ll. 16-17 (EG 192)]

In sum, Barlow's passionate interest for native Mexican cultures both in his scholarly activity and in his poetic efforts aims at the fulfillment of a double goal:

1. to keep memory alive: the study of the past of native cultures represents an attempt to preserve memory, and to provide nature with the capacity to remember;
2. to respect nature, since Barlow's poetry shows the deep connections existing between the cultures, traditions, and religions of Mesoamerican natives and their profound, reverential, almost sacred respect for the natural environment and its hidden, spiritual forces.

But what actually were the motives and the sources of Barlow's concern and estimation for Mexican native cultures? Those related with nature and the "ingenuity" of their civilizations are only some of the reasons that led him to dedicate important parts of both his scholarship and his literature to native Mesoamerican cultures.

Kenneth Faig provides an illuminating insight on the deepest intellectual as well as emotional roots of Barlow's inclination and fondness for Mexican ancient cultures. As it will result clear, Lovecraft's influence on this aspect of his pupil's formation is undeniable:

> ... As Hart observes, while Barlow was an utterly up-to-date and innovative poet, his vision of the world was still a romantic, backward-looking one—with an aura of felt but inexpressible tragedy. His heavy use of Aztec and Maya images reflected not only his preoccupying intellectual interests but also his love of lost peoples and times—and the consequent enigma of adjustment in the Machine Age. Recall his estimate of Lovecraft's greatness not as a creator of weird tales, however skilled HPL may have been in the art, but as a man who lived a life of meaning in the increasingly meaningless age.[64] There are often references to long-lost peoples and more meaningful ways of life ... (Faig, UL 212)

like those envisioning a genuine and devout respect for Nature.

When Barlow was advised by Barbara Mayer to enroll in a course in anthropology, he willingly accepted. And this was very predictable, since "his love for archaic races and lost languages is clear from such early pieces as the 'Annals of the Jinns'" (UL 217). Faig advances a further intriguing suggestion in order to better explain Barlow's love for the cultures and the ways of life of the Culhua-Mexica peoples:

> ... Barlow identified the native peoples of Mexico with Lovecraft's Old Ones or perhaps with the numerous "lost races" of fantasy fiction in general. Lovecraft had even adopted Mexican gods for use in the Cthulhu Mythos in a few stories—including "The Curse of Yig" and "The Mound" [...] Many other pulp writers of the 1930s [...] wrote stories with at least an Hispanic background—in most of which the Spaniard was depicted as the convention evil and sensual villain, as witnessed in Munn's story "The Wheel" (*Weird Tales*, May 1933). Indeed, Barlow's sympathies in his research and writing seem to have been with the native peoples in the struggle to maintain their culture against the Spanish influx ... (UL 217)

Barlow's love for these peoples, as well as his scorn of war, can thus be understood also in connection with a "sociopolitical" issue, that of preserving the memory and the integrity of traditions easily "westernized" and subdued to a cultural brainwashing by the dominant and colonizing civilizations—those of the modern Machine Age, war, and respect *manqué* for nature. However, there is no better way to understand Barlow's position on this key issue than directly resorting to his own and Smisor's words, in the introduction to the first issue of their journal *Tlalocan*. Addressing a 1943 war-torn world, their effort to foster a rediscovery and appreciation of the native, "natural" Mexican cultures acquires the

---

64. "The fantasies he wrote have become models. As an unobtrusive guide treads knowingly the stair to an Etruscan tomb or a Zapotec chamber, HPL conducts us by means of his dexterous prose to doorways of awe and wonder and flings them suddenly wide to us. But he was much more than a story writer [...] He is more important as a man who had the integrity to ignore the Machine Age and its levelling-out-to-rubble of life's rich irregularities, who had the courage to study and think and converse and write, in accordance with the deeper traditions of a more orderly age [...] His intimate acquaintance with astronomy, history, and literature, as well as a host of other interests, made him a civilizer among barbarians" (WG 362-63).

symbolic acceptation of an intellectual, scholarly answer to the nonsense of the "unnatural" world massacre perpetrated by the Machine Age: "What we are after are materials which will contribute to an understanding and appreciation of the Indian peoples who have been so often libeled, grotesquely romanticized, or ignored by even their own ashamed descendants" (quoted in Faig, *UL* 221).

Barlow's interest in Indian peoples pertained to their customs, languages, and history: "so intense was his love of the native languages that he often spoke Nahuatl instead of Spanish with those of his associates who also had a mastery of the tongue" (*UL* 225). And he did not stop at simply studying the native cultures at the time of the Spanish conquest: he became a friend of his contemporary Indians, among whom he spent most of the time during the Mexican period of his life, for scholarly reasons as well as for personal preference and inclination: "Barlow did not achieve his tremendous erudition from books and codices alone. Although the native texts were his chief scholarly interest, he also did field work among the Mexican Indians—observing their culture and language and gathering examples of their myths and legends" (*UL* 225). Observation, participation, and immersion seem the key concepts showing the intensity and extent of Barlow's personal concern with the Indian peoples. In return for his respect and appreciation for the cultures of the Mexican natives,[65] he was paid back by his same coin: "in time, Barlow became a sort of minor folk hero among the Indians of his region" (*UL* 226), and quite fitting and moving was the tribute to his memory written by his secretary, Lieutenant Antonio E. Castaneda, in a letter addressed to George Smisor upon Barlow's death:

> He lived among us, savoring our languages with humility, and loved the Mexican Indian to such an extent that he lived alongside of them with complete pleasure; but at the same time that he was relishing their languages, their food, and their customs, he urged them toward the progress which would set them free from the conditions in which they live. I consider myself highly privileged to have been in the service of that genius in science and goodness. My gratitude as a Mexican towards him will prove imperishable, because in truth foreigners like him who dedicate himself in body and soul to everything that was Mexican, are extremely rare. (Quoted in Faig, *UL* 232)[66]

---

65. In 1945 RHB was even appointed by the Mexican government as "director of the literacy campaign among the Indians of Morelos" (Faig, *UL* 225), and the publication of the journal *Mexihkayotl* was intended by RHB as a means to provide the descendants of the Indians with a newspaper in Nahuatl, since at that time they had nothing to read in that language (one can scarcely imagine a more truly *memory-preserving* endeavor on a scholar's part). Moreover, RHB "brought Indians from remote corners of the republic to his Azcapotzalco home to be educated in their native tongues while working for him in the house and the print shop" (*UL* 226).

66. Originally published in George T. Smisor, "R. H. Barlow and 'Tlalocan,'" *Tlalocan*, 3, No. 2 (1952): 97–102. Translation from Spanish by Donald Sidney-Fryer.

Cover of Barlow's journal, Leaves.

Conclusion

Far from aspiring to provide an exhaustive analysis of Robert Barlow's work, my study has traced some paths of investigation for those interested in the challenging, controversial, and deserving figure of this member of the Lovecraft circle.

I hope my study may constitute a stepping-stone for further studies on Barlow's writing: the indication of the seven "themes" of his fiction and the five thematic areas specific to his poetry (with the several interconnections that my occasional references have striven to demonstrate), as well as the analysis of his personality—particularly in connection with Lovecraft's influence—will hopefully serve for other scholars.

Much work is left to do. Both Barlow's fiction and his poetry seem deserving of further, focused interpretative efforts. In particular, a psychoanalytic interpretation of the images of his poetry calls for attention, as well as a study grounded in the tenets of the anthropological studies conducted by Gilbert Durand on the archetypal roots of imagination.

Robert H. Barlow had a complex, sensitive, versatile, and, under many viewpoints, genial personality. His interests were manifold, his intellect amazingly brilliant, his creativity unrestrained. But if Barlow the academic scholar and researcher has been widely recognized and appreciated so far, what is still missing is an academic evaluation of his literary work that, though scarce in quantity, truly qualifies for substantial interpretative study.

The Barlow homestead c. 2006.

Bibliography

I. Primary

Books

Poems for a Competition. Sacramento: The Fugitive Press, 1942.
View from a Hill. Azcapotzalco: [no publisher given], 1947.
Accent on Barlow: A Commemorative Anthology. Ed. Lawrence Hart. San Rafael, CA: Lawrence Hart, [1962].
The Annals of the Jinns. West Warwick, RI: Necronomicon Press, 1978.
The Night Ocean (as by H. P. Lovecraft). West Warwick, RI: Necronomicon Press, 1978, 1982.
A Dim-Remembered Story. West Warwick, RI: Necronomicon Press, 1980.
The Battle That Ended the Century and Collapsing Cosmoses (with H. P. Lovecraft). West Warwick, RI: Necronomicon Press, 1992.
On Lovecraft and Life. Ed. S. T. Joshi. West Warwick, RI: Necronomicon Press, 1992.
The Hoard of the Wizard-Beast and One Other (with H. P. Lovecraft). Ed. S. T. Joshi. West Warwick, RI: Necronomicon Press, 1994.
Eyes of the God: The Weird Fiction and Poetry of R. H. Barlow. Ed. S. T. Joshi, Douglas A. Anderson, and David E. Schultz. New York: Hippocampus Press, 2002.

Books Edited

H. P. Lovecraft. *The Notes & Commonplace Book Employed by the Late H. P. Lovecraft Including His Suggestions for Story-Writing, Analyses of the Weird Story, and a List of Certain Basic Underlying Horrors, &c., &c., Designed to Stimulate the Imagination.* [Ed. R. H. Barlow.] Lakeport, CA: The Futile Press, 1938; rpt. West Warwick, RI: Necronomicon Press, 1978.
George Sterling. *After Sunset.* San Francisco: John Howell, Publisher, 1939. Compiled by R. H. Barlow.

Publisher

Dragon-Fly. 15 October 1935; 15 May 1936.
Leaves. Summer 1937; Winter 1938/39.
Frank Belknap Long, Jr. *The Goblin Tower.* Cassia, FL: Dragon-Fly Press, 1935.
H. P. Lovecraft. *The Cats of Ulthar.* Cassia, FL: Dragon-Fly Press, 1935.

II. Secondary

Benjamin, Walter. "Der Erzähler" (1936-37). In *Schriften*. Ed. Theodor W. Adorno and Gretel Adorno. 2 vols. Frankfurt am Main: Suhrkamp, 1955. Eng. trans.: "The Storyteller." In *Illuminations: Essays and Reflections*. New York: Shocken, 1969.

Bloch, Robert. "Heritage of Horror." In *The Dunwich Horror and Others* by H. P. Lovecraft. Sauk City, WI: Arkham House, 1984. ix-xxvi.

Cavendish, Richard. *The Powers of Evil in Western Religion, Magic, and Folk Belief.* 1975. New York: Dorset, 1993.

Cuddon, J. A. *Dictionary of Literary Terms and Literary Theory*. 3rd ed. Harmondsworth, UK: Penguin, 1999.

Dansky, Richard E. "Transgression, Spheres of Influence, and the Use of the Utterly Other in Lovecraft." *Lovecraft Studies* No. 30 (Spring 1994): 5-14.

de Camp, L. Sprague. *Lovecraft: A Biography*. Garden City, NY: Doubleday, 1975.

Derleth, August. *Some Notes on H. P. Lovecraft*. Sauk City, WI: Arkham House, 1959.

Durand, Gilbert. *The Anthropological Structures of the Imaginary*. Brisbane: Boombana, 1999.

Eckhardt, Jason. "The Cosmic Yankee." In Schultz and Joshi, 78-100.

Faig, Kenneth W., Jr. "HPL: The Book That Nearly Was." *Xenophile* No. 11 (March 1975): 118-23.

———. "R. H. Barlow." In Faig's *The Unknown Lovecraft*. New York: Hippocampus Press, 2009. 194-234.

———. *R. H. Barlow: An Account of the Life and Career of the Most Controversial Member of the Lovecraft Circle*. Columbia, SC: Dragonfly Press, 2000.

———. "Robert H. Barlow as H. P. Lovecraft's Literary Executor: An Appreciation." *Crypt of Cthulhu* No. 60 (Hallowmas 1988): 52-62. In Faig's *The Unknown Lovecraft*. New York: Hippocampus Press, 2009. 235-48.

Gray, Martin. *A Dictionary of Literary Terms*. Harlow, UK: Longman; Beirut: York Press, 1984.

Hart, Lawrence. *Ideas of Order in Experimental Poetry*. San Francisco: George Leite, 1945.

———. "A Note on Robert Barlow." *Poetry* 78 (May 1951): 115-16.

Hummel, Franklin. "In Memory of Robert H. Barlow." *Gaylactic Gazette* 5, No. 3 (Winter 1991): 25-29.

Humphreys, Brian. "'The Night Ocean' and the Subtleties of Cosmicism." *Lovecraft Studies* No. 30 (Spring 1994): 14-21.

Jordan, Stephen J. "H. P. Lovecraft in Florida." *Lovecraft Studies* Nos. 42/43 (Fall 2001): 32-45.

Joshi, S. T. *A Dreamer and a Visionary: H. P. Lovecraft in His Time*. Liverpool: Liverpool University Press, 2001.

———. *H. P. Lovecraft: A Life*. West Warwick, RI: Necronomicon Press, 1996.

———. "H. P. Lovecraft: The Decline of the West." In *The Weird Tale*. Austin: University of Texas Press, 1990. 168–229.

———. *H. P. Lovecraft: The Decline of the West*. Mercer Island, WA: Starmont House, 1990.

———. "Lovecraft's Contribution to 'Till A' the Seas.'" *Crypt of Cthulhu* No. 17 (Hallowmas 1983): 33–39.

———. *Primal Sources: Essays on H. P. Lovecraft*. New York: Hippocampus Press, 2003.

———. "R. H. Barlow and the Recognition of Lovecraft." *Crypt of Cthulhu* No. 60 (Hallowmas 1988): 45–51.

———. *A Subtler Magick: The Writings and Philosophy of H. P. Lovecraft*. San Bernardino, CA: Borgo Press, 1996.

———. "Textual Problems in Lovecraft: A Preliminary Survey." *Lovecraft Studies* No. 6 (Spring 1982): 18–32.

Joshi, S. T., and Marc A. Michaud, ed. *H. P. Lovecraft in "The Eyrie."* West Warwick, RI: Necronomicon Press, 1979.

Joshi, S. T., and Schultz, David E. *An H. P. Lovecraft Encyclopedia*. Westport, CT: Greenwood Press, 2001.

Kermode, Frank. *The Sense of an Ending: Studies in the Theory of Fiction*. New York: Oxford University Press, 1967.

Lovecraft, H. P. *The Ancient Track: The Complete Poetical Works*. Ed. S. T. Joshi. San Francisco: Night Shade, 2001.

———. *The Annotated Supernatural Horror in Literature*. Ed. S. T. Joshi. New York: Hippocampus Press, 2000.

———. *The Call of Cthulhu and Other Weird Stories*. Ed. S. T. Joshi. New York: Penguin, 1999.

———. *Collected Essays*. Ed. S. T. Joshi. New York: Hippocampus Press, 2004–06. 5 vols.

———. *The Dreams in the Witch House and Other Weird Stories*. Ed. S. T. Joshi. New York: Penguin, 2004.

———. *Essential Solitude: The Letters of H. P. Lovecraft and August Derleth*. Ed. David E. Schultz and S. T. Joshi. New York: Hippocampus Press, 2008. 2 vols.

———. *Letters to Alfred Galpin*. Ed. S. T. Joshi and David E. Schultz. New York: Hippocampus Press, 2003.

———. *Marginalia*. Ed. August Derleth and Donald Wandrei. Sauk City, WI: Arkham House, 1944.

———. *Miscellaneous Writings*. Ed. S. T. Joshi. Sauk City, WI: Arkham House, 1995.

———. *O Fortunate Floridian: H. P. Lovecraft's Letters to R. H. Barlow*. Ed. S. T. Joshi and David E. Schultz. Tampa, FL: University of Tampa Press, 2007.

———. *Selected Letters*. Ed. August Derleth and James Turner. Vols. 4–5. Sauk City, WI: Arkham House, 1976.

———. *The Shadow out of Time: The Corrected Text*. Ed. S. T. Joshi and David E. Schultz. New York: Hippocampus Press, 2001.

———. *The Shuttered Room and Other Pieces.* Ed. August Derleth. Sauk City, WI: Arkham House, 1959.

Montelone, Paul. "The Vanity of Existence in 'The Shadow out of Time.'" *Lovecraft Studies* No. 34 (Spring 1996): 27–35.

Mooser, Clare. "A Study of Robert Barlow: The T. E. Lawrence of Mexico." *New Mexico Quarterly Review* 3, No. 2 (1968): 5–12.

Mosig, Dirk W. *Mosig at Last: A Psychologist Looks at H. P. Lovecraft.* West Warwick, RI: Necronomicon Press, 1997.

Moskowitz, Sam. *A. Merritt: Reflections in the Moon Pool.* Philadelphia: Oswald Train, 1985.

Murfin, Ross, and Supryia M. Ray. *The Bedford Glossary of Critical and Literary Terms.* 2nd ed. Boston: Bedford, 2003.

Nelson, Dale J. "Lovecraft and the Burkean Sublime." *Lovecraft Studies* No. 24 (Spring 1991): 2–5.

Pouillon, Jean. *Temps et Roman.* Paris: Gallimard, 1946.

Ruber, Peter, ed. *Arkham's Masters of Horror: A 60th Anniversary Anthology Retrospective of the First 30 Years of Arkham House.* Sauk City, WI: Arkham House, 2000.

Schultz, David E., and Joshi, S.T., ed. *An Epicure in the Terrible: A Centennial Anthology of Essays in Honor of H. P. Lovecraft.* Rutherford, NJ: Fairleigh Dickinson University Press, 1991.

Sigurdson, Kirk. "A Gothic Approach to Lovecraft's Sense of *Outsideness.*" *Lovecraft Studies* No. 28 (Spring 1993): 22–34.

Smisor, George T. "R. H. Barlow and Tlalocan." *Tlalocan* 3, No. 2 (1952): 97–102.

Smith, Clark Ashton. *Out of Space and Time.* Sauk City, WI: Arkham House, 1942.

———. *Selected Letters.* Ed. David E. Schultz and Scott Connors. Sauk City, WI: Arkham House, 2003.

Spengler, Oswald. *The Decline of the West.* Trans. Charles Francis Atkinson. New York: Knopf, 1926–28. 2 vols.

Todorov, Tzvetan. *The Fantastic: A Structural Approach to a Literary Genre.* Trans. Richard Howard. 1973. Ithaca, NY: Cornell University Press, 1978.

Wetzel, George T. "Lovecraft's Literary Executor." *Continuity* 3, No. 1 (October 1976): 30–41. Rpt. *Fantasy Commentator* 4, No. 1 (Winter 1978–79): 34–43.

Wilson, Edmund. "Tales of the Marvellous and the Ridiculous" (1945). Rpt. in *H. P. Lovecraft: Four Decades of Criticism,* ed. S. T. Joshi. Athens: Ohio University Press, 1980.

www.ingramcontent.com/pod-product-compliance
Lightning Source LLC
Chambersburg PA
CBHW060105170426
43198CB00010B/777